# A Woman Rides the Beast

## DAVE HUNT

**HARVEST HOUSE PUBLISHERS**

EUGENE, OREGON

*Cover by Garborg Design Works, Savage, Minnesota*

**A WOMAN RIDES THE BEAST**
Copyright © 1994 by Dave Hunt
Published by Harvest House Publishers
Eugene, Oregon, 97402
www.harvesthousepublishers.com

Library of Congress Cataloging-in-Publication Data

Hunt, Dave
    A woman rides the beast: the Catholic Church and the last days / Dave Hunt.
        p.m.
    ISBN 978-1-56507-199-5
    1. Catholic Church—Controversial literature.  2. Bible—Prophecies.
3. Bible. N.T. Revelation—Criticism, interpretation, etc.  4. End of the world.  I. Title.
BX1765.2H85    1994
282—dc 20                                                              94-10726
                                                                            CIP

**Printed in the United States of America**

15  / VP /  23  22

# Contents

*To the nearly 1 billion Roman Catholics
misinformed by their hierarchy;
to the 400 million Protestants equally ignorant
of the facts; and to the genuine martyrs
on both sides, this book is dedicated.*

# Overturning
# the Reformation

The most significant event in nearly 500 years of church history was revealed as a *fait accompli* on March 29, 1994. On that day leading American evangelicals and Catholics signed a joint declaration titled "Evangelicals and Catholics Together: The Christian Mission in the 3rd Millennium " The document, in effect, overturned the Reformation and will unquestionably have far-reaching repercussions throughout the Christian world for years to come.

This startling development was the culmination of careful planning and negotiations over the previous two years. Each step was continuously monitored and approved by the Vatican. The *New York Times* release making the announcement, which was carried in newspapers across the country on March 30, said in part:

> They toiled together in the movements against abortion and pornography, and now leading Catholics and evangelicals are asking their flocks for a remarkable leap of faith: to finally accept each other as Christians. In what's being called a historic declaration, evangelicals including Pat Robertson and Charles Colson [one of the chief originators] joined with conservative Roman Catholic leaders today in upholding the ties of faith that bind the nation's largest and most politically active religious groups. They urged Catholics and evangelicals . . . to stop aggressive proselytization of each other's flocks.
>
> John White, president of Geneva College and former president of the National Association of Evangelicals, said the statement represents a "triumphalistic moment" in American religious life after centuries of distrust. . . .
>
> Other evangelical endorsers include the heads of the Home Mission Board and Christian Life Commission of the Southern Baptist Convention [who acted in an inde-

pendent capacity], the nation's largest Protestant denomination, and Bill Bright, founder of Campus Crusade for Christ.... Mark Noll of Wheaton University... [Os Guinness, Jesse Miranda (Assemblies of God), Richard Mouw (President, Fuller Theological Seminary), J.I. Packer and Herbert Schlossberg].

Robert Simonds, Southern California chairman of the National Association of Evangelicals, "applauded the declaration" and said he hoped it would bring "increased cooperation between evangelicals and Catholics...." Other evangelical leaders have since signed the declaration, while still others have denounced it as a betrayal of the Reformation. Ironically, this bold move to "unite Catholics and evangelicals" will divide evangelicals as nothing else could—and as its endorsers must have realized.

The 25-page document acknowledges, without compromise, some key differences between Catholics and evangelicals (such as the significance of baptism and the authority of Scripture). Unfortunately, the most important difference— *what it means to be a Christian*—is not mentioned. In fact, that such a difference even exists is denied. This compromise of the gospel lies at the heart of the agreement.

The key element behind this historic joint declaration is the previously unthinkable admission on the part of leading evangelicals that active participation in the Catholic Church makes one a Christian. If that is indeed the case, then the Reformation was a tragic mistake. The millions who were martyred (during a thousand years before the Reformation and since then to the present time) for rejecting Catholicism as a false gospel have all died in vain. If, however, the Reformers were right, then this new agreement between Catholics and evangelicals could well be the cleverest and deadliest blow struck against the gospel in the entire history of the church. Either way, the consequences are staggering. In praising the joint declaration, one leading evangelical declared:

[This document] has the potential to recast all the ecumenical discussions that have gone on through the years.... This is a new day. Our closest friends, as evangelicals, in the cultural task and in the fundamental theological task, are Roman Catholics.[1]

The theological differences between Catholics and Protestants were once considered to be so great that millions died as martyrs rather than compromise them, and their Catholic executioners were equally convinced of the importance of such differences. How have these differences been dissolved? What has happened to cause leading evangelicals to declare that Catholicism's gospel, which the Reformers denounced as heretical, is now biblical? That gospel hasn't changed. Has conviction been compromised to create a huge coalition among conservatives for social and political action?

Evangelicals would decry the complacent attitude that everyone actively involved in a Protestant church is a Christian. How then did evangelical leaders consent to the view that all active Catholics are Christians and not to be evangelized? The document explains that both Catholics and evangelicals endorse the Apostles' Creed: that Christ "suffered under Pontius Pilate, was crucified, died, and was buried." That creed, however, like the Nicean and other creeds, does *not* express the gospel that saves (Romans 1:16): that "Christ died *for our sins* (1 Corinthians 15:1-4). Mormons affirm the Apostles' Creed, but they aren't biblical Christians. Nor does embracing the Creed make Catholics (or Protestants) Christians. Furthermore, what Catholics mean by Christ dying for their sins is entirely different from an evangelical understanding of this truth, as we shall see in later pages.

Whereas Roman Catholicism was once the official state religion and the practice of all others was prohibited throughout Latin America and most of Europe, that is no longer the case. Therefore Rome uses other strategies. In some countries, such as France, the Catholic Church is pressuring the government to make it illegal to "proselytize"—exactly what the endorsers of this joint pact have agreed upon. In other places the Catholic Church is demanding that evangelicals sign an agreement similar to the one just signed here in the United States. A recent news report declared:

> Stunned by the staggering growth of evangelical "sects" in Brazil, leaders of the Roman Catholic Church have threatened to launch a "holy war" against Protestants unless they stop leading people from the Catholic fold. . . . At the 31st National Conference of the Bishops of Brazil . . . Bishop Sinesio Bohn [called] evangelicals a serious threat to the Vatican's influence in his country.
>
> "We will declare a holy war; don't doubt it," he announced. "The Catholic Church has a ponderous structure, but when we move, we'll smash anyone beneath us." . . . According to Bohn, an all-out holy war can't be avoided unless the 13 largest Protestant churches and denominations sign a treaty . . . [that] would require Protestants to stop all evangelism efforts in Brazil. In exchange, he said, Catholics would agree to stop all persecution directed toward Protestants.[2]

The bishop admits that persecution of Protestants is still official policy. The extent of that persecution throughout history (which we will document) would greatly surprise both Catholics and Protestants. It is important to note that the concern at the bishops' conference was not the truth of the gospel or the salvation of souls, but *maintaining the influence of the Vatican and keeping people in the Catholic Church.*

Note too that the very treaty which Bishop Bohn demands under threat in Brazil has been granted in the United States by Colson, Packer, Bright, Robertson, et al! That Bohn's threats influenced American evangelical leaders is evident from Colson's statement in an interview that he and the other signatories to the document had become "distressed by the clashes arising from the growth of evangelical Protestantism in traditionally Catholic Latin America. . . ."[3]

While evangelicals sign a truce, Rome is stepping up its evangelization of Protestants into the Catholic Church. Rome's "Evangelization 2000" has six evangelism training conferences scheduled just for 1994 across America involving such groups as "Paulist Evangelization Training Institutes" (in Washington D.C. during June 26-30 and July 24-28) and "The Association of Coordinators of Catholic Schools of Evangelization" (during August 3-6, also in Washington). These are serious training sessions for leaders in what they specify as "Catholic evangelism." Charles Colson was a featured speaker at the "John Paul II and the New Evangelization: Implementing the Vision" conference in Ypsilanti, Michigan, held during May 11-14. He shared the podium with Catholic leaders such as Fr. Tom Forrest, who heads "Evangelization 2000" out of the Vatican.[4]

The evangelical leaders who signed the joint declaration apparently imagined a spiritual partnership with Catholics to win the world to Christ. "Evangelism" for evangelicals means leading people to Christ. For Catholics, however, it means bringing people *into the Roman Catholic Church*—something which the joint agreement neglected to state. Consider the following explanation of "Catholic evangelism" by Fr. Tom Forrest to a group of Catholic charismatics:

> Our job is to make people as richly and as fully Christian as we can make them by bringing them *into the Catholic Church*. So evangelization is never fully successful, it's only partial, until the convert is made a member of Christ's body by being led into the [Catholic] Church.
>
> Now listen again to the words of [Pope] Paul VI. Now this is a document every one of you should have in your homes . . . called "On Evangelization in the Modern World." This is what the Pope says: "The commitment of someone newly evangelized cannot remain abstract ('Oh, I'm a Christian,' now that's, too abstract) . . . it must be given concrete and visible form through entry . . . into the [Catholic] Church our visible sacrament of salvation."
>
> I like saying those words; I'm going to say them again: "Our visible sacrament of salvation!" That's what the Church is, and if that is what the Church is, we have to be evangelizing into the Church! . . .
>
> No, you don't just invite someone to become a Christian, you invite them *to become Catholics* . . . Why would this be so important? First of all, there are seven sacraments, and the Catholic Church has all seven. . . . On our altars we have the body of Christ; we drink the blood of

10

Christ. Jesus is alive on our altars, as offering. . . . We become one with Christ in the Eucharist. . . .

As Catholics we have Mary, and that Mom of ours, Queen of Paradise, is praying for us till she sees us in glory.

As Catholics we have the papacy, a history of popes from Peter to John Paul II . . . we have the rock upon which Christ did build His Church.

As Catholics—now I love this one—we have purgatory. Thank God! I'm one of those people who would never get to the Beatific Vision without it. It's the only way to go. . . .

So as Catholics . . . our job is to use this remaining decade evangelizing everyone we can *into the Catholic Church,* into the body of Christ and into the third millennium of Catholic history.[5]

Yet in spite of such clear explanations of Roman Catholic "evangelism," evangelicals are participating with Catholics in joint evangelistic efforts. For the Catholic, salvation does not come through personally receiving Christ as Savior but is a lengthy process that begins with baptism and thereafter depends upon one's continued relationship to the Church. Salvation comes through participation in the sacraments, penance, good works, suffering for one's sins and the sins of others here and/or in purgatory, indulgences to reduce time in purgatory, and almost endless masses and Rosaries said on one's behalf even after one's death. Catholic "evangelism" is by works, the very antithesis of "the gospel of the grace of God" (Acts 20:24).

Nevertheless, many Catholics, when they hear the true biblical gospel of God's grace, are receiving Christ as personal Savior. Such Catholic Christians eventually struggle with the conflict between Roman Catholicism and what they now realize the Bible teaches—a conflict so marked that the vast majority find it impossible to remain in the Catholic Church. Many Protestants are equally in doubt over the question of what their relationship to Catholics ought to be.

Confusion now surrounds the issues which were involved at the Reformation. The purpose of this book is to present vital, factual information which throws essential light upon the whole question of Catholic/Protestant relationships. The vast majority of both Catholics and Protestants are ignorant of the pertinent facts. It is our hope and prayer that the following pages will help to clarify the issues and dispel the confusion.

—————— **A WOMAN** ——————

*He carried me away in the spirit into the wilder-*
*ness, and I saw a woman sit upon a scarlet*
*colored beast full of names of blasphemy, hav-*
*ing seven heads and ten horns.*

—Revelation 17:3

—————— **R I D E S   T H E   B E A S T** ——————

# 1

## A Woman
## Rides the Beast!

The most astounding prophecies in the Bible are found in its last book, known as "The Revelation" or "The Apocalypse" and recorded by the apostle John about A.D. 95. He claimed to have received from the resurrected Christ Himself this series of visions of God's final judgment upon mankind which would close human history. This, the Bible's last and most awesome panoramic view into the future, embodies revelations of climactic events—some already fulfilled, most still future, but all both incredible and terrifying.

Of all the glimpses of "things which must shortly come to pass" (Revelation 1:1) which John reveals, none is as intriguing and staggering as the vision recorded by John in chapter 17. There we see a fearsome, scarlet-colored beast with seven heads and ten horns. This is not the first time it has appeared to biblical prophets. From the description, it is obviously the same terrifying creature whose description has already been recorded three times. John himself had seen it twice. Daniel saw it as well, 600 years earlier. But in this last glimpse, suddenly something has changed.

In its previous appearances in Scripture the beast has always been the total focus of attention, and invariably presented alone. Now, however, it appears with a rider on its back. That anyone would dare, much less be able, to mount such an incredible beast seems beyond imagination. Yet there she

13

sits, quite at ease and obviously in control, astride a world-devouring creature defying description. *She?* Yes, *she.* A *woman* rides the beast!

For 1900 years the beast itself has been a major focus of attention for students of prophecy. Its identity, the frightening role it will play in the last days, and its ultimate end have been debated through the centuries. In the last 200 years, however, many evangelical Christians have held to a fairly clear consensus: The beast represents both the revived Roman Empire (Satan's worldwide counterfeit of God's kingdom), and the satanically empowered Antichrist who will rule it. Whether that interpretation is correct or not will become apparent in the following pages.

## A Woman Who Can't Be Ignored

The woman is a far more enigmatic figure. The leaders of the Reformation were certain that she represented the Roman Catholic Church in general and the pope in particular. That belief, however, has been rejected lately by most Protestants as provocative and demeaning to a body of fellow Christians with whom evangelicals desire to work together in the task of winning most of the world for Christ before the year 2000. In fact, the subject of the woman is generally avoided today as too divisive to discuss.

Still, the woman, so vividly protrayed by John, cannot be dismissed so easily. There she is. Two of the final chapters in the Bible are devoted to her. What will we do with her? It would be dishonest to ignore such an important prophetic figure. The entire Bible is God's Word. We have no more right to close our eyes to Revelation 17 and 18 than to John 3:16.

Unquestionably, the woman is the central figure in these two important chapters, a major player in the drama of the last days. John gives far more attention to *her* than to the beast she rides. And the fact that she *rides the beast*—a beast of such importance that it literally holds the central position in Bible prophecy—demands our special attention. It could not be clearer that the secret of this woman's identity and the role she will play is a major key to understanding biblical prophecies concerning the reign of Antichrist and events leading up to Christ's second coming.

## The Most Stunning Prophecy in Scripture

In the following pages we will show that the woman's identity is established meticulously and beyond any reasonable doubt by John himself. We will see that the vision of the woman is one of the most remarkable and significant prophecies in Scripture. The insights John was given by the Holy Spirit concerning this woman staggered him. These insights are no less breathtaking in our day.

Much of John's vision has already been fulfilled in history and can therefore be verified beyond question. Based upon the insights John provides, our identification of the woman will be determined carefully and unequivocally. Although many readers may denounce our conclusions, no one will be able to refute them.

The truth about the woman astride the beast is one of the most stunning prophecies in Scripture. We say specifically "in *Scripture*" because significant prophecies which have been on record for centuries and were later fulfilled are unique to the Bible. These are not cheap guesses by psychics but involve major world events of sweeping importance and irrefutable historic record.

The vision of the woman riding the beast, as we shall see, provides insights into occurrences which have shaped world history in the past and which will profoundly determine human destiny in the future. She sits, in fact, not only astride the beast but upon the culmination of centuries of related Bible prophecy.

## A Question of Credibility

Are we simply sensationalizing John's vision? Why should anyone today be concerned with its interpretation? The question of validity can be settled quite easily. Most prophecies in the Bible have already been fulfilled. It is therefore a rather simple and straightforward matter to examine that record. For the sake of any doubters and to strengthen the faith of those who already believe, we must take a brief excursion into the amazing world of biblical prophecy. We will prove that past prophecies have been impeccably accurate, and that their fulfillment could not be explained by chance. That evidence will assure us that we are not wasting our time by examining prophecies concerning the future. And the woman on the beast does indeed have much to tell us about the future.

That goal accomplished, we will turn our attention to Revelation 17 and 18 and address the question of the identity and future role of the woman riding the beast, confident that the vision will be fulfilled exactly as John reveals it.

Much of the information we will present will not make pleasant reading. Disturbing, stretching the reader's credulity, denied by many, it will nevertheless be the fully documented truth. Moreover, it is a truth which every person on planet Earth, and especially all who consider themselves to be Christians—and most of all, Roman Catholics—need desperately to understand.

Our sympathy is particularly with sincere Roman Catholics who have such confidence in their Church that they have accepted what the hierarchy has told them without studying history to learn the full truth. It is our hope and prayer that the historic facts we present will be thoroughly checked against the record so that many devout followers of Rome will be able to face the evidence.

*Remember the former things of old, for I am God, and there is none else . . . declaring the end from the beginning, and from ancient times the things that are not yet done, saying, My counsel shall stand, and I will do all my pleasure.*

—Isaiah 46:9,10

# 2

# Reason to Believe

B iblical prophecy is the key to understanding both the past and the future. While to skeptics that may seem a preposterous claim, it is easily proved. Because most prophecy recorded in Scripture has already been fulfilled, it is therefore a simple matter to determine whether or not the prophecies in the Bible are reliable.

Two major themes of prophecy run consistently throughout all of Scripture: 1) Israel; and 2) the Messiah who comes to Israel and through Israel to the world as the Savior of all mankind. Around these two central themes almost all other prophecies revolve and find their meaning, whether it be the rapture of the church, Antichrist, his coming world government and religion, the battle of Armageddon, Christ's second coming, or any other prophesied occurrence. The Bible is absolutely unique in presenting these prophecies, which it records in specific detail, beginning more than 3000 years ago.

About 30 percent of the Bible is devoted to prophecy. That fact validates the importance of what has become a neglected subject. In marked contrast, prophecy is completely absent from the Koran, the Hindu Vedas, the Baghavad Gita, the Ramayana, the sayings of Buddha or Confucius, the Book of Mormon, or any other writings of the world's religions. This fact alone provides an undeniable stamp of divine approval upon the Judeo-Christian faith, which all other faiths lack. Biblical prophecy's unblemished record of fulfillment is sufficient to authenticate the Bible, in distinction to all other writings, as the one and only inerrant Word of God.

## Prophecy—The Great Proof

There are many important reasons for Bible prophecy. First of all, prophecy fulfilled provides irrefutable proof for the existence of the very God who inspired the prophets. By foretelling major events of world history centuries and even thousands of years before they happen, the God of the Bible proves that He is the only true God, the Creator of the universe and mankind, the Lord of history—and that the Bible is His infallible Word given to communicate His purposes and way of salvation to all who will believe. Here is a proof so simple that a child can understand it, yet so profound that the greatest genius cannot refute it.

Prophecy thus plays a vital role in revealing God's purpose for mankind. It also provides foolproof identification of God's true Messiah, or Christ, and unmasks Satan's impostor, the Antichrist, so that no one who heeds God's Word need be deceived by him.

Just as prophecy is unique to the Bible, so it is unique to Christ. No prophecies foretold the coming of Buddha, Muhammad, Zoroaster, Confucius, Joseph Smith, Mary Baker Eddy, the currently popular Hindu gurus who have invaded the West, or any other religious leader, all of whom lack the credentials which distinguish Jesus Christ. Yet there are more than 300 Old Testament prophecies which identify Israel's Messiah. Centuries before His coming, the Hebrew prophets set forth numerous and specific criteria which had to be met by the Messiah. The fulfillment of these prophecies in minute detail in the life, death, and resurrection of Jesus of Nazareth demonstrates indisputably that He is the promised One, the true and only Savior.

Inasmuch as these two major themes of Bible prophecy, Israel and the Messiah, have been dealt with in some of my other books, principally in *How Close Are We?*, we will only summarize them briefly here. In Isaiah 43:10 the God of Israel declares that the Jews are His witnesses to the world that He is God. Such is the case in spite of the fact that 30 percent of today's Israelis claim to be atheists and most Jews worldwide would never think of telling the world that God exists. Yet they are the witnesses, both to themselves and to the world, of His existence because of the astonishing fulfillment in history of precisely what God said would happen to these special people.

## The Chosen People—Their Land and Destiny

Though much that the prophets foretold concerning Israel is yet future, *nine* major prophecies involving specific and historically verifiable details have already been fulfilled precisely as foretold centuries beforehand. 1) God promised a land of clearly defined boundaries (Genesis 15:18-21) to Abraham (Genesis 12:1; 13:15; 15:7; etc.). He renewed that promise to Abraham's son Isaac (Genesis 26:3-5), to his grandson Jacob (Genesis 28:13), and to their descendants after them forever (Leviticus 25:46; Joshua 14:9; etc.). 2) It is a historical fact that God brought these "chosen people" (Exodus 7:7,8; Deuteronomy 7:6; 14:2; etc.) into the "Promised Land," an amazing story of miracles in itself. 3) When the Jewish people entered the Promised Land, God warned them that if they practiced the idolatry and immorality of the land's previous inhabitants, whom He had destroyed for their evil (Deuteronomy 9:4), He would cast them out as well (Deuteronomy 28:63; 1 Kings 9:7; 2 Chronicles 7:20; etc.). That this happened is, again, an indisputable fact of history.

So far the story is hardly remarkable. Other peoples have believed that a certain geographic area was their "Promised Land" and after entering it have later been driven out by enemies. The next six prophecies, however, and their fulfillment, are absolutely unique to the Jews. The occurrence of these events precisely as prophesied could not possibly have happened by chance. 4) God declared that His people would be scattered "among all people, from the one end of the earth even unto the other" (Deuteronomy 28:64; cf.1 Kings 9:7; Nehemiah 1:8; Amos 9:9; Zechariah 7:14; etc.). And so it happened. "The wandering Jew" is found everywhere.

The precision with which prophecies fit the Jews alone

becomes increasingly remarkable as fulfillment follows fulfillment, until the case for God's existence through His dealings with His chosen people is irrefutable. 5) God warned that
wherever they wandered the Jews would be "an astonishment,
a proverb, a byword . . . a curse and a reproach" (Deuteronomy
28:37; 2 Chronicles 7:20; Jeremiah 29:18; 44:8; etc.). Amazingly, this has been true of the Jews all down through history,
as even the present generation knows full well. The maligning,
the slurs and jokes, the naked hatred known as anti-Semitism,
not only among Muslims but even among those who call
themselves Christians, is a unique and persistent fact of history
peculiar to the Jewish people. Even today, in spite of the
haunting memory of Hitler's holocaust which once shocked and
shamed the world, and in defiance of logic and conscience,
anti-Semitism is still alive and is once again increasing worldwide.

## History of Persecution

Furthermore, the prophets declared that these scattered
peoples would not only be slandered, denigrated, and discrimi-
nated against, but 6) they would be persecuted and killed as no
other peoples on the face of the earth. History stands as
eloquent witness to the fact that this is precisely what has
happened to the Jews century after century wherever they
were found. The historical record of no other ethnic or national group of people contains anything that even approaches
the nightmare of terror, humiliation, and destruction which the
Jews have endured down through history at the hands of the
peoples among whom they have found themselves.

Shamefully, many who claimed to be Christians and thus
followers of Christ, who was Himself a Jew, were in the
forefront of Jewish persecution and slaughter. Having gained
full citizenship in the pagan Roman Empire in A.D. 212 under
the Edict of Caracalla, the Jews became second-class citizens
and the object of increasing persecution after the emperor,
Constantine, supposedly became a Christian. Thereafter, it
was those who called themselves Christians who were far
more cruel to the Jews than pagans had ever been.

The Roman Catholic popes were the first to develop anti-
Semitism to a science. Hitler, who remained a Catholic to the

end, would claim that he was only following the example of both Catholics and Lutherans in finishing what the Church had begun. Anti-Semitism was a part of his Catholicism from which Martin Luther was never freed. He advocated burning down Jews' homes and giving them the choice between conversion and having their tongues torn out.[1] When Rome's Jews were released from their ghetto by the Italian army in 1870, their freedom at last ended about 1500 years of unimaginable humiliation and degradation at the hands of those who claimed to be the vicars of Christ.

No pope hated Jews more than Paul IV (1555-59), whose cruelties defy the bounds of human reason. Catholic historian Peter de Rosa confesses that a whole "succession of popes reinforced the ancient prejudices against Jews, treating them as lepers unworthy of the protection of the law. Pius VII [1800-23] was followed by Leo XII, Pius VIII, Gregory XVI, Pius IX [1846-78]—all good pupils of Paul IV."[2] Historian Will Durant reminds us that Hitler had good precedent for his sanctions against the Jews:

> The [Roman Catholic] Council of Vienne (1311) forbade all intercourse between Christians and Jews. The Council of Zamora (1313) ruled that they must be kept in strict subjection and servitude. The Council of Basel (1431-33) renewed canonical decrees forbidding Christians to associate with Jews . . . and instructed secular authorities [as the church had herself long enforced in Rome and the papal states] to confine the Jews in separate quarters [ghettos], compel them to wear a distinguishing badge [it had previously been a yellow hat], and ensure their attendance at sermons aimed to convert them.[3]

## Preservation and Rebirth

God declared that in spite of such persecution and the periodic wholesale slaughter of Jews, 7) He would not let His chosen people be destroyed, but would preserve them as an identifiable ethnic, national group (Jeremiah 30:11; 31:35-37; etc.). The Jews had every reason to intermarry, to change their names and hide their identity by any possible means in order to escape persecution. Why preserve their bloodline when they had no land of their own, when most of them didn't take the Bible literally, and when racial identification imposed only the cruelest disadvantages?

To refrain from intermarrying made no sense. Absorption by those among whom they found themselves would have seemed inevitable, so that little trace of the Jews as a distinct people should have remained today. After all, these despised exiles have been scattered to every corner of the world for 2500 years since the destruction of Jerusalem by Nebuchadnezzar in 586 B.C. Could "tradition" be that strong without real faith in God?

Against all odds, the Jews remained an identifiable people after all those centuries. That fact is an astonishing phenomenon without parallel in history and absolutely unique to the Jews. For most of the Jews living in Europe, Church law made it impossible to intermarry without converting to Roman Catholicism. Here again the Roman Catholic Church played an infamous role. For centuries it was a capital offense under the popes for a Jew to marry a Christian, preventing intermarriage even for those who desired it.

The Bible declares that God determined to keep His chosen people separated to Himself (Exodus 33:16; Leviticus 20:26; etc.) because 8) He would bring them back into their land in the last days (Jeremiah 30:10; 31:8-12; Ezekiel 36:24,35-38; etc.) prior to the Messiah's second coming. That prophecy and promise, so long awaited, was fulfilled in the rebirth of Israel in her Promised Land. It happened at last in 1948, nearly 1900 years after the final Diaspora at the destruction of Jerusalem in A.D. 70 by the Roman armies of Titus. This restoration of a nation after 25 centuries is utterly astonishing, a phenomenon without parallel in the history of any other peoples and inexplicable by any natural means, much less by chance.

Even more remarkable, 9) God declared that in the last days before the Messiah's second coming, Jerusalem would become "a cup of trembling . . . a burdensome stone for all people" (Zechariah 12:2,3). At the time Zechariah uttered this prophecy 2500 years ago, Jerusalem lay in ruins and was surrounded by wilderness. And so it remained century after century. Zechariah's prophecy seemed to be utter madness even after Israel's rebirth in 1948. Yet today, exactly as foretold, a world of nearly 6 billion people has its eyes upon Jerusalem, fearful that the next world war, if it breaks out, will be fought over that tiny city. What an incredible fulfillment of prophecy!

## No Ordinary Explanation

Israel occupies about one-sixth of 1 percent of the land area which the Arabs possess. The Arabs have the oil, the wealth, and the worldwide influence which such seemingly inexhaustible resources command. Not only is Israel's postage-stamp piece of land scarcely discernible on a world map, but it lacks all the essentials to make it the center of worldwide concern. In defiance of all reason, however, it is the focus of world attention, precisely as prophesied.

Jerusalem is a small city of neither commercial importance nor strategic location. Yet the eyes of the world are upon it as upon no other city. Jerusalem is indeed a "burdensome stone" around the necks of all nations of the world, the most vexing and volatile problem the United Nations faces today. There is no ordinary explanation for this. What the Hebrew prophets declared thousands of years ago and what seemed utterly fantastic in their time is being fulfilled in our day. This is only part of the evidence, as we shall see, that the prophesied "last days" are upon us and that our generation will likely see the remainder of Bible prophecy fulfilled.

The prophecies outlined above (to say nothing of scores of others) have been a matter of public record on the pages of Scripture and available for careful examination for centuries. That they have been fulfilled in specific detail cannot be the result of mere chance but is in fact more than sufficient proof for the existence of the God who inspired the Bible and of that Book's authenticity and inerrancy. In view of such clear and overwhelming evidence, one can only charitably assume that no agnostic or atheist has bothered to read the biblical prophecies and check them personally against history and current events.

There are additional prophecies concerning Israel and Jerusalem which pertain to the last days and still await future fulfillment. We may be certain, on the basis of the prophecies which have already come true, that these too will surely be realized, and in the not-too-distant future. The most appalling time of utter destruction both for Jews and for the entire population of the world lies yet ahead. It is called "the time of Jacob's trouble" (Jeremiah 30:7).

With astonishing accuracy, the Bible does not single out Damascus, Cairo, London, or Paris as the center of action in the last days, but two other specific cities: Jerusalem and Rome. They are diverse, have been enemies since the days of the Caesars, and remarkably are still rivals today for spiritual supremacy. Catholic Rome claims to be the "Eternal City" and the "Holy City," titles which the Bible has given to Jerusalem. Rome also claims to be the "New Jerusalem," putting her in direct conflict with God's promises concerning the true City of David.

There have been 2000 years of tension and antagonism between Rome and Jerusalem. For nearly 46 years after Israel's rebirth in 1948 the Vatican refused to acknowledge her right to exist. That animosity has not been erased by the recent overtures which the Vatican has found it expedient to make toward Israel. Rome wants to influence the future of Jerusalem, which she still insists must be an international city over which Israel will have no more say than any other nation.

With awesome precision, the Bible identifies Jerusalem and Rome as the focal points of prophesied last-days events. Both will come in for their share of God's judgment. It requires little more than casual attention to the daily news to recognize the accuracy of that forecast. Here too, in what the Bible says about Rome and Vatican City, we have additional evidence that this book is God's Word—evidence that we will be examining in detail.

*Ye men of Israel, hear these words: Jesus of Nazareth . . . being delivered by the determinate counsel and foreknowledge of God, ye have taken, and by wicked hands have crucified and slain.*

—Peter in his first sermon
Acts 2:22,23

*Paul . . . [for] three sabbath days reasoned with them [the Jews in their synagogue] out of the [Old Testament] Scriptures . . . that Christ must needs have suffered and risen again from the dead, and that this Jesus, whom I preach unto you, is Christ [the Messiah].*

—Paul in a typical sermon
Acts 17:2,3

# 3

# A Passover Plot?

The prophecies concerning the second major theme of the Bible, the coming of the Messiah, are even more numerous and detailed than those pertaining to Israel. These prophecies have also been dealt with at some length in my previous books, so we will only summarize a few of them briefly here. Even the most anti-Christian critics who deny categorically that Jesus of Nazareth is the Savior of the world admit that many specific messianic prophecies were fulfilled in His life and crucifixion. In the attempt to explain away the significance of that fact some bizarre theories have been invented.

Typical of such attempts was a book and movie (neither very successful) some years back entitled *The Passover Plot*. Its thesis was that Jesus, knowing some of the messianic prophecies in the Old Testament, conspired with Judas to fulfill them in order to make it appear that He was the promised Messiah.

## Irreconcilable Contradiction?

Obviously it would have been ludicrous for Jesus to get Himself crucified in order to convince a small band of uneducated, inept followers that He was the Christ. In fact, neither His disciples nor any other Jew, including even John the Baptist, could believe (though the prophecies were clear, as Christ

29

explained often) that the Messiah was to be crucified. His death rather seemed proof that he was *not* the Messiah, so fulfilling the prophecies concerning His crucifixion to the letter, as He did, would not have been the way to gather a following. In fact, Christ's death in fulfillment of Scripture was in order to pay the penalty for our sins.

The prophecies concerning His death (Psalm 22:16; Isaiah 53:5,8-10,12; Zechariah 12:10; etc.) were avoided by the Jews as impenetrable mysteries because they seemed totally at odds with other prophecies declaring plainly that the Messiah would ascend David's throne and rule over a magnificent kingdom. How could the Messiah establish a kingdom and a peace that would never end (Isaiah 9:7) and yet be rejected and crucified by His own people? It seemed impossible for both to be true, so the Jewish interpreters simply ignored what didn't seem to make sense to them.

That the Jews were able to crucify Jesus was the final triumphant proof to the rabbis, and it served as the disappointing but undeniable evidence to the Jewish masses and His most devoted disciples that Jesus of Nazareth couldn't possibly have been the Messiah. The prophesied messianic kingdom had not been established, nor had He brought peace to Israel by delivering her from her enemies, so at best He could only have been a well-meaning impostor, and at worst a deliberate fraud. Such remains the argument of most Jews today.

There was, however, one way to reconcile the apparent contradiction: The Messiah had to come twice, the first time to die for man's sins, the second time to reign on the Davidic throne. But even when Jesus explained that fact ahead of time, no one could understand it. It would take His resurrection to open blind eyes.

## Beyond a Mere Man

Yes, there were a few prophecies which Jesus of Nazareth could have conspired with Judas or others to fulfill. Most prophecies, however, were beyond the control of any mere man. For example, being born in Bethlehem and of the seed of David were major requirements for the Messiah. The timing of the Messiah's birth, too, as foretold was obviously beyond the influence of any ordinary mortal. His birth had to occur before the scepter departed from Judah (Genesis 49:10), while the temple was standing (Malachi 3:1), while the genealogical records were available to prove His lineage (2 Samuel 7:12; Psalm 89; etc.), and shortly before the temple and Jerusalem were destroyed (Daniel 9:26).

There was a narrow window of time during which the Messiah had to come—and He did. As the apostle Paul, a former rabbi, so eloquently put it, "But when the *fullness of time* was come, God sent forth his Son, made of a woman [i.e. virgin born] . . ." (Galatians 4:4). It is too late for the Messiah to make His *first* appearance now. There can only be a *second* coming, as the Bible declares. Yet the Jews still await the first appearing of the one whom they will imagine is their Messiah but who will in fact be the Antichrist.

The scepter departed from Judah about A.D. 7, when the rabbis lost the right to exact the death penalty. This right was crucial to the practice of their religion because death was the penalty for certain religious offenses. When Pilate told the rabbis he wanted nothing to do with Jesus and for them to judge Him themselves, they replied, "It is not lawful for us to put any man to death" (John 18:31). The Messiah had to be born before that power was lost, and He had to be put to death afterward, for He was not to die by stoning, the Jews' manner of execution, but by *Roman crucifixion*. Amazingly, His crucifixion was prophesied centuries before that means of execution was even known: "They pierced my hands and my feet" (Psalm 22:16).

Obviously, too, the Messiah had to be born while the genealogical records still existed, or there could be no proof that He was of the seed of David. Those records were lost with the destruction of Jerusalem and the temple in A.D. 70, an event which both Daniel (in 9:26) and Christ prophesied (Matthew 24:2). Since then it has been too late for the Messiah to come, though the majority of Jews still await His first advent. Christians, on the other hand, expect the *second* coming, which also was foretold by the Hebrew prophets.

## Amazing Fulfillments

Had Jesus conspired to fulfill the prophecies, He would have had to bribe Pilate to condemn the two thieves to be crucified with Him in fulfillment of Isaiah 53:9. He also would have had to know what soldiers would be on duty that day in order to bribe them ahead of time to divide His clothes among them and gamble for His robe (Psalm 22:18), to give Him vinegar to drink mingled with gall (Psalm 69:21), and to pierce His side with a spear (Zechariah 12:10) instead of breaking His legs as was the custom, but which could not be done to the Messiah (Exodus 12:46; Psalm 34:20).

Were the rabbis also part of the plot? Was that why they paid Judas exactly 30 pieces of silver to betray Him as prophesied by Zechariah (11:12), then used the money to buy a "potter's field" for burying strangers when Judas threw it down at their feet in the temple, again as foretold (Zechariah 11:13)? Is that why they crucified Him precisely when the Passover lambs were being slain all over Israel, in fulfillment of Exodus 12:6? The "Passover plot" scenario becomes increasingly ridiculous the more one examines it.

Where did Jesus get the money to pay off the multitude that lined the road into Jerusalem and hailed Him as the Messiah when He rode in on a donkey—the last beast one would expect a triumphant king to choose—precisely as foretold in Zechariah 9:9? It was Nisan 10 (April 6), A.D. 32, the very day the prophets had declared that this amazing event would occur—483 years to the day (69 weeks of years as Daniel 9:25 foretold it) after Nehemiah, in the twentieth year of the reign of Artaxerxes Longimanus (465-425 B.C.) had received (on Nisan 1, 445 B.C.) authority to rebuild Jerusalem (Nehemiah 2:1)! The fulfillment by Jesus of these and many other messianic prophecies in minute detail cannot be explained away.

## Missing Body, Empty Tomb

Furthermore, if Jesus had successfully "plotted" to get Himself crucified on the precise date and time that was prophesied—in spite of the determination of the rabbis to the contrary (Matthew 26:5; Mark 14:2)—Jesus still had to rise from the dead. No "Passover plot," no matter how many conspirators were involved, could accomplish that! A fake "resurrection" wouldn't be sufficient basis for His followers to launch Christianity. Only if He really died and came back to life would they have the motivation and courage to proclaim His gospel in the face of persecution and martyrdom.

Roman soldiers didn't sleep on duty. Had they done so while the disciples had stolen the body, they would have been on crosses the next day, and so would the disciples for their crime in breaking the Roman seal on the tomb. And if the disciples had stolen the body and somehow managed to keep it a secret, why would they die for a lie? They were such cowards that none of them had been willing to die for what they had once believed to be the truth. Yet they almost all went to their deaths as martyrs, declaring to the very end that they were eyewitnesses of the fact that Jesus had risen from the dead. None of them tried to save his life in exchange for revealing where the body had been hidden. There is simply no way to explain the undeniably empty tomb except by resurrection.

Neither Hinduism, Buddhism, Islam, nor any of the world's other religions makes any pretense that its founder is still alive. For Christianity, however, the resurrection is the very heart of its gospel. If Christ did not rise from the dead, then the whole thing is a fraud. Nor did Jesus tell His disciples to go to far-off Siberia or South Africa to preach His resurrection where no one could challenge that claim. He told them to begin in *Jerusalem*, where, had He not risen from the dead, a short walk to the grave just outside the city wall could have proven that He was still dead. How the rabbis and Roman rulers would have loved to discredit Christianity before it could gather momentum! The surest way would have been to put the dead body of Jesus on display, but they could not. The closely guarded grave was suddenly empty!

**Enter Saul of Tarsus**

The proofs for the resurrection are numerous and irrefutable, but having dealt with them elsewhere we will mention only one—a proof often overlooked. That Christ had indeed risen from the dead is the only explanation for the fact that Saul of Tarsus, the chief enemy of Christianity, became its chief apostle. A popular young rabbi, Saul was on his way to great honors for his leadership role in pursuing this aberrant sect with arrest, imprisonment, and martyrdom. Then suddenly he became one of the despised and persecuted Christians himself, and for this he was repeatedly arrested, beaten, and imprisoned. On one occasion he was even stoned and left for dead. Finally he was beheaded. This stunning turnabout made no sense . . . unless.

Why voluntarily trade popularity for suffering and eventual martyrdom? Paul explained that he had met the resurrected Christ, and that the One who had died for the sins of the world was alive and had revealed Himself to him. That testimony, however, was not sufficient in itself to prove that Christ was indeed alive. Something more was needed.

No one could doubt Paul's sincerity. That was demonstrated by his willingness to suffer and even die for Christ. A sincere belief, however, that Christ was alive was not sufficient proof. It was possible that Paul had hallucinated and simply imagined that Christ had appeared to him and spoken to him and was indeed alive.

The Roman governors Felix and Festus, as well as King Agrippa, heard Paul's account of this supernatural encounter and were convinced that he was sincere but deluded (Acts 24–26). That explanation, however, did not fit the facts. Paul's sudden intimacy with Christ's teachings provided proof of the resurrection that could not be explained away by any means.

## Conclusive Evidence

Paul, who had not known Christ before He was crucified, was suddenly the chief authority on what Christ had privately taught His inner circle of disciples. He had to have met Him! The apostles, who had been personally instructed by Christ for several years, had to acknowledge that their onetime enemy, Paul, without consulting any of them, knew all that Christ had taught them, and indeed had even deeper insights than they. When Paul rebuked Peter for going astray, the latter submitted to the correction (Galatians 2:11-14).

"I have *received of the Lord* that which also I delivered unto you" (1 Corinthians 11:23) was how Paul began his explanation to the Corinthian church of what happened at the Last Supper and what Christ had taught His disciples on that occasion. Yet Paul had not been present, nor had he consulted any of those who had been there. "I conferred not with flesh and blood; neither went I up to Jerusalem to them which were apostles before me, but I went into Arabia" (Galatians 1:16,17) was Paul's sworn testimony. That he was suddenly the chief apostle and authority on what Christ had taught could be explained in no other way than that he had been instructed by the resurrected Christ, exactly as he claimed.

Without consulting any of those who had been Christ's disciples during His earthly ministry, Paul had become the chief authority on Christian doctrine, as all the church had to acknowledge. He wrote most of the New Testament epistles. "I certify you, brethren, that the gospel which was preached of me is not of man. For I neither received it of man neither was I taught it but by the revelation of Jesus Christ" (Galatians 1:11,12) was Paul's solemn testimony. There is no other explanation than that Christ had indeed been resurrected and had personally instructed Paul.

## Reason for Confidence

The fulfillment of the prophecies mentioned above as well as scores of others in the life, death, and resurrection of Christ prove beyond any possible doubt that He is the Messiah of Israel, the Savior of the world. No one can examine the facts and remain an honest doubter. Those who refuse to believe in the face of such overwhelming evidence are without excuse.

We have taken these few pages to establish the validity of biblical prophecy for a purpose. Having seen that what the Bible prophesied concerning past events was fulfilled with 100 percent accuracy, we have valid reason for believing that what it tells us concerning the future will likewise be fulfilled.

With confidence, then, we can now consider the insight into the future given to us in Revelation 17 and 18 and address the important question of the identity of the woman riding the beast. First of all, our attention must be directed to the beast itself.

**A WOMAN**

*Four great beasts came up from the sea. . . . The first was like a lion . . . a second like a bear . . . and, lo another, like a leopard . . . and behold a fourth beast, dreadful and terrible . . . it had ten horns . . . and the ten horns out of this kingdom are ten kings. . . .*

—Daniel 7:3-7,24

**RIDES THE BEAST**

# 4

# An Unfolding Revelation

John's vision in Revelation 17 of the woman riding the beast is not the first time that this ominous creature has been seen. It is in fact the culmination of a series of visions which began 600 years earlier. The first vision was the dream King Nebuchadnezzar had in which he saw an image with "head . . . of fine gold, his breast and his arms of silver, his belly and his thighs of brass, his legs of iron, his feet part of iron and part of clay" (Daniel 2:32,33).

The interpretation given to Daniel by God revealed that the image with its four parts of different metals depicted four world empires: Babylonian, Medo-Persian, Grecian, and Roman. The Babylonian empire existed at the time. That it was succeeded by the other three and in that order is a matter of history.

Why are only four empires seen? What of the many others which history records and which have occupied territories at least as great as any of these four? The Bible ignores them all. Why? Time has passed them by. They will not rise again. Only Rome will be revived, its "deadly wound" healed (Revelation 13:3).

For centuries the seat of world power was Egypt. There were great dynasties in China. There was Genghis Khan's far-ranging empire, and the vast Mayan and Aztec kingdoms of Central and South America. At one time the Arabs controlled most of North Africa, the Middle East, and much of Europe. None of these empires, however, will rise again. Only Rome will recover its greatness. As she controlled the ancient world, so will she be the headquarters for the new world order, the dream of the United Nations.

The United States has been the dominant industrial and military world force for the last 50 years. That dominance, however, is waning and is doomed. The prophecies are clear: The *Roman Empire* will be revived, with Antichrist's seat in Western Europe and the world religion's headquarters in Rome, as we shall see. So the Bible has said for the past 1900 years in the New Testament and for centuries more in the Old. The United States is not mentioned.

## An Empire Divided

The two legs in the image foretold the division of the fourth empire, the Roman, into East and West, and so it occurred. In A.D. 330 Constantine established Constantinople (today's Istanbul) as his new imperial capital, leaving the Bishop of Rome in charge in the West and setting the stage for the later political and religious division of the empire. The final break came religiously in 1054 when the Orthodox Church in the East broke off from the Roman Catholic Church in the West and Pope Leo IX excommunicated Michael Cerularius, Patriarch of Constantinople. That division between Roman Catholicism and Eastern Orthodoxy remains to this day and is at the root of the current bloodshed in the Croatia-Sarajevo-Bosnia-Herzegovina region of Yugoslavia, as we shall document.

Politically the Roman Empire was several times revived in the West—for example, in A.D. 800 under Charlemagne. The Eastern and Western kingdoms, however, were never united again. The full Roman Empire passed away altogether as a political entity, but religiously it grew larger, to extend around the entire world. Today the Roman Catholic Church has some 980 million members worldwide. Eastern Orthodoxy has something less than half as many. The breach between it and Roman Catholicism will be healed under Antichrist.

Protestants of various denominations comprise the remainder of what has become known as Christendom, a total of about 1.7

billion persons, nearly 30 percent of the world's population today. According to Revelation 13:8, "All that dwell upon the earth shall worship him [the beast, or Antichrist]. . . ." This indicates that not only Roman Catholicism and Eastern Orthodoxy will be united, but that Protestants will join together with them, along with all of the world's religions, including even the Muslims, to form one new world religion. It will involve emperor worship, as in the days of the Caesars, with the death penalty for those who refuse to comply (Revelation 13:14,15).

This revival of Rome's religion will undoubtedly be a blend of Christianity and paganism, as occurred under Constantine and continued thereafter. That perverted and paganized form of Christianity eventually became known as Roman Catholicism. Claiming to be infallible and unchangeable (*semper eadem*, "always the same"), the Roman Catholic Church stands poised today to become the vehicle for the final ecumenical union of all religions.

## The Importance of Prophecy

The ten toes on King Nebuchadnezzar's image represented ten future kings, concerning whom Daniel 2:44 declares in the most straightforward and unmistakable language: "And *in the days of these kings* shall the God of heaven set up a kingdom which shall never be destroyed. . . ." Inasmuch as ten kings have never ruled the Roman Empire, that simple statement tells us that it *must be revived under ten heads*, to be ruled of course by Antichrist.

That one verse of Scripture told Christ's disciples (and John the Baptist and the rabbis as well) that it was not the time for Christ to take His father David's throne. The reason was obvious: Ten kings were not ruling the Roman Empire at that time. Failure to understand this prophecy caused those in Christ's day to become disillusioned when He didn't immediately set up His earthly kingdom. Here again we see the importance of an accurate understanding of prophecy.

In his vision, Nebuchadnezzar saw a "stone . . . cut out without hands." It "smote the image upon his feet" and smashed it to a powder that was blown away in the wind. "And the stone that smote the image became a great mountain, and filled the whole earth" (Daniel 2:34,35). The interpretation is clear: The true church will not gradually take over the world, but God's kingdom will be established suddenly by a cataclysmic intervention from heaven. Christ will return to destroy Antichrist and his revived Roman Empire, and He will then set up His millennial kingdom to rule the world from Jerusalem on David's ancient throne as reinstituted by God Himself.

That interpretation is confirmed by other Scriptures, notably 2 Thessalonians 2:8, which clearly says that Christ will destroy Antichrist at His *"coming"*: "Then shall that wicked [one] be revealed, whom the Lord shall consume with the spirit [breath] of his mouth, and shall *destroy with the brightness of his coming*. . . ." Thus the second coming (as distinct from the rapture of Christians) will not occur until Antichrist has been revealed and has established his one-world government. Only then will Christ return, in the midst of Armageddon (with the believers He has previously raptured to heaven—Zechariah 14:5; Jude 14) to rescue Israel from the armies of Antichrist which are about to destroy her, to execute judgment upon the earth, and to establish His messianic kingdom by ruling the world from David's throne in Jerusalem. (See Zechariah 12–14.)

## History Written in Advance

Some time after Nebuchadnezzar had his dream, Daniel was given a vision of his own as the next stage in the unfolding revelation from God concerning Antichrist's coming world kingdom. In it Daniel saw the same four world empires once again, this time depicted as ferocious beasts. The fourth beast, representing the Roman Empire, had ten horns, which signified, like the ten toes on the image, ten kings or regional rulers who would arise in the future (Daniel 7:24).

Daniel's vision included remarkable details concerning the Medo-Persian and Grecian empires, so astonishingly accurate that skeptics have sought desperately but without success to show that the book of Daniel was written after the fact. Otherwise it would have to be admitted that valid prophecies had been made. Of course, the Bible is filled with valid prophecies given centuries before their fulfillment. Unquestionably, the prophecies we mentioned briefly in the previous chapter concerning Israel and the Messiah were all written many centuries before their remarkable fulfillment.

As for Daniel, he clearly foretold the division of Alexander the Great's Grecian empire into four parts (Daniel 8:20-22; 11:4). The next 16 verses give amazing details of the wars of Ptolemy (the Grecian general who took possession of Egypt after Alexander's death) and the wars of his successors against the Seleucids of Syria. That prophecy climaxed with details concerning Seleucid ruler Antiochus Epiphanes (Daniel 11:21-36), a type or foreshadowing of Antichrist. It is this history, declared in advance, that the critics have desperately tried to prove was written after it already occurred.

That the book of Daniel was in fact written during the Babylonian captivity, long before these events took place, has been thoroughly authenticated. Moreover, Daniel 9:25 specifies the very day the Messiah would ride into Jerusalem on the colt of an ass and be hailed as the promised One. Even the most skeptical critics must acknowledge that Daniel was written long before that event.

Between the writing of the Old and New Testaments there were four centuries of silence before God spoke again through His prophets. And not until we come to Revelation 12:3 do we see Daniel's fourth beast again, this time without any reference to the other three, which will be seen no more. Furthermore, from this point onward the fourth beast is seen only in its future revived form.

## Enter the Dragon

As the prophecy unfolds, Daniel's fourth beast appears to John as "a great red dragon, having seven heads and ten horns and seven crowns upon his heads" (Revelation 12:3). This is Satan, for a few verses later we are shown a future "war in heaven: [Archangel] Michael and his angels fought against the dragon. . . . And the great dragon was cast out, that old serpent, called the devil and Satan, which deceiveth the whole world" (verses 7, 9).

The interpretation is clear: The revived fourth world empire under Antichrist will be so utterly evil that it is seen as Satan himself. What horror lies ahead for this world after Christ has taken His own to His Father's house in the rapture!

The same "fourth beast" is seen again in chapter 13:1 rising "up out of the sea," as all four beasts did in Daniel 7:3. Here again it has the telltale "seven heads and ten horns," but now with "ten crowns, and upon his heads the name of blasphemy." The beast is described in the next verse as "like a leopard . . . a bear, and . . . a lion. . . ." So although the other three beasts no longer appear, we are not allowed to forget the continuity that exists between the revived Roman Empire and the three world empires which preceded it all the way back to Babylon. Remember, the beasts representing these three previous world empires were described as like a leopard, a lion, and a bear (Daniel 7:4-6).

In Revelation 13, the fourth beast clearly depicts both the revived Roman Empire and Antichrist, whom "all that dwell upon the earth shall worship" (verse 8). In this remarkable vision of the future, the world also "worshiped the dragon which gave power unto the beast" (verse 4). So Satan is again shown to be the power behind Antichrist and his kingdom: "The dragon [Satan] gave him [Antichrist] his power and his seat and great authority" (verse 2).

During His temptation in the wilderness, Christ was shown by Satan "all the kingdoms of the world and the glory of them" (Matthew 4:8). The devil then offered it all to Christ, saying: "All these things will I give thee if thou wilt fall down and worship me" (verse 9). The love of the world and the lust for power ultimately lead to partnership with Satan and his worship. Of course, Christ refused Satan. Tragically, a persecution-weary church would fall for the same offer when it would later be made through Constantine.

Christ did not dispute Satan's claim to ownership of the world: "For that is delivered unto me, and to whomsoever I will I give it" (Luke 4:6). As John reminds us, "The whole world lieth in [the hands of] wickedness [i.e., the wicked one, Satan—see verse 18 and 2 Thessalonians 2:8]" (1 John 5:19). It is Satan, permitted by God for His own purposes, who delivers to Antichrist the world which Christ refused.

## Coming World Religion

An image will be made of the beast, and all who do not bow

down and worship it, and through it the Antichrist as God, will be slain (Revelation 13:15). Such was the practice in the ancient Roman Empire. We are thus being told that the religion of Rome with its emperor worship will be revived as well. Religion must, in fact, not only be *involved* in Antichrist's new world government, but it must be *preeminent*, for Satan, who controls both Antichrist and the revived Roman Empire, is "the god of this world" (2 Corinthians 4:4) and desires its worship with a passion. The woman who rides the beast in chapter 17 undoubtedly represents that world religion, as we shall see.

Religion was always the dominant element in ancient world empires, including the four depicted by Nebuchadnezzar's image and Daniel's four beasts. Priests, soothsayers, and sorcerers were the closest advisers to rulers for thousands of years, and in most instances were the real power behind the throne, manipulating sovereigns by their "magic" and devious counsel. Science itself had its roots in occultism, beginning in astrology and alchemy. Materialism, skepticism, and atheism are of fairly recent origins and will be submerged in the tidal wave of renewed interest in "spirituality," which is already gathering momentum exactly as Jesus foretold for the last days (Matthew 24:4,5,11,24).

Atheism is not Satan's major weapon in his campaign to deceive mankind into following him. He himself is not an atheist, for his great ambition, "I will be like the Most High [i.e., God]" (Isaiah 14:14), itself acknowledges God's existence. Satan wants to be worshiped as God, but since he is a nonphysical being without a body of his own he will have to be satisfied in receiving this worship through the man who represents him, the Antichrist.

As "the god of this world," Satan's weapon is *false religions and the deceitful promises they present,* which turn aside those who believe them from knowing God's truth. The fact that religion will play a dominant role in the revived Roman Empire, as in ancient times, is clearly portrayed by the fact that the woman, who represents the new world religion, has mounted the beast and is holding the reins.

## Satanic Resurrection?

In the further unfolding of the revelation of the fourth beast, John saw "one of his heads as it were wounded to death; and his deadly wound was healed, and all the world wondered after the beast" (Revelation 13:3). To many interpreters this vision means that the Antichrist himself will be killed and raised to life again. Others believe that an Antichrist figure from the past, such as Hitler or Nero, will come back to life and rule the new world order. On the contrary, neither a past evil ruler nor the future Antichrist will come back from the grave because Satan does not have power to create life. (This does not eliminate the possibility that the world may be deceived into believing that a resurrection has taken place. However, the language in Revelation 13:3 does not encourage that idea.)

That "one of his heads" received a deadly wound would not indicate that the *entire beast* was dead but rather that he was mortally wounded *in one aspect of his being*. Although the heads are said to represent kings, it could not be a literal king who was killed and raised to life for the reasons already given. The beast and its heads represent several things at once: kings, kingdoms, Satan, the Antichrist, and the revived Roman Empire. The latter has within it the elements of death and apparent resurrection. The Roman Empire did indeed "die," though not completely, inasmuch as the fragments remained along with the perpetual hope of ultimate resurrection. When that "resurrection" does take place under Antichrist it will be as though an empire—not a person—came back from the dead.

That God intends to establish His own kingdom on earth and that the revived Roman Empire stands in its way and must be destroyed for God's kingdom to appear is clear as well. This was shown at the very beginning of this progressive revelation in the stone smashing the image and filling the earth. It is equally clear that Antichrist is Satan's counterfeit of Christ and that the revived Roman Empire is a counterfeit of the kingdom of God on earth.

## The First and Future Antichrist

The prefix "anti" comes from the Greek language and has

two meanings: 1) opposed to, and 2) in the place of or a substitute for.[1] Antichrist will embody both of these meanings. He will indeed oppose Christ, but in the most diabolically clever way it could be done: by pretending to be Christ and thus perverting "Christianity" from within. Indeed, Antichrist will "sit in the temple of God showing himself that he is God" (2 Thessalonians 2:4).

If Antichrist pretends to be Christ and is worshiped by the world (Revelation 13:8), then his followers are of course "Christians." Not Communism but Christianity will take over the world, and not real Christianity but an Antichrist counterfeit thereof. Thus the great apostasy precedes the revelation of Antichrist (2 Thessalonians 2:3). Part of the apostasy is the ecumenical movement, which is literally setting the stage for a union between all religions and even influences evangelicals as well. An Antichrist "Christianity" must be created which embraces all religions and which all religions will embrace— precisely what is occurring today with astonishing speed. We have documented this development in other books, such as *Global Peace and the Rise of Antichrist*, and will have much more to say about it later.

The Latin equivalent of the Greek "anti" is "vicarius," from which comes "vicar." Thus "vicar of Christ" literally means Antichrist. Although the Roman Catholic popes have called themselves vicar of Christ for centuries, they were not the first to do so, but inherited that title from Constantine (see below). His future counterpart, the coming world ruler over the revived Roman Empire, will be *the* Antichrist.

As already noted, in the ancient Roman Empire the Emperor was worshiped as God. As such he was the leader of the pagan priesthood and of the official, state-sponsored pagan religion of the empire. An image was made to the Caesars, before which the citizens were required to bow in worship. Those who refused to acknowledge the emperor as God were killed. And so it will be when the Roman Empire is revived under Antichrist. This fact is clearly presented in the extensive vision Christ gave to John:

> And he . . . causeth the earth and them which dwell
> therein to worship the first beast . . . saying to them that

dwell on the earth that they should make an image to the
beast . . . and cause that as many as would not worship
the image of the beast should be killed (Revelation
13:12-15).

## The Paganization of Christianity

When Emperor Constantine supposedly became a Christian
in A.D. 313 (really a clever political maneuver), he gave freedom to Christians as well as official status alongside paganism
to the Christian church. Since the church was now a recognized religious body in the empire, Constantine, as emperor,
had to be acknowledged as its de facto head. As such, he
convened the first ecumenical council, the Council of Nicea, in
A.D. 325, set its agenda, gave the opening speech, and presided
over it as Charlemagne would over the Council of Chalon 500
years later, Interested not in the truth of the gospel but in
unifying the empire, Constantine was the first ecumenist and
introduced that error into the persecution-wearied church.

While heading the Christian church, Constantine continued
to head the pagan priesthood, to officiate at pagan celebra-
tions, and to endow pagan temples even after he began to build
Christian churches. As head of the pagan priesthood he was
the *Pontifex Maximus* and needed a similar title as head of the
Christian church. The Christians honored him as "Bishop of
Bishops," while Constantine called himself *Vicarius Christi*,
Vicar of Christ. He meant that he was "another Christ" acting
in the place of Christ. When translated into Greek, however,
as we have seen, *Vicarius Christi* literally means *Antichrist*.
Constantine was the prototype of the Antichrist prophesied in
Scripture and who is yet to come.

In the Middle Ages, the bishops of Rome began to claim that
they were the sole representatives of Christ upon earth.
Demanding that the entire church worldwide must be subject
to their rule, they forbade any other bishops to be called
"papa" or pope and took to themselves the three titles of
Constantine—Pontifex Maximus, Vicar of Christ, and Bishop
of Bishops—which they retain to this day.

As the popes' claims to absolute power over kingdoms,

people, and property were realized, great corruption entered the Roman Catholic Church. The Reformers and their creeds were unanimous in identifying each pope as the Antichrist. Scripture, however, does not support that claim. The Antichrist is a *unique* individual without predecessors or successors. He will be the new "Constantine," the ruler of the revived worldwide Roman Empire.

## A Staggering New Insight

The final revelation of the fourth beast comes in the vision which God gave John as recorded in Revelation 17. This time, in a staggering new insight, a *woman* sits astride this horrible creature! That this is the same beast which Daniel saw and which is presented to us in chapters 12 and 13 of Revelation is quite clear, for it has the now-familiar "seven heads and ten horns" (verse 3). One other identifying feature is recorded: The beast is "full of names of blasphemy," an obvious elaboration upon what was seen in chapter 13, "and upon his heads the name of blasphemy."

There is a remarkable change of perspective this last time the beast is seen. The woman riding it rather than the beast itself is now the focus of attention. The description of the beast is brief, only sufficient to let us know that it is the same one we have seen before. No further insights into the nature or meaning of this horrible creature are given. A new figure has taken center stage, and two entire chapters of Revelation, 17 and 18, are devoted to detailed discussion of the woman—far more space than has been given to the beast itself in all its prior appearances.

John has never indicated in any of the three times he has seen the frightening creature that he was shocked or even amazed by it. But now, at last, he expresses great astonishment—not for the beast, however, but for the *woman* on its back. It is the sight of *her* that staggers John.

How did this woman mount such a fearsome creature? Why should it allow her to sit on its back, holding the reins and controlling it? Obviously, she will play a key role in the revival of the Roman Empire, the reign of Antichrist, and future world events leading to Christ's second coming.

What will that role be? When will it be revealed? Who is this woman? To answer such questions and more is the purpose of this book.

*Upon her forehead was a name written, MYS-TERY, BABYLON THE GREAT....*

—Revelation 17:5

*Thus, as the moon receives its light from the sun ... so the royal power [state] derives from the Pontifical authority the splendor of its dignity.... The state of the world ... will be restored by our diligence and care ... for the pontifical authority and the royal power ... fully suffice for this purpose....*

—Pope Innocent III (1198-1216)

# 5

# Mystery, Babylon

Why "mystery"? That Babylon, an ancient city whose ruins have been covered by the desert sands for at least 2300 years, should be mentioned so prominently in prophecies pertaining to the last days does indeed seem an enigma. It is popularly taught that the woman represents ancient Babylon revived. The fact that Iraq's sadistic ruler, Saddam Hussein, began its reconstruction some years ago is therefore seen as contributing to the fulfillment of this vision.

Ancient Babylon, however, even if it again becomes an inhabited and functioning city, could not possibly be the Babylon to which the writing on the woman's forehead refers. Saddam's rebuilt Babylon simply doesn't meet the criteria John sets forth. Those criteria, which we will be examining in detail, establish the woman's identity—and, as we shall see, she is not ancient Babylon.

Saddam imagines himself to be a modern Nebuchadnezzar, perhaps even the reincarnation of that emperor of ancient Babylon. What Saddam admires most about Nebuchadnezzar is that he destroyed Jerusalem and killed or carried away captive Israel's inhabitants into Babylon, leaving the land of Israel desolate. As the new Nebuchadnezzar, he dreams of wreaking the same destruction upon today's Israelis, whom he sees as his chief enemies. Of course, Babylon itself was then conquered by the Medes and Persians. For that depredation

Saddam views Iran (the successor of ancient Persia) as his other great enemy and fought an eight-year war against her.

Saddam has proudly imprinted his name on every brick being used in the reconstruction of ancient Babylon. As much hated as feared by his own people, one day Saddam will be deposed, as eventually happens to all tyrants. It would not be surprising if the Iraqis, in order to erase the last vestige of Saddam's loathsome memory, thereafter bulldozed the proud structures he has erected at the site of ancient Babylon. Whether that happens or not, there is no way that this city, rebuilt after lying in ruins for more than 2000 years, could be mistaken for the Babylon which is the major subject of Revelation chapters 17 and 18.

## The Babel Connection

There is, of course, a connection to ancient Babylon. The name on the woman's forehead establishes that fact. What could that name mean in the world of the "last days" just prior to the second coming of Christ? Obviously it must refer to a dominant feature common to all four world empires—a major element of the first empire, Babylon, which is still dominant in the fourth empire, Rome.

A paramount feature common to all was the unity between throne and altar, between prince and priest. "Separation of church and state" was as yet unheard of; in fact, the opposite was true. The pagan priests—astrologers, magicians, sorcerers, soothsayers—were the emperor's close advisers and often the hidden influence controlling the empire. Thus a principle characteristic of this woman, who is both a city and a spiritual entity, will be her adulterous relationships with secular governments.

The unity of church and state persisted from the days of Babylon until beyond the ascendancy of Rome, the fourth world empire in Daniel's vision. As we have seen, Roman emperors, like other ancient rulers, headed the pagan priesthood and were worshiped as gods. Inasmuch as religion was the dominant factor in every empire, we do well to take a closer look at the religion of Babylon.

## Tower to Heaven

Nebuchadnezzar's Babylon was built around the ruins of the Tower of Babel, which was erected shortly after the flood by the descendants of Noah under the leadership of Nimrod (Genesis 10:8-10; Micah 5:6). Its original purpose was clearly stated by its builders: "Let us build us a *city* and a *tower* whose top may reach unto heaven; and let us make us a name, lest we be scattered abroad upon the face of the whole earth" (Genesis 11:4).

The *city* was a political/civil union of earth's inhabitants at that time. The *tower* was clearly a religious enterprise, the means of reaching heaven. Babel thus represents the unity of state and church, involving the entire world in the attempt to elevate man to God's level. That this would be accomplished through a tower built by human genius and energy obviously represents man's religion of self-effort. Inasmuch as the entire world was united in this effort, we have the first example of world government and world religion joined as one. As man began in this unity, so he must end in it as well; such is the clear message on the woman's forehead.

The tower was the obsession of the city's inhabitants, the purpose of life that both united and enslaved. Thus religion dominated the partnership of church and state. That such will be the case in the new world order of Antichrist, at least for a time, is clearly depicted by the fact that the woman rides the beast.

Babel's tower stood in stark contrast to the way of salvation which God had consistently declared from Abel onward. The rebellion of Adam and Eve in the Garden had separated man from God by sin. No reconciliation to God and no entrance into heaven was possible apart from the full payment of sin's penalty. For man, a finite creature, payment of the infinite penalty demanded by God's infinite justice was impossible. One day, in mercy and grace, God Himself would come as a sinless, perfect man to die for the sins of the world in payment of the full penalty demanded by His own justice. He would be "the Lamb of God" (John 1:29,36), the only acceptable sacrifice. In anticipation of the coming Messiah, animals were to be sacrificed as types of that Holy One who would "put away sin by the sacrifice of himself" (Hebrews 9:26).

The only interim approach to God that He approved had been stated clearly (Exodus 20:24-26). Animal sacrifices were to be offered upon an altar of earth. If the ground was too rocky to scrape sufficient earth together, the altar could be made of stones heaped up, but *not carved or fashioned in any way by tools*. Nor was it to be elevated so that one approached the altar by steps.

No human effort could play any part in man's salvation. It must be a gift from God, unmerited and unearned. Human pride, however, has always resisted God's grace. We see the clear violation of God's Word continuing today in the ornate cathedrals and gilded, elevated altars of both Protestants and Catholics as well as in the rituals and good works which man foolishly imagines will help to make him acceptable to God. It all began with Babel.

## A Pattern Followed by Rome

The city and tower of Babel set the pattern of the unholy alliance between civil government and a religion of self-effort and ritual which continued for thousands of years and was exemplified both in pagan Rome and in "Christian" Rome following Constantine's "conversion." The "separation of church and state" is a concept of recent origin, largely since the Protestant Reformation, and one which the Roman Catholic Church, as the religious continuation of the Roman Empire, has consistently and even viciously opposed. Dr. Brownson, highly regarded nineteenth-century Catholic journalist, expressed Catholicism's position in the *Brownson Quarterly* journal:

> No civil government, be it a monarchy, an aristocracy, a democracy . . . can be a wise, just, efficient, or durable government, governing for the good of the community, without the Catholic Church; and without the papacy there is and can be no Catholic Church.[1]

The Vatican has consistently fought every democratic advance from absolute monarchies toward government by the people, beginning with England's Magna Carta (June 15, 1215), "the mother of European Constitutions." That vital document was denounced immediately by Pope Innocent III (1198-1216), who "pronounced it null and void and excommunicated the English barons who obtained it"[2] and absolved the king of his oath to the barons.[3] Encouraged by the pope, King John brought in foreign mercenaries to fight the barons, bringing great destruction upon the country. Subsequent popes did all in their power to help John's successor, Henry III, overturn the Magna Carta, impoverishing the country with papal taxes (salaries to the numerous imported Italian priests were three times the crown's annual revenue). Nevertheless, the barons finally prevailed.

Pope Leo XII reproved Louis XVIII for granting the "liberal" French Constitution, while Pope Gregory XVI denounced the Belgian Constitution of 1832. His outrageous encyclical, *Mirari vos*, of August 15, 1832 (which was later confirmed by Pope Pius IX in his 1864 *Syllabus Errorum*), condemned freedom of conscience as "an insane folly" and freedom of the press as "a pestiferous error, which cannot be sufficiently detested."[4] He reasserted the right of the Church to use force and like countless popes before him demanded that civil authorities promptly imprison any non-Catholics who dared to preach and practice their faith. One eminent historian of the nineteenth century, commenting upon the Vatican's denunciation of the Bavarian and Austrian constitutions, paraphrased its attitude thus:

> Our absolutist system, supported by the Inquisition, the strictest censorship, the suppression of all literature, the privileged exemption of the clergy, and arbitrary power of bishops, cannot endure any other than absolutist governments...[5]

The history of Latin America has fully demonstrated the accuracy of that appraisal. In Catholic countries the popes' hatred of freedom and their partnership with oppressive regimes which they often succeeded in manipulating to their own ends is a matter of historical record. Whatever her true motives, history bears full witness to the fact that whenever she has been able to do so, the Roman Catholic Church has suppressed and openly condemned such basic human rights as freedom of the press, speech, religion, and even conscience.

Prior to the revolution led by Benito Juarez in 1861, Roman Catholicism had dominated the lives of the Mexican people and controlled the government for 350 years. It was the state religion and no other was allowed. As one author has stated after an exhaustive investigation of the records:

> The oppression by Spain and the oppression by the Church of Rome were so intermeshed as to be indistinguishable by the people. The [Roman Catholic] hierarchy supported the Spanish regime and excommunicated, through its New World Inquisition, anyone resisting the power of the state. . . . The government in turn enforced Church laws and, as the "secular arm," functioned as disciplinarian and even as executioner for the Church.[6]

## Consequences of a State Religion

After Napoleon III's French army defeated Juarez and installed Maximilian as Emperor of Mexico, the latter saw that there could be no return to the old totalitarian ways. Pope Pius IX was outraged and wrote indignantly to Maximilian demanding that "the Catholic religion must, above all things, continue to be the glory and the mainstay of the Mexican nation, to the exclusion of every other dissenting worship," that "instruction, whether public or private, should be directed and watched over by the [Roman Catholic] ecclesiastical authority," and that the Church must not be "subject to the arbitrary rule of the civil government."[7]

The poverty and instability that has plagued Latin America resulted from the union between church and state and the power over government which Rome, having enjoyed in Europe for centuries, brought to the new world in the name of Christ. The Roman clergy were like little gods lording it over the natives, who became their servants. The revolutions in Latin American countries have been in large measure created by the contrast between the poverty of the people and the wealth of the Roman Catholic Church and the evil dictatorships it supported. Liberation Theology was spawned in Latin

America by radical Catholic priests and nuns whose aroused consciences could no longer justify the oppression of the masses by both Church and state.

Scores of other examples could be given but must be deferred until later. The point is that the roots of the unholy alliance between church and state, with the church in dominance, go back to Babel. Nimrod founded the first world empire; church and state were one. Such is the ideal empire which Roman Catholicism has always striven with all its might to establish and maintain whenever possible. As *The Catholic World* stated at the time of Vatican I:

> While the state has some rights, she has them only in virtue and by permission of the superior authority... [of] the Church....[8]

The antipathy of Roman Catholicism to basic human freedoms later created unholy alliances with the totalitarian governments of Hitler and Mussolini, who were praised by the pope and other Church leaders as men chosen by God. Catholics were forbidden to oppose Mussolini and were urged to support him. The Church virtually put the Fascist dictator in office (as it would Hitler a few years later). In exchange, Mussolini (in the 1929 Concordat with the Vatican) made Roman Catholicism once again the official state religion, and any criticism of it was made a penal offense. The Church was granted other favors, including a vast sum in cash and bonds.

### Roots of a Modern Delusion

Satan's promise to Eve that she could become one of the gods became the foundation of pagan religion worldwide. To achieve that goal man would have to assert himself and labor mightily. Thus was born the religion of self-effort. In fact, works instead of grace has always been and still is religion, of which Roman Catholicism is a prime example. The rising Tower of Babel seemed to give credence to the grandiose delusion that man could reach heaven by his own efforts. Nimrod was very likely the first emperor to be deified, and thus was a forerunner of Antichrist.

Babel (and the city of Babylon later constructed around her ruins) was the cradle of the belief in a "higher destiny" for all mankind. Later that dream would be limited to special races, such as the Aryans, a claim which Hitler's Nazism would pursue to the destruction of 6 million Jews. Echoing the serpent's lie, Hitler would say, "Man is becoming God. . . . We need free men who feel and know that God is in themselves." The Jews, however, were not men at all in Hitler's estimation, but *Untermenschen* (subhumans), whom he determined to exterminate for the good of the Aryan race.

Hitler's theory of the "purity of blood," which he sought to maintain through extermination of the Jews (unopposed by the Vatican), had its roots in ancient occultism involving a mythical Nordic Garden of Eden in the far North known as Hyperborea. There an Aryan race of god-men had allegedly been spawned by gods visiting earth. Nietzsche, whose writings heavily influenced Hitler, began his key work, *Anti-Christ*, with the sentence, "Let us see ourselves for what we are. We are Hyperboreans [gods] all." It was the lie of the serpent from the Garden of Eden once again.

Pulitzer-Prize-winning historian Peter Viereck finds the roots of the Nazi dream of a master race of god-men ruling the world not only in Hegel and Nietzsche but in Wagner and a host of romantic writers who all echoed the serpent's lie to Eve. The following excerpt is from the 1940 conclusion of Viereck's remarkable book *Meta-Politics: The Roots of the Nazi Mind*— an ending which the original publisher refused to include as being too extreme, but which hindsight now reveals was amazingly accurate:

> *Mein Kampf* was a best-seller long before the German people, voting uncoerced in the free Reichstag election of September 1930, increased the Nazi seats from 12 to 107 and made them the biggest party in Germany. By then, Hitler had said in *Mein Kampf* (to pick a typical threat at random): "If at the start [of World War I] we had *held under poison* twelve or fifteen thousand of these Hebrew subverters of our people . . . then the sacrifice of a million Germans at the front would not have been in vain. . . . The timely elimination of 12,000 bums. . . ."

The German enigma is: just what kind of behavior could those millions of pro-Hitler voters, from 1930 on, expect of the monster-mentality that composes such "held under" threats? . . . his book is no classified secret document . . . millions of Germans own it . . . a few must have browsed in it. These few must have included some of the cheering public and also some influential dignitaries with access to press, radio, and other means of warning the public. . . .

Some day the same Germans, now cheering Hitler's strut into Paris, will say . . . "We did not know what went on . . ." and when that day of know-nothing comes, there will be laughter in hell.[9]

## Adolf Hitler, Chosen by God?

Surely *Mein Kampf* must also have been known to many of the 30 million Roman Catholics in Germany as well as to the leaders of the Roman Catholic Church both there and in Rome. Yet the Church hierarchy praised Hitler, sometimes in the most extravagant terms. Pope Pius XI told Vice-Chancellor Fritz von Papen, himself a leading Catholic, "how pleased he was that the German Government now had at its head a man uncompromisingly opposed to Communism. . . ."[10] No word of reproof against the evil that Hitler had loosed upon Germany.

Bishop Berning published a book stressing the link between Catholicism and patriotism and sent a copy to Hitler "as a token of my devotion." Monsignor Hartz praised Hitler for having saved Germany from "the poison of Liberalism . . . [and] the pest of Communism." Catholic publicist Franz Taeschner praised "the Fuehrer, gifted with genius" and declared that he had "been sent by providence in order to achieve the fulfillment of Catholic social ideas."[11]

Most German Catholics were in a state of euphoria after the 1933 concordat between Hitler and the Vatican was signed. Catholic young men were ordered "to raise their right arm in salute, and to display the swastika flag. . . . The Catholic Youth organization, *Neudeutsche Jugend* . . . called for the full and close cooperation between the totalitarian state and the

totalitarian Church." The German bishops together pledged
their solidarity with National Socialism. Addressing a gathering of Catholic youth in the Cathedral of Trier, Bishop
Bornewasser declared, "With raised heads and firm step we
have entered the new Reich and we are prepared to serve it
with all the might of our body and soul."[12]

Bishop Vogt of Aachen in a congratulatory telegram promised Hitler that "diocese and Bishop will gladly participate in
the building of the new Reich." Cardinal Faulhaber, in a
handwritten note to Hitler, expressed the wish "coming from
the bottom of our heart: May God preserve the Reich Chancellor for our people." A picture appeared in a German-American
paper showing Vicar General Steinmann leading Catholic
youth organizations in a parade past Hitler and returning the
Fuehrer's raised arm salute. Replying to the criticism from
outraged American Catholics, Steinmann declared that "German Catholics did indeed regard the government of Adolph
Hitler as the God-given authority" and that someday the world
would "gratefully acknowledge that Germany . . . erected a
bulwark against Bolshevism. . . ."[13] What of *Mein Kampf* and
the evil of Nazism?

University of Massachusetts Associate Professor of Government Guenter Lewy fled his native Germany as a boy of fifteen
in 1939. He returned in 1960 to spend years researching
official files. Lewy writes in *The Catholic Church and Nazi
Germany*:

> Pius XI in 1933 called the Chancellor of the German
> Reich [Hitler] the first statesman who, together with the
> Pope, had clearly recognized the Bolshevik danger. . . .
> Bishop Landersdorfer praised "the harmonious collab-
> oration of Church and State [though the Nazis had
> already imprisoned many priests and nuns for 'political'
> reasons]."
>
> On March 29 [1936], 45,453,691 Germans, or 99 per
> cent of those entitled to vote, went to the polls. Of these,
> 44,461,278, or 98.8 per cent of those voting, voiced their
> approval of Hitler's leadership. [The Catholic vote ap-
> proving Hitler was virtually unanimous.]
>
> A joint pastoral letter [from all the German bishops]
> was read from the pulpits . . . January 3, 1937 [stating

that] "the German bishops consider it their duty to support the head of the German Reich by all those means
which the Church has at its disposal. . . . We must mobil-
ize all the spiritual and moral forces of the Church in
order to strengthen confidence in the Fuehrer."[14]

By this time no one could have been ignorant of Hitler's
ruthlessness and of his real goals. Yet Catholic leaders (like
most Protestant clergy) in Germany continued to heap praise
upon their fellow Catholic. Two books on *Reich und Kirche*,
published with ecclesiastical permission, called "deepening
the understanding [of] the great work of German renewal to
which the Fuehrer has summoned us" the "biggest spiritual
task of contemporary German Catholicism." Karl Adam,
world-renowned Catholic theologian, argued that National
Socialism and Catholicism, far from being in conflict, "belonged together as nature and grace" and that in Adolf Hitler
Germany had found at last "a true people's chancellor."[15]

A minority of brave men (both Catholics and Protestants)
opposed Hitler, some openly, others in secret plots. A few
voices were raised in public protest. One belonged to a priest, a
Fr. Muckermann, who dared to express his amazement and
consternation that—

> . . . despite the inhuman brutalities perpetrated in the
> concentration camps . . . despite the personal insults
> against individual princes of the Church, against the
> Holy Father and the entire Church . . . the bishops find
> words of appreciation for what (next to Bolshevism) is
> their worst enemy. . . .[16]

### Answer to an Enigma

The enigma of Germany remains the enigma of Russia,
China, Vietnam, Cuba, Haiti, Yugoslavia, South Africa, and
the entire world of our day. On the other hand, it is not an
enigma at all if one accepts the testimony of Scripture. We find
the answer in Babel—a tower which has never ceased to be
under construction. Only the location and outward form

change from time to time, but the perverted ambition, impossible dream that it is, remains steadfast.

The end result—the judgment of God that will come upon mankind—is foretold clearly in biblical prophecy. Make no mistake: We are hastening to that day. In the meantime, the woman who rides the beast, whose name is MYSTERY, BABYLON, has a key role to play. As a result she will taste God's judgment before the rest of the world knows its full and awesome power as well.

In his important analysis in 1940, Viereck warned that Nazism was a religion that had infected Germany's youth. It was pagan worship of nature, yet its claim to be "Christian" deceived millions (as is happening in the United States today by the same means). That perversion surfaced in the twisted thinking of Nazi Minister of Propaganda Joseph Goebbels, who admired Christ "as one of a long line of Aryan heroes, ranging from Wotan and Siegfried to Wagner and Hitler."[17] The "shell game switch" was echoed by Dr. Ley, head of the Nazi Labor Front: "Our faith . . . is National Socialism . . . !"[18] Hans Kerrl, Nazi Minister of Church Affairs, furthered the lie that was embraced by the majority of both Catholics and Protestants: "True Christianity is represented by the Party . . . the Fuehrer is the herald of a new revelation. . . ."[19]

New? Viereck called Nazism a "new paganism." Actually, only the veneer was new, but underneath it was still Babel. John's vision of the woman on the beast makes that fact abundantly clear.

## Religion of Self-Effort

God confounded the language of Babel's builders into numerous tongues so they couldn't understand one another and thus were scattered. But the proud religion of self-effort leading to deification of a master race persisted, evidenced by the ruins of similar towers, called ziggurats, found throughout that area of the world. None of the towers, however, attained great height with that day's primitive technology. Heaven was still beyond man's reach. So the ziggurats became occultic altars of every perversion. On their pinnacles astrology began, with the worship of heavenly bodies believed to have mystical power to control the destinies of men.

Far from dying out, Babel's religion of self-effort was institutionalized in Babylon and throughout its vast empire. This is paganism, the perennial world religion that persists to this day. It lives on not only among primitive peoples who worship nature spirits, but flourishes among university professors who attribute similar intelligence to nature's "forces."

Paganism has been characterized worldwide throughout the centuries by mysterious rituals celebrated around ornately carved and decorated altars atop structures such as the pyramids that one finds from Egypt to Central and South America. Though warned of God through His prophets against this evil, Israel also succumbed to pagan seduction. This corruption of the truth He had taught them eventually brought God's judgment upon His chosen people.

The Old Testament has many references to "high places" that were constructed in Israel. Violating the prohibition against "going up by steps" to God's altar, they became the centers of Jewish idolatry (Leviticus 26:30; Numbers 22:41; etc.). At times of repentance and revival these "high places," with their idols, were destroyed by godly kings and priests, but Israel never rid itself of this evil. Both Orthodox and Catholics and even some Protestants have embraced the same corruption by their stately structures, elevated and gilded altars, and ornate vestments and intricate liturgies, which presumably please God and help open the doors to heaven.

The bricks and mortar which were involved remind us that Babel was not only a religious and political enterprise but that it engaged the most advanced technology/science of its day. Today's science still represents an attempt to elevate man to godhood by conquering space, the atom, disease, and eventually death.

## Babel/Babylon Is Alive and Well

At Babel, God scattered mankind and confounded their language so they could not communicate their evil designs to one another. On Mars Hill in Athens Paul declared that God separated races and nations so they could concentrate upon seeking Him (Acts 17:26,27). The consensus of opinion today is that we need just the opposite: The solution to mankind's ills will come about through unscrambling the languages and uniting all nations in scientific enterprises which will ultimately turn planet Earth into a paradise once again.

Such was the declaration of a recent Lockheed Corporation ad in *Scientific American* featuring an illustration of the ancient Tower of Babel. Touting Lockheed's technological accomplishments, the ad boasted that its scientific advancements were "undoing the Babel effect" by bringing mankind together and making it possible for all to speak one language. In other words, Lockheed was countering God, the One responsible for what it called "the Babel effect."

The Tower of Babel fills the official poster for the 12-nation United Europe (whose new currency depicts a woman riding a beast). Circling above the unfinished tower are 12 stars. Unlike those on the American flag, however, these are upside down, thus forming the pentagram of classic occultism. The pentagram, with its two "horns" pointing upward and its "beard" downward, is also known as the Goat of Mendes, or Baphomet, a symbol of Satan.

International Business Machines has also used an artist's depiction of the Tower of Babel in some of its ads, with modern high-rise buildings protruding from the half-finished structure. Why this nostalgic return to what most people today dismiss as a myth? There seems to be an innate sympathy with Babel, a recognition that modern man is carrying on where Babel left off and is pursuing the same ambition of achieving immortality by human effort.

God scattered the builders of Babel, but today's determination is the opposite: to unite all nations into one new world order. God confounded the languages, but today's technology is aimed at breaking down every language barrier. Soon there will be phones on the market which will allow English spoken into the receiver in Los Angeles to come out the other end in Tokyo as Japanese.

Dare we suggest that something is wrong? Why not encourage and enjoy what intellect and talent can accomplish? Even God acknowledged the limitless bounds of human capabilities when He said, "Whatever they imagine they will be able to perform."

God, however, had already declared that "the imagination of man's heart is evil from his youth" (Genesis 8:21). Thus human ingenuity, as God foresaw, would create ever-increasing evil until the very survival of mankind would hang in the balance. Surely today's threats to survival have all come from scientific genius. Honesty would also force us to admit that the rise of urbanization, even in ancient times, has contributed to the escalating tide of evil that threatens to engulf our world today.

John's vision indicates that Babel/Babylon will be very much alive in the last days. Emblazoned across the forehead of the woman riding the beast are the words "MYSTERY, BABYLON." That she represents revived paganism is clear.

Most interesting of all, however, is the fact that she embodies paganized *Christianity*. The woman represents a worldwide religious system which is based in Rome and claims to be Christian but which has its roots in Babel and Babylon. That conclusion will become unassailable as we examine further the vision John received.

**A WOMAN**

*The woman which thou sawest is that great city,
which reigneth over the kings of the earth. . . .*

*Here is the mind which hath wisdom: The seven
heads are seven mountains [or hills] on which
the woman sitteth.*

—Revelation 17:18,9

**RIDES THE BEAST**

# 6

# A City
# on Seven Hills

A woman rides the beast, and that woman is a city built on
seven hills that reigns over the kings of the earth! Was
ever in all of history such a statement made? John immediately
equates the readers' acceptance of this revelation with "wisdom." We dare not pass over such a disclosure casually. It
merits our careful and prayerful attention.

Here is no mystical or allegorical language but an unam-
biguous statement in plain words: "The woman . . . is that
great city." There is no justification for seeking some other
hidden meaning. Yet books have been written and sermons
preached insisting that "Mystery Babylon" is the United
States. That is clearly not the case, for the United States is a
country, not a city. One might justifiably refer to the United
States as Sodom, considering the honor now given to homosexuals, but it is definitely not the Babylon that John sees in this
vision. The woman is a *city*.

Furthermore, she is a city built on *seven hills*. That specifi-
cation eliminates ancient Babylon. Only one city has for more
than 2000 years been known as the city on seven hills. That
city is Rome. The *Catholic Encyclopedia* states: "It is within
the city of Rome, called the city of seven hills, that the entire
area of Vatican State proper is now confined."[1]

There are, of course, other cities, such as Rio de Janeiro,
that were also built on seven hills. Therefore, John provides at

least seven more characteristics to limit the identification to Rome alone. We will examine each one in detail in subsequent chapters. However, as a preview of where we are going, we will list them now and discuss each one briefly. As we shall see, there is only *one* city on the earth which, in both historical and contemporary perspectives, passes every test John gives, including its identification as Mystery Babylon. That city is Rome, and more specifically, Vatican City.

Even Catholic apologist Karl Keating admits that Rome has long been known as Babylon. Keating claims that Peter's statement "The church here in Babylon ... sends you her greeting" (from 1 Peter 5:13) proves that Peter was writing from Rome. He explains further:

> Babylon is a code word for Rome. It is used that way six times in the last book of the Bible [four of the six are in chapters 17 and 18] and in extrabiblical works such as *Sibylling Oracles* (5, 159f.), the *Apocalypse of Baruch* (ii, 1), and 4 *Esdras* (3:1).
>
> Eusebius Pamphilius, writing about 303, noted that "it is said that Peter's first epistle ... was composed at Rome itself; and that he himself indicates this, referring to the city figuratively as Babylon."[2]

As for "Mystery," that name imprinted on the woman's forehead is the perfect designation for Vatican City. Mystery is at the very heart of Roman Catholicism, from the words *"Mysterium fide"* pronounced at the alleged transformation of the bread and wine into the literal body and blood of Christ to the enigmatic apparitions of Mary around the world. Every sacrament, from baptism to extreme unction, manifests the mysterious power which the faithful must believe the priests wield, but for which there is no visible evidence. Rome's new *Catechism* explains that liturgy "aims to initiate souls into the mystery of Christ (It is 'mystagogy.')" and that all of the Church's liturgy is "mystery."[3]

## Who Is the Whore?

The first thing we are told about the woman is that she is a "whore" (Revelation 17:1), that earthly kings "have committed fornication" with her (verse 2), and that "all the inhabitants of the earth have been made drunk with the wine of her fornication" (verse 3). Why would a *city* be called a *whore* and be accused of having committed *fornication* with *kings?* Such an indictment would never be made of London or Moscow or Paris—or any other ordinary city. It wouldn't make sense.

Fornication and adultery are used in the Bible in both the physical and the spiritual sense. Of Jerusalem God said, "How is the faithful city become a harlot!" (Isaiah 1:21). Israel, whom God had set apart from all other peoples to be holy for His purposes, had entered into unholy, adulterous alliances with the idol-worshiping nations about her. She had "committed adultery with stones and with stocks [idols]" (Jeremiah 3:9); "and with their idols have they committed adultery" (Ezekiel 23:37). The entire chapter of Ezekiel 16 explains Israel's spiritual adultery in detail, both with heathen nations and with their false gods, as do many other passages.

There is no way that a *city* could engage in literal, fleshly fornication. Thus we can only conclude that John, like the prophets in the Old Testament, is using the term in its spiritual sense. The city, therefore, must claim a spiritual relationship with God. Otherwise such an allegation would be meaningless.

Though it is built on seven hills, there would be no reason to accuse Rio de Janeiro of spiritual fornication. It makes no claim of having a special relationship with God. And though Jerusalem has that relationship, it cannot be the woman riding on the beast, for it is not built on seven hills. Nor does it meet the other criteria by which this woman is to be identified.

Against only one other *city* in history could a charge of fornication be leveled. That city is Rome, and more specifically *Vatican City*. She claims to have been the worldwide headquarters of Christianity since its beginning and maintains that claim to this day. Her pope enthroned in Rome claims to be the exclusive representative of God, the vicar of Christ. Rome is the headquarters of the Roman Catholic Church, and in that too she is unique.

Numerous churches, of course, are headquartered in cities, but only one city *is* the headquarters of a church. The Mormon

Church, for example, is headquartered in Salt Lake City, but there is much more to Salt Lake City than the Mormon Church. Not so with Vatican City. It is the heartbeat of the Roman Catholic Church and nothing else. She is a spiritual entity that could very well be accused of spiritual fornication if she did not remain true to Christ.

## In Bed with the Rulers

Not only does Rome's pope call himself the vicar of Christ, but the Church he heads claims to be the one true Church and the bride of Christ. Christ's bride, whose hope is to join her Bridegroom in heaven, is to have no earthly ambitions. Yet the Vatican is obsessed with earthly enterprise, as history proves; and in furtherance of these goals it has been, exactly as John foresaw in his vision, engaged in adulterous relationships with the kings of the earth. That fact is acknowledged even by Catholic historians.

Christ said to His disciples, "If ye were of the world, the world would love his own; but because ye are not of the world, but I have chosen you out of the world, therefore the world hateth you" (John 15:19). The Catholic Church, however, is very much of this world. Her popes have built an unrivaled worldwide empire of property, wealth, and influence. Nor is empire-building an abandoned feature of the past. We have already seen that Vatican II clearly states that the Roman Catholic Church today still ceaselessly seeks to bring under its control *all mankind* and *all their goods.*

Popes have long claimed dominion over the world and its peoples. Pope Gregory XI's papal bull of 1372 (*In Coena Domini*) claimed papal dominion over the entire Christian world, secular and religious, and excommunicated all who failed to obey the popes and to pay them taxes. *In Coena* was confirmed by subsequent popes and in 1568 Pope Pius V swore that it was to remain an eternal law.

Pope Alexander VI (1492-1503) claimed that all undiscovered lands belonged to the Roman Pontiff, for him to dispose of as he pleased in the name of Christ as His vicar. King John II of Portugal was convinced that in his Bull *Romanus Pontifex* the pope had granted all that Columbus discovered exclusively to him and his country. Ferdinand and

Isabel of Spain, however, thought the pope had given the same lands to them. In May 1493 the Spanish-born Alexander VI issued three bulls to settle the dispute.

In the name of Christ, who had no place on this earth that He called his own, this incredibly evil Borgia pope, claiming to own the world, drew a north-south line down the global map of that day, giving everything on the east to Portugal and on the west to Spain. Thus by *papal grant*, "out of the plenitude of apostolic power," Africa went to Portugal and the Americas to Spain. When Portugal "succeeded in reaching India and Malaya, they secured the confirmation of these discoveries from the Papacy. . . ." There was a condition, of course: "to the intent to bring the inhabitants . . . to profess the Catholic Faith."[4] It was largely Central and South America which, as a consequence of this unholy alliance between church and state, had Roman Catholicism forced upon them by the sword and remain Catholic to this day. North America (with the exception of Quebec and Louisiana) was spared the dominance of Roman Catholicism because it was settled largely by Protestants.

Nor have the descendants of Aztecs, Incas, and Mayas forgotten that Roman Catholic priests, backed by the secular sword, gave their ancestors the choice of conversion (which often meant slavery) or death. They made such an outcry when John Paul II in a recent visit to Latin America proposed elevating Junipero Serra (a major eighteenth-century enforcer of Catholicism among the Indians) to sainthood that the pope was forced to hold the ceremony in secret.

Christ said, "My kingdom is not of this world; otherwise my servants would fight." The popes, however, have fought with armies and navies in the name of Christ to build a huge kingdom which is very much of this world. And to amass their earthly empire they have repeatedly engaged in spiritual fornication with emperors, kings, and princes. Claiming to be the bride of Christ, the Roman Catholic Church has been in bed with godless rulers down through history, and these adulterous relationships continue to this day. This spiritual fornication will be documented in detail later.

## Rome Equals Vatican

Some may object that it is Rome, and not that small part of it known as Vatican City, which is built on seven hills, and that the Vatican can hardly be called a "great city." Though both objections are true, the words "Vatican" and "Rome" are universally used interchangeably. Just as one would refer to Washington and mean the government that runs the United States, so one refers to Rome and means the hierarchy that rules the Roman Catholic Church.

Take for example a placard carried by a demonstrator outside the November 15-18, 1993, meeting in Washington D.C. of the National Conference of Catholic Bishops. Protesting any deviation from the pope's wishes, it read: "ROME'S WAY OR THE HIGHWAY."[5] Obviously by "Rome" it meant the Vatican. Such is the common usage. So closely are Catholicism and Rome linked that the Catholic Church is known as the *Roman* Catholic Church, or simply the *Roman* Church.

Moreover, for more than a thousand years the Roman Catholic Church exercised both religious and civil control over the entire city of Rome and its surroundings. Pope Innocent III (1198-1216) abolished the secular Roman Senate and placed the administration of Rome directly under his command. The Roman Senate that had governed the city under the Caesars had been known as the *Curia Romana* (Roman Curia). That name, according to the *Pocket Catholic Dictionary*, is now the designation of "the whole ensemble of administrative and judicial offices through which the Pope directs the operations of the Catholic Church."[6]

The popes' authority even extended to large territories outside Rome acquired in the eighth century. At that time, with the help of a deliberately fraudulent document manufactured for the popes known as *The Donation of Constantine*, Pope Stephen III convinced Pepin, king of the Franks and father of Charlemagne, that territories recently taken by the Lombards from the Byzantines actually had been given to the papacy by the Emperor Constantine. Pepin routed the Lombards and handed to the pope the keys to some 20 cities (Ravenna, Ancona, Bologna, Ferrara, Iesi, Gubbio, etc.) and the huge chunk of land joining them along the Adriatic coast.

Dated 30 March 315, *The Donation* declared that Constantine had given these lands, along with Rome and the Lateran Palace, to the popes in perpetuity. In 1440 this document was proven to be a forgery by Lorenzo Valla, a papal aide, and is so recognized by historians today. Yet allegedly infallible popes continued for centuries to assert that *The Donation* was genuine and on that basis to justify their pomp, power, and possessions. That fraud is still perpetuated by an inscription in the baptistry of Rome's St. John Lateran, which has never been corrected.

Thus the Papal States were literally stolen by the popes from their rightful owners. The papacy controlled and taxed these territories and derived great wealth from them until 1848. At that time the pope, along with the rulers of most of the other divided territories of Italy, was forced to grant his rebellious subjects a constitution. In September 1860, over his raging protests, Pius IX lost all of the papal states to the new, finally united Kingdom of Italy, which left him, at the time of the First Vatican Council in 1870, still in control of Rome and its surroundings.

The point is that, exactly as John foresaw in his vision, a spiritual entity that claimed a special relationship with Christ and with God became identified with a city that was built on seven hills. That "woman" committed spiritual fornication with earthly rulers and eventually reigned over them. The Roman Catholic Church has been continuously identified with that city. As "The most definitive Catholic encyclopedia since Vatican II" declares:

> ... hence, one understands the central place of Rome in the life of the Church today and the significance of the title, Roman Catholic Church, the Church that is universal, yet focused upon the ministry of the Bishop of Rome. Since the founding of the Church there by St. Peter, Rome has been the center of all Christendom.[7]

## Wealth from Ill-Gotten Gain

The incredible wealth of this woman caught John's attention next. She was dressed "in purple and scarlet color, and decked with gold and precious stones and pearls, having a golden cup in her hand full of abominations and filthiness of her fornication" (Revelation 17:4). The colors of purple and scarlet once again identify the woman with both pagan and Christian Rome. These were the colors of the Roman caesars with which the soldiers mockingly robed Christ as "King" (see Matthew 27:28 and John 19:2,5), which the Vatican took to itself. The woman's colors are literally still the colors of the Catholic clergy! The same *Catholic Encyclopedia* quoted above states:

**Cappa Magna**
A cloak with a long train and a hooded shoulder cape . . . [it] was purple wool for bishops; for cardinals, it was scarlet watered silk (for Advent, Lent, Good Friday, and the conclave, purple wool); and rose watered silk for Gaudete and Laetare Sundays; and for the pope, it was red velvet for Christmas Matins, red serge at other times.

**Cassock (also Soutane)**
The close-fitting, ankle-length robe worn by the Catholic clergy as their official garb. . . . The color for bishops and other prelates is purple, for cardinals scarlet. . . .[8]

The "golden cup [chalice] in her hand" again identifies the woman with the Roman Catholic Church. Broderick's edition of *The Catholic Encyclopedia* declares of the chalice: "[It is] the most important of the sacred vessels. . . . [It] may be of gold or silver, and if the latter, then the inside must be surfaced with gold."[9] The Roman Catholic Church possesses many thousands of solid gold chalices kept in its churches around the world. Even the bloodstained cross of Christ has been turned to gold and studded with gems in reflection of Rome's great wealth. *The Catholic Encyclopedia* says: "The pectoral cross [suspended by a chain around the neck and worn over the breast by abbots, bishops, archbishops, cardinals, and the pope] should be made of *gold* and . . . decorated with gems . . ."[10]

Rome has practiced evil to gather her wealth, for the "golden cup" is filled with "abominations and filthiness." Much of the wealth of the Roman Catholic Church was acquired through the confiscation of the property of the pitiful victims of the Inquisitions. Even the dead were exhumed to face trial and property was taken from their heirs by the Church. One historian writes:

> The punishments of the Inquisition did not cease when the victim was burned to ashes, or immured for life in the Inquisition dungeons. His relatives were reduced to beggary by the law that all his possessions were forfeited. The system offered unlimited opportunities for loot. . . .
>
> This source of gain largely accounts for the revolting practice of what has been called "corpse-trials." . . . That the practice of confiscating the property of condemned heretics was productive of many acts of extortion, rapacity and corruption will be doubted by no one who has any knowledge either of human nature or of the historical documents. . . . no man was safe whose wealth might arouse cupidity, or whose independence might provoke revenge.[11]

Most of Rome's wealth has been acquired through the sale of salvation. Untold billions of dollars have been paid to her by those who thought they were purchasing heaven on the installment plan for themselves or loved ones. The practice continues to this day—blatantly where Catholicism is in control, less obviously here in the United States. No greater deception or abomination could be perpetrated. When Cardinal Cajetan, sixteenth-century Dominican scholar, complained about the sale of dispensations and indulgences, the Church hierarchy was indignant and accused him of wanting "to turn Rome into an uninhabited desert, to reduce the Papacy to impotence, to deprive the pope . . . of the pecuniary resources indispensable for the discharge of his office."[12]

In addition to such perversions of the gospel which have led hundreds of millions astray, there are the further abominations of corrupt banking practices, laundering of drug money, trading in counterfeit securities, and dealings with the Mafia (fully documented in police and court records), which the Vatican and her representatives around the world have long employed. Nino Lo Bello, former *Business Week* correspondent in Rome and Rome bureau chief for *New York Journal of*

*Commerce*, writes that the Vatican is so closely allied with the Mafia in Italy that "many people . . . believe that Sicily . . . is nothing more than a Vatican holding."[13]

The Roman Catholic Church is by far the wealthiest institution on earth. Yes, one hears from Rome periodic pleas for money—persuasive appeals claiming that the Vatican cannot maintain itself on its limited budget and needs monetary assistance. Such pleas are unconscionable ploys. The value of innumerable sculptures by such masters as Michelangelo, paintings by the world's greatest artists, and countless other art treasures and ancient documents which Rome possesses (not only at the Vatican but in cathedrals around the world) is beyond calculation. At the World Synod of Bishops in Rome, England's Cardinal Heenan proposed that the Church sell some of these superfluous treasures and give the proceeds to the poor. His suggestion was not well-received.

Christ and His disciples lived in poverty. He told His followers not to lay up treasure on this earth but in heaven. The Roman Catholic Church has disobeyed that command and has accumulated a plethora of riches without equal, of which "the Roman Pontiff is the supreme administrator and steward. . . ."[14] There is no church, no city which is a spiritual entity, no religious institution past or present which even comes close to possessing the wealth of the Roman Catholic Church. A recent newspaper article described only a fraction of that treasure at one location:

> The fabulous treasure of Lourdes [France], whose existence was kept secret by the Catholic Church for 120 years, has been unveiled. . . . Rumours have been circulating for decades about a priceless collection of gold chalices, diamond-studded crucifixes [a far cry from the bloodstained cross on which Christ died], silver and precious stones donated by grateful pilgrims.
>
> After an indiscreet remark by their press spokesman this week, church authorities agreed to reveal part of the collection . . . [some] floor-to-ceiling cases were opened to reveal 59 solid gold chalices alongside rings, crucifixes, statues and heavy gold brooches, many encrusted with precious stones.

Almost hidden by the other treasures is the "Crown" of Notre Dame de Lourdes, made by a Paris goldsmith in 1876 and studded with diamonds.

Church authorities say they cannot put a value on the collection. "I have no idea," says Father Pierre-Marie Charriez, director of Patrimony and Sanctuaries. "It is of inestimable value." . . .

Across the road is a building housing hundreds of [antique] ecclesiastical garments, robes, mitres and sashes—many in heavy gold thread. . . .

"The Church itself is poor," insists Father Charriez. "The Vatican itself is poor."[15] [The treasure described here is only part of that which is kept in one location, the small town of Lourdes, France!]

## The Mother of Harlots and Abominations

The more deeply one probes into the history of the Roman Catholic Church and its current practices, the more impressed one becomes with the amazing accuracy of the vision John received centuries before it would all be lamentable reality. John's attention is drawn to the inscription boldly emblazoned upon the woman's forehead: "MYSTERY, BABYLON THE GREAT, THE MOTHER OF HARLOTS AND ABOMINA-TIONS OF THE EARTH" (Revelation 17:5). Sadly enough, the Roman Catholic Church fits the description "mother of harlots and abominations" as precisely as she fits the others. Much of the cause can be traced to the unbiblical demand that her priests be celibates.

The great apostle Paul was a celibate and recommended that life to others who wanted to devote themselves fully to serving Christ. He did not, however, make it a condition for church leadership as the Catholic Church has done, thereby imposing an unnatural burden upon all clergy that very few could bear. On the contrary, he wrote that a bishop should be "the husband of one wife" (1 Timothy 3:2) and set the same requirement for elders (Titus 1:5,6).

Peter, whom the Catholics erroneously claim was the first pope, was married. So were at least some of the other apostles.

This fact was not the chance result of their having been married before Christ called them, but it was accepted as an ongoing norm. Paul himself argued that he had the right to marry like the rest: "Have we not power [Greek *exousia*, the right or privilege or authority] to lead about a sister, a wife, as well as other apostles and as the brethren [half-brothers, sons of Mary and Joseph] of the Lord, and as Cephas [Peter]?" (1 Corinthians 9:5).

The Roman Catholic Church, however, has insisted upon celibacy even though many popes, among them Sergius III (904-11), John X (914-28), John XII (955-63), Benedict V (964), Innocent VIII (1484-92), Urban VIII (1623-44), and Innocent X (1644-55), as well as millions of cardinals, bishops, archbishops, monks, and priests throughout history, have repeatedly violated such vows. Not only has celibacy made sinners of the clergy who engage in fornication, but it makes harlots out of those with whom they secretly cohabit. Rome is indeed "the mother of harlots"! Her identification as such is unmistakable. No other city, church, or institution in the history of the world is her rival in this particular evil.

History is replete with sayings that mocked the church's false claim to celibacy and revealed the truth: "The holiest hermit has his whore" and "Rome has more prostitutes than any other city because she has the most celibates" are examples. Pius II declared that Rome was "the only city run by bastards" [sons of popes and cardinals]. Catholic historian and former Jesuit Peter de Rosa writes:

> Popes had mistresses of fifteen years of age, were guilty of incest and sexual perversions of every sort, had innumerable children, were murdered in the very act of adultery [by jealous husbands who found them in bed with their wives]. . . . In the old Catholic phrase, why be holier than the pope?[16]

As for abominations, even Catholic historians admit that among the popes were some of the most degenerate and unconscionable ogres in all of history. Their numerous outrageous crimes, many of which are almost beyond belief, have been recited by many historians from preserved documents that reveal the depths of papal depravity, some of which we will cover in later chapters. To call any of these men "His Holiness, Vicar of Christ" makes a mockery of holiness and of Christ. Yet the name of each one of these unbelievably wicked popes— mass murderers, fornicators, robbers, warmongers, some guilty of the massacre of thousands—is emblazoned in honor on the Church's official list of popes. These abominations that John foresaw not only occurred in the past but continue to this very day, as we shall see.

## Drunk with the Martyrs' Blood

John next notices that the woman is drunk—and not with an alcoholic beverage. She is drunk with "the blood of the saints, and with the blood of the martyrs of Jesus . . ." (Revelation 17:6). The picture is a horrible one. It is not merely her *hands* that are red with this blood, but she is *drunk* with it! The slaughter of innocents who, for conscience' sake, would not yield to her totalitarian demands has so refreshed and exhilarated her that she reels in ecstasy.

One thinks immediately of the Inquisitions (Roman, Medieval, and Spanish) which for centuries held Europe in their terrible grip. In his *History of the Inquisition*, Canon Llorente, who was the Secretary to the Inquisition in Madrid from 1790-92 and had access to the archives of all the tribunals, estimated that in Spain alone the number of condemned exceeded 3 million, with about 300,000 burned at the stake.[17] A Catholic historian comments upon events leading up to the suppression of the Spanish Inquisition in 1809:

> When Napoleon conquered Spain in 1808, a Polish officer in his army, Colonel Lemanouski, reported that the Dominicans [in charge of the Inquisition] blockaded themselves in their monastery in Madrid. When Lemanouski's troops forced an entry, the inquisitors denied the existence of any torture chambers.
>
> The soldiers searched the monastery and discovered them under the floors. The chambers were full of prisoners, all naked, many insane. The French troops, used to cruelty and blood, could not stomach the sight. They

emptied the torture-chambers, laid gunpowder to the monastery and blew the place up.[18]

To wring out confessions from these poor creatures, the Roman Catholic Church devised ingenious tortures so excruciating and barbarous that one is sickened by their recital. Church historian Bishop William Shaw Kerr writes:

> The most ghastly abomination of all was the system of torture. The accounts of its cold-blooded operations make one shudder at the capacity of human beings for cruelty. And it was decreed and regulated by the popes who claim to represent Christ on earth. . . .
>
> Careful notes were taken not only of all that was confessed by the victim, but of his shrieks, cries, lamentations, broken interjections and appeals for mercy. The most moving things in the literature of the Inquisition are not the accounts of their sufferings left by the victims but the sober memoranda kept by the officers of the tribunals. We are distressed and horrified just because there is no intention to shock us.[19]

The remnants of some of the chambers of horror remain in Europe and may be visited today. They stand as memorials to the zealous outworking of Roman Catholic dogmas *which remain in force today*, and to a Church which claims to be infallible and to this day justifies such barbarism. They are also memorials to the astonishing accuracy of John's vision in Revelation 17. In a book published in Spain in 1909, Emelio Martinez writes:

> To these three million victims [documented by Llorente] should be added the thousands upon thousands of Jews and Moors deported from their homeland. . . . In just one year, 1481, and just in Seville, the Holy Office [of the Inquisition] burned 2000 persons; the bones and effigies of another 2000 . . . and another 16,000 were condemned to varying sentences.[20]

Peter de Rosa acknowledges that his own Catholic Church "was responsible for persecuting Jews, for the Inquisition, for slaughtering heretics by the thousand, for reintroducing torture into Europe as part of the judicial process." Yet the Roman Catholic Church has never officially admitted that these practices were evil, nor has she apologized to the world or to any of the victims or their descendants. Nor could Pope John Paul II apologize today because "the doctrines responsible for those terrible things still underpin his position."[21] Rome has not changed at heart no matter what sweet words she speaks when it serves her purpose.

## More Blood Than the Pagans

Pagan Rome made sport of throwing to the lions, burning and otherwise killing thousands of Christians and not a few Jews. Yet "Christian" Rome slaughtered many times that number of both Christians and Jews. Beside those victims of the Inquisition, there were Huguenots, Albigenses, Waldenses, and other Christians who were massacred, tortured, and burned at the stake by the hundreds of thousands simply because they refused to align themselves with the Roman Catholic Church and its corruption and heretical dogmas and practices. Out of conscience they tried to follow the teachings of Christ and the apostles independent of Rome, and for that crime they were maligned, hunted, imprisoned, tortured, and slain.

Why would Rome ever apologize for or even admit this holocaust? No one calls her to account today. Protestants have now forgotten the hundreds of thousands of people burned at the stake for embracing the simple gospel of Christ and refusing to bow to papal authority. Amazingly, Protestants are now embracing Rome as Christian while she insists that the "separated brethren" be reconciled to her on her unchangeable terms!

Many evangelical leaders are intent upon working with Roman Catholics to evangelize the world by the year 2000. They don't want to hear any "negative" reminders of the millions of people tortured and slain by the Church to which they now pay homage, or the fact that Rome has a false gospel of sacramental works.

"Christian" Rome slaughtered Jews by the thousands—far more than pagan Rome ever did. The land of Israel was seen as belonging to the Roman Catholic Church, not to the Jews. In 1096 Pope Urban II inspired the first crusade to retake Jerusalem from the Muslims. With the cross on their shields and armor, the Crusaders massacred Jews across Europe on their way to the Holy Land. Almost their first act upon taking Jerusalem "for Holy Mother Church" was to herd all of the Jews into the synagogue and set it ablaze. These facts of history cannot be swept under the carpet of ecumenical togetherness as though they never happened.

Nor can the Vatican escape considerable responsibility for the Nazi Holocaust, which was thoroughly known to Pius XII in spite of his complete silence throughout the war on that most important of subjects.[22] The involvement of Catholicism in the Holocaust will be examined later. Had the pope protested, as representatives of Jewish organizations and the Allied Powers begged him to do, he would have condemned his own church. The facts are inescapable:

> In 1936, Bishop Berning of Osnabruch had talked with the Fuehrer for over an hour. Hitler assured his lordship there was no fundamental difference between National Socialism and the Catholic Church. Had not the church, he argued, looked on Jews as parasites and shut them in ghettos?
>
> "I am only doing," he boasted, "what the church has done for fifteen hundred years, only more effectively." Being a Catholic himself, he told Berning, he "admired and wanted to promote Christianity."[23]

There is, of course, another reason why the Roman Catholic Church has neither apologized for nor repented of these crimes. How could she? The execution of heretics (including Jews) was decreed by "infallible" popes. The Catholic Church herself claims to be infallible, and thus her doctrines could not be wrong.

## Reigning over the Kings of the Earth

Finally, the angel reveals to John that the woman "is that great city which reigneth over the kings of the earth" (Revelation 17:18). Is there such a city? Yes, and again only one:

Vatican City. Popes crowned and deposed kings and emperors, exacting obedience by threatening them with excommunication. At the time of the First Vatican Council in 1869, J.H. Ignaz von Dollinger, Professor of Church History in Munich, warned that Pope Pius IX would force the Council to make an infallible dogma out of "that pet theory of the Popes—that they could force kings and magistrates, by excommunication and its consequences, to carry out their sentences of confiscation, imprisonment, and death. . . ." He reminded his fellow Roman Catholics of some of the evil consequences of papal political authority:

> When, for instance, [Pope] Martin IV placed King Pedro of Aragon under excommunication and interdict . . . then promised indulgences for all their sins to those who fought with him and [tyrant] Charles [I of Naples] against Pedro, and finally declared his kingdom forfeit . . . which cost the two kings of France and Aragon their life, and the French the loss of an army. . . .
>
> Pope Clement IV, in 1265, after selling millions of South Italians to Charles of Anjou for a yearly tribute of eight hundred ounces of gold, declared that he would be excommunicated if the first payment was deferred beyond the appointed term, and that for the second neglect the whole nation would incur interdict. . . . [24]

Though John Paul II lacks the power to enforce such brutal claims today, his Church still retains the dogmas which authorize him to do so. And the practical effects of his power are no less than those of his predecessors, though exercised quietly behind the scenes. The Vatican is the only city which exchanges ambassadors with nations, and she does so with every major country on earth. Ambassadors come to the Vatican from every major country, including the United States, not out of mere courtesy but because the pope is the most powerful ruler on earth today. Even President Clinton journeyed to Denver in August 1993 to greet the pope. He addressed him as "Holy Father" and "Your Holiness."

Yes, ambassadors of nations come to Washington D.C, to Paris, or to London, but only because the national government has its capital there. Nor does Washington, Paris, London, or any other city send ambassadors to other countries. Only Vatican City does so. Unlike any other city on earth, the Vatican is acknowledged as a sovereign state in its own right, separate and distinct from the nation of Italy surrounding it. There is no other *city* in history of which this has been true, and such is still the case today.

Only of the Vatican could it be said that a *city* reigns over the kings of the earth. The phrase "the worldwide influence of Washington" means the influence not of that city but of the United States, which has its capital there. When one speaks, however, of the influence of the Vatican around the world, that is exactly what is meant—the *city* and the worldwide power of Roman Catholicism and its leader the pope. Vatican *City* is absolutely unique.

## Forget a Rebuilt Babylon

Some suggest that the Vatican will move to Babylon in Iraq when it is rebuilt. But why should it? The Vatican has been fulfilling John's vision from its location in Rome for the past 15 centuries. Moreover, we have shown the connection to ancient Babylon which the Vatican has maintained down through history in the paganized Christianity it has promulgated. As for ancient Babylon itself, it wasn't even in existence during the past 2300 years to "reign over the kings of the earth." Babylon lay in ruins while pagan Rome and later Catholic Rome, the new Babylon, was indeed reigning over kings.

One eighteenth-century historian counted 95 popes who claimed to have divine power to depose kings and emperors. Historian Walter James wrote that Pope Innocent III (1198-1216) "held all Europe in his net."[25] Gregory IX (1227-41) thundered that the pope was lord and master of everyone and everything. Historian R.W. Southern declared: "During the whole medieval period there was in Rome a single spiritual and temporal authority [the papacy] exercising powers which in the end exceeded those that had ever lain within the grasp of a Roman emperor."[26]

That the popes reigned over kings is an undisputed fact of history that we will more fully document later. That in so doing horrible abominations were committed, as John foresaw, is also indisputable. Pope Nicholas I (858-67) declared: "We [popes] alone have the power to bind and to loose, to absolve Nero and to condemn him; and Christians cannot, under penalty of excommunication, execute other judgment than ours, which alone is infallible." In commanding one king to destroy another, Nicholas wrote:

> We order you, in the name of religion, to invade his states, burn his cities, and massacre his people. . . .[27]

The qualifying information which John gives us under the inspiration of the Holy Spirit for identifying this woman, who is a *city*, is specific, conclusive, and irrefutable. There is no *city* upon earth, past or present, which meets all of these criteria except Catholic Rome and now Vatican City. That inescapable conclusion will become increasingly clear as we proceed to uncover the facts.

*Every cleric must obey the Pope, even if he commands what is evil; for no one may judge the Pope.*

— Pope Innocent III (1198-1216)

*The First See [Rome/papacy] is judged by no one. It is the right of the Roman Pontiff himself alone to judge . . . those who hold the highest civil office in a state. . . .*

*There is neither appeal nor recourse against a decision or decree of the Roman Pontiff.*

— From today's *Code of Canon Law*[1]

# 7

# Fraud and Fabricated History

The Roman Catholic pope has often been the most powerful religious and political figure on earth. This is true today, even though the pope no longer has at his disposal the armies and navies of past Roman pontiffs. The papacy is crucial to Roman Catholicism, which is destined to play a vital role in the last days prior to Christ's second coming. Therefore we must take time to understand the papacy in relation to both the Church and the world. How did the papal office arise? What is its significance today?

The Vatican's constituency of 980 million followers is at least three times the number of citizens in any Western democracy and is exceeded only by the population of China. Even more important, these 980 million people are scattered throughout the world, many of them holding high political, military, and commercial positions in non-Catholic countries. Moreover, the pope has thousands of secret agents worldwide. They include Jesuits, the Knights of Columbus, Knights of Malta, *Opus Dei*, and others. The Vatican's Intelligence Service and its field resources are second to none.

Politically the pope's power is exercised mostly behind the scenes, at times in cooperation with and at other times in opposition to the CIA, British Intelligence, Israeli Mossad, and other intelligence services. Remember, the pope's 980 million subjects are bound to him by *religious* ties, which are far stronger than any political loyalties could ever be. No secular government can compete with the motivational power of religious belief.

The typical Roman Catholic, though he may disagree with his church on such issues as homosexuality, abortion, extramarital sex, contraceptives, and the necessity for confession, nevertheless believes that, when it comes time for him to die, Rome holds his only hope. The pope as Christ's Vicar gives a visible reality and practical expression to that hope. The extraordinary position of the pope in relation to members of the Church was expressed succinctly in Rome's *La Civilta Cattolica*, which a papal brief described in the midnineteenth century as "the purest journalistic organ of true Church doctrine"[2]:

> It is not enough for the people only to know that the Pope is the head of the Church . . . they must also understand that their own faith and religious life flow from him; that in him is the bond which unites Catholics to one another, and the power which strengthens and the light which guides them; that he is the dispenser of spiritual graces, the giver of the benefits of religion, the upholder of justice, and the protector of the oppressed.[3]

Similar words have been spoken by the followers of Joseph Smith, Sun Myung Moon, and other cult leaders. The pope is "another Christ" and "God on earth" to his followers, and, as Vatican II says, he can be judged by neither man nor tribunal.[4]

## Check Your Mind at the Door

The pope, and therefore the Church through him as its head, both claim to be infallible. Ordinary Catholics must not question anything the pope or Church have to say concerning faith and morals. The councils and catechisms have for centuries declared the need for such total submission and still insist upon it today. *The Catholic World* reminded all Roman Catholics in the United States at the time of the First Vatican Council:

> Each individual must receive the faith and law from the Church . . . with unquestioning submission and obedience of the intellect and the will. . . . We have no right

> to ask reasons of the Church, any more than of Almighty
> God. . . . We are to take with unquestioning docility
> whatever instruction the Church gives us.[5]

Here we have as clear a denial of individual moral responsibility as can be found in any cult. The same requirement of unthinking submission is demanded in Vatican II. *The Code of Canon Law* likewise reasserts the same rule:

> The Christian faithful, conscious of their own responsibility, are bound by Christian obedience to follow what the sacred pastors, as representatives of Christ, declare as teachers of the faith or determine as leaders of the Church.[6]

When it comes to faith and morals and the way of salvation, Catholics must check their minds at the door and accept whatever the Church says. They can't even study the Bible for themselves because only the Magisterium can interpret it. Obviously, this prohibition against freedom of conscience is related to the total suppression of basic human rights for all mankind everywhere, which is the unchanging goal of Roman Catholicism.

To understand Roman Catholicism one must ignore the public posturing and public-relations-motivated profile offered by the Catholic Church. The face that Rome shows to the world varies from country to country depending upon the control it has and what it can effect. Instead, we must look to Catholicism's official doctrines, which never change.

Vatican II is thought by most Catholics and non-Catholics to have liberalized Catholicism. In fact, it reaffirmed the canons and decrees of previous key councils: "This sacred council accepts loyally the venerable faith of our ancestors . . . and it proposes again the decrees of the Second Council of Nicea, of the Council of Florence, and of the Council of Trent."[7] The Council of Trent denounced the Reformation and damned evangelicals' beliefs with more than 100 anathemas. All of these condemnations of the gospel of God's grace are endorsed and reaffirmed by Vatican II. As for the pope, Vatican II clearly states:

The Roman Pontiff, head of the college of bishops, enjoys this infallibility in virtue of his office [not the holiness of his life], when, as supreme pastor and teacher of all the faithful . . . he proclaims in an absolute decision a doctrine pertaining to faith or morals. For that reason his definitions are rightly said to be irreformable . . . in no way in need of the approval of others, and do not admit of appeal to any other tribunal.

. . . the faithful, for their part, are obliged to submit to their bishops' decision, made in the name of Christ, in matters of faith and morals, and to adhere to it with a ready and respectful allegiance of mind. This loyal submission of the will and intellect must be given, in a special way, to the authentic teaching authority of the Roman Pontiff, even when he does not speak ex cathedra in such wise, indeed, that his supreme teaching authority be acknowledged with respect, and that one sincerely adhere to decisions made by him, conformably with his manifest mind and intention. . . . [8]

*Obliged to submit to their bishops' decision . . . submission of the will and intellect must be given . . .* ! That gives Rome incredible power over devout Catholics. That every Catholic does not obey is not the point; the point is that such wording is the *unchangeable teaching and intent of the Church,* not only for its members but for all mankind.

While many Catholics rebel against certain Church doctrines, they remain nominally attached to the Church, though they may only attend on Christmas or Easter. When it comes, however, to their hope of someday being released from purgatory and getting to heaven, no Catholic can question the Church or he would cease to be under its protection and thus be damned. Vatican II clearly says:

This holy Council teaches . . . that the Church . . . is necessary for salvation. . . . Hence, they could not be saved who, knowing that the Catholic Church was founded as necessary by God through Christ, would refuse either to enter it, or to remain in it.[9]

Remember that Hitler and Mussolini remained Catholics to the end and were never excommunicated from the Church. So did thousands of the worst Nazi war criminals, whom the Vatican smuggled out of Europe into safe havens in South America. Such archcriminals are honored with Catholic funerals and, like Mafia members, die with the assurance that their Church will continue to say Masses in order to get them out of purgatory and eventually into heaven. It is an insurance policy that very few allow to lapse completely.

## "Impeccability" Versus "Infallibility"

The required blind faith in the pronouncements of the pope and the clergy seems to make sense because the Roman Church is the largest and oldest. Surely so many billions of religious people couldn't be wrong for the past 1500 years! Faith is also bolstered by the assurance that the Roman Catholic Church is the one true church, the one which alone can be traced back to the original apostles, and that its papal authority comes directly from Christ through Peter by a long and unbroken line of apostolic succession.

As proof, the Church provides a list of its popes (thus far 263) all the way back to Peter. Few Catholics know that popes quarreled and fought with one another, excommunicated one another, and sometimes even killed each other. It is difficult to find even a few among the popes after the fifth century who exhibited the basic Christian virtues. Their lives as recorded in the *Catholic Encyclopedia* read like an unbelievable soap opera of lust, madness, mayhem, and murder. Nevertheless, all of these master criminals, poisoners, adulterers, and mass murderers are considered to have been infallible when they spoke ex cathedra—that is, made dogmatic pronouncements upon faith and morals to the whole church.

Catholic apologists argue that there is a difference between *impeccability* in character and conduct, which the popes certainly did not have, and *infallibility* in faith and morals, which every Catholic must believe they had.[10] What folly to believe that a man who in his life denies the faith and is habitually immoral is nevertheless infallible when he *speaks* of faith and morals!

Knowledgeable Catholics readily admit that many popes were incredibly evil. But that fact, it is argued, simply proves they were human and allows one to disagree with them in good conscience. To the Catholic it makes good sense that, in spite of the undeniable wickedness of her clergy, the Roman Catholic Church *must* be mankind's only hope. After all, it was established by Christ Himself, who made Peter the first pope. That is supposedly proved by the Scripture "Thou art Peter, and upon this rock I will build my church" (Matthew 16:18), which we will deal with in detail later.

## The Unknown Dogma

Contrary to what Roman Catholics are taught, the papal office did not originate with Peter. It was centuries before the Bishop of Rome attempted to dominate the rest of the Church, and many centuries more before this primacy was generally accepted. Leo the Great's letter to Flavian in 449 was not accepted until the Council of Chalcedon had approved it. "[Pope] Leo [I] himself acknowledged that his treatise could not become a rule of faith till it was confirmed by the bishops."[11]

There were eight councils of the Church before the schism in 1054 split it into Roman Catholicism and Eastern Orthodoxy, when the Bishop of Rome and the Patriarch of Constantinople excommunicated each other. None of these eight councils was called by the Bishop of Rome, but by the emperor, who also put his stamp of approval upon their decrees. As for papal authority, one Catholic historian reminds us:

> Pope Pelagius (556-60) talks of heretics separating themselves from the Apostolic *Sees*, that is, Rome, Jerusalem, Alexandria plus Constantinople. In all the early writings of the hierarchy there is no mention of a special role for the Bishop of Rome, nor yet the special name of 'Pope.' ... Of the eighty or so heresies in the first six centuries, not one refers to the authority of the Bishop of Rome, not one is settled by the Bishop of Rome. ... No one attacks the [supreme] authority of the Roman pontiff, *because no one has heard of it.*[12]

The Easter Synod of 680 called by Pope Agatho was the first ecclesiastical body that asserted the primacy of Rome over the rest of the Church, but this was not an ecumenical council of the entire Church, so its decision was not generally accepted. As Catholic historian Peter de Rosa points out:

> ... not one of the early Fathers of the church saw in the Bible any reference to papal jurisdiction over the church. On the contrary, they take it for granted that bishops, especially metropolitans, have the full right to govern and administer their own territory without interference from *anyone*. The Eastern church *never* accepted papal supremacy; Rome's attempt to impose it led to the schism.
>
> ... one looks in vain in the first millennium for a single doctrine or piece of legislation imposed by Rome *alone* on the rest of the church. The only general laws came out of Councils such as Nicaea. In any case, how *could* the Bishop of Rome have exercised universal jurisdiction in those early centuries when there was no [Roman] Curia, when other bishops brooked no interference in their dioceses from *anyone*, when Rome issued no dispensations and demanded no tribute or taxation, when all bishops, not just the Bishop of Rome, had the power to bind and loose, when no bishop or church or individual was censured by Rome?
>
> Further, for centuries, the Bishop of Rome was chosen by the local citizens—clergy and laity. If he had jurisdiction over the universal church, would not the rest of the world want a say in his appointment? When he *was* believed to have [universal] supremacy the rest of the church *did* demand a say in his election. This came about only in the Middle Ages.[13]

## From Calvary to Regal Pontiff

It requires ingenious interpolation to derive from the simple statement "On this rock I will build my church" a Petrine office, apostolic succession, papal infallibility, and all the pomp, ceremony, and power surrounding the pope today. As one Catholic writer rather sarcastically points out: "... it required [great] skill to take statements made by a poor Carpenter to an equally poor fisherman and apply them to a regal pontiff who was soon to be called Lord of the World."[14]

Yet such is the only biblical foundation upon which the entire superstructure of the Roman Catholic Church has been built. It includes an infallible papacy, apostolic succession, an intricate hierarchy of priests, bishops, archbishops, cardinals et al, the magisterium of bishops which alone can interpret the Bible, the requirement that for his alleged infallibility the pope must speak ex cathedra to the entire Church on matters of faith or morals, etc. etc. That none of these concepts is even remotely suggested, much less specifically stated, either in Matthew 16:18 or elsewhere in Scripture is dismissed by Catholic apologists, who then look to "tradition" for support. There they enter a maze of deceit and actual fraud.

It took centuries of developing ingenious arguments to finally arrive at the theory that the Christ who had "nowhere to lay his head" (Matthew 8:20), who lived in poverty and was crucified naked, was to be represented by a regal pontiff who possessed more than one palace containing in excess of 1100 rooms each, was waited upon day and night by scores of servants, and wore the finest gold-embroidered silk robes! That Christ passed on to Peter such pomp and luxuries, which neither of them knew, is both ludicrous and blasphemous.

The glories and powers enjoyed by popes are not even remotely related to Peter's life of purity and poverty. This fisherman-apostle said, "Silver and gold have I none" (Acts 3:6). Nor were papal luxuries and pompous claims of authority over kings and kingdoms known in the Church until centuries later as ambitious popes gradually extended and solidified their authority and control over earthly rulers. Popes began to call themselves by such titles as "supreme ruler of the world" and "king of kings." Others claiming to be "God on earth," even the "redeemer" who "hung on the cross as Christ did," asserted that "Jesus put the popes on the same level as God."[15] Peter would have denounced such pretentious fraud as blasphemy.

Rome had been the capital of the empire before Constantine moved his palace to the East, and it continued to be regarded as the capital of the western half of the empire. With the Emperor Constantine installed in the city of Constantinople (Istanbul today), the pope developed near absolute power, not only as the head of the Church but as the emperor of the West.

When the empire later fell, it was the papacy which gave the fragmented remains its continuity. Thomas Hobbes would say, "The papacy is no other than the ghost of the deceased Roman Empire, sitting crowned upon the grave thereof."

W.H.C. Frend, Emeritus Professor of Ecclesiastical History, in his classic *The Rise of Christianity*, points out that by the middle of the fifth century the Church "had become the most powerful single factor in the lives of the peoples of the empire. The Virgin and the saints had replaced the [pagan] gods as patrons of cities."[16] Pope Leo I (440-61) boasted that St. Peter and St. Paul had "replaced Romulus and Remus as the city's [Rome's] protecting patrons."[17] Frend writes that "Christian Rome was the legitimate successor of pagan Rome ...Christ had triumphed [and] Rome was ready to extend its sway to the heavens themselves."[18]

## Shameless Revision of History

Such was the ambition of most of those who were scrambling onto the alleged throne of Peter and at times warring with one another to gain it. Using the name of Christ and piously making the sign of the cross, they labored mightily to satisfy their lust for power and pleasure and wealth. No justification for making themselves the absolute and infallible rulers over the Church, much less the world, could be found in the writings of the early Fathers and certainly not in Scripture. Therefore the popes had to find other support. The means they chose was to rewrite history by manufacturing allegedly historical documents. The first of these bold forgeries was *The Donation of Constantine*, which we have already mentioned. It was followed by pseudo-*Isidorian Decretals*, which were early papal decrees allegedly compiled by Archbishop Isidore (560-636) but actually fabricated in the ninth century. These frauds became the foundation for much "tradition" still relied upon today.

Catholic historian J.H. Ignaz von Dollinger writes that prior "to the time of the *Isidorian Decretals* no serious attempt was made anywhere to introduce the neo-Roman theory of infallibility. The popes did not dream of laying claim to such a privilege."[19] He goes on to explain that these fraudulent *Decretals* would—

gradually, but surely, change the whole constitution and government of the Church. It would be difficult to find in all history a second instance of so successful and yet so clumsy a forgery.

For three centuries past [he wrote in 1869] it [the fabrication] has been exposed, yet the principles it introduced and brought into practice have taken such deep root in the soil of the Church, and have so grown into her life, that the exposure of the fraud has produced no result in shaking the dominant system.[20]

The *Isidorian Decretals* involved about a hundred concocted decrees allegedly promulgated by the earliest popes, along with counterfeit writings of supposed Church authorities and synods. These fabrications were just what Nicholas I (858-67) needed to justify his claims that the popes "held the place of God on earth" with absolute authority over kings, including even the right to "command massacres" of those who opposed them—all in the name of Christ.

The popes who followed Nicholas were only too happy to emulate his ways, and each of them used his predecessors' actions to justify his own, thus building an ever-larger case for infallibility, but upon a fraudulent foundation. Writing in the nineteenth century, Church historian R.W. Thompson, himself a Catholic, comments:

Such times as these were adapted to the practice of any kind of imposture and fraud which the popes and clergy considered necessary to strengthen the authority of the papacy. . . . the personal interest [and] ambition of Innocent III led him to preserve all these forgeries with care, so that . . . the "pious fraud" might become sanctified by time . . . The result he hoped and sought for has been accomplished. . . .

[These] false *Decretals*, which are now universally considered to have been bold and unblushing forgeries . . . constitute the cornerstone of that enormous system of wrong and usurpation which has since been built up by the papacy, to revive which Pope Pius IX has now put forth his Encyclical and *Syllabus* [*of Errors*]. . . .[21]

Devout Catholics would be shocked to learn that much of the "apostolic tradition" they have been told supports Roman Catholicism (and is to be regarded upon the same level as Scripture) was actually a deliberately manufactured fraud. The doctrines built upon these forgeries became so interwoven into Catholicism that even after the hoax was exposed the popes were reluctant to make the necessary corrections. Pope after infallible pope endorsed the counterfeit. To make a clean break from centuries of accumulated lies would tear apart the very fabric of Roman Catholicism.

Pope Pius IX relied upon the fraud, though it had already been exposed for three centuries, to build his case for pressuring the bishops to make papal infallibility an official dogma at Vatican I. But the testimony of history conclusively refutes both apostolic succession and papal infallibility.

*This is the sole Church of Christ which in the creed we profess to be one, holy, catholic and apostolic, which our Saviour, after his resurrection, entrusted to Peter's pastoral care, commissioning him and the other apostles to extend and rule it. . . .*

*The Roman Pontiff, as the successor of Peter, is the perpetual and visible source and foundation of the unity both of the bishops and of the whole company of the faithful.*

—Vatican II[1]

# 8

# Unbroken Line
# of Apostolic Succession?

The claim that the popes are the successors of the apostle Peter is the cornerstone of Roman Catholicism, without which that Church would lose its uniqueness and could not function. We must therefore spend further time to examine this claim carefully. Is there actually an unbroken line of 262 popes succeeding Peter?

For apostolic succession to occur, each pope must choose his own successor and personally lay hands on him and ordain him. This was the procedure when Paul and Barnabas were sent forth by the church at Antioch on their first missionary journey (Acts 13:3). Timothy's appointment to the ministry was also by the elders laying hands upon him (1 Timothy 4:14), as did Paul when he imparted a special spiritual gift to Timothy (2 Timothy 1:6). This biblical procedure, however, has never been followed with regard to successors of the bishops of Rome or the popes. A pope's successor is chosen not by him, but after his death by others; and it has most often been done in the most ungodly manner, as we shall see.

Furthermore, there is no record that Peter was ever Bishop of Rome, and therefore no Bishop of Rome could possibly be his successor. Irenaeus, Bishop of Lyons (178-200), provided a list of the first 12 Bishops of Rome. Linus was the first. Peter's name does not appear. Eusebius of Caesaria, the Father of church history, never mentions Peter as Bishop of Rome. He simply says that Peter came to Rome "about the end of his days" and was crucified there. Paul, in writing his epistle to the Romans, greets many people by name, but not Peter. That would be a strange omission if Peter had been living in Rome, and especially if he were its bishop!

## Missing Links in the "Unbroken Line"

The Vatican puts out an official list of the popes, arbitrarily beginning with Peter and continuing to the present. There have been several such lists which were apparently considered accurate at one time but subsequently had to be revised—and now conflict with each other. The earliest lists come from *Liber Pontificalis* (Book of Popes), presumably first composed under Pope Hormisdus (514-23), yet even the *Catholic Encyclopedia* casts doubt upon its authenticity, and most scholars today agree that it mixed fact with fiction. Who the actual Bishops of Rome were cannot be known with any certainty at this late date. Even the *New Catholic Encyclopedia*, published by the Catholic University of America, acknowledges this fact:

> But it must be frankly admitted that bias or deficiencies in the sources make it impossible to determine in certain cases whether the claimants were popes or antipopes.[2]

The simple truth is that the Roman Catholic Church itself, with all of its archives, cannot verify an accurate and complete list of the popes. The alleged "unbroken line of succession back to Peter" is therefore a mere fiction. Anyone who takes the time to seriously attempt a verification of its accuracy will conclude that the Church has fabricated an official list of popes in order to justify the papacy and its pretensions. Nor was the Bishop of Rome considered to be the pope of the universal Church until about a thousand years after Pentecost!

## Apostolic Succession?

For centuries the citizens of Rome considered it their right to elect the Bishop of Rome. This custom is proof that the

Bishop of Rome had jurisdiction *only over that territory*, for if he had had jurisdiction over the whole Church, then all of the Church would have been involved in choosing him, as it is today. When at times the right to elect their own Bishop was denied them, the citizens of Rome revolted and forced their will upon the local civil and religious authorities. How could such pressure by mob violence be called apostolic succession by the direction of the Holy Spirit?

Feuds were carried on between powerful families (Colonna, Orsini, Annibaldi, Conti, Caetani, et al), who fought wars for the papacy for centuries. For example, Boniface VIII, a Caetani, had to battle the Colonna to remain in power. At the height of his success he had all of Western Christendom coming to Rome for the great Jubilee in 1300. But in 1303 he was seized by emissaries of Philip the Fair of France, and Rome fell into French possession. As a consequence, the papacy was moved to France, and from 1309-77 the popes were French and resided at Avignon. Such political maneuverings could hardly constitute apostolic succession!

Popes were both installed and deposed by imperial armies or Roman mobs. Some were murdered. More than one pope was executed by a jealous husband who found him in bed with his wife—hardly apostolic succession. Money and/or violence most often determined who would be "Peter's successor." No wonder that in the Concordat of Worms (between Pope Calixtus II and the Emperor Henry V, September 23, 1122) the pope was made to swear that the election of bishops and abbots would take place "without simony and without any violence,"[3] which all too often decided Church affairs.

At times there were several rivals each claiming to have been legally voted in by a legitimate council. One of the earliest examples of multiple popes was created by the simultaneous election by rival factions of Popes Ursinus and Damasus. The former's followers managed, after much violence, to install him as pope. Later, after a bloody three-day battle, Damasus, with the backing of the emperor, emerged the victor and continued as vicar of Christ for 18 years (366-84). So "apostolic succession" by an "unbroken line from Peter" operated by armed force? Really?

Ironically, Damasus was the first who, in 382, used the phrase "Thou art Peter and upon this rock I will build my church" to claim supreme spiritual authority. Bloody, wealthy, powerful, and exceedingly corrupt, Damasus surrounded himself with luxuries that would have made an emperor blush. There is no way to justify any connection between him and Christ, yet he remains one link in that chain of alleged unbroken succession back to Peter.

## Violence, Intrigue, and Simony

Stephen VII (896-7), who exhumed Pope Formosus and condemned the corpse for heresy at a mock trial, was soon thereafter strangled by zealots who opposed him. His party promptly elected a Cardinal Sergius to be pope, but he was chased out of Rome by a rival faction which had elected Romanus as its "vicar of Christ." Of the strange manner in which popes followed one another in an "unbroken line of apostolic succession from Peter," one historian writes:

> Over the next twelve months four more popes scrambled onto the bloodstained [papal] throne, maintained themselves precariously for a few weeks—or even days—before being *hurled* themselves into their graves.
>
> Seven popes and an anti-pope had appeared in a little over six years when . . . Cardinal Sergius reappeared after seven years' exile, backed now by the swords of a feudal lord who saw a means thereby of gaining entry into Rome. The reigning pope [Leo V, 903] found his grave, the slaughters in the city reached a climax, and then Cardinal Sergius emerged as Pope Sergius [III, 904-11], sole survivor of the claimants and now supreme pontiff.[4]

Attempting to establish stability in selecting popes, in 1059 Nicholas II (1059-61) "defined the role of the cardinals in the [papal] electoral process. During the Third Lateran Council in 1179, Alexander III (1159-81) restricted papal elections to the cardinals."[5] It was hardly an improvement. As one nineteenth-century historian pointed out, "Few papal elections, if any, have been other than simoniacal [bought off for money]. . . . The invention of the Sacred College [of cardinals] has been, on the whole, perhaps the most fertile source of corruption in the Church. Many cardinals went to Rome for the conclave with their bankers."[6]

Much insight into such corruption comes from the diaries of John Burchard. Master of Ceremonies at the conclave that elected Rodrigo Borgia (Pope Alexander VI [1492-1503]), Burchard concludes that only five votes were not bought in that election. "The young cardinal Giovanni de' Medici, who had refused to sell his vote, thought it prudent to leave Rome immediately."[7] In those days a cardinal's hat sold for a king's ransom, so it took a fortune to enter the polluted stream of "apostolic succession." Money flowed in from all over Europe to back favorite candidates. Borgia bought the papacy with "villas, towns and abbeys . . . [and] four mule-loads of silver to his greatest rival, Cardinal Sforza, to induce him to step down." Peter de Rosa remarks facetiously:

> It is instructive to see, by way of Burchard's diaries, how the Holy Spirit goes about choosing St. Peter's successor.[8]

## Sex and Succession

Some popes were put in office by their mistresses—*six* by a mother-and-daughter pair of prostitutes. Theodora of Rome (wife of a powerful Roman Senator) was most successful at this strategy. She manipulated Roman politics by exploiting the fact that her daughter, Marozia, was the mistress of Pope Sergius III. Known as "the mistress of Rome," Marozia did not hesitate at murder to accomplish her ambitions. Theodora herself was mistress to two ecclesiastics whom she maneuvered in quick succession, after Sergius's death, onto "Peter's throne"—popes Anastasius III (911-13) and Lando (913-14). Falling in love with a priest from Ravena, she maneuvered him also onto the papal throne.

That prostitutes determined who would be pope could hardly be "apostolic succession"! Of this remarkable mother and daughter Edward Gibbon wrote in his *Decline and Fall of the Roman Empire*:

> The influence of two prostitutes, Marozia and Theodora, was founded on their wealth and beauty, their political and amorous intrigues. The most strenuous of their lovers were rewarded with the Roman mitre. . . . The bastard son, the grandson, and the great grandson of Marozia—a rare genealogy—were seated in the Chair of St. Peter.[9]

Alberic, another of Marozia's sons, with his armed thugs, literally controlled Rome. He made the Roman leaders swear to elect his son (Marozia's grandson), Octavian, not only as his successor to the Imperial throne but, upon the death of the pope, to that supreme religious office as well. And so it happened that Octavian called himself Pope John XII, while at the same time retaining the name Octavian as prince. Thus both the civil and ecclesiastical thrones were joined in one man.

John XII (955-63) was obsessed with illicit sex even more than he was with power. Though he had many regular mistresses, they were not enough. It was no longer safe for any woman to come into St. Peters! Bishop Liudprand of Cremona, papal observer and chronicler of that time, tells that the pope "was so blindly in love with [one mistress] that he made her governor of several cities—and even gave to her the golden crosses and cups of St. Peter himself." Roman mobs that had supported him and cared nothing about his amorous affairs were angered by the loss of properties which Romans had looked upon as part of their heritage.

Surrounded by mobs who were now eager to remove him, and besieged by the new King of Italy with his armies from without, Octavian abandoned his position as civil ruler but would not give up the even more lucrative and influential papacy, though he made no pretense of being a religious man, much less a true Christian. The papacy still had the power to crown emperors, so the pope summoned Otto, King of Germany and Europe's most powerful monarch, to Rome to be crowned Emperor of the Holy Roman Empire. Otto came in haste with his army to the aid of the besieged pontiff.

After his coronation by John XII, Otto attempted to lecture the young pope about his dissolute life. John XII pretended to heed the advice. But after Otto and his armies had left, the pope, unwilling to abandon his sexual exploits, offered the Imperial crown to Berenger, the very enemy whose armies had plundered northern Italy and because of whose threats he had appealed to Otto.

Tempted by the prize that was now dangled in front of him, Berenger nevertheless declined, knowing that his forces were no match for Otto's army. The frantic pope then appealed to everyone from Saracens to Huns to rescue him from the man he had just crowned emperor of the Holy Roman Empire and with whom he had sworn to revive the ancient partnership between crown and papacy that had once worked so well between Leo III and Charlemagne!

## Papal Musical Chairs

When Otto returned with his army to settle accounts, John XII fled from Rome to Tivoli with what Vatican treasures he could carry. Otto opened a synod to decide John's fate. Bishop Liudprand presided in the emperor's name and recorded the proceedings. Witnesses were called and the crimes of the pope established, from fornication with numerous women who were named, to blinding Benedict, his spiritual father, to the murder of a Cardinal John, to toasting Satan at St. Peter's altar. But before Otto could execute justice, Pope John XII was killed by a husband who found the unrepentant pontiff bedded with his wife. Yet John XII is on the official Roman Catholic list of popes, each known as "His holiness, Vicar of Christ."

Not long after Otto's death in Germany, the papacy fell under the control of a powerful family of warlords in the Alban hills. The leader of the clan, Gregory of Tusculum, through wealth and the power of the sword succeeded in placing two of his three sons and a grandson (one succeeding the other) on the supposed throne of St. Peter. The Alberics of Tusculum could eventually boast of 40 cardinals, 3 antipopes, and 13 popes issuing from that one family. It would be a mockery to say that the wealth and power that produced this remarkable familial network of popes had anything to do with apostolic succession.

Of this period, Church historian von Dollinger, himself a devout Catholic, writes:

> ...the Roman Church was enslaved and degraded, while the Apostolic See became the prey and the plaything of rival factions of the nobles, and for a long time of ambitious and profligate women. It was only renovated for a brief interval (997-1003) in the persons of Gregory V and Silvester II, by the influence of the Saxon emperor.
>
> Then the Papacy sank back into utter confusion and moral impotence; the Tuscan Counts made it hereditary in their family; again and again dissolute boys, like John XII [age 16 when he became Pope] and Benedict IX [at age 11], occupied and disgraced the Apostolic throne, which was now bought and sold like a piece of merchandise, and at last three Popes fought for the tiara, until the Emperor Henry III put an end to the scandal by elevating a German bishop to the See of Rome.[10]

Chased by mobs from Rome in 1045, Pope Benedict IX (1032-44; 1045; 1047-8) fled to the protection of his uncle, Count Gregory, whose army controlled the hill country of Tusculum. In his absence, John, Bishop of the Sabine Hills, entered Rome and installed himself as pope under the name Sylvester III (1045). He occupied the "throne of Peter" a mere three months until Benedict stormed back with more swords than Sylvester could summon and ruled as pope once again. Yet both of these men are on the official Vatican list of those considered worthy of the titles "His Holiness" and "Vicar of Christ."

Tiring of the burdens of his office and eager to devote himself entirely to his favorite lover, Benedict sold the papacy for 1500 pounds of gold to his godfather, Giovanni Gratiano, archpriest of St. John's Church at the Latin Gate. Giovanni took over the papacy in May 1045 under the name of Pope Gregory VI (1045-6). With fresh resolve, Benedict returned to Rome in 1047 and set himself up as pope once again. So did Sylvester III. Now there were three popes, each ruling over that portion of Rome which his private army controlled, each claiming to be the vicar of Christ and possessor of the keys of heaven by virtue of apostolic succession.

Growing weary of the charade, the disillusioned and angry Roman citizens appealed to Emperor Henry III. He marched into Rome with his army and presided over a synod that deposed all three "popes" and installed the emperor's choice. He called himself Clement II (1046-7). But Benedict was not so easily dispatched. As soon as the Imperial army withdrew, he returned to Rome and managed by force of arms to rule as pope for another eight months (1047-8), until Henry returned and chased him back to the Alban hills for the last time.

One would think the Roman Catholic Church would be ashamed of such fiascos and blot out the memory of evil popes and their fraudulent and often violent means of gaining and losing and recovering the papal throne. Yet in spite of such godless rivalry and in spite of the fact that their papacies overlapped (at times all three claimed to be pope), each of these adversarial claimants to Peter's throne is found on the Vatican's official list of popes today. (For further history of the popes see Appendix D.)

*It is beyond question that he [the pope] can err even in matters touching the faith. He does this when he teaches heresy by his own judgment or decretal. In truth, many Roman Pontiffs were heretics.*

—Pope Adrian VI, 1523[1]

# 9

# Infallible Heretics?

The great importance of the papacy warrants yet further investigation as to its legitimacy. Vital is the claim that the popes are infallible when they speak on morals and dogma to the entire Church. If they are not infallible, the Roman Catholic Church has lost its unique leadership and apostolic authority. Yet popes themselves (Adrian VI quoted on the facing page and others) have denied that they or any other popes were infallible. Why not believe them?

Pope Adrian VI's declaration goes even further. If many popes have been heretics, then we have another reason why there cannot be an unbroken line of "apostolic succession back to Peter." Besides proving that a person is *not* infallible, espousing heresy is a mortal sin in Roman Catholic theology. Its immediate consequence, so says the official Roman Catholic *Code of Canon Law* (a codification of the canons and decrees of the Church councils) is instant and automatic excommunication.[2] A heretic has denied the faith and placed himself outside the Church.

A heretical pope is therefore no longer even a member of the Church, much less its head. Consequently, a heretic, though pope, could not possibly provide a channel of apostolic authority to a successor. Yet the list of popes contains numerous heretics who were denounced as such by councils and by other popes.

No wonder the theories of apostolic succession and papal infallibility were not proposed until many centuries after Peter's death! It was as the popes grasped after more power, and began to command monarchs and entire nations, that they needed to justify their arrogant and oppressive imperialism. Already they claimed to be "God on earth" and the vicars of Christ, but that was not enough. They necessarily began to assert *infallibility* as well.

## The Roots of Infallibility

Kings and emperors had once claimed to be gods, but their luster faded as they fought among themselves and their subjects began to chafe for more freedom. What was needed was an infallible representation of deity on earth to whom the civil rulers could look to settle their disputes. The popes began to fill that need, and by the thirteenth century they had established themselves as the supreme authority all across Europe. A leading nineteenth-century Catholic historian wrote that this authoritarianism encouraged despotism:

> ... the Catholic Church [developed] an hostile and suspicious attitude towards the principles of political, intellectual, and religious freedom and independence of judgment... [so that the] ideal of the Church [became] an universal empire... of force and oppression, where the spiritual authority is aided by the secular arm in summarily suppressing every movement it dislikes.
> ... we could not, therefore, avoid bringing forward ... a very dark side of the history of the Papacy.[3]

Much of the "dark side of the history of the Papacy" involving that "empire of force and oppression" resulted from the popes' claim to infallibility. People eagerly embraced the idea in spite of the popes' wickedness. After all, the pagan gods stole one another's wives and lived riotously, so why not the popes? But the idea that a pope could be thought *infallible* even while blatantly contradicting himself was remarkable. Yet that fraud was maintained.

Such was the case, for example, when Pope Clement XI (1700-21) confirmed King Philip V of Spain and then shortly thereafter King Charles III of Germany, both with the same titles and privileges, including the highly prized Bull of the Crusade. As a result, Charles went to war with Philip to claim the crown which the pope seemingly had given him. Clement even confirmed two different candidates, one proposed by each sovereign, for the same bishopric.

One would think that such blatant contradictions would be proof enough that the pope was *not* infallible. Yet the bishops arguing the case for Charles III, according to a contemporary observer, "did allege the Pope's infallibility, and that every Christian is obliged in conscience to follow the last declaration of the Pope, and blindly to obey it, without inquiring into the reasons that did move the Pope to it."[4] Such is the illogical and unbiblical but absolute and infallible papal authority which had long been claimed by the popes and which became official Roman Catholic dogma at Vatican I. That Council was coerced by Pius IX (1846-78) even to make submission to the pope a requirement of salvation:

> If anyone therefore shall say that blessed Peter the Apostle was not appointed the prince of all the apostles and the visible head of the whole church militant or that the same directly and immediately received from our Lord Jesus Christ a primacy of honor only and not of true and proper jurisdiction [over the whole church], let him be anathema [excommunicated and thus damned]!

Nearly 300 years earlier, in 1591, the Jesuit Cardinal Robert Bellarmine, whose loyalty to the pope was absolute, had declared that whatever the Roman Pontiff commanded must be believed and obeyed no matter how evil or ludicrous. Of course, he could show neither biblical, logical, nor traditional support for such an extreme view, a view which did away with the individual moral accountability to God so clearly taught in Scripture and recognized in every conscience.

Peter Olivi, a Franciscan priest, made one of the earliest attempts to establish papal infallibility. His motive was primarily selfish. Pope Nicholas III (1277-80) had favored the Franciscans by declaring that "communal renunciation of property was a possible way to salvation."[5] (Roman Catholicism had long taught salvation by works, as it teaches even today.)

Desiring to make the pope's decision in favor of himself and his fellow Franciscans unassailable, Olivi proposed that such papal pronouncements were infallible. A pope could live the most wicked life, murdering rivals, plundering cities, massacring their inhabitants (as many popes did), and denying Christ daily in abominable deeds. Yet if and when he made a pronouncement to the Church on faith and morals he would be under the guidance of the Holy Spirit to such an extent that whatever he said would be infallible.

Olivi's astonishing proposal was a radical departure from Church tradition. Until then few popes had dared to look upon themselves as infallible, though the temptation to the human ego to embrace such folly is especially great for those who are so highly revered and venerated. Catholic theologian Hans Kung writes:

> With regard to the origin of the Roman Doctrine of infallibility: . . . [it] did not slowly "develop" or "unfold," but rather was created in one stroke in the late 1200s [by] an eccentric Franciscan, Peter Olivi (d. 1298), repeatedly accused of heresy. At first no one took Olivi's notion seriously. . . . The medieval canonists . . . had never claimed that the Church needed an infallible head to preserve its faith. . . . [And] the modern critical attack on the principles of infallibility has the backing of Scripture and the body of Catholic tradition.[6]

## "A Work of the Devil"

Olivi's theory was soon denounced by a pontiff, who would take awful vengeance upon the Franciscans. Pope John XXII (1316-34) had his own selfish reasons for denying papal infallibility. Had the Franciscans not been the champions of it, John might have accepted the idea as useful for his own purposes. However, he hated the Franciscans for taking vows of poverty that condemned his own lavish lifestyle. He had amassed a huge fortune "by duping the poor, by selling livings, indulgences and dispensations."[7] Angrily, John XXII condemned as heresy both the Franciscan way of life and Nicholas III's commendation thereof.

To justify contradicting another pope, John produced his Bull *Qui quorundam* (1324), a dogmatic assertion of doctrine made to the entire Church and thus infallible by today's rules. In it John XXII reviled the doctrine of papal infallibility as "the work of the devil."

Though often offered as an example of the consummate heretic, John XXII continued in the "holy office" for 18 wicked years, and his name remains today unashamedly displayed on the Vatican's official list of the vicars of Christ. This pope is described by one Catholic historian as "full of avarice, more worldly than a pimp, and with a laugh that crackled with unimprovable malice."[8] Yet he is an essential link in the alleged apostolic succession back to Peter upon which John Paul II's legitimacy depends today.

## Papal Heretics' Heretic

John XXII's predecessor, Clement V, had given away all of the Church's wealth to his relatives, leaving a bare treasury. That condition the new pope went about to cure with a vengeance. He sold everything for a price, including absolution from sin and eternal salvation. Thus the golden chalice held by the woman riding the beast was refilled with filthy lucre gained by abominable means exactly as the apostle John foresaw in his remarkable vision.

John XXII published a list of crimes and gross sins, together with the individual price for which he, as vicar of Christ, head of the one true Church, would absolve transgressors from each of them. The list left nothing out, from murder and piracy to incest, adultery, and sodomy. The wealthier one was, the more one could sin; the more Catholics sinned, the richer the Church became.

Much of the wealth thus acquired was spent to further John XXII's passion for wars. One of his contemporaries wrote: "The blood he shed would have incarnadined the waters of Lake Constance [an extremely large lake], and the bodies of the slain would have bridged it from shore to shore."[9]

John XXII's pet doctrine was like that of many who are popular on Christian radio and TV today: that Christ and His apostles had been men of great wealth. So he declared in a papal bull, *Cum inter nonnullos* (1323). To deny this dogma was heresy punishable by death. John demanded that secular rulers burn at the stake Franciscans who had taken vows of poverty. Those who refused to do so were excommunicated. During his pontificate he handed over 114 Franciscans to the Inquisition to be consumed by the flames for the heresy of purposely living in poverty as Christ had. Thus it became official Roman Catholic dogma that Christ and His disciples were men of considerable wealth, and that all Christians ought to be so—a dogma repudiated by other popes.

Such papal heretics and their condemnations of one another are part of the history of the popes, a history which Catholics must honestly face. And Protestants as well, those who admire John Paul II, must realize that the position he holds and the special authority he claims come to him through a long line of criminals and heretics whom he and his Church still honor as past vicars of Christ.

## The Holy Heretic

Millions of Catholics from whom the historical truth has been hidden have looked upon John XXII as an exceptionally holy man. Was he not favored above all popes by "Our Lady of Mount Carmel" with one of her rare personal appearances? John swore that the "Virgin Mary" appeared to him to present the Great Promise: that she would personally go into purgatory the Saturday after their death and take to heaven all those who, having met certain other conditions, died wearing her brown scapular. In reliance upon this special Sabbatine [Saturday] Privilege, which was confirmed by other popes, untold millions of Roman Catholics have since worn (and still wear today) the brown scapular of "Our Lady of Mount Carmel" as their ticket to heaven.

John XXII was eventually denounced as a heretic by Emperor Louis of Bavaria, who deposed him and appointed another pope in his place. But the emperor's purging of the papacy turned embarrassing when, shortly after the new pope took office, his wife appeared on the scene. The emperor quickly decided that John XXII wasn't so bad after all. For, as de Rosa sarcastically remarks, although John, like most of the other popes, had illegitimate children, at least he "had never committed the sin of matrimony." Such sarcasm, though it comes from a Catholic historian, may seem unfair at first but is in fact fully warranted. Today's *Code of Canon Law*, Canon 1394, refers to marriage as a "scandal" for a priest, whereas it has no such harsh words for sins of which priests are frequently guilty even today, such as child molestation, keeping a mistress, homosexuality, etc.

Reinstated as pope, John XXII's heretical pronouncements became so outrageous that only his death saved him from removal again from the papacy. Yet he remains on that long list of alleged successors of Peter through whom Pope John Paul II received his authority.

In 896 Stephan VII (896-7) had the corpse of the previous Pope Formosus (891-6) exhumed eight months after burial. Dressed in its former papal vestments and propped on a throne in the council chamber, the cadaver was "tried" and found guilty of having crowned as emperor one of Charlemagne's many illegitimate descendants. In fact, there have been a number of popes who were themselves the illegitimate sons of previous popes. They were thus illicit claimants to the alleged throne of Peter and therefore hardly capable of passing on to their successors apostolic authority.

Having been condemned by Pope Stephan VII, the former Pope Formosus's corpse was stripped, the three fingers of benediction on the right hand were hacked off, and the remains thrown to the mob outside, who dragged it through the streets and threw it into the Tiber. Fishermen gave it a decent burial. Pope Stephan VII then declared all of Formosus's ordinations invalid, creating a most serious problem which haunts the Roman Catholic Church to this day.

Formosus had ordained many priests and bishops, who in turn ordained multitudes of others, who also did the same. Thus an open and insoluble question remains concerning which priests, bishops, et al, down to the present time may be in the line of those ordained by Formosus and are therefore without genuine apostolic authority. And what of those who were ordained by the many other heretical popes? And what of the fact that Formosus, too, remains on that official Vatican list of vicars of Christ, as does the pope who exhumed his body and denounced him posthumously?

Pope Sergius III agreed with Stephan VII in pronouncing all ordinations by heretical popes invalid—which, of course, is only logical in view of the automatic excommunication which we have already noted accompanies heresy. In *Cum ex Apostolatus officio*, Pope Paul IV declared "by the plenitude of papal power" that all of the acts of heretical popes were null and void. That infallible declaration leaves "apostolic succession" in ruins.

## Councils Above Popes

A former unscrupulous Roman official, Vigilius, as pope (537-55) became an even more tragic figure. He changed his mind on doctrine each time the emperor demanded it. Vigilius was finally declared a heretic and excommunicated by the Fifth General Council (553), called at Constantinople by the Emperor Justinian. (No one doubted that a council's authority was above that of a pope.)

Exiled by the emperor, Vigilius confessed his errors and pleaded that he had been deceived by the devil. Yet the reign of this man on Peter's alleged throne was among the longest of any of the popes. More than one pope was condemned as a heretic by a Church council. The Council of Constance [1414-18] deposed three popes who each claimed to be the one true vicar of Christ and had each "excommunicated" the other two. (See Appendix D.)

Pope Honorius (625-38) was condemned as a heretic by the Sixth Ecumenical Council (678-87). For centuries each new pope taking office was required to swear by an oath that Honorius had been a heretic and that the council had acted properly in condemning him. Yet he too remains on the official list of Peter's successors!

The action of the Sixth Ecumenical Council, affirmed by subsequent popes, was considered proof for centuries that popes were not infallible. Yet a strong-willed despot, Pope Pius IX, through threats and manipulation, would engineer an affirmation of papal infallibility by the First Vatican Council in 1870.

## Contradictions, Contradictions

Two persons holding opposite opinions can't both be right. Yet popes have almost made a business of contradicting one another on key issues. Agapetus (535-6) burned the anathema which Boniface II (530-2) had solemnly issued against Dioscorus (530). The latter is shown as an antipope, but Agapetus, who sided with him, is shown as a true pope. Adrian II (867-72) said civil marriages were valid; Pius VII (1800-23) declared them invalid. Both men are shown as legitimate popes. Nicholas V (1447-55) voided all of Eugenius IV's (1431-47) "documents, processes, decrees, and censures against the Council [of Basle] . . . to be regarded as having never existed,"[10] yet both remain on the official list of popes today.

On July 21, 1773, Pope Clement XIV issued a decree suppressing the Jesuits, only to have it reversed by a decree restoring them, issued by Pope Pius VII on August 7, 1814. Eugenius IV condemned Joan of Arc (1412-31) to be burned as a witch and heretic, but she was beatified by Pius X (1903-14) in 1909 and canonized by Benedict XV (1914-22) in 1920. Today inside Paris's Cathedral of Notre Dame, one of the most popular images is that of *Saint* Joan of Arc, France's "national heroine," with a profusion of candles always burning before it. How could an "infallible pope" condemn a *saint* to death as a witch and heretic? Yet Eugene IV remains on the list of allegedly infallible "successors of Peter."

History conclusively denies both apostolic succession and papal infallibility. And in fact many popes denied the latter also, among them Vigilius (537-55), Clement IV (1265-8), Gregory XI (1370-8), Adrian VI (1522-3), Paul IV (1555-9) and even Innocent III (1198-1216), who ruled Europe with an iron hand. Then why was Pope Pius IX so determined to immortalize this obvious fraud as official dogma?

There was a very special reason: Infallibility was the final desperate prop which Pius IX hoped would support the collapsing structure of Roman Catholic domination over the governments of the world and their citizens. To establish that dogma once for all, he convened the First Vatican Council December 8, 1869.

*These false and perverse opinions [of democracy and individual freedom] are so much the more detestable, by as much as they . . . hinder and banish that salutary influence which the Catholic Church, by the institution and command of her Divine Author, ought freely to exercise, even to the consummation of the world, not only over individual men, but [over] nations, [over] peoples, and [over] sovereigns.*

—Pope Pius IX, *Quanta Cura*
December 8, 1864

*I come to proclaim . . . the message of human dignity, with its inalienable human rights . . . [as] a pilgrim in the cause of justice and peace . . . as a friend of the poor . . . who are seeking . . . the deep meaning of life, liberty and the pursuit of happiness.*

—Pope John Paul II at Miami,
September 10, 1987, in the
initial speech of his "Second
Pastoral Visit" to the U.S.[1]

# 10

# Infallibility
# and Tyranny

Which of the contradictory statements on the facing page from the two popes are we to believe? Pius IX is only reaffirming the suppression of basic human rights which his predecessors have consistently enforced before him in order to bring all mankind under the absolute authority of the Roman Catholic Church. John Paul II would have us believe that his Church has always championed basic freedoms and does so today. He sounds so sincere. Yet he contradicts the consistent voice of the papacy and the dogmas of his Church down through the centuries, dogmas which are still in force today.

The American form of government, which John Paul II frequently praised during his U.S. tour,[2] was repeatedly denounced by previous popes. Has Rome changed? She boasts that she never changes. While lauding freedom, John Paul II also said that to be a good Catholic "it is necessary to follow the teaching of our Lord *expressed through the Church*" (emphasis added).[3] Sincere Catholics cannot learn directly from Christ's own words, but must accept the *Church's* explanation thereof. It is the same denial of freedom of conscience and individual moral accountability to God which Rome has consistently practiced throughout history.

John Paul II would have us believe that he and his Church are the champions of freedom. Yet we have already cited numerous

121

examples to show that Rome has consistently stood against basic human rights. If a change has been made, we need to hear a clear apology for the centuries-long suppression of elementary human rights by previous popes and their Church. How can the present pope pose as the friend of the downtrodden without denouncing as grievous error the slaughter of millions of people simply because they embraced the gospel of God's grace and for that "heresy" were anathematized by Rome?

## Consistent Record of Suppression

In contrast to his praise of basic freedoms in North America, to solidly Catholic audiences in Latin America John Paul II denounces Protestants and the idea that men ought to be free to profess any religion. The oppression, persecution, and even martyrdom of those who refused allegiance to Rome has been her consistent policy. For example, the Concordat between Pius IX and Ecuador of September 26, 1862, established Roman Catholicism as the state religion and forbade other religions. All education was to be "strictly controlled by the Church." A later law declared that "only Catholics might be regarded as citizens of Ecuador."[4]

The following year neighboring Colombia took the opposite course, establishing religious freedom and curtailing the monopoly on education and the privileged position that had long been enjoyed by the Roman Catholic Church. Pope Pius IX reacted angrily. On September 17, 1863, in an encyclical titled *Incredibili Afflictamur*, he lashed out at the "nefarious and most iniquitous" laws that Colombia had enacted, citing especially the evil of allowing "the worship of non-Catholic sects." His papal pen asserted his authority over that entire nation, including the right to rescind its laws:

> We with Apostolic Authority denounce and condemn
> all such laws and decrees with all their consequences,
> and by the same authority we abrogate those laws and
> declare them entirely null and without binding power.

Colombia ignored the pope at that time. In 1948, however, a new pro-Catholic government came into power. Its concordat with the Vatican instituted the very suppression which Pius IX had earlier demanded. Within ten years, scores of Christians had been slain for their faith, scores of Protestant churches had been burned down, about 200 Protestant schools were closed, and evangelistic work by Protestants was forbidden in most of the country.[5] Today Protestants are still being killed for their faith in Mexico and other parts of Latin America. Homes and churches are being destroyed, with as many as ten thousand Indian believers driven from their villages and fields in the Chiapas region of Mexico alone. Rome has not changed, though its opportunities for despotism are somewhat limited today.

John Paul II is not being honest with us. Historic evidence (and not only from the distant past) is abundant in testifying that Roman Catholicism suppresses basic freedom whenever, wherever, and however she can. The claim of papal infallibility becomes the justification for such tyranny, a tyranny which Roman pontiffs have repeatedly expressed and enforced in Christ's name and as His alleged vicars. As von Dollinger, himself a devout Catholic, has pointed out:

> The whole life of such a man [the pope], from the moment when he is placed on the altar to receive the first homage by the kissing of his feet, will be an unbroken chain of adulations.
>
> Everything is expressly calculated for strengthening him in the belief that between himself and other mortals there is an impassable gulf, and when involved in the cloud and fumes of a perpetual incense, the firmest character must yield at last to a temptation beyond human strength to resist.[6]

Pope Gregory XVI's (1831-46) *The Triumph of the Holy See and the Church over the Attacks of the Innovators* is one example among many. Its major thesis was that popes had to be infallible in order to fulfill the office of a true monarch. As absolute monarch over Church and state, Gregory rejected freedom of conscience, not only within the Church but in society as a whole, as "a false and absurd concept." Freedom of the press was equal madness.

Gregory's successor was Pius IX, convener of Vatican I. He was of the same mind with regard to the most elementary human freedoms. Popes had openly declared Rome's opposition to the United States and its freedom-granting constitution from the moment of that nation's birth. Pius IX did the same. The *Catholic World* frankly expressed the Roman Catholic view of the U.S. form of government:

> ... we do not accept it, or hold it to be any government at all.... If the American Republic is to be sustained and preserved, it must be by the rejection of the principle of the Reformation, and the acceptance of the Catholic principle....[7]

## Contempt for Human Life

It is a matter of incontrovertible historical record that many of the popes were as contemptible of human life as they were of freedom. Pope Gregory IX (1227-41) declared it the duty of every Catholic "to persecute heretics." A heretic was anyone who did not give complete allegiance to the Roman Catholic Church. Such persons were to be tortured, imprisoned, and slain. Disloyalty to the pope was the same as treason, so closely were state and Church allied. "Of eighty popes in a line from the thirteenth century on," writes de Rosa, "not one of them disapproved of the theology and apparatus of Inquisition. On the contrary, one after another added his own cruel touches to the workings of this deadly machine."[8]

Nor was it only the Inquisition that trampled human rights and life. Even before that evil institution, de Rosa reminds us, "for more than six centuries without a break, the papacy was the sworn enemy of elementary justice." Nearly 400 years before the Inquisition would be established by Gregory IX, Pope Nicholas I (858-67) encouraged the King of Bulgaria, a new convert to what he thought was "Christianity," to force Rome's religion upon his subjects:

> I glorify you for having maintained your authority by putting to death those wandering sheep who refuse to

> enter the fold; and . . . congratulate you upon having
> opened the kingdom of heaven to the people submitted to
> your rule.
>
> A king need not fear to command massacres, when
> these will retain his subjects in obedience, or cause them
> to submit to the faith of Christ; and God will reward him
> in this world, and in eternal life, for these murders.[9]

Such a statement may seem an incredible relic from the Dark Ages, but we could cite *many* like it from other popes. Remember that the popes who condoned and practiced the persecution, torture, and massacre of all who refused to give them allegiance were the allegedly infallible successors to Peter, the predecessors of today's Pope John Paul II, essential links in the long papal line from whom he received his authority and power. Nor has the Vatican ever acknowledged the evil of past popes or apologized for it.

By the time of Pius IX, the tide of public opinion was turning against the popes because of their ruthless totalitarianism. The revolutionary ideas of freedom of the press, of religion, of conscience, of the people's right to choose their rulers, and of the separation of church and state, having been established by the United States Constitution, were also gaining momentum across Europe. This new breath of freedom threatened Rome and had to be smothered in Christ's name. Pius IX was determined to continue Rome's autocratic rule in partnership with autocratic governments. To protect Rome's dictatorial powers, papal infallibility had to be established as an official and universally held doctrine.

## Contempt for Truth and Freedom

In his *La Inquisicion Espanola* (*The Spanish Inquisition*), Gerard Dufour reminds us that "the first article of the first heading of the [Spanish] constitution proclaimed that "the Roman Catholic Apostolic religion, in Spain and in all the Spanish possessions, will be the religion of the King and of the nation and no other one shall be permitted."[10] So it became in Latin America. Comte Le Maistre, in his defense of the Spanish Inquisition, writes that in a "Catholic country, a man may *entertain* [in his mind] whatever religious or irreligious opinions he likes" but "he must keep them to himself," or else "he is brought before the Tribunal [Inquisition]."[11]

The Constitution of the United States was condemned by the papacy because it separated church and state and prohibited the establishment of any religion by the government. The popes, on the other hand, had long required governments to make Roman Catholicism the official religion and to prohibit the practice of any other. In his 1864 *Syllabus of Errors*, which, in all fairness, contained some truth, Pius IX soundly condemned the belief that "every man is free to embrace and profess the religion he shall believe true. . . ."[12] His *Syllabus* decreed the union of Church and state, that Roman Catholicism must be the state religion everywhere, that the Church may use force to compel obedience, that there is no hope of salvation outside the Roman Catholic Church, etc. The *Syllabus* has never been rejected or amended and remains the belief of the Roman Catholic Church today, though unenforceable in most countries.

Let us take a typical example of enforcement of the Catholic-inspired Spanish constitution. In April 1863 three Spaniards, Matamoras, Trigo, and Alhama, were tried and found guilty of attending Protestant services. The sentence was harsh: nine years each for Alhama and Matamoras and seven for Trigo, to be served without time off *in the galleys*! Here was but one of thousands of instances of the church using its "secular arm" to enforce its decrees in the suppression of the common human right to worship God according to one's own conscience. To be true to its basic and unchangeable dogmas, Rome would today enforce a similar denial of civil rights everywhere if it had the power to do so.

A living death in the galleys, with at least the hope of eventual release if one could survive, was not the ultimate punishment. Popes had long decreed the death penalty for deviation from "the faith," not only through the Inquisitions in religious matters, but as part of their civil rule over the vast territories known as the papal states. For example, Clement XII (1730-40) had specifically prescribed the death penalty for membership in the Freemasons, or even for "rendering aid, succor, counsel, or a retreat to one of its members."[13]

## Pretentions to Omnipotence

The Roman Catholic Church fought the Protestant Reformation for more than religious reasons. The Reformation was now spreading on a grand scale what had previously been successfully suppressed for more than a thousand years: freedom of conscience and basic human rights. The desire for civil liberty among the common people was taking root and spreading everywhere. Nothing was more hateful to the Vatican, for civil liberty threatened its very foundations. As one nineteenth-century historian wrote concerning Pope Clement XII (1730-40):

> As soon as he was seated on the throne of the apostle, like his predecessor [Benedict XIII (1724-30)], he declared himself to be an enemy of the democratic ideas which were filtering through all classes of society, announced his pretensions to omnipotence, and set himself up as a pontiff of the Middle Ages.[14]

Fifty years later Thomas Jefferson congratulated the citizens of the United States for having abolished "religious intolerance under which mankind so long bled and suffered." He urged that "public reason, freedom of religion, and freedom of the press" be preserved. Such freedoms were a fruit of the Reformation. One hundred years after Jefferson, Pius IX was still hoping for exactly the opposite: for a growth of Roman Catholicism there which would eventually turn the United States into a Catholic country so that all its citizens could enjoy the blessings of Roman rule.[15]

The Second National Council of the Roman Catholic Hierarchy of the United States met in Baltimore in October 1866. Presided over by Archbishop Spalding of Baltimore as "apostolic delegate" representing the pope, the Council pointed out the difference between a *Protestant* form of government as in the United States, and a *Catholic* form of government as in most Latin American countries. The former, it was noted, derived its direction and power by a vote of *the people*, whereas the latter looked entirely to *the pope* in obedience to his direction and authority. One commentator noted:

The two systems stand in direct antagonism with each other. The Protestant has separated the State from the Church; the papal proposes to unite them again. The Protestant has founded its civil institutions upon the *will of the people*; the papal proposes to reconstruct and found them upon the *will of the pope*. The Protestant secures religious freedom; the papal requires that every man shall give up his conscience to the keeping of ecclesiastical superiors.[16]

The National Council of the Roman Catholic Hierarchy, though comprised of presumably loyal Americans, unanimously expressed its preference for the *Catholic* form of government and its absolute submission to papal authority. It sent a cable to Pius IX, wishing him "long life, with the preservation of all the ancient and sacred rights of the Holy See." So pleased was the pope by this expression of loyalty from America that he had it published in Italy as an example for his own rebellious subjects to consider.[17] Even as Pius IX planned Vatican I with its declaration of papal infallibility, however, the papal empire in Italy was crumbling.

## The Winds of Freedom

In 1861 the newly formed Kingdom of Italy with King Victor Emmanuel II at its head had declared Rome its capital, though the pope and his military forces still held and ruled it. It was the first time ever that Italy, so long the pawn of European powers, had been united under an Italian head of state. A crowd gathered along the Corso, shouting, *"Viva Italia! Viva Vittorio Emanuele!"* The papal police immediately fired upon them.

Absolute power had corrupted the papacy absolutely and the people of Italy were determined to throw off that yoke. A leading Italian at the time wrote that the Tribunal of the Holy Inquisition was still very much alive and that its "secret power ... was felt not only in religious questions, but in every other. ... Under such a system, the man who had murdered or plundered another had nothing to fear from Papal justice" if he did not espouse basic human freedoms "and were a firm adherent of the temporal [papal] power."[18] In 1864, in *Quanta Cura*, Pius IX denounced what he called—

> that erroneous opinion most pernicious to the Catholic Church, and to the salvation of souls, which was called by our Predecessor, Gregory XIV, the insanity (*deliramentum*): namely, "that the liberty of conscience and of worship is the peculiar (or inalienable) right of every man, which should be proclaimed by law, and that citizens have the right to ... openly and publicly express their ideas, by word of mouth, through the press, or by any other means."[19]

One might again ask how this statement by a predecessor could be reconciled with John Paul II's claims that Rome is and always has been the champion of human freedom. Into what mental black hole do people today consign the obvious facts in order to believe that the Church nourishes basic human rights? How many sincere Catholics are deceived because Church authorities sound so convincing? When an article in *The Catholic World* credited the Catholic Church with giving England that great charter of human rights, the Magna Carta, how many readers knew that Rome had in fact done everything she could to destroy it?[20]

## Backlash Against Dictatorship

The French and American revolutions in the previous century had ignited a spark of resentment against autocratic rulers that was being fanned into flame across Europe. No monarch was more dictatorial than the pope himself. Pius IX still reigned as "King of Rome" and its environs, as his predecessors had for centuries reigned over the entire Papal States. The growing sentiment for democracy was a threat to papal authority, a threat which Vatican I would surely put down by its dogmatic declaration of papal infallibility. That would, the pope hoped, settle the matter.

The year before the encyclical of Pius IX (in preparation for Vatican I), partially quoted above, Abraham Lincoln had addressed himself at Gettysburg to the same issues. No two

men could have been more at odds. Lincoln's words, intended
to pull the nation together in that crisis, were at the same time
a rebuke, though probably unintended, to the basic dogmas
underlying Roman Catholicism and papal tyranny. Nor could
Pius IX have been ignorant of the famous Gettysburg Address,
so that his words could only be regarded as a harsh response to
these of Lincoln:

> that from these honored dead we take increased de-
> votion to that cause for which they gave the last full
> measure of devotion—that we here highly resolve that
> these dead shall not have died in vain—that this nation,
> under God, shall have a new birth of freedom—and that
> government of the people, by the people, for the people,
> shall not perish from the earth.

Lincoln's ideal was the antithesis of Roman Catholicism.
Popes had sought to prevent such freedom, but nothing could
stop it in America or elsewhere. The Italian people, too, long
the pawns of tyrannical monarchs from France, Germany, and
Austria, were in a struggle for independence. Nor was it lost
upon them, in spite of their religious fervor, who was the worst
enemy of freedom. A military hero in the fight for independence appealed to his fellow Italians:

> Before fighting against this external enemy [the
> French and Austrians], you have internal enemies to beat
> down; and I will tell you that the chief of them is the
> Pope. . . .
> I am a Christian as you are; yes, I am of that religion
> which has broken the bonds of slavery, and has pro-
> claimed the freedom of men. The Pope, who oppresses
> his subjects, and is an enemy of Italian independence, is
> no Christian; he denies the very principle of Chris-
> tianity; he is Antichrist.[21]

The people of the province of Rome, where the pope still
ruled, endorsed this view in a resounding vote of 133,681 to
1507 for an independent Italy free of foreign influence and
papal control. Pius IX fought back viciously. He executed

hundreds of Italians who held the heretical views of civil government free from Church domination. About 8000 were confined to the papal jails under intolerable conditions, "many chained to the wall and not released even for exercise or sanitary purposes. The English ambassador called the dungeons of Pius IX 'the opprobrium of Europe.' "[22] An eyewitness described this monument to the pope's infallibility:

> From dawn till nightfall, the miserable captives would cling to the iron bars of their horrible dwellings, and perpetually call upon the passer-by for alms in the name of God. A Papal prison! how I shudder in writing the words. . . . human beings were heaped confusedly together, covered with rags, and swarming with vermin.[23]

Rome's Palace of the Inquisition still stands next to the Vatican, the headquarters of that same infamous institution, now called the Congregation for the Doctrine of the Faith. That hated structure would have been burned to the ground by a mob when Pius IX was deposed as King of Rome, had not the new government persuaded the people to keep it for "some charitable purpose." It was opened to the public to "let the citizens see with their own eyes the secret mechanisms of the papal system." An eyewitness, describing the horror of those who came to that "open house," wrote:

> They did not need any evidence to know that the only crime of serious moment in the States of the Church was liberal thought [advocacy of basic human freedoms] in religion and politics. That their friends and relations had been spirited away, and immured in prison, they also knew too well. And when the prison doors were open these emaciated heretics had a sad tale to tell of cruel suffering and ingenious torture.[24]

## Denying History to Build a Lie

The fall of papal Rome was still almost a year in the future when Pius IX formally opened Vatican I on December 8, 1869.

Yet even prior to that grandiose event, the opposition to papal infallibility (which all now knew the pope intended to push through the Council) had built to enormous proportions among bishops and lay members alike. It was no longer the Middle Ages with forged documents to bolster papal authority. The bishops well knew that papal infallibility had never been accepted by the Church but had been repeatedly denied. To accept it now would be to go against centuries of Church tradition as well as the Scriptures.

Those in favor of infallibility when the Council began were a small minority. Nevertheless, they had a concrete plan of action for taking control of the key positions in the Council bureaucracy and the Church's news media. In this they were aided by "the Pope, most of the Curia and the Jesuits." To gain votes, this pressure group "did not flinch from intrigues, promises, and threats."[25]

"Everything is in readiness here for the proclamation of papal infallibility," Lord Acton wrote to Great Britain's Prime Minister, William E. Gladstone, on November 24, 1869, two weeks before the Council officially convened. The English chargé d'affaires to the Holy See commented that preparations to push through infallibility had been so well organized that—

> . . . foreign bishops find it quite impossible to express their own opinions freely. They will be unpleasantly surprised to find themselves forced to sanction something which they actually wished to condemn.[26]

Much of what we know about the sinister intrigue behind the scenes and the dishonest conclusion of Vatican I is owing to the work of Swiss historian and scholar August Bernhard Hasler. During his five years in the Vatican Secretariat for Christian Unity, Hasler had access to the Vatican secret archives. What he learned thereby about Vatican I was so disturbing ("The whole business amounted to a clear manipulation of the Council") that he felt compelled to write *How the Pope Became Infallible*.[27] Hasler met an "untimely death" just after the manuscript was finished. For writing the book's introduction, Catholic theologian Hans Kung was "stripped of his ecclesiastical teaching privileges."[28]

## No Discussion Allowed

Devout Catholics today have sincerely believed the deceitful impression given by their Church that Vatican I's declaration of infallibility represented the mind and will of the attending bishops. On the contrary, many bishops were strongly opposed to affirming infallibility both on scriptural and traditional grounds. Some left in protest before the final vote was taken and only affirmed it later under Vatican threats and for the sake of Church unity. Bishop Lecourtier was so distressed by the fraud that he "threw his conciliar documents into the Tiber and left Rome. . . ." For that act he was removed from his bishopric.[29]

Attending bishops were virtual prisoners. Exit visas were deliberately withheld to prevent anyone from leaving. Among those fleeing Rome were two Armenian bishops, one of whom was Placidus Casangian, Abbot-General of all Armenian Antonite monks. From the other side of the Roman border, outside papal jurisdiction, he wrote both the pope and the Council that under "the constant threat of imprisonment and owing to his serious illness, he had feared for his life and thought his only safety lay in flight."[30]

Oppressive rules were imposed which were designed to stifle opposition and to eliminate free discussion. "There was to be no discussion in small groups, speeches at the Council could not be printed . . . [making] it impossible to study the arguments and give a careful response to them . . . and bishops were forbidden, under pain of mortal sin, to say anything about what took place in the great hall of the Council."[31] Such was the cultlike control over Council members. In the main sessions, those who dared to voice any opposition were interrupted, "often with the explanation that no one was allowed to speak so negatively about the Holy See."[32]

Sincere Catholics believe papal infallibility was passed down from Peter to his successors. But in fact it was foisted upon the Church by a ruthless cadre of Vatican insiders who conspired to stifle discussion, rigged elections, and literally intimidated bishops into voting, out of fear, for a proposition which they opposed. "The elections are dishonest," was entered December 20, 1869, in Archbishop Georges Darboy's diary. Another bishop complained of "the utter worthlessness of these elections."[33]

## Licensing Dictatorial Powers

"The pressure was felt, in particular, by bishops financially dependent on the Vatican" was the earnest complaint of more than one Council member. Many felt they "had a knife at their jugular," forcing them to approve what the vast majority actually opposed.

When the Armenian bishops, in the face of dire threats, remained steadfast in their refusal to support infallibility, the pope commanded their leaders "to perform compulsory spiritual exercises in a monastery." When Bishop John Stephanian refused to comply, the papal police arrested him on the street. His resistance provoked a riot by a mob, which rescued him.

To aid in the intimidation of the bishops in attendance, the papal police instituted surprise house searches. "Msgr. Lorenzo Randi, papal minister of police and later a cardinal, had all letters from newspaper correspondents intercepted at the [Vatican] post office and suppressed the most negative reports."[34]

As for J.H. Ignaz von Dollinger, one of the most eminent Catholic historians and theologians at the time, his reward for 47 years of teaching Roman Catholic theology and history was to be excommunicated.[35] His crime had been to point out that the pope's claim to infallibility lacked support either from Scripture or from Church tradition. Such was certainly the predominant view of Catholic historians and even of most bishops within the Church of Rome at that time. Von Dollinger's monumental work *The Pope and the Council*, published just prior to Vatican I, was immediately placed on the Index of forbidden reading. Pius IX could not afford to have the bishops read such facts from history as the following:

> Tertullian, Cyprian, Lactantius know nothing of special Papal prerogative, or of any higher or supreme right of deciding in matters of doctrine. In the writings of the Greek doctors, Eusebius, St. Athanasius, St. Basil the great, the two Gregories, and St. Epiphanius, there is not one word of any prerogatives of the Roman bishop. The

most copious of the Greek Fathers, St. Chrysostom, is
wholly silent on the subject, and so are the two Cyrils;
equally silent are the Latins, Hilary, Pacian, Zeno,
Lucifer, Sulpicius, and St. Ambrose. . . .

St. Augustine has written more on the Church, its
unity and authority, than all the other Fathers put together. . . . He urges all sorts of arguments to show that
the Donatists are bound to return to the Church, but of
the Papal Chair, as one of them, he knows nothing.[36]

## No Support in History

Bishop Joseph Hefele of Rottenburg, a former professor of
church history, addressed these words to the First Vatican
Council: "Forgive me if I speak simply: I am very familiar with
the old documentary sources of the history and teaching of the
Church, with the writings of the Fathers, and the acts of the
Councils, so that I can say . . . I have had them in my hands
night and day. But in all those documents I have never seen the
doctrine [of papal infallibility from a credible source]." Hasler
informs us further:

[Archbishop] Thomas Connolly . . . of Halifax, Nova
Scotia, had come to Rome as a convinced adherent of
infallibility. After thorough study he became one of its
declared opponents. . . . he repeatedly challenged the
Infallibilists in the Council hall to come up with clear
texts from the first three centuries—always in vain. He
made a private offer of one thousand pounds (perhaps
thirty thousand dollars today) to anyone who could provide the text he wanted. All he got was a forgery.[37]

Von Dollinger, one of that day's great authorities on church
history, agreed entirely with Hefele. His book (banned by
Rome) warned of Pius IX's coming attempt to push through the
dogma of infallibility and reminded the bishops who would
gather to deliberate this vital decision:

None of the ancient confessions of faith, no catechism, none of the patristic writings composed for the

> instruction of the people, contain a syllable about the
> Pope, still less any hint that all certainty of faith and
> doctrine depends on him.
>
> For the first thousand years of Church history not a
> question of doctrine was finally decided by the Pope.
> ... Even the controversy about Christ kindled by Paul of
> Samosata, which occupied the whole Eastern Church for
> a long time, and necessitated the assembling of several
> Councils, was terminated without the Pope taking any
> part in it. ...
>
> In three controversies during this early period the
> Roman Church took an active part—the question about
> Easter, about heretical baptism, and about the penitential
> discipline. In all three the Popes were unable to carry out
> their own will and view and practice, and the other
> Churches maintained their different usage. ... Pope Vic-
> tor's attempt to compel the Churches of Asia Minor to
> adopt the Roman usage, by excluding them from his
> communion, proved a failure.[38]

It is a fully established fact of history that for many centuries after Christ the Church had no notion that the Bishop of
Rome had the final word on all disputes or that he was infallible. Moreover, when the popes began to assert their alleged
infallibility, as we have already seen, they often used it wick-
edly. Furthermore, according to a 1987 *Time* poll, 93 percent
of today's Catholics hold the opinion that "it is possible to
disagree with the pope and still be a good Catholic." So much
for the practical effect of infallibility. No wonder the Church
got along without it for 1800 years!

## A Tragic Farce

There is no doubt that the claim of infallibility further
encourages the despotism which is already so much a part of
the papacy. Despotism in turn leads to contempt for truth
because the despot's power over others must be maintained at
all cost. That defect of character in Pius IX was evident to many
observers. Though the pope had personally approved an article
in *La Civilta Cattolica* which in February 1869 began his

campaign for infallibility, he denied any knowledge of it in an audience with foreign ambassadors. The deceit was blatant, but the pope seemed blind to the fact that anyone with common sense knew he was lying.

The pope wrote articles under another name and then denied knowing of them. When Bishops Clifford, Ramadie, and Place protested the demeaning language that Pius IX had publicly used concerning them, "he denied the whole thing." Before many witnesses, Bishop Henri Maret, dean of the Sorbonne in Paris, called Pius IX "false and a liar."

Pius IX constantly applied pressure and threats, engineered behind-the-scenes intrigue, and denounced in vicious terms any who opposed infallibility. Yet to the very end he insisted that he desired to "leave the Council completely free." "The facts proving the opposite are too numerous and too obvious," wrote Count Trauttmansdorff to Vienna on June 22, 1870. In view of these and many other evidences of blatant dishonesty, Cardinal Gustav von Hohenlohe remarked, "I need no other argument [against papal infallibility] than this single one, that in my entire life I never met a man who was less particular about the truth than Pius IX."[39]

Such was the man who used the power of his despotic office to force the bishops to approve a dogma which the majority of them opposed. Bishop Dupanloup noted on April 15, 1870, that several bishops had said to him, "I'd rather die than see all that." Some of the bishops grew "bitter from vexation and despair, or fell sick." For many the Council looked like a degrading game, a tragic farce. Bishop Georg Strossmayer complained that Vatican I had not had "the freedom necessary to make it a true Council and to justify its passing resolutions binding the conscience of the entire Catholic world. The proof of this was perfectly self-evident."[40]

## Infallibility or Instability?

As we have already noted, more than a few members "left the Council in disgust before it ended." On July 17, 1870, the day before the vote was to be taken, 55 bishops who were opposed declared that "out of reverence for the Holy Father they did not wish to take part [in the vote]. They then left Rome in protest."[41]

On July 18, 1870, the last day of the Council, there were
only 535 "yes" votes, less than half of the 1084 original
members entitled to vote. Yet the Vatican newspapers deceitfully wrote it up as though the assent had been unanimous.
Through threats of demotion and job loss and other pressures,
the pope managed eventually to obtain the submission of most
of those opposed. Such was the unbiblical and scandalously
dishonest manner in which papal infallibility became a dogma
of the Roman Catholic Church! Unfortunately, far too few
Catholics know the facts.

Bishop Dupanloup entered in his diary on June 28, 1870:
"I'm not going to the Council anymore. The violence, the
shamelessness, and even more the falsity, vanity, and continual
lying force me to keep my distance." On August 26, 1870, 14
German theologians declared, "Freedom from every sort of
moral coercion and from influence through superior force is a
*sine qua non* for all ecumenical councils. Such freedom was
missing from this gathering. . . ."[42]

Further insights into the character and behavior of Pius IX
which Hasler, during years of research, gleaned from the
secret Vatican archives and other documents are tragically
revealing:

> The unhealthy mysticism, the childish tantrums, the
> shallow sensibility, the intermittent mental absences, the
> strangely inappropriate language even in strictly official
> speeches, and the senile obstinacy all indicate the loss of
> a solid grip on reality. . . .
>
> Beyond this there are instances of near megalomania
> which are still hard to evaluate. In 1866 . . . Pius IX ap-
> plied Christ's saying, "I am the way, the truth, and the
> life," to himself. On April 8, 1871, Count Harry von
> Arnim-Suckow reported to the imperial chancellor,
> Prince Otto von Bismarck, of Pius IX's attempt to work a
> miracle: " . . . as he was passing by the church of Trinita
> dei Monti, the pope bade a cripple who was lying out in
> front, 'Rise up and walk!' But the experiment failed."
>
> The historian Ferdinand Gregorovius had previously
> noted in his diary on June 17, 1870: "The pope recently
> got the urge to try out his infallibility. . . . While out on a

walk he called to a paralytic: 'Get up and walk.' The poor devil gave it a try and collapsed, which put God's vice-regent very much out of sorts. The anecdote has already been mentioned in the newspapers. I really believe that he's insane." . . .

Pius IX gave the impression that he was suffering from delusions of grandeur in other ways as well. Some, even bishops, thought he was mad, or talked about pathological symptoms. The Catholic Church historian Franz Xaver Kraus noted in his diary: "Apropos of Pius IX, Du Camp agrees with my view that ever since 1848 the pope has been both mentally ill and malicious."[43]

## The Bitter Fruit of Papal Tyranny

While Pius IX, living in his fantasy world of omnipotence, was forcing the incredible concept upon the Church and the world that the magic of an office could render a mere human infallible, the Italian people, chafing under the pope's depravity and barbarism, were planning his overthrow. Accusing the papacy of erecting a "fortress of usurped power upon the corpses of passing generations," Italian patriot Giuseppe Mazzini denounced Pius IX and his predecessor popes eloquently:

> The Gospel whispers universal love and brotherhood, but you have sown discord, you have inspired hatred. . . . You who should have protected the weak against the oppressor, you who should have encouraged peace among citizens, you have summoned the paid assassins [from Spain, France, Austria and Naples] to whet their murderous daggers upon the very stone of the altar, while you have warned your citizen slaves "do not dare to arise."[44]

In 1861 the Parliament of the newly created Kingdom of Italy declared Rome to be its capital, even though the pope was still its tyrant. When the time came to enforce that verdict, those fighting for Italian independence would not be denied. The combined papal, French, and Austrian armies were not able to withstand the forces fighting for Italian freedom and unity. On September 20, 1870, almost two months to the day after Vatican I had confirmed the pope's infallibility, he was finally deposed as the ruler of the province of Rome. Overwhelming the defending papal army, the troops of General Cadorna battered their way through Rome's walls near the Porta Pia. The plebiscite, to which we have already referred, confirmed by an overwhelming vote Rome's annexation to a United Italy.

Pius IX withdrew into the Vatican in self-imposed imprisonment, and from that sanctuary loosed a veritable bombardment of words upon his enemies. His damnation of King Victor Emmanuel—"wherever he may be, whether in the house or in the field . . . in all the faculties of his body . . . damned in his mouth, in his breast, in his heart . . . may heaven, with all the powers that move therein, rise up against him, curse him and damn him!"—ran to more than 130 words. As for the rest of his enemies, which according to the vote must have been about 99 percent of the Italian population, the pope thundered, "With the authority of Almighty God, of the holy apostles Peter and Paul . . .

> all those . . . who have perpetrated the invasion, usurpation and occupation of the provinces of our domain, or of this dear City [Rome] . . . have incurred major excommunication and all the rest of the censures and ecclesiastical penalties, covered by the sacred canons, apostolic constitutions and decrees of all the general Councils, especially the Council of Trent.[45]

Of course, the pope's frustrated fulminations, at least on this occasion, were in vain. The Italians were not impressed with the new dogma of infallibility. Rome has continued under the control of the Italian government to this day. As we have already mentioned, the Concordat with Mussolini in 1929 would salvage for the popes their autonomy over a city-state, the Vatican, which has thereafter enjoyed equal status with the nations of the world.

The Vatican did not die. Nor did the Roman Catholic Church shrivel up. It has grown worldwide to nearly 1 billion members. The pope's influence around the globe, though effected more subtly, is now greater than ever. John's vision is still remarkably accurate, though much remains to be fulfilled.

## Pomp and Adulation

Peter declared that Christ had left us "an example that [we] should follow his steps" (1 Peter 2:21). He wrote that church leaders were not to act as "lords over God's heritage" but, like Christ, were to be "examples to the flock" (1 Peter 5:1-3). That the popes have disobeyed both Christ and Peter, whom they claim was the first pope, is abundantly clear. How could any ordinary member of the flock follow the example of the autocratic, luxurious, and highly privileged papal lifestyle? The popes, in defiance of the one whom they say was the first pope, are literally "lords" over those under them. This fact has been manifest for centuries in their tyrannical conduct, which has been rendered even more offensive by the idea of infallibility becoming a Roman Catholic dogma.

The *Donation of Constantine*, though a fraud (as we have seen elsewhere), and from which the popes claimed to get their authority and power, reveals a great deal about the way popes dressed, lived, and functioned during the Middle Ages. As de Rosa puts it:

> From the Donation, it is plain that the Bishop of Rome looked like Constantine, lived like him, dressed like him, inhabited his palaces, ruled over his lands, had exactly the same imperial outlook. The pope, too, wanted to lord it over church and state.
>
> Only seven hundred years after Peter died, the popes had become obsessed with power and possessions. Peter's [alleged] successors [became] not the servants but the masters of the world. They . . . dress in purple like Nero and call themselves Pontifex Maximus.[46]

The unbiblical nature of the papal office gives the man holding it a power greater than even that of a political tyrant. And both the opportunity and temptation for abuse is immeasurably increased when the man is considered to be infallible— something which no civil ruler would dare to claim today.

To see the devastating effect of ascribing such supreme authority to a mere man, one need only watch the obsequious reaction of those who find themselves fortunate enough to meet the pope in person, to shake his hand or reach out and touch him. Observe the wild enthusiasm of the tens of thousands who gather when the pope makes a personal appearance. In their fawning acknowledgment of infallibility there is an unwholesome identification of the Roman Catholic faithful with papal power. It is an identification which breeds even among common Church members a blinding and destructive pride at belonging to "the oldest and largest . . . the one true Church, outside of which there is no salvation." That conceit makes devout Catholics insensitive to what would otherwise be obvious failings in their Church, and it keeps them in its power.

The Church has become the Savior in the place of Christ, leading to the seductive and appealing belief that no matter what happens, that institution with the good offices of the pope, the saints, and especially Mary will eventually get one to heaven if surviving relatives pay for enough Masses to be said in one's name. It is a deadly delusion which is promoted in catechisms taught from childhood to all Catholics. Such destructive deceit is made plausible by the teaching that although Christ paid for our sins on the cross, the Church is the dispenser of the "graces and merits" He won. Add to that the ruinous conceit that subtly ensnares members of a Church whose head is "infallible," and one has the elements to create craven superstition and, finally, tragedy.

Yet the Roman Catholic Church has changed her mind enough times on important issues to demonstrate even to herself that she is not infallible. It used to be a mortal sin to eat meat on Friday, but that is no longer the rule. One used to see medals and statues of St. Christopher, patron saint of travelers, displayed not only on dashboards but even in elevators for protection. But this popular Catholic saint was declared a myth. The millions who for centuries thought he protected them were deluded, according to the latest ruling by the hierarchy. As ex-nun Patricia Nolan Savas puts it:

> Any organization that can, with the stroke of its sacerdotal pen, remove the pain of eternal punishment

from a Friday hot dog and pluck St. Christopher from
millions of dashboards can surely admit that it has erred
in other matters.[47]

One would think so, but so far there has been no admission
of wrongdoing by Rome even regarding the Inquisition, the
mistreatment and massacre of tens of thousands of Jews, the
martyrdom of millions of Christians, the slaughter of 1 million
Serbs during World War II, and the smuggling of tens of
thousands of Nazi war criminals into safe havens.

*Simon Peter answered and said, Thou art the Christ, the Son of the living God. . . . And I [Jesus] say also unto thee, That thou art Peter [Petros], and upon this rock [petra] I will build my church; and the gates of hell shall not prevail against it.*

—Matthew 16:16,18

*Feed my lambs . . . feed my sheep . . . feed my sheep.*

—John 21:15-17

*After Peter's confession of faith, he [Christ] determined that on him he would build his Church; to him he promised the keys of the kingdom of heaven. . . .*

—Vatican II[1]

# 11

# Upon This Rock?

An infallible pope as Peter's successor who holds the keys to heaven as vicar of Christ? Once the boast was that papal pomp and powers were inherited from Constantine. Today it is claimed that Christ's statement to Peter quoted on the facing page made him the first pope, the rock on which the "one true Church" was built, and that all who have followed in that office, no matter how violent or fraudulent their acquisition thereof nor how evil their deeds, have been his successors. The pope's authority today and the Catholic religion over which he presides stand or fall upon that assertion.

The pope is the Church. Without him it couldn't function and wouldn't even exist. Hence the importance of pursuing this subject even further. It matters little what Mr. or Mrs. Average Catholic thinks or does. But the doctrines and deeds of the hierarchy and primarily of the popes make or break the Church. That is where our focus must be, not on the opinions of someone's Catholic neighbor who says he doesn't believe half of what his Church teaches. (Then he shouldn't call himself a Catholic. Why trust a Church for one's eternal salvation if it is not trustworthy in lesser matters?)

What about Christ's statement to Peter "Upon this rock I will build my church" (Matthew 16:18)? Protestants argue that there is a play on words in the key verse above: In the Greek, "Peter" is *petros*, a small stone, while "rock" is the Greek

145

*petra*, a huge rock like Gibraltar. Such a huge *petra* could only be Christ Himself and the confession that Jesus is the Christ as Peter had just expressed it.

Modern Catholic apologists respond that Christ was likely speaking Aramaic, which eliminates the play on words and leaves Peter the rock upon which the church was built. That position, however, actually denies one of the basic tenets of Roman Catholicism, the Tridentine profession of faith. It has required all clergy, since the days of Pope Pius IV (1559-65), to vow to interpret Holy Scripture only in accord with the unanimous consent of the Fathers.

## The Testimony of the Church Fathers

How did the so-called Church Fathers (the leaders up to the time of Pope Gregory the Great, who died in 604) interpret this passage? It so happens that in this regard they are unanimously in agreement with the Protestant position. Not one of them interprets this passage as Catholics are taught to understand it today.

To be in agreement with the unanimous teaching of the Church Fathers, a Catholic would have to reject the dogma that Peter was the first pope, that he was infallible, and that he passed his authority on to successors. Devout Catholic historian von Dollinger reminds us of the undeniable facts:

> Of all the Fathers who interpret these passages in the Gospels (Matthew 16:18; John 21:17), *not a single one applies them to the Roman bishops as Peter's successors.* How many Fathers have busied themselves with these texts, yet not one of them whose commentaries we possess—Origen, Chrysostom, Hilary, Augustine, Cyril, Theodoret, and those whose interpretations are collected in catenas—has dropped the faintest hint that the primacy of Rome is the consequence of the commission and promise to Peter!
>
> Not one of them has explained the rock or foundation on which Christ would build His Church as the office given to Peter to be transmitted to his successors, but they understood by it either Christ Himself, or Peter's confession of faith in Christ; often both together.[2]

In other words, contrary to what the average Catholic has been told, the so-called Fathers of the Roman Catholic Church stood unanimously against the current Catholic interpretation. And it is a devout Roman Catholic authority on Church history, one who loves his Church, who points out these facts.

Other Catholic historians agree with von Dollinger. Peter de Rosa, also a devout Catholic, just as ably punctures the balloon of papal supremacy and an unbroken line of succession back to Peter:

> It may jolt them [Catholics] to hear that the great Fathers of the church saw no connection between it [Mattthew 16:18] and the pope. Not one of them applies "Thou art Peter" to anyone but Peter. One after another they analyse it: Cyprian, Origen, Cyril, Hilary, Jerome, Ambrose, Augustine. They are not exactly Protestants.
>
> Not one of them calls the bishop of Rome a Rock or applies to him specifically the promise of the Keys. This is as staggering to Catholics as if they were to find no mention in the Fathers of the Holy Spirit or the resurrection of the dead. . . .
>
> For the Fathers, it is Peter's faith—or the Lord in whom Peter has faith—which is called the Rock, not Peter. All the Councils of the church from Nicaea in the fourth century to Constance in the fifteenth agree that Christ himself is the only foundation of the church, that is, the Rock on which the church rests.
>
> . . . not one of the Fathers speaks of a transference of power from Peter to those who succeed him. . . . There is no hint of an abiding Petrine office.
>
> So the early church did not look on Peter as Bishop of Rome, nor, therefore, did it think that each Bishop of Rome succeeded Peter. . . . The gospels did not create the papacy; the papacy, once in being, leaned for support on the gospels [though it wasn't there].[3]

That the popes for centuries relied upon fraudulent documents (*The Donation of Constantine* and the *False Decretals*) to justify their pomp and power even after their exposure as deliberate counterfeits betrays how little these "vicars of Christ" cared for truth. It also tells us that in those days the popes didn't rely for justification of their papal authority upon Matthew 16:18 and alleged apostolic succession from Peter, or they would not have needed false documents to authenticate their position. Such an application of "thou art Peter" was invented much later.

## Who Is the Rock?

The truth of the matter does not depend upon a disputable interpretation of a few verses but upon the totality of Scripture. God Himself is clearly described as the unfailing "Rock" of our salvation throughout the entire Old Testament (Deuteronomy 32:3,4; Psalm 62:1,2; etc.). In fact, the Bible declares that God is the *only* Rock: "For who is God save [except] the Lord? or who is a rock save [except] our God?" (Psalm 18:31).

The New Testament makes it equally clear that Jesus Christ is the Rock upon which the church is built and that He, being God and one with the Father, is therefore the *only* Rock. The rock upon which the "wise man built his house" was not Peter but Christ and His teachings (Matthew 7:24-29). Peter himself points out that Christ is the "chief cornerstone" upon which the church is built (1 Peter 2:6-8) and quotes an Old Testament passage to that effect.

Paul likewise calls Christ "the chief cornerstone" of the church and declares that the church is also "built upon the foundation of [all] the apostles and prophets" (Ephesians 2:20). That statement clearly denies to Peter any special position in the Church's foundation.

## No Unique Promise to Peter

When Christ gave Peter "the keys of the kingdom of heaven" (Matthew 16:19), He explained what that meant: "Whatsoever thou shalt bind on earth shall be bound in heaven, and whatsoever thou shalt loose on earth shall be loosed in heaven." That same promise was renewed to all of the disciples in Matthew 18:18, as it was in John 20:23, with the special application there to forgiveness of sins.

Clearly the keys of binding and loosing and remitting or retaining sins were given to all, not just to Peter. Therefore it is unwarranted to claim that Peter had special power and authority over the other apostles. Such a concept cannot be found anywhere in the New Testament and was unknown even in the Roman Catholic Church until centuries later. Peter was given the special *privilege* of presenting the gospel first to the Jews (Acts 2:14-41) and then to the Gentiles (Acts 10:34-48), but no special *authority*.

Catholic apologists claim that Christ's words to Peter in John 21:15-17 ("Feed my lambs...my sheep") gave him unique authority. On the contrary, Peter himself applied that command to all elders (1 Peter 5:2) and so did Paul (Acts 20:28). Again von Dollinger informs us:

> None of the ancient confessions of faith, no catechism, none of the patristic writings composed for the instruction of the people, contain a syllable about the Pope, still less any hint that all certainty of faith and doctrine depends on him. . . .
>
> The Fathers could the less recognize in the power of the keys, and the power of binding and loosing, any special prerogative or lordship of the Roman bishop, inasmuch as—what is obvious to any one at first sight—they did not regard a power first given to Peter, and afterwards conferred in precisely the same words on all the Apostles, as any thing peculiar to him, or hereditary in the line of Roman bishops, and they held the symbol of the keys as meaning just the same as the figurative expression of binding and loosing. . . .
>
> The power of the keys, or of binding and loosing, was universally held to belong to the other bishops just as much as to the bishop of Rome.[4]

## No Special Power to Peter

The special authority which has been claimed by the Roman Catholic popes as Peter's alleged successors was *never* exercised by Peter. In his epistles Peter exhorts equals; he does not command subordinates: "The elders which are among you I exhort, who am also an elder" (1 Peter 5:1). He offers as the basis for his writings no official and exalted ecclesiastical position or power. He simply declares himself "a witness of the sufferings of Christ" (1 Peter 5:1) along with all the apostles, who were "eyewitnesses of his majesty" (2 Peter 1:16). He makes no unique claim for himself, but simply takes his place with the other apostles.

The gathering of "apostles and elders" at Jerusalem around A.D. 45-50 described in Acts 15:4-29 was convened on Paul's initiative, not Peter's. (It was not "the first church council," as some claim. There was no church hierarchy, no delegates from afar, all present being resident in Jerusalem.) Furthermore, it was James and not Peter who seemed to take the leadership. While Peter made an important statement, it was not doctrinal. It was mainly a summation of his experience in first bringing the gospel to the Gentiles. James, however, drew upon the Scriptures and argued from a doctrinal point of view. Moreover, it was James who said, "Wherefore my sentence [judgment] is . . ." and it was his declaration that became the basis of the official letter sent back to Antioch.

There is no evidence that Peter intimidated others, but James intimidated him. Fear of James and his influence and leadership caused Peter to revert to Jewish traditional separation from Gentiles. As a result, Paul, who wrote far more of the New Testament than Peter and whose ministry was obviously much broader, publicly rebuked Peter for his error (Galatians 2:11-14). Certainly Peter neither acted like a pope nor was so treated by others.

## The Apostles' True Successors

Christ told the apostles to make disciples through preaching the gospel. He added that each person who believed the gospel was to be taught to obey everything that He had taught the original twelve: "Teaching them [the disciples you make through the gospel] to observe all things whatsoever I have commanded you" (Matthew 28:20). This statement can't be applied exclusively to a leadership hierarchy. *All* of those who became Christ's disciples through the preaching of the original disciples were expected to obey *everything* Christ had commanded the twelve. And in order to do all that the twelve were commanded to do, every ordinary disciple must have the same authority and power from Christ as did the apostles.

Whatever commands and empowerment the apostles received from Christ were passed on to all who believed the gospel (e.g., their own disciples), who in turn passed on this command to their converts, and so on down to the present time. Obviously, then, not some special class of bishops, archbishops, cardinals, popes, or a *magisterium*, but *all* Christians are the successors of the apostles.

The history of the early Church given in the New Testament bears out the above. The apostles did what Christ commanded them to do: They made disciples by the thousands and passed on to them all of Christ's commands; and Christ Himself, from heaven, empowered these new disciples to carry on this great commission. Christians multiplied and churches were established throughout the Roman Empire.

There were no cathedrals. The local church met in homes. Leadership was by a group of godly elders who were older and more mature in the faith and who lived exemplary lives. There was no hierarchy, locally or over a wider territory, which had to be obeyed because of title or office. There was no select class of priests who had special authority to act as intermediaries between God and the people. Such had been the Jewish priesthood, which was a shadow of things to come (Hebrews 7:11-28; 10:1-22) and became terribly corrupted, only to be done away at the cross.

Every believer was encouraged to pray and prophesy in the church gatherings. Paul made that very clear:

> When ye come together [as a church], every one of you hath a psalm, hath a doctrine, hath a tongue, hath a revelation, hath an interpretation. Let all things be done unto edifying.
> If any man speak in an unknown tongue, let it be by two, or at the most by three, and that by course [i.e., one at a time]; and let one interpret. . . .
> Let the prophets speak two or three, and let the others [those listening] judge. If anything be revealed to another that sitteth by, let the first hold his peace [so the other can speak]

> For ye may all prophesy one by one, that all may learn
> and all may be comforted. . . .
>
> Wherefore, brethren, covet [earnestly desire] to
> prophesy, and forbid not to speak with tongues. Let all
> things be done decently and in order (1 Corinthians
> 14:26-40).

## No Elite Class

None of Christ's promises to the apostles were only for them
or for some elite class. For example: "If two of you shall agree
on earth as touching anything that they shall ask, it shall be
done for them of my Father which is in heaven" (Matthew
18:19); "Whatsoever ye shall ask in my name, that will I do"
(John 14:13); and yet again, "Whatsoever ye shall ask the
Father in my name, he will give it you" (John 16:23). All
Christians pray in Christ's name, yet this promise was originally given to His inner circle of twelve. All Catholics take the
bread and wine at Mass, yet it was to the twelve that Christ
said, "This do in remembrance of me" (Luke 22:19).

It is clear that everything Christ stated to His inner circle of
disciples applied to their converts and to all Christians today.
Does that mean that if two ordinary Christians agree on
something it will be given to them, or whatever an ordinary
Christian asks the Father in Christ's name will be given? Yes.
Then why isn't every prayer answered? They all are, but for
some the answer is "no" and for others "later." Christ's
"name" is not a magic formula which, if added to a prayer,
assures an automatic answer in the affirmative. To ask in His
name means to ask as He would ask, for His goals and glory,
not for our own.

On this point the Church has badly deceived sincere Catholics. Every prayer a Catholic priest asks is not automatically
answered any more than those of ordinary Catholics or Protestant ministers or laypersons. That is obvious. Yet it is claimed
that a member of the Catholic clergy has a special power so
that whatever he pronounces in Christ's name—whether binding or loosing, or forgiving sins—automatically occurs. Not
so. It is dishonest to say that loosing from sin (which can't be

verified) happens each time a Catholic priest pronounces it, when loosing from disease or a debt (which can be verified) rarely happens when pronounced.

The implication is clear: Whether it is obtaining an answer to prayer from the Father in the name of Christ, or obtaining some blessing that two or more Christians agree upon, or binding and loosing or forgiving sins, it does not occur automatically by the mere expression of a formula but is only done by Christ working through chosen vessels when, where, and as *He* pleases.

None of these promises worked automatically at the sole discretion of Peter or any of the other apostles. Nor do they attach automatically to a member of the Roman Catholic Church or any other religious hierarchy. Such false dogmas have placed those who believe them under the power of Rome, causing them to look to a priest for that which is the heritage of every true disciple of Christ.

## Past Tyranny and the Magisterium Today

The great apostle Paul wrote that, insofar as civil rulers do not command that which is against God's will, every Christian, including the apostles themselves, is to obey those rulers (Romans 13:1-7). We are to pray "for kings and for all that are in authority" (1 Timothy 2:1-3). Every Christian is to be "subject to principalities and powers, to obey magistrates..." (Titus 3:1).

Peter wrote to the Christians, "Submit yourselves to every ordinance of man for the Lord's sake: whether it be to the king as supreme; or unto governors..." (1 Peter 2:13,14). The popes taught just the opposite: that they were the supreme sovereigns and that only their laws were to be obeyed, even by kings. The total submission that Rome requires has been expressed by many popes, but none said it more clearly than Nicholas I (858-67):

> It is evident that the popes can neither be bound nor unbound by any earthly power, nor even by that of the apostle [Peter], if he should return upon the earth; since Constantine the Great has recognized that the pontiffs

held the place of God upon earth, the divinity not being able to be judged by any living man. We are, then, infallible, and whatever may be our acts, we are not accountable for them but to ourselves.[5]

That Nicholas was not expressing merely his own fanaticism but the view of the popes which eventually became Roman Catholic doctrine is clear both from history and from the official Church dogmas which are still in effect. According to Vatican II, no one is allowed even to question the *magisterium* in matters of faith and morals. Only the hierarchy can interpret the Bible, and the faithful must accept that interpretation as from God. And everyone must obey the pope even when he doesn't speak ex cathedra. Such requirements of blind faith are today's vestiges of the tyrannical rule of the popes down through the centuries.

## The Failure of the "First Pope"

If Christ's words to Peter in Matthew 16:18 made him the first infallible pope, then we have another serious problem. The next words out of Peter's mouth denied the very heart of the Christian gospel by declaring that Christ need not go to the cross: "Be it far from thee, Lord; this [death on the cross] shall not be unto thee" (verse 22). The Lord responded immediately, "Get thee behind me, Satan!" (verse 23). Here was Peter's initial ex cathedra declaration to the whole church (it is recorded in the Bible) on faith and morals (it deals with the means of salvation)—and it was not infallible but heresy!

In the next chapter Peter seriously errs again, with another heretical pronouncement. He puts Christ on the same level with Moses and Elias: "Let us make here three tabernacles: one for thee, and one for Moses, and one for Elias" (Matthew 17:4). This time it is God Himself from heaven who rebukes the "new pope": "This is my beloved Son, in whom I am well pleased, hear ye him" (verse 5).

Later, fearing for his life, Peter denies "with oaths and curses" that he knew Christ—again a declaration on "faith and morals" to the entire church in denial of Christ Himself. Even if the popes were his successors, Peter could hardly pass on to them an infallibility which he himself obviously did not possess!

## A Biblical Basis for Infallibility?

A current leading Catholic theologian, Hans Kung, recently pointed out: "The main proof text cited at Vatican I for papal infallibility, Luke 22:32 ('I have prayed for you that your faith may not fail') was never used even by medieval canonists to document this dogma—and rightly so. In this passage Jesus does not promise Peter freedom from error but the grace to persevere in the faith till the end."[6] Von Dollinger was in complete agreement:

> Everyone knows the one classical passage of Scripture on which the edifice of Papal Infallibility has been reared: "I have prayed for thee, that thy faith fail not; and when thou art converted, confirm thy brethren" [Luke 22:32]. But these words manifestly refer only to Peter personally, to his denial of Christ and his conversion. . . .
>
> It is directly against the sense of the passage . . . to find in it a promise of future infallibility to a succession of Popes. . . . No single writer to the end of the seventh century dreamt of such an interpretation; all without exception—and there are eighteen of them—explain it simply as a prayer of Christ that his Apostle might not wholly succumb and lose his faith entirely in his approaching trial.[7]

Many other leading Catholic historians and theologians could be cited in the same vein. Peter de Rosa adds his own insight:

> According to the [Church] Fathers, Peter as such had no successor. They see all bishops as succeeding to the apostles, not an individual bishop succeeding to an individual apostle, in this case Peter. They, therefore, could not possibly have accepted the claim that "Peter's successor" had to rule the See of Rome.
>
> We have seen, too, that all the great doctrinal statements, especially the creeds, came not from popes but

from Councils. In the early centuries, it never occurred to the Bishops of Rome that they could define doctrine for the whole church.[8]

## Unstable Rocks

After promising Christ at the Last Supper that he would die rather than deny Him, Peter does exactly what he said he wouldn't do: "Then began he to curse and to swear, saying, I know not the man" (Matthew 26:74). Here is a complete denial of Christ Himself and thus of Christianity in its entirety. Peter was a very unstable "rock" for Christ to build His Church upon! His alleged successors, however, were guilty of far worse failings.

We have mentioned a number of these already. Consider one more brief example: Pope Julius II (1503-13), syphilitic, an infamous womanizer, father of a number of bastards. He bribed his way into the papacy. At Lent, when good Catholics were on a strict diet, he gorged himself on the richest fare. Clad in armor, Julius often led his army to conquer cities and territories in the expansion of the Papal States. How could he possibly be the "vicar" of the Christ who said His kingdom was not of this world and therefore His servants didn't fight? To say he was mocks Christ and His teachings.

## Successors to the Emperors

Remember that in the early days of the Church, infallibility was not attributed to the Bishop of Rome, but to his superior, the emperor. Pope Leo I (440-61), for example, ascribed to a godless emperor the very infallibility which Pius IX would persuade the members of Vatican I to declare had always been the exclusive power of the popes: "By the Holy Spirit's inspiration the emperor needs no human instruction and is incapable of doctrinal error."[9]

The following extravagant praise, which sounds like that given to popes today, is from a speech by Eusebius honoring the pagan Emperor Constantine after he had assumed leadership of the Church:

Let then our emperor . . . be declared alone worthy . . .
who alone is free . . . above the thirst of wealth, superior
to sexual desire . . . who has gained the victory over
those passions which overmaster the rest of men: whose
character is formed after the Divine original of the
Supreme Sovereign, and whose mind reflects, as in a
mirror, the radiance of His virtues. Hence is our emperor
perfect in prudence, in goodness, in justice, in courage,
in piety, in devotion to God. . . . [10]

That this praise was to the emperor *alone* placed him above
the Bishop of Rome, who was subservient to him. Thus Constantine called himself "Bishop of Bishops." Today's popes,
who bear Constantine's titles and wear his regalia, are *his*
successors, not Peter's. Historian Will Durant points out that
"throughout his reign he [Constantine] treated the bishops as
his political aides; he summoned them, presided over their
councils, and agreed to enforce whatever opinion their majority should formulate."[11]

Doctrine meant nothing to Constantine—only that the
bishops should agree for the sake of imperial unity. De Rosa
quotes a fourth-century bishop that "the church [at that time]
was part of the state." He goes on to explain:

Even the Bishop of Rome—not to be called *"the
pope"* for many centuries—was, in comparison [to Con-
stantine], a non-entity. In civic terms he was vassal of the
emperor; in spiritual terms, he was, compared with Constantine, a second-class bishop. . . .

Not the pope but he [Constantine], like Charlemagne
later, was the head of the church, its source of unity,
before whom the Bishop of Rome had to prostrate himself and pledge his loyalty. All bishops agreed that he [the
emperor] was "the inspired oracle, the apostle of Church
wisdom."

It was, therefore, Constantine, not the Bishop of
Rome, who dictated the time and place of church synods
and even how the votes were cast. Without his approval,
they could not pass into law; he alone was legislator of
the Empire.[12]

## The Papacy's Pagan Heritage

The very idea of a Church Council was invented by Constantine, who, in spite of his professed "conversion" to Christ, remained a pagan. He never renounced his loyalty to the many pagan gods. He abolished neither the pagan Altar of Victory in the Senate nor the Vestal Virgins; and the sun-god, not Christ, continued to be honored on the imperial coins. He was not baptized until just before his death, and that by a heretical Arian priest, Eusebius. Durant reminds us that throughout his "Christian" life Constantine used pagan as well as Christian rites and continued to rely upon "pagan magic formulas to protect crops and heal disease."[13]

That Constantine murdered those who might have had a claim to his throne (notably his son, Crispus, a nephew and brother-in-law) is further evidence that his "conversion" to Christianity was, as historians have suggested, a clever political maneuver. Historian Philip Hughes, himself a Catholic priest, reminds us, "In his manners he [Constantine] remained, to the end, very much the Pagan of his early life. His furious tempers, the cruelty which, once aroused, spared not the lives even of his wife and son, are . . . an unpleasing witness to the imperfection of his conversion."[14]

The three "Christian" sons of Constantine (Constantine II, Constantius II, and Constans) secured, after their father's death, their separate regions of the empire by a merciless family massacre. They then took the "Christianization" of the empire to new heights. Such (not Peter) were the forerunners of today's popes.

As already mentioned, Constantine convened, set the agenda for, gave the opening address at, and played a dominant part in the first ecumenical council of the Church, the Council of Nicaea, and a number of other councils as well, as would Charlemagne 500 years later. Inasmuch as the emperors called the councils, it is not surprising that no council for the first thousand years acknowledged the Bishop of Rome as head of the Church.

Christ exemplified humility and service to others. He told His disciples: "The kings of the Gentiles exercise lordship over them. . . . But ye shall not be so; but he that is greatest among you, let him be as the younger; and he that is chief, as he that doth serve" (Luke 22:25,26). Forgetting that admonition, the popes emulated the pagan emperors from whom they inherited their position and power.

Christ also condemned the authoritarian position which had been taken by the rabbis in His day. His words to the Jewish religious leaders are quite appropriate for the Roman Catholic hierarchy:

> [They] love the uppermost rooms at feasts, and the chief seats in the synagogues, and greetings in the markets, and to be called of men, Rabbi, Rabbi.
>
> But be not ye called Rabbi, for one is your Master, even Christ; and all ye are brethren. And call no man your father upon the earth; for one is your Father, which is in heaven. . . .
>
> Woe unto you, scribes and Pharisees, hypocrites! For ye are like unto whited sepulchres, which indeed appear beautiful outward, but are within full of dead men's bones, and of all uncleanness . . . within ye are full of hypocrisy and iniquity (Matthew 23:6-9,27,28).

*Upon her forehead was a name written . . .
MOTHER OF HARLOTS AND ABOMINA-
TIONS. . . .*
— Revelation 17:5

*The history of celibacy makes for reading so
black. . . . A large part [of it] is the story of the
degradation of women. . . . Ivo of Chartres
(1040-1115) tells of whole convents with inmates who were nuns only in name . . . [but]
were really prostitutes.*
— Peter de Rosa, *Vicars of Christ*

*The recent disclosures of widespread sexual mis-
conduct on the part of certain members of the
Roman Catholic clergy come as no surprise to
most of us who were once priests or nuns.*
— Ex-nun Patricia Nolan Savas in
*USA Today*[1]

# 12

# Unholy Mother

Let there be no misunderstanding: We are not suggesting that Catholic popes, priests, and nuns are inherently more prone to promiscuity than the rest of mankind. Our hearts are all the same. Many of these tragic individuals no doubt began with high moral and spiritual aspirations and in that spirit set out upon what they sincerely intended to be a life of purity and devotion to Christ. It was the system of hierarchical privilege, power, and authority over the laity which perverted and destroyed them.

That system, as we have seen, gathered momentum through the centuries by the lust and greed of popes whose natural propensity for evil (innate in us all) found occasion through the unusual opportunities afforded by their office. To enhance their power they issued a host of false documents which purported to be the writings of early Church Fathers and decrees of early synods. One self-serving theme of these forgeries was the claim that the popes had inherited "innocence and sanctity from Peter" and could not be judged by any man. Von Dollinger writes:

> A saying ascribed to Constantine, at the Council of Nice, in a legend recorded by Rufinus, was amplified till it was fashioned into a perfect mine of high-flying pretensions. Constantine, according to this fable, when the

written accusations of the bishops against each other were laid before him, burned them, saying...that the bishops were gods, and no man could dare to judge them.[2]

If one is on the level of the gods, what privileges could not one claim? Gods are above the law. No wonder, then, that the popes began to declare openly that they had power over kings and kingdoms and all persons, and power to behave like tyrants. The added pretense of infallibility only made matters worse.

Each priest and nun, by association, shares (though to a lesser extent) this same corrupting absolutism and elevation above laypersons. Add to this pretended Godlike authority the unnatural rule of celibacy (an intolerable burden which only a small minority of persons could possibly bear) and the stage is set for all manner of evil. A sincere Catholic historian writes:

> The fact is that priestly celibacy has hardly ever worked. In the view of some historians, it has probably done more harm to morals than any other institution in the West, including prostitution....
>
> The proof of the harm done by celibacy comes not from bigoted anti-Catholic sources; on the contrary, it includes papal and conciliar documents and letters of reforming saints. They all point in one direction: far from being a candle in a naughty world, priestly celibacy has been more often than not a stain on the name of Christianity.[3]

## Celibacy's Roots and Fruits

One must understand that mandatory celibacy is not taught in the Bible, nor was it practiced by the apostles. This teaching developed as an integral part of the evolving papal system and gradually became essential to it. The concern was not morality, for celibacy proved to be a veritable cornucopia of evil. In fact, the rule of celibacy was not the prohibition of *sex* but of *marriage*. Pope Alexander II (1061-73), for example, refused to discipline a priest who had committed adultery with his father's second wife because he hadn't committed the *sin of matrimony*. That was the great evil which had to be eliminated for the priesthood to be totally devoted to the Church.

All down through history not only priests and prelates but popes as well had their mistresses and visited prostitutes. Many were homosexuals. No member of the clergy was ever excommunicated for having sex, but thousands have been put out of the priesthood for the scandal of getting married. Why then the strict insistence upon celibacy, even to the present day, if it really doesn't mean abstinence from sex? It is because *the rule of celibacy has a very practical and lucrative result for the Church:* It leaves priests and especially bishops and popes without families to whom to bequeath property and thereby impoverish the Church. The clergy must have no heirs.

Pope Gregory VII, bemoaning the difficulty in stamping out marriage among priests, declared: "The Church cannot escape from the clutches of the laity unless priests first escape from the clutches of their wives." Here is another vital reason for celibacy: to create a priesthood without the encumbrance (and loving loyalties) of wives and children. Thus fornication and adultery, though forbidden in theory, were preferable to a marriage relationship. Nineteenth-century historian R.W. Thompson explains:

> It was considered absolutely necessary to the perfect working of the papal system that there should be organized a compact body of ecclesiastics, destitute of all those generous sympathies which grow alone out of the family relation, that they might be the better fitted to do the work of the popes.... [4]

Though married men in those early days were allowed to enter the priesthood, they were required to live celibate lives. Pope Leo I (440-61) decreed that married clergy were to treat their wives "as sisters." Few if any Catholics realize that as late as the reign of Pope Gregory VII (1073-85) it was accepted for priests to be married and supposedly live in celibacy with their wives.

Such a requirement was both unnatural and unrealistic. Who could keep such a rule? All over Italy the clerics openly had large families and no discipline was enacted against them. After all, many of the popes had large families as well and sometimes made no secret of it. De Rosa comments:

> This theological confusion in an age of depravity led the clergy, in fifth-century Rome in particular, to become a byword for everything that was gross and perverted. . . . When Pope Sixtus III (432-40) was put on trial for seducing a nun, he ably defended himself by quoting Christ's words, "Let him who is without fault among you throw the first stone."
>
> . . . roving monks were proving to be a social menace . . . there were long periods when many monasteries were nothing but houses of ill repute. . . . The second Council of Tours in the year 567 . . . publicly admitted there was hardly a cleric anywhere without his wife or mistress. . . . [5]

## A System Made for Prostitution

For centuries the priesthood was largely hereditary. Most priests were the sons of other priests and bishops. More than one pope was the illegitimate son of a previous and supposedly celibate pope. For example, Pope Sylverius (536-7) was fathered by Pope Hormisdas (514-23), and John XI (931-5) by Sergius III (904-11) of his favorite mistress, Marozia, to whom we referred earlier.

Among the other bastards who ruled the Church were Popes Boniface I (418-22), Gelasius (492-6), Agapitus (535-6), and Theodore (642-9). There were more. Adrian IV (1154-9) was the son of a priest. No wonder Pope Pius II (1458-64) said Rome was "the only city run by bastards." Pius himself admitted to fathering at least two illegitimate children, by different women, one of them married at the time. The rule of celibacy literally created prostitutes, making Rome the "Mother of Harlots," as the apostle John foresaw.

In his fiery sermons, Savonarola of Florence, Italy (soon to be martyred), called Rome "a harlot ready to sell her favors for coin"[6] and accused the priests of bringing "spiritual death upon all . . . their piety consists in spending their nights with harlots." He cried, "One thousand, ten thousand, fourteen thousand harlots are few for Rome, for there both men and women are made harlots."[7]

Pope Alexander VI threatened to "lay an interdict upon Florence" if it did not silence Savonarola. The city rulers obeyed for fear that as a result of the interdict all "the Florentine merchants in Rome would be thrown into jail."[8] The pope wanted Savonarola brought to Rome for trial as a heretic, but the Signory of Florence wanted to execute him themselves. After signing confessions that had been wrung out of them by the cruelest of torture, Savonarola and two comrade friars were hanged and burned to ashes.[9] Yet this man who preached against the Church leaders' immorality and was slain by Roman Catholics is now celebrated by the Vatican as "a giant of our faith, martyred May 23, 1498."[10] What revision of history!

Visiting Germany in the eighth century, St. Boniface found that *none* of the clergy honored their vows of celibacy. He wrote to Pope Zachary (741-52): "Young men who spent their youth in rape and adultery were rising in the ranks of the clergy. They were spending their nights in bed *with four or five women*, then getting up in the morning . . . to celebrate mass." Bishop Rathurio complained that if he excommunicated unchaste priests "there would be none left to administer the sacraments, except boys. If he excluded bastards, as canon law demanded, not even boys [would be left]."[11]

Even idealists became unprincipled rogues because the priesthood was one of the surest and fastest ways to wealth and power and afforded unique opportunities for the most profligate pleasure. Today's pope, John Paul II, in his recent encyclical, *Veritatis Splendor (Splendor of Truth)*, soundly condemns promiscuity. One might respect such a treatise if he would admit that his predecessors in the papacy have been some of the worst offenders; that the clergy, because they can't marry, have been more prone to illicit relationships than the laity; and that promiscuity is still widespread among the Roman Catholic clergy. Otherwise *Splendor of Truth* has a hollow sound.

## Vicars of Christ?

John XII (955-64), to whom we referred earlier, became pope at age 16, ran a harem in the Lateran Palace, and lived a life of evil that passes imagination, even toasting the devil in front of St. Peter's altar. Spiritual leader of the Church for eight years, John XII slept with his mother and any other woman he could get his hands on. Women were warned not to venture into St. John Lateran church. Of this man Liutprand wrote in his journal:

> Pope John is the enemy of all things. . . . the palace of the Lateran, that once sheltered saints and is now a harlot's brothel, will never forget his union with his father's wench, the sister of the other concubine Stephania. . . .
> Women . . . fear to come and pray at the thresholds of the holy apostles, for they have heard how John a little time ago took women pilgrims by force to his bed, wives, widows and virgins alike. . . . [12]

St. Peter Damian's eleventh-century record of the incredible evils caused by the pledge of celibacy made such scandalous reading that the pope with whom he shared it preserved it in the papal archives. In fact, it "proves that profligacy among the clergy of the time was universal. After six centuries of strenuous efforts to impose celibacy, the clergy were a menace to the wives and young women of the parishes to which they were sent."[13]

Pope Innocent IV (1243-54), forced to leave Rome by Emperor Frederick II, took refuge along with his *Curia* in Lyons, France. Upon the pope's return to Rome after Frederick's death, Cardinal Hugo wrote a letter thanking the people of Lyons. He reminded them that they also owed a debt to the pope and his court. His remarks provide a glimpse of the shameless depravity of the papal court:

> During our residence in your city, we [the Roman *Curia*] have been of very charitable assistance to you. On our arrival, we found scarcely three or four purchasable

sisters of love, whilst at our departure we leave you, so to say, one brothel that extends from the western to the eastern gate.[14]

## The Enforcement of Celibacy

Celibacy was hardly known in England before it was at last enforced by Innocent IV in about 1250. Most priests there were married, a practice long accepted by the Church. But Rome determined that it had to end all familial devotion for priests and nuns; their loyalty must now be given solely to Mother Church and the Pope. R.W. Thompson explains why celibacy was forced upon England:

> The celibacy of the Roman clergy has been, since its introduction, considered one of the most effective means of establishing the supremacy of the popes; and for this purpose the attempt was made to introduce it into En gland, after the Norman conquest.[15]

Pope Honorius II (1124-30) sent Cardinal John of Crema to England to see that his decree against marriage for clergy was carried out. The cardinal gathered the senior clerics and chided them vigorously for their evil ways, declaring that "'twas a horrible crime to rise from the side of a harlot, and then to handle the consecrated body of Christ." The clergy whom he had lectured, however, surprised him in his room later that night in bed with one of the local prostitutes.[16] At least he wasn't married.

In the thirteenth-century St. Bonaventure, cardinal and general of the Franciscans, had said that Rome was just like the harlot of the Apocalypse, exactly as John foresaw and as Luther would see to his sorrow three centuries later. Pope Boniface VIII (1294-1303) did not hesitate to have both a mother and daughter as his mistresses together. It was Luther's visit to Rome which completed his growing disillusionment with his Church.

By the fourteenth century the Church had lost all credibility as an example of Christlike living. Cynicism was rampant. It was no secret that Pope John XXII (1316-34) had a son who was raised to cardinal. Like Luther, England's John Colet had been shocked at the brazen ungodliness of the pope and cardinals when he visited Rome. From his pulpit in London's St. Paul's Cathedral, of which he was the dean, Colet thundered his disapproval:

> Oh, the abominable impiety of those miserable priests, of whom this age contains a great multitude, who fear not to rush from the bosom of some foul harlot into the temple of the Church, to the altars of Christ, to the mysteries of God![17]

## Life in the Papal Court

For years it had been a common saying that "Rome has more prostitutes than any city in the world because it has the most celibates." Pope Sixtus IV (1471-84) turned that fact into a source of considerable profit by charging Rome's numerous brothels with a Church tax. Then he gathered more wealth still by charging a tax on mistresses kept by priests. Will Durant reports:

> There were 6800 registered prostitutes in Rome in 1490, not counting clandestine practitioners, in a population of some 90,000. In Venice, the census of 1509 reported 11,654 prostitutes in a population of some 300,000. An enterprising printer published a "Catalogue of all the principal and most honored courtesans of Venice, their names, addresses, and fees."[18]

Upon becoming Pope Alexander VI (1492-1503), Rodrigo Borgia, who had committed his first murder at age 12, cried triumphantly, "I am Pope, Pontiff, Vicar of Christ!" Gibbon calls him "the Tiberius of Christian Rome." Though he scarcely pretended to be a Christian, he was, like all the popes, deeply devoted to Mary. Of him a leading Florentine scholar wrote:

> His manner of living was dissolute. He knew neither shame nor sincerity, neither faith nor religion. Moreover,

he was possessed by an insatiable greed, an overwhelming ambition and a burning passion for the advancement
of his many children who, in order to carry out his iniquitous decrees, did not scruple to employ the most
heinous means.[19]

Like his predecessor, Pope Innocent VIII (1484-92), Borgia
as a fond father admitted who his children were, baptized them
personally, gave them the best education, and proudly offici-
ated at their weddings in the Vatican, which were attended by
Rome's leading families. Alexander VI had ten known illegitimate children, four of them (including the notorious Cesare
and Lucrezia) by Vannozza Catanei, his favorite mistress.
When Vannozza faded, Borgia, then 58, took newly-married,
15-year-old Giulia Farnese. She obtained a cardinal's red hat
for her brother (thereafter known as "the Petticoat Cardinal"), who later became Pope Paul III (1534-49) and convened
the Council of Trent to counter the Reformation.

## The Record in Art and Architecture

Papal promiscuity has been immortalized in the very structures and statuary of the Vatican, St. Peter's, and other of
Rome's most famous churches and basilicas. The magnificent
Sistine Chapel, for example, was built by and named after
Sixtus IV, who taxed others for keeping a mistress but paid
none for his own. Here the cardinals meet to elect the next
pope. Sixty-five feet above them the huge ceiling bears the
incredible artwork of Michelangelo.

Admiring visitors are not aware that this, the world's greatest work of art, was commissioned by Julius II (1503-13), who
bought the papacy with a fortune and didn't even pretend to be
religious, much less a Christian. A notorious womanizer who
sired a number of bastards, Julius was so eaten up with syphilis
that he couldn't expose his foot to be kissed. The Sistine
Chapel thus stands as one of Rome's many monuments to the
fact that the church which owns and proudly displays it is, as
John foresaw, the "Mother of Harlots."

Known as "the most important church dedicated to Mary in
Western Christendom," Santa Maria Maggiore is the fruit of

the combined efforts of a number of promiscuous popes. Sixtus III (432-40), another notorious womanizer, built the main structure. The "golden wood ceiling over the nave was commissioned by the Borgia Pope Alexander VI [1492-1503],"[20] who paid for it with gold from America received as a gift from Spain's Ferdinand and Isabella, to whom he had given the new world. Borgia's unbelievable wickedness, including his devotion to torture, his mistresses, and his illegitimate children, have been mentioned briefly. He "launched the first censorship of printed books . . . the *Index*, which [lasted] over four hundred years."[21]

Inside St. Peter's basilica, the burial monument of Pope Paul III (1534-49) is adorned with reclining female figures. One figure, representing Justice, was naked for 300 years until Pius IX had clothes painted on her. She was modeled after Paul III's sister, Giulia, a mistress of Alexander VI. Thus is immortalized the promiscuity of "celibate" popes.

## Today's Unbiblical Tolerance

The gross immorality among Roman Catholic clergy is not confined to the past but continues on a grand scale to this day. Such wickedness was rare and a cause for excommunicating the offending party in the days of the apostles. The faithful were not even to associate with fornicators (1 Corinthians 5:8,9) who claimed to be Christians, so the world would know that such conduct was condemned by the church and all disciples of Christ. Of a sexually profligate man at Corinth, Paul wrote to the church: "Therefore put away from among yourselves [excommunicate] that wicked person" (verse 13).

Yet popes, cardinals, bishops, and priests without number have been habitual fornicators, adulterers, homosexuals, and mass-murderers—ruthless and depraved villains who pursued their degenerate lifestyles immune from discipline. Far from being excommunicated, such popes remain proudly displayed on the list of past "vicars of Christ." Today a priest who engages in sexual misconduct is rarely expelled from the priesthood or excommunicated from the Church. Instead, he is reassigned elsewhere and perhaps given psychological counseling. Priests pronounced cured by such treatment centers (for example, Servants of the Paraclete in Jemez Springs, New Mexico) have been reassigned to parishes only to abuse more victims.[22]

While Rome officially condemns fornication, thousands of its priests engage in sex outside of marriage. A national Catholic newspaper recently reported: "Seven French women... companions of priests who... are forced to 'live clandestinely, for a lifetime, the love they share with a priest' [and who] represent thousands of women in similar relationships ... arrived at the Vatican August 20. [They] asked the pope to... look into the reality faced by 'thousands of priests' companions who live in the shadows, often with the approval of church superiors, and by the children who... are raised by their mothers alone or are abandoned."[23]

The fraud and hypocrisy persist. Ex-nun Patricia Nolan Savas, author of *Gus: A Nun's Story*, writes:

> During my ten years as Sister Augusta... I witnessed situations that ranged from compromising to aberrant. ...In theory, we were forbidden by the Rule to ever touch another person, male or female. "Particular friendships," considered serious violations of the vow of chastity, were to be avoided at all costs. And the cost of imposed asexuality and corporeal denial was always high and often tragic.
>
> With the exception of a few select eunuchs, many of the priests and nuns I knew eventually rejected that intolerable burden and either abandoned the religious life altogether or formed liaisons with their fellow clerics or with outsiders.
>
> There were the valiant ones who continued in their sincere attempts to murder the flesh and often fell victim to serious psychogenic disorders. Some still remain seriously damaged in mind and body, sequestered in institutions referred to as "retreats" or other such euphemisms. A tragic number became alcoholics and quietly drank themselves to death.
>
> A major cause of this apalling waste of lives? Celibacy—a virtuous state when freely entered into but an overwhelming millstone when imposed as dogma on the

entire clergy, as it was by the Roman Catholic Church nine centuries ago.[24]

Early in 1994, "Terence German, 51 [former Jesuit priest], filed a $120-million lawsuit in New York State Supreme Court against the Church, Pope John Paul II, and Cardinal John O'Connor." He accused them "of turning a blind eye to his repeated reports of other priests' sexual misconduct and misuse of church funds." German's formal complaint explains that—

> he gave up all of his "worldly goods" when he took his vows in 1964 in exchange for a promise that the church would care for him until his death. The underlying assumption was that he would "live a life guided by the established principles" of the Roman Catholic Church. . . .
> "The church—by acquiescing to pervasive sexual and financial misconduct—broke its part of the established principals. . . . The Church wasn't enforcing its own rules, so [I wasn't] able to live according to the Church's rules . . . with people stealing and in sexual alliances with small boys."[25]

Today's "celibate" fornicators, pedophiles, and perverts are almost always quietly transferred. In their new parishes they continue to celebrate Mass and to perform priestly functions. Should they commit the much more serious sin of marrying, however, they are forbidden ever to function as priests again.

## Exposed at Last

Twentieth-century misconduct by the Roman Catholic clergy, covered up for decades, is now being exposed. Increasing numbers of victims are coming forward to sue the Church. An estimated billion dollars has been paid by the Church so far in the United States in out-of-court settlements. The Santa Fe, New Mexico, Archdiocese is on the brink of bankruptcy due to nearly 50 lawsuits against which it is now defending itself. "More than 45 priests are believed to have [sexually] abused some 200 people over a 30-year period."[26] Nor is Santa Fe the only area where the Church faces such lawsuits. In 1994 the Archdiocese of Chicago expects to pay out more than the 2.8 million dollars it had paid for settlements in 1993. The problem is widespread.

The Franciscan boy's seminary in Santa Barbara, California, has just been shut down because of the sexual involvement of the majority of its priests with students. Across the United States women who have brought paternity suits are being paid child support by the Church "in return for their agreement to maintain silence about the fatherhood."[27] In the Santa Fe Archdiocese cases, the 12 insurance companies which held liability coverage, including Lloyds of London, have refused to pay claims. They argue that "they should not have to pay out because diocesan officials continued to give parish assignments to priests with a history of sexual abuse."[28]

Organizations such as ten-year-old "Good Tidings," which helps priests and women who are sexually involved, have sprung up around the world. Good Tidings, headquartered in Canadensis, Pennsylvania, has branches in Canada, Australia, and England. It is "developing ties with similar organizations in other countries, hoping to create a federation that can present a united front to the Church of Rome, which has dismissed sexual liaisons between priests and women as merely an American problem." Many priests "develop patterns of repeated involvement with women." Some of the priests' lovers consider themselves married, "in heart if not legally," and some relationships amount to "common-law marriage. . . ." But "when the responsibility of a child comes, the priest is gone."[29]

## Brazen Hypocrisy

The Church's insistence upon the unnatural and unworkable rule of celibacy has led to a priesthood of hypocrites who profess one thing and live another. According to *National Catholic Reporter*, about "10 percent of priests report a sexual approach from a priest while they were in training. . . . Spiritual directors, novice masters, seminary professors often introduce sexual contact into the context of their spiritual office."[30]

Bishops from western Canada visiting Rome in September 1993 asked the pope in a series of meetings to "grant an exception on cultural grounds and allow married priests among the Inuit and Dene peoples of northern Canada." The pope was polite but unbending. Fifteen centuries of "infallibility" can't be changed that easily.[31]

St. John's Abbey, Collegeville, Minnesota, was the scene during August 12 and 13, 1993, of a groundbreaking conference on "Sexual Trauma and the Church" sponsored by two Benedictines, Abbot Timothy Kelly and Br. Dietrich Reinhart, President of St. John's University. Protestants were involved as well. Dominated by the search for psychological rather than spiritual solutions, participants included psychologists and psychiatrists such as Jesuit Fr. James Gill, psychiatrist and editor of *Human Development*.

Conferees noted that accurate numbers of sexual-abuse cases are not available because of the widespread suppression of such information by the Church. One canon lawyer, Fr. Thomas Doyle, coauthor of the 1985 Doyle-Moulton-Peterson report on abuse in the clergy, estimated that in 1990 about 3000 of the 50,000 priests in America were "currently involved sexually with minors." It is estimated that "four times as many priests involve themselves sexually with adult women and twice the number of priests involve themselves with adult men as those involved with children."[32] The situation is out of hand, as it has been for centuries. Of his fellow clergymen, William Hogan wrote after leaving the priesthood in the early nineteenth century:

> I am sorry to say, from my knowledge of them, since my infancy to the present moment, that there is not a more corrupt, licentious body of men in the world.[33]

At Vatican II Paul VI used the dogma of papal infallibility to take out of the Council's hands critical issues such as celibacy and birth control, upon which he pronounced his own opinions. He demanded that all priests renew their vow of celibacy on Holy Thursday in 1970. Rome can't possibly reverse itself on celibacy without admitting that its infallible popes and councils have been wrong on this point, out of touch with the

Scriptures and the Holy Spirit for centuries, while Protestants have been right all along.

Rome's hypocrisy is monumental. She continues to lecture the rest of the world on high moral standards and to pose as the arbiter and paragon of virtue, while tens of thousands of her clergy violate the very morals she proclaims. Consider the 179 pages of *Veritatis Splendor*, produced by John Paul II over six years and published late in 1993. This weighty theological treatise condemns contraception, illicit sex, and homosexuality as "intrinsically evil." Conspicuous by its absence, however, is any admission that a high percentage of the Roman Catholic clergy practice all three.

## Sad Proof of Failure

Catholic theologian Hans Kung echoes the belief of the majority of Roman Catholics when he calls John Paul II's entire pontificate too "hard line" on sexual morality and suggests that such harshness, rather than preventing sexual misconduct, has actually contributed to it. Kung, who continues under a cloud of Vatican disapproval, calls *Veritatis Splendor* (which church leaders hailed as "a call to holiness"), "the testimony of his [John Paul II's] failure. Wojtyla's point of view, after having been voiced in hundreds of speeches all over the world, has fallen on deaf ears. This is the crowning fiasco of his 15-year-old pontificate."[34]

In his 120-million-dollar lawsuit against the Church, former Jesuit priest Terence German, a Vatican troubleshooter from 1978 to 1981 at Rome's Jesuit headquarters, claims that "the pope turned a deaf ear to his complaints of sexual improprieties." And when the facts could no longer be denied, the pope tried to say that such things were only occurring in the United States. "But that's hogwash," says German. "It's going on right in Rome, and he knows it."[35]

Chicago's Joseph Cardinal Bernardin boasts that *Veritatis Splendor* "reaffirms the moral vision that has sustained the Catholic community since the time of Christ."[36] Can he really be that ignorant of both the history and current condition of his Church?

Rome is beyond question that city which is the "Mother of

Harlots" of Revelation 17, having created them around the world and down through history literally by the millions. No other city on earth even comes close to rivaling her in this regard.

*Upon her forehead was a name written . . .
THE MOTHER OF . . . ABOMINATIONS OF
THE EARTH.*

—Revelation 17:5

*The Church . . . teaches and commands that the
usage of indulgences—a usage most beneficial
to Christians and approved by the authority of
the Sacred Councils—should be kept in the
Church; and it condemns with anathema those
who say that indulgences are useless or that the
Church does not have the power to grant them.*

—Vatican II[1]

*From the very earliest days of the Church there
has been a tradition whereby images of our Lord,
his holy Mother, and of saints are displayed in
churches for the veneration of the faithful.
. . . The practice of placing sacred images in
churches so that they be venerated by the faithful is to be maintained.*

—Vatican II[2]

# 13

# Seducer of Souls

Look at the fruit of the Reformation, with its many divisions and denominations among the Protestants," is the frequent cry from Catholic apologists. "How can such confusion be of God!" The implication is that only Protestants have doctrinal differences among themselves, while the Roman Catholic Church is a unity of 980 million faithful adherents who all believe and practice the same thing. That is, of course, far from the truth. Catholicism gives a false impression of unity because wide disagreements in doctrine and practice are retained under its broad cloak. As *Fidelity* editor E. Michael Jones, a leading Catholic writer, puts it, the faithful—

> [do not abandon] the Catholic Church . . . [because it] is the only barque of Christ . . . no matter what waves of heresy buffet its sides, one is never justified in jumping ship, not even during the fiercest storms.[3]

## Serious Divisions

As we have already seen, popes disagreed with and excommunicated one another as heretics (yet those excommunicated remain on the list of popes today); councils disagreed with one another and there were even serious differences of opinion within the same council. There were many dissenters at the

179

Council of Trent—a council which did not represent the mind of the Church at large, yet remains the major fount of official dogma today. At Vatican I many bishops were opposed to papal infallibility and only later confirmed the vote to spare themselves the pope's wrath. It was much the same at Vatican II, with Pope Paul VI smothering opposition.

The English version of the new Universal Catechism had been held up for more than a year because of serious differences among the bishops. Some of these were aired at the November 15-18, 1993, National Conference of Catholic Bishops held in Washington D.C. Many bishops expressed doctrinal concerns. Archbishop Rembert Weakland of Milwaukee told the Conference, "There is enormous unrest and unease about liturgy right now."[4]

The numerous divisions within the Roman Catholic Church range all the way from archconservatism to beliefs and practices of priests and nuns deeply involved in Hinduism or Buddhism to Hans Kung's liberalism. The latter is so far from Rome's official party line that in 1979 the Vatican revoked his status as a theologian. Yet he remains a powerful influence within the Catholic Church. Or take Fr. Matthew Fox, silenced for one year by the Vatican but vocal thereafter with views that can only be called pagan and New Age. Expelled from the Dominican order for insubordination but not excommunicated from the Church for his gross heresies, Fox has since become an Episcopalian. A wide range of other theologians and clergy remain in the Church, from Maryknoll priests and nuns advocating Marxism and Liberation Theology to Society of St. Pius X zealots who are scandalized by John Paul II's ecumenism.

## The Great Schism

There have been at least as many divisions among Roman Catholics through the centuries as among Protestants, and there still are to this very day. Some of these disagreements were fought with sword and spear. Consider, for example, the Great Schism when France and Italy struggled for possession of the lucrative papacy. In 1378, Urban VI, a Neapolitan, became pope. Trying to effect some much-needed reform,

Urban excommunicated the cardinals who had purchased their benefices. It was a well-intentioned but politically foolish move. As von Dollinger explains:

> Simony had long been the daily bread of the Roman *Curia* and the breath of its life; without simony the machine must come to a stand-still and instantly fall to pieces. The Cardinals had, from their own point of view, ample ground for insisting on the impossibility of subsisting without it. They accordingly revolted from Urban and elected Clement VII, a man after their own heart.
>
> And thus it came to pass that from 1378 to 1409 Western Christendom was divided into two Obediences.[5]

In 1409, Pisa was the scene of a synod from all Europe that was called to heal the breach. It was the first time in 300 years that those attending such a gathering dared to speak openly and vote freely. There was a sense of relief, even of triumph when the two reigning popes, Gregory XII and Benedict XIII, were deposed as heretics and a third pope, Alexander V, was elected. Of course neither of the two "popes" yielded to the synod's decision. Now there were three "vicars of Christ" instead of a mere two, just as there had been 350 years before. That situation lasted from 1409-15.[6]

Could it be that one of the "abominations" to which this woman in John's vision would give birth was a man claiming to be "vicar of Christ," and even worse, three men each claiming to be Christ's true and only representative on earth, each damning those who followed either of the other two? Catherine of Siena, who persuaded Gregory XI, seventh of the Avignon popes, to return to Rome, is recognized today as a Catholic saint. She was a staunch supporter of Urban VI, but he is shown on the lists as an anti-pope.

## The Worst Abominations

Just before her death, Catherine, who had lengthy trances in which she allegedly saw heaven, purgatory, and hell, received permission from God (so she said) to allow her "to bear the punishment for all the sins of the world. . . ."[7] Yet Christ's death had already paid the full penalty for sin. Was she excommunicated as a heretic for such blasphemy? No, she was so admired for her "sacrifice" that the Roman Catholic Church made her a saint.

Five hundred years later the Church would accept the claim that the sufferings (evidenced by the stigmata bleeding in hands, feet, and side where Christ was pierced) endured for 50 years[8] by a monk named Padre Pio were also in payment for the sins of the world. Pio claimed that more spirits of the dead than living persons visited him in his monastery cell. The spirits came to thank him for paying for their sins with his sufferings so they could be released from purgatory and go to heaven. Other monks testified that they heard multitudes of voices talking with Padre Pio at night.[9]

The Bible, however, repeatedly assures us that Christ suffered the full penalty for sin: "In whom we have redemption through his blood, the forgiveness of sins, according to the riches of his grace" (Ephesians 1:7; cf. Colossians 1:14). There is nothing left for sinners to pay in order to receive the pardon offered by God's grace. The debt has been paid in full. "It is finished!" Christ cried in triumph just before He died upon the cross (John 19:30). To suggest otherwise is the most serious heresy.

John the Baptist hailed Christ as "the Lamb of God which taketh away the sin of the world" (John 1:29). All others (including Pio, et al), being sinners ("all have sinned"— Romans 3:23) would have to die for their own sins and therefore could not also pay for sins of another person. Peter declared that Christ once for all time "suffered for sins, the just [sinless one] for [us] the unjust, that he might bring us to God" (1 Peter 3:18).

Yet Catherine of Siena, Padre Pio, and other such "suffering saints" are revered and prayed to by millions of Catholics, including the current pope, for having suffered for the sins of others. They are greater than Christ in the sense that His suffering leaves good Catholics still in purgatory, whereas Padre Pio's suffering releases multitudes to heaven. Vatican II declares that believers have always "carried their crosses to make expiation for their own sins and the sins of others . . . [to] help their brothers obtain salvation from God. . . ."[10]

Such blasphemy is one of the abominations to which the Roman Catholic Church has given birth and which she still nurtures today. Can there be any greater abomination than teaching that sinners for whom Christ paid the full penalty of sin need yet to "make expiation for their own sins and the sins of others"?

## Idols of Thy Abominations

In the Bible the word "abomination" is a spiritual term associated with idolatry. God condemned Israel for the "idols of thy abominations" (Ezekiel 16:36). Occult practices are also called abominations, along with illicit and perverted sex. Since the woman astride the beast is "the mother of harlots and abominations," it seems clear that these evil practices rooted in Babel will, under Antichrist, characterize the world religion which this woman represents. She is called the "Mother" of these things because she has fostered and encouraged them. The description fits exactly both the history and the present practice of the Roman Catholic Church.

The biblical prohibition against making images for religious purposes and bowing down before them (and God's abhorrence of this pagan practice) is clearly set forth in the second of the Ten Commandments and in numerous other passages of Scripture. For example: "Ye shall make you no idols nor graven image . . . to bow down unto it. . . . Cursed be the man that maketh any graven or molten image, an abomination unto the Lord" (Leviticus 26:1; Deuteronomy 27:15). Yet Vatican II commends images in churches and says they are to be "venerated by the faithful." In Catholic churches and cathedrals around the world one sees the faithful on their knees in front of images of this or that "saint," most often "Mary."

The second of the Ten Commandments that God gave to Israel states: "Thou shalt not make unto thee any graven image, or any likeness of anything that is in heaven above, or that is in the earth beneath. . . . Thou shalt not bow down thyself to them, nor serve them" (Exodus 20:4,5; cf. Deuteronomy 5:8,9). How does the Roman Catholic Church get around this clear prohibition? She does worse than ignore it; she literally hides it from the people.

The "Ten Commandments" shown in Catholic catechisms leave out the second commandment prohibiting images and divide the last one, prohibiting covetousness, into two. It is a flagrant rejection of a clear command by God. Moreover, that rejection is dishonestly covered up by pretending the command doesn't exist. It is a deliberate deception practiced upon the members of the Church, most of whom know nothing of the Bible except what the clergy tell them.

When Emperor Leo III issued an edict from Constantinople calling for forcible baptism of Jews, he was praised. But when, in 726, he demanded that all images be broken, there was a great outcry from citizens and clergy. Pope Gregory II claimed that images were not worshiped but reverenced. The truth slipped out, however, in his letter to the emperor: "But as for the statue of St. Peter himself, which all the kingdoms of the West esteem as a god on earth, the whole West would take a terrible revenge [if it were destroyed]."[11] A bloody war was fought around Ravena over this issue and a synod in Rome excommunicated all who dared attack the images.

Christians had not used images until Constantine became the de facto head of the Church. The door that was opened to paganism at that time has never been shut. The Church attempted to accommodate the pagans joining it by retaining their idols under Christian names. That practice is still part of Santeria, voodoo, etc. today.

Catholic apologists insist that veneration is not of the image itself but of the "saint" it represents. Yet John Paul II openly promotes the pagan belief that images have power. Recently at St. Peter's Basilica the Pope declared:

> A mysterious "presence" of the transcendent Proto-type seems as it were to be transferred to the sacred image. . . . The devout contemplation of such an image thus appears as a real and concrete path of purification of the soul of the believer . . . because the image itself, blessed by the priest . . . can in a certain sense, by analogy with the sacraments, actually be considered a channel of divine grace.[12]

Such idolatry the Bible repeatedly condemns as spiritual adultery or fornication! Rome is the "Mother of Harlots" in this way as well, having led untold millions into idolatry.

## Salvation for Sale

The Roman Catholic Church has been in the business of selling salvation to the naive, with much of her great wealth accumulated from that source. And she does this in the name of the Christ, who offers salvation as a free gift! He told His disciples, "Freely ye have received, freely give" (Matthew 10:8)! There could be no greater abomination than selling salvation, yet Rome has never repented of this evil but continues similar practices to this day.

Under Pope Leo X (1513-21)—who cursed and excommunicated Martin Luther—specific prices were published by the Roman Chancery to be paid to the Church for absolution from each imaginable crime. Even murder had its price. For example, a deacon guilty of murder could be absolved for 20 crowns. The "anointed malefactors," as they were called, once pardoned in this way by the Church, could not be prosecuted by civil authorities.

Leo's sale of salvation was nothing new. Two hundred years earlier John XXII (1316-34) had done the same, setting a price for every crime from murder to incest to sodomy. The more Catholics sinned the richer the Church became. Similar fundraising schemes had been in operation for years.

Innocent VIII (1484-92), for example, had granted the 20-year *Butterbriefe* indulgence. For a certain sum one could purchase the privilege of eating favorite dishes during Lent and at other times of fasting. It was a way to be credited with fasting while indulging oneself in the richest of foods. The people believed that the popes had such power. After all, wasn't whatever the vicars of Christ bound or loosed on earth similarly bound or loosed in heaven? The proceeds from this enterprising scheme built the bridge over the Elbe. Julius III (1550-5) renewed this indulgence (for a handsome fee) for another 20 years after he came to office.

Leo X tore down Constantine's basilica and built St. Peter's, largely with monies paid by people who thought they were thereby gaining forgiveness of sins and entrance to heaven. That magnificent structure stands as one more piece of evidence that Rome is the "Mother of abominations."

As Giovanni de Medici, Leo had been made an abbot at age seven for his first communion and a cardinal at age 13. Though he was the youngest cardinal to that time, Pope Benedict IX ascended to Peter's throne at age 11. Imagine an 11-year-old solemnly pronouncing forgiveness of sins as Christ's one true representative on earth! It was Leo X who commissioned the Dominican Friar Tetzel to sell indulgences, which it was promised would free those in purgatory or release the purchaser, if bought in his own name, from having to spend any time in that intermediate place of torment.

Tetzel's infamous sales pitch went, "As soon as the coin in the coffer rings, a soul from purgatory springs!" How could anyone be so naive as to believe that the forgiveness of sins for which Christ had to endure the full wrath of God upon the cross could be purchased with money? This "God" of Catholicism who moves in response to whatever regulations a corrupt Church invents is clearly not the God of the Bible. (It was this particular abomination of selling salvation that scandalized Martin Luther and sparked the Reformation.)

Well-meaning Protestants, wanting to believe the best, imagine that Roman Catholicism has rid itself of past abominations, including indulgences. Charles Colson's book *The Body* contains examples of such incorrect information. Though the book eloquently speaks much truth, it erroneously presents Roman Catholicism as biblical Christianity and calls for union therewith on the part of evangelicals. Colson writes: "The Reformers, for example, assailed the corrupt practices of indulgences; today they [indulgences] are gone (save for the modern-day equivalent practices by some unscrupulous television hucksters, ironically mostly Protestants, who promise healing and blessing for contributions)."[13]

We endorse his condemnation of "unscrupulous television hucksters," but wonder at his incorrect interpretation of Rome. A major document of Vatican II devotes 17 pages to explaining indulgences and how to obtain them and excommunicates and damns any who deny that the Church has the right to grant indulgences today *for salvation*.[14] The rules are complex and ludicrous as well as abominable. Try to imagine God honoring such regulations as granting certain indulgences "only on set days appointed by the Holy See" or that a "plenary indulgence, applicable only to the dead, can be gained in all churches ... on November 2,"[15] etc. The entire teaching on indulgences denies the sufficiency of Christ's redemptive sacrifice for sins upon the cross. (See Appendix B for further details.)

Some ancient indulgences even remain in force today. A recent notice in *Inside the Vatican* reminded Catholics that on August 28 and 29, 1994, an unusual opportunity for obtaining a special indulgence would occur:

> Pope Celestine V gave a Holy Door to the Cathedral of Maria Collemaggio in his Bull of 29 September, 1294. To obtain this "perdonanza" indulgence, it's necessary to be in the Cathedral between 18:00 (6 P.M.) 28 August and 18:00 (6 P.M.) 29 August, to truly repent of one's sins, and to confess and go to mass and communion within 8 days of the visit. The Holy Door is open every year, but this year, 1994, is the *700th anniversary* of the Bull of Pardon. Go there![16]

## Warning: Reformation Ahead

Inside the door of the Wittenberg castle church to which Martin Luther nailed his 95 theses were relics (including an alleged lock of the Virgin Mary's hair) offering 2 million years in indulgences to those venerating them according to prescribed rules. Never has the Roman Catholic Church apologized for having led multitudes astray in this manner. And how does one apologize to souls now in hell for having sold them a bogus "ticket to heaven"?

For both ingenuity and infamy, no money-grabbing scheme of the past or of today's unscrupulous television hucksters even comes close to the sale of indulgences. It provided much cash for the popes at the time of the Reformation. In A.D. 593 Pope Gregory I had first proposed the unbiblical (but ultimately very profitable) idea that there was a place called "purgatory" in which the spirits of the dead suffered in order to be purged of their sins and fully delivered from "the debt of eternal punishment." This fabrication was declared to be a Church dogma by the Council of Florence in 1439 and remains an important part of Roman Catholicism today.

It was not such abominable heresies, however, that divided Roman Catholics. All seemed content with the promise that the Church would somehow get them to heaven, no matter how repugnant to common sense and justice the methods were. As Chamberlin has said, "the eye of faith was blind to the incidental discrepancies."[17] It was the division caused by rival popes, each claiming to be in charge of the machinery of salvation, that stirred the Church to action.

By deposing all three rivals who each claimed to be the Vicar of Christ, and then appointing a new pope, Martin V, the Council of Constance (1414-18) reunited the Church. (See Appendix D for more details.) Many bishops were convinced that a reformation was desperately needed. To move the Church toward reformation, Constance decreed that there should be another ecumenical council each ten years. Pope Martin V dutifully—

> summoned the Council in 1423 to meet, first at Pavia, then at Sienna. But the moment any signs of an attempt at reform manifested themselves, he dissolved it "on account of the fewness of those present." However, shortly before his death, he summoned the new Council to meet at Basle.
>
> Martin V's successor, Eugenius IV, could not avoid carrying out the duty he had inherited from his predecessor, to which he was already pledged in conclave.[18]

## The Struggle for Supremacy

Eugenius ordered the council disbanded almost immediately upon a pretext, but the assembly refused and a contest with the pope began, at first with the backing of the general populace of Europe and King Sigismund. In vain the pope excommunicated the prelates involved. Support for reform poured in to the council from kings, princes, bishops, prelates and universities. Under pressure the pope was forced to give the council his full sanction, an acknowledgment once again of the superiority of council over pope (which Pius IX would manage to reverse at Vatican I).

The council deposed Eugenius, calling him "a notorious disturber of peace and unity of God's Church, a simoniac, a perjurer, an incorrigible man, a schismatic, an apostate from the Faith, an obstinate heretic, a squanderer of the Church's rights and property, incapable and harmful to the administration of the Roman Pontificate. . . ."[19] (Yet his name remains on today's official list of the vicars of Christ.) With great courage the council decreed:

> All ecclesiastical appointments shall be made according to the canons of the Church; all simony shall cease . . . all priests whether of the highest or lowest rank shall put away their concubines, and whoever within two months of this decree neglects its demands shall be deprived of his office, though he be the Bishop of Rome.
>
> . . . the popes shall neither demand nor receive any fees for ecclesiastical offices. From now on, a pope should think not of this world's treasures but only of those of the world to come.

That medicine proved too strong, and the tide of opinion turned against the council.[20] The people wanted reformation, but not that much; and the last thing the pope and the *Curia* wanted was to be required to live as true Christians with a council making certain they did. Pope Eugenius summoned his own council at Florence, deposed and anathematized the members of Basle, "laid Basle under interdict, excommunicated the municipal council, and required every one to plunder the merchants who were bringing their wares to the city, because it is written, 'The righteous hath spoiled the ungodly.' "[21] The pope then bribed King Frederick with 100,000 florins "together with the imperial crown, assigned tithes to him from all the German benefices and . . . gave full power to his confessor to give him twice a plenary absolution from all sins." Such is the abominable manner in which the popes dispensed their favors, including forgiveness of sins.

The Council of Basle could not compete with the power and wealth of the pope. Eugenius now had the backing he needed. Von Dollinger comments, "The victory of Eugenius was complete. When on his deathbed he received the homage of the German ambassadors, the event was celebrated (February 7 1447) in Rome with ringing of bells and bonfires. Even the slight concessions the pope had made to the Germans he thereupon recalled in secret Bulls." In 1443 an anonymous German Catholic, in mourning for his Church, seemed to echo the very vision God had given John in Revelation 17:

> The Roman harlot has so many paramours drunk with the wine of her fornications, that the Bride of Christ, the Church, and the Council representing her, scarcely receive the loyal devotion of one among a thousand.[22]

As he died, having triumphed over the council and Germany, Eugenius cried in agony of conscience, "How much better were it for thy soul's salvation hadst thou never become Cardinal and Pope!"[23] The next pope, Nicholas V (1447-55), voided Eugenius's decrees against the Council of Basle (yet both remain on the official list of popes today). It was the last chance for the papacy to be reformed, but it would not happen. In only a short while the *Curia's* diligent forgers were at work again producing more false documents to prove the popes' infallibility and dominance over all.

## Corruption of the Era

Rome's dominance of Church and world for more than a thousand years through excommunication, torture, and death had led to corruption of such proportions that even the secular world recoiled in shame and horror. The cry resounded throughout Christendom for a reformation of the Church. All knew, however, that it was impossible as long as the Court of Rome remained what it was: "There every mischief is fostered and protected, and thence it spreads, but there, unless by a miracle, there is no hope of reformation."[24]

Among the popes who followed Nicholas on Peter's alleged throne were some whose evil was beyond imagination. Von

Dollinger says of Paul II, Sixtus IV, Innocent VIII, and Alexander VI that each tried "to exceed the vices of his predecessor." One contemporary said that Paul II had "made the Papal Chair into a sewer by his debaucheries."[25] Pilgrims who went to Rome with high hopes returned disillusioned, like Martin Luther, to declare that "in the metropolis of Christendom, and in the bosom of the great mother and mistress of all Churches, the clergy, with scarcely an exception, kept concubines."[26] And the Church made a profit from it.

Sixtus IV (1471-84), who had licensed Rome's brothels for an annual fee and taxed the clergy for their mistresses, invented an even more ingenious method of filling the Church's coffers. It would be used by the popes after him to full advantage. Sixtus decided that he, as Christ's vicar, could apply indulgences to the dead as well as to the living. It was a novel idea which no one had thought of before, and one which turned out to be incredibly profitable.

What surviving relative could refuse to purchase the release of a deceased mother, father, aunt, uncle, or child from the tortures of purgatory? And of course the richer the living relatives were the more it invariably cost to transfer the deceased from purgatory to heaven. One marvels that anyone would take the word of such an evil pope, but Sixtus was no worse than many others, and after all, evil or not, he *was* Christ's vicar and the successor of Peter, was he not? Again Chamberlin put it so well: "No lay monarch, no matter how powerful or virtuous, could hope to attract to himself the deep instinctive reverence that men felt for the successor of St. Peter, no matter how unworthy. . . ."[27] The few bold souls, such as Savonarola, of Florence, who dared to criticize Rome's abominations, were consigned to the flames for their zeal.

## The Council of Trent

Such was the state of the Roman Catholic Church at the time of the Reformation. Remember, Luther and Calvin were devout Catholics. There were no Protestants. That word had not been invented. Multitudes had been crying for reformation for at least 200 years. No one, however, Calvin and Luther included, wanted to leave the Church. They desired to see it reformed from within.

Furious at the challenge to their power, the popes would have consigned Luther and Calvin to the flames, but, unable to get their hands on them because of the protection afforded by certain German princes, the hierarchy threw them summarily out of the Church. Sick to death with the arrogant despotism of the papacy, with its oppression and slaughter of any who would not bow to its imperious demands, multitudes followed Luther and Calvin and the other Reformation leaders out of the Church, giddy with the first gasping breaths of spiritual freedom they had ever drawn.

Suddenly Protestantism, this upstart clamor of "heresy," was thriving and on the march everywhere. Pope Paul III saw his empire dwindling and his influence over kings coming to an end. A despotic, Renaissance pope who had "bestowed the red hat on his nephews, aged fourteen and seventeen, and promoted them despite their notorious immorality,"[28] Paul III acted decisively on two fronts. He convened a council in Trent (northern Italy) that would condemn the Reformation theologically; and he went to work behind the scenes to organize a holy war that was intended to militarily wipe Protestantism from the face of the earth in Christ's name.

Rome's popularity was at a low ebb when the Council of Trent met in 1545 to consider its response to the menace of Protestantism which threatened the Church in much of Europe. There were still many clergy within the Catholic Church who realized the need for a reformation and hoped that Trent would bring it about, thereby making it possible to welcome those who had left the Church back into its fold. The pope and his *Curia*, however, had other plans.

The opening speech at the council, by Bishop Coriolano Martorano, encouraged those who hoped for reform. Unfortunately, very few so minded were present, for the pope had stacked the deck with his own men. Von Dollinger describes that stirring oration:

> The picture he [Martorano] drew of the Italian Cardinals and bishops, their bloodthirsty cruelty, their avarice, their pride, and the devastation they had wrought of the Church, was perfectly shocking. An unknown writer, who has described this first sitting in a letter to a friend, thinks Luther himself never spoke more severely.[29]

In fact, this lone cry for a return to genuine Christianity was followed by a chorus supporting the very evil which Martorano had exposed. The Council of Trent, controlled by Italians, was to prove itself incapable of facing the facts. When once again a non-Italian delegate dared to bring up charges that reflected badly upon the papacy, the Italian bishops shouted, stamped their feet, and cried that this "accursed wretch must not speak; he should at once be brought to trial."[30] The "freedom of speech" at Trent was similar to what it would be 325 years later in Rome at Vatican I.

A famous eyewitness wrote shortly after the council opened that nothing beneficial was to be hoped for from the "monstrous bishops" attending; there was "nothing episcopal about them except their long robes . . . [they] had become bishops through royal favor, through solicitation, through purchase in Rome, through criminal arts, or after long years spent in the *Curia*." They "must all be deposed" if Trent was to produce anything worthy, but that was impossible.[31] Another contemporary, Pallavicini, wrote:

> The Italian bishops knew of no other aim than the upholding of the Apostolic See and its greatness. They thought that in working for its interests they showed themselves at once good Italians and good Christians.[32]

## The Catholic-Protestant Wars

Not satisfied with damning the Protestants theologically (the canons and decrees of the Council of Trent contain more than 100 anathemas against Protestant beliefs), Pope Paul III wanted to destroy them physically. He offered the Holy Roman Emperor, Charles V of Spain, "1,100,000 ducats, 12,000 infantry, 500 horses, if he would turn his full force against the heretics." The Catholic emperor was only too happy to have a reason to bring the rival Protestant princes of Germany into subjection and "to crush Protestantism and give to his realm a unified Catholic Faith that would, he thought, strengthen and facilitate his government."[33]

Nearly ten years of war across Europe ensued. Paul III "issued a bull excommunicating all who should resist Charles

and offering liberal indulgences to all who should aid him."
After heavy losses on both sides and much treachery among
the rival rulers, the Protestants remained strong enough to
force the emperor into a compromise. Will Durant explains the
settlement that created the state churches which still exist in
Europe today:

> In order to permit peace among and within the states
> each prince was to choose between Roman Catholicism
> and Lutheranism; all his subjects were to accept "his
> religion whose realm" it was; and those who did not like
> it were to emigrate. There was no pretense on either side
> to toleration; the principle which the Reformation had
> upheld in the youth of its rebellion—the right of private
> judgment—was as completely rejected by the Protestant
> leaders as by the Catholics. . . .
> The Protestants now agreed with Charles and the
> popes that unity of religious belief was indispensable to
> social order and peace . . . the princes [were to] banish
> dissenters instead of burning them. . . . The real victor
> was not freedom of worship but the freedom of the princes.
> Each became, like Henry VIII of England, the supreme
> head of the Church [whether Catholic or Protestant] in
> his territory, with the exclusive right to appoint the
> clergy and the men who should define the obligatory
> faith.
> The "Erastian" principle—that the state should rule
> the Church—was definitely established. As it was the
> princes, not the theologians, who had led Protestantism
> to its triumph, they naturally assumed the fruits of vic-
> tory—their territorial supremacy over the emperor, their
> ecclesiastical supremacy over the Church. . . . In effect
> the Holy Roman Empire died not in 1806 but in 1555.[34]

The story of the Reformation has been told elsewhere.
There were evils perpetrated on both sides, which we lack the
space to recount. We are pursuing one objective primarily in
this book: to identify the woman riding the beast in Revelation
17. In this chapter we are demonstrating the fact that "Mother
of abominations" was inscribed on her forehead. Let us now
move from the past to the present.

"Abomination" is a spiritual term. There is no greater abomination than rejecting the sacrifice Christ made on the cross for our sins—unless it is leading others astray also. That abomination in varying forms continues in Roman Catholicism to this day. Another of Rome's great deceptions relates to marriage and divorce.

## Divorce by Another Name

The Roman Catholic Church is known for its adamant stand against divorce. Yet at the same time she is a veritable and unique divorce mill, hiding this fact by deceitfully calling it by another name. The Church grants in the United States alone "annulments" by the tens of thousands each year.[35] Her use of psychology is particularly perverse. Many annulments are granted for "psychological" reasons such as being raised in a "dysfunctional" family or being "psychologically unprepared" for a marriage that occurred decades before and produced numerous children. It is the ultimate in hypocrisy and cynicism, another of the abominations Rome has birthed.

Here is an excerpt from a typical letter from a Catholic diocese justifying to a distraught woman an annulment granted to her husband of 30 years (five children, husband and wife both Catholics):

> This investigation by a court of the Catholic Church determines whether an essential element of the Sacrament of Matrimony was missing at the time the marriage was entered. If a careful investigation should determine that such an element as perceived by the Church was lacking, then your marriage does not bind you or Mr. _____ so far as the Catholic Church is concerned. This decision does not have civil implications and does not make your children illegitimate.

Of course there are no "civil implications." As unjust as the courts may be at times, civil judges are not yet ready to pretend a marriage didn't actually occur because one of the parties now claims that he or she was not psychologically prepared at the time or held some mental reservation as to whether it would work out. Sadly enough, some Catholics now file secret letters with their attorneys at the time of marriage, expressing doubts, just in case they want an annulment later. Common sense would say that if there are doubts, then the vows should not be taken; and once the promise is made to be faithful "for better or worse," it should be kept. If couples can make solemn vows of fidelity and later break them without penalty and with the blessing of the Church, then all interpersonal relationships break down, whether business or private. No one can be trusted anymore to keep any promise.

The *PrimeTime* television show of January 6, 1994, dealt with the issue of Catholic annulments. A Catholic priest remembered hearing a Church canon lawyer tell him, "Charlie, there isn't a Catholic marriage in the United States that we couldn't annul." A number of women guests told of their ex-husbands, after a divorce, seeking annulments so they could remarry in the Church: Barbara Zimmerman, married 27 years and mother of five children; Pat Cadigan, married 23 years; Sheila Rauch Kennedy, married to Congressman Joseph P. Kennedy II, Bobby Kennedy's eldest son, for 12 years and mother of his twin sons.

A Catholic priest on the program, Fr. Patrick Cogan, explained that annulments are granted even though the Church doesn't believe in divorce, because "the Catholic Church believes that it must hold onto a higher principle." Really? He explained that an annulment means "there was never a marriage from the very beginning." Mrs. Kennedy responded angrily, "To say that a marriage that lasted . . . close to 13 years . . . that took place after a nine-year courtship and a marriage that created two wonderful children never happened is, to me, outrageous." Joseph Kennedy had explained to her, "But you have to understand that nobody believes this anyway. It's—it's just Catholic gobbledygook. It's the way the Church requires that you say these things, so don't take it so seriously."[36]

While claiming to stand for holiness, Rome corrupts her followers. On *PrimeTime* Barbara Zimmerman declared: "For my Church to say, 'Well, you know, you can't get a divorce, but we'll annul it and that'll take care of it'—it's—it's slimy. It's sleazy. It's dishonest. It's saying, 'We'll get around our own rules.' "

The implications for eternity are solemn indeed. If the Catholic Church can't be trusted to tell the truth about marriage and divorce, then how can it be trusted when it comes to salvation? To be cheated in this life is costly enough, but to be cheated for eternity is a loss from which there is no recovery.

The golden chalice held by the woman riding the beast was filled with "the abominations and filthiness of her fornication" (Revelation 17:4). There is not and never has been a city on earth except "Christian" Rome which perfectly fits that description. She has been the seducer of souls, leading multitudes into the abominations of idolatry, sexual immorality, the denial of the sufficiency of Christ's redemptive work upon the cross, and the sale of counterfeit salvation in its place—and has done it while posing as the one true Church acting in the name of Christ.

*I saw the woman . . . and when I saw her, I wondered with great admiration.*

—Revelation 17:6

*The man who enters [a fourth-century church] is bound to see drunkards, misers, tricksters, gamblers, adulterers, fornicators, people wearing amulets, assiduous clients of sorcerers, astrologers. . . .*

*He must be warned that the same crowds that press into the churches on Christian festivals, also fill the theatres on pagan holidays.*

—St. Augustine[1]

# 14

# An Incredible
# Metamorphosis

That a gorgeously clad *woman* should be holding the reins
astride such a terrifying, world-devouring beast was just
cause for astonishment. John appears, however, to have been
dumbfounded by more than that fact—indeed, by the woman
herself ("when I saw *her*, I wondered with great admiration
[amazement]"). Why? Was it because the woman was a *religious* figure? Hardly.

That *religion* should wield great authority was a universal
fact of John's day. Church and state were one, with religion
playing the dominant role. If the woman merely represented
pagan world religion, John would hardly have been surprised.
What could there have been about this woman that astonished
him? Had he known her before and was shocked by the unbelievable transformation?

Beneath the luxurious attire, the priceless jewelry, the
heavy cosmetics, and the shamelessly impudent stare there
was a haunting familiarity. It couldn't be possible! How had
Christ's chaste bride become this brazen whore? What diabolical mutation had transformed that small, despised flock of
humble followers of the Lamb into this notorious prostitute
toasting Satan with the blood of the martyrs in a golden
chalice! How could the church, hated and persecuted by the
world, as Christ had said she would be—how could she have

become this powerful worldwide institution that reigned over the kings of the earth?

John was staggered. What he was being shown seemed impossible: that those who belonged to Christ would find themselves in a false church, a whore. There would be no possibility of reforming her from within. The cry would come from the Lord Himself in heaven, "Come out of her, my people, that ye be not partakers of her sins" (Revelation 18:4).

History authenticates John's vision. It has become quite clear that the world religion under Antichrist will not be atheism, Hinduism, Islam, Buddhism, or even New Age. It will be *Christianity*, but in a paganized form—exactly what it became under the leadership of Constantine and his successors, the popes. The coming world religion will have its headquarters in Rome.

## The Persecuted Early Church

For more than two centuries, as Tertullian said, the blood of the martyrs was the seed of a heavenly-minded church without earthly ambition, a church whose members had increased to about 10 percent of the Roman Empire. The church that Christ had established seemed to thrive under persecution. Mistreatment by the world kept her pure, detached from earthly desires, and longing to be with Christ in heaven. Christians were radically different from pagans; they were misfits, despised and blamed for every disaster because their refusal to worship the idols had presumably brought down the wrath of the gods. Early in the third century Tertullian wrote:

> If the Tiber reaches the walls, if the Nile does not rise to the fields, if the sky doesn't move or the earth does, if there is famine, if there is plague, the cry is at once: "The Christians to the lions!"[2]

A successful Roman lawyer and convert to Christianity from Stoicism, Tertullian was one of the church's first and most prominent theologians and apologists. He openly attacked every facet of pagan culture and religion. Needling the pagans who debated him, Tertullian declared: "Day by day you groan over the ever-increasing number of Christians. Your constant cry is that your state is beset by us, that Christians are everywhere."[3] An early church leader described Christians with these words:

> But while they dwell in Greek or barbarian cities according as each man's lot has been cast, and follow the customs of the land in clothing and food, and other matters of daily life, yet the condition of citizenship which they exhibit is wonderful, and admittedly strange.
>
> They live in countries of their own, but simply as sojourners . . . endur[ing] the lot of foreigners. . . .
>
> They exist in the flesh, but they live not after the flesh. They spend their existence upon earth, but their citizenship is in heaven. They obey the established laws, and in their own lives they surpass the laws. They love all men, and are persecuted by all.[4]

The persecutions of the third century were far more severe than the earlier ones. Clement reported "roastings, impalings and beheadings" of Christians in Alexandria before he fled that city around 203.[5] Persecutions came in waves, punctuated by periods of relative tolerance and tranquility. The totalitarian system of the Caesars made the pagan view of the emperor as deity (he had absolute control over life and death) seem all the more credible. Loyalty to the traditional pagan cults, headed by the emperor as *Pontifex Maximus*, was a form of patriotism. The Christian rejection of the pagan gods and emperor worship was seen as treason and fueled popular hatred against this "unpatriotic" minority.

Aroused by the fact that "the heathen temples began to be forsaken and the Christian churches thronged,"[6] the Emperor Decius, around A.D. 250, martyred thousands of people, including the bishops of Rome, Antioch, and Jerusalem as well as a number of the emperor's own soldiers who refused to sacrifice to idols.[7] "Not a town, not a village of the Empire escaped," historian Philip Hughes informs us, then adds significantly, "but the emperor's intention was not so much the massacre of Christians as their conversion to the old religion . . . [through] long drawn-out trials . . . repeated interrogations and the extensive use of torture in the hope of gradually breaking down the resistance."[8] Chadwick further explains:

> [Decius required] that everyone should possess a certificate (*libellus*) that he had sacrificed to the gods before special commissioners. . . . They [the certificates] were a deliberate attempt to catch people, and were the gravest attack hitherto suffered by the Church.
>
> Especially among property-owners the number of apostates [those denying their faith to save their lives and possessions] was immense. . . .[9]

It sounds like a foretaste of what it will be like when the Roman Empire is revived under Antichrist. Following a brief respite, the persecution directed by Emperor Valerian (253-60) forbade all Christian worship and specifically focused on the execution of church leaders. Among ordinary Christians as well, the martyrs were innumerable. The worst, however, was yet to come.

The Great Persecution, as it came to be called, began in 303 under the Emperor Diocletian and his coemperor, Galerius. All Bibles had to be surrendered to the authorities, all churches were to be destroyed, all Christian worship was forbidden, all clergy were to be imprisoned, and all citizens of the empire were to sacrifice to the pagan gods on pain of death. In many places it was a bloodbath. For example, in Phrygia, "where the whole population was Christian, a whole town was wiped out."[10]

## Setting the Stage for Apostasy

At the height of the most devastating persecution, deliverance came from an astonishing direction in the form of a new emperor, Constantine. A brilliant military commander, he took control of the empire in the West, while his ally, Licinius, conquered the East. Together they signed the Edict of Milan in 313, restoring to Christians full rights as citizens.

Freedom at last from persecution seemed like a gift from God. Unfortunately, it set the stage for an apostasy that would envelop Christendom for more than a millennium. Christ's bride had been wedded to paganism. No wonder John was shocked!

The only Christianity John knew was the "little flock" (Luke 12:32) of those who, hated by the world, were following in Christ's path of rejection and suffering. The Lord had promised: "If ye were of the world, the world would love his own; but because ye are not of the world, but I have chosen you out of the world, therefore the world hateth you.... If they have persecuted me, they will also persecute you..." (John 15:19,20). And so it happened.

That this despised little band, persecuted by the world for its holiness and fidelity to Christ, could ever metamorphose into an evil institution sitting astride the very seat of worldly power and ruling over earthly kings and kingdoms seemed impossible to John, but there she was in that vision of the future.

With the at-first-reluctant but increasingly enthusiastic consent and participation of the bishops, the church entered upon an apostasy which led to Roman Catholicism and has lasted until the present time. In fact, it is now gaining momentum for God's final judgment upon the great whore. Will Durant, a purely secular historian with no religious axe to grind, comments upon the marriage of Christianity and paganism that came about through Constantine's pretended "conversion" and assumption of church leadership:

> Paganism survived... in the form of ancient rites and customs condoned, or accepted and transformed, by an often indulgent Church. An intimate and trustful worship of saints replaced the cult of pagan gods.... Statues of Isis and Horus were renamed Mary and Jesus; the Roman Lupercalia and the feast of purification of Isis became the Feast of the Nativity; the Saturnalia were replaced by Christmas celebration... an ancient festival of the dead by All Souls Day, rededicated to Christian heroes; incense, lights, flowers, processions, vestments, hymns which had pleased the people in older cults were domesticated and cleansed in the ritual of the Church ...soon people and priests would use the sign of the cross as a magic incantation to expel or drive away demons....

> [Paganism] passed like maternal blood into the new religion, and captive Rome captured her conqueror. ...the world converted Christianity....[11]

## From Persecuted to Persecutor

Referring to developments after Constantine, Peter Brown writes: "Far from being a source of improvement, this alliance [with the state] was a source of 'greater danger and temptation' [than persecution had been].... The spread of Christianity in Africa, by indiscriminately filling the churches, had simply washed away the clear moral landmarks that separated the 'church' from the 'world.'"[12] Political considerations began to subtly influence Christian life and doctrine (just as today), because what was best for the state loomed large in ecclesiastical affairs and the emperor was now in charge of both. With the fall of the Roman Empire, the popes would assume the emperor's role and the marriage with the world would be complete.

In its new role as the favored (and eventually official) religion of the empire, "Christianity" became polluted by its avid pursuit of secular power. The purity and spiritual power of the early church had been so awesome that unbelievers dared not join it (Acts 5:13). In contrast, what the Church would become after Constantine has been described eloquently by Peter de Rosa:

> The time is not far off [after Constantine] when Peter's [alleged] successors will be not the servants but the masters of the world. They will dress in purple like Nero and call themselves Pontifex Maximus. They will refer to the Fisherman as "the first pope" and appeal not to the authority of love but to the power invested in him to act as Nero acted.
>
> In defiance of Jesus, Christians will do unto others what was done unto them, and worse will they do. The religion that prided itself on triumphing over persecution by suffering will become the most persecuting faith the world has ever seen....

They will order in Christ's name all those who disagree with them to be tortured, and sometimes crucified
over fire. They will make an alliance between throne and
altar; they will insist that the throne is the guardian of the
altar and the guarantor of faith.

Their idea will be for the throne (the state) to impose
the Christian religion on all its subjects. It will not
trouble them that Peter fought against such an alliance
and died because of it.[13]

From being persecuted, the Church became the chief persecutor, not only of religious faith but, as we have seen, of any
form of freedom of conscience. Hasler explains how the metamorphosis occurred: "Once Christianity became the state
religion, deviations from orthodoxy threatened both the unity
of the empire and of the Church. And it was the emperor who
had the greatest interest in settling doctrinal disputes. He
convened ecumenical councils and largely dictated their results."[14] The popes, however, had the trump card—the keys to
heaven—and used it to intimidate kings and emperors into
becoming the secular arm which did their bidding, especially
the executions during the Inquisitions.

In 1864, Pius IX's *Syllabus of Errors* condemned "the whole
existing view of the rights of conscience and religious faith and
profession." The *Syllabus* said it was "a wicked error to admit
Protestants to equal political rights with Catholics, or to allow
Protestant immigrants the free use of their worship; on the
contrary, to coerce and suppress them is a sacred duty, when it
has become possible . . . the Church will, of course, act with
the greatest prudence in the use of her temporal and physical
power, according to altered circumstances. . . ."[15]

The Bible was the most dangerous Book in the world and
had to be kept from the common people. The clergy would give
them selected readings and tell them what it meant. The
Protestant view that anyone could read and understand the
Bible would destroy Catholicism. Pope Clement XI's Constitution *Unigenitus* (1713) denounced the following Jansenist
propositions presented by Pasquier Quesnel:

"Christians are to sanctify the Lord's Day with reading godly books, more particularly the Holy Scriptures." Clement's judgment: "CONDEMNED!"

"To pull the New Testament out of the hands of Christians is to shut the mouth of Christ against them." "CONDEMNED!"

"To forbid Christians the reading of the Holy Scriptures and especially of the Gospel is to forbid the use of the light by the children of light and to punish them with a kind of excommunication." "CONDEMNED!"

## Freedom—Roman Style

The Vatican can't enforce its edicts today in the totalitarian manner it once employed. So it professes to stand for freedom of religion and conscience because it wants such rights for its own people where Catholics are in the minority. Vatican II has an entire section titled "Declaration on Religious Liberty" which contains such statements as "the human person has a right to religious freedom."[16] What it promotes, however, is *freedom from government interference or discrimination in religion*. The dishonest impression is given that Rome advocates full freedom of religion. There is no mention of, much less repentance for, the millions of people who were martyred and massacred century after century simply because they would not accept the Roman Catholic interpretation of the Bible.

Nor does Vatican II concede genuine freedom of conscience. Yes, it says everyone is free to pursue truth. But it declares that truth exists only within the Roman Catholic Church. Nor does the Council point to the Bible, God's Word, as the source of truth, to be read and understood by all. As in the Middle Ages, the Church alone can interpret the Bible. She alone has the sacraments and is the means of salvation. The Church possesses the truth and is its guardian and sole dispenser for all time.

Therefore, for all the talk about freedom of religion and conscience in this section of Vatican II, there is no true freedom because this same document makes it clear that the truth can only be known and the soul saved by complete and blind submission to Rome. Consider the following from this section on "Religious Liberty":

We believe that this one true religion continues to exist in the Catholic Church, to which the Lord Jesus entrusted the task of spreading it among all men. . . .

So while the religious freedom which men demand in fulfilling their obligation to worship God has to do with freedom from coercion in civil society, it leaves intact the traditional Catholic teaching on the moral duty of individuals and societies towards the true religion and the one Church of Christ. . . .

Throughout the ages she [the Roman Catholic Church] has preserved and handed on the doctrine which she has received from her Master and the apostles. . . . in forming their consciences the faithful must pay careful attention to the sacred and certain teaching of the Church. For the Catholic Church is by the will of Christ the teacher of truth. It is her duty to proclaim and teach with authority the truth which is Christ and, at the same time, to declare and confirm by her authority the principles of the moral order which spring from human nature itself.

So while in theory there is freedom of conscience, in fact there is not. One is free to pursue truth, but truth exists not in the Bible in a form which the conscience can recognize and is available to all mankind, but resides only within the Roman Catholic Church, and her prelates alone can recognize it and dispense it. No one may judge her "truth" by conscience or God's Word, but her dogmas must be accepted blindly because she is the one true Church founded by Christ upon Peter, and her popes are Peter's successors.

Antichrist will himself acknowledge this fantastic claim (the woman will ride the beast), but with no more sincerity than did Constantine. It will be a ploy to use the Church to his own ends until finally he puts his image in the temple and demands that all people worship him as god. At that point the beast will turn upon the woman and devour her (Revelation 17:16).

## Shepherds Deceiving the Sheep

Remember, it was the totalitarian papal system which, first of all, destroyed those men who became part of it, and then through them destroyed the Church. The shepherds became corrupted with the lust for power and then corrupted all of the clergy, who in turn corrupted the people. Cardinal Sadolet said of Clement VII, whom he knew intimately, that before his election he studied the Bible constantly, but afterward his character deteriorated and his pontificate was "a series of mistakes, a perpetual dodging to evade the Council which he hated and feared." Before he became pope, Paul IV favored Church reformation, but afterward he avidly pursued his own selfish interests and the advancement and enrichment of his nephews. A contemporary described Pius IV before his pontificate as "humane, tolerant, beneficent, gentle and unselfish," but just the reverse as pope. He "abandoned himself to vulgar sensuality and lusts, ate and drank immoderately, became imperious and crafty," and even stopped attending "Divine service in the chapel." So it was with Innocent X, Alexander VII, and a host of others.[17]

With his usual clarity, de Rosa provides further insight. "In the tenth century, for all its adolescent, adulterous and murderous popes, the papacy was a local phenomenon. The head of a powerful Roman family put his cherished teenaged son on the throne; the lad made hay for a few frantic months or years and was ambushed by members of a rival family whose hour had come. But since the eleventh century Gregory VII had put his stamp upon the papacy. It had grown in stature and prestige; it was able to control the entire church, from the simplest country curate to the most powerful archbishop. What emerged was the most appalling corruption that Christianity has ever seen or is likely to see. It began at the top. The papacy was auctioned off in conclave to the highest bidder, irrespective of a candidate's worth."[18] Von Dollinger extended the blame to the entire *Curia*:

> When the Cardinals said, in the letter they addressed to their Pope, Gregory XII, in 1408, that there was no soundness in the Church from the sole of the foot to the crown of the head, they should have added, if they wished to tell the whole truth, "It is we and our colleagues, and your predecessors, it is the *Curia*, who have gone on saturating the body of the Church with moral poison, and therefore is it now so sorely diseased."[19]

St. Bonaventure declared that in Rome "Church dignities were bought and sold, there did the princes and rulers of the Church assemble, dishonoring God by their incontinence, adherents of Satan, and plunderers of the flock of Christ. . . . the prelates, corrupted by Rome, infect the clergy with their vices; and the clergy, by their evil example of avarice and profligacy, poison and lead to perdition the whole Christian people." Others "called the *Curia* the utterly corrupt 'carnal Church.' . . ." Those who still had some hope for a reformation of the Church, writes von Dollinger, "predicted a great renewal and purification through a holy Pope, the *Papa Angelicus*, long looked for, but never willing to appear."[20]

Petrarch, close observer for many years of the Roman *Curia*, came to the conclusion that Rome was the fulfillment of John's vision in Revelation 17. She was "the Apocalyptic woman drunken with blood, the seducer of Christians, and plague of the human race." Von Dollinger says that Petrarch's descriptions of the papacy and the *Curia* "are so frightful that one would suppose them the exaggerations of hatred, were they not confirmed by all his contemporaries. . . . Augustinian monk of Florence, Luigi Marsigli, [said] the Papal Court no longer ruled through hypocrisy—so openly did it flaunt its vices—but only through the dread inspired by its interdicts and excommunications."[21]

The popes had loaded St. Bonaventure with honors. As a cardinal and General of his Order, he was bound by the closest ties to Rome. Yet in his *Commentary on the Apocalypse* he declares that Rome was "the harlot who makes kings and nations drunk with the wine of her whoredoms." Dante, too, applied to the popes the apocalyptic prophecy of the harlot on the seven hills who is drunk with the blood of men and seduces princes and peoples.[22] It was a metamorphosis that John found hard to believe could ever occur—but it has been fulfilled exactly as Christ revealed it.

## Some Contrasts to Ponder

The Church holds a position for the average Catholic that is entirely different from the relationship between an evangelical and whatever denomination to which he or she may belong. For the evangelical, Christianity involves a personal relationship between the believer and God and Jesus Christ. Many Protestants lack that personal relationship and thus are not real Christians. The lack of that personal relationship, however, is not because they have been taught to look to a Baptist or Methodist or Presbyterian or some other denominational church for salvation; at least that is not generally the teaching of any Protestant church.

In contrast, a Mormon is taught that salvation comes by belonging to and remaining in good standing with the Church of Jesus Christ of Latter-day Saints. The same is true of a Jehovah's Witness, a Christian Scientist, or a member of most other cults, whether "Christian" or Hindu or Buddhist. Rome, too, decrees that the individual can only receive "the merits and graces of Christ" through the Church. The essential personal relationship with Christ apart from any institution, and the accompanying assurance of being with Him the moment one dies, is denied to individual Catholics. Their hope is in the Church: They hope that its continued efforts even after their death will eventually bring them to heaven.

While the Bible teaches submission to Church leaders, it also insists that this submission go *only as far as the leaders are following Christ Himself*. Paul wrote, "Follow me as I follow Christ" (from 1 Corinthians 11:1). He didn't suggest that all Christians must follow him because of his high office, but only as he was true to Christ and His Word. Obviously, to make that judgment the individual must know Christ and His Word for himself.

Paul says that each believer, and not just a special clergy class, is free to present God's truth to the church, and that when leaders speak to the church those who hear them are to judge for themselves the validity of what is said (1 Corinthians 14:29-32). In contrast, Catholicism's *Code of Canon Law* says, "The First See (papacy) is judged by no one."[23] Vatican II declares that pronouncements by the pope on faith or morals are infallible, irreformable, "in no way in need of the approval of others, and do not admit of appeal to any other tribunal."[24] The same is said of "the body of bishops when, together with Peter's successor [the pope], they exercise the supreme teaching office."[25]

John says that all true believers have the anointing of the Holy Spirit and thus must not follow anyone blindly (1 John 2:20-27), but must discern whether a doctrine is biblical by following the leading of God through His Word and the Holy Spirit. How else could each of us judge whether those who preach and teach are presenting God's truth, as Paul says we must? In Catholicism, however, it is explicitly declared that no one may come to his or her own personal opinion concerning biblical truth but must accept whatever the Church hierarchy teaches.

## Great Responsibility, Great Privilege

As we have already seen from the language of Matthew 28:19,20 ("teaching them to observe *all things whatsoever I have commanded you*"), several conclusions are inescapable: 1) An unbroken chain of command flows from our Lord through successive generations of disciples down through history to Christians today; 2) every ordinary Christian is to obey every applicable command that Christ gave His original disciples and to do what He trained and commanded them to do, including preaching the gospel in all the world and making disciples; 3) each Christian has been given by the Lord the same privileges, responsibilities, authority, and power which the original twelve received. How else could each generation of new disciples obey every command Christ had given the original twelve?

The early Christians followed these instructions. Not even the knowledge that they would be killed deterred them. After the death of Stephen the Christians were scattered, and we are told that everywhere they went they preached the gospel (Acts 8:4). We must do the same. Each individual Christian is a full-fledged successor of the apostles, called and empowered by the Holy Spirit to carry on the task of representing Christ and bringing His gospel to the world. Charged with the Great Commission to preach the gospel to "every creature," each disciple at every moment in history is a soldier of the cross and an ambassador of the King of kings. What an awesome responsibility—but what a great privilege!

Unfortunately, many Christians are unwilling to take this responsibility. They want to leave it to a special class of professionals, many of whom are only too eager to lord it over the flock. Every Christian has the authority to resist the devil and see him flee, to "bind and loose" as Christ empowered His first disciples, and to be His ambassador to mankind. In the metamorphosis in the centuries following Constantine, the Roman hierarchy claimed for itself the exclusive right to do what Christ had intended to be the task of all His disciples.

## Vital Distinctions

Christ made a clear distinction between Caesar and God: "Render to Caesar the things that are Caesar's, and to God the things that are God's" (Mark 12:17). This is foundational. The Catholic Church wedded God to Caesar. Church and state became one, with the Church in control and the state doing its bidding. That situation is still much the same in Catholic countries today.

Christ made a clear distinction between His kingdom, which is not of this world, and the kingdoms of this world (John 18:36). In disobedience to the Christ whom they claim to represent, the popes have built a kingdom which is very much of this world, yet they claim it is *God's* kingdom. And they have done it in unholy alliance with secular rulers.

Christ made a clear distinction between His Church, which He has called out of the world, and the world itself (John 17:18-20). John declared, "Love not the world, neither the things that are in the world. If any man love the world, the love of the Father is not in him" (1 John 2:15).

The distinctions that Christ made must be adhered to by those who belong to Him: "If a man love me, he will keep my words. . . . He that loveth me not keepeth not my sayings" (John 14:23,24); "Why call ye me Lord, Lord, and do not the things which I say?" (Luke 6:46).

*Come hither; I will show unto thee the judgment of the great whore that sitteth upon many waters, with whom the kings of the earth have committed fornication, and the inhabitants of the earth have been made drunk with the wine of her fornication.*

—Revelation 17:1,2

*You [Pope Pius IX] have stooped to unite in political fornication with the civil government of any and all despotic countries; you have prostituted the cross, the symbol of sacrifice and salvation into the symbol of tyranny and ruin.*

*Those who call themselves the Vicars of God on earth have become the Vicars of the genius of evil.*

—Giuseppi Mazzini
Italian patriot, 1863[1]

# 15

# Unholy Alliances

A *city* built on seven hills is accused of committing fornication with the kings of the earth! We have noted that the term "fornication" is used often in the Bible in a spiritual sense signifying unfaithfulness to God. Ezekiel 16 is devoted entirely to denouncing Jerusalem for her unfaithfulness to God, likening her to "a wife that committeth adultery, which taketh strangers instead of her husband" (verse 32). Jerusalem had violated her spiritual relationship to God through idolatry and alliances with pagan nations. That meaning is clear from many passages in Scripture.

Jerusalem, however, can't be this woman because, as we have seen, she isn't built upon seven hills and doesn't meet any of the other criteria. Obviously, then, the city which this woman represents must claim a faithful relationship to God *similar* to Jerusalem's. In fact, Rome claims to have replaced Jerusalem in God's affection. And she has violated that relationship by entering into unholy alliances with godless earthly kings. Rome alone meets this and the many other criteria that John sets forth.

History is replete with the record of unholy alliances between the Vatican and secular governments. Much of the evidence remains today in Rome's churches and monuments. For example, the Vatican museum is filled with priceless ancient paintings, sculptures, tapestries, gold, and jewels once worn or treasured by despotic rulers. Most were given to popes by kings, queens, emperors, or governments in token of papal partnerships with these worldly figures—relationships which the Bible condemns and which would be unthinkable for the true bride of Christ.

## The Witness of History

Driven from Rome by a popular uprising against his oppressive reign, Pope Leo III fled to the Frankish court of Charlemagne to enlist his help in recovering those territories over which the popes reigned. That bloodthirsty warrior's armies recaptured Rome and, in the name of Christ, restored Leo to the papal throne. While Charlemagne knelt at Mass in St. Peter's on Christmas day of A.D. 800, the pope placed a crown on his head and proclaimed him emperor of the West. The title was eventually recognized by both the eastern emperor in Constantinople and the Caliph of Baghdad. As Maurice Keen reminds us, "The restoration of the worldwide dominion of Rome was the dream not only of medieval popes and emperors but also of many of their subjects and servants."[2] This dream will be fully achieved at last under Antichrist.

The pope's move was a shrewd one. Charlemagne's power had threatened to overshadow the authority of the papacy. After his coronation by the pope in St. Peter's, however, Charlemagne, in solid partnership with the papacy, "worked for some forty years to create a Christian commonwealth such as St. Augustine had earlier outlined."[3] The emperor's brutal military campaigns in northern Europe were accompanied by the forcible conversions of the heathen. Charlemagne was the popes' secular arm that Christianized the pagans with the sword and thereby enlarged the Roman Catholic domain as the Spanish conquistadors would later do in America.

Charlemagne's father, Pepin, as we have previously noted, on the basis of a fraudulent document, *The Donation of Constantine*, had subdued and turned over to the popes the huge territories thereafter known as the papal states and ruled by the papacy. Charlemagne, too, was deceived by this fraud. Based upon the *Donation*, he formally drew up a charter which acknowledged the papacy as both spiritual and temporal ruler over "all the regions of Italy and the West." Thereafter Charlemagne acted as the popes' protector and partner, much as Constantine had at the very beginning of the developing coalition between Church and state. Such an arrangement, totally contrary to the teachings of Christ, is only one example of the spiritual fornication which this woman would be involved in, exactly as John foresaw it in his vision.

Eventually the Church and the state became so closely allied that there was scarcely any distinction between them. Emperors convened and presided over the great councils of the Church and looked upon the popes and the rest of the Church hierarchy as their partners in governing the masses. Such unholy papal alliances, soon to become commonplace, would have been anathema to the early church; they made a mockery of Christ's rejection and crucifixion by the world. Consider another excerpt from the shamelessly flattering speech by Eusebius (a different portion of which we previously quoted) in praise of Constantine. He attributes to the pagan emperor the very spiritual qualities and ecclesiastical authority and functions now claimed by the popes:

> Our Emperor, His [Christ's] friend, acting as interpreter to the Word of God, aims at recalling the whole human race to the knowledge of God; proclaiming clearly in the ears of all, and declaring with powerful voice the laws of truth and godliness to all who dwell on the earth. . . . invested as he is with a semblance of heavenly sovereignty, he . . . frames his earthly government according to the pattern of that Divine original . . . the monarchy of God.[4]

There can be no doubt as to the amazing accuracy of John's vision of a city that claims to belong to Christ yet prostitutes herself to the kings of the earth. To have pagan rulers enforcing "Christianity" by military might upon an ever-widening papal empire was a blasphemous travesty of the truth that Christ proclaimed. It was such a gross misrepresentation of the gospel and such a confusing identification of the state with the Church that eventually Christ was considered the true ruler of Byzantium! Coins depicted Him wearing the Imperial crown and icons represented Him clothed in the vestments of the emperor. The emperor's own throne sat next to another one, empty except for a copy of the Gospels, indicating that Christ was the coemperor of Byzantium. Such was the spirit of the times that prevailed in the West as well.

Eventually, as we have already noted, Pope Innocent III abolished the Roman Senate and placed the administration of Rome directly under his control with a single senator as his deputy. In 1266 Clement IV gave this function to Charles of Anjou, who founded the University of Rome. The papacy continued to be at the heart of almost every political intrigue; and its armies were allied with the forces of many a king in the continual wars that plagued Europe.

In the New World the Church was the partner of the Spanish conquistadors and of the Portuguese in Africa. Recently Native American activists called on Pope John Paul II to formally revoke a papal bull, *Inter Cetera*, issued in 1493, which declared that "barbarous nations discovered and yet to be discovered should be subjugated to the Catholic faith in order to propagate the Christian empire."[5] Examples of "fornication with the kings of the earth" from ancient history could be multiplied, but we need to move on to modern times.

## The 1929 Concordat with Mussolini

We have already referred to the fact that in 1870 the independence of Italy was declared and what remained of the Papal States was absorbed by the new united nation. We have also noted that the Italian people voted overwhelmingly against the pope's rule and for the new independence. The temporal powers of the popes were ended, including their prestige and alliances with earthly regimes. The popes' civil authority was limited to the Vatican, where they remained in self-imposed exile for nearly 60 years until, in 1929, Mussolini and Pope Pius XI signed the Lateran Treaty.

This Concordat made Roman Catholicism once again, by national law, "the sole religion" of Italy. Neither Peter nor Paul, and surely not Christ, would ever have entered into such an arrangement with any government, let alone with a Fascist dictatorship. The Vatican, which claimed to be the true and only Church, the bride of the Christ who said His kingdom was not of this world, was acknowledged once again as a sovereign state with the status of a secular nation able to send and receive political ambassadors.

For having seized the papal territories in 1870, Italy paid to the Holy See 750 million lire in cash and 1 billion lire in state bonds. Some of these funds would be used to start the Vatican Bank, now infamous for its corruption. Some would end up in rather strange investments for Holy Mother Church, such as "an Italian firearms factory and a Canadian pharmaceutical company that manufactured contraceptives."[6]

There is no doubt that the Roman Catholic Church put Mussolini in power. In order to obtain the Lateran Treaty, the pope required Catholics to withdraw from participation in politics (many had been socialists actively opposing Mussolini and his Fascist party) and gave the Church's backing to Il Duce. The pope made public statements so strongly in support of Mussolini—e.g., "Mussolini is the man sent by Providence"—that Catholics had no choice but to support the aspiring Fascist dictator. Without that help Mussolini would not have been voted in and history might have been much different.

## Quid Pro Quo

On his part, after the Concordat was signed, Mussolini declared: "We recognize the preeminent place the Catholic Church holds in the religious life of the Italian people—which is perfectly natural in a Catholic country such as ours, and under a regime such as the Fascist." All the cardinals in Rome, in an address to the pope, hailed Mussolini as "that eminent statesman [who rules Italy] by a decree of the Divine Providence." Looking back, one wonders how men who claimed to be the emissaries of the Holy Spirit could have been so wrong. There was, however, a selfish reason for their folly.

It was a *quid pro quo* that promised much for both parties. Mussolini needed the Church to establish his hold on Italy, and on its part the Church was willing to support him in exchange for restoration of at least some of its former prestige and power. With the solid backing of the Church, Mussolini was established as dictator. And with the Treaty, the Roman pontiff once again achieved the status of right-hand man to the emperor, a position which the popes had earlier enjoyed, beginning with Constantine and continuing with his successors. "Fornication with kings," after a brief interruption, had begun again.

The Church remained, throughout World War II, the loyal partner of an oppressive dictatorship which had been only too happy to give the pope what he wanted: the suppression of basic human rights. With Catholicism now the state religion, religious education was made compulsory in the schools, teachers and textbooks had to be approved by the Church, religious marriage became compulsory, and divorce was forbidden. Criticism of Catholicism either oral or in print was made a penal offense.

As Avro Manhattan puts it in *The Vatican and World Politics*, "Thus the Church became the religious weapon of the Fascist State, while the Fascist State became the secular arm of the Church." No such arrangement with any secular government could be entered into by any other church (Baptist? Methodist? Lutheran?) even if it so desired. Only Vatican City is capable of spiritual fornication, and surely its concordats with Mussolini, later with Hitler and with a variety of other governments, are exactly that. There is simply no mistaking this woman's identity.

On June 3, 1985, the Vatican and Italy signed a new concordat that ended "a number of privileges the Catholic Church had in Italy, including its status as the state church. . . . the new treaty guarantees religious freedom for non-Catholics and ends Rome's status as a 'sacred city' [but] still recognizes the 'particular significance' of Rome to Roman Catholicism."[7]

## The 1933 Concordat with Hitler

One of the key figures in negotiating the 1929 Concordat with Mussolini was Solicitor Francesco Pacelli, brother of Cardinal Eugenio Pacelli, who later became Pope Pius XII. The latter, as the Vatican's Secretary of State, would play a key role in negotiating the lucrative (for the Church) 1933 Concordat with Hitler. One of the benefits of the Concordat was the hundreds of millions of dollars that would flow to the Roman

Catholic Church through the *Kirchensteuer* (church tax) throughout the entire war. In return, Pius XII would never excommunicate Hitler from the Catholic Church nor would he raise his voice to protest the slaughter of 6 million Jews.

Leading Catholic prelates and theologians were ecstatic at the signing of the 1933 Concordat. Catholic theologian Michael Schmaus wrote in praise of the authoritarianism of the Nazi regime and compared it to that of the Church: "The strong emphasis on authority in the new government is something essentially familiar to Catholics. It is the counterpart, on the natural level, to the Church's authority in the supernatural sphere. Nowhere is the value and meaning of authority so conspicuous as in our holy Catholic Church." Of course that was true. The papacy had for centuries worked in close partnership with autocratic kings and emperors in the suppression of basic human rights.

Today's Catholics need to face the fact that the totalitarianism of their Church was a major factor in preparing German Catholics to embrace the Nazi regime. Catholic professor of church history Joseph Lortz "never tired of speaking of 'the *fundamental kinship* between National Socialism and Catholicism, a kinship which runs amazingly deep. . . .' " In the same year, 1933, a well-known prelate from Cologne, Robert Grosche, wrote in *Die Schildgenossen*:

> When papal infallibility was defined in the year 1870, the Church was anticipating on a higher level the historical decision which has now been made on the political level: a decision for authority and against discussion, for the pope and against the sovereignty of the Council, for the Fuehrer and against the Parliament.[8]

Drawing upon years of study of secret documents in the Vatican archives, its curator of some years, August Bernhard Hasler, noted: "Both in Italy and in Germany the *Curia* took the opportunity to secure from a dictatorial regime what seemed impossible under parliamentary government, namely, a concordat." He then quotes German Catholic leader Ludwig Kaas: "The 'authoritarian state' necessarily understood the basic principles of the 'authoritarian church' better than others had." Indeed, they were partners who were made for each other. Hitler received the following warm note of congratulations from Cardinal Michael Faulhaber six months after he came to power:

> What the old parliaments and parties failed to achieve in sixty years your broad statesman's vision has made a reality of world history in six months. This handclasp with the papacy, the greatest moral force in the history of the world, signifies a mighty deed full of immense blessing and an increase in German prestige East and West, in the sight of the entire world.[9]

Pulitzer-prize-winning journalist John Toland points out that the leaders of the Roman Catholic Church were eager to curry Hitler's favor. After an audience with Pope Pius XI, even though Hitler had just outlawed the Catholic Party, its leader, Monsignor Ludwig Kaas (in words obviously intended to impress the Fuehrer), told the press: "Hitler knows how to guide the ship. Even before he became Chancellor I met him frequently and was greatly impressed by his clear thinking, by his way of facing realities while upholding his ideals, which are noble." Toland goes on to explain:

> The Vatican was so appreciative of being recognized as a full partner that it asked God to bless the Reich. On a more practical level, it ordered German bishops to swear allegiance to the National Socialist regime. The new oath concluded with these significant words: "In the performance of my spiritual office and in my solicitude for the welfare and the interest of the German Reich, I will endeavor to avoid all detrimental acts which might endanger it."[10]

## Drawn into the Maelstrom

When Hitler, over the objections of Mussolini, announced that Germany was withdrawing from the League of Nations, a telegram came quickly from Catholic Action pledging its support. Shrewdly, Hitler made this move subject to a vote of the people, then put pressure upon them to back him. The Catholic Church gave him its enthusiastic support and made it clear to Catholics that they were to vote in favor of Hitler's decision. Cardinal Faulhaber, with the approval of every bishop in Bavaria, declared that by voting yes, Catholics would "profess anew their loyalty to people and fatherland and their agreement with the farsighted and forceful efforts of the Fuehrer to spare the German people the terror of war and the horrors of Bolshevism, to secure public order and create work for the unemployed."

When Hitler moved his troops into Austria, after the usual promises that he wouldn't, he was astonished at the enthusiasm of the crowds of Austrians, almost all Catholics, who greeted him. After addressing a crowd of about 200,000 in the Heldenplatz, he led a parade past the Winter Palace with Austrian generals joining on horseback. Later Cardinal Innitzer greeted Hitler "with the sign of the cross and gave assurance that so long as the [Roman Catholic] Church retained its liberties Austrian Catholics would become 'the truest sons of the great Reich into whose arms they had been brought back on this momentous day.'" Der Fuehrer shook the Cardinal's hand warmly and "promised him everything."[11]

On Hitler's fiftieth birthday "Special votive masses were celebrated in every German [Roman Catholic] church 'to implore God's blessing upon Fuehrer and people.' The Bishop of Mainz called upon Catholics in his diocese to pray specifically for 'the Fuehrer and Chancellor, the inspirer, enlarger and protector of the Reich.'" Nor did the pope fail to send his congratulations.[12]

The Catholic press throughout Germany almost unanimously declared that Hitler's narrow escape from the 1939 attempt upon his life was the miraculous protection of God. Cardinal Faulhaber instructed that a *Te Deum* be sung in the cathedral of Munich "to thank Divine Providence in the name of the archdiocese for the Fuehrer's fortunate escape." Having failed to condemn Germany's liquidation of Poland, the pope did not neglect to send his special personal congratulations to Hitler for his miraculous survival of the assassination attempt.

Even when Hitler's evil had been fully revealed, the Church continued to support him. When German troops launched their offensive against the Soviet Union, the pope again "made it clear that he backed the Nazi fight against Bolshevism, describing it as 'high-minded gallantry in defense of the foundations of Christian culture.' A number of German bishops, predictably, openly supported the attack. One called it 'a European crusade,' a mission similar to that of the Teutonic knights. The pope exhorted all Catholics to fight for 'a victory that will allow Europe to breathe freely again and will promise all nations a new future.'"

We could go on with page after page of documentation. However, this should be enough to establish the fact that from the pope and bishops on down Roman Catholics felt a kinship with Hitler and backed him even after his ruthless expansionist ambitions and crimes against humanity were well known. Unholy alliance? Spiritual fornication? There can be no doubt.

## Today's Continuing Alliances

The cover of *Time* magazine of February 24, 1992, carried the pictures of former President Ronald Reagan and Pope John Paul II together with this startling caption: "HOLY ALLIANCE: How Reagan and the Pope conspired to assist Poland's Solidarity movement and hasten the demise of Communism." The lead story told how Reagan had "believed fervently in both the benefits and the practical applications of Washington's relationship with the Vatican. One of his earliest goals as President, Reagan says, was to recognize the Vatican as a state 'and make them an ally.'"

And allies they became in one of the most amazing exploits in history. It brought down the Berlin Wall, ended the Cold War, and completely unraveled Soviet Communism. It was a story of intrigue and cooperation between the CIA and the apparently even more effective agents of the Vatican. Reagan and John Paul II, both survivors of assassination attempts, shared "a unity of spiritual view and a unity of vision on the Soviet empire: that right or correctness would ultimately prevail in the divine plan."

A five-part strategy emerged during the first half of 1982 "that was aimed at bringing about the collapse of the Soviet economy, fraying the ties that bound the U.S.S.R. to its client states in the Warsaw Pact and forcing reform inside the Soviet empire." In the outworking of the plan, former Secretary of State Alexander Haig acknowledged that "the Vatican's information was absolutely better and quicker than ours in every respect. [The] Vatican liaison to the White House, Archbishop Pio Laghi, kept reminding American officials, "Listen to the Holy Father. We have 2000 years' experience of this."[13]

That the pope played a key role, both Reagan and later Gorbachev frankly admitted. A major newspaper article coming out three weeks after the *Time* story reported: " 'Pope John Paul II played a major political role in the collapse of communism in Eastern Europe,' said Mikhail Gorbachev, former leader of the Soviet Union. Gorbachev predicted that the pope will continue to play 'a great political role' in the current 'very delicate transition' taking place in Europe. . . . the events in Eastern Europe 'might not have been possible without the presence of this pope, without the great role—including political—which he knew how to play on the world scene,' said Gorbachev."[14]

At this point we will leave it to the reader to consider the Vatican's motivation in such heavy political intervention. The fact remains that such a role on the world scene, with its unholy alliances, political intrigues, and earthly goals, would be anathema to Christ's true bride.

The Vatican has long been involved in clandestine activities and self-serving partnerships with many nations. According to the Knights of Columbus magazine, "the history of diplomatic ties between the United States and the Holy See goes back nearly 200 years." The article pictured the then American ambassador to the Vatican, Thomas Melady, and his wife, Margaret, with the pope and quoted Melady:

> Pope John Paul II is at the high point of respect as a
> world leader . . . our government is cooperating as one
> government to another government, the government of
> the Holy See. It is a great honor for me to be there,
> representing our government to the Holy See, at this
> significant time in world history.

Apparently Christ, whose kingdom at the beginning was

"not of this world," had changed His mind. He who commissioned His disciples to call converts out of the world to heavenly citizenship with His gospel of redemptive grace has apparently decided to work with the nations of this world to create a paradise down here. The Knights of Columbus article went on to exult in the fact that—

> Diplomatic relations between the U.S. and the Holy See began in the 18th century when the Papal States (before their absorption into Italy) agreed to open several Mediterranean ports to U.S. shipping. In 1797 John B. Sartori, an Italian, was named U.S. Consul....
>
> In 1847, at the request of President James K. Polk, the U.S. Senate established a diplomatic post in the Papal States . . . until 1867 when anti-Catholic elements in the United States succeeded in getting the diplomatic mission eliminated.
>
> Informal relations resumed in 1939 when President Franklin D. Roosevelt appointed Myron C. Taylor as his "personal envoy" to the Holy See....
>
> In 1981, President Reagan named William A. Wilson, a Catholic, to the post. Wilson served until 1984, when the Vatican and the U.S. began full diplomatic relations and Wilson was made the first U.S. Ambassador to the Holy See.[15]

Consider the following from a recent brochure advertising "The Catholic Event of the Year": "Pope Leo XIII compared the proper relation between Church and State to 'the union of the soul and the body in man.' Imagine a nation without a soul! As recent events have confirmed with frightening clarity, America today is such a nation. America was discovered by a Catholic [Columbus], who claimed her for Christ the King. If America is to be rediscovered and reclaimed for our King—if she is to find her missing soul—it is Catholics who must act, and act now."[16]

Rome has not changed. Her ambitions remain very much of this world. Of course, it is in Christ's name that she wants to reestablish her "reign over the kings of the earth." It is for "the good of mankind and the glory of Christ," as she perceives it, that "the Catholic Church ceaselessly and efficaciously seeks for the return of all humanity and all its goods"[17] back under her control. Vatican II couldn't be clearer on this point.

*Fear, then, our wrath and the thunders of our vengeance; for Jesus Christ has appointed us [the popes] with his own mouth absolute judges of all men; and kings themselves are submitted to our authority.*

—Pope Nicholas I (858-67)[1]

*The Italians are exalted above all nations by the special grace of God, who gives them in the Pope a spiritual monarch, who has put down from their thrones great kings and yet mightier emperors, and set others in their place, to whom the greatest kingdoms have long paid tribute, as they do to no other, and who dispenses such riches to his courtiers that no king or emperor has ever had so much to give.*

—Padua Provost and
Professor Carrerio, 1626[2]

*It is the office of the Papacy to tread under foot kings and emperors.*

—J.H. Ignaz von Dollinger[3]

# 16

# Dominion over Kings

The last identifying characteristic that John was given concerning the woman astride the beast was that she was a city "which reigneth over the kings of the earth" (Revelation 17:18). Could there be a *city* that actually *reigns* over the governments of the world? History bears witness that there was indeed such a city, and only one. That city was, of course, Rome after its bishops began to call themselves popes and, claiming to be the successors of the Caesars, took upon themselves the imperial powers of worldwide sovereignty.

Consider, for example, the arrogant imperialism of Pope Alexander III (1159-81). Declaring that "the power of the popes is superior to that of princes," Alexander excommunicated Frederick I, Holy Roman Emperor, King of Germany and Italy. Attempting to chastise the pope, Frederick's forces were defeated by the pope's army. The chastened emperor came to Venice to beg forgiveness and absolution, promising to "submit always to the Roman Church." Imagine a *church* ruling the world by military might! Fortunatus Ulmas, a Catholic historian, enthusiastically described the scene:

> When the emperor arrived in the presence of the pope, he laid aside his imperial mantle, and knelt on both knees, with his breast on the earth. Alexander advanced and placed his foot on his neck, while the cardinals

> thundered forth in loud tones, "Thou shalt tread upon
> the cockatrice, and crush the lion and the dragon." ...
>
> The next day Frederick Barbarossa ... kissed the feet
> of Alexander, and, on foot, led his horse by the bridle as
> he returned from solemn mass, to the pontifical pal-
> ace....
>
> The papacy had now risen to a height of grandeur and
> power which it had never reached before. The sword of
> Peter had conquered the sword of Caesar![4]

As a swordsman, Peter had been signally inept: Aiming to
cut off a head, he had instead severed an ear. Christ rebuked
His erring disciple, healed the ear, and then allowed the armed
band to lead Him captive on His way to the cross. The early
church knew full well that Christians did not wield sword or
spear in the defense of Christ. His kingdom, which is "not of
this world," must first be established in the hearts of those
who believe in Him as the Savior who died for their sins. These
true disciples follow in His path of rejection, suffering, and
death. How then did those who called themselves vicars of
Christ reach such a worldly pinnacle whereby they could
command emperors, defeat their armies with the sword, and
place a foot upon the neck of a vanquished sovereign?

## The Path to Earthly Glory

Some years after Constantine had moved the imperial headquarters to the East, the Roman Empire in the West broke up.
The vacuum created by the absence of a central authority in
Rome was filled by the Church, the only Roman institution
capable of doing so. The Church played the major role in
education and charity. Gradually, however, the popes took over
the civil government of Rome and its surroundings; and then
by fraud (as we have seen) they added the large territories of
the Papal States to their domain. As their ambitions grew, the
new Roman pontiffs took upon themselves the titles and much
of the flavor and function of emperor.

The popes, some of whom were exceptionally capable military leaders, had armies and navies at their command to extend
and to hold their territories. They wielded, however, a greater

power than the force of arms: "The keys of heaven" were theirs. Temporal rulers were compelled, no matter how unwillingly, to bow the knee to the popes. Only the "heretics" (true Christians) doubted that the Church determined who entered heaven and could bar its gate to any who opposed her.[5] The most powerful civil rulers trembled when threatened with excommunication, for it was almost universally believed that outside the Church there was no salvation. Historian Walter James writes:

> The Papacy controlled the gateway to heaven which all the faithful, including their rulers, hoped earnestly to enter. Few in those days doubted the truth of this and it gave the Popes a moral authority which has never been wielded since.[6]

The fraudulent *Donation of Constantine* mentioned earlier was followed by a veritable library of forged documents. It was these false decretals that traced papal authority back to the early bishops of Rome and through them to Peter. Even Thomas Aquinas, the Roman Church's greatest theologian, was deceived by these fraudulent assertions into believing that "there is no difference between Christ and the Pope...." So blinded was Aquinas by the pomp and power of the popes that he "made the Fathers say that in fact the rulers of the world obey the Pope as though he were Christ."[7]

On the contrary, Christ had nothing to do with the rulers of this world; and far from obeying Him, "the princes of this world . . . crucified the Lord of glory" (1 Corinthians 2:8). Yet the Catholic heresy stuck and became the central principle of the popes in fulfilling John's vision by literally ruling over the kings of the earth.

## Papal Dominion over England and Ireland

During the Middle Ages the awesome power which the popes wielded over the kings of the earth continued to grow. Gregory VI (1045-6) had declared that the pope commanded blind obedience to his every word, even from sovereigns. Alexander II (1061-73), with the counsel of the great Hildebrand (later Gregory VII), issued a decree declaring Harold, the lawful King of England, a usurper and excommunicated his followers. The pope decreed that William, Duke of Normandy, was the lawful claimant to the English crown.

With the pope's blessing, William the Conqueror killed Harold in battle, took England, and was crowned in London on Christmas Day, 1066. William accepted the crown "in the name of the Holy See of Rome." It was another triumph for the papacy and greatly increased Roman Catholic influence in England. Freeman, in *The Norman Conquest*, elaborates on the arrangement:

> William was authorized [by the pope] to go forth as an avenger of Heaven. He was required to teach the English people "due obedience to Christ's Vicar," and, what the papacy never forgets, "to secure a more punctual payment of the temporal dues of his apostle."[8]

In 1155 Pope Adrian IV gave the crown of Ireland to the King of England. Thus, by his authority as "Christ's vicar," he subjugated Ireland to English rule and consigned Ireland's "peaceful and Christian people to the merciless cruelties of Henry II, upon the ground that it was a portion of 'the patrimony of St. Peter and of the Holy Roman Church.' "[9] Subsequent popes affirmed this decree.

So long as England remained Catholic the arrangement was tolerable. But when England turned Protestant its continued control of Catholic Ireland and Protestant persecution of Catholics planted the seeds of a problem that continues to this day. While Catholic Ireland has many legitimate grievances too complex to relate here, she needs to remember that it was, after all, the Roman Catholic popes who gave Ireland to England in the first place.

In fact, the popes were to blame for many of England's trials and tribulations as well. The Roman pontiffs treated "its kings [as] their vassals, and its people as having no rights of any value whatsoever when they came in conflict with the demands of the papacy. . . . The Catholic clergy, as the popes' emissaries, ran England, disregarding the laws of the land, as though the popes were the sovereigns of the country. Civil courts had no jurisdiction over priests. Thompson elaborates:

> It would be impossible to enumerate . . . the outrages
> and enormities practiced in England during this gloomy
> period by kings and popes, who considered the assertion
> of any single popular right as a crime which God had
> appointed them to punish! More than a hundred murders
> were committed by ecclesiastics during the reign
> of Henry II, in which the parties were not even pun-
> ished. . . .
> The clergy had absolute power over their own body,
> and no appeal was allowed from their decisions. A lay-
> man forfeited his life by the crime of murder, but an
> ecclesiastic went unpunished. This was called one of the
> immunities of the clergy! [When the king tried to change
> the law to deal with clergy] the pope refused his sanction
> and denounced it as "prejudicial to the Church, and
> destructive of her privileges!"[10]

Looking back from today's perspective, such overt papal
dominion over sovereigns seems inconceivable, but it was in
fact the norm for that day. The popes literally ruled the entire
known world for centuries, exactly as John's vision foretold.

## Pope Gregory VII (1073-85)

Before he became pope, as the famous Hildebrand, Gregory
VII was the manipulating genius behind five other popes,
including Alexander II. Gregory began his pontificate "by
asserting the right to dispose of kingdoms, in imitation of the
example set by Pope Gregory I [the Great], nearly four hundred years before." He declared that the power to "bind and
loose" granted by Christ to Peter gave the popes "the right to
make and unmake kings, to construct and reconstruct governments, to wrest from those who disobeyed all the territory held
by them, and to bestow it upon those who would hold it subject
to papal authority." Had he not read Revelation 17:18?

Gregory was the first pope to literally dethrone kings. If he
decided to depose the German emperor, Gregory simply said,
"To me is given power to bind and loose on earth and in
heaven." If he set his heart upon some property that belonged
to others, Gregory simply declared, as he had at his Roman

Synod of 1080: "We desire to show the world that we can give or take away at our will kingdoms, duchies, earldoms, in a word, the possession of all men; for we can bind and loose."[11]

Picture, for example, in 1077, the humbled Henry IV, supreme head of the Holy Roman Empire and heir to Charlemagne (whom Pope Leo III had crowned emperor in 800), crossing the Alps and forced to wait, in penitence, barefoot in a haircloth shirt in the snow outside the castle at Canossa to make his peace with Gregory VII! Claiming to be "King of kings," Gregory, because of a quarrel with Henry, had declared: "On the part of God omnipotent, I forbid Henry to govern the kingdoms of Italy and Germany. I absolve all subjects from every oath they have taken and I excommunicate every person who shall serve him as king." Henry had no defense against that superweapon of the popes.

Thus was established that magnificent "whore" portrayed by John in Revelation 17—headquartered in a city located upon seven hills (verse 9) and which "reigneth over the kings of the earth" (verse 18). One eighteenth-century historian counted 95 popes who claimed to have divine power to depose kings.[12] There is no other city which meets these criteria. John's vision had been remarkably accurate.

## The Bloodiest Pontiff

Of Innocent III (1198-1216), whom he says "encompassed Christendom with terror... for close on twenty years," de Rosa writes: "He crowned and deposed sovereigns, put nations under interdict, virtually created the Papal States across central Italy from the Mediterranean to the Adriatic. He had not lost a single battle. In pursuit of his aims, he shed more blood than any other pontiff."[13] Desiring to put Otho of Saxony on the German throne, Innocent wrote:

> By the authority which *God has given us in the person of St. Peter*, we declare you king, and we order the people to render you, in this capacity, homage and obedience. We, however, shall expect you to subscribe to all our desires as a return for the imperial crown.[14]

Innocent III's "proud spirit chafed at the thought that any earthly potentate should equal him either in greatness or authority. Therefore he required that 'all disputes between princes' should be referred to him; and if either party should refuse 'to obey the sentence of Rome, he was to be excommunicated and deposed,' and a like penalty was to be visited upon those who refused to attack whatsoever 'refractory delinquent' he should point out."[15] As Ehler and Morrall remind us, "The Papacy became not only the highest authority in respect of international jurisdiction, being entitled to judge kings and princes, but secular potentates also sought the Pope's sanction in major changes of their international position, such as acquisition of new territories or titles."[16]

John Lackland, King of England, made the mistake of having a violent quarrel with Pope Innocent III. "After attempting resistance he completely submitted to Rome, surrendered his royal crown to Pope Innocent III and received it back from him as a vassal of the Holy See."[17] The document, dated May 15, 1213, is known as "King John Lackland's Infeodation to Pope Innocent III."[18] (See Appendix C.) R.W. Thompson adds his insight:

> Forfeitures, interdicts, excommunications, and every other form of ecclesiastical censure and punishment were of almost daily occurrence. Even such monarchs as Philip Augustus and Henry IV quailed before him [Innocent III], and Peter II of Aragon and John of England ignominiously consented to convert their kingdoms into spiritual fiefs and to hold them in subordination to him, upon the condition of paying an annual tribute.[19]

## Yet More Evidence

Gregory IX (1227-41), who established the Inquisition and the handing of heretics to the secular power for execution, thundered that the pope was lord and master of everyone and everything. Innocent IV (1243-54) agreed because, as he argued, the popes did not get their dominion merely from *The Donation of Constantine* but already had it from God. Boniface VIII went further and, in his Bull *Unam Sanctam* in 1302, in which he claimed authority over all temporal powers, made absolute obedience to the pope a condition of salvation.

By the time of the death of Roman Emperor Frederick Barbarossa (upon whose neck Pope Alexander III had placed his conquering foot) it had long been understood that "nobody could acquire [the Imperial crown] without coronation by the Pope. . . ."[20] "Emperor Charles IV secured peace and final harmony with the Papacy by renouncing any Imperial activity in the whole of Italy [leaving the popes to govern there] and this self-restriction was observed by subsequent Emperors until the end of the Middle Ages."[21]

Pope Julius II (1503-13), furious because Louis XII of France wouldn't support him in his military campaigns, drew up a papal bull depriving him of his kingdom and giving it to Henry VIII of England, provided he proved his piety by supporting the pope in his wars. Julius died before the bull was published. That pope's passion for fighting "holy wars" to extend the papal territories inspired Michelangelo, whom he hired to paint the ceiling of the Sistine Chapel, to pen the famous lines so apropos of Julius and many other popes:

> Of chalices they make helmet and sword
> And sell by the bucket the blood of the Lord.

In a recent article in a national Catholic newspaper, a priest confessed, "The church . . . was subverted by the ambitions of such men as Gregory VII, Innocent III and Boniface VII into a politico-ecclesiastical institution wielding totalitarian power in both sacred and secular fields."[22] He fails to mention that the dogmas and claims of Rome remain the same today as they were then. The Church has not changed; only circumstances force her to vary her tactics.

The open threats and aggression of a Gregory VII won't work in today's world. Though wielded more subtly, however, the Vatican's power is no less effective today than it ever was. One author who spent a lifetime analyzing and writing about the Vatican concluded:

> The Vatican is . . . the paramount superpower of our times. Its adherents . . . nearing a billion, can be made to operate in every corner of the world. . . . Hence the importance [for every government] of having the Pope as

a partner in the pursuance of any given world policy.
. . . Vatican policies are directed by the Pope. . . [who]
has neither Parliament, Congress or Senate, or any similar democratic body . . . limiting his decisions, powers or
policies. He is an absolute autocratic ruler, in the fullest
meaning of that word.[23]

## A Golden Cup in Her Hand

Kings dwell in palaces, are waited upon by servants, and,
because of their absolute authority over their subjects, accu-
mulate great wealth. It would therefore be expected that a city
which reigns over the kings of the earth would be the wealthiest of all. Such is the case with the woman astride the beast.
That fact is surely signified by the "gold and precious stones
and pearls" with which she is adorned as well as by the
"golden cup in her hand" (Revelation 17:4).

That the golden cup is "full of abominations and filthiness"
indicates that her wealth has been acquired through abominable means. Cardinal Baronius, though a defender of the
papacy, confessed that in St. Peter's Chair have sat monsters
"filled with fleshly lusts and cunning in all forms of wickedness [having] prostituted the Chair of St. Peter for their min-
ions and paramours." In his sixteenth-century *Ecclesiastical
Annals* he wrote:

> The Roman Church was. . . covered with silks and
> precious stones, which publicly prostituted itself for
> gold. . . . Never did priests, and especially popes, com-
> mit so many adulteries, rapes, incests, robberies, and
> murders. . . [as in the Middle Ages].[24]

Petrarch, poet laureate of the empire, described the papal
court in Avignon scornfully as "the shame of mankind, a sink
of vice, a sewer where is gathered all the filth of the world.
There God is held in contempt, money alone is worshipped and
the laws of God and men are trampled under foot. Everything
there breathes a lie: the air, the earth, the houses and above all
the bedrooms." Referring to Avignon as "the Babylon of the
West," Petrarch declared:

> Here reign the successors of the poor fishermen of
> Galilee . . . loaded with gold and clad in purple, boasting
> of the spoils of princes and nations. Instead of holy
> solitude we find a criminal host . . . instead of soberness,
> licentious banquets . . . instead of the bare feet of the
> apostles . . . horses decked in gold and fed on gold, soon
> to be shod with gold, if the Lord does not check this
> slavish luxury.[25]

Of Rome's wealth in the Middle Ages de Rosa says: "The
cardinals had huge palaces with countless servants. One papal
aide reported that he never went to see a cardinal without
finding him counting his gold coins. The *Curia* was made up of
men who had bought office and were desperate to recoup their
enormous outlay. . . . For every benefice of see, abbey and
parish, for every indulgence there was a set fee. The pallium,
the two-inch-wide woollen band with crosses embroidered on
it . . . paid for by every bishop . . . brought in . . . hundreds of
millions of gold florins to the papal coffers. . . . [T]he Council
of Basle in 1432 was to call it 'the most usurious contrivance
ever invented. . . .'" De Rosa continues:

> Dispensations were another source of papal revenue.
> Extremely severe, even impossible, laws were passed so
> that the Curia could grow rich by selling dispensations
> . . . [such as] from fasting during Lent. . . . Marriage in
> particular was a rich source of income. Consanguinity
> was alleged to hold between couples who had never
> dreamed they were related. Dispensations from consan-
> guinity in order to marry amounted to a million gold
> florins a year.[26]

## An Eyewitness Account from Spain

D. Antonio Gavin, author of *A Master-Key to Popery*, was
born and educated in Spain at the end of the 1600s. As a
Roman Catholic priest he had become thoroughly disillusioned by the evil in which he found himself entangled. Fleeing
the Spanish Inquisition disguised in an army officer's uniform,

Gavin made his way to safety in England. His book gives a clear picture of Roman Catholicism in his day and has much to say about her incredible wealth and the part it played in the practice of Rome's paganized Christianity:

> In the cathedral of St. *Salvator* [in Zaragoza] there are ten thousand ounces of silver in plate, part of it gilt, to adorn the two corners of the altar on great festivals [and an] . . . abundance of rich ornaments for Priests, of inexpressible value. Eighty-four chalices, twenty of pure gold, and sixty-four of silver, gilt on the inside of the cup; and the rich chalice which only the Archbishop makes use of in his pontifical dress.
>
> All these things are but trifles in comparison with the great *custodia* they make use of to carry the great Host through the streets on the festival of *Corpus Christi:* . . . [solid gold set with diamonds, emeralds and other precious stones it is] five hundred pound weight. . . . Several goldsmiths have endeavoured to value this piece, but nobody could set a certain sum on it.[27]

The most famous church in Zaragoza is called Our Lady of the Pillar because of an alleged appearance of the Virgin there. Gavin describes the crown on the image of the Virgin: "twenty-five pounds weight, set all over with large diamonds, so that nobody can see any gold in it, and everybody thinks it is all made of diamonds. Beside this rich one, she has six crowns more of pure gold, set with rich diamonds and emeralds. . . ." He goes on to say:

> The roses of diamonds and other precious stones she has to adorn her mantle are innumerable; for though she [the image of the "Virgin"] is drest every day in the colour of the church's festival, and never useth twice [in a year] the same mantle, which is of the best stuff imbroidered with gold, she has new roses of precious stones every day for three years together, she has three hundred and sixty-five necklaces of pearls and diamonds, and six chains of gold set with diamonds, which are put on her mantle on the great festivals of Christ.[28]

A visitor to Zaragoza today may enter the treasure room to see some of the wealth. The Virgin has a different skirt for each day of the year embroidered with gold and set with diamonds and other precious stones. Another image of silver five feet high is set with precious stones and wears a diamond-studded crown of pure gold. In the early 1700s "the Right Honorable Lord *Stanhope*, then General of the *English* forces," was shown the treasure. Gavin was present and heard the General exclaim, "If all the Kings of Europe should gather together all their treasures and precious stones, they could not buy half of the riches of this treasury." Such was the wealth 280 years ago in one cathedral in one small city of Spain!

The Vatican's incredible riches have been accumulated at the expense of the people in even the poorest countries. At the time of Mexico's Civil War the Roman Catholic Church there owned "from one-third to one-half of all the land of the nation [and about one-half of all the property of Mexico City]. Its revenues from tithes, Masses, and the sale of devotional articles such as statues, medals, rosaries, and the like, amounted to between six and eight million dollars annually, while its total revenues reached the astronomical figure of twenty million dollars.... This drain on the poor country of Mexico was equal to the operating expense of the entire United States government during these same years."[29]

We bring this lamentable recital to a close. There can be no doubt that John's remarkable vision had come to pass: A *city on seven hills* sated with wealth, which claimed a special relationship to God and Christ, literally ruled over the kings of the earth. As with the other identifying criteria John provides, there is only one city in history (and only one today) which passes this test. Peter de Rosa reminds us of what must have shocked John:

> Jesus renounced possessions. He constantly taught: "Go, sell all thou hast and give to the poor, then come and follow me." He preached doom to the rich and powerful.... Christ's Vicar lives surrounded by treasures, some of pagan origin. Any suggestion that the pope should sell all he has and give to the poor is greeted with derision as impractical. The rich young man in the gospel reacted in the same way.
>
> Throughout his life, Jesus lived simply; he died naked, offering the sacrifice of his life on the cross.

When the pope renews that sacrifice at pontifical high mass, no greater contrast could be imagined. Without any sense of irony, Christ's Vicar is clad in gold and the costliest silks.

... the pope has a dozen glorious titles, including State Sovereign. The pope's aides also have titles somewhat unexpected in the light of the Sermon on the Mount: Excellency, Eminence, Your Grace, My Lord, Illustrious One, Most Reverend, and so on....

Peter, always penniless, would be intrigued to know that according to canon 1518... his successor is "the supreme administrator and manager of all church properties." Also that the Vatican has its own bank.... [30]

The Vatican has gathered its incalculable fortune through the most abominable means: selling bogus tickets to heaven. Nino Lo Bello, former Rome correspondent for *Business Week*, calls the Vatican "the tycoon on the Tiber" because of its incredible wealth and worldwide enterprises. His research indicates that it owns fully one-third of Rome's real estate and is probably the largest holder of stocks and bonds in the world, to say nothing of its ownership of industries from electronics and plastics to airlines and chemical and engineering firms. [31]

In his September 1993 trip to the Baltic countries "the pope was an unusually stern critic of unbridled capitalism. In a speech that hinted of more to come, the pope said capitalistic ideology was responsible for 'grave social injustices'—and that Marxism's 'kernel of truth' lay in seeing capitalism's faults." [32] One marvels at the hypocrisy of such statements coming from the head of a Church which is the biggest capitalist in the world! Lo Bello suggests that the Church shed its "mantle of piety; then at last the Vatican will expose the full extent of its financial interests." [33]

The woman riding the beast has used her wealth and power to subdue kings and kingdoms and to slaughter millions who, though they were subject to civil authority, could not accept her heresies. To this day that gold cup overflows with the blood of those who, for conscience' sake, were martyred for their faith.

*The horrid conduct of this Holy Office [Inquisition] weakened the power and diminished the population of Spain by arresting the progress of arts, sciences, industry and commerce, and by compelling multitudes of families to abandon the kingdom; by instigating the expulsion of the Jews and the Moors, and by immolating on its flaming shambles more than three hundred thousand victims.*

—Jean Antoine Llorente
Secretary to the Spanish
Inquisition, 1790-92[1]

*The Inquisition is, in its very nature, good, mild, and preservative. It is the universal, indelible character of every ecclesiastical institution; you see it in Rome, and you can see it wherever the true Church has power.*

—Comte Le Maistre, 1815[2]

*It would be better to be an atheist than believe in the God of the Inquisition.*

—Anonymous Catholic[3]

# 17

# Blood
# of the Martyrs

The quotations on the facing page present two opposing viewpoints, both by Catholics. Only one is right. We learn the truth from John's vision and from history. The woman astride the beast is "drunken with the blood of the saints, and with the blood of the martyrs of Jesus" (Revelation 17:6). It is a horrible picture, but one which history fully authenticates for Rome alone and no other city.

Every citizen in the empire was required to be a Roman Catholic. Failure to give wholehearted allegiance to the pope was considered treason against the state punishable by death. Here was the basis for slaughtering millions. As Islam would be a few centuries later, a paganized Christianity was imposed upon the entire populace of Europe under the threat of torture and death.

Thus Roman Catholicism became "the most persecuting faith the world has ever seen . . . [commanding] the throne to impose the Christian [Catholic] religion on all its subjects. Innocent III murdered far more Christians in one afternoon . . . than any Roman emperor did in his entire reign."[4] Will Durant writes candidly:

> Compared with the persecution of heresy in Europe
> from 1227 to 1492, the persecution of Christians by

243

> Romans in the first three centuries after Christ was a
> mild and humane procedure.
>
> Making every allowance required by an historian and
> permitted to a Christian, we must rank the Inquisition,
> along with the wars and persecutions of our time, as
> among the darkest blots on the record of mankind,
> revealing a ferocity unknown in any beast.[5]

Of course not all dissenters openly proclaimed their disloyalty to Rome. There were secret heretics who had to be sought
out diligently. The method devised was the Inquisition, in the
opinion of Egyptian author Rollo Ahmed, "the most pitiless
and ferocious institution the world has ever known" in its
destruction of lives, property, morals, and human rights. Lord
Acton, a Catholic, called the Inquisition "murderous" and
declared that the popes "were not only murderers in the great
style, but they made murder a legal basis of the Christian
Church and the condition of salvation."[6]

## No Absolution for Rome

Roman Catholic apologists deceitfully try to absolve their
Church of any responsibility in the actual burnings of heretics.
They claim that the Inquisition was the work of the state. On
the contrary, "The binding force of the laws against heretics
lay not in the authority of secular princes, but in the sovereign
dominion of life and death over all Christians claimed by
the Popes as God's representatives on earth, as Innocent III
expressly states it."[7]

The penalties were executed by the civil authorities, but
only as the secular arm of the Church. Innocent III commanded the archbishop of Auch in Gascony: "We give you a
strict command that, by whatever means you can, you destroy
all these heresies . . . you may cause the princes and people to
suppress them with the sword." The pope offered "a plenary
indulgence to the king and nobles of France for aid in suppressing the Catharist heresy. To Philip Augustus, in return for such
aid, the pope offered the lands of all who should fail to join in a
crusade against the Albigensians."[8]

Comte Le Maistre, in his letters written in 1815 to justify
the Spanish Inquisition, states that it existed "by virtue of the

bull of the sovereign pontiff" and that the Grand Inquisitor "is always either an archbishop or bishop."[9] If the authorities refused to execute the condemned, they would themselves be brought before the Tribunal and consigned to the flames.

It was the popes themselves who invented the Inquisition and saw that it was carried out. "Gregory IX, in 1233, handed over the office [of the Inquisition] in permanence to the Dominicans, but always to be exercised in the name, and by the authority of, the Pope."[10] As already noted, "Of eighty popes in a line from the thirteenth century on not one of them disapproved of the theology and apparatus of the Inquisition. On the contrary, one after another added his own cruel touches to the workings of this deadly machine."[11] We are not quoting Protestants or even ex-Catholics, but Catholic historians. Listen to the leading nineteenth-century Catholic professor of Church history:

> Through the influence of Gratian . . . and unwearied activity of the Popes and their legates since 1183, the view of the Church had been . . . [that] every departure from the teaching of the Church, and every important opposition to any ecclesiastical ordinances, must be punished with death, and the most cruel of deaths, by fire. . . .
>
> Innocent III declared the mere refusal to swear, and the opinion that oaths were unlawful, a heresy worthy of death, and directed that whoever differed in any respect from the common way of life of the multitude should be treated as a heretic.
>
> Both the initiation and carrying out of this new principle must be ascribed to the Popes alone. . . . It was the Popes who compelled bishops and priests to condemn the heterodox to torture, confiscation of their goods, imprisonment, and death, and to enforce the execution of this sentence on the civil authorities, under pain of excommunication.
>
> From 1200 to 1500 the long series of Papal ordinances on the Inquisition, ever increasing in severity and cruelty, and their whole policy towards heresy, runs on without a break. It is a rigidly consistent system of

legislation; every Pope confirms and improves upon the devices of his predecessor. All is directed to the one end, of completely uprooting every difference of belief. . . .

It was only the absolute dictation of the Popes, and the notion of their infallibility in all questions of Evangelical morality, that made the Christian world . . . [accept] the Inquisition, which contradicted the simplest principles of Christian justice and love to our neighbor, and would have been rejected with universal horror in the ancient Church.[12]

Far from being its originators, civil authorities often tried to resist the Inquisition, but they could not. Forced to carry out the sentence, executioners sometimes "strangled the condemned before lighting the flames."[13] Such acts of deficient mercy were, unfortunately, the rare exception. A few compassionate voices were raised within the Church: "St. Bernard pointed out that Christ had expressly forbidden the line of conduct afterwards prescribed by the Popes, and that it could only multiply hypocrites and confirm and increase the hatred of mankind against a bloodthirsty and persecuting Church and clergy."[14] But most clergy agreed with the popes.

## Papal Decrees

We often learn of secular resistance from papal decrees overruling it. Will Durant informs us that in 1521 Leo X issued the bull *Honestis* which "ordered the excommunication of any officials, and the suspension of religious services in any community, that refused to execute, without examination or revision, the sentences of the inquisitors."[15] Consider Clement V's rebuke of King Edward II:

We hear that you forbid torture as contrary to the laws of your land. But no state law can override [the Church's] canon law, our law. Therefore I command you at once to submit those men to torture.[16]

Pope Urban II (1088-99), inspirer of the first Crusade, decreed that all heretics were to be tortured and killed. That became a dogma of the Church. Acclaimed as the 'angelic doctor,' even St. Thomas Aquinas taught that non-Catholics, or heretics, could, after a second warning, be legitimately killed. His exact words are: *"they have merited to be excluded from the earth by death."*[17]

Pope Martin V (1417-31) commanded the King of Poland in 1429 to exterminate the Hussites (sympathizers with the martyred Jan Hus), who had fought back and had routed the pope's army. The following from the pope's letter to the king reinforces what we know of the evil of papal totalitarianism and tells us why popes hated the Hussites and other independent Christians and wanted them destroyed:

> Know that the interests of the Holy See, and those of your crown, make it a duty to exterminate the Hussites. Remember that these impious persons dare proclaim principles of equality; they maintain that all Christians are brethren, and that God has not given to privileged men the right of ruling the nations; they hold that Christ came on earth to abolish slavery; they call the people to liberty, that is to the annihilation of kings and priests.
>
> While there is still time, then, turn your forces against Bohemia; burn, massacre, make deserts everywhere, for nothing could be more agreeable to God, or more useful to the cause of kings, than the extermination of the Hussites.[18]

The popes themselves were the authority behind the Inquisitions. They wielded the power of life and death even over emperors. Had any pope opposed the Inquisition, he could have stopped it during his papacy at least. Where do we read that the popes thundered anathemas against the secular authorities who imposed so many and such gruesome deaths upon their victims? Never! Civil magistrates would have desisted from these loathsome murders in order to save their own souls, but papal orders to stop the Inquisitions never came.

On the contrary, the Roman pontiffs, who originated and directed the Inquisitions, threatened excommunication against any who failed to carry out the inquisitors' decrees.

Today's Catholic apologists deny the facts of history and accuse those who present the truth of being "unscholarly." D. Antonio Gavin, a Catholic priest and eyewitness to the Spanish Inquisition, tells us:

> The Roman Catholics believe there is a Purgatory, and that the souls suffer more pains in it than in Hell: But I think that the Inquisition is the only Purgatory on earth, and the holy Fathers [priests/popes] are the judges and executioners in it. The reader may form a dreadful idea of the barbarity of that tribunal by what I have already said, but I am sure it never will come up to what it is in reality, for it passeth all understanding. . . . [19]

## The Dogmas Remain Today

Had Rome ever confessed the evil of her ferocious slaughter of millions of those whom she called heretics, and had she renounced the centuries of plunder and murder and wiped those doctrines from her books, then we could forget that horror. That she has not done so, however, requires us to face, no matter how unpleasant, the facts of history. Far from expressing shame for the execution of heretics, a popular American Catholic weekly in 1938 declared:

> Heresy is an awful crime against God, and those who start a heresy are more guilty than they who are traitors to the civil government. If the state has a right to punish treason with death, the principle is the same that concedes to the spiritual authority [Roman Catholic Church] the power of life and death over the archtraitor [heretic]. [20]

Infallibility can never admit it was wrong. As John Fox reminds us in his *Book of Martyrs*, "A Church which pretends to be infallible will always seek the destruction of those who dissent from it. . . ." [21] De Rosa points out that Pope John Paul II—

> knows the church was responsible for persecuting Jews, for the Inquisition, for slaughtering heretics by the thousand, for reintroducing torture into Europe as part of the

judicial process. But he has to be careful. The doctrines
responsible for those terrrible things still underpin his
position.[22]

Disobedience to the pope became the epitome of heresy.
Those guilty of it immediately lost any normal human rights
and were summarily put to death. Consider Urban VIII's 1627
Bull *In Coena Domini*. Gregory XI had first brought it out in
1372, and Gregory XII reconfirmed it in 1411, as did Pius V in
1568 (who said it was to remain an eternal law in Christendom). Each pope added new touches until it was well-nigh
impossible for an admitted non-Catholic to exist in Europe,
much as it will be worldwide under Antichrist for any who do
not submit totally to him. The bull "excommunicates and
curses all heretics and schismatics as well as all who favor or
defend them, [including] all princes and magistrates...."[23]

*This bull is still in force today.* Nor could it be otherwise,
with the ex cathedra pronouncements of four infallible popes
behind it. The absolutism remains even though Rome is not
presently able to enforce it so blatantly. *The Code of Canon
Law*, Canon 333, par 3, declares: "There is neither appeal nor
recourse against a decision or decree of the Roman Pontiff."
Vatican II, of course, says the same.

The woman rides the beast, holding the reins! Incredible,
but it happened. Heresy in the Church's eyes was treated as
treason against the crown. The Church sought out the heretics,
found them guilty, and handed them to the civil authorities for
execution. As its secular arm, the state did the Church's
bidding in the execution of heretics, the confiscation of their
property, and the enforcement of the Church's decrees against
them and their heirs.

### The Use of Torture

Remember, it is not that the woman's hands are red with
blood but that she is *drunk* with the blood of the martyrs. Her
condition depicts a Church that not only kills but tortures its
pitiful victims for days and even weeks. The inquisitors seemed
to be drugged into insensibility until their normal sense of
horror and sympathy had been numbed. Indeed, to be able to

impose the most extreme torture without a twinge of conscience or compassionate thought became a mark of holiness and fidelity to the Church.

Try to imagine being suddenly arrested in the middle of the night and taken to an unknown location kept secret from family and friends. You are not told the charges against you or the identity of your accusers, who remain unknown and thus immune from any examination to discover whether they are telling the truth. Whatever the accusation, it is accepted as fact and you are guilty without trial. The only "trial" will be by the most ingeniously painful torture that continues until you confess to that unnamed crime or heresy of which you have been accused. Imagine the torment of dislocated joints, torn and seared flesh, internal injuries, broken bones on the rack and other devices, mended by doctors so they could be torn asunder again by fresh torture. Eventually you would confess to anything to end the torment, but no matter what you confess it never fits the secret accusation, so the torture continues until at last you expire from the unbearable trauma.

Such was the fate of *millions*. These were real people: mothers, fathers, brothers, sisters, sons, and daughters—all with hopes and dreams, with passions and feelings, and many with a faith that could not be broken by torture or fire. Remember that this terror, this evil of such proportions that it is unimaginable today, was carried on for *centuries* in the name of Christ by the command of those who claimed to be the vicars of Christ. They are still honored with that title by this Church, which has never admitted that the Inquisitions were wrong. She has not repented or apologized, and she dares to pose even today as the supreme teacher and example of morals and truth. Remember also that the doctrines which supported the Inquisitions remain in force within the Roman Catholic Church even at the present time.

With the use of torture, there was no limit to what the accused would confess. At least one poor creature said he would admit having killed God if his inquisitors would stop torturing him. Women accused of being witches confessed, under torture, to having had sex with Satan and even to having borne him children, children who remained invisible and were thus all the greater menace to Catholics. Pope Innocent VIII made such hysterical nonsense official Catholic dogma in his 1484 Bull, *Summis desiderantes affectibus*:

> Men and women straying from the Catholic faith have abandoned themselves to devils, *incubi* and *succubi* [male and female demonic sexual partners], and by their incantations, spells, conjurations . . . have slain infants yet in the mother's womb, as also the offspring of cattle, have blasted the produce of the earth. . . .[24]

Torture was considered to be essential because the church felt duty-bound to identify from the lips of the victims themselves any deviance from sound doctrine. Presumably, the more excruciating the torture, the more likely that the truth could be wrung from reluctant lips. The inquisitors were determined that it was "better for a hundred innocent people to die than for one heretic to go free." This horrendous doctrine was maintained under every pope for the next three centuries. Durant suggests:

> The inquisitors appear to have sincerely believed that torture was a favor to a defendant already accounted guilty, since it might earn him, by confession, a slighter penalty than otherwise; even if he should, after confession, be condemned to death, he could enjoy priestly absolution to save him from hell.[25]

Another author, Gerard Dufour, quotes a 1552 book by Simancas stating that "the inquisitors should be more inclined to the use of torture than regular judges because the crime of heresy is concealed and very difficult to prove." The openly stated purpose of torture was "to cause the most intense pain to the prisoner. And for that the inquisitors exchanged recipes [techniques]." Other authorities of that time are quoted to the effect that torture was not expected to rescue the accused from his heresy, but its main purpose was to terrorize the masses,[26] which in fact it did.

Catholic apologists are quick to say that Pope Sixtus IV attempted to stop the Inquisition. That is not true. He issued a bull in 1482 declaring that the inquisitors *in Aragon, Spain*, seemed more interested in getting wealthy than defending the faith and accusing them of imprisoning, torturing, and burning faithful Catholics on the basis of false accusations from their enemies or slaves. He decreed that a representative of the local bishop must always be present, that the accused must know the names of the accusers, and that appeals to the Holy See ought to be allowed.

This bull, however, was *only for Aragon*, and when King Ferdinand defied it Sixtus backed off and five months later suspended it. In the meantime he was taking money for granting dispensations and absolutions (which the inquisitors never honored) from the sentences of the Inquisition in Aragon. Nor did he give any refunds. If the pope had been seriously concerned for justice rather than money, he would have forced the king to comply and have made the bull effective everywhere instead of only in Aragon.[27]

## The Modus Operandi

When the inquisitors swept into a town an "Edict of Faith" was issued requiring everyone to reveal any heresy of which they had knowledge. Those who concealed a heretic came under the curse of the Church and the inquisitors' wrath. Informants would approach the inquisitors' lodgings under cover of night and were rewarded for information. No one arrested was ever acquitted.

"Heretics" were committed to the flames because the popes believed that the Bible forbade Christians to shed blood. The victims of the Inquisition exceeded by hundreds of thousands the number of Christians and Jews who had suffered under pagan Roman emperors.

The Inquisition, established and repeatedly blessed by the popes, was an open assault upon truth and justice and basic human rights. It was the perfect setup for bigots, villains, enemies, and crazies with overworked imaginations to seek revenge, rid themselves of a rival, or gain personal satisfaction of having become important to the Church. De Rosa writes:

> Whenever one of the Papal States fell to the armies of
> the new Italy and the prisons were opened, the prisoners'

conditions were said to be indescribable. . . . for more than six centuries without a break, the papacy was the sworn enemy of elementary justice.[28]

The property of heretics was confiscated and divided between the inquisitors and the popes. That the corpse of Pope Formosus had been twice disinterred, condemned, and excommunicated set a pattern. In 680 the Sixth General Council decreed that even dead heretics should be tried and condemned. Corpses that had lain in the grave for decades were dug up, tried, and found guilty. At that point the past assets of the deceased were confiscated, causing heirs to lose everything, including, in many cases, all civil rights.

Roman Catholic apologists pass off the Inquisitions as a necessity at the time to keep the Church doctrinally pure. They suggest that any excesses were the work of overly patriotic Spaniards who were concerned that many "converted" Moors and Jews were not really loyal to the Church. Seemingly forgotten is the "barbaric cruelty of the pious priestly inquisitors in Italy, France, Germany, the Low Countries, England and the Scandinavian lands." Besides the Spanish Inquisition there were the Roman and Medieval Inquisitions as well. Emmet McLoughlin, who spent years researching relevant historical records in the New World, writes:

> There were no Moors and few Jews in Peru, where I saw the Hall of the Inquisition, the dungeons of imprisonment, and the gorgeously carved door with . . . an opening made at mouth height so that the witness could testify against the accused heretic without being seen or identified. . . .[29]

As an eyewitness in the early eighteenth century in Spain, Gavin tells us, "This tribunal is composed of three Inquisitors, who are absolute judges . . . from their judgment there is no appeal. . . . The first Inquisitor is a divine, the second a casuist, and the third a civilian; the first and second are always Priests. . . . The third sometimes is not a Priest. . . . The Inquisitors have a despotic power to command every living soul; and no excuse is to be given, nor contradiction to be made, to their orders. . . ."[30]

## The Pilgrim Church

Catholic apologists admit that the Church "made some mistakes," but insist that Rome couldn't be the whore in Revelation 17. Why? Because Christ promised that the gates of hell would not prevail against the church (Matthew 16:18), and Roman Catholicism was *the* Church. Even many evangelicals are deceived by this argument.

The truth is that Roman Catholicism *did not represent Christ and was not His Church.* For at least a thousand years before the Reformation the true church was composed of *multitudes of simple Christians who were not part of the Roman system.* That such believers existed, refused to be called "Catholics," and worshiped independently of the Roman hierarchy is history. It is a fact that they were pursued to imprisonment and death since at least the end of the fourth century. Among the evidence in ancient records stands the "Edict of the Emperors Gratian, Valentinian II, and Theodosius I" of February 27, 380, which established Roman Catholicism as the state religion. In part it said:

> We order those who follow this doctrine to receive the title of Catholic Christians, but others we judge to be mad and raving and worthy of incurring the disgrace of heretical teaching, nor are their assemblies to receive the name of churches. They are to be punished not only by Divine retribution but also by our own measures, which we have decided in accordance with Divine inspiration.[31]

These non-Catholic Christians had, out of conscience before God and in obedience to His Word, separated themselves from what they sincerely called even in that day "the whore of Babylon." Concerning them, Bishop Alvaro Palayo, an official of the *Curia* in Avignon, wrote grudgingly: "Considering the Papal Court has filled the whole Church with simony, and the consequent corruption of religion, it is natural enough the heretics should call the Church the whore."[32] E.H. Broadbent calls these Bible-believing Christians *The Pilgrim Church* in his book of that name:

In the Alpine valleys of Piedmont there had been for
centuries congregations of believers calling themselves
brethren, who came later to be widely known as Waldenses, or Vaudois. . . . In the South of France . . . the
congregations of believers who met apart from the Catholic Church were numerous and increasing. They are
often called Albigenses [and] had intimate connections
with the brethren—whether called Waldenses, Poor
Men of Lyons, Bogomils, or otherwise—in the surrounding countries, where churches spread among the
various peoples.

In 1209 [Pope Innocent III] proclaimed a crusade
against [them]. Indulgences, such as had been given to
the [Holy Land] Crusaders . . . were now offered to all
who would take part in the easier work of destroying the
most fruitful provinces of France. This, and the prospect
of booty and license of every kind, attracted hundreds of
thousands of men. Under the presidence of high clerical
dignitaries and led by Simon de Montfort, a military
leader of great ability . . . the most beautiful and culti-
vated part of Europe at that time was ravaged. . . .[33]

These simple believers were burned at the stake or slain
with the sword (and most of their records were destroyed)
when their towns and villages were razed by papal armies.
Catholic apologists falsely accuse them of heresies and abominable practices which they denied. The accounts we have of
their trials reveal that they held beliefs similar to evangelicals
of today. Though some of the worst tales are told about the
Cathari, one can only agree with their beliefs as described by
Durant:

[They] denied that the [Roman Catholic] Church was
the Church of Christ; [declared that] St. Peter had never
come to Rome, had never founded the papacy; [and that]
the popes were successors to the emperors, not to the
apostles. [They taught that] Christ had no place to lay His
head, but the pope lived in a palace; Christ was property-
less and penniless, but Christian prelates were rich; surely
. . . these lordly archbishops and bishops, these worldly
priests, these fat monks, were the Pharisees of old

returned to life! The Roman Church, they were sure, was the Whore of Babylon, the clergy were a Synagogue of Satan, the pope was Antichrist. They denounced the preachers of crusades as murderers . . . laughed at indulgences and relics . . . they called the churches "dens of thieves" and Catholic priests seemed to them "traitors, liars, and hypocrites."[34]

Nineteenth-century Roman Catholic author du Pin writes: "The pope [Innocent III] and the prelates were of opinion that it was lawful to make use of force, to see whether those who were not reclaimed out of a sense of their salvation might be so by the fear of punishments, and even of temporal death." Almost everyone knows that crusades were organized of tens of thousands of knights and foot soldiers to retake Jerusalem from the Muslims. Very few have ever heard that similar crusades involving huge armies were fought against Christians who could not in good conscience submit to Rome. Yet such was the case, beginning with Pope Innocent III.[35]

A major crime of these Christians was believing in freedom of conscience and worship—biblical concepts which the popes hated, for such beliefs would put Rome out of business. Though no exact figures are available, the slaughter of these Christians by the popes probably ran into the millions during the thousand years before the Reformation. In the city of Beziers alone about 60,000 men, women, and children were wiped out in one crusade.[36] Innocent III considered the annihilation of these particular heretics the *crowning achievement of his papacy!* Broadbent writes:

> When the town of Beziers was summoned to surrender, the Catholic inhabitants joined with the Dissenters in refusing. . . . The town was taken, and of the tens of thousands who had taken refuge there, none were spared [alive].[37]

In spite of periodic massacres, groups of independent Christians were growing in numbers long before Martin Luther was born. They would seemingly be wiped out in one area only to be found in another. As Ulric Zwingli would later state in 1522 in a letter to his brothers, who were fearful that he would be burned at the stake:

> O, my beloved brethren, the Gospel derives from the blood of Christ this wondrous property, that the fiercest persecutions, far from arresting its progress, do but hasten its triumph![38]

Rome could not allow independence from her iron grip. Thus the French Vaudois incurred the wrath of Pope Innocent VIII (1484-92) "for daring to maintain their own religion in preference to that of Rome." In 1487 the pope raised a crusade against them in which he promised "the remission of all sins to everyone who should slay a heretic,"[39] and ordered any bishop removed who neglected to purge his diocese from heretics. No wonder these Christians thought of the popes as Antichrists, for what they suffered was far worse than Roman emperors meted out to the early church and seemed so much like the persecution under Antichrist prophesied in Revelation 13.

In 1838 George Stanley Faber wrote *An Inquiry into the History and Theology of the Ancient Valdenses and Albigenses*. Nearly 200 years earlier, in 1648, Samuel Morland had published his *History of the Evangelical Churches of Piedmont* (an area in France populated by the Albigenses and other "heretics"). The investigation of both of these authors drew on a number of other works going back into the thirteenth century. From written and public testimony at their trials, it is quite clear that the Vaudois, Albigenses, Waldenses, and other similar groups were heretics to Rome only. In fact, their beliefs were much like those of the Reformers, of whom they were, in a sense, the forerunners. Martin Luther acknowledged his debt to them when he wrote:

> We are not the first to declare the papacy to be the kingdom of Antichrist, since for many years before us so many and such great men (whose number is large and whose memory is eternal) have undertaken to express the same thing so clearly and plainly.[40]

## The Mennonites

One of the worst heresies in Rome's eyes was to reject infant baptism. That ritual supposedly removed the stain of original sin, made the infant a child of God and member of the Church, and started the process of salvation, which consisted in obeying Rome's ordinances and participating in her sacraments. Those who managed to find a copy of the Bible (which Rome did her best to keep from the people) discovered that it contradicted Rome's doctrines. Salvation came not through baptism but by faith in Christ. Baptism was for those who believed in Him as their personal savior. No infant was capable of such understanding and faith.

Those who believed the gospel they found in the Bible wanted to be baptized as believers. The Dutch Catholic priest Menno Simons relates his own confusion before he became a Christian:

> On March 20, 1531, a certain tailor by the name of Sicke Freerks Snijder was executed in [Leeuwarden] for the strange reason that he had been baptized a second time. "It sounded strange in my ears," says Menno, "that a second baptism was spoken of."
>
> It seemed still more strange when Menno learned that Freerks was a pious, God-fearing man, who did not believe the Scriptures taught that infants should be baptized but rather that baptism should be administered only to adults upon confession of a personal faith.[41]

Many of the growing numbers of Protestants, such as Lutherans, continued to baptize infants and do so today—one of several elements of Roman Catholicism from which many Reformers were unable to shake free. Thus Protestants, too, began to persecute and in some cases even to execute those who had been baptized a second time. These "heretics" came to be known as Anabaptists.

The Catholic Inquisition in Holland, where most of the Anabaptists were, burned tens of thousands at the stake for espousing the baptism of adults who had come to personal faith in Christ. Those who gave the heretics help or shelter shared their fate. The largest group of Anabaptists followed the teachings of Menno Simons and became known as Mennonites. Menno writes:

> [About 1539] a very pious and God-fearing man, Tjard Reynders, was apprehended in the place where I sojourned for the reason that he had received me, a homeless man, out of compassion and love, into his house, although in secret. . . . he was, after a free confession of his faith [in Christ alone], broken on the wheel and executed as a valiant soldier of Christ, according to the example of his Lord, although he had the testimony, even of his enemies, that he was an unblamable and pious man.[42]

The stories of the martyrs who, because they placed their faith in Christ alone and were devoted to Him, were tortured and slain, many in the flames, present a picture which in its pathos and tragedy is almost unbelievable. We learn both of the terror they faced bravely at the hands of those who claimed to be serving Christ, and of their faith, from letters they wrote while awaiting execution. Consider this brief excerpt from a letter that Hans Van Munstdorp wrote to his wife when they were both in prison at Antwerp:

> An affectionate greeting to you, my beloved wife, whom I love from the heart . . . and must now forsake for the truth [for] which we must count all things loss and love Him above all. . . . my mind is still unwaveringly fixed to adhere to the eternal truth. [I hope] by the grace of the Lord that this is also the purpose of your mind, which I would be rejoiced to hear. I herewith exhort you my beloved lamb, with the apostle: "As you have received Christ Jesus the Lord, so walk in Him, rooted and built up in Him, and established in the faith, and suffer yourself not to be moved from your purpose. . . ."[43]

On September 19, 1573, after her husband's death and after she had in prison given birth, Janneken Munstdorp wrote a farewell letter to her baby daughter. It was a lengthy exhortation to live for Christ, filled with Scripture references and teachings from God's Word to guide her child as she grew up. This brief excerpt from that letter reveals a young mother's and martyr's love and faith:

> The true love of God and wisdom of the Father strengthen you in virtue, my dearest child. . . . I commend you to the Almighty, great and terrible God, who only is wise, that He will keep you and let you grow up in His fear . . . you who are yet so young and whom I must leave here in this wicked, evil, perverse world. Since . . . you are here deprived of father and mother, I will commend you to the Lord; let Him do with you according to His holy will. . . .
>
> My dear lamb, I who am imprisoned . . . can help you in no other way; I had to leave your father for the Lord's sake. . . . [W]e were apprehended . . . [and] they took him from me. . . . And now that I have . . . borne you under my heart with great sorrow for nine months, and given birth to you here in prison, in great pain, they have taken you from me. . . .
>
> Since I am now delivered up to death, and must leave you here alone, I must through these lines cause you to remember that when you have attained your understanding you endeavor to fear God and examine why and for whose name we both died; and be not ashamed . . . of us; it is the way which the prophets and the apostles went, and the narrow way which leads into eternal life. . . . [44]

Perhaps the greatest tragedy is that these martyrs have been forgotten. Or, worse yet, their faithfulness to Christ in torture and death is being mocked today by evangelical leaders who say that the truths for which they gave their lives are not important. They died to bring the gospel to lost souls because Rome's gospel was sending multitudes to eternal judgment. But even though Rome's gospel has not changed, many evangelical leaders today are saying that Catholics who follow Rome are saved, and they are now looking upon the Roman Catholic Church (a Church that burned people at the stake for giving out the Scriptures!) as a partner in evangelizing the world for Christ. The martyrs must weep in heaven—not for themselves but for the lost—if Christ allows them to know of this uncaring betrayal of the faith for which they died.

## The Inquisition Today

The Medieval Inquisition had flourished for centuries when Pope Paul III, in 1542, gave it permanent status as the first of Rome's Sacred Congregations, the Holy, Catholic and Apostolic Inquisition. Known more recently as the Holy Office, its name was changed in 1967 to the Congregation for the Doctrine of the Faith—quite appropriate inasmuch as the public burnings were known as *autos-da-fe* or acts of faith. The persecution, torture, and killing of heretics has never been repudiated by the Roman Catholic Church and has continued into modern times, as we shall see.

Rome is faced with a clear choice: Either her zealous torture and slaughter of so many innocent victims is something to be proud of or it is something to be ashamed of. Of course, Rome will neither repent of its sins nor give up its claim to infallibility. Therefore it is not surprising that the Office of the Inquisition still occupies the Palace of the Inquisition adjacent to the Vatican, though under its new name, the Congregation for the Doctrine of Faith. Its current Grand Inquisitor, who reports directly to the pope, is the former Archbishop of Munich, Joseph Cardinal Ratzinger, whom *Time* has called "the world's most powerful cardinal [and] the Catholic Church's chief enforcer of dogma. . . ."[45] That enforcement may be brutally direct or dealt with a gloved hand through another person, as was the case in late 1993 in the muzzling of Fr. Joseph Breen by Nashville's Bishop Edward Kmiec. In a letter to the nation's bishops, Breen, pointing to "the vast difference between what is said in Rome and what actually happens" pleaded for "optional celibacy." He was forced to sign a pledge "that he will not speak to media . . . [and] not criticize what bishops do."[46]

While it no longer immolates its victims, the Congregation still attempts to maintain the Vatican's cultlike control over the thinking of its clergy and Church members. For example, on June 9, 1993, Ratzinger published "Instructions . . . in Promoting the Doctrine of the Faith." The document demands that "prior permission is required . . . for what is written by clerics and members of religious institutes for newspapers, magazines or periodicals which are accustomed to attack openly the Catholic religion or good morals. The instruction also warns Catholic publishing houses to conform to church law. And bishops are obliged to prevent the sale and display in their churches of publications on religion and morals that lack church approval. . . ."[47] It is the Index of Forbidden Books again!

## Monumental Hypocrisy

The Roman Catholic Church has been the greatest persecutor of both Jews and Christians the world has ever seen, and has martyred far more Christians than even pagan Rome or Islam. She has been exceeded only by Mao and Stalin, but they hardly claimed to be acting in Christ's name. Catholic Rome has no rival among religious institutions in qualifying as the woman who is "drunk with the blood of the saints and the martyrs of Jesus."

Yet John Paul II, in his recent treatise, *Veritatis Splendor*, has the audacity to speak of Catholic saints "who bore witness to and defended moral truth even to the point of enduring martrydom. . . ."[48] What of the millions whom his Church massacred because their moral conscience and understanding of God's Word did not coincide with Rome's! The silence from the Vatican concerning its infamous and innumerable crimes against God and humanity is deafening. Even worse is the hypocrisy that allows this murderous woman to pose as the great teacher and exemplar of obedience to Christ.

" 'Blessed are those who are persecuted for the sake of righteousness, for theirs is the kingdom of heaven (Matthew 5:10).' Thus John Paul II began today's [October 10, 1993] solemn mass in honor of the beatification of 11 [Catholic] martyrs of the Spanish Civil War and two Italian religious."[49] So reported the influential Catholic magazine *Inside the Vatican*. As always, while Catholic martyrs are lauded, there is no admission of and no apology for the millions of Christians and Jews who have been martyred by the Roman Catholic Church. The hypocrisy is monumental.

*God's holy providence has provided that in a decisive hour he [Hitler] be entrusted with the leadership of the German people.*

—From an article in *Klerusblatt*, organ
of the Bavarian Association of
Diocesan Priests, honoring
Hitler on his fiftieth birthday,
April 20, 1939[1]

*The [Nazi] movement for freeing the world from the Jews is a movement for the renaissance of human dignity. The all-wise and Almighty God is behind this movement.*

—Fr. Franjo Kralik in a Zagreb
Catholic newspaper, 1941[2]

# 18

# Background to the Holocaust

The approval of Hitler by Catholic prelates and their statements about "freeing the world from the Jews" seem shocking. Yet they only reflect Catholicism's historic treatment of the Jews. Hitler justified his "final solution" by pointing out that the Church had oppressed and killed Jews for centuries. How amazing that those who claimed to be the followers of Christ and successors of Peter could "persecute the race from which Peter—and Jesus—sprang"!3 Yet they did it in the name of Christ and felt justified thereby.

Roman Catholics were taught they had replaced the Jews as God's chosen people. The land of Israel, promised by God to the descendants of Abraham, Isaac, and Jacob, now belonged to "Christian" Rome. She became the "new Zion," the "Eternal City," and "The Holy City," titles which God had given to Jerusalem alone. Papal armies fought to expand "the Kingdom of God." As a nineteenth-century historian reminds us, "The territory under the immediate dominion of the Pope was enlarged whenever war or treaty could increase it; and the inhabitants had to pay the utmost taxes they could bear."4

## A Great Reproach upon Christ

Those who called themselves vicars of Christ have brought

great reproach upon the name of Christ by their treatment of the Jews. The latter mistakenly equate Catholicism with Christianity. The Jews who were persecuted through the centuries by the Roman Catholic Church didn't realize that there were millions of Christians outside that Church—Christians who did not persecute God's chosen people and were themselves persecuted and killed by Catholics in far greater numbers than were the Jews.

Consider the following indictment of "Christianity" from a scholarly rabbinical treatise on the Holocaust. Note that Roman Catholicism is critiqued, not evangelical Christianity, which the author and his Jewish readers may not even know exists. This is from the chapter titled "The Christian Role [in the Holocaust]":

> . . . without Christianity, the success of Nazism would not have been possible. . . . Were it not for the fact that dozens of generations in Europe had been imbued with religious hatred, the growth of racist hatred towards Jewry in modern times could not have taken place.
>
> Furthermore, [all] through the Holocaust, the Vatican refrained from protesting the murder, and by and large stood aside, rescuing only a tiny few. To this day the Vatican refuses scholars full access to the documents of the period. It has been established, however, that the Vatican was among the first in the world to know about the genocide, and it did nothing to publicize the information (see Walter Laquer, *The Terrible Secret*). . . .
>
> [I]t is difficult to avoid the conclusion that the Pope's inaction indicated tacit approval. . . . Even when the Church engaged in isolated rescue activities, the motive seems to have been to bring the rescued Jews into the bosom of Christianity. Thousands of Jewish children were taken into monasteries, and after the war, many were not returned to their people and faith even after relatives pleaded for their release.
>
> With unparalleled cynicism, many Christians still see the Holocaust as a heavenly punishment for the Jews' failure to accept Christianity.[5]

The rabbi continues to analyze "Christianity" as he sees it (all he knows is Roman Catholicism) in his attempt to understand the reason for its moral failure in relation to the Holocaust. His observations and arguments are devastating, yet he doesn't know that there are millions of true Christians who would agree with his critique of the false religion of Rome. One would think he had never heard of the Reformation and Protestants who don't have "monks" and whose ministers marry:

> The priests of Christianity [Catholicism] are forbidden to marry, and its monks, living lives of self-affliction, isolate themselves from human society. The religion is not one which can easily be put into practice. . . . The notion that it can be, leads to incomparable hypocrisy. . . .
>
> Over the years, Christianity [Catholicism] gave rise to a number of mystic cults, some of which distinguished themselves by their affinity for the lowest forms of moral abomination. The Christian [Catholic] process of repentance also led to the commission of grave crimes. When automatic atonement is offered to those who confess before a priest, the temptation to sin is greatly increased. . . .
>
> While murder, robbery, and rape were all but unheard of within medieval Jewish communities, these acts were commonplace within devoutly Christian [Catholic] Europe. The spiritual salvation promised by Christianity found no concrete expression.[6]

## Anti-Semitism at Work

The rabbi's critique of *Catholicism* is right on the mark. The tragedy is that he thinks he is dealing with *Christianity*. From the time the popes ruled Rome, the Jews' plight—in the name of Jesus Christ the Jew—was far more grievous than it had ever been at the hands of pagan rulers. Pagans had blamed every disaster upon Christians. Now the Roman Catholic Church blamed all on the Jews. Accused of causing the Black Death, Jews were rounded up and hanged, burned, and drowned by the thousands in revenge.

A rare pope now and then sought to ameliorate the Jews' situation. Gregory I "forbade the compulsory conversion of Jews, and maintained their rights of Roman citizenship in lands under his rule. . . . To the bishop of Naples he wrote: 'Do not allow the Jews to be molested in the performance of their [religious] services." Alexander III was "friendly to Jews, and employed one to manage his finances." Innocent III "led the Fourth Lateran Council in its demand for a Jewish badge, and laid down the principle that all Jews were doomed to perpetual servitude because they had crucified Jesus." Yet "he reiterated papal injunctions against forcible conversions, and added: 'No Christian shall do the Jews any personal injury . . . or deprive them of their possessions. . . .'" (Yet he massacred tens of thousands of Christians.) Gregory IX, though the founder of the Inquisition, "exempted the Jews from its operation or jurisdiction except when they tried to Judaize Christians, or attacked Christianity, or reverted to Judaism after conversion to Christianity. In 1235 he issued a bull denouncing mob violence against Jews." Innocent IV "repudiated the legend of the ritual murder of Christian children by Jews."[7]

In spite of the above, the general picture was one of persecution of Jews by the Church. Numerous councils and papal bulls dealt with this issue, as the following will illustrate:

> The Council of Vienna (1311) forbade all intercourse between Christians and Jews. The Council of Zamora (1313) ruled that they must be kept in strict subjection and servitude. The Council of Basel (1431-33) renewed canonical decrees forbidding Christians to associate with Jews . . . and instructed secular authorities to confine the Jews in separate quarters, compel them to wear a distinguishing badge, and ensure their attendance at sermons aimed to convert them.
>
> Pope Eugenius IV (1431-47) . . . added that Jews should be ineligible for any public office, could not inherit property from Christians, must build no more synagogues, and must stay in their homes, behind closed doors and windows, in Passion Week (a wise provision against Christian violence). . . .

In a later bull Eugenius ordered that any Italian Jew found reading Talmudic literature should suffer confiscation of his property. Pope Nicholas V commissioned St. John of Capistrano (1447) to see to it that every clause of this repressive legislation should be enforced, and authorized him to seize the property of any Jewish physician who treated a Christian.[8]

More than 100 anti-Semitic documents were published by the Roman Catholic Church between the sixth and twentieth centuries. Anti-Semitism became official Church doctrine. The rationale was that "Christ crucifiers" had no rights in God's holy kingdom, the land of Israel no longer belonged to the Jews but to Christians, and the Church had to wrest the land from the possession of both Arabs and Jews.

The Catholic Church has no comprehension of Bible prophecies concerning the return of Jews to Israel and of the Messiah returning to reign from the throne of His father David. Rome calls itself the New Jerusalem; old Jerusalem and the Jews are no longer part of God's plan. In 1862, *La Civilta*, the semiofficial voice of the Vatican, echoed a belief held for centuries by declaring: "As the Jews were formerly God's people, so are the Romans [Catholics] under the New Covenant."[9] It was only natural that such teaching would nurture and sustain anti-Semitism.

## The Historical Record

To raise an army for the First Crusade, Pope Urban II promised instant entrance into heaven without purgatory for all who fell in that great cause. The knights and knaves who responded with enthusiasm to that deceitful promise left a trail of mayhem, plunder, and murder on their way to Jerusalem, where they massacred all Arabs and Jews. One of the first acts after their triumphal entry into Jerusalem was to herd the Jews into the synagogue and set it ablaze. On their way to the Holy Land, the Crusaders gave the Jews the choice of baptism or death. De Rosa recounts:

> In the year 1096 half of the Jews of Worms were slaughtered as the Crusaders passed through the town.

The rest fled to the bishop's residence for protection. He agreed to save them, on condition that they asked to be baptized. The Jews retired to consider their decision. When the doors of the audience chamber were opened, all 800 Jews inside were dead. Some were decapitated; fathers had killed their babes before turning their knives on their wives and themselves; a groom had slain his bride. The first-century tragedy of Masada was repeated everywhere in Germany and, later, throughout France.[10]

During the brief pontificate of Pope Paul IV (1555-9), the population of Rome was decimated by almost half, with the Jews the main victims. Three hundred years earlier the church had put Jews in ghettos and "obliged them to wear on their chest, to their public shame, a yellow circle of cloth,"[11] but enforcement of that edict had become lax. Pope Paul IV issued, on July 17, 1555, a landmark anti-Semitic bull, *Cum nimis absurdum*. It returned Jews to their ghettos, forced them to sell their properties at huge losses, and reduced them to the status of slaves and rag merchants.

Marriage between a Christian and a Jew was punishable by death. One synagogue was allowed in each city; the others were destroyed, seven out of the eight in Rome suffering that fate. While still a cardinal, Paul IV had burned the Jews' books, including the Talmud, and no replacements were allowed. These are only some of the indignities and crimes the Jews suffered by this bull, which set a pattern that lasted for another three centuries.

Pope Gregory XIII declared that the guilt of Jews in crucifying Christ "only grows deeper with successive generations, entailing perpetual slavery." Subsequent popes continued the persecution:

A succession of popes reinforced the ancient prejudices against Jews, treating them as lepers unworthy of the protection of the law. Pius VII followed by Leo XII, Pius VIII, Gregory XVI, Pius IX—all good pupils of Paul IV.

Eleven days after Rome fell, on 2 October 1870, the Jews, by a royal decree, were given the freedom which the papacy had denied them for over fifteen hundred years. The last ghetto in Europe [at that time] was dismantled.[12]

## Forced Conversions

Catholicism's doctrine of infant baptism destroyed the truth that one becomes a Christian not by any work or ritual but by responding to the offer of God's grace through personal faith in Christ. Since baptism automatically saved, Pope Leo III decreed forcible baptism of Jews. At times, Jews were given the option of professing to believe in Christ, or death—or in some cases merely imprisonment or expulsion from the region. The famous rabbinical authority, philosopher, and physician Maimonides fled Spain to Morocco to escape such an edict, and then to Egypt in 1135. Today's visitors to the former Jewish quarters in Spain receive pamphlets providing some of the tragic history, such as the following from the city of Girona:

> On March 31, 1492, Ferdinand and Isabel of Castile and Aragon, known as the Catholic Monarchs, issued the edict expelling the Jews from Spanish territory ... [they had] no other choice but renunciation of religious belief or compulsory expatriation. Those who chose to convert to Christianity in order to avoid expulsion faced the full fury of the Inquisition, which had already begun to prosecute heretics in Girona in 1490.... Some Jewish families were virtually wiped out at the hands of the Inquisitors.

Baptizing an infidel assured one's passage to heaven. Jewish children were sprinkled forcibly with water and declared to be "Christians" by those who imagined they had thereby guaranteed themselves a heavenly abode. Benedict XIV (1740-58) supported this terror by ruling that a child, though baptized against its own and its parents' will, was nevertheless a Roman Catholic. If these unwilling "converts" thereafter denied their new "faith" they were then heretics, with the dire consequences attached to that label.

Similar crimes continued for centuries. For example, in 1858 Pius IX ordered his papal police to take the seven-year-old son of wealthy Jewish parents from them and put him into a Catholic boarding school. A Catholic maid had, without the parents' knowledge or consent, baptized the boy, Edgar Mortara, shortly after his birth, thus allegedly making him a member of the Roman Catholic Church.

When the parents pleaded with the pope to return their child, he replied in typical papal fashion (referring to the adverse publicity the case had aroused in newspapers), "I don't care a rap for the whole world!" Hasler continues the story:

> The pope treated the young secretary of the Jewish community, Sabatino Scazzocchio, with particular cruelty and humiliated him so badly that he suffered a protracted nervous breakdown.
>
> Two years later Pius IX displayed Edgar Mortara, now dressed in a seminarian's robe, to the Jews of Rome.[13]

## Foundation for the Holocaust

Surely *Shoah*'s authors, rabbis Schwartz and Goldstein, are accurate in saying that Roman Catholicism's (though they think it is Christianity's) centuries-long persecution of the Jews laid the foundation for what was yet to come, the Nazi Holocaust. The Catholic Church bears a large responsibility for that horrendous crime. Most of the overseers of the massacre of the Jews were Catholics. The longtime persecution and slaughter of Jews by the Church undoubtedly helped Catholic persecutors to justify their actions.

Shock waves went through the international media on May 26, 1994, when these headlines came across the Associated Press wire: "VATICAN TO TAKE HOLOCAUST BLAME." The amazing article, datelined Jerusalem, stated: "The Roman Catholic Church is drafting a document that acknowledges the church fostered centuries of anti-Semitism and failed to stop the Holocaust, a report released Wednesday said. . . . Rabbi David Rosen, an Israeli negotiator with the Vatican, gave the report on the draft document to Israel during talks this week in Jerusalem. . . . 'It's not just important,' Rosen said. 'It's mind-boggling.' . . . The report also says the document will declare that 'the tradition of theological and church anti-Judaism was an important element on the way toward the Holocaust.' "[14]

The following day a denial came from the Vatican, reminding the world that while "Pope John Paul II has repeatedly denounced anti-Semitism . . . he has always defended previous popes against accusations they were silent about the Holocaust." Chief Vatican spokesman Joaquin Navarro explained that the document referred to in the news report the day before was "not in any way a draft of a document prepared by the Holy See, but rather by the Polish and German Episcopal Conferences."[15] Thus the Vatican continues to deny what the rest of the world knows is the truth.

Numerous examples could be given showing that Catholicism prepared the way for the Holocaust, but we must confine ourselves to just a few. A Catholic Church in Deggendorf, Bavaria, had for centuries displayed a picture commemorating that town's historic slaughter of all Jews "out of legitimate zeal pleasing to God." The inscription under the picture read: "God grant that our fatherland be forever free from this hellish scum."[16] The display offended neither people nor prelates, being consistent with Roman Catholicism's historic treatment of Jews. A French Jewish scholar concluded that the Church had actually prepared the German Catholics for Hitler:

> Without centuries of Christian [Roman Catholic] catechism, preaching and vituperation, the Hitlerian teachings, propaganda and vituperation would not have been possible.[17]

## Hitler's Rise to Power

At first the Church was opposed to Hitler. "After the smashing election victory of the Nazis in 1930, representatives of all important Catholic organizations met . . . to discuss ways of halting the threatening brown tide."[18] But after the July 1932 Reichstag elections, during which "the National Socialists polled 37.4 percent of the popular vote and elected 230 deputies . . . [making] them the largest single party in the Reichstag," the Catholic Bishops began to ease their criticism.

In spite of the fact that "all dioceses had declared membership in the Nazi party to be inadmissible," hundreds of thousands of Catholics had joined and probably several million were supporting it with their votes. Why chase these good Catholics from the Church? After all, the pope and cardinals in Italy praised and supported Mussolini's Fascist party there, so why not in Germany?

On March 13, 1933, at a conference of Bavarian bishops, Cardinal Faulhaber, just back from Rome, reported that "the Holy Father, Pius XI, had publicly praised the Chancellor Adolf Hitler for the stand which he had taken against Communism. . . . [R]eports were circulating again that the Vatican was anxious for the friendly co-operation of German Catholics with the Hitler government. . . . "

On March 23, Hitler announced that "the government of the Reich, [which] regards Christianity [Catholicism] as the unshakable foundation of the morals and the moral code of the nation, attach[es] the greatest value to friendly relations with the Holy See and [is] endeavoring to develop them." Five days later the German bishops publicly withdrew their previous opposition to the Nazi Party.[19] The strategy that Hitler had earlier outlined to Rauschning was working:

> We should trap the priests by their notorious greed and self-indulgence. We shall thus be able to settle everything with them in perfect peace and harmony. . . . Why should we quarrel? They will swallow anything in order to keep their material advantages.[20]

## The Church and the Third Reich

Catholics in increasing numbers rallied to the support of Hitler's Third Reich. Organizations such as *Kreuz und Adler* (Cross and Eagle) were formed with leading Catholic professors of theology such as Otto Schilling and Theodor Brauer, newspapermen like Emil Ritter and Eugen Kogon, and other

Catholic leaders pledged to support the new Nazi Regime.[21] Hitler assured the Church it had nothing to fear from National Socialism so long as it cooperated fully. The bishops "called for the support of the government's program of 'spiritual, moral and economic rejuvenation.'"[22]

That Hitler was a Catholic in good standing made his promises of peaceful partnership with the Church believable. He had been raised in a traditional Catholic family, had regularly attended Mass, had served as an altar boy, had hoped at one time to become a priest, and had attended school as a boy in a Benedictine monastery at Lambach. The abbot was heavily involved in the occult and Eastern mysticism, and it was at this monastery that Hitler first encountered the Hindu swastika which he later adopted. Nor did Hitler neglect to attend Catholic Church services from time to time even after he came to power.

G.S. Graber, a specialist on the history of the SS, informs us that "Himmler's Catholicism was very important to him. He attended church regularly, took Communion, confessed, and prayed."[23] Himmler's December 15, 1919, entry in his diary read: "Come what may, I shall always love God, shall pray to Him, shall remain faithful to the Catholic Church, and shall defend it. . . ."[24]

After the war, escape was the paramount aim for SS members, of which nearly one-quarter were Catholics.[25] Many would be successful in eluding Allied justice and reaching havens, mainly in South America. Tens of thousands of the worst Nazi war criminals—most of them Catholics—would travel the secret "Ratlines" to a new life. The principle agent in their escape would be the Vatican.

Himmler was able to compartmentalize his life so that, as head of the infamous SS, he could oversee the murder of millions of people with the stroke of a pen or by verbal orders to his underlings through his vast organization, but could not pull the trigger himself. He was willing to wipe out the Jews or any other elements in society that he deemed undesirable. However, "he did not want to see [with his own eyes] the blood flow . . . because this would induce soul-searching, not to mention stomach cramps."[26]

An audio and typed copy with authenticated handwritten notes of Himmler's October 4, 1943, speech in Posen, Poland, to 100 German secret police generals was recently discovered and is on display in the new Holocaust Museum in Washington D.C. In it Himmler said:

> I also want to talk to you, quite frankly, on a very grave matter. Among ourselves it should be mentioned quite frankly, and yet we will never speak of it publicly.
> I mean . . . the extermination of the Jewish race. This is a page of glory in our history which has never been written and is never to be written.[27]

SS Colonel Rudolf Hoess, Commandant of Auschwitz and one of the greatest mass murderers in history, was also raised in a devoutly Catholic family that hoped to see him become a priest. He was devoted to his family, fond of animals, and a fanatical believer in Hitler's Nazi religion. In his autobiography he said, "Let the public continue to regard me as the bloodthirsty beast, the cruel sadist . . . [they] could not understand that [the Commandant of Auschwitz] had a heart and that he was not evil."[28]

The SS, in many respects, was patterned after the Jesuit Order, which Himmler had studied and admired. Amazingly, the SS oath ended "So help me God." Its catechism "consisted of a series of questions and answers along the following lines: Q: Why do we believe in Germany and the Fuehrer? A: Because we believe in God, we believe in Germany which He created in His world and in the Fuehrer Adolf Hitler, whom He has sent to us."

The Jews could be exterminated in the name of God by good Catholics because for centuries their Church had demonstrated this to be God's will by its relentless persecution and slaughter of those despised "Christ-rejecters."

From the very beginning Hitler, who was "well aware of the [Catholic] Church's long anti-Jewish record,"[29] made no secret of his plans for the Jews. Meeting with Church representatives Bishop Berning and Monsignor Steinmann on April 26, 1933, "he reminded his visitors that the [Catholic] Church for 1500 years had regarded the Jews as parasites, had banished them into ghettos, and had forbidden Christians to work for them. . . . He, Hitler, merely intended to do more effectively what the Church had attempted to accomplish for so long."[30]

There is no indication that the two Catholic prelates disagreed with him. How could they without denouncing numerous infallible popes and their own infallible Church?

*Above all I have learned from the Jesuits. And so did Lenin too, as far as I recall. The world has never known anything quite so splendid as the hierarchical structure of the Catholic Church. There were quite a few things I simply appropriated from the Jesuits for the use of the Party.*

—Adolf Hitler[1]

*Soldiers returning from the Eastern Front were telling horrible stories, how in occupied Russia Jewish civilians—men, women and children— were being lined up and machine-gunned by the thousands.*

*... In the spring of 1942 the leaflets of the "White Rose," composed by a group of students and a professor of philosophy at the University of Munich, told of the murder of 300,000 Jews in Poland and asked why the German people [about 43 percent were Catholic] remained so apathetic in the face of these revolting crimes.*[2]

# 19

# The Vatican, the Nazis, and the Jews

Hitler's intention to exterminate the Jews was known by the Vatican before it signed the concordat, yet the Holocaust never became a factor in the Church's subsequent dealings with the Fuehrer. On April 1, 1933, about four months *before* the Vatican would sign its concordat with him, Hitler began his systematic program with a boycott against the Jews. He justified it with these words: "I believe that I act today in unison with the Almighty Creator's intention. By fighting the Jews I do battle for the Lord." When the Italian ambassador, speaking for Mussolini, asked Hitler to reconsider his harsh attitude toward the Jews, Hitler "predicted 'with absolute certainty' that in five or six hundred years the name of Hitler would be honored in all lands 'as the man who once and for all exterminated the Jewish pest from the world.'"[3]

Hitler had the backing of many German psychiatrists who would later declare that Himmler, Hoess, and the other Nazi mass murderers were quite "normal." As for the German psychiatrists' feelings about the Jews, Carl Jung expressed the view of many when, as president of the New German Society of Psychotherapy, he wrote:

> The Arian unconscious has a higher potential than the Jewish. . . . Freud [a Jew] . . . knew the German soul as little as his idolators knew it. Did they learn something

from the powerful appearance of National Socialism upon which the world looks with amazed eyes...?[4]

SS Lieutenant Colonel Adolph Eichmann's role as director of the extermination of Jews from all over Nazi-occupied Europe was just a job and had nothing to do with God or religion. Unlike Catholics, he had no quarrel with Jews. Even Simon Wiesenthal, who devoted his life to tracking down Nazi war criminals, said that Eichmann had "no motive, no hatred [against Jews in particular]. . . . He would have done the same job if he had been ordered to kill all men whose name began with P or B, or all who had red hair."[5]

For Hitler, however, the Holocaust was a highly spiritual undertaking. In line with his conviction that he was doing God's will in exterminating the Jews, Hitler ordered that the Final Solution be executed "as humanely as possible." In spite of his persecution of the Church whenever he perceived that it stood in his way, Hitler insisted to the very end, "I am now as before a Catholic and will always remain so." He was convinced that the plan he had conceived as a good Catholic would complete the massacre of "those Christ killers" which the Catholic Church had begun during the Middle Ages but had executed so poorly. John Toland explains:

> The extermination, therefore, could be done without a twinge of conscience since he was merely acting as the avenging hand of God—so long as it was done impersonally, without cruelty. Himmler was pleased to murder with mercy. He ordered technical experts to devise gas chambers which would eliminate masses of Jews efficiently and "humanely," then crowded the victims into boxcars and sent them east to stay in ghettos until the killing centers in Poland were completed.[6]

## Church Support of Nazi Anti-Semitism

Hermann Goering and Franz von Papen on their mission to work out a concordat were well-received at the Vatican. Rome's friendly attitude toward the Nazi regime was made clear. Had no one read *Mein Kampf*? Of course they had, but

Rome and Berlin had much in common, including persecution and killing of Jews. There was no lack of Catholic leaders who openly supported the purge of Jews. During the years 1933-39, the writings of leading Catholics, "all published in journals edited by priests or in books bearing the *Imprimatur*" presented ideas such as the following:

> The Jews had a "demoralizing influence on religiosity and national character." [They] had brought the German people "more damage than benefit." The Jews had displayed "a mortal hatred for Jesus, while the Aryan Pontius Pilate would gladly have let him go free." ... The Jews ... "in their boundless hatred of Christianity were still in the forefront of those seeking to destroy the Church."[7]

Curate Roth, who became an official in the Nazi Ministry of Ecclesiastical Affairs, called the Jews "a morally inferior race who would have to be eliminated from public life." Dr. Haeuser, in a book with the *Imprimatur* of the diocese of Regensburg, called the Jews "Germany's cross, a people disowned by God and under their own curse [who] carried much of the blame for Germany having lost the [First World] War. . . ." Father Senn called Hitler "the tool of God, called upon to overcome Judaism." Nazism, he said, provided "the last big opportunity to throw off the Jewish Yoke."[8]

The Church cooperated fully with the Nazis "in sorting out people of Jewish descent. . . ." A priest wrote in the *Klerusblatt*, "We shall do our best to help in this service to the people." The Church continued this diabolical "cooperation" all through the war, even when being Jewish meant "deportation and outright physical destruction."[9] The Church was well aware of the Jews' dread fate. In a speech on January 30, 1939, only months before his attack upon Poland began the war, Hitler had declared that if war broke out it would result in "the extermination of the Jewish race."[10]

Hitler's totalitarianism was approved by the Church so long as it could be his partner. Guenter Lewy's extensive sifting through the relevant documents of the entire Nazi period indicates that "the Holy See was no more opposed to the central political doctrines of Nazism than the German bishops themselves."[11] Cardinal Faulhaber "went out of his way to make clear that he was not concerned with defending his Jewish contemporaries." One had to distinguish, he said, between the Jews before the crucifixion of Christ and afterward. In 1939, Archbishop Grober declared that—

> Jesus Christ...had been fundamentally different from the Jews of his time—so much so that they had hated him and demanded his crucifixion, and "their murderous hatred has continued in later centuries."
>
> Jesus had been a Jew, admitted Bishop Hilfrich of Limburg...in 1939, but "the Christian religion has... had to make its way against this people."
>
> Theologian Karl Adam defended the preservation of the German people's pure blood as a justified act of self defense, for... "the myth of the German, his culture and his history are decisively shaped by blood."
>
> An article on the revolution of 1918 in the paper of the Bavarian priests exposed the role of the Jews in this stab in the back of the undefeated German army [and on and on it went in similar vein].[12]

Cardinal Bertram, head of the East German church province, and Archbishop Grober, head of the Upper Rhenish province, along with other bishops, expressed concern for the dismissals of Catholic civil servants by the new government. At the same time, however, the bishops rejected reports of brutality in the new concentration camps. Grober even became a "promoting member" of the SS and kept up his financial contributions to the bitter end.

## What the Vatican and German Bishops Knew

Nazism was opposed by Catholic leaders only where it conflicted with "Church matters and interests." Thus while remaining silent regarding the Holocaust as a whole, the Church spoke up for and attempted to protect Jewish converts to Catholicism. That fact makes its failure to oppose the Nazi extermination of Jews all the more reprehensible.[13] "There were 30 million Catholics in Germany. Although Jews were helped secretly [by some Catholic individuals], the Church never publicly recognized that the defense of the Jews was a Christian duty."[14] The Vatican sternly banned other books, but it never put *Mein Kampf* or the poisonous anti-Semitic works of numerous Church leaders on its *Index* of forbidden reading.[15]

Joseph Muller, a military intelligence officer and confidant of Cardinal Faulhaber, "kept the episcopate well informed about the systematic atrocities committed in Poland." So did Hans Globke, a Catholic high official in the Ministry of the Interior "entrusted with handling racial matters." The Vatican and the German bishops, along with most of the German population, knew full well that Jews were being rounded up and exterminated. Viereck reminds us:

> Hitler's extermination-expert, R[udolf] Hoess, wrote in *Commandant of Auschwitz*: "When a strong wind was blowing, the stench of burning flesh was carried for many miles and caused the whole neighborhood to talk about the burning of the Jews." He notes, of still another camp, that whenever a bus with victims drove past, even the German children chortled in the street: "There comes the murder box again!"[16]

The Church well knew what was happening but closed its eyes as well as its lips. Kurt Gerstein, a covert member of the evangelical opposition to Hitler, became an SS officer in order to discover the secret of the extermination camps and tell it to the world. He brought his report to the pope's personal representative in Berlin, who refused to see him when he explained his errand.

"There were tens of thousands of priests in cities, towns, and villages throughout Europe. They saw houses emptied, villagers deported; they heard confessions. They were unusually well informed." Catholic soldiers returned periodically from the Russian front with tales of the wholesale massacres. "The Vatican was among the first to know of the genocidal programs. Authoritative information on the killing was sent to the Vatican by its own diplomats in March 1942."[17]

Hitler flaunted his evil intentions and deeds to the world. The Vatican had no excuse for its Nazi partnership or for its continued commendation of Hitler on the one hand and its thunderous silence regarding the Jewish question on the other hand. As the evil mounted, the Roman Catholic Church continued to work with the Fuehrer and even to praise him. Even after Hitler's troops, in spite of promises to the contrary, marched in and took over the demilitarized Rhineland, Catholic leaders all over Germany lauded him, among them Cardinal Schulte in Cologne's cathedral. [18]

The concordat with Hitler was nothing new. The popes had been partners with evil rulers for centuries. Would Jesus make a deal with Pilate or the apostle Peter with Nero? Yet those who claimed to be Peter's successors had been in unholy alliances with pagan emperors from Constantine onward, and continued in the alliance with Hitler until the end of the war, reaping hundreds of millions of dollars in payments from the Nazi government to the Vatican.

## The Moral Failure of Silence

Pius XII was known for his outspoken warnings to the faithful against the "abuse of human rights,"[19] yet he was silent about the Holocaust. He never spoke a public word against Hitler's systematic extermination of the Jews, because to do so would have condemned his own Church for its similar deeds. This silence, historians agree, encouraged Hitler and added to the unspeakable genocide.

The pope boasted that he was the moral watchdog for the world, yet said nothing in the face of the worst crime in human history. In his first encyclical, issued in October 1939, Pius XII declared that his office as Christ's vicar demanded that he "testify to the truth with Apostolic firmness." He went on to explain:

> This duty necessarily entails the exposition and confutation of errors and human faults; for these must be made known before it is possible to tend and to heal them. . . .
> In the fulfillment of this our duty we shall not let ourselves be influenced by earthly considerations nor be

held back by mistrust or opposition, by rebuffs or lack of appreciation of our words, nor yet by the fear of misconceptions and misinterpretations.[20]

These were high-sounding words, but proved to be absolutely empty. The very day Pius XII commenced his pontificate, Mussolini expelled Italy's 69,000 Jews and the pope said nothing. A few weeks later Italy invaded Albania. The pope protested, but "not because a country had been wantonly attacked, but because the aggression had been carried out on a Good Friday."[21] This was Christ's "vicar"?

Like their pope, the German bishops repeatedly promised "fearlessly to condemn injustice." In 1936 Cardinal Faulhaber declared that a bishop could not be God's servant "if he were to speak to please men or remain silent out of fear of men." In July 1941, Bishop Galen claimed to be the defender of every man's God-given "basic rights and liberties" and that his duty was to "courageously . . . brand as an injustice crying to heaven the condemnation of defenseless innocents." Similar empty rhetoric was thundered from pulpits by other bishops, all of whom remained silent while 6 million Jews were systematically exterminated like so much vermin. The continued hypocrisy more than proves this is not the true Church.

Joseph Cardinal Ratzinger, now in his third five-year term as head of the modern equivalent of the Holy Inquisition, served in the military in Germany during the war, though he saw no combat. By his own admission he was aware of the Holocaust. No German could have been totally ignorant. "The abyss of Hitlerism could not be overlooked," Ratzinger now confesses.[22] Yet he overlooked it when it would have cost him something to speak out against it.

Surely now, as the watchdog of orthodoxy and the longest-serving and most powerful official in the Vatican next to the pope, Ratzinger could make amends both for his own silence and that of his Church all during the Holocaust. Why not offer genuine repentance and sorrowful apology to the Jews? But Ratzinger and John Paul II continue Pius XII's stony silence. And how could they apologize without admitting that their popes and Church have sinned grievously against Christ's natural brethren, and thus that the very claim to infallibility and being the one true Church is a fraud?

## No Escape from Guilt

It has been argued that had the pope protested, as many begged him to, it would only have made things worse for the Jews. Could it have been any worse? Did the Vatican's silence save anyone? Obviously not. De Rosa puts it so well: "There was one man in the world whose witness Hitler feared, since many in his armies were Catholics. That one man did not speak. In the face of what Winston Churchill was to call 'probably the greatest and most horrible single crime ever committed in the whole history of the world' he chose to stay neutral."[23]

The Church minced no words in opposing the Nazi euthanasia program and succeeded in stopping it. The bishops spoke out against the mistreatment of Jews who had become Catholics and against classifying as Jews Catholics who were only partially Jewish. It opposed the forced divorce of Jews married to Catholics and the subsequent deportation of the Jewish partner. But it never spoke out against the destruction of the Jews. As Guenter Lewy said:

> When thousands of German anti-Nazis were tortured to death in Hitler's concentration camps, when the Polish intelligentsia was slaughtered, when hundreds of thousands of Russians died as the result of being treated as Slavic Untermenschen [subhumans], and when 6,000,000 human beings were murdered for being "non-Aryan," Catholic church officials in Germany bolstered the regime perpetrating these crimes. The Pope in Rome, the spiritual head and supreme moral teacher of the Roman Catholic Church, remained silent.
>
> In the face of these greatest of moral depravities which mankind has been forced to witness in recent centuries, the moral teachings of a Church [allegedly] dedicated to love and charity could be heard in no other form but vague generalities.[24]

When, in February 1943, the Gestapo in the process of deporting the last German Jews to the East for death "seized several thousand Christian non-Aryans in mixed marriages [about 6,000 in Berlin alone] . . . something unexpected and unparalleled happened. Their Aryan wives followed them to the place of temporary detention and there they stood for hours screaming and howling for their men. With the secrecy of the whole machinery of destruction threatened, the Gestapo yielded and the non-Aryan husbands were released. Here was an example of what an outraged conscience could achieve, even against Hitler's terror apparatus."[25]

When Edoardo Senatro, *L'Osservatore Romano* corresponaent in Berlin, "asked Pius XII whether he would not protest the extermination of the Jews, the pope reportedly answered, 'Do not forget that millions of Catholics serve in the German armies. Shall I bring them into conflicts of conscience?'" Guenter Lewy sums it up:

> The Pope knew that the German Catholics were not prepared to suffer martyrdom for their Church; still less were they willing to incur the wrath of their Nazi rulers for the sake of the Jews whom their own bishops for years had castigated as a harmful influence in German life.
>
> In the final analysis . . . the Vatican's silence only reflected the deep feeling of the Catholic masses of Europe—those of Germany and eastern Europe in particular. The failure of the Pope was a measure of the Church's failure to convert her gospel of brotherly love and human dignity into living reality.[26]

## While the World Turned Its Back

Pope Pius XII's silence concerning the Holocaust was, at the first, condoned and encouraged by the United States (President Roosevelt was silent as well), Britain, and "neutral" Switzerland. These countries literally turned fleeing Jews back to the Nazis and certain death. In the crucial months when there was still a chance for many Jews to leave Germany, the U.S. State Department deliberately blocked the immigration of Jews and delayed processing valid papers until the applicants were hauled off to Nazi extermination camps.

Such was the fruit of the anti-Semitism which was rampant in the 1920s and 1930s across America. It was one of the blackest pages of American history. The horrifying facts of America's complicity in the Holocaust at the highest levels of government were presented in part on April 6, 1994, on television by the Public Broadcasting System:

> [Senators and Congressmen] openly spewed anti-Semitic poison in the very halls of the nation's capital. ...There were anti-Semitic campaigns conducted by over 100 organizations across America....
>
> Father Charles Coughlin, a Catholic priest, was the most influential anti-Semitic spokesman in the country. His radio broadcast reached more than 3 million people.[27]

Documents recently uncovered prove that both the United States and England were unwilling to take Jews in and obstructed their emigration. Far from pressuring Hitler to stop the killings, England and America feared that the Fuehrer, if unduly pressed, might dump thousands of Jews on the Americans and British. It was the last thing those hypocritical governments wanted in spite of their public hand-wringing about Nazi atrocities. The Western powers, like the Vatican and in partnership with it, were actually accomplices in the Holocaust. The truth is almost too terrible to face.

No less significant is the fact that the Church never excommunicated Hitler, Mussolini, Himmler, or any of the other key players in the Holocaust. They remained Catholics to the end under the shelter of Mother Church. Moreover, the Church has deliberately lied about its role, spreading "a legend of resistance" to the Nazis that needs to be corrected.[28] Except in rare instances of a few individuals, there was collaboration, not resistance. Furthermore, those who worked with the Nazis, far from being reprimanded, were rewarded by Rome. Guenter Lewy provides a few examples:

> This concealment [of the truth about Catholic cooperation] has been so bold and successful that in Germany . . . not a single bishop had to resign his office [for cooperation with the Nazis].
>
> Quite the contrary, Bishop Berning, who had served until the downfall of Hitler in Goering's Prussian State

Council, in 1949 was given the honorary title of Archbishop. Herr von Papen [who helped negotiate the 1933 concordat] was made Papal Privy Chamberlain in 1959.

Such rewards for men deeply involved with the Nazi regime represent a mockery of heroic figures ... who died fighting Hitler.[29]

Pius XII claimed that his encyclicals were just as binding upon the Church as ex cathedra declarations.[30] Therefore, had he given a directive to the members of his Church the chances are that he could have brought down Hitler at the very beginning. The sequence of events, with the Roman Catholic Church literally putting Hitler in power and supporting him thereafter, disproves the claim by the popes that they are Christ's vicars and led of the Holy Spirit.

## Anti-Semitism on the Rise

Memories are short and deceitful, and the conscience of the world is easily hardened, necessitating a recent ad by the United Jewish Appeal which has appeared in major magazines. It displays a picture of a black-shirted, unofficial military unit in today's Russia (apparently connected with the surprising rise to power of Fascist fanatic, Vladimir Zhirinovsky), giving the Fascist extended arm salute. Headlined "FOR JEWS IN THE FORMER SOVIET UNION, THE EXIT SIGNS ARE CLEARLY MARKED," the appeal goes on to state:

> The signs are all too familiar. Black-shirted Fascists march. Synagogues mysteriously go up in flames. Right-wing extremist Vladimir Zhirinovsky rants against Jews and "Zionist plots." And his party wins more votes than any other in Russia.
>
> Once again, opportunists blame terrible conditions on their traditional scapegoat—the Jews.
>
> And for Jews, anti-Semitism just adds to the misery of life in the former Soviet Union: severe economic hardship. Political instability. The depressing lack of opportunity for an education, for a better life.

**But there is hope. Operation Exodus.**

So far, the UJA-Federation Operation Exodus Campaign has helped rescue 500,000 Jews from the former Soviet Union—69,132 in 1993 alone. And brought them home to Israel.

Yet 1.4 million Jews remain. With your support, they can leave the hatred and despair behind. Before it's too late.

Please give generously to Operation Exodus and the Annual Campaign. This time we can clearly see what's happening over there. And all the signs point in the same direction. Out.

**Call Operation Exodus now at 1-800-880-1426. Or call your local Jewish Federation.**

The former Soviet republics are not the only places where there is an obvious renewed threat to Jewish life and culture. Anti-Semitism is on the rise everywhere, including the United States. A recent Associated Press dispatch reported:

> Anti-Semitic assaults, threats and harassment jumped 23 percent in the United States last year. . . . The ADL (Anti-Defamation League) reported 1867 anti-Semitic acts overall in 1993, the second-highest number in the survey's 15-year history. The highest was 1879 in 1991. The 1992 total was 1730.
>
> The survey found 1079 reports of anti-Semitic assaults, threats and harassment, compared with 874 in 1992. The worst incidents included an arson and a bombing. No deaths or serious injuries resulted. . . .
>
> Alan Swartz, ADL research director, also cited renewed efforts by a Holocaust revisionist to place ads in college newspapers stating that the Holocaust never happened.[31]

The Hebrew prophets foretold such hatred and abuse of God's chosen people and that (except for periodic times of apparent relief) it would not end until Jesus Christ returns to this earth to rescue His people (Zehariah 12:10). Behind much of the anti-Jewish propaganda and violence worldwide it is only logical to suspect the machinations of the anti-Semitic war criminals to whom the Vatican, by smuggling them out to South America, gave a new opportunity to carry on their evil work.

The callous indifference to the Holocaust when it was in process and the desire to have it fade into the forgotten past is what one might expect from those who make no pretense of knowing God. The Vatican, however, claims to represent Christ and to set the moral standard for the world. The pope periodically preaches peace and love and lectures others for their moral failures, yet his Church's hands are stained with the blood of millions of innocent victims.

## The Duplicity Continues

In 1986, John Paul II went to Rome's synagogue, not far from his palace. In his speech there he deplored the crimes of the past committed against the Jews "by anyone." When he repeated that last phrase, spontaneous applause broke out. The pope and chief rabbi Elio Toaff embraced. However, the implied regret for abuse of the Jews by his Church was a weak ploy. What was needed was a specific admission of exactly what the Church had done to the Jews, from their confinement in ghettos and slaughter throughout history to its partnership with the Nazis in the Holocaust. Without such an admission and full apology all other polite gestures are deceptive.

On December 30, 1993, after 18 months of intensive negotiations, Msgr. Claudio Maria Celli, undersecretary for foreign states at the papal Secretariat of State, and Dr. Yossi Beilin, Israel's deputy foreign minister, signed a 14-article "Fundamental Agreement" establishing full diplomatic relations between the Vatican and Israel. Its preamble refers to "the unique nature of the relationship between the Catholic Church and the Jewish people" as well as the "historic process of reconciliation" and the "growth in mutual understanding and friendship between Catholics and Jews."[32]

The "unique nature of the relationship between the Catholic Church and the Jewish people" has been that of persecutor and persecuted, slayer and slain. As for the "historic process of reconciliation," the repentance by Rome to start the process is still missing. How can a meaningful reconciliation take place unless the party which has so horribly abused the other is willing to make a full confession, a sincere apology, and serious restitution?

Since the establishment of the Jewish state in 1948, Rome had for nearly 46 years refused to even acknowledge Israel's existence. Even now it insists that Jerusalem must be an international city not governed by Israel. Why then the current "agreement"? With Israel's borders and relationship to the PLO being redefined, the Vatican realizes that to have a say in Israel's future it must establish diplomatic relations with her. And it wants that influence.

Present Israeli leaders apparently have forgotten that it took the Italian army to liberate the Jews from Rome's Vatican-imposed ghetto. Forgotten, too, must be Pius X's statement which Golda Meir quotes in her *Autobiography*: "We cannot prevent the Jews from going to Jerusalem, but we would never sanction it. . . . The Jews have not recognized our Lord; we cannot recognize the Jews." It is dangerous to trust those whose past words and consistent deeds for centuries give the lie to the "agreement" now being reached.

In the agreement the Vatican requires Israel's pledge "to observe the human right to freedom of religion and conscience." What unmitigated gall! Rome has never been willing to grant such rights to others whenever it has been in control. We have thoroughly documented that Roman Catholicism is the sworn enemy of freedom of speech, religion, and the press, and that popes have consistently suppressed these freedoms whenever they had the power to do so.

The agreement, furthermore, commits Israel and the Vatican to work together against anti-Semitism. Of what value is such an agreement without Rome's admission that she has. practiced the most vicious anti-Semitism for centuries, and without her sincere apology for having done so? Without that minimal gesture, the agreement is cause for weeping rather than rejoicing on Israel's part.

## History Still Cries Out

Rome's deceitful attempt to cover its anti-Semitism is found also in Vatican II. There the Jews, though not named, are alluded to as those "from which Christ was born according to the flesh" and are called "most dear for the sake of the fathers. . . ."[33] That statement hardly squares with the way

Rome has treated God's chosen people throughout history. One despairs of hearing truth from such a source. The next sentence presents a lie no less brazen:

> But the plan of salvation also includes those who acknowledge the Creator, in the first place amongst whom are the Moslems; these profess to hold the faith of Abraham, and together with us they adore the one, merciful God, mankind's judge on the last day.[34]

What blasphemy to call Islam's Allah the Creator and thus identify the ancient Kaaba's chief pagan deity (the god of Muhammad's Quraish tribe) with Jahweh, the God of the Bible. Islam specifically denies that Allah is a father or has a son or that he is a triune being of Father, Son, and Holy Spirit; Islam thus has no explanation for "Let *us* make man in *our* image" (Genesis 1:26). Allah is merciful only to those who do good and he hates sinners, whereas the true God *is love* and He loves all. Allah is a distant god with whom it is impossible to have a personal relationship, since he lacks the attributes of holiness, grace, and love, and he authors evil. Allah is the very antithesis of the God of Abraham, Isaac, and Jacob.

As for holding "the faith of Abraham," that patriarch looked forward to the coming of Christ as God's Lamb who would die for our sins (Genesis 22:8; John 1:29; 8:56)—a truth which Muslims adamantly oppose. Islam denies that Jesus is God or God's Son, denies that He died on the cross for our sins (someone else allegedly died in His place), and of course it denies His resurrection. Yet this section in Vatican II suggests that the Muslims are nevertheless included in "the plan of salvation." We will come back to Rome's incredible ecumenism in a later chapter.

Allah is Jahweh and Islam is the "faith of Abraham"? Is Rome being generous to the Muslims in order to curry their favor? In fact, this section in Vatican II suggests that everyone, even idol worshipers, will eventually come under the saving umbrella of the Roman Catholic Church—everyone, that is, except Protestants. There are limits to Rome's generosity, though her iron fist is now clothed in a velvet glove. Israel is being wooed at the moment, but common sense tells us that the motives are less than pure. History still cries for our attention.

Jerusalem has its *Yad Vashem* (Holocaust Museum) to keep ever before the world's conscience the 6 million Jews killed by Hitler. In contrast, there is no memorial to the untold millions of both Jews and Christians murdered by Holy Mother Church. The deceptively sweet words emanating from the Vatican cannot eliminate the haunting question from recent history which Guenter Lewy raises:

> When Hitler set out on his murderous campaign against the Jews of Europe, truth and justice found few defenders. The Deputy [Vicar] of Christ and the German [Catholic] episcopate were not among them. Their role gives a special relevance to the question the young girl in Max Frisch's *Andorra* asks her priest: "Where were you, Father Benedict, when they took away our brother like a beast to the slaughter, like a beast to the slaughter, where were you?"
>
> This question still waits for an answer.[35]

*A good Ustashi is one who can use a knife to cut a child from the womb of its mother.*

— Ante Pavelic, Croatian Fuehrer[1]

*Ante Pavelic, as* poglavnik *(Fuehrer) of the nation of Croatia, and Stejpan Hefer, as governor-general of Baranja County, assured their places in history atop the mutilated bodies of nearly a million victims. . . .*

*Both were middle-aged Roman Catholics . . . members of parliament [and] participated in the genocide of their countrymen, in murders carried out with sadism that would shock even their Nazi allies [and] both would escape [after the war] to Argentina [via the Vatican Ratlines] to resurrect their movement in exile.*

— Scott and Jon Lee Anderson
*Inside The League*

# 20

# The Slaughter
# of the Serbs

The Vatican's backing of Hitler and Mussolini and the Nazi puppet regime in France during the Second World War was consistent with its desire to resurrect the Holy Roman Empire with secular leaders doing Rome's bidding. Such has long been the Vatican dream and still is. France (which Pius XI called "the first-born of the great Catholic Family"), together with Italy and Germany, were Europe's principal Catholic countries where the Church held great power. Their governments were willing to work with the Church and even to establish formal relations through concordats.

Soviet Communism's aggressive atheism and its ruthless destruction of churches made it the foremost enemy which Catholicism had yet encountered in its long existence. Capitalist democracies, too, with their penchant for freedom of conscience, religion, and press, were incompatible with Roman Catholicism. So it was that Fascism in the 1920s and 1930s seemed to offer the best hope of uniting Catholic Europe as a bulwark against the rising red tide of world Communism and the growing threat of democracies.

The Vatican realized it was in a war to the death against Marxism-Leninism. It seemed essential to join in partnership with the emerging forces of Fascism in Western Europe. The 1929 concordat with Mussolini and the 1933 concordat with Hitler were part of this policy. These important alliances reflected the skillful diplomacy of Eugenio Maria Giuseppe Giovanni Pacelli, who was Vatican Secretary of State, on his way to succeeding Pius XI as Pope Pius XII just before World War II would break out in 1939. Both Mussolini and Hitler were Catholics and their leadership would strengthen European Catholicism. The Vatican's imperialism could grow side by side with Italy's and Germany's.

## The Intermarium

In the closing days of World War I, Pacelli, already a rising star in the Vatican's eyes, had been the Papal Nuncio in Munich. He had negotiated secretly for the Vatican with the Central Powers to save Germany and Austria-Hungary from defeat. These Catholic countries were vital to the Vatican's interests in Europe. Their breakup into smaller states would mean the formation of countries in which Catholics would be a minority and the Church would thus lose its dominant position, so important to its ambitions.

President Wilson, however, had been determined to grant independence to the Southern Slavs. Thus were born the independent states of Czechoslovakia and Yugoslavia. Suddenly the Catholic Croatians found themselves a minority in a new country controlled by the Eastern Orthodox Church. To change this unhappy situation, the Vatican launched a campaign to destroy Orthodoxy in Yugoslavia and to counter the growing threat of Communism in that land.

In pursuit of these twin goals, the Vatican made contact in the 1920s with a group of "White" Russian intelligentsia who had fled the Bolshevik takeover and were determined to return to defeat "the Reds." As this coterie of conspirators grew it became known as Intermarium—an international underground committee to liberate and unite the peoples of the "Intermare" region bounded by the Baltic, Black, Aegean, Ionian, and Adriatic Seas. This buffer zone of more than a dozen states would theoretically seal off the Communists to the East from a new united Catholic Europe. As Intermarium's potential grew so did its support from the Vatican, even though by the 1930s it was clearly a Fascist group involved in international terrorism. Among its most vicious and sadistic leaders was a man named Ante Pavelic, who was destined to be of great service both to Hitler and the Vatican as the head of a Nazi puppet regime in Yugoslavia known as the Ustasha.

World Communism has been an evil beyond imagination, responsible for the slaughter of untold millions and the unlawful imprisonment and torture of multitudes more. Unfortunately, many of those who made it their lifework to oppose Communism were its equals in savagery. After World War II the World Anti-Communist League was infiltrated by "terrorists, Nazis, and Latin American [former Ustasha] death squads."[2] The Ustasha's background is important.

## Ante Pavelic and the Catholic Croatian Underground

The lawful leaders of Croatia, though Catholics, were suspicious of the political ambitions of the Vatican and justifiably unwilling to aid its efforts. Thus it was necessary to form an illegal army of pro-Vatican terrorists. This group of Ustashi was led by Intermarium leader Ante Pavelic in partnership with Croatian Archbishop Aloysius Stepinac. These two arch-criminals were responsible for numerous assassinations including Yugoslavian King Alexander and French Foreign Minister Barthou (1934), as well as Croat Peasant Party leader Radich (1928). (The latter had warned against and opposed the machinations of the Vatican and thus had to be removed.)

As the mastermind behind the murders in France of Alexander and Barthou, Pavelic was sentenced to death by the French but managed to escape. He had already been condemned to death in absentia by the Yugoslavian government five years earlier. Mussolini, out of loyalty to the Vatican, gave Pavelic asylum in Italy and refused both French and Yugoslavian demands for his extradition.

All over Europe, under Pavelic's leadership, the Ustashi were responsible for murders, bombings in public places, blackmail, threats, and other acts of terror aimed at disruption of order in Yugoslavia and the formation of an independent Catholic Croatian state. Vatican diplomacy did its part to further the same goal. Backed with funds from both Mussolini and the Vatican, the Ustasha grew in numbers and power; thus, when Hitler moved into Yugoslavia, it was ready to operate a Nazi puppet regime headed by Pavelic.

Ante Pavelic and his Ustashi had a propaganda machine which turned out Nationalistic Croatian historical revisionism and racial hatred calculated to appeal to the lowest level of prejudice and superstition. Croatia's population in the late 1920s was comprised of about 3 million Roman Catholics, nearly 2 million Serbians of Eastern Orthodox faith, a million Muslims, and about 50,000 Jews. The Ustashi held out an appealing solution for those who wanted the Croatians in control of their country: All non-Catholics and non-Croatians would be removed either by deportation or liquidation.

In order to achieve that goal, Croatia had to gain its independence from Yugoslavia. To that end, Pavelic had already in 1929 established training camps for his Ustashi guerrillas in Hungary and Italy. From these bases the Ustashi sallied forth to commit their acts of terror against the Yugoslavian government. The Ustashi guerrillas were trained by the Italian Fascist militia, wore their black uniforms, aped the goose-step and outstretched-arm salute, and eagerly awaited the day when they would "liberate" their country. That moment came when the German army entered the Croatian capital of Zagreb and summoned Pavelic from Italy.

The Nazis, fulfilling the Vatican's desire, declared Croatia to be an independent nation and set up Ante Pavelic as the head of their puppet regime. Pavelic immediately launched his extermination program. His friend Stejpan Hefer was made governor-general of the county of Baranja, where he zealously enforced the Ustasha creed. "It meant that the slaughter of Serbs and the deportation of Jews [to Nazi death camps] was official state policy carried out by vigilante bands of Croatian terror squads that traveled the hills and valleys in search of [non-Catholic] families."[3]

Pavelic reprimanded Hitler for being too lenient in his treatment of the Jews and boasted that in Croatia he had completely solved the "Jewish problem." The approximately 50,000 Jews who had been resident there upon the outbreak of war were quickly either liquidated or shipped to the Nazi killing camps, mainly Auschwitz.

## The Catholic Connection

Most of Croatia's Catholic clergy were fanatically behind Pavelic and his unbelievably evil regime. Medals were even given by Pavelic to nuns and priests, thus betraying the fact that many of them played active roles alongside the Ustashi military. Franciscan monks in particular joined Ustashi battalions. Concerning Pavelic's relationship to top clergy, two investigators write:

> When the Ustashi were ushered into Zagreb by the Germans, Archbishop Stepinac of Croatia immediately offered his congratulations to the *poglavnik* and held a banquet to celebrate the founding of the new nation. [As head of the Croatian Bishops] he ordered the proclamation of the independent state to be delivered from all pulpits of the Catholic Church in Croatia on Easter Sunday and arranged to have Pavelic received by Pope Pius XII [in Rome].[4]

Said Archbishop Stepinac, "God, who directs the destiny of nations and controls the hearts of Kings, has given us Ante Pavelic and moved the leader of a friendly and allied people, Adolf Hitler, to use his victorious troops to disperse our oppressors. . . . Glory be to God, our gratitude to Adolf Hitler and loyalty to our Poglavnik, Ante Pavelic."[5] It was an open partnership between Church and state such as the Vatican loved but had not enjoyed for 300 years. Pavelic's birthday was the occasion for special ceremonies honoring him in all the Catholic churches. Former BBC commentator Avro Manhattan, an expert on Vatican policies, has written:

> . . . here the Catholic Church [erected] a State in complete accord with all her tenets. The result was a monster standing upon the armed might of twin totalitarianisms: the totalitarianism of a ruthless Fascist State and the totalitarianism of Catholicism. . . .
>
> What gives to such a creature of Vatican diplomacy its peculiar importance is that here we have an example of the Catholic Church's implementing all her principles, unhampered by opposition, or by fear of world opinion.

The uniqueness of the Independent Catholic State of Croatia lies precisely in this: that it provided a model, in miniature, of what the Catholic Church, had she the power, would like to see in the West and, indeed, everywhere. As such it should be carefully scrutinized. For its significance... is of the greatest import to all the freedom-loving peoples of the world.[6]

Once Pavelic took power, Archbishop Stepinac issued a Pastoral Letter ordering the Croatian clergy to support the new Ustasha State. The involvement of Catholic clergy either in active participation or in blessing the Ustashi-run holocaust is well-documented. One Franciscan monk, Miroslav Filipovic, headed the Jasenovac concentration camp for two years, during which time he directed the extermination of no less than 100,000 victims, mostly Serbian Orthodox. Archbishop Stepinac headed the committee which was responsible for forcible "conversions" to Roman Catholicism under threat of death and was also the Supreme Military Apostolic Vicar of the Ustashi Army, which effected the slaughter of those who failed to convert. Stepinac was known as the "Father Confessor" to the Ustashi and continually bestowed the blessing of Holy Mother Church upon its members and actions.

After the opening of the Ustasha Parliament, Pavelic attended the Zagreb cathedral, where Archbishop Stepinac offered special prayers for his good friend and ordered a solemn *Te Deum* to be sung in thanks to God for the establishment of the new regime. The reaction of the Catholic Bishop of Mostar to the subsequent slaughter of the Serbs and Jews was to lament not that hundreds of thousands of innocent persons had been tortured and sadistically slaughtered, but that they weren't converted to Catholicism: "If the Lord had given to the authorities more understanding to handle the conversions to Catholicism with skill and intelligence... the number of Catholics would have grown at least [by] 500,000 to 600,000."[7]

Among the most infamous Church officials involved, in addition to Archbishop Stepinac, were Father Vilim Cecelja (later a key figure in the Vatican's escape route for Nazi war criminals), who presided as priest at Pavelic's swearing-in ceremony, and bishops Gregory Rozman of Lubljana and Ivan

Saric of Sarajevo. Cecelja served as Deputy Military Vicar to the Ustashi militia, in which he held the rank of Lieutenant Colonel. Known in Bosnia and Herzegovina as "the hangman of the Serbs," Saric declared that Almighty God was behind the Ustashi movement and that His blessing was specifically upon their determination to free the world of the Jews.

As a reward by the Vatican for his work, Stepinac was later made a cardinal. Though his crimes were well-known, Pavelic was received at the Vatican and blessed by Pope Pius XII. "When the British Minister to the Vatican, in private audience, ventured to draw his [Pius XII's] attention to events in Croatia, the pope referred to Pavelic as 'a much maligned man.'"[8]

## The Slaughter of the Serbs

Unlike the Germans, who were interested only in the quickest and most efficient means of mass extermination, the Catholic Ustashi, with priests and bishops participating and giving their blessing, took great pleasure from "torturing before killing. Most of their victims were not shot but were strangled, drowned, burned, or stabbed to death. Serbs were herded into Orthodox churches by Ustashi [as the crusaders had done with Jews in an earlier age], who then barred the doors and torched the timbers. One captured photograph shows Ustashi smiling for the camera before a table displaying the body of a Serbian businessman whom they had castrated, disemboweled, carved with knives, and burned beyond recognition."[9]

Estimates of the number of victims exceed a million. This is probably a realistic figure. Yugoslavia in its war-crimes trials estimated that from 700,000 to 900,000 victims were "tortured and put to death... [in] the two dozen concentration camps" within Croatia,[10] and tens of thousands never reached the camps. Many were Jews, but most were Serbians of Orthodox faith who were given the choice of conversion to Roman Catholicism or death.

Both in Yugoslavia and the Ukraine, Roman Catholic priests, bishops, and cardinals, with the full knowledge of the Vatican, participated in and gave their blessing to some of the bloodiest and most barbaric massacres of the war, aimed at giving Roman Catholicism control of these regions. Fitzroy Maclean, Britain's military liaison to the anti-Ustasha partisans, wrote in a report:

> The massacres began in earnest at the end of June [1941] and continued throughout the summer, growing in scope and intensity until in August the terror reached its height. The whole of Bosnia ran with blood. Bands of Ustase roamed the countryside with knives, bludgeons and machine guns, slaughtering Serbian men, women and little children, desecrating Serbian churches, murdering Serbian priests, laying waste Serbian villages, torturing, raping, burning, drowning. Killing became a cult, an obsession.
>
> The Ustashi competed among themselves on how many of "the enemy" they could kill. In order to impress the *poglavnik*—Pavelic—and be promoted or singled out for "heroism," the bands would pose with their victims before cameras. Captured photographs—they are too grisly to reproduce—show Ustashi beheading a Serb with an axe, driving a saw through the neck of another, carrying a head through the streets of Zagreb. In all of them, the Ustashi are smiling and crowding themselves into the picture, as if to prove they had a role in the atrocity. Some Ustase collected the eyes of Serbs they had killed, sending them, when they had enough, to the Poglavnik for his inspection or proudly displaying them and other human organs in the cafes of Zagreb.[11]

Even the Nazis were eventually sickened by the atrocities of the Ustashi and intervened on occasion to rescue their victims, disbanding one Ustashi regiment in 1942 to prevent further atrocities. Some Italian troops hid Jews and Serbs from Ustashi bands. Hefer, however, as governor-general of a large area, was able to facilitate the continued killings.

## Postwar Escapes and Misinformation

After the war Archbishop Aloysius Stepinac was arrested by the Yugoslav government and sentenced to 17 years in prison for war crimes. The Vatican propaganda machine portrayed Stepinac as a brave victim of Communist persecution—a portrayal which has continued in the secular media, including such magazines as *Newsweek*.[12] Pope Pius XII elevated Stepinac to cardinal after the war. In Croatian communities around the world, "Cardinal Stepinac Associations" were formed to lobby for the release of this "suffering martyr." Such pressures succeeded in obtaining Stepinac's release from prison after only a few years.

Andrija Artukovic, the admitted Ustashi Minister of Interior and later Minister of Justice under Ante Pavelic,[13] was in charge of the Croatian government's genocide policies, supervised its extermination camps, and in 1986 was described as "probably the most important war criminal still alive and unpunished today."[14] Nevertheless, having been mistakenly released by British Intelligence in Austria in 1945, he entered the United States illegally under the name Alois Anich and lived unmolested in Southern California under his own name until his arrest for a deportation hearing in 1984. Artukovic was defended by fellow Catholics, such as Croatian priest Fr. Cuturic, quoted in a Chicago newspaper:

> And what are they trying to do to one of our real leaders, Andrija Artukovic—Croatian and Catholic—who is being defended by the real champions of freedom, justice, and truth against the godless Jews, Orthodox, communists, protestants everywhere? They call our leader, Andrija Artukovic, a "murderer." No, we Ustashi must keep our dignity.[15]

Finally returned to Yugoslavia in 1985, Artukovic was tried and found guilty of numerous war crimes, including "ordering the killing of the entire population of the town of Vrgin Most and its surrounding villages...."[16] Sentenced to death by firing squad, he died January 16, 1988, at the age of 88 before the sentence could be carried out. To the end, his defenders portrayed Artukovic as the innocent victim of Communist propaganda and persecution.

Names such as Bosnia-Herzegovina and Sarajevo have become known to the world. The Serbs are properly castigated for their aggression and atrocities; yet news reports never mention the 1941-43 massacres of Serbian civilians by the Catholic Ustashi, for which the Serbs are seeking revenge. A *Reader's Digest* article by a journalist authority on Yugoslavia mentions the Ustashi without a word about their slaughter of Serbs. It refers to "Christian Croats and Serbs,"[17] and ignores the fact that the Croats are Catholics and the Serbs Orthodox and that a deep hatred exists between them.

Just prior to this new war, inside Croatia the Serbs had begun to fear another purge. "Ethnic Serbs, accounting for 12 percent of Croatia's 4.75 million people, accuse[d] the nationalist administration of resurrecting the spirit and policies of the Ustasha regime."[18] The newspaper *Slobodna Dalmacija* was put under strict censorship in January 1993 for claiming that "in the new state of Croatia, it is forbidden not to be Croatian [Catholic]."[19]

We mourn with Archbishop Vinko Puljic the deliberate destruction of Catholic churches and slaughter of Catholics by the Serbs, which he publicized during a three-week tour of the United States in April 1994.[20] However, it is dishonest for him not to mention the Catholic Ustashi massacres of nearly a million Serbs. The sins on both sides must be admitted and repented of for there to be peace.

The Vatican, which played a major role in the Ustashi's massacre of Serbs and then smuggled most of the mass murderers to freedom, denies the blood on its hands and lectures the world on truth and morality. In his "state of the world address" for January 1993, the pope said "that the war in Bosnia-Herzegovina has humiliated Europe and that the international community has a duty to 'disarm the aggressor' if other means fail." Though he didn't mention Serbia directly, he implied that it was the aggressor to which he referred.[21] Clearly the Vatican's hypocrisy knows no bounds.

In the last days of World War II, as Soviet troops closed in, Pavelic made his escape. Disguised as a Catholic priest, Hitler's puppet ruler eluded both the Soviet and Allied intelligence search teams and made his way to Rome, where he was hidden by the Vatican. There he met frequently with Pius XII's Assistant Secretary of State, Montini, who later became Pope

Paul VI. Montini had known for years what the Ustashi were doing. As early as September 1941, a Yugoslavian named Branko Bokun had turned over to Montini a huge file of evidence including gruesome photos and eyewitness accounts which documented the Ustashi atrocities. The Vatican saw no reason to change its policy, but continued to back their man in Croatia and his Ustashi regime and deeds.

After Vatican officials had learned all that Pavelic could tell them about Soviet Communism, Catholicism's archenemy, he was sent down its Ratlines to Argentina. There this sadist and mass murderer surfaced once again, this time as security adviser to Juan Peron, the Catholic dictator who welcomed fugitive Catholic war criminals for Mother Church.

*I gather that ... some arrangement has been worked out with Vatican and Argentina ... protecting not only Quislings but also [those] ... guilty of terrible crimes committed in Yugoslavia. I presume we must protect our agents even though it disgusts me ... we are conniving with Vatican and Argentina to get guilty people to haven in latter country.*

—John Moors Cabot
American Ambassador to Belgrade
June 1947[1]

*The Vatican's [Ratlines] were supposed to remain hidden forever. But beneath the sleepy town of Suitland, Maryland, there are twenty underground vaults, each an acre in size, crammed ... with classified documents ... hidden from public scrutiny. As the decades passed, the successors to the original custodians had no idea what awful secrets lay buried ... until piece by piece they lifted the veil of Vatican secrecy.*

*By the time the intelligence chiefs read this book it will be too late. ... The Vatican's Ratlines have passed from secrecy to history. It is an ugly legacy of spies, scandals, and Nazi smuggling.*

—From the preface to
*Unholy Trinity: The Vatican,
The Nazis and Soviet Intelligence*[2]

# 21

# The Vatican Ratlines

With the collapse of German resistance at the end of World War II, the great fear of the peoples living in Eastern Europe was that the advancing Soviet troops would not liberate but enslave them. Whole countries would become part of the spoils of war with which Roosevelt would reward Stalin. Freedom would be lost and citizens once used to traveling freely from country to country would become virtual prisoners of Communist regimes behind closed borders.

Escape from Communist rule, if it was to occur, had to be effected immediately. With this realization, multitudes of refugees began streaming west ahead of the advancing Red Army. Mingling among those fleeing, and hoping to hide their identity in the confusion, were tens of thousands of war criminals from the Ukraine, Hungary, Romania, Yugoslavia, Czechoslovakia, and Germany. Ironically, many of them would receive faster and better aid than the legitimate refugees, some of whom they had imprisoned and tortured.

Pius XII's defenders insist that his wartime silence in the face of the Holocaust was dictated by the necessity for the Church to remain neutral. As the war neared its end, however, the pope was far from neutral. He pleaded with the Allied Forces to go easy on both Mussolini and Hitler. Their countries had to remain strong as a buffer against Soviet Communism.

The Allies, of course, turned a deaf ear to the pope's surprising intercession for mass murderers.

Having failed to do anything on a significant scale to rescue the Jews, the pope would exert great effort to save their murderers. The rationale was that the Fascists who had fought Communism must be rescued from prosecution as war criminals in order to carry on the battle from other Catholic countries. Though unable to rescue Hitler and Mussolini, the pope let it be known in the refugee camps "that the Vatican would shelter Fascist fugitives."[3]

## The Great Escape West

It is almost uncanny how quickly that word reached the "right people" while remaining unknown to the rest. A steady stream of Nazi war criminals began to flow through an underground escape route which was quickly set up by the Vatican. The network would be known as the Ratlines. Investigative reporters Mark Aarons and John Loftus, having sifted through thousands of hitherto secret documents, write in their remarkable book *Unholy Trinity*:

> Under the direction of Pope Pius XII, Vatican officials such as Monsignor Giovanni Montini (later Pope Paul VI) supervised one of the greatest obstructions of justice in modern history . . . facilitat[ing] the escape of tens of thousands of Nazi [war criminals] to the West, where they were supposed to be trained as "freedom fighters" . . . [as well as] Central European Fascist [war criminals] from Russia, Byelorussia, and the Ukraine.[4]

Most Catholics would have been shocked to know what the Vatican was secretly doing—and most of all to know that the escaping war criminals included a large number of clergy, from priests to archbishops. Nor was the Vatican ignorant of their crimes but had actually given them its blessing with full knowledge of the awful facts. How tragic that a similar effort had not been put forth to rescue millions of Jews from the Nazi death machine!

Thousands of the Ustashi retreated with the Nazi troops in face of the Russian advance and attempted to surrender to

British forces at the Austrian border but were refused. It was therefore necessary to get past the British lines secretly, and to do so they were aided by fellow Ustasha, Father Vilim Cecelja. A Lieutenant Colonel in the Ustashi militia, he "spoke with pride of his leading role in organising 800 peasants to fight alongside the Nazi invaders" of Yugoslavia. He had been part of Pavelic's entourage when the latter had been blessed by Pius XII in Rome on May 17, 1941.

In anticipation of the Nazi defeat, Cecelja had gone to Vienna in May 1944 "to prepare the Austrian end of the escape network" and to found "the Austrian branch of the Croatian Red Cross, which provided ideal cover for his illegal work."[5] As for Pavelic himself, Western intelligence records indicate:

> Ante Pavelic clipped his recognizable bushy eyebrows, donned a beard, and, with an Argentine passport, slipped into Austria under the name "Ramirez." He hid in the Convent of St. Gilgin until picked up by British occupation forces. [By arrangement with the Vatican] he was released and surfaced two years later in Italy dressed as a priest and secreted in another convent . . . [until] he sailed to Buenos Aires in 1948.[6]

## The Early Ratlines Operation

One of the early key figures directing the escape of Nazi war criminals (and especially Catholic clergy) was Bishop Alois Hudal, rector of a seminary for German priests in Rome and a close associate of both Monsignor Giovanni Montini (later Pope Paul VI) and Alcide de Gasperi (later Italian Premier). Confidant also of Eugenio Pacelli both before and after he became Pius XII, Hudal was as fanatical in his support of Hitler and Nazi policies as he was in his hatred of anything Communist. An unrepentant anti-Semite to his death, Hudal worked closely in Rome with the Holy Office (successor to the Inquisition), watchdog over Catholic doctrine.

Hudal saw no conflict between his beloved Roman Catholicism and his equally beloved Nazism. During the war he proudly drove around Rome displaying a "Greater Germany" flag on his car, until an allied victory was inevitable. Then it was hastily removed.

Hudal's pro-Nazi speeches in Rome, his pro-Nazi book, *The Foundations of National Socialism* (given the imprimatur by Cardinal Theodore Innitzer, primate of the Austrian Catholic Church, who welcomed Hitler enthusiastically when he invaded Austria), far from being frowned upon by the Vatican, seemed rather to earn its approval. Close associate of the Vatican's Secretary of State, Cardinal Eugenio Maria Pacelli (who became Pope Pius XII on March 2, 1939), Hudal was elevated to Titular Bishop in 1936 in a ceremony presided over by Cardinal Pacelli himself. Equally favored by the Nazis, Hudal held a Golden Nazi Party membership badge.

Among the war criminals that Hudal helped escape were major figures such as Franz Stangl, commandant of the infamous extermination camp at Treblinka; he had presided over the efficient murder of about 900,000 inmates, mostly Jews. After his arranged "escape" from prison camp in Austria, Stangl made his way down the pipeline to Rome along with tens of thousands of others. "Hudal" was the name they all whispered, the password that opened secret sanctuaries. As Stangl told it, shortly after he had arrived at a Vatican property in Rome where he would be sheltered, Bishop Hudal "came into the room where I was waiting and he held out both his hands and said, 'You must be Franz Stangl. I was expecting you.'"[7]

Stangl was finally located and recaptured in Brazil in 1967 by Simon Wiesenthal's Nazi hunters, who learned of the Ratlines. This underground network of Catholic offices, seminaries, monasteries, convents, and residences provided not only shelter on the escape route but false identities and passage to South America and other safe havens. The most infamous mass murderer of them all, Adolf Eichmann, atheistic head of the SS Department for Jewish Affairs and in charge directly under Hitler of the entire Holocaust, was among the tens of thousands who were carefully smuggled by Catholic officials with Vatican blessing down the Ratlines.

Israeli Intelligence eventually tracked down Eichmann in Argentina and kidnapped him. He was tried in Jerusalem and executed in 1962. The Israelis were careful to look upon this remarkable exploit not as revenge but as a triumph for truth and justice. Eichmann could have been murdered in Buenos Aires by Israeli agents. Instead he was, at great risk and effort, brought to trial where his victims could face him in open court and the whole world could hear the evidence of the Holocaust. The "wandering Jews," without a national home, whom Eichmann had systematically put to death by the millions, but now in their own land, heard the testimony. After hearing Eichmann's own admissions (though he justified obedience to his "god" Hitler), the jurists weighed the evidence, rendered the verdict, and hanged him.

Most of the other Nazi war criminals, however, were able to melt into the German communities in Latin America. Having escaped the arm of human justice, they eventually faced a Higher Court—as we all must someday. There perfect justice is meted out in spite of the corruption of those who claim to represent that Court on earth.

## An Incredible Obsession

The Ratlines began with diplomatic pressure applied by Pius XII to allow his personal representatives to visit prisoner-of-war camps "to minister religiously to Catholics." The real purpose was to identify and smuggle out Nazi war criminals. It can hardly be a coincidence that the man Pius XII chose to head this outrageous obstruction of international justice was his close adviser, Bishop Hudal, whom almost all of Rome knew was a fanatical anti-Semite and pro-Nazi. As Hudal himself later frankly admitted:

> I thank God that He [allowed me] to visit . . . prisons and concentration camps and [to help prisoners] escape with false identity papers. . . . I felt duty bound after 1945 to devote my whole charitable work mainly to former National Socialists [Nazis] and Fascists, especially to so called "war criminals."[8]

What an admission! Do not forget that Hudal was a Roman Catholic bishop, close friend, and confidant of more than one pope. He dedicated his life to serving Holy Mother Church in obedience to its spiritual leader, whom he believed to be the vicar of Christ. He would not have done anything that was contrary to the dictates of the one whom he called Holy Father. And he was rewarded with position and titles for that faithful service.

Remember, the war had ended. Hitler's evil and its horrendous consequences in destroyed cities and millions of lives lost was a matter of undisputed history. The massacre of 6 million Jews was fully documented public record. The criminality of the Hitler regime had so outraged the world that an international tribunal had been assembled in Nuremburg to try those responsible for "war crimes." Yet Bishop Hudal, knowing the facts, declared with the conviction of a man who believes he has served God well that his "charitable work" had mainly consisted in rescuing "war criminals" from the justice the rest of the world wanted to impose upon them!

Did Hudal act alone? Indeed not. He faithfully carried out a secret mission in service of the pope and his beloved Church. After he was replaced, that work continued under Vatican sponsorship. The new men in charge were even more overtly evil than Hudal. Like him, they were Catholic clergy who believed they were serving God and knew they had the pope's blessing. Thus Hudal's incredible words about "charitable work" in rescuing "war criminals" are really the words of the Vatican that was behind the operation.

## All to the Glory of God?

Some of the most valuable assistance that Hudal received in setting up his infamous escape routes came from an old friend, Walter Rauff, himself a Nazi war criminal and mass murderer of Jews. The tangled web of evil implicates other powers as well with whom the Vatican covertly worked, including the United States. The OSS (predecessor to the CIA) "borrowed" Rauff from the Vatican long enough to debrief this former SS Intelligence chief of everything he knew about Communist agents operating in the West, then allowed him to return to his apartment in Milan, from which he ran the northern end of the Ratlines.

To help finance the Vatican's escape network, Rauff enlisted a former SS colleague, Frederico Schwendt, one of the most talented counterfeiters of all time. His genius supplemented Vatican funds during the early days of the Ratlines. Later operations were supported in large measure from the sale of some of the Nazis' ill-gotten treasures, including hundreds of pounds of gold smuggled out to the West and laundered by Catholic prelates.

Even the International Red Cross, especially the Rome office, but others as well, was duped into aiding the operation by providing the false identity papers that enabled multitudes of war criminals to board ships in Genoa for South America. That end of the operation was overseen by Croatian Archbishop Siri, who hid such infamous monsters as Eichmann in a monastery during his flight from justice.[9] As for Pavelic's old friend from Intermarium and one of the mass killers of Serbs and Jews in Croatia, Stejpan Hefer, the records indicate:

> Stejpan Hefer also escaped into Austria. He was there on August 19, 1946, when the Yugoslav government filed documents asking for his return to Yugoslavia to stand trial for war crimes [but] sailed to join his *poglavnik* in Argentina.
>
> Hefer was helped out of Europe by the most important Croatian escape route, which operated out of the Instituto de Santa Jeronimus (Institute of St. Jerome) at 132 Tomaselli Street in Rome. This [Vatican-financed] Catholic foundation, run by Fathers Draganovic and Levasic, facilitated the escape of thousands of Ustashi to South America. . . .
>
> In Buenos Aires, the refugees could receive assistance from a group of exiled Croatian Catholic monks. In this way, as many as five hundred Ustashi a month were able to slip away.[10]

By what rationale could torturers and mass murderers be protected from justice? The accumulated evidence indicates that being pro-Catholic and anti-Communist was all that mattered. Absolution was possible for any crime. Moreover, killing heretics and Jews had been a well-established practice for centuries by the Church and had been confirmed by numerous popes as an act of faith to the glory of God. When one considers the Vatican's history, the rescue of Nazi war criminals who were Catholics and had faithfully followed the example of Mother Church seems gruesomely understandable.

Supporting the Roman Catholic Church in its struggle against its archenemies (Communism and Protestantism) and propagating the Catholic faith worldwide was seen as doing God's will. It was therefore to be pursued by any means, at any cost, and with any partners of convenience. The Vatican's determination to see Europe become once again a Catholic Federation of States in opposition to Stalin's Communism was the overriding factor, with which all else had to fall in line. The Western Allies were willing to be limited partners in such an enterprise to whatever extent it served their own selfish interests. It was the very unholy alliance ("fornication with kings") all over again, of which the woman whom John had seen astride the beast would be guilty down through history.

Catholic countries were duty-bound to do their part in furthering the Vatican's interests. Part of that duty included providing safe haven for those sons of Mother Church whom she wished to protect in the pursuit of her great mission to create God's kingdom on earth. Those in far-off Latin America were strategically located to best perform that service, and they did so.

## A New Director for the Ratlines

Hudal's open espousal of Nazism, his outspoken admiration for Hitler, and his unabashed anti-Semitism continued even after the war ended and the unfathomable evil of the Holocaust had been revealed to a horrified world. As a result, the bishop eventually became an embarrassment to the Vatican. He was drawing public attention which threatened exposure of the Ratlines. Consequently, his superiors brought pressure upon Hudal to step out of the picture. Reluctantly he retired from his ecclesiastical positions and faded into the background.

Thereafter the supervision of the Ratlines fell upon the shoulders of a resourceful Croatian Catholic priest, Father Krunoslav Draganovic. In Croatia he had been a close assistant to Bishop Saric of Sarajevo, a notorious anti-Semite known as the "hangman of the Serbs." Church officials had called Draganovic to Rome in August 1943, where he became Intermarium's most influential contact in the Vatican. That he had also maneuvered himself into becoming the Croatian Red Cross representative in Rome was of invaluable help after the war in obtaining false documents for fugitives.

Draganovic was director of the Croatian Confraternity of San Girolamo, founded in Rome by Pope Nicholas V in 1453. The monastery's labyrinthian interior on Tomaselli Street soon sheltered many a fugitive from international justice. San Girolamo became, in fact, the nerve center for the continued smuggling of Nazi war criminals to South America and elsewhere. Many of Draganovic's former associates in the Ustashi, including a number of Catholic priests such as Father Vilim Cecelja (listed as "war criminal number 7103" by Tito's government and unsuccessfully sought for extradition), were key figures in operating the Ratlines. Cecelja, already referred to as responsible for the Austrian end of the Ratlines, "had served as a military chaplain and performed absolution for Ustashi forces during the height of the massacres of Serbs and Jews."[11]

Immediately after the war, Father Cecelja, ostensibly for the purest humanitarian reasons but without any affiliation or approval of the International Red Cross, founded the Croatian Red Cross, a strategic move which was to prove extremely useful for the Ratlines.[12] Receiving temporary permission to run his "refugee camp" in Austria until the International Red Cross could set up its own authorized affiliate, Cecelja gained access to Red Cross identity cards. He was thereby able to provide false papers certified by the Red Cross[13] for his fellow Ustashi as they escaped into Austria and then made their way down the Vatican pipeline through Rome to Genoa and on to freedom in South America. This Catholic Father often boasted of his initiation into the Ustashi in a secret ritual involving candles, a crucifix, and crossed dagger and revolver.

## A Staggering Contempt for Truth

When rumors of the smuggling operation began to circulate, both the Vatican and Draganovic disclaimed any involvement in the Ratlines. Such denials by the Roman Catholic hierarchy continue to this day, usually datelined Vatican City and carried in major newspapers around the world. Here is a recent protest of innocence:

> Rebutting an old accusation, the Vatican yesterday rejected . . . allegations that it aided Nazi war criminals to flee Europe to South America after World War II.
>
> The assertion . . . was triggered by reports from Argentina that newly declassified archives there show that Nazi officials arrived in Buenos Aires after the war on passports provided by the Vatican, the Red Cross and Spain. . . .
>
> Vatican archives for the period are closed, despite requests from Jewish groups for access to them. . . .
>
> Vatican press chief Joaquin Navarro, the spokesman for Pope John Paul II . . . said, "The idea that the Holy See . . . helped Nazi criminals, persecutors of the Jews, to flee from Europe . . . is historically false."[14]
>
> [A later article declares]:
>
> Almost two years after President Carlos Saul Mennen announced that he would open Argentina's "Nazi files," investigators here say they have . . . probably gathered one of the most exhaustive archives documenting the movement of Nazis after the war that exists. . . .
>
> The documents show, for example, that Ante Pavelic . . . entered Argentina after the war with eight Croatian aides . . . but not previously known was the entry of Pavelic associates accused of war crimes, including . . . [a list of names follows].[15]

Such periodic outbursts of self-righteous indignation only betray the Vatican's flagrant disregard for truth. The facts, hidden for decades in secret vaults, can no longer be denied. Some of the records that Aarons and Loftus uncovered, which establish beyond question the Vatican's active involvement, were originally acquired by "a daring burglary of Draganovic's office which obtained photographs of many of Draganovic's top secret records." Those records provide conclusive proof that Girolamo was "the centre of the Vatican's smuggling operation."[16]

Photocopied documents from the burglary also confirm that Ante Pavelic himself "was living inside the Vatican along with other wanted war criminals."[17] In those days the former Croatian Fuehrer was disguised as a Catholic priest. While being hidden at the Vatican, Pavelic became a good friend of Monsignor Giovanni Battista Montini, the Vatican's under secretary of state. Montini became Pope Paul VI in 1963 in the midst of John XXIII's Vatican Council II. As already mentioned, Paul VI would take control of and impose his will upon Vatican II much as Pius IX had done with Vatican I in 1870.

Vatican sponsorship of the Ratlines was also thoroughly established through constant surveillance by Allied intelligence teams.[18] Consider the following brief excerpt from a report by Counter Intelligence Corps (CIC) Agent Robert Mudd:

> These Croats [war criminals] travel back and forth from the Vatican several times a week in a car with a chauffeur whose license plate bears the two initials CD, "Corps Diplomatic." It issues forth from the Vatican and discharges its passengers inside the Monastery of San Geronimo [at San Girolamo]. Subject to diplomatic immunity, it is impossible to stop the car. . . .
>
> Draganovic's sponsorship of these Croat Quislings definitely links him up with the plans of the Vatican to shield these ex-Ustashi nationalists until such time as they are able to procure for them the proper documents to enable them to go to South America.[19]

Western intelligence was spectacularly inept in its opposition to "the very well organized and successful Ratline run by Father Krunoslav Draganovic and an array of Croatian clerics." One of the few moments of triumph came when "the British arranged an ambush at San Girolamo itself, arresting about one hundred men as they left a meeting."[20] One reason for the lack of success was the fact that both "Washington and London had entered into arrangements with the Holy See to assist many Nazi collaborators to emigrate via Draganovic's smuggling system."[21]

## American and British Involvement

The frustrated American and British agents who were attempting to capture elusive war criminals were not aware that Draganovic was being tipped off by certain elements within their own agencies. Thus the "good Father" continued to snatch his fellow Ustashi out of refugee camps just before they were about to be arrested. This was the case, for example, with Ljubo Milos, a senior official at the Jasenovac concentration camp where about 300,000 people were killed. Milos had enjoyed the "ritual killing of Jews," slitting throats, sheering ribs, and ripping open bellies with a special knife, or having prisoners thrown alive into the brick factory furnace, or simply having them bludgeoned to death.[22] Tipped off that Milos was about to be arrested, Draganovic snatched him out from under the noses of his would-be captors and whisked him away to safety.

Another Catholic priest/Ustashi member and war criminal who worked underground on the Ratlines was Father Draggutin Kamber. A mass murderer, Draggutin had even set up and commanded a concentration camp for Serbs and Jews, whom he declared had to be exterminated because they were harmful to the Ustashi state. Now he worked diligently to help his fellow Ustashi war criminals elude Soviet and Allied intelligence and make their way to freedom, where the Ustashi movement could make a fresh start. The OSS even cooperated in the effort because it was hopeful that these Croatian patriots would become a formidable foe to the Communist Tito, who had become President of Yugoslavia.

The CIC was actually working against itself. While one section, under orders from Washington, was seeking to arrest war criminals, another was under secret orders from Washington to shelter and use Nazi war criminals to its own ends. Take, for example, the infamous Klaus Barbie, the Gestapo chief in Lyons, France. The United States CIC 66th headquarters in Stuttgart, Germany, sheltered Barbie and his family for more than five years while it used him as an informer—then helped him escape. While many of the Barbie files have been removed from State Department archives, "it appears that the High Commissioner's Office issued Barbie with Allied Control

Board travel documents, and sent him down the Vatican Ratline." Aarons and Loftus continue:

> Draganovic promptly shipped him [Barbie and his family] off to South America under the name of Klaus Altmann. In Bolivia, Barbie was received by Draganovic's local representative, Father Rocque Romac, another Fascist Croatian priest and wanted war criminal, whose real identity was Father Stjepan Osvaldi-toth. . . .
>
> A close examination of the badly copied Barbie documents reveals that the State Department co-ordinated his passage down the Ratline. Indeed, almost all of the early passengers on the American Ratlines were handled by the State Department's Office of Policy Co-ordination (OPC) through their contact man in Rome.
>
> In fact, many of Draganovic's phoney exit papers were arranged through Robert Bishop, an American ex-OSS agent who was then in charge of the eligibility office of the International Refugee Organization (IRO) in Rome according to CIC records.[23]

Thus the Vatican's infamous Ratlines were operated in unholy alliances with Western intelligence agencies—up to a point. At the same time that Allied intelligence was helping Draganovic to smuggle out certain war criminals he was going behind their backs to rescue many thousands more. Recently released secret documents reveal an almost unbelievable web of intrigue and evil—payoffs, doublecross, murder—that eventually implicated CIA chiefs such as Allen Dulles and William Casey as well as United States presidents, and laid the foundation for later scandals such as Watergate and the Iran-Contra affair. Infamous war criminals who should have been tried at Nuremburg were even brought into the Pentagon as special consultants in preparation for what seemed an inevitable war with the Soviet Union. Ironically, the policy opened the door to Soviet agents who infiltrated the entire Ratline system and the related Western intelligence agencies—but that is another story.

The Vatican not only rescued tens of thousands of war criminals from justice but set them up to continue their terrorism anew after the war. It was Intermarium all over again, a fresh start to build a Catholic Europe in opposition to Soviet Communism. For example, Draganovic sheltered within the San Girolamo monastery Vilko Pecnikar, "organiser of Pavelic's pre-war terrorist groups [and] a General in Pavelic's Personal Body Guard," who also commanded "the brutal Gendarmerie, which worked in close collaboration with the Gestapo." Both Britain and America had agreed to hand him over to Tito's Yugoslavian government for prosecution as a major war criminal. But Draganovic rescued Pecnikar and gave him access to "the treasure he had collected for his Ratline" to use "in re-organizing the Ustashi movement [abroad]."[24]

## The Death of Ante Pavelic

In due time, when he had given Vatican and Western intelligence all the information he possessed, Pavelic was passed down the Ratline to safety under the identity of Pablo Aranyos. The Aranyos identity papers were provided by yet another Croatian Catholic Priest, Fr. Josip Buzanovic, himself a wanted war criminal who later escaped to Australia.

Pavelic was welcomed to Argentina by its dictator, Juan Peron, himself a Bailiff Grand Cross of Honor and Devotion of the Roman Catholic secret order, Knights of Malta. It is still required that the head of Argentina be a Roman Catholic. Pavelic was assured that Peron had already approved the continuation of the Ustashi movement from Argentina as its new base. That arrangement had been negotiated by a Vatican representative, Daniel Crljen, another priest who had also played a key role in the slaughter of Serbs.

Waiting for Pavelic in Buenos Aires was a host of his former ministers, police, and military officers, most of them wanted war criminals. Virtually the entire leadership of the Ustashi had escaped intact and had safely preceded their *poglavnik* down the Ratlines in their flight from justice. His old friend Stejpan Hefer had also joined the Ustashi Fuehrer there to give the movement a fresh start in new locations around the world.[25]

The exiled Ustashi members managed to portray themselves as victims of Communist terrorism who had fled from persecution brought about because they were Croatian patriots who opposed Tito's Communist regime. Having experienced Communism's evil firsthand, they said, they now wanted to warn the world and were dedicated to fighting this monster and eventually freeing the oppressed. Thus they claimed to merit the backing of freedom-loving people. Anticommunist front groups were set up, such as the Croatian Liberation Movement (HOP), founded by Ante Pavelic and headquartered in Buenos Aires. Stejpan Hefer was named to its supreme council.

But there is no honor among murderers, and it was not long until rival Croatians attempted to assassinate Pavelic, and the *poglavnik* went into hiding in Spain. He lived quietly and reclusively in Madrid until his death from natural causes in December 1959. On that day, Pope John XXIII pronounced his personal benediction upon that incredibly evil and sadistic mass murderer!

Pavelic is buried in a secret grave outside Madrid. "On Pavelic's death, the leadership of the HOP passed to Stejpan Hefer."[26] Archbishop Saric died a year later, in 1960, also in Spain.

## The Pitiful Denials

In tracing the history of the Vatican and the popes, we have found a consistent pattern of suppression of the most elementary human rights, a pattern which has included torture and murder on a grand scale. Such behavior, supported by infallible pronouncements and unchangeable dogmas, has not been confined to the Middle Ages but continues to the present as circumstances allow. The operation of the Ratlines, which we have only been able to summarize briefly, provides additional proof that Rome has not changed.

We have also seen a consistent pattern of denial of the facts which betrays a staggering contempt for truth. The irrefutable historic record provides no basis for confidence in the pledges of peace and goodwill either toward Jews or evangelicals which are currently issuing forth from Rome. Recent newspaper articles reveal that there are still Catholic clergy who would support the Holocaust and run Ratlines today:

> One of France's most notorious Nazi collaborators
> was arrested Wednesday [May 24, 1989] at a Roman

> Catholic priory and charged with crimes against humanity, after spending most of four decades in hiding.
>
> The 74-year-old fugitive, Paul Touvier, was head of intelligence for a pro-Nazi militia in Lyons. . . .
>
> His protection during the early postwar period by senior members of the Roman Catholic hierarchy has been extensively documented. . . .[27]
>
> The hierarchy of France's Roman Catholic Church supported the pro-Nazi government of Vichy France. . . . Despite individual acts of bravery and heroism [by Catholics], much of the church hierarchy collaborated wholeheartedly . . . for decades French cardinals, monks and nuns helped . . . Paul Touvier elude justice.[28]

On May 5, 1994, *PrimeTime Live* with Sam Donaldson presented a television documentary titled "The Last Refuge." The program, shot in both Argentina and Rome, offered some of the same information we have just presented above. The entrance into Argentina of Nazi war criminals coming down the Vatican Ratlines was documented from the recently released archives in Buenos Aires: for example, the recorded entry of Jose Mengele (known as "the Angel of Death" of Auschwitz). It was shown that the Argentine government, which was both pro-Catholic and pro-Nazi, knew Mengele's true identity and whereabouts and protected him in spite of demands for his extradition. He died of natural causes in Brazil in 1979.

The most fascinating part of the film was Sam Donaldson's street encounters with elderly surviving Nazi war criminals interviewed for the first time ever on camera. Initial denials were followed with grudging admissions of identity after Donaldson showed copies of SS membership documents and photos of the individuals in SS uniform. Acknowledgment of involvement in atrocities was also elicited but with the excuse that "I was only following orders." One ex-Nazi acknowledged that he had had an office *in the Vatican*.

Interviewed also were ex-military intelligence agents who confirmed that the Vatican had run the Ratlines. Donaldson then went to Rome to interview Father Robert Graham, a Church historian who is an authority on the immediate postwar period as reflected in the Vatican archives. In view of the overwhelming hard evidence we now have that the Vatican ran the Ratlines, it was both humorous and maddening to hear the pitiful denials from Graham of any Vatican involvement whatsoever. He did acknowledge that the Vatican facilitated the passage through Italy and into South America of thousands of what he insisted were "simple refugees," with maybe "one or two" war criminals sneaking through unrecognized.

"One or two?" exclaimed Donaldson in surprise. "There were thousands!"

"Oh, please! Please!" returned Graham patronizingly. "Don't be ridiculous. A thousand? That's absurd!"

When Donaldson persisted, giving additional evidence, Graham, now visibly upset, responded, "Please! Are you all so simple and unsophisticated as to believe that stuff? Please! Be more intelligent than that. Give the Pope some credit. . . ."

But the evidence is ironclad, and the Vatican denials only serve to demonstrate once again its contempt for truth. While many individual Catholics showed compassion and concern and even risked their lives to rescue Jews, the Church as an entity did not. It is only fitting that Aarons and Loftus concluded their book with this moving indictment of the Roman Catholic Church at its highest levels:

> Instead of smuggling homeless Jews to Argentina, the Ratlines smuggled Eichmann, Pavelic and Stangl, among many others. Instead of denouncing Bishop Hudal, the Vatican replaced him with a less conspicuous but far more efficient and effective operative in the form of Father Draganovic. Instead of international justice, there was Intermarium and a host of *emigre* Nazi fronts. . . .
>
> What the Vatican did after World War II was a crime. The evidence is unequivocal: the Holy See aided the flight of fugitives from international justice. The Ratlines were intentionally created to aid and abet the escape of wanted Nazi war criminals. . . .
>
> We find no defense of ignorance: Pius XII was fully aware of Ante Pavelic's crimes. Nor was he the only case. The Ratlines operated with reckless disregard for the fugitives' crimes against humanity. If the Pope wanted to

know their real names, he had only to ask Father Draganovic. The burglary of his office revealed that he kept
lists of the fugitives' true and false identities.

The Pope's diplomatic messages reveal a pattern of
protection and intercession for war criminals. . . . the
Vatican knew they were sheltering Nazis.

We find no defense of unauthorised conduct: the Ratlines were an official extension of covert Vatican diplomacy. . . . There was virtually unanimous agreement
among the surviving witnesses that Draganovic operated
with the highest official sanction. . . . The intelligence
files of several nations confirm that the Vatican's top
leaders authorized and directed the smuggling of fugitive
war criminals.[29]

No matter how much and how convincing the evidence,
however, Rome persists in its denials of culpability. The absolute, infallible, and unchallengeable authority of the Roman
Pontiff must be maintained at all cost.

*Wherewithal shall a young man cleanse his way? By taking heed thereto according to thy Word. . . . Thy Word is a lamp unto my feet and a light unto my path.*

—Psalm 119:9,105

*That from a child thou hast known the Holy Scriptures, which are able to make thee wise unto salvation through faith. . . .*

—2 Timothy 3:15

*It is evident, from experience, that the Holy Scriptures, when circulated in the vulgar tongue, have produced more harm than benefit [paraphrasing Trent[1]]. . . . We have deliberated upon the measures proper to be adopted, by our pontifical authority, in order to remedy and abolish this pestilence . . . this defilement of the faith so imminently dangerous to souls.*

—Pope Pius VII
encyclical letter of 1816 addressed
to the primate of Poland

*If I am cast into prison . . . it will be easier to transport a rock from our Alps than to move me as much as a hand's breadth from the Word of Jesus Christ.*

—Ulric Zwingle, August 13, 1522[2]

# 22

# Sola Scriptura?

The well-known axiom that power corrupts and absolute power corrupts absolutely is just as true in religion as in politics. In fact, religious power is even more corrupting than political power. Absolutism reaches its ultimate abusive pinnacle when it claims to act for God. Vatican II requires "loyal submission of the will and intellect" to the Roman Pontiff "even when he does not speak ex cathedra. . . . "[3] No Catholic can presume to obey God and His Word directly but must give that absolute obedience to the Church, which acts for God and thus stands between the individual and God.

The corruption of power reaches its greatest height in Catholicism's bold claim that its members cannot understand the Bible for themselves but must accept unquestioningly the Church's interpretation: "The task of giving an authentic interpretation of the Word of God . . . has been entrusted to the living teaching office of the Church alone."[4] With that edict, God's Word, the one repository of truth and liberty which is capable of destroying despotism, is kept under Church control and shrouded in mystery. This leaves devout Catholics at the mercy of their clergy, a clergy which, as we have seen, is all too readily corrupted.

## Blind Acceptance

To escape that destructive enslavement, the Reformers urged submission to God's pure Word as the ultimate authority rather than to the Church or the pope. The basic issue that sparked the Reformation (and which remains the basic issue today) was whether to continue in blind submission to Rome's dogmas, even though they contradicted the Bible, or to submit to God's Word alone as the final authority. Menno Simons's biographer relates the conflict he faced:

> The real problem came when Menno, having dared to open the lids of the Bible, discovered that it contained nothing of the traditional teaching of the Church on the Mass. By that discovery his inner conflict was brought to a climax, for he now was compelled to decide which of two authorities was to be supreme in his life, the Church or the Holy Scriptures.[5]

The Reformers made that choice in favor of Scripture and their central cry became *Sola Scriptura!* That liberating truth was rejected at the Council of Trent by bishops who were unwilling to surrender control of the people under them. It was even considered to be harmful for the people to possess the Bible in their own tongue because they might take it literally, which Rome argues even today must not be done. From her viewpoint only a specially trained elite can understand the Bible:

> The interpreter must...go back wholly in spirit to those remote centuries...with the aid of history, archaeology, ethnology, and other sciences, accurately determine what modes of writing the authors of that ancient period would be likely to use, and in fact did use.[6]

Trent's view that the authority for the Catholic is the Church, not the Bible, remains in force today. *Only Scripture scholars trained at the Pontifical Biblical Institute in Rome* with "a degree in theology [and] mastery of six or seven languages (including Hebrew, Aramaic, and Greek...)" are capable of understanding the Bible. Having earned "a Licentiate in Sacred Scripture...the Catholic Church's license to teach Scripture,"[7] they alone can teach the Bible. No layman is qualified. Vatican II insists:

> It is for the bishops, with whom the apostolic doctrine resides, suitably to instruct the faithful entrusted to them

in the correct use of . . . the New Testament . . . by giving
them translations of the sacred texts which are equipped
with necessary and really adequate explanations.[8]

## What the Bible Says

The Bible was given by God to all mankind, not to an elite
group to explain it to others. It is to be a lamp on the path
(Psalm 119:105) of all who heed it. Moses proclaimed that man
shall not live by bread alone but by every word that proceeds
from the mouth of God (Deuteronomy 8:3)—and not a whis-
per about that word being interpreted by an elite hierarchy.
Psalm 1 speaks of the blessed man who meditates upon God's
Word (variously called the law, statutes, judgments, commandments, etc.) day and night. "Man" surely includes
woman, but cannot possibly be interpreted to mean *only* a
special class of highly educated experts.

We get the impression from reading Paul's epistles that
those to whom they were written were expected to understand
them. The epistles are not addressed to a bishop or select group
of leaders but to *all* of the Christians at Corinth, Ephesus, etc.
Each Christian is given an understanding by the indwelling
Holy Spirit of the words which the same Spirit inspired "holy
men of God" to write (2 Peter 1:21).

Even a "young man" is expected to "heed" God's Word
(Psalm 119:9). Again, not a hint is given that it must be
explained to him by a rabbi. Christ, quoting Moses, affirmed
that man is to feed upon the Bible for his very life (Deuteronomy 8:3; Matthew 4:4). Job considered God's Word "more
than my necessary food" (Job 23:12). Never a word about
consulting a hierarchy for its meaning!

## Trusting the Church Instead of the Bible

The pope, in his August 15, 1993, "address to representa-
tives of the Vietnamese community" at Denver, told them:
"The challenge before you is to keep pure and lively your
Catholic identity. . . ."[9] One seldom if ever hears Catholic
leaders exhorting the flock to be true simply to Christ or to
God's Word, but always to the Church. *Veritatis Splendor*, John

Paul II's 1993 treatise on morals, refers to the truth taught by Christ and *mediated by the Church*. Without that mediation the Catholic cannot know God's truth simply by reading God's Word. Only by such a doctrine can Rome keep its adherents blindly following its corrupt and unbiblical teachings.

Cardinal Ratzinger, watchdog of orthodoxy, exemplifies this blind faith in Catholicism. He tells of a theology professor who admitted that the Assumption of the Virgin Mary, declared a Roman Catholic dogma in 1950 by Pope Pius XII, could not be supported by Scripture, yet decided to believe it because "the Church is wiser than I." Sadly, he is actually acknowledging the Church to be wiser than the Bible and thus capable of contradicting it!

Ratzinger has that same unwarranted total trust in Catholicism and pledges "to follow the Catholic faith and not my own opinions."[10] Thus he guards the "faith" not by making certain that what is taught in Catholic seminaries, universities, and pulpits around the world agrees with the Word of God, but that it conforms to Catholic tradition taught by popes, councils, and church fathers—and much of it in *false decretals*. Vatican II says that "both Scripture and Tradition must be accepted and honored with equal feelings of devotion and reverence."[11] The new universal *Catechism of the Catholic Church* recently released by the Vatican states:

> The Church to which is confided the transmission and the rendering of the Revelation does not draw solely from the Holy Scriptures her certainty on all points of Revelation [but also from Tradition and the *magisterium*]. . . .[12]

## The Church Stands in the Way of Truth

Christ declared, "If ye continue in my word, then are ye my disciples indeed; and ye shall know *the truth* [no hint of another source of truth]" (John 8:31,32). He did not make that statement to the 12 apostles, but to common people who had just "believed on him" (verse 30). He said nothing of His truth having to be interpreted by the rabbis, and of course the Roman Catholic hierarchy didn't even exist then. God's Word was available to and was to be understood, believed, and obeyed by even the newest converts. That was what Christ expected of His followers then and it is what He expects of us today as well.

Rome blocks the individual's access to the truth. The Catholic can't learn directly from Christ's words, but only from the *interpretation thereof by the Church*. Christ said, "Come unto *me . . . I* will give you rest" (Matthew 11:28). Rome allows no one to come directly to Christ, but has set itself up as the intermediary channel of God's grace necessary for knowing God's truth and for salvation. On this point Rome is adamant. Otherwise she would lose her hold on the people, who could then do without her.

Would God inspire infallible Scripture and then deny to all except an elite few the ability to understand it, requiring billions of people to surrender their minds to a hierarchy by blindly accepting their interpretation of His Word? If the Holy Spirit can convince *the world* "of sin, and of righteousness, and of judgment" (John 16:8), then surely He can teach all those in whom He dwells. John says that the Christians to whom he writes don't have to look to some special class of men for teaching but have an "anointing [of the Holy Spirit which] teacheth you of all things" (1 John 2:27).

If all Christians are "led by the Spirit of God" (Romans 8:14), then surely all must be able to understand the Scriptures which the Spirit of God has inspired. Christians "have received . . . the Spirit which is of God, that we might know the things that are freely given to us of God" (1 Corinthians 2:12). There is no hint that a group of clergy must interpret the Scriptures for everyone else. And why should they? All Christians "have the mind of Christ" (verse 16). Rome dare not acknowledge this truth, for then those under her would be set free.

Rome is still searching for truth *outside God's Word*. Consider Rome's Pontifical University of St. Thomas Aquinas (the Angelicum). Pope John Paul II is a graduate. Its 1200 students from 135 countries have made "the search for truth" through the thousands of volumes on theology and philosophy in its library and elsewhere their "life-objective."[13] Contrast Christ's statement, that by obeying His Word one knows the truth, with the complexity of the "search for truth"by Catholic scholars. Both can't be right.

## A Deadly Spiritual Bondage

Ordinary Bereans checked Paul's teachings not with a hier-archy in Rome, which didn't even exist, but against the Bible (Acts 17:11). That practice was commended then and it is still each individual's responsibility to know God's Word and to test every spiritual leader by it, no matter who he may be. This is what the Bible declares.

Roman Catholics, however (like Mormons, Jehovah's Witnesses and members of various cults), must *accept*, not *check*, their Church's teachings. The very Book that would bring life, light, and freedom to individuals and nations is spiritually chained out of reach even as it was once literally chained. Of course, such withholding of God's Word from the laity is consistent with Catholicism's persistent suppression of the basic human freedoms of conscience, religion, and the press.

Among the crimes for which believers were committed to the flames in the Spanish Inquisition was the distribution and reading of the Bible. Smuggling Bibles into Communist or Muslim countries such as China or Iran is understandable, but imagine having to smuggle Bibles into a "Christian" country such as Spain, and being put to death for doing so! Yet in an *Auto de Fe* in Seville on December 22, 1560, Julian Hernandez, one of those burned at the stake on that occasion, was declared to be an arch-heretic because—

> through his great efforts and incomprehensible stealth he introduced into Spain prohibited books [Bibles and New Testaments] that he brought from far away places [Germany] where they give protection to the ungodly [Protestants]. . . . He firmly believes that God, by means of the Scriptures, communicates to the laity just the same as He communicates to the priest.[14]

To believe that God could communicate His truth through the Bible not only to the clergy but to ordinary believers was a crime punishable by death! Rome has not changed, though the

Bible is no longer banned overtly as in the past. To do so today would be the wrong tactic and likely create the opposite reaction to the one desired. There is a better way: Let the people have the Bible in their *hands*, and even encourage them to read it, but keep it from their *hearts* by insisting that only the Church can interpret it.

At the same time, confidence in Scripture is undermined by Rome's teaching that the Bible is not trustworthy in its pronouncements on history or science. Catholicism takes a symbolic meaning from the book of Jonah concerning "the universality of salvation" and denies that a literal prophet named Jonah was swallowed by a literal fish.[15] The early chapters of Genesis are likewise viewed as symbolic rather than accounts of actual creation of the world and man, leaving the door open to evolution. Even the rapture is seen as symbolic and not referring to a literal catching up of Christians to heaven, an idea which Catholics consider to be a delusion.[16] The 1964 Instruction of the Biblical Commission declared that the literalist view of the Bible adopted by Fundamentalists "actually invites people to a kind of intellectual suicide."[17]

## Did the Catholic Church Give Us the Bible?

It is claimed that only the Church can interpret the Bible because it was the Church which gave it to us. That is like saying that because Paul wrote his epistles we need him to interpret them. Furthermore, the Church did *not* give us the Bible—certainly not the Old Testament, for there was no Church in those days. And if the Roman Catholic Church was not needed to give us the Old Testament, then clearly it was not needed to give us the New either.

A favorite question of Catholic apologists is, "How do you know that Luke wrote the Gospel of Luke or that Matthew wrote the Gospel of Matthew?" They claim that Roman Catholic tradition contains this information. Yet no tradition proves who wrote Hebrews, Job, Esther, or various Psalms. Nor does it matter. *That the authors were inspired by the Holy Spirit is* what counts. This inspiration bears witness within readers who are themselves indwelt by the same Holy Spirit who inspired the writing of Scripture.

Catholicism's claim that the New Testament comes from the Church by decision of the councils is false. No early council even ruled on what was canonical; yet in these councils, to support their arguments, both sides quoted the New Testament, which had obviously been accepted by general consensus *without any conciliar definition of the canon.* The Synod of Antioch, in A.D. 266, denounced the doctrine of Paul of Samosata as "foreign to the ecclesiastical canon." The Council of Nicea in 325 refers to "the canon"; and the Council of Laodicea in 363 exhorted that "only the 'canonized' books of both Old and New Testaments be read in the church." Yet none of those councils deemed it necessary to list the canonized books, indicating that they were already well-known and accepted by the common consent of Christians indwelt by the Holy Spirit.

Not until the Third Council of Carthage, in A.D. 397, do we have the first conciliar decision on the canon.[18] That is rather late if without it Christians didn't know what books were in the New Testament and therefore couldn't use them, as Rome claims today! History proves that the books of the New Testament were known and accepted by Christians and in wide circulation and use at least 300 years before Carthage listed them. Historian W.H.C. Frend writes:

> The Gospels and epistles were circulating in Asia, Syria, and Alexandria (less certainly in Rome), and being read and discussed in the Christian synagogues there by about 100. In Polycarp's short letter there is an astonishing amount of direct and indirect quotation from the New Testament: Matthew, Luke, and John, Acts, the letters to the Galatians, Thessalonians, Corinthians, Ephesians, Philippians, Colossians, Romans, the Pastorals, 1 Peter particularly, and 1 and 2 John are all used....
>
> The Christian Scriptures were quoted so familiarly as to suggest that they had been in regular use a long time.[19]

No rabbinical body decided upon the canon of the Old Testament. That canon was recognized by Israel and available as it was being written. Daniel, a captive in Babylon, had a copy of Jeremiah written only a few years earlier and was studying it as Scripture (Daniel 9:2). We are certain that the entire Old Testament was well-known when Christ was here and undoubtedly long before, for every Israelite was required to meditate upon it day and night.

## God's Word Speaks Directly to All

In Old Testament times the common people were expected to know God's Word, not through rabbinical interpretation but for themselves, and were able to know it. That fact, as well as its availability to all, is very clear from Christ's rebuke of the two disciples on the road to Emmaus: "O fools, and slow of heart to believe *all* that the prophets have spoken . . ." (Luke 24:25). He would not have used such harsh language in holding these two ordinary people responsible for their ignorance of prophecies had not *all* of the Old Testament Scriptures been readily available, familiar, and understandable to the ordinary Jew. He then expounded unto them in *all* the Scriptures (which must therefore have been known) "the things concerning himself" (Luke 24:25-27). *All* of the Scriptures were even available to the faraway Bereans north of Greece, who, as we have seen, "searched the Scriptures daily" (Acts 17:11).

The same evidence is found in the fact that Timothy knew the Old Testament from early childhood (2 Timothy 3:15) and that it was taught to him not by the rabbis in the synagogue but at home by his mother and grandmother, who themselves were women of faith (2 Timothy 1:5). It is certainly clear that no one in Old Testament times looked to any hierarchy for an official interpretation of Scripture. Nor did the early church. Nor should we today.

The plain words of the Bible, without Rome's domineering interpretation, give the lie to the hierarchical structure of the Roman Catholic Church and the authoritarianism of its clergy. Priscilla and Aquila were an ordinary husband and wife who labored daily at tentmaking (Acts 18:3). Yet a "church [met] in their house" (1 Corinthians 16:19) and they were capable teachers of God's Word, even instructing a man so eloquent as Apollos (Acts 18:26). Paul referred to them as "my helpers in Christ Jesus" (Romans 16:3). They had never been to seminary and were not part of a clerical hierarchy (which didn't exist), but they knew God and His Word by the Holy Spirit indwelling them. So should all Christians today.

According to Paul, ordinary Christians are to judge whether a preacher is speaking God's truth. Paul submitted his writings to the same criteria, inviting his readers to judge by the Holy Spirit within them whether his epistles were from God or not: "If any man think himself to be a prophet or spiritual, let him acknowledge that the things that I write unto you are the commandments of the Lord" (1 Corinthians 14:37). It was by the same witness of the Holy Spirit within each individual believer that the first-century church decided which books were canonical. In exactly the same way Christians today recognize the Bible as God's inspired Word.

## The Sad Consequences

Unfortunately, the average Catholic has been taught to look to the Church hierarchy for the instruction which the Holy Spirit desires to give directly to believers. To Rome, to suggest that the Holy Spirit speaks to individuals through the words of the Bible is anathema. Karl Keating, one of the leading Catholic lay apologists, writes:

> The Catholic believes in inspiration because the Church tells him so—that is putting it bluntly—and that same church has the authority to interpret the inspired text. Fundamentalists have no interpreting authority other than themselves.[20]

In fact, "Fundamentalists" look to the guidance of the Holy Spirit. Catholicism also claims that guidance, but only for its hierarchy, who alone can be led of the Spirit to understand the Bible. Yet the Bible says *every* Christian is indwelt, empowered, and led of the Holy Spirit. In fact, one is not even a Christian without this inner witness and leading of the Holy Spirit:

> Now if any man have not the Spirit of Christ, he is none of his. . . . For as many as are led by the Spirit of God, they are the sons of God. . . . The Spirit itself beareth witness with our spirit, that we are the children of God . . . (Romans 8:9,14,16).

> But God hath revealed them [the "things of God"]
> unto us by his Spirit; for the Spirit searcheth all things,
> yea, the deep things of God. . . . the things of God know-
> eth no man but [by] the Spirit of God.
> Now we have received, not the spirit of the world, but
> the Spirit which is of God, that we might know the things
> that are freely given to us of God.
> Which things also we speak, not in the words which
> man's wisdom teacheth, but which the Holy Spirit teach-
> eth (1 Corinthians 2:10-13).

Having been convinced that he cannot understand the Bible
for himself, the devout Catholic is at the mercy of his Church
and must believe whatever it teaches. The *Convert's Catechism
of Catholic Doctrine* bluntly declares:

> Man can obtain a knowledge of God's Word [only]
> from the Catholic Church and through its duly consti-
> tuted channels.
> When he has once mastered this principle of divine
> authority [residing in the Church], the inquirer is pre-
> pared to accept whatever the divine Church teaches on
> faith, morals and the means of grace.[21]

Here again, brazenly stated, is the first principle of every
cult: "Check your mind at the door and believe whatever the
group or church or guru or prophet in charge says." The idea
appeals to those who think that by thus surrendering their
minds to an infallible authority they escape their individual
moral responsibility to God. Others are afraid to think for
themselves because that would put them outside the Church,
where "there is no salvation."[22] By this means God's Word,
which should speak powerfully to each individual, is held just
out of reach of individual Catholics by their Church.

### When Was the New Testament Canon Established?

That the New Testament canon, exactly like the Old, was
accepted and recognized by a consensus of the believers as it
was being written is clear from the historic evidence we have
given above. Further proof comes from the testimony of Peter:

> Even as our beloved brother Paul also according to the
> wisdom given unto him hath written unto you, as also in
> *all his epistles*, speaking in them of these things, in which
> are some things hard to be understood, which they that
> are unlearned and unstable wrest [twist], as they do also
> *the other Scriptures*, unto their own destruction (2 Peter
> 3:15,16).

Peter acknowledges Paul's writings to be Scripture. So has,
apparently, the entire body of believers at this time. "The
other Scriptures" by that time would have included most of the
remainder of the New Testament. Furthermore, these books
were so readily available and well-known by common consensus already at this early date (about A.D. 66) that Peter
didn't even need to name them. Christians knew what writings
were inspired of God in the same way a native in the jungle
knows that the gospel is true: by the convicting power of the
Holy Spirit.

Tragically, Catholicism not only teaches that the Church
hierarchy *alone* can interpret the Bible, but that *no one can
believe it without the Church attesting to its authenticity.* Keating suggests that the gospel itself has no power without this
endorsement. He quotes St. Augustine: "I would not believe in
the Gospel if the authority of the Catholic Church did not move
me to do so."[23] If that is true, then no one prior to the Third
Council of Carthage in A.D. 397 could have believed or preached
the gospel!

Yet the gospel was preached from the very beginning. Paul
turned the world upside down with the gospel (Acts 17:6).
Within the first two centuries about 10 percent of the Roman
Empire became Christians and studied, meditated upon,
believed, and were led by both the Old and New Testament
Scriptures exactly as we have them today. If they could know
what books were inspired and could be guided by them without
the authenticating stamp of the Roman Catholic Church
(which didn't yet exist), then so can we today.

The absurdity and destructiveness of the view that God's
Word must have Rome's endorsement is immediately apparent. It is a blasphemous denial that the gospel in itself has
power to save or that the Holy Spirit can use the Bible to speak

directly to hearers' hearts. Under this view, one must first prove that the Roman Catholic Church is the one true Church, that it is infallible, that it says the Bible is true, and that therefore the Bible and the gospel must be believed; only then can the gospel be preached. How absurd! Yet to a Catholic this view makes perfect sense because the Church is the vehicle of salvation. One's eternal destiny depends not upon one's relationship to Christ, who is revealed in His Word, but upon one's relationship to that Church and participation in its sacraments.

This theory, of course, is refuted by the Bible itself. Christ and His disciples preached the gospel before *any* church was established. Early in His ministry, before even saying anything about establishing His church, Christ sent His disciples forth, "and they departed, and went through the towns, preaching the gospel" (Luke 9:6). Eleven times in the four Gospels we are told that Christ and His disciples were engaged in preaching the gospel, a gospel which is "the power of God unto salvation" to those who believe it (Romans 1:16). Yet there was no Roman Catholic Church in existence to verify that the gospel was true. Nor does today's preaching need Rome's endorsement any more than it did in the beginning.

Three thousand souls were saved on the day of Pentecost without Peter saying one word about an infallible Church putting its approval on what he preached. Even after Pentecost we find no attempt by Christians, who "went everywhere preaching the Word" (Acts 8:4), to prove that an infallible Church existed and endorsed the gospel. We read of the preaching of Philip in Samaria and of Paul in many places, where multitudes believed; yet not once is the gospel supported by the statement that Christ established an infallible Church and that the bishops of this Church had put their official stamp of approval upon what was being preached. If the endorsement of the Roman Catholic Church wasn't needed then, neither is it needed now, for the Word of God is "living and powerful . . . a discerner of the thoughts and intents of the heart" (Hebrews 4:12).

## The Sufficiency of Scripture

"Show us one verse in the Bible that clearly declares *Sola Scriptura*, that the Bible is sufficient in itself," is the specious challenge thrown out by Catholic apologists. One might as well demand "just one verse that states that God is a triune being of Father, Son, and Holy Spirit." No single verse says so, yet the doctrine of the trinity is accepted by both Catholics and Protestants as biblical. Nor is there a single verse which contains the words "the Bible is sufficient." However, when we put together the many verses in the Bible on this topic it is clear that the Bible teaches its own sufficiency both to authenticate itself to the reader and to lead to spiritual maturity and effectiveness all who are indwelt by the Holy Spirit and read it with open hearts.

Paul declared that Scripture was given for "doctrine, for reproof, for correction, for instruction in righteousness" and that the Bible itself makes the man or woman of God "perfect [i.e., mature, complete, all that God intended], thoroughly furnished [equipped] unto all good works" (2 Timothy 3:16,17). In other words, the Bible contains all the doctrine, correction, and instruction in righteousness that is needed for those who heed it to become complete in Christ.

Catholic apologists quote nineteeth-century Cardinal John Henry Newman to the effect that if this passage proves the above, then it "proves too much," that "the Old Testament *alone* would be sufficient as a rule of faith, the New Testament unnecessary" because all Timothy had was the Old Testament.[24] The argument is fallacious for several reasons.

First of all, Timothy had more than the Old Testament. This is Paul's *second* epistle to him, so he has at least two epistles from Paul in addition to the Old Testament. Paul goes on to say that he is about to be martyred (2 Timothy 4:6-8), making this the *last* epistle Paul wrote. So Timothy, obviously, has *all* of Paul's epistles. The date is probably around A.D. 66, so he also has the first three Gospels and most of the rest of the New Testament.

Furthermore, when Paul says "all Scripture" it is clear that he means the entire Bible, not merely that which had been written up to that time. Similar expressions are often used in Scripture, but they never mean only the Bible written to that time. When Jesus said, "The word that I have spoken, the same shall judge him in the last day" (John 12:48), He didn't mean only what He had spoken *to that time*. Likewise, when He said, "Thy Word is truth" (John 17:17) He obviously meant *all* of God's Word, though all had not yet been written.

When the writer of Hebrews said, "The Word of God is living and powerful, sharper than any two-edged sword," he didn't mean only that part of the Word of God that had been written to that time. Nor did Paul by "all Scripture" mean only that which had been written *to that time*. He clearly meant *all* Scripture. So Cardinal Newman was wrong, and naively so. Yet Catholic apologists confidently quote his folly to disprove the sufficiency of Scripture.

"That the man of God may be perfect" simply means that the Word of God is all one needs to be "perfect" in the sense of being mature and all that God wants a Christian to be. Catholic apologists refer to other verses where the word "perfect" is used, such as: "If you would be perfect, sell all you have and give to the poor," or "Let patience have its perfect work, that ye may be perfect and entire," etc. They then contend that if it can be argued from 2 Timothy 3:17 that the Bible is sufficient to perfect believers, then selling everything one has and giving it to the poor or being patient is also sufficient to make one perfect.

Again the argument fails. Suppose an athletic trainer offers a perfect diet with all the nutritional elements one needs to produce a perfect body. This doesn't mean that other things, such as exercise, aren't necessary. Paul is saying that the doctrine, reproof, correction, and instruction in righteousness contained in Scripture is sufficient teaching for the man (or woman) of God to be all God desires. This does not mean that one doesn't have to exercise patience, faith, obedience, charity, etc., which themselves are taught by Scripture. It *does* mean that in the area of doctrine, reproof, correction, and instruction in righteousness the Bible needs no supplementation from tradition or any other source.

Moreover, Paul goes on to say that the man (or woman) of God is, by the Scriptures themselves, "thoroughly prepared unto every good work." The Bible never makes such a statement about patience or love or charity or tradition or anything else. Paul is clearly teaching *Sola Scriptura*. This doctrine was not invented by the Reformers; they derived it from Scripture.

344 • *Dave Hunt*

## The Central Issue—A Clear Choice

When Thomas Howard, brother of Elizabeth Elliot (wife of martyred missionary Jim Elliot), became a Catholic, Gordon College removed him from its faculty. Among the reasons given was the fact that the statement of faith which all faculty had to sign affirmed the Bible as "the only infallible guide in faith and practice"—impossible for a Catholic to sign. Howard acknowledged that "the sole authority of Scripture is a principle unique to Protestantism, and that he, as a Catholic, could not subscribe to it."[25]

*Sola Scriptura* remains the central issue at the heart of the Reformation. One must choose between submitting to the authority of the Bible or to that of the Roman Catholic Church. One cannot do both because of the clear conflict between the two.

The choice one must make is obvious. Blind submission to *any* earthly hierarchy in itself contradicts the Bible. Moreover, we have given more than sufficient evidence from history to show that the Roman Catholic Church, from the pope down, has forfeited any claim it may ever have had to be trusted.

The most tragic consequence of the blind faith in their Church as the sole interpreter of God's Word for mankind is that hundreds of millions of Catholics consequently trust it for their eternal destiny. The question of salvation, therefore, is also a key issue necessarily separating Catholics and evangelicals.

*Though we or an angel from heaven preach any other gospel unto you than that which we have preached unto you, let him be accursed. . . . a man is not justified by the works of the law but by the faith of Jesus Christ . . . for by the works of the law shall no flesh be justified.*

—Galatians 1:8; 2:16

*For by grace are ye saved through faith, and that not of yourselves: It is the gift of God, not of works, lest any man should boast.*

—Ephesians 2:8,9

*If anyone says that the sacraments of the New Law [of the Roman Catholic Church] are not necessary for salvation but . . . that without them . . . men obtain from God through faith alone the grace of justification . . . let him be anathema.*

—Council of Trent, 7, General, 4[1]

*From the most ancient times in the Church good works were also offered to God for the salvation of sinners . . . [by] the prayers and good works of holy people . . . the penitent was washed, cleansed and redeemed . . .*

*Following in Christ's steps, those who believe in him have always . . . carried their crosses to make expiation for their own sins and the sins of others . . . [to] help their brothers to obtain salvation from God. . . .*

—Vatican II, Apostolic Constitution
on the Revision of Indulgences
II 5., III 6.[2]

# 23

# A Question of Salvation

Sacred Tradition and sacred Scripture make up a single sacred deposit of the Word of God," says Vatican II.[3] When its tradition and the Bible conflict, Rome goes by tradition. Thereby is created the widest difference between Protestants and Catholics: the question of salvation. That vast chasm of division, recognized for 400 years by both Protestants and Catholics, neither of whom has changed basic beliefs, is now denied by leading evangelicals. Charles Colson, for example, in response to questions concerning his embracing Catholics as Christians, says:

> We have differences, but on the ancient creeds and the core beliefs of Christianity we stand together.[4]

Not so. Agreement on the *creeds,* yes, but the creeds say nothing about *how one is saved.* Salvation is the one most important core belief in Christianity. And on that point the difference between evangelicals and Catholics is as great as the difference between eternal life and eternal judgment.

## The "Saved" and the "Unsaved"

The Bible says there are two classes of people: those who are *saved* and those who are *unsaved* or *lost.* Christ Himself declared that His mission was to save a world of lost people: "The son of man is come to seek and to save that which was lost" (Luke 19:10); "I came... to save the world" (John 12:47). God sent Him "that the world through him might be saved" (John 3:17). Paul testifed, "Christ Jesus came into the world to save sinners" (1 Timothy 1:15). Save them from what? From the judgment of God eternally separating them from God's presence because of sin:

> He that believeth on the Son hath everlasting life, and he that believeth not the Son shall not see life, but the wrath of God abideth on him (John 3:36).

> In flaming fire taking vengeance on them that know not God, and that obey not the gospel... who shall be punished with everlasting destruction from the presence of the Lord.... That they all might be damned who believed not the truth (2 Thessalonians 1:8,9; 2:12).

> Whosoever was not found written in the book of life was cast into the lake of fire (Revelation 20:15).

The gospel declares "that Christ died for our sins according to the Scriptures, and that he was buried, and that he rose again the third day" (1 Corinthians 15:3,4). Evangelicals believe the gospel not merely as a fact of history but as offering them forgiveness for their sin and eternal life as a free gift of God's grace. Paul said this is the gospel "by which also ye are *saved*" (1 Corinthians 15:2). On that basis the evangelical *knows* he is *saved*.

One "gets saved" the moment one believes the gospel. To the earnest cry, "What must I do to be saved?" (Acts 16:30) Paul responded, "Believe on the Lord Jesus Christ and thou shalt be saved" (verse 31). It's that simple. The moment faith is placed in Christ one is saved, never to be lost again. One has "passed from death unto life" and is no longer under God's judgment (John 5:24). Heaven is now one's home, and death means to be "absent from the body and... present with the Lord" (2 Corinthians 5:8). The Bible says:

> For God so loved the world that he gave his only begotten Son, that whosoever believeth in him should not

perish but have *everlasting life* (John 3:16); I am the door [said Jesus]; by me if any man enter in he shall be *saved* (John 10:9); My sheep hear my voice, and I know them, and they follow me; and I give unto them *eternal life*, and they shall never perish (John 10:27,28); Unto us which are *saved* (1 Corinthians 1:18); It pleased God by the foolishness of preaching to *save* them that believe (1 Corinthians 1:21); by which also ye are *saved* (1 Corinthians 15:2); By grace are ye *saved* (Ephesians 2:8); Who will have all men to be *saved* (1 Timothy 2:4); [God] who hath *saved* us (2 Timothy 1:9); According to his mercy he *saved* us (Titus 3:5); the nations of them which are *saved* (Revelation 21:24); etc.

The evangelical believes that, having accepted Christ's offer of pardon and eternal life, he is a Christian, born of the Holy Spirit into God's family. He is certain that as a child of God he will "never perish" (John 10:28) nor "come into condemnation" (John 5:24). His salvation is secure because, by God's wonderful grace, Christ's death paid the penalty for his sin. So says God's Word:

He that believeth on the Son of God hath the witness in himself [the assurance of the Holy Spirit in his heart]; he that believeth not God hath made him a liar, because he believeth not the record that God gave of his Son.

And this is the record, that God hath given to us eternal life, and this life is in his Son.

He that hath the Son hath life, and he that hath not the Son of God hath not life.

These things have I written unto you that believe on the name of the Son of God, that ye may *know* that ye *have* eternal life, and that ye may believe on the name of the Son of God (1 John 5:10-13).

## The Evangelical Goal: Salvation of Sinners

While growing up in an evangelical home and church one may believe the gospel intellectually from childhood yet realize that he is not yet saved. Merely mentally assenting to all that the Bible says does not save; one must *personally receive*

*Christ as Savior.* In that *act of faith* one is saved: "For by grace are ye saved, through faith" (Ephesians 2:8). Everything is now different. One has become a "new creature" in Christ; "old things are passed away; behold, all things are become new" (2 Corinthians 5:17).

The person is now "saved," a member of the universal church—not through joining a Baptist, Lutheran, Methodist, Catholic, or other church, but through the Spirit of God having placed him in the body of Christ: "The Lord added to the church daily such as should be [were being] saved" (Acts 2:47). "For by one Spirit are we all baptized into one body, whether we be Jews or Gentiles" (1 Corinthians 12:13). This is the "good news" of the gospel.

Christ told His disciples to "go into all the world and preach the gospel" (Mark 16:15) so that His mission of saving sinners would be accomplished. The primary goal of evangelicals is to preach the gospel to the lost so they might be saved. Peter said we "must be saved" (Acts 4:12) through Jesus, since there is no other way of salvation. Paul's passion for his fellow Jews was "that they might be saved" (Romans 10:1). Such is the desire of the evangelical for all mankind.

## Catholics Aren't "Saved" But Are "Lost"

The Reformers were Catholic priests who realized that they were not saved but were lost because Catholicism was not the biblical gospel that saves, but a false one. People were not being brought into a personal relationship with Christ as Savior but into bondage to the Church, hoping it would eventually get them to heaven if they followed its rules. In Catholicism, salvation is not an accomplished fact resulting from faith in Christ but an ongoing process of works and ritual in obedience to the Church.

Having believed the biblical gospel, the Reformers knew they were saved, rejoiced in that fact, and preached the good news of "the gospel of the grace of God" (Acts 20:24) to their fellow Catholics, hoping to reform the Church from within. For that they were excommunicated and persecuted, multitudes of them to the point of death.

The Council of Trent was convened to confront the issues raised by the Reformation. It rejected everything for which the

Reformers stood, from the authority of the Word of God to salvation by grace through faith and the priesthood of all believers. And it cursed with more than 100 anathemas anyone who accepted the doctrines which evangelicals hold. Not one of these curses has been removed even to this day.

These are the simple facts of history. Nothing has changed in the beliefs of either evangelicals or Catholics. Oddly, evangelicals who try to point out the errors in Catholicism because they love Catholics and want them to be saved are accused of "Catholic bashing." What of the more than 100 anathemas damning Protestants? Is that not the real "bashing"?

It is popularly imagined that Vatican II changed a great deal. In fact, only a few cosmetic changes were made, such as allowing the Mass to be in the language of the people rather than in Latin. Nothing of the core doctrines of Rome has been changed at all. Vatican II continually quoted from the Council of Trent and other councils and simply reaffirmed the established Catholic dogmas of the past. To make that abundantly clear, Vatican II states:

> This sacred council accepts loyally the venerable faith of our ancestors in the living communion which exists between us and our brothers who are in the glory of heaven or who are yet being purified [in purgatory] after their death; and it proposes again the decrees of the Second Council of Nicea [787], of the Council of Florence [1438-42], and of the Council of Trent [1545-63].[5]

## "Salvation" in Catholicism

Yes, the Catholic Church preaches salvation, but in direct opposition to Scripture and to what evangelicals believe. Salvation is through obeying the Church, not on the basis of the finished work of Christ upon the cross. No Catholic could say that he is saved and knows for certain that upon death he will go to heaven. To say that would bring automatic excommunication and the curse of Rome:

> If anyone says that in order to obtain the remission of sins it is necessary . . . to believe with certainty and without any hesitation . . . that his sins are forgiven him, let him be anathema (Council of Trent, Six, XVI, 13).

> If anyone says that he will for certain . . . have that
> great gift of perseverance even to the end [i.e. knows he
> is saved as the Bible promises] . . . let him be anathema
> (Council of Trent, Six, XVI, 16).[6]

The Roman Catholic Church is adamant in insisting that the work necessary for our salvation was not all finished by Christ upon the cross and that the sinner cannot be saved by simple faith in Him. It insists that salvation is an ongoing process of works, ritual, and suffering decreed by the Church that continues throughout life and more than likely requires one to suffer in purgatory as well:

> If anyone says that after the reception of the grace of
> justification the guilt is so remitted and the debt of
> eternal punishment so blotted out to every repentant
> sinner, that no debt of temporal punishment remains to be
> discharged either in this world or in purgatory before the
> gates of heaven can be opened, let him be anathema.[7]

Trent thus affirms that a "repentant sinner" is justified by "grace." That sounds biblical and deceives many. Though the *words* may be the same as evangelicals use, the Catholic *meaning* is entirely different. Trent insists that a "repentant sinner" who has been justified by "grace" must still suffer to be "purged" of his sins, either here or in purgatory, and most likely in both. That dogma denies the sufficiency of Christ's suffering for sin upon the cross. It is a false gospel, which Paul cursed (Galatians 1:8).

The Bible declares repeatedly that salvation is *not of works* and *not by the deeds of the law*. Yet Rome insists that salvation is indeed through works in obedience to its "New Law." Vatican II declares that "preaching the gospel" (the task of the bishops) is to help all men "attain to salvation through faith, baptism and *the observance of the commandments*"[8] (emphasis added). Instead of salvation by faith alone, as the Bible states, Vatican II declares "that God himself has made known to the human race how men *by serving him can be saved* . . . [9] (emphasis added).

## Redemption: Continuing Process or Accomplished Fact?

The most important part of "serving him" and "observance of the commandments" *for salvation* involves participation in the sacraments, principally baptism and the Mass. The long work of salvation is begun through baptism and continues for life through participation in other sacraments, good works, and suffering. The Catholic is never certain of the outcome or how long it will take. One hopes not to die in mortal sin, which sends the soul not to purgatory but to hell, from which there is no escape. Again Vatican II decrees:

> For it is the liturgy through which, especially in the divine sacrifice of the Eucharist, the work of our redemption is accomplished. . . .[10]
> But He [God] also willed that the work of salvation which they [the apostles] preached should be set in train through the sacrifice and sacraments, around which the entire liturgical life revolves. . . . The liturgy is . . . the fount from which all her [mother church's] power flows.[11]

According to God's Word, redemption (or salvation) was accomplished by Christ in His sacrifice upon the cross and is received by faith: "In whom we *have redemption through his blood*" (Ephesians 1:7; Colossians 1:14); "By his own blood he entered in once into the holy place [heaven], *having obtained eternal redemption for us*" (Hebrews 9:12). Rejecting God's Word, Rome insists that redemption remains yet to be accomplished by the Church's liturgy. Catholicism's contradiction of Scripture on this point is a blatant and fatal one.

In the gospel of God's grace preached by Christ's apostles for the salvation of souls there is nothing about liturgy, much less that it is the means of accomplishing redemption or the "fount" from which "all the Church's power flows." Those ideas were formulated later as part of Rome's "Apostolic Tradition," none of which can be traced back to the apostles. (See Appendix F.)

Evangelical leaders who accept Catholics as Christians often say, "I found that I had more in common with Catholics than with liberal Protestants." True, and one could have more in common politically or ethically even with conservative atheists or Buddhists than with *liberal Protestants*. But *salvation* has nothing to do with politics, ethics, or social action. A Catholic may be very moral and/or politically conservative, but when it comes to salvation, his Church's dogmas are the very antithesis of what the Bible teaches.

An ex-Catholic, cut off by his family (who won't even discuss the issues), explains what Catholics trust in for salvation:

> I am so grieved over what the Catholic Church is doing to members of my own family. It is sending my mother to hell. She sees no need to know Jesus or to read the Bible because of her belief that as long as she is in right standing with Jesus' Church that's all that is needed.
>
> After all, she attends Mass every Sunday and holy day of obligation. She is up on her confession and penance and she regularly performs corporal works of mercy and recites many prayers to saints and Mary for indulgences.
>
> Her good deeds and the administration of so-called sacraments are her passbook through the pearly gates once she's spent her allotted time burning in Purgatory to pay for what sins might remain. And Peter himself has the keys to give her entrance into heaven and he passed those keys on to the popes, so she thinks she's got it made.[12]

## Salvation: By Grace or by Works?

There is nothing in the gospel Paul preached about the "work of salvation" being "set in train" through Catholic liturgy, as Vatican II declares. Salvation is totally a work of God and Christ, finished once and for all upon the cross, with nothing for man to do because there is nothing man can do. "Work out your own salvation with fear and trembling" (Philippians 2:12) cannot possibly mean that we are to work *for* our salvation (a concept soundly condemned in Scripture); it can only mean that, having been saved, we are now to live the *outworking of that salvation* as those "created in Christ Jesus unto good works, which God hath before ordained that we should walk in them" (Ephesians 2:10).

A sinner (which we all are) can no more save himself than a corpse can give itself a blood transfusion. By nature we are "dead in trespasses and in sins" (Ephesians 2:1; cf. Colossians 2:13). In Catholicism, however, man has only "been *wounded* by sin,"[13] but is not *dead* in sin. Thus he can work for his salvation:

> Man gains such [God-given] dignity when, ridding himself of all slavery to the passions, he presses forward towards his goal by freely choosing what is good, and, by his diligence and skill, effectively secures for himself the means suited to this end.[14]

On the contrary, the Bible teaches that even the "righteousness" of a sinner is but "filthy rags" in God's sight (Isaiah 64:6). Only after being saved can we, in the power of the Holy Spirit, do good works—not to earn our salvation, but because we love Him who saved us. To be saved, man must acknowledge his guilt and helplessness to save himself and must believe in what Christ has done, accepting His substitutionary payment of the penalty for sin. The Bible repeatedly states that salvation is by grace through faith and not of works: "Through the grace of the Lord Jesus Christ we shall be saved" (Acts 15:11); "By grace ye are saved" (Ephesians 2:5); "The grace of God that bringeth salvation" (Titus 2:11).

Grace cannot be granted on the basis of a mere bookkeeping entry in heaven, but by the debt having been paid in full by Christ: "Being justified freely by his grace *through the redemption that is in Christ Jesus*" (Romans 3:24). The Catholic gospel of salvation by works and ritual stands in the fullest opposition to God's grace. It is, in fact, a rejection of God's offer of salvation by grace through faith in what Christ has done. It requires that Christ's sacrifice be supplemented by our works and/or suffering.

The gospel that we must believe to be saved is called "the gospel of the grace of God" (Acts 20:24) because "by grace are ye saved." Grace by its very nature excludes works. Paul argues: "If by grace, then is it no more of works; otherwise grace is no more grace. But if it be of works, then is it no more grace; otherwise work is no more work" (Romans 11:6). One cannot earn, merit, or pay for grace or else it would no longer be grace. Salvation can only be received from God as a gift of His grace by those who admit they neither deserve it nor can do anything to earn or merit it.

Vatican II repeatedly teaches salvation by works. Any active Catholic is earning his salvation. Some priests and nuns even today put stones in their shoes, wear haircloth shirts, and flagellate themselves to earn their salvation. Go to any Catholic country on Church holidays and see penitents beating themselves, pilgrims crawling upon their knees toward some Marian shrine, others staggering under heavy crosses, and still others hoping to better their chances of salvation by purchasing candles to burn before an image of "our lady" of this or that or some other "saint." In some places, such as the Philippines, a few zealots even have themselves nailed to crosses to hang in agony for a time to pay at least part of the price for their own salvation and for others as well. Far from rebuking these efforts, Rome encourages them. Salvation by works is so clearly taught in Rome's dogmas and so widely practiced by the faithful that none can deny it.

Remember Julian Hernandez, burned at the stake on December 22, 1560, in Seville, Spain, for bringing Bibles into that country from Germany? He was also immolated for believing that "whoever has faith in Jesus Christ, and trusts only in the merits of Him, is certain of going to heaven. . . ."[15] Imagine being condemned to the flames for believing the gospel of God's grace! Yet hundreds of thousands of others were slain by Rome for this reason.

## The Gospel According to Rome

One must carefully define terms in discussion with a Catholic. Catholicism employs many biblical words (grace, redemption, salvation, etc.), but with an unbiblical meaning. Catholicism affirms that Christ is the only begotten Son of God, one with the Father, who died for our sins, rose the third day, and will return to earth to reign. To that truth, however, have been added dogmas which pervert the gospel. Ignorant of these additions, many evangelicals think Catholics are Christians and pass that delusion on to others.

Catholic apologists such as InterVarsity author Peter Kreeft encourage such confusion by insisting that Catholics "are saved by God's free grace, not by working their way to heaven."[16] Yet Catholicism is all about "working one's way to heaven"! Kreeft hides the fact that "saved by God's free grace" means to the Catholic that original sin is wiped clean by baptism and that one may now earn one's way to heaven through good deeds, penance, eating Christ's body and blood in the Eucharist, prayers to Mary and the saints, qualifying for indulgences, and a host of other means. Furthermore, "grace" is not available to the Catholic directly from Christ or God but comes through the Church and its sacraments and especially through Mary, who is called "the dispenser of all grace."

The Catholic Church has long taught that "all grace is passed from God to Jesus, from Jesus to Mary, and from Mary to us. The grace of God, cure for our ills, comes to us through Mary like water through an aqueduct."[17] St. Bernadine said:

> [A]ll gifts, all virtues, and all graces are dispensed by the hands of Mary to whomsoever, when, and as she pleases. O Lady, since thou art the dispenser of all graces, and since the grace of salvation can only come through thy hands, *our salvation depends on thee*.[18]

## Mary's Role in Salvation

Mary plays the key role in salvation. St. Bernard said: "All men, past, present, and to come should look upon Mary as the means and negotiator of salvation. . . ."[19] Here is a sample of what the chief Catholic saints have said about Mary's role in salvation:

> St. Bonaventure says, "the gates of heaven will open to all who confide in the protection of Mary." St. Ephrem calls devotion to the divine Mother "the unlocking of the gates of the heavenly Jerusalem." Blosius also says, "To thee, O Lady, are committed the keys and the treasures of the kingdom of heaven." And therefore we ought constantly to pray to her, in the words of St. Ambrose, "Open to us, O Mary, the gates of

paradise, since thou hast its keys." Nay more, the Church says, "Thou art its gate."

"For," says the saint [Fulgentius], "by Mary God descended from heaven into the world, that by her man might ascend from earth to heaven." "And thou, O Lady," says St. Athanasius, "wast filled with grace, that thou mightest be the way of our salvation and the means of ascent to the heavenly kingdom." ...

"Blessed are they who know thee, O Mother of God," says St. Bonaventure; "for the knowledge of thee is the high road to everlasting life, and the publication of thy virtues is the way of eternal salvation." "Mary, in fine," says Richard of St. Laurence, "is the mistress of heaven; for there she commands as she wills, and admits whom she wills."

... Hence, says the Abbot Guerric, "he who serves Mary and for whom she intercedes, is as certain of heaven as if he was already there ... [and] those who do not serve Mary will not be saved. ..." St. Bonaventure exclaims, "Give ear, O ye nations; and all you who desire heaven, serve, honor Mary, and certainly you will find eternal life."

"It suffices, O Lady," says St. Anselm, "that thou willest it, and our salvation is certain." And St. Antoninus says that "souls protected by Mary, and on which she casts her eyes, are necessarily justified and saved."[20]

Another more recent author also quotes saints from the past: "The Church and the saints greet her thus: 'You, O Mary, together with Jesus Christ, redeemed us. ... O Mary, our salvation is in your hands. ... She is co-Redemptrix of the human race, because with Christ she ransomed mankind from the power of Satan. Jesus redeemed us with the blood of His body, Mary with the agonies of her heart ... suffer[ing] in her heart whatever was lacking in the passion of Christ."[21] A popular tract titled "Heaven Opened by the Practice of the THREE HAIL MARYS" promises:

One of the greatest means of salvation and one of the surest signs of predestination is unquestionably the devotion to the Most Blessed Virgin. All the holy doctors of the Church are unanimous in saying with St. Alphonsus of Liguori: "A devout servant of Mary shall never perish. ..."

I consecrate to Thee [Mary] my heart with all its affections, and beseech Thee to obtain for me from the Most Holy Trinity all the graces necessary for salvation.[22]

## "Graces" or Grace?

That Mary is the one to whom Catholics primarily look for "the graces necessary for salvation" cannot be denied. This fact is passed off by Catholic apologists as the practice of simple Catholics who don't know any better. On the contrary, the quotes above are from Catholic *saints*. Liguori was one of the great authorities in the Church, a cardinal and *saint*. Maryolatry is not rebuked by the Church hierarchy but is taught and encouraged by them. Bishops, cardinals, and popes themselves have been among the most devoted to Mary, none more so than John Paul II. "Our Lady of Mt. Carmel," who, it was said, had given The Great Promise to St. Simon Stock in 1251 ("Whosoever dies wearing this Scapular shall not suffer eternal fire") allegedly appeared to Pope John XXII in 1322 and reconfirmed the Sabbatine (Saturday) Privilege for those who wore her scapular: "I, the Mother of Grace, shall descend on the Saturday after their death and whomsoever I shall find in Purgatory, I shall free."[23] Confirmed by popes Alexander V, Clement VII, Pius V, Gregory XIII, and Paul V,[24] this promise has been relied upon by tens of millions of scapular-wearing Catholics since then. De Liguori explained further:

> [Pope Paul V] in a Bull of the year 1613, says that "Christian people [who wear the scapular] may piously believe that the blessed Virgin will help them after death by her continual intercession, her merits, and special protection. . . ."
>
> Why should we not hope for the same graces . . . of this good Mother? And if we serve her with more special love, why can we not hope to go to heaven immediately after death, without even going to purgatory?[25]

Many Catholics continue to pray to "Our Lady of Mt. Carmel" the prayer of St. Simon Stock: "Patroness of all who wear the Scapular, Pray for us! Hope of all who die wearing the Scapular, Pray for us! O Sweet Heart of Mary, be our salvation!"[26] Notice that salvation is through Mary and that Catholicism speaks of "graces," not merely "grace." The Mass is said to be the means of "applying" and "confer[ring] gradually and continually" the "graces needed for salvation" which Christ won on the cross.[27] *"Graces"?* The plural of grace is not found even *once* in Scripture.

The Bible says we are "saved by *grace*." Pardon of sin and eternal life is imparted by grace to all who believe God's promise through the gospel. The Catholic idea of "graces" indicates that salvation cannot be received all at once but only in installments a little at a time, principally through participation in the sacraments, which literally confer graces. Thus one never receives pardon and eternal life as a completed transaction. There are always more "graces" to be earned on the road to salvation. Yes, *earned*. Biblical grace is unmerited by man. Catholic "graces" are earned.

In Catholicism there is much to accomplish in order to receive "graces." In biblical contrast, all one must do to receive God's grace is to believe His offer in the gospel and accept His free gift of forgiveness and eternal life. To obtain "graces," however, there are many rules to follow, many ways by which they may be accumulated. Six hundred years later "Our Lady of Fatima" allegedly appeared in Portugal and promised to "assist at the hour of death with all the graces necessary for salvation" all who would follow certain prescribed rules for five consecutive months (which we will explain in detail later). There can be no doubt that Roman Catholicism teaches salvation through works and Mary plays the largest part and the key role. Vatican II says that to "gain indulgences the work prescribed must be done."[28]

Here we see clearly the great difference between Roman Catholicism and the biblical gospel of God's grace. In the former, graces come from God (through the mediation of Mary) in response to *what the devout Catholic does*; in the latter, grace comes from God in response to *what Christ has done*. It is an insult to God's justice to suggest that He can forgive sins because someone prays the Rosary or goes to Mass or does something else which the Church has prescribed. *God can only forgive sins and save the soul on the basis of Christ having paid the full penalty demanded by God's justice.* That having been done, God can be "just, and [at the same time] the justifier of him which believeth in Jesus" (Romans 3:26).

## A Semantic Misunderstanding?

In his book on apologetics, Peter Kreeft makes the outrageous claim that what Luther discovered of justification by faith was a Catholic doctrine that had all along been taught and is still taught by Rome.[29] Surely Kreeft knows that Catholic "justification by faith" is entirely different from what Luther came to believe from Scripture and from what evangelicals believe today. Otherwise, Luther and the other Reformers must have been mentally deficient indeed. And the inquisitors must have been even more cruel than we thought not to have told the poor souls they committed to the flames that it was all a semantic misunderstanding, that Rome taught their "heresy" and was even its originator.

Keith Fournier in his book *Evangelical Catholics* equates Catholicism with the biblical gospel of God's grace. That some Catholics use D. James Kennedy's *Evangelism Explosion* materials is offered as proof that they are evangelical. When asked about this usage, however, Fournier replied:

> . . . there were a couple of things in James Kennedy's process [of evangelism] that we as Catholics couldn't accept because it wasn't Catholic teaching. For example, too obvious was the total assurance of salvation . . . and the other one is salvation by faith alone.
>
> For Catholics we are saved by faith and also through obedience to Christ . . . there are acts of obedience and cooperation in God's Spirit that are tied up with salvation.[30]

Paul wrote: "Though we or an angel from heaven preach any other gospel unto you than that which we have preached unto you, let him be accursed" (Galatians 1:8). He was referring to those of his day who "pervert the gospel of Christ" (verse 7).

These "Judaizing" legalists, while partly affirming the true gospel, also declared that, in addition, one had to be circumcised and keep the law (Acts 15:24). That addendum perverted the gospel and brought Paul's curse upon them. Catholicism has had 15 centuries to add things to the gospel that the Judaizers never imagined. It merits Paul's curse.

## Contrast with the Biblical Gospel

Paul made it very clear that salvation results from believing the gospel: "I am not ashamed of the gospel of Christ, for it is the power of God unto salvation to everyone that believeth [it] . . ." (Romans 1:16). Salvation is that simple, and has nothing to do with the opinions of a Roman pontiff and his colleagues in a hierarchy which didn't even exist until centuries after the gospel was first preached and had resulted in the salvation of millions.

Paul didn't tell the desperate jailer mentioned above: "Believe on Christ and that will get you started on a long road of good deeds, church membership, sacraments, prayers to saints, etc. If you stick with it, eventually, after excruciating suffering in the flames of purgatory and if enough Masses and Rosaries are said for you, heaven's gates will at last open." But that is the gospel of Rome. These ideas are all later inventions which give Rome incredible power over those who look to her for salvation. That hundreds of millions are still being led astray concerns us deeply.

Roman Catholic salvation is not what the Bible teaches. Christ said, "Come unto *me*" (Matthew 11:28); Rome says, "Come unto *Mother Church*." Catholics can't reach Christ directly but must come through the Church, which offers for salvation, in addition to Christ's finished work, the merits of the saints plus credit for one's own penance and good works, the suffering of others on one's behalf, submission to the popes, obedience to the Church's decrees, etc. Vatican II states very clearly that the Catholic Church "is necessary for salvation."[31] This dogma is stated in numerous papal decrees like that of Pope Boniface VIII:

> There is one holy Catholic and apostolic church, outside of which there is no salvation. . . . it is altogether

necessary for salvation for every creature to be subject to the Roman Pontiff.[32]

The Church is the key to salvation for the Catholic, and through her the faithful are kept on a treadmill of Church-directed self-effort. The new universal *Catechism of the Catholic Church* refers to "all the ways of salvation" which the Church administers[33] and declares that "salvation comes from Christ the head through the Church, his body . . . [which] is necessary for salvation."[34] Vatican II affirms that there are many "means of salvation" dispensed by the Church:

> Fully incorporated into the Church are those who, possessing the Spirit of Christ, accept all the means of salvation given to the Church together with her entire organization, and who—by the bonds constituted by the profession of faith, the sacraments, ecclesiastical government, and communion—are joined in the visible structure of the Church of Christ, who rules her through the Supreme Pontiff and the bishops.[35]

Instead of looking to Christ alone and having a personal relationship with Him, the Roman Catholic looks to the Church and must be in a proper relationship with it when he or she dies in order to be saved. This is taught to the Catholic from childhood, is found in every catechism, and is recited for confirmation. Hear Vatican II: "Basing itself on Scripture and tradition, it [the Church] teaches that the Church, a pilgrim now on earth, is necessary for salvation. . . . He [Christ] himself explicitly asserted . . . the necessity of the Church which men enter by baptism as through a door."[36] The Vatican's new universal catechism explicitly states that salvation flows from Christ *through the Church.*[37] Canon 992 calls the Roman Catholic Church "the minister of redemption."[38]

The Roman Catholic apologist will argue that one need not be in the Church to be saved and will cite Vatican II to the effect that even idolaters can be saved without belonging to the Church:

> Nor is God remote from those who in shadows and images seek the unknown God, since . . . the Saviour

wills all men to be saved. Those who, through no fault of their own, do not know the Gospel of Christ or his Church, but who nevertheless seek God with a sincere heart, and, moved by grace, try in their actions to do his will as they know it through the dictates of their conscience—those too may achieve eternal salvation.[39]

The preceding sections, however, explicitly declare that "in different ways to it [the Roman Catholic Church] belong, or are related: the Catholic faithful, others who believe in Christ, and finally all mankind, called by God's grace to salvation."[40] Moreover, the next paragraph states that salvation is denied to "those who, knowing that the Catholic Church was founded as necessary by God through Christ, would refuse either to enter it, or to remain in it."[41] In other words, pagan idolaters somehow are in the Church, though unaware of that fact, and will be saved through her, but Protestants and especially ex-Catholics are anathematized.

## What's Wrong with Good Works?

A critical distinction must be made between good works *to merit salvation* (an impossible task) and the good works (called the "fruit of the Spirit"—Galatians 5:22,23) which *result from being born again* by the Holy Spirit. A sinner can no more become a saint by doing good works than a crab apple tree can become a Golden Delicious apple tree by pinning Golden Delicious apples upon its branches. The fruit results from the kind of tree it already is. Only after a sinner is saved by grace and thereby miraculously turned into a saint by God can good works acceptable to God result. "Not by works of righteousness which we have done, but according to his mercy he saved us" (Titus 3:5).

Moreover, what seems "good" from our perspective is badly flawed in God's eyes. Jesus said, "There is none good but one, that is God" (Mark 10:18). By God's perfect standard, "there is none that doeth good, no not one" (Romans 3:12; cf. Psalm 14:1,3). "All have sinned and come short of the glory of God" (Romans 3:23). So what seems like "good works" to us is unacceptable to God.

As for keeping the law, "by the deeds of the law there shall no flesh be justified in his sight" (Romans 3:20). Imagine a person arrested for speeding who thinks he should escape the penalty because he has driven that same road within the speed limit more times than he has broken it. That plea won't work in any earthly court, yet multitudes hope their good deeds will exceed their bad and thus merit heaven. Suppose the guilty party tells the judge, "Let me off this time and I promise never to break the law again." The judge replies, "If you never break the law again, you're only doing what the law demands. You get no *extra credit* for perfect performance." Thus to live a perfect life in the future (even if we could) could not make up for having committed even one sin in the past.

Furthermore, salvation is a gift: "The *gift* of God is eternal life" (Romans 6:23); "God hath *given* to us eternal life, and this life is in his Son" (1 John 5:11). One cannot earn or merit or pay for a gift. It must be received gratis or it is not a gift. Jesus said, "I *give* them eternal life" (John 10:28). Salvation and the eternal life which accompanies it must be received as a *gift* from God. Any attempt to offer works is to reject the gift.

Is there no place for good works? Most decidedly. Good works *follow* salvation as surely as fruit is produced in nature and light accompanies the rising of the sun. Christians are exhorted to be "rich in good works" (1 Timothy 6:18) and to be "careful to maintain good works" (Titus 3:8). Christians are "new creatures" (2 Corinthians 5:17) "created in Christ Jesus unto good works" (Ephesians 2:10), of which we are to be "zealous" (Titus 2:14).

### Aren't Some Catholics Saved?

"But surely some Catholics are saved!" is often the response to the truth about Catholicism. I am more charitable than Rome, which anathematizes those who say they are saved. Yes, some Catholics may be saved, but only by believing the same gospel whereby other lost souls are saved. Nor can one believe two contradictory propositions simultaneously. One can't believe that Christ obtained redemption through His blood and also believe that redemption is being accomplished through works, suffering, ritual, and indulgences; one can't believe that salvation is by faith and *"not of works"* and at the same time believe that good works earn salvation.

It is often said in its defense that the Roman Catholic Church professes the orthodox creeds and therefore that all Catholics are Christians. The ancient creeds, however, do not contain the gospel. Certainly neither the Apostles' nor the Nicene creeds do. They declare the deity of Christ, His virgin birth, and that He "suffered under Pontius Pilate," but they do not specify that He died for our sins and that we have eternal life through faith in Him. So it is fallacious to suggest that the Roman Catholic Church is evangelical because it subscribes to "the ancient church creeds."

In a recent survey of 2000 homes in Spain only two persons knew clearly what the gospel was, and they were Protestants. The other 1998 were Catholics who thought good works, church attendance, etc. would get them to heaven. In 15 years of evangelizing in Spain, missionary friends of the author have never met even one Catholic who was saved or knew how to be saved. Knowing that Catholics are lost causes evangelicals to work day and night to bring them the gospel!

This author has contacted a multitude of Catholics who were saved and left that Church. *Not one* had ever heard the true gospel preached there; all were saved by believing a gospel that is anathema to Catholicism. It is love and compassion for Catholics, *that they might be saved*, that motivates a book such as this.

*This do in remembrance of me. . . . For as often as ye eat this bread and drink this cup, ye do show [proclaim] the Lord's death till he come.*

—1 Corinthians 11:24,26

*There should be no doubt in anyone's mind "that all the faithful ought to show to this most holy sacrament [wafer which allegedly has been transformed into Christ's body] the worship which is due to the true God, as has always been the custom of the Catholic Church. Nor is it to be adored any the less because it was instituted by Christ to be eaten." [quoting Trent] . . . he is to be adored there because he is substantially [physically] present there . . . whole and entire, God and man . . . permanently . . . through that conversion of bread and wine which, as the Council of Trent tells us, is most aptly named transubstantiation*

*. . . in the Eucharist we become partakers of the Body and Blood of God's only Son . . . [and] the partaking of the Body and Blood of Christ has no less an effect than to change us into what we have received.*

—Vatican II[1]

# 24

# "Sacrifice" of the Mass

We have come to the very heart of Roman Catholicism, that unique element which separates it from all other religions and especially from evangelical Christianity: the *sacrifice* of the Mass. In it "the sacrifice of the cross is perpetuated. [It is] the source and the summit of the whole of the Church's worship and of the Christian life."[2] Declared present on the altar through the miracle of transubstantiation (which only the Catholic priest can perform) is the "true Body and Blood of Jesus Christ, who is really and substantially present under the appearance of bread and wine in order to offer himself in the sacrifice of the Mass and to be received as spiritual food in Holy Communion."[3]

Christ said from the cross just as He died, "It is finished" (John 19:30). But to the Catholic it isn't finished. Christ's sacrifice continues to this day, being endlessly repeated on Catholic altars: "Each time Mass is offered, the Sacrifice of Christ is repeated. A new sacrifice is not offered, but by divine power, one and the same sacrifice is repeated. . . . In the Mass Christ continues to offer Himself to the Father as He did on the Cross"[4] but in an "unbloody manner under the appearance of bread and wine."[5]

Calvary was a very bloody scene. How there could be an unbloody repetition thereof is not explained. Furthermore, the Bible distinctly says that "without shedding of blood is no remission [of sins]" (Hebrews 9:22). Yet the "unbloody" Mass is deemed to bring remission of sins—a remission which is not needed, for Christ already obtained it on the cross. The Bible says:

> And he took the cup . . . saying . . . this is my blood of the new testament, which is shed [on the cross] for many for the remission of sins (Matthew 26:27,28).
> To him [Christ] give all the prophets witness, that . . . whosoever believeth in him shall receive [as a gift of God's grace] remission of sins (Acts 10:43).

### Many Sacrifices or Only One?

The Mass is called a *propitiatory sacrifice* in which "Christ offers himself [perpetually] for the salvation of the entire world . . . [and] the work of our redemption is accomplished."[6] In contrast, the Bible repeatedly emphasizes that the full penalty for sin was paid upon the cross and on that basis the resurrected Christ "entered in *once* into the holy place [heaven], having obtained eternal redemption for us" (Hebrews 9:12). There He is seated at the Father's right hand, our Great High Priest (Hebrews 4:14), representing those He has redeemed, where "he ever liveth [dies no more] to make intercession for them":

> Who needeth not daily, as those [Old Testament] high priests, to offer up sacrifice . . . for this he did *once*, when he offered up himself [on the cross] (Hebrews 7:27).

The contrast between Catholicism and what the Bible teaches could not be greater than with regard to the alleged "sacrifice" of the Mass. That difference is exposed with stark clarity in the distinction which the Bible emphasizes between the *one* sacrifice Christ made of Himself and the continual Old Testament sacrifices which had to be *repeated daily*. The repetition of those offerings is given as proof that they could not pay the penalty for sin; and the fact that Christ was offered only *once* is given as proof that His sacrifice was sufficient and never needed to be repeated. That the Mass must be *repeated* proves its ineffectiveness. If once is not enough, then neither would be a billion repetitions; nor can Rome say how many masses it takes to get anyone out of purgatory.

The *many* Old Testament sacrifices of animals were anticipatory types of the *one* sacrifice of Christ upon the cross which would accomplish what they could not. The Bible allows no misunderstanding:

> Nor yet that he [Christ] should offer himself often, as the [Jewish] high priest entereth into the holy place every year with blood of others; for then must he often have suffered since the foundation of the world; but now *once* in the end of the world hath he appeared to put away sin by the sacrifice of himself.
>
> And as it is appointed unto men *once to die*, but after this the judgment, so Christ was *once offered* to bear the sins of many. . . .
>
> For the law . . . can never with those sacrifices which they offered year by year continually make the comers thereunto perfect. For then would they not have ceased to be offered? . . .
>
> But this man [Christ], after he had offered *one sacrifice for sins forever*, sat down on the right hand of God . . . for by *one offering* he hath perfected *forever* them that are sanctified. . . .
>
> [God says] their sins and iniquities will I remember no more. Now where remission of these is, there is *no more offering for sin* (Hebrews 9:25–10:2; 10:12-18).

Scripture could not be clearer. Christ's sacrifice took place *once for all time* upon the cross and is never to be repeated because it paid the full penalty for sin. That the Mass is Christ being sacrificed over and over on Catholic altars is the heart of Catholicism; and the repetition of the Mass is the Catholic's main hope of eventual release from purgatory. That doctrine directly contradicts the Bible. Vatican II declares: "In the sacrifice of the Mass . . . the body which is given for us and the blood which is shed for the remission of sins are offered to God by the Church for the salvation of the whole world."[7] If this is true, then Christ's death upon the cross was not sufficient but only a partial payment for sin. Yet the Bible assures us that He paid the *full* penalty for our sins.

## The Impossibility

What is claimed for the "sacrifice of the Mass" (whether it is called a renewal, repetition, reenactment, or re-presentation) is impossible. Christ's sacrifice upon the cross occurred at a specific time and accomplished its purpose. This historic event may be (and should be) *remembered* and *honored*, but it can no more be "perpetuated," repeated, or "re-presented" than yesterday's news or any other past occurrence. And why should it be, since by that *one offering* He "perfected forever them that are sanctified"?

The Christian's faith is in Christ's sacrifice upon the cross. The Catholic's faith is in the Church's alleged ability to repeat that sacrifice upon its altars. Yet even the pope can't say how many such repetitions may be needed. Thus many Catholics designate large sums in their wills so that after their decease hundreds and even thousands of Masses will be said on their behalf. This doctrine breeds uncertainty, not the calm assurance that Christ offers in Scripture. The *Pocket Catholic Dictionary* declares, ". . . the more often the sacrifice [of the Mass] is offered the more benefit is conferred." How much "benefit" in each Mass? No one knows.[8]

Furthermore, Christ is now in a resurrected, glorified, immortal body at the Father's right hand, never to die again. He cannot be "sacrificed" in the Mass. Christ declared: "I am he that liveth, and was dead; and, behold, I am *alive forevermore*" (Revelation 1:18). Moreover, his body, which now lives in "the power of an *endless life*" (Hebrews 7:16), contains no blood, which is the life of mortal flesh. His resurrection body is immortal.

## "Flesh and Bone"—A Resurrected Body Without Blood

When Christ first came to His disciples that resurrection evening they thought they were seeing a spirit. To prove He was alive, He said, "Handle me and see, for a spirit hath not flesh and bones [not "flesh and *blood*"], as ye see me have"

(Luke 24:39). Doubting Thomas, absent on that occasion, declared skeptically, "Except I shall . . . put my finger into the print of the nails, and thrust my hand into his side, I will not believe" (John 20:25).

When Christ returned a week later He invited Thomas to do just that: "Reach hither thy hand and thrust it into my side, and be not faithless, but believing" (John 20:27). Clearly Christ's wounds had not "healed" but remain as memorials. The gaping hole in Christ's side into which Thomas could thrust his whole hand is further evidence that there is no blood in His body.

Blood is the life of mortal flesh, and Christ's blood was poured out upon the cross for our sins: "For the life of the flesh is in the blood, and I have given it to you upon the altar to make an atonement for your souls, for it is the blood that maketh an atonement for the soul" (Leviticus 17:11). Yet the wine is said to become Christ's blood upon Catholic altars—the blood of His precrucifixion body that was resurrected immortal.

To repeat or to perpetuate the sacrifice of Christ, His precrucifixion body must be reconstituted. This stunning feat is allegedly accomplished through the "miracle" of transubstantiation: changing bread and wine into the body and blood of Christ. Therefore, "the priest is indispensable, since he alone by his powers can change the elements of bread and wine into the body and blood of Christ. . . ."[9]

## The Vital Role of Transubstantiation

Due to the alleged miracle of transubstantiation, the host (or wafer) which is eaten at Mass is worshiped as Christ Himself. The same devotion is directed to additional blessed wafers reserved in a tabernacle (a small, boxlike receptacle covered with a veil and with a light perpetually burning nearby). The devout come and pray to the wafers therein as though to Christ, believing they are in His holy presence. Mother Teresa expresses this belief:

> It is beautiful to see the humility of Christ . . . in his permanent state of humility in the tabernacle, where he has reduced himself to such a small particle of bread that the priest can hold him in two fingers.[10]

A large wafer is exhibited for adoration in a *monstrance*—a gold or silver vessel with a transparent center for displaying the wafer. Seeing the sacrament "stimulates the faithful to an awareness of the marvelous presence of Christ, and is an invitation to spiritual communion with him. It is therefore an excellent encouragement to offer him [in the wafer] that worship in spirit and truth which is his due."[11] An ex-Catholic writes:

> [Catholics] bow down to a wafer that sits in a "tabernacle" on an altar and believe that it is actually Christ Himself. . . . That's why as a child I was taught to make the sign of the cross whenever passing a Catholic church.

There is a revival across America of "perpetual adoration of the Blessed Sacrament." Parish families sign up for an hour or more each week so that some devout are "keeping Christ company" in worship of the host almost around the clock every day. "Pope John Paul II approves enthusiastically of perpetual adoration . . . establishing exposition of the Blessed Sacrament in St. Peter's in 1981." He has said:

> How great is the value of conversation with Christ in the blessed sacrament. There is nothing more consoling on earth, nothing more powerful for advancing along the road to holiness.[12]

## Pagan Pageantry to Honor Christ?

Enclosed in a *monstrance*, the wafer is also carried in processions. It is astonishing with what extravagant pageantry the host is paraded through the streets on special festivals. An early eighteenth-century eyewitness and participant in the grand procession in Zaragoza, Spain, on the annual festival of *Corpus Christi* writes:

> The Dean of the cathedral summons all the communities of Friars, all the clergy of the parish churches, the Viceroy, Governor and Magistrates, the judges of the civil and criminal council, with the Lord chancellor of the kingdom and all the fraternities, brotherhoods, or corporations of the city to meet

together . . . in the Metropolitan cathedral church of St. Salvator, with all the standards, trumpets, giants [huge wooden figures 15 feet tall dressed colorfully] in their respective habits of office or dignity; and all the clergy of the parish churches and Friars of convents, to bring along in a procession all the silver bodies of saints on a base or pedestal, which are in their churches and convents. The inhabitants are to clean the streets, which the sacrament is to go through, and cover the ground with greens, and flowers, and to put the best hangings in the fronts of balconies and windows.

The Viceroy goes in state with the Governor, Judges, Magistrates, and officers to meet the Archbishop in his palace, and to accompany his Grace to church, where all the communities of Friars, Clergy, and Corporations, are waiting for them. . . . After the Archbishop has made a prayer before the great altar, the musick begins . . . while the Archbishop takes out of the tabernacle the Host upon the rich [solid gold] chalice, and placeth it on the great *custodia*, on the altar's table.

The Archbishop in his pontifical habit officiateth . . . his Grace giveth the blessing to the people with the sacrament in his hands. Then the Archbishop, with the help of the Dean, Archdeacon, and Chanter, placeth the *custodia* on a gilt pedestal, which is adorned with flowers and the jewels of several ladies of quality, and which is carried on the shoulders of 12 Priests, drest in the same ornaments they say Mass in. This being done, the procession begins to go out of the church in the following order.

First of all the bagpipe, and the great and small giants [colorful figures], dancing all along the streets [followed by] the big silver Cross of the cathedral. . . . [Next come 30 corporations of tradesmen, the smallest is 30 people, then] the boys and girls of the blue hospital with their master, mistress, and the chaplain. . . . [Then all the religious orders, led by the Franciscans because they are the youngest, in all about 70 orders] drest in the ornaments they use at the altar. . . . There are 20 convents of Friars . . . about 2000 present on this solemn occasion; 16 convents of Nuns . . . [about] 1500 . . . [and the 1200 parish priests] . . . [in all] 4700 ecclesiastical persons [and] the inhabitants come to 15,000 families.

[Then come] the clergy of the cathedrals of St. *Salvator* and the lady of *Pilar*, with all their sacerdotal ornaments and the musicians of both the cathedrals which go before the *custodia* or sacrament, singing all the way. Then the 12 Priests more, that carry the canopy, under which the sacrament goes. . . . The Archbishop in his pontifical habit goes at the Subdeacon's right hand, the Viceroy at the Archbishop's, and the Deacon and Subdeacon one at the right and the other at the left all under the canopy.

Six Priests with incense and incensaries on both sides of the *custodia* go incensing the sacrament without intermission; while one kneels down before the great Host and incenses it three times the other puts incense in his incensary . . . and thus they do from the coming out of the church till they return back again to it.

The great Chancellor, Presidents, and councils follow after [with] all the nobility, men and women, with lighted candles. This procession lasts four hours from the time it goes out, till it comes into the church again. All the bells of the convents, and parishes ring all this time. . . .

The riches of that procession are incredible. . . . With this magnificence they carry the sacrament through the principal streets of the city, and all the people that are in the balconies and lattice windows throw roses and other flowers upon the canopy of the sacrament as it goes by.[13]

If this wafer is the literal precrucifixion body of Jesus Christ being offered on Catholic altars around the world, then the pageantry is not overdone—or is it? How did that one body become millions of bodies each in the form of a tiny wafer, *each one literally and physically* Jesus Christ "whole and entire"? How did the bloodied "old rugged cross [with] its shame and reproach" transmute into gold and become encrusted with diamonds? And how can bishops in their ornately embroidered robes of finest silk represent that One who hung naked on the cross and whose lifeless, battered body wrapped in graveclothes was laid in a tomb? Has the "perpetuation" of Christ's death become an incongruous farce?

What does such pagan pageantry with its gold and jewels have to do with *Calvary*? How blasphemous is this parading before the world of the Church's boasted power to hold the precrucifixion body of Christ in its hands and offer Him again upon its altars!

This dogma breeds fanaticism, not faith. The slaughter of the Jews in Deggendorf to which we earlier referred had been in revenge for their allegedly stealing and "torturing" a consecrated wafer.[14] Those conditioned to believe that wine had become Christ's blood were able to believe Hitler's myth of blood as well.

## Reality or Fraud?

This alleged power of the priests to re-create upon Catholic altars the literal body of Christ and then to offer Him to God in "the sacrifice of the Mass [in which] Our Lord is immolated . . . [and] Christ perpetuates in an unbloody manner the sacrifice offered on the cross"[15] is the distinctive mark of Roman Catholicism. It is thereby, as we have noted, separated by an impassable gulf from all other religions and especially from evangelical Christianity. What we have here is either the most vital and miraculous reality or the most diabolical fraud. There is no middle ground.

The Catholic cannot deny that on the face of it the claim of transubstantiation seems preposterous. There is no detectable change in wafer or wine after they presumably have been transformed through the priest's unique power into Christ's literal body and blood. How then can one be certain that this "miracle" has occurred? As with so much else in Catholicism, assurance comes only by blindly accepting whatever the Church says.

Yes, some Bible verses are offered in support of this dogma, but the Catholic must accept the Church's interpretation of these, though common sense and proper exegesis would reject it. There are two main passages from which the doctrine of transubstantiation is derived: John 6:51-57 and Matthew 26:26-28 (compare also Luke 22:19,20 and 1 Corinthians 11:24,25). Let us consider them.

## Literalism or Symbolism?

Referring to His impending crucifixion, Christ told the Jews in John 6, " . . . the bread that I will give is my flesh, which I will give for the life of the world. . . . Except ye eat the flesh of the Son of man and drink his blood, ye have no life in you" (verses 51,53). Catholicism takes these words *literally* and faults Protestantism for interpreting them *symbolically*. Christ also said, "I am the bread of life" (verse 35). Why not take Him literally there, making Him a loaf of bread? Is it any more foolish to say Christ is bread than to say a piece of bread is Christ? The Bible should be taken literally wherever that is its meaning—but not when analogy or symbolism is meant and literalism would violate logic or God's laws.

The psalmist said, "He [God] shall cover thee with his feathers, and under his wings shalt thou trust" (Psalm 91:4). Are we to picture God as a big bird? Jesus wept over Jerusalem: "How often would I have gathered thy children together, as a hen doth gather her brood under her wings, and ye would not!" (Luke 13:34). Surely He wasn't speaking literally, though He was identifying Himself as the very One of whom Moses wrote in Psalm 91.

Jesus called mankind to *believe* on Him. He told Nicodemus that those who *believed* on Him would "not perish but have everlasting life" (John 3:16), and that *believing* on Him would bring about a new birth. He didn't mean a physical birth, however, but a *spiritual* birth, a fact which even Catholics acknowledge. He promised to give the woman at the well "living water" and even "a well of water" springing up within her (John 4:10-14), but He surely didn't mean physical water. He told the Jews that whoever would believe on Him, "out of his belly shall flow rivers of living water" (John 7:38), but He meant neither a physical belly nor literal physical rivers.

In John 6 Jesus said: "I am the bread of life; he that cometh to me shall never hunger and he that believeth on me shall never thirst" (verse 35). That He didn't mean He was literal, physical bread or that those who believed on Him would thereafter never have the need for physical food or drink is clear—but they would never hunger or thirst *spiritually* again. He was of course speaking spiritually and illustrating His ideas with analogies from things familiar to all. Then why should He be taken literally when a few moments later He says that one must "eat" His body and blood?

Based on that crucial interpretive mistake, the Catholic insists that the bread and wine is literally Christ. Let us follow that to its logical conclusion. If Christ was speaking literally about His body, then He must have been speaking literally when He said, "I am the bread of life; he that cometh to me shall never hunger and he that believeth on me shall never thirst" (verse 35). Since the Catholics claim to literally eat Christ's physical body, they should never physically hunger or thirst—but of course they do. Yet if "hungering and thirsting" are spiritual terms, then so must be the eating of His body. Obviously, Christ is saying that those who believe on Him receive eternal life and don't have to keep coming back to Him for another installment.

Catholicism insists that the faithful eat the body and drink the blood of Christ frequently. The more Masses said the better, yet even then one can't be sure of making heaven without suffering in purgatory. *The Code of Canon Law*, Canon 904, says, "Remembering that the work of redemption is continually accomplished in the mystery of the Eucharistic sacrifice, priests are to celebrate frequently; indeed daily celebration is strongly recommended. . . ."[16] The Bible, however, assures us in numerous verses which we have already quoted that the work of redemption was accomplished once for all on the cross and that Christ's sacrifice is never to be repeated.

Christ said, "This is the will of him that sent me, that everyone which seeth the Son and *believeth* on him may have everlasting life" (John 6:40). Clearly this believing on Christ (which He likens to eating Him) is a once-for-all act. He doesn't say it must be done 20 times, a thousand times, once a day, or once a week. *The moment a person believes on Christ, he or she receives forgiveness of sins and everlasting life as a free gift of God's grace.* Clearly, a person who has received eternal life by once believing/eating need never repeat that act. Otherwise everlasting life is misnamed, for something that is everlasting must last forever and need not be renewed or reinforced. Consider Christ's words in this same chapter again:

> Verily, verily, I say unto you, He that believeth on me *hath* [present possession] everlasting life. I am that bread of life. Your fathers did eat manna in the wilderness and are dead. This is the bread which cometh down from

heaven that a man may eat thereof and not die. I am the
living bread which came down from heaven; if any man
eat of this bread he shall live forever, and the bread that I
will give is my flesh, which I will give for the life of the
world (John 6:47-51).

Where did Christ give His flesh? Not at the Last Supper, as
Catholicism teaches, but *on the cross*. That interpretive error is
again a fatal one. For if when Christ said, "This is my body
... this is my blood" at the Last Supper it was literally true,
then He sacrificed Himself before He went to the cross! This
is, in fact, the strange teaching of Catholicism: "Our Saviour
at the Last Supper on the night when he was betrayed instituted
the eucharistic sacrifice of his Body and Blood so that he might
perpetuate the sacrifice of the cross throughout the centuries
till his coming."[17]

We repeat: If Christ is speaking physically of His body and
blood in John 6, then those who eat of Him will never physically die. But all of the apostles themselves are dead. If He did
not mean that eating of Him would prevent physical death,
then neither did He refer to physically eating Him. He is
obviously speaking spiritually *all through that chapter,* as
elsewhere.

Tragically, the Catholic is prevented from receiving the
spiritual eternal life that Christ offers by the dogma that He is
speaking physically. Rome claims to control "the merits
Christ won" and to dispense another installment thereof each
time the Catholic (so it is imagined) physically ingests Christ's
literal body and blood. The Mass must be repeated endlessly.

## Parables to the Multitudes

When Jesus said, "I am the door; by me if any man enter in
he shall be saved" (John 10:9), not even Catholics take that to
mean that Christ is a *physical* door through which one must
*literally* walk one's *physical* body to be saved. He is using this
analogy to illustrate that in *believing on Him* one walks through
a door into a new state of spiritual being, eternal life. When
Jesus said, "I am the light of the world; he that followeth me
shall not walk in darkness" (John 8:12), He was not speaking of

*physical* light but of the *spiritual* light which those who believe on Him receive, in contrast to the spiritual darkness in which this world dwells.

Further examples could be given but would be superfluous. Jesus continually called mankind to *believe* on Him. Whatever He spoke about, whether the new birth, water, sheep, shepherd, seed, sower, plants, fruit, bread, or a door, was meant to convey a *spiritual truth* through the *physical object* of which He spoke and was not to be taken literally. We are told specifically that *whenever* Jesus spoke to the multitude, He *always* spoke to them in parables: "All these things spake Jesus unto the multitude in parables; and *without a parable spake he not unto them"* (Matthew 13:34).

Christ was speaking to the multitude in John 6. We know, therefore, that He was, as always to them, speaking in parables, using figurative and spiritual, not literal and physical, language. There are, of course, other reasons for knowing this.

## Further Compelling Arguments

It was and still is against the law for a Jew to partake of blood (Leviticus 7:26,27; 17:10,11; etc.), and under the inspiration of the Holy Spirit the apostles urged Gentile believers also, as something "necessary," to abstain "from blood" (Acts 15:28,29). Surely, then, Christ would not require Christian or Jew to drink His literal, physical blood. And eating His physical body would be cannibalism, an act He would not approve of, much less advocate. That He was referring to *believing on Him* and illustrating it by the symbol of eating and drinking is clear:

> I am the bread of life; he that *cometh* to me shall never hunger, and he that *believeth* on me shall never thirst. But . . . ye also have seen me and *believe* not. . . .
> He that *believeth* on me hath everlasting life. I am that bread of life. . . . The bread that I will give is my flesh, which I will give for the life of the world. . . .
> Except ye eat the flesh of the Son of man and drink his blood, ye have no life in you. Whoso eateth my flesh and

drinketh my blood hath eternal life (John 6:35,36,47, 48,51,53,54).

Is Jesus really saying that in order to receive eternal life one must literally eat and drink his physical body and blood? Or is He saying that we must *believe on Him* and is using the analogy of eating and drinking to illustrate that truth? He says very clearly that *believing* gives eternal life. Yet He says that only by *eating* Him can one have life. Here is an irreconcilable contradiction—unless, of course, *eating* is a synonym for *believing*.

There is an obvious reason why Christ used the symbol of eating. In the Old Testament the priests ate of the sacrifice: "The priest that offereth it for sin shall eat it . . . all the males among the priests shall eat thereof" (Leviticus 6:26,29; cf. 6:16,18; 7:6,15; etc.). Christ was thus telling the Jews that He was the fulfillment of the Old Testament sacrifices and that His body and blood would be given for the sins of the world. He was also introducing the priesthood of all believers. Only the priests ate of the sacrifice under the law, but now all must partake of Him by faith to receive the gift of eternal life by God's grace. All must believe that the Son of God had become a literal flesh-and-blood man in order to die for mankind.

There are numerous other reasons why Christ could not have meant the literal eating and drinking of His physical body and blood. His sacrifice for sin occurred only once. If there were any physical eating, it should have taken place at that time. The body that was sacrificed and laid in the grave, as already noted, was resurrected and glorified. Christ's new body in which He now resides at the Father's right hand in heaven has no blood and cannot die. The old body whose life was in the blood no longer exists. Paul said, "Yea, though we have known Christ after the flesh, yet now henceforth know we him [as He was before the cross] no more" (2 Corinthians 5:16). To suggest that the precrucifixion body of Christ has been re-created on Catholic altars to be offered again for sin is a clear contradiction of both Scripture and logic.

## The Bounds of Reality

The Catholic rests his entire case upon the plea that he is taking Christ literally. It is not literalism, however, but fantasy to suggest that each one of millions of wafers is the complete, whole, and entire physical, precrucifixion body of Christ—while at the same time Christ is in heaven in His resurrected body. "But God is omnipresent," is the response. That is true, and because He is God, by His Spirit, Christ is everywhere at once. But when Christ became a man He voluntarily subjected Himself to certain limitations. A physical body occupies space and therefore can only be in one place at a time. Never is there a hint in the Bible that Christ was *bodily* present in more than one place at a time.

Yes, Christ said, "Where two or three are gathered together in my name, there am I in the midst of them" (Matthew 18:20). Christians believe this promise, but no one imagines that Christ is at one and the same time *physically* present in the midst of thousands of different groups of believers around the world. In fact, none of them imagines He is present *physically* at all, for that would mean He could be seen, but He is not. To suggest that millions of wafers are each Christ's physical body, whole and entire, is to depart from reality and engage in fantasy.

Nor does Christ's language at the Last Supper support transubstantiation: "[He] took bread . . . broke it, and said, Take, eat; this is my body which is broken for you; this do *in remembrance* of me. . . . This cup is the new testament in my blood; this do ye, as oft as ye drink it, *in remembrance* of me" (1 Corinthians 11:23-25). He wants Christians to *remember* His death on the cross and to take bread and wine as a *reminder* thereof. His language contains no thought of a repetition of His sacrifice on the cross.

Notice His words, "This *is* my body." He didn't say that one day pieces of bread would *become* His body through the miraculous power of transubstantiation wielded by Catholic priests, but that the bread at that moment *was* His body. No one could take that statement literally, for he was sitting there in His physical body and holding the bread in His hands. Obviously the bread was symbolic.

We may be sure that none of Christ's disciples imagined that the bread He held was His literal body. That it could be His literal body and at the same time Christ be there in His literal body was impossible. Such a fantasy did not enter the minds of those present and was not invented until much later. It was certainly not conveyed by Christ's words, nor do we have any reason to believe that the disciples derived from them such a meaning. It was Pope Innocent III who made the Mass as a "sacrifice" official dogma in A.D. 1215.

## Lutheranism's Similar View

Martin Luther was unable to shake free from much of his Roman Catholicism (infant baptism, etc.), and it remains within the church that bears his name to this day. While denying that they teach transubstantiation, Lutherans declare:

> The true, real body and blood of Christ are somehow present, in a unique way, in, with, and under the bread and wine which are set aside, blessed, and consumed in the holy Supper. That is the plain meaning [?] of Scripture (Matthew 26:26-28; 1 Corinthians 10:16; 11:23-32). . . .
>
> The Lutheran doctrine is that the bread and wine in the holy Supper are the body and blood of Christ. How that can be, we do not know and do not understand. But . . . Christ . . . said that the bread is His body and that the wine is His blood. We simply echo His words. . . .
>
> Those who do not believe Christ's Words about this Sacrament, do not discern or recognize His body—or His blood—in the Supper and so can receive the Sacrament only in an unworthy way. . . .[18]

It is not a question of whether one *believes* Christ's words, but of how those words are *understood*. There is no more reason to take Him literally when He said "This is my body" than when He said "I am the door." To take Him literally violates common sense, consents to breaking God's law through cannibalism and partaking of blood, and leads to the foolish heresy that in spite of Christ being in heaven in a resurrected and glorified immortal body, His precrucifixion body of mortal flesh and blood is being ingested again and again by Catholics and Lutherans. It also leads to the fantasy of imagining that millions of bits of bread or wafers can each one simultaneously be the entire physical body of Christ.

At least Luther did not teach that Christ's sacrifice was being repeated endlessly and that forgiveness of sins and eternal life are received in installments by eating the bread and wine. That delusion fostered by transubstantiation prevents the Catholic from *believing* in Christ. The Eucharist is the very heart of the false gospel of works promulgated by Catholicism.

Sadly, the devout Catholic has been turned from simple *faith* in Christ as his Savior to what he thinks is the *physical eating* of Christ's body and blood. Thus salvation comes not through *faith* but *works*; not by *believing* but by *eating*. No wonder it is so difficult for a Catholic to accept the biblical gospel! He has been taught that each time he ingests the alleged body and blood of Christ he takes another step toward salvation and heaven. Obviously such a person finds it very difficult to accept that through *one act of faith*—receiving Christ by faith into his heart—he is saved eternally and at the moment of death passes instantly into Christ's presence, not into purgatory.

The gospel of God's grace is denied by the teaching that the "merits and graces" won by Christ are dispensed to the faithful in installments through Catholic liturgy, especially through the Mass. The alleged power of the priest to turn the tiny wafer and the wine into the literal body and blood of Christ is the heart of the lie. Thus the Catholic, ignorant of the biblical teaching that Christ's *one* sacrifice suffices and that there is "no more offering for sin" (Hebrews 10:18), has been convinced by his Church that repeated sacrifices of Christ on Catholic altars are paying for his sin:

> The Mass is a truly propitiatory sacrifice [by which] the Lord is appeased [and] pardons wrongdoings and sins. . . .[19]

## A "Miracle"?

Those who reject the fantasy of transubstantiation are accused of not believing in miracles. Yes, "with God all things are possible" (Matthew 19:26; Mark 10:27). Even that statement, however, must be defined by the nature of God and of reality. God cannot become a demon or Satan, nor can He lie

(Titus 1:2). Nor could God become the universe, for by His very nature He is separate and distinct from the universe and pantheism is therefore impossible.

Likewise a miracle must function within the bounds of verifiable reality. A wafer which has been "turned into" Christ's body and blood yet retains all its original qualities and characteristics lacks an essential of a miracle: to be recognizable and thereby bring glory to God. Since the wafer and wine remain unchanged, the alleged miracle remains unseen. But a miracle must be observable (the lame walk, the blind see, the storm is instantly calmed, the dead come to life upon command, etc.), or else no one can know that it has taken place and thus no one can give God glory for it.

Of course God would be able to turn a wafer into human flesh. John the Baptist said that God could "of these stones . . . raise up children unto Abraham" (Matthew 3:9; Luke 3:8). But if He did it, the stones which had been changed into human beings would not continue to look like stones and have all the qualities of stones. To turn a wafer into human flesh and blood would deny neither the nature of God nor of reality. But transubstantiation is not such a miracle. The wafer becomes Christ's body "under the appearance of a wafer."

There is no such "miracle" in the Bible. The opening of the Red Sea so that the Israelites could walk through it on dry land was a feat that both Jews and Egyptians observed and that both understood had occurred by God's power. Suppose it had been a "transubstantiation kind of miracle"—the Red Sea "opened" under the appearance of remaining closed and the Israelites had "walked" across on dry land "under the appearance" of having to swim across. Suppose Christ healed a blind man "under the appearance" of his not being able to see, or raised the dead "under the appearance" of lifelessness. Such suppositions are ludicrous, yet that is exactly the nature of the "transubstantiation miracle."

Let's take the miracle of the water turned to wine at Cana of Galilee. When the governor of the feast tasted it he exclaimed to the groom, "Thou hast kept the good [best] wine until now" (John 2:10). Suppose instead he had said, "This isn't *wine*, it's *water!*" The servants reply sincerely, "No, sir, it's *wine*." The governor's voice rises in anger: "Don't mock me! It looks like water, it tastes like water, it *is* water!" The servants insist, "Sir, it is *wine.* Jesus miraculously turned water into wine *under the appearance of it remaining water.*" There is no such "miracle" in the Bible, and for Rome to make such a claim is a lame attempt to cover obvious fraud.

## Decay, Condemnation, and Death

Let us consider only one further reason why transubstantiation is a hoax. The psalmist declared (and Peter quoted this prophecy in his Pentecost sermon, as did Paul later): "Thou wilt not . . . suffer thine Holy One to see corruption" (Psalm 16:10; cf. Acts 2:27; 13:35). Christ's body did not decay in the grave. Yet the consecrated and transubstantiated host reserved for administering to the sick or displayed for adoration breeds worms and mold if it isn't disposed of soon enough. If it were really Christ's body, it could not corrupt.

Tragically, the Mass becomes a cause of condemnation for Catholics, who "are obliged under penalty of serious [mortal] sin to hear Mass on Sundays and holy days. . . ."[20] According to a recent poll, only 33 percent of American Catholics attend Mass "on a given Sunday"[21] and far less do so *every* Sunday as required. Only 12 percent of the Catholics in France (which is 90 percent Catholic) can be found in Mass on any Sunday. This works out to a very high percentage of Catholics who are habitually in mortal sin and thus deprived of "sanctifying grace" and "the right to heaven."[22]

So important is this transubstantiation dogma to Rome that multitudes who could not accept it were burned at the stake. It was for this reason that most of the 288 English martyrs were consigned to the flames during the five-year reign of Bloody Queen Mary, who brought Catholicism back into England after a brief time of tenuous freedom from the papal tyranny.

Many a sincere and devout Roman Catholic desired to save England for beloved Mother Church and rejoiced when the Reformation was turned back. Today it is leading evangelicals who are only too happy to undo the Reformation and thereby deny Christ and His gospel. And in the process, they mock those who did not count their lives dear in order to preserve that gospel for us.

*The burning of the Marian martyrs is an act that the Church of Rome has never repudiated ...Never has she repented of her treatment of the Vaudois and the Albigenses...of the wholesale murders of the Spanish Inquisition ...of the burning of the English Reformers.*

*We should take note of that fact and let it sink down in our minds. Rome never changes.*

—Anglican Bishop J.C. Ryle, 1885

*The Roman Catholic Church is a counter-feit...of the worst and most diabolical kind ...a form of the antichrist...to be rejected and denounced....*

—D. Martin Lloyd-Jones

*I don't know anyone more dedicated to the great fundamental doctrines of Christianity than the Catholics.*

—W.A. Criswell, former president
Southern Baptist Convention[1]

*I've found that my beliefs are essentially the same as those of orthodox Roman Catholics.*

—Billy Graham[2]

# 25

# The Reformation Betrayed

There is a growing trend among today's evangelicals to embrace and promote a benign view of Romanism that contradicts the convictions held by Protestants for more than 400 years. The Reformation, if remembered at all, is being portrayed as an unnecessary separation from a Church which was biblical and evangelical. Statements by various evangelicals today impugn the faith and convictions of the millions of martyrs who died rather than accept transubstantiation, purgatory, indulgences, worship of saints, and the remainder of Rome's false and destructive gospel of ritual and works. If Catholicism stands solidly for "the great fundamental doctrines of Christianity," then what was the Reformation all about?

If the view held by many of today's evangelicals is right, then those millions put to death by Rome throughout the centuries died not for their faith but for a semantic misunderstanding. How tragic! If evangelical and Catholic doctrines are "essentially the same," then the Reformation was based upon an incredible mistake which is only now being recognized after more than four centuries. But if that is not the case, and there were indeed clear and vital differences between Catholic and Protestant views on essential doctrines at the time of the Reformation, why not today? Has Catholicism changed?

We have seen that the dogmas of Roman Catholicism which the martyrs could not embrace have not changed. Nor have evangelicals as a whole opted for a different gospel from salvation by grace through faith alone as it was preached by the Reformers. Certainly men such as Billy Graham and W.A. Criswell have demonstrated through long lives of service to Christ and winning thousands to Him that they would not knowingly compromise the gospel of God's grace through Jesus Christ. This makes it difficult to understand how they and other evangelical leaders profess a commonality of faith with Roman Catholicism which would have been unthinkable to past generations of Protestants.

A major reason for this book is to dispel the gross misunderstandings about Catholicism. Rome adeptly covers her real intentions with sweet words and hides her true character behind beautiful art and moving manifestations of piety. Much of what we have revealed thus far—even the truth behind events so current as the war in Yugoslavia, widespread sexual promiscuity of priests, and marriage annulments by the tens of thousands—has likely shocked, perhaps offended, many readers. This is because through its media dominance, Rome projects an image that makes the truth difficult to believe.

Having joined forces in political and social action, why shouldn't Catholics and Protestants evangelize the world together as well? At least they subscribe to the same creeds and many of the same morals. Whatever "slight differences in doctrine" exist can hardly be of any great importance and should not be allowed to separate Christians. Such is the thinking of many evangelical leaders, and their followers, through the same misconceptions, gladly accept it.

## History Forgotten, Truth Suppressed

The Reformation is so far removed in time that its issues have been forgotten. We need to be reminded of all of the facts, no matter how unpleasant, in order to dispel the misconceptions which the new ecumenism is based upon and promotes. Most Protestants have only the sketchiest idea of what was "protested" so long ago and even less understanding of its significance today. Even so staunch an evangelist as Billy Graham, like so many other leading evangelicals, seems to have been persuaded by Rome's new posture. Having visited Pope John Paul II three times, and apparently based upon the pope's representations to him, Graham calls him "the world's greatest evangelist"[3] and says that any differences in their theology "are not important as far as personal salvation is concerned."[4] That the Pope has been less than honest with Graham is clear from what we have seen is the official teaching of Rome, a teaching about which so many evangelicals seem to be poorly informed.

So eager are many evangelicals to work with Catholics that they accept Rome's self-serving revision of history without checking the facts for themselves. Surely Rome's protestations of peace, love, and brotherhood in Christ are sincere, so let us forgive and forget the past.

Even well-meaning evangelical organizations and leaders at times have suppressed the facts in order not to offend the Catholics whom they hope to evangelize. Wilson Ewin gives a classic example:

> The BGEA [Billy Graham Evangelistic Association] acquired the printing rights [for a special edition] of ... the classic Henry H. Halley Bible Commentary entitled, *Pocket Bible Handbook.* . . . [It] described [Rome's] martyrdom of millions. . . . [In its 1962 Billy Graham Crusade Edition] the Graham Association . . . removed all these pages. . . .[5]

The same deletions were made from the additional special Crusade editions in 1964 and 1969. As a result, readers were denied dozens of pages of vital historical fact. Those pages recited the evil of some of the popes as well as of Rome's persecution and slaughter of Christians for centuries even before the Reformation. The following is a sample of facts carefully presented by Halley and still found in copies sold in bookstores today, but which were eliminated from the special Crusade editions:

> [The Albigenses] preached against the immoralities of the [Catholic] priesthood, pilgrimages, worship of

saints and images ... opposed the claims of the Church
of Rome; made great use of the Scriptures. ... By 1167
they embraced possibly a majority of the population of
South France. ... In 1208 a crusade was ordered by Pope
Innocent III; a bloody war of extermination followed,
scarcely paralleled in history; town after town was put to
the sword and the inhabitants murdered without distinction of age or sex ... within 100 years the Albigenses
were utterly rooted out.

[Two centuries later] between 1540 and 1570 no fewer
than 900,000 Protestants were put to death in the Pope's
war for the extermination of the Waldenses. Think of
monks and priests directing, with heartless cruelty and
inhuman brutality, the work of torturing and burning
alive innocent men and women, and doing it in the Name
of Christ, by the direct order of the "Vicar of Christ"!

... on the night of August 24, 1572, 70,000 Huguenots, including most of their leaders, were massacred
[St. Bartholemew's massacre]. Some 200,000 [more]
perished as martyrs ... [and] 500,000 fled to Protestant
countries.[6]

## Why the Reformation?

We have already noted that for centuries before the Reformation simple Christian fellowships existed outside the Catholic Church. These believers abhorred the heresies and hypocrisy of Rome and refused to honor the pope. For this they were
hounded to terrible deaths by the hundreds of thousands.
Crusades to exterminate these "heretics" were organized just
as they were for driving Jews and Muslims from the Holy
Land. Remember, in one day Innocent III massacred 60,000
people in the "crowning achievement of his papacy."

Through the testimony of these persecuted Christians and
from the Bibles they gave out, men like John Wyclif (1329-84),
Jan Hus (1373-1415), and Johannes Geiler von Kaysersberg
(1445-1510) believed the gospel and began preaching it to their
fellow Catholics. Multitudes of them believed and remained
true to their faith in the flames. These were the forerunners of
the Reformation.

Though in the Western world today the death penalty cannot lawfully be exacted against heretics, it is still difficult to be an evangelical in parts of Latin America and in Catholic strongholds of Europe. There the truth is suppressed and the average Catholic will likely never be confronted with the biblical gospel in his or her entire lifetime. When visiting such areas one sees firsthand the antagonism of Rome against the gospel and is able to appreciate better what it must have been like in Reformation times.

Talking with acquaintances in Spain recently, I asked them what life had been like as Roman Catholics, what they had believed, and how they had become Christians. The stories would make one weep! They went to confession and Mass, prayed to the images of Mary and the saints, lit candles, crossed themselves frequently, and hoped the Church would somehow get them to heaven. They could only trust that after they died friends and relatives would continue to have Masses said to get them out of purgatory.

One man heard the gospel in a cemetery, where Catholics went on holy days to pray to the saints and their ancestors. Knowing this pagan custom, a small group of despised evangelicals had come there to give out literature. Another young man learned the gospel from a tract which a friend had torn up in anger and thrown to the ground. So starved was this devout Catholic for truth that he laboriously pieced the tract back together, read it, and was saved.

Even long after the Reformation had gained a foothold, becoming a Christian could cost one's life in a Catholic country such as Spain or Italy or in the large areas of Europe which remained fanatically Catholic. Having dealt mainly with Europe in previous chapters, we turn our attention to England to see how the Reformation came to that land and how it is dishonored today.

England was unique. The entire country eventually came under Protestant control. It therefore became a refuge for those who could reach it. D. Antonio Gavin, a Spanish Catholic priest who escaped to England after becoming a Christian in the early eighteenth century, wrote:

> [When] it had pleased God by his grace to overcome in
> me the prejudices . . . in favour of that corrupt church, in
> which I had been bred . . . I [had to] immediately quit
> Spain, where all persons who did not publicly profess the
> Romish religion were condemned to death.[7]

## Henry VIII, England's New "Pope"

Even before Martin Luther's awakening, England had its
own Reformers who called the consecrated host "merely
bread," denied that the priests had special power to absolve
sin, that "the sacraments were necessary to salvation" or that
"pilgrimages, holy shrines and prayers for the dead" had any
value. They testified that "man can be saved by faith alone . . .
[and] the Bible, not the Church, should be the sole rule of
faith. . . ." For their deviation from Catholicism, many of
these "heretics" were consigned to the flames even before the
Reformation began in Germany in 1517.[8]

In contrast to the holy lives of these martyrs, the corruption
of the English clergy and their Church was all the more
obvious to the common people. Even some Church leaders
spoke out against the rampant immorality. In 1489 Archbishop
Morton denounced abbots "living publicly and continuously
with harlots and mistresses" in their abbeys and accused
monks of "a life of lasciviousness . . . nay, of defiling the holy
places, even the very churches of God, by infamous intercourse with nuns. . . ."[9] The Church was hated for its taxes and
great wealth that had impoverished the people. By 1500 the
supposedly "heavenly-minded" Church, the largest landowner
by far in Europe, owned about a fifth of all property in
England.[10]

Thus popular sentiment favored Henry VIII when he confronted the pope over the matter of a divorce from his Spanish
consort. A staunch Catholic, Henry had been honored by the
pope with the title "Defender of the Faith" (still retained,
oddly, by England's Protestant monarchs) for his fervent
polemic, *Assertion of the Seven Sacraments Against Martin
Luther*. The King wanted an annulment of his marriage to
Catherine of Aragon so he could marry the younger, more
beautiful, and hopefully more fertile Anne Boleyn. Rome had

recently granted Henry's sister, Margaret, Queen of Scotland, an annulment. But Pope Clement VII, held captive and pressured by Catherine's nephew, Emperor Charles V, refused to grant Henry's wish. So Henry VIII broke with Rome and declared himself head of England's Catholic Church.

Backing the King, the House of Commons pronounced numerous valid accusations against the Roman hierarchy: "that the clergy exacted payment for the administration of the sacraments; that the bishops gave benefices to 'certain young folks [their bastard sons], calling them their nephews' . . . that the episcopal courts greedily exploited their right to levy fees and fines; that these courts arrested persons, and imprisoned them, without stating the charges against them [etc]." The document ended by "begging the King for 'reformation' [in no way Protestant] of these ills."[11]

Parliament eventually voted the Statute of Supremacy (November 11, 1534) which effectively put Henry VIII, who was still every inch a Catholic, in the pope's place as head of the Church of England. Ironically, England's Protestant monarchs still retain that position. Will Durant writes:

> Henry was now the sole judge of what, in religion and politics, the English people were to believe. Since his theology was still Catholic in every respect except the papal power, he made it a principle to persecute impartially Protestant critics of Catholic dogma, and Catholic critics of his ecclesiastical supremacy. . . .
>
> Theological bonfires continued to the end of the reign . . . One [engulfed] a young woman, Anne Askew, who kept to her heresy through five hours of questioning.
>
> "That which you call your God," she said at her trial, "is a piece of bread; for proof thereof let it lie in a box three months, and it will be moldy."
>
> She was tortured till nearly dead to elicit from her the names of other heretics; she remained silent in her agony, and went to her death, she said, "as merry as one that is bound toward heaven."[12]

For the burning of Protestant heretics the Bishop of Lincoln even offered "an indulgence of forty days to good Christians who would carry a faggot to feed the fire."[13] The reign of England's royal pope became one of terror. Henry's subjects never knew whose head would roll next, Catholic or Protestant. Catholics (such as Bishop John Fisher and Thomas More) were executed for opposing the King as head of England's Church. Protestants, too, would oppose later Protestant monarchs for holding such a position, but no Protestant monarch would execute any subject on those grounds.

## Preparation for a Unique Role

Henry's tyrannical rule prepared England to play a unique role. Her religion thereafter would be that of her monarch. When the Protestant Reformation finally came to England it became the religion of the entire country, thus making that island a refuge for those fleeing Catholic persecution elsewhere. The Huguenots, escaping from Catholic France, where they were being massacred, transformed English industry and brought great prosperity. Evangelical missionaries sent out from England's shores would take the gospel to every corner of the earth. Durant summarizes it well:

> [Henry] thought to replace the pope while leaving unchanged the old faith . . . but his successful defiance of the papacy, his swift dispersal of monks and relics, his repeated humiliation of the clergy, his appropriation of Church property, and his secularization of the government so weakened ecclesiastical prestige and authority as to invite the theological changes that followed in the reigns of Edward and Elizabeth. . . .
>
> The elimination of the papacy from English affairs left the people for a time at the mercy of the state; but in the long run it compelled them to rely on themselves in checking their rulers and claiming, decade after decade, a measure of freedom. . . . Perhaps Elizabeth and Shakespeare could not have been had not England been set free by her worst and strongest king.[14]

The major preparation for the Reformation in England, however, would be through the circulation of Scripture. Even during the reign of Henry VIII, copies of William Tyndale's English New Testament were smuggled in from Germany, where it was printed. The Bishop of London gathered all the copies he could find and publicly burned them at St. Paul's Cross. Nothing, however, not even a government ban on "importation or possession of heretical works," could stop the influx of Scripture or the flame of redemption and freedom that its truth ignited in hungry hearts.

When reproved by an ardent Catholic for his desire to translate and print the Bible in English, Tyndale had replied earnestly, "If God spare me life, ere many years I will cause the boy that driveth the plow to know more of the Scripture than you do." That prayer was answered and the smoldering embers of truth in England were fanned into a conflagration that nothing could extinguish.

Tyndale was burned at the stake in 1536. Henry VIII was still on the throne. The martyr's last words were, "Lord, open the King of England's eyes." Henry died in 1547, eyes still unopened. He "left a large sum to pay for Masses for the repose of his soul."[15]

## England's Reformation Martyrs

Henry VIII's death opened the door to a weak Protestantism. His son, Edward VI, was but a boy of ten when he succeeded his father to the throne. He became the pawn of unscrupulous counselors in a struggle between selfish landlords and nobles still in power and tenants and peasants being ground into poverty. Real freedom in either politics or religion was still a dream.

Sickly since childhood, Edward died at age 15, still too young to be blamed for his unfortunate reign. Lady Jane Grey, a devout Protestant, was forced onto the throne against her will in 1553 and was removed five days later when popular opinion swept the rightful heir, Mary Tudor, into power. A fervent Catholic faith had sustained Mary during years of illness and exile. She soon earned the name by which history still remembers her—Bloody Mary.

By law, Catholic worship became the official religion again. "Protestantism and other 'heresies' were made illegal, and all Protestant preaching or publication was prohibited."[16] One of the first unfortunate victims was Jane Grey, who, before laying her head on the executioner's block, testified to the watching crowd:

> I do look to be saved by no other means, but only by the mercy of God in the blood of His only Son Jesus Christ; and I confess that when I did know the Word of God, I neglected the same, loved myself and the world . . . and yet I thank God, that of His goodness He hath given me respite to repent. . . . Lord, into thy hands I commit my spirit.[17]

At first much of England favored the return to Catholicism. (Most of the people did not understand the issues.) Ironically, the persecution of dissenters during Bloody Mary's five-year reign would make the truth known. "The sufferers looked upon their trials and executions as providentially ordained forms of public witness to the gospel."[18] Church historian R. Tudor Jones writes:

> The majority of the martyrs were ordinary people, including many women. . . . The lengthy interrogations of scores of these people have survived and they concentrate on such topics as their beliefs about the Bible and its authority, transubstantiation, their attitude towards such Roman Catholic practices as the cult of saints, prayers for the dead and purgatory.
> One cannot but be impressed by the vigour and ability with which [simple] people . . . defended themselves, as well as by the immense courage of the sufferers in the face of unspeakable agony.[19]

John Foxe was an eyewitness and earnest historian of this fierce persecution. His *Book of Martyrs* gives detailed accounts of many public trials and executions. After Queen Mary's demise a copy of that classic was chained to every pulpit in England to make it available to all. Foxe tells how imprisoned Archbishop Thomas Cranmer, out of fear, signed a submission to Rome and affirmed transubstantiation. On March 21, 1556, he was brought before an overflow crowd at St. Mary's Church in Oxford to publicly recant of his "heresies." Gathering the courage he had previously lacked, Cranmer turned the tables on his oppressors by boldly declaring:

> And now forasmuch as I am come to the end of my life . . . I see before mine eyes either heaven ready to receive me, or else hell ready to swallow me up; I shall therefore declare unto you my very faith how I believe. . . .
>
> And now I come to the great thing which so much troubleth my conscience, more than any thing that ever I did or said in my whole life, and that is the setting abroad of a writing contrary to the truth, which now here I renounce . . . as written for fear of death. . . .
>
> And forasmuch as my hand hath offended, writing contrary to my heart, therefore my hand shall first be punished; for when I come to the fire it shall first be burned.
>
> And as for the pope, I refuse him as Christ's enemy, and Antichrist, with all his false doctrine.[20]

The shocked papists shouted him down and led him off to his execution outside Oxford University's Balliol College, at the same spot where Bishops Hugh Latimer and Nicholas Ridley had been burned six months before. Foxe relates that Cranmer made good his pledge: "stretching out his right hand, he held it unshrinkingly in the fire until it was burnt to a cinder, even before his body was injured, frequently exclaiming, 'This unworthy right hand!' . . . as long as his voice would suffer him" interspersed with the words of Stephen, " 'Lord Jesus, receive my spirit,' [until] in the greatness of the flame, he gave up the ghost."[21]

In front of Balliol College in Oxford there is a stone cross built into the cobblestone street and a small plaque on the wall of the building opposite. It marks the place where Cranmer, Ridley, and Latimer were burned for rejecting transubstantiation. Around the corner on a larger avenue a weathered monument has stood in silent witness for 153 years. It is scarcely noticed or visited these days. Those few who pause read these words:

To the glory of God and in grateful commemoration of his servants Thomas Cranmer, Nicholas Ridley and Hugh Latimer, prelates of the Church of England, who near this spot yielded their bodies to be burned, bearing witness to the sacred truths which they had affirmed and maintained against the errors of the Church of Rome, and rejoicing that to them it was given not only to believe on Christ but also to suffer for his sake. This monument was erected by public subscription in the year of our Lord God MDCCCXLI.

Durant writes that "as the holocaust advanced it became clear that it had been a mistake. Protestantism drew strength from its martyrs as early Christianity had done, and many Catholics were disturbed in their faith, and shamed in their Queen, by the sufferings and fortitude of the victims." As for "Bloody Mary," she "showed to an England still Catholic the worst side of the Church she served. When she died England was readier than before to accept the new faith that she had labored to destroy."[22]

## Rewriting History

Mary was succeeded on the throne by her half-sister Elizabeth, who turned England back to Protestantism, ending the pope's power on English soil. A refreshing breath of freedom was blowing across that land and had to be stopped. The pope vented his rage from Rome, confident that his vast army of loyal subjects, reinforced with promises of plenary indulgences, would do his bidding.

As already mentioned, in February 1570, Pope Pius V pronounced Queen Elizabeth a heretic, deprived her of her kingdom, forbade her subjects to obey her, and excommunicated all who remained loyal to her.[23] But Elizabeth and most of England simply ignored the pope's fulminations. Many of Rome's fanatical zealots, however, were inspired to attempt to overthrow the Queen.

The plot was uncovered, the conspirators were arrested, and about 120 priests and 60 laity were executed. These were not persecuted believers martyred for their faith, but revolutionaries executed for treason. Ironically, these traitors are honored each year as the "English Martyrs," while the hundreds consumed in the flames for their faith in Christ under Catholic monarchs are forgotten.

To mention evangelicals martyred for their faith would offend Catholics and threaten the ecumenical dialogue with Rome. So history is being rewritten. The martyrs of the Reformation are, in effect, being mocked by evangelical leaders who now join with Rome in a new spirit of mutual trust and cooperation. Author Michael de Semlyen writes with passion from England:

> Many of us were brought up to believe that the martyrs of our faith were those who died in the fire unable and unwilling to compromise their trust in the Scriptures ...But in November 1987, in uncharacteristic fashion, the serious newspapers, TV and radio were giving prominent coverage to "the honouring of English martyrs."
>
> [We were] startled to discover that they referred to 85 Roman Catholic "heroes of resistance to the Protestant Reformation." These men were beatified by the Pope in Rome in the presence of Anglican Bishop of Birmingham, Mark Santer.[24]

De Semlyen informs us that "at the time of the extensive press coverage of the 1987 beatification of the 85 'English martyrs,' the London-based United Protestant Council" sent the following to all of England's national newspapers, yet *none printed any part of it*:

> No one who is concerned for historical truth can be satisfied with the claim, by the Church of Rome, that the 85 English subjects that have been "beatified" by the Pope were martyrs, which means that they suffered for their faith alone. The 288 martyrs who were put to death during Mary I's five year reign suffered solely for their faith. They were condemned on purely religious charges, being principally that they refused the doctrine of transubstantiation. ... They never denied that Mary was the lawful Queen of England, nor maintained any of her

open and foreign enemies, nor procured any rebellion or civil war. They did not sow sedition in secret places. . . .

Such charges of treason, however, were legitimately brought against those Roman Catholics who were put to death under the reign of Elizabeth and succeeding monarchs, and whose names are included in the recent list of those "beatified" by the Pope in Rome. . . .

No Roman Catholic was executed in the first eleven years of Elizabeth I's reign, prior to Pope Pius V inciting all Roman Catholics to rebellion, commanding them not to obey her, on pain of excommunication. It is an unchallengeable fact that no Roman Catholic was executed solely on account of his religious beliefs. The truth is that most of those laymen "beatified" were put to death for assisting the "seminary priests" in their design to bring down the throne; 63 out of the 85 "English martyrs" were "seminary priests," trained abroad and sent back to further the plots of the Pope to undermine the English throne. These had been stepped up after Pope Gregory XIII's sanctioning of the assassination of Elizabeth in 1580 and the organising of the [Spanish Armada] invasion [of England] of 1588. . . .

With this background in mind it is impossible to agree that these men were martyrs in any proper sense of the word. On the contrary, what the Church of Rome is engaged in doing is glorifying traitors, spies and conspirators.[25]

## The Reformation Betrayed

It seems inexplicable that the English, of all people, carefully avoid any mention of genuine martyrs and instead honor seditious traitors. When George Carey was enthroned as the new Archbishop of Canterbury in April 1991, he reached far back into England's pre-Reformation past to praise by name some of the Catholic archbishops of Canterbury. In doing so he deliberately passed over many of his predecessors in that office who had firmly stood against the evils of Rome. Most conspicuous by its absence was any mention of the first Protestant Archbishop of Canterbury, Thomas Cranmer, martyred for the very faith which Carey had sworn to defend.

History is sacrificed on the altar of ecumenism as an oblation to Rome. No sacrifice is too great to further the "unity" movement that is drawing the non-Catholic church back under the pope. Recently the Duchess of Kent, seven Anglican bishops, and more than 700 English clergymen converted to Catholicism.[26] The same historical revisionism is being practiced by American evangelical leaders who dishonor the memories of those who preserved the gospel with their blood.

Catholic apologists in America promote the same revisionism. Peter Kreeft writes of the noble "Catholic martyrs" but doesn't explain that they were executed for treason, not for their faith. And he never mentions the far more numerous martyrs slain by Catholics—an omission all the more inexcusable when found in a book that purports to argue for the truth.[27] Such an omission is scarcely recognized by one in a thousand Protestants for the misinformation it is, and is instead passed on as truth by evangelical leaders.

While Rome pretends to have changed and thereby deceives many evangelicals, Catholic apologists such as Karl Keating, Jerry Matatics, Scott Hahn, Thomas Howard, and others are stepping up their efforts to educate Catholics *against* what they boldly proclaim are the errors of the evangelical gospel. The pope himself is in the forefront of the denunciation of the evangelical faith to Catholic audiences,[28] while he tells the "separated brethren" of his love and desire for unity with them.

### Love and Dialogue?

We are told to love one another as Christ has loved us. Pop psychology trivializes that command by equating it with a "positive" attitude. Forgotten is the first duty of love: to speak the truth (Ephesians 4:15). Real love does not flatter or soothe when correction is needed but points out the error which is blinding and harming the loved one. Christ said, "As many as I love, I rebuke and chasten; be zealous, therefore, and repent" (Revelation 3:19). Instead, the idea is now current that love excludes rebuke, ignores the truth, and seeks unity at any price. Only disaster can result.

Eugene Daniels, World Vision International's senior adviser for church relations, recently said, "We discovered that we could work with the Catholic Church in terms of the spiritual needs of the people in much the same way that we have traditionally worked with the Protestant churches."[29] Other major evangelical ministries that have been working with Catholics as fellow Christians include the Billy Graham Evangelistic Association, Charles Colson's Prison Fellowship, InterVarsity Christian Fellowship, Campus Crusade for Christ, Full Gospel Businessmen's Fellowship, Youth With A Mission, Wycliffe Bible Translators, and others.[30] Obviously this recent development, peculiar to our generation, is extremely significant and is gaining momentum as Rome increases its campaign to present itself as "evangelical."

A Christian with the love of Christ in his heart would be willing to forgive past history, even of oppression, torture, and death. But forgiveness has not been asked nor has any wrong been admitted. As for the present, Rome's dogmas have not changed and her false gospel is still sending souls to eternal judgment by the millions. The salvation of souls is the great issue: how man can be forgiven and assured of eternity in heaven. All else is secondary. Catholicism is a counterfeit gospel. No amount of dialogue can change that fact but only sets the stage for eventual compromise.

"Dialogue" is a popular folly unheard of in the days of the martyrs. *Dialogue?* It was either bow to Rome's imperious authority and accept her false gospel without question or else die at her hand. Nor has Rome changed in her dogmas, though she has had to change her tactics. Vatican II clearly states that Rome's teachings are "irreformable."[31] Her agents in these "dialogues" insist that in the final analysis the Roman Catholic Church is the only true Church, that it has the sacraments which lead to salvation, and that it can never share this distinction with others.[32]

The purpose of dialogue is to draw the "separated brethren" back under the pope—clearly the road upon which evangelicals have set foot. In January 1986 the Roman Catholic Church and 29 Protestant denominations announced "plans for a nationwide evangelistic effort called Congress '88." The steering committee included members from many Protestant denominations.[33] Would the apostle Paul have joined the Judaizers in evangelism? In 1992 an ecumenical team of 19 U.S.

religious leaders met with Pope John Paul II "to explore possibilities for an international interfaith effort to combat child and hardcore pornography."[34] Would Luther and Calvin have joined the papists to fight immorality? Of course not, because morals and even the solution to social ills cannot be divorced from the gospel.

Two major articles (13 pages) in the February 1992 *Bookstore Journal*, the "Official Publication of the Christian Booksellers Association," urged members to cultivate Catholic customers as "brothers and sisters in Christ." Tragically, this will prevent the gospel Catholics need to hear from being given to them. Even some leading evangelical watchdog groups, which otherwise do a commendable job of warning the church of false doctrines and cults, lose their cutting edge when it comes to Roman Catholicism, and Christian media is becoming a major promoter of compromise.

On Trinity Broadcasting Network, the largest Christian television network, network founder Paul Crouch and popular televangelist and faith healer Benny Hinn declared that Roman Catholic doctrine is no concern, for, after all, Catholics "love Jesus." So did Ghandi; so do many Muslims, to say nothing of Mormons and Jehovah's Witnesses. But what "Jesus"? The Bible warns of "another Jesus" and "another gospel" (2 Corinthians 11:4; Galatians 1:6,7), and Rome surely has both. On another program Crouch told two priests and a leading Catholic laywoman who were guests:

> In the essentials our theology is basically the same: some of these even so-called doctrinal differences... are simply matters of semantics. One of these things that has divided us [referring to transubstantiation] all of these years shouldn't have... we were really meaning the same thing but just saying it a little differently....
> So I say to the critics and theological nitpickers, "Be gone, in Jesus' name!" Let's come together [with Rome] in the spirit of love and unity.... [Audience applause.][35]

Even such admired evangelicals as J.I. Packer and Os Guinness have embraced Roman Catholicism as basically Christian and advocate working with Catholics in evangelizing the world together as is evidenced by their recent signing of the *Evangelicals and Catholics Together* document. One of the most highly regarded evangelical apologists, Norman L. Geisler, stated recently that Catholics "believe in justification by grace" and that differences between Catholics and evangelicals "are not as great as generally perceived and they are not crucial . . . [nor do they] involve heresy . . . the whole theological core of historic Christianity is held in common."[36] We have demonstrated that not to be the case.

## The Unchanging Issue—Salvation of Souls

Some evangelists, including Billy Graham and Luis Palau, have long pledged not to attempt to proselytize Catholics, who "usually make up the largest single denominational group" at Graham's crusades.[37] That certainly makes sense if Catholics are now considered to be Christians. The names of Catholics who come forward are turned over to local Catholic churches for followup. Catholic bishops across the country announce that such crusades are the best means they know of to bring lapsed Catholics back into the Church once again.[38] Says Graham, "We're delighted that the Roman Catholic Church now cooperates with us wherever we go."[39] That cooperation involved about 400 Catholic "counselors" in Graham's mid-September 1990 crusade at Nassau Coliseum, Long Island. The local Catholic Charismatic Renewal Office announced that the crusade would "provide opportunities for Catholics who attend to be reconnected to their parishes via Catholic Bible study."[40] The 1991 St. Louis crusade was cosponsored by the St. Louis Archdiocese and involved 300 to 400 parish volunteers.[41]

Upon receiving an honorary doctorate at Belmont Abbey (a Jesuit college), Graham said, "The gospel that built this School and the gospel that brings me here tonight is still the way of salvation."[42] Certainly both those who were martyred and those who consigned them to the flames were convinced there was a great difference between the Catholic and Protestant view of salvation.

Charles Dullea, a Jesuit and Vatican official, assures Catholics attending Graham's crusades, "A Catholic will hear no slighting of his Church's teaching authority, nor of papal or episcopal prerogatives, no word against Mass or Sacraments or Catholic practice."[43] (Yet the pope and his apologists denounce Fundamentalism and the evangelical gospel. The Vatican has financed construction of the most powerful radio transmitter in South America to be used specifically to combat evangelicals.) Other evangelists have adopted the same stance toward Rome. A Southern California newspaper recently noted:

> Puerto Rican-born evangelist Dr. Raimundo Jimenez is back on television in Los Angeles with a unique multi-lingual Gospel outreach to both the Spanish and English-speaking communities of this huge area of some 17 million people. . . .
>
> The broadcaster says that he realizes that most His-panics are nominally Roman Catholic. "In fact, in Southern California, out of six million Hispanics, there are said to be less than 200,000 [about 3 percent] evan-gelicals," said Jimenez. "However, we do not allow any attacks on the Catholic Church. . . . We just present the positive Gospel of Jesus Christ."[44]

Catholicism is a counterfeit Christianity which in some respects so closely resembles the truth that, unless a clear distinction is made, one presents "the positive Gospel of Jesus Christ" in vain. A major problem is that while Catholics believe so much of the gospel, they also believe much that has been added which destroys the truth. Paul "disputed in the synagogue with the Jews, and with devout persons, and in the market daily with them that met with him" (Acts 17:17). Jesus firmly corrected the rabbis and those deluded by them in His day. Shouldn't we do the same? It is no kindness to Catholics to leave them doomed in their error.

## More Than a Misunderstanding

Even worse than not pointing out Catholicism's errors can-didly and with love is accepting Catholics as Christians and denying that they need the gospel at all. Such is the grievous error of the joint declaration to which we referred at the opening of this book, titled "Evangelicals and Catholics Together: The Christian Mission in the 3rd Millennium." That historic document, signed by evangelical leaders, implies that the Reformers must have been deluded, that all active Catholics then as presumed today were saved but didn't know it, and that Rome's gospel of transubstantiation, sacramental rituals, prayers to the saints, good works, indulgences, and purgatory saves souls.

If that is true, then the martyrs mistakenly opposed a gospel they were convinced came from hell but which we are now assured is actually from heaven. The tens of millions of Catholics who since the Reformation have received Christ by faith alone and left the Catholic Church have also been deceived. The whole evangelical church of today is equally deluded about what it means to be a Christian. Rome has been correct all along and we must join her in evangelism. Yet even Catholic apologist Peter Kreeft admits:

> Over the past twenty-five years I have asked hundreds of Catholic college students the question: If you should die tonight and God asks you why he should let you into heaven, what would you answer? The vast majority of them simply do not know the right answer to this, the most important of all questions, the very essence of Christianity. They usually do not even mention Jesus![45]

Here we have an admission that the Catholic Church does not teach "salvation by grace through faith" in such a manner that most Catholics understand it. Luther, Calvin, and the other Reformers did not come to know the biblical gospel from their many years as devout Catholics. In fact, they claimed that Rome didn't teach this truth, and they appealed to her to do so. Her answer? "No!"

In the same book, Kreeft claims that Rome has always taught and still teaches the true gospel and that the Reformation was based upon an unfortunate misunderstanding. Yet that "misunderstanding," by his own admission, persists to this day in the minds of intelligent college students who have grown up in the Catholic Church. Why? Because it is not a misunderstanding: *Rome has added to justification by faith a complex system of religion by which Catholics embrace a false gospel.* This is the very perversion of the gospel that Paul cursed in Galatians 1:6-9.

A missionary friend of the author who has spent years in door-to-door and street evangelism in Spain related sadly:

> I have yet to talk to a single Catholic over here who can explain what the gospel is, or just what it takes to be saved. . . . they are incredulous when I explain that I am assured of going to heaven after I die because the Scriptures say so and God doesn't lie. None of them would say that it is sufficient only to believe in Jesus to be saved, or that the blood of Jesus alone is, in itself, a sufficient price paid to redeem them from the curse of sin. The more involved they are in Roman Catholicism, the more firmly it seems that they hold to the necessity of works added to their "faith."

## A Flickering Candle of Truth

If we truly love the lost souls about us, no matter what their religious affiliations, we will increase our efforts to bring them the truth of the gospel before it is forever too late. Such was the passion of Bishop Hugh Latimer, England's most powerful preacher in his day. He had dared to explain the errors of transubstantiation and of Rome's false gospel even during the reign of Henry VIII, for which he was imprisoned in the Tower of London. Released when Edward came to power, Latimer continued his passionate preaching of the gospel of salvation by grace through faith in the finished work of Christ until, under Bloody Mary, he was imprisoned again and burned at Balliol College on October 16, 1555.

Bound back-to-back with iron chain at the same stake with Bishop Nicholas Ridley, Latimer was heard to call out to his companion in martyrdom as the flames engulfed them:

> Be of good courage, Master Ridley, and play the man. We shall this day, by God's grace, light such a candle in England as I trust will never be put out![46]

Such is the heritage of today's Protestants, which evangelical leaders are now dishonoring and even repudiating. Christian leaders who likely would not have known the gospel but for the martyrs who bravely stood up to Rome are now joining in an unholy partnership with that very institution which shed the martyrs' blood!

Yes, the woman rides the beast, and part of that ride is in unholy alliance with those who ought to know better. Let us stand firmly against the descending darkness as that candle ignited by the immolated bodies of countless martyrs flickers ever more dimly in our day.

*It is the bounden duty of every Christian to pray against Antichrist, and as to what Antichrist is no sane man ought to raise a question. If it be not the Popery in the Church of Rome there is nothing in the world that can be called by that name.*

*It wounds Christ, robs Christ of His glory, puts sacramental efficacy in the place of His atonement, and lifts a piece of bread in the place of the Saviour. . . .*

*If we pray against it, because it is against Him, we shall love the persons though we hate their errors; we shall love their souls though we loathe and detest their dogmas. . . .*

—Charles Haddon Spurgeon[1]

*I'm eradicating the word Protestant even out of my vocabulary. . . . I['m] not protesting anything . . . [it's] time for Catholics and non-Catholics to come together as one in the Spirit and one in the Lord.*

—Paul Crouch on TBN[2]

*It's time for Protestants to go to the shepherd [the pope] and say, "What do we have to do to come home?"*

—Robert Schuller[3]

# 26

# Apostasy
# and Ecumenism

The statements with which we introduce this and the previous chapter indicate a dramatic change in the thinking of Christian leaders regarding Roman Catholicism from the days of Spurgeon to the present time. For 350 years most Protestant creeds identified the papacy as the system of Antichrist. That identification is now being dropped. The world's foremost evangelist has called Pope John Paul II "the greatest religious leader of the modern world. . . ."[4] One of America's foremost "experts on the family" considers the pope to be "the most eminent religious leader who names the name of Jesus Christ."[5] One frequently hears of leading evangelicals who have visited the pope and come away convinced that he is "born again." If so, how could he continue in that fraudulent office heading that corrupt religious system with its false gospel of works and ritual that is sending multitudes to condemnation?

Increasing numbers of today's evangelicals are accepting Catholics as Christians and seem to find no problem in joining with them in the evangelization of the world. That fact is made clear by the very title of the historic joint declaration (referred to earlier) by Catholic and evangelical leaders: *Evangelicals and Catholics Together: The Christian Mission in the 3rd Millennium.* Evangelicals and Catholics are declared to be full partners in the *Christian mission* of taking the gospel to the world, and they are not to evangelize one another. "It is neither theologically legitimate nor a prudent use of resources for one Christian community [evangelicals] to proselytize among active adherents of another Christian community [Catholics]."[6] Some of the leading Protestant evangelists are now conducting their crusades in partnership with Catholics. However, D. Martyn Lloyd-Jones explains why he could not support such crusades in England:

> I remind you that the Protestant Reformers were not just bigoted zealots or fools. Their eyes were opened by the Holy Spirit. . . . They saw this horrible monstrosity depicted in the Bible and they warned against it. At the risk of even losing their lives they stood up and protested. . . .
>
> A Christianity that merely preaches "Come to Christ" or "Come to Jesus" cannot stand before Rome. Probably what that will do ultimately will be to add to the numbers belonging to Rome. People who hold evangelistic campaigns and say, "Are you Roman Catholics? Go back to your church," are denying New Testament teaching. We must warn them!

We have shown that the beast of Revelation 13 and 17 represents both the revived Roman Empire and the Antichrist. The false church, headquartered in Rome, is the woman riding the beast. But that identification of the woman, which for centuries was almost unanimous among Protestants, is accepted by only a few evangelical leaders today. A new spirit of ecumenism is sweeping the Christian world. Consider the following from a *Christianity Today* editorial:

> As we [Catholics and evangelicals] discussed the meaning of the gospel and what Christ meant to us, it became abundantly evident that we shared a common faith. . . . Traditional Roman Catholics accept the doctrine of grace alone. . . . They [Catholics and evangelicals] share the promise of the Father that they have been accepted by Him, and so they, His children, had better accept each other.[7]

Nothing could be further from the truth, as we have thoroughly demonstrated. The Catholic view of grace, faith, and salvation is not at all what the Bible teaches. Yet misinformation about Catholicism persists. For example, Tom Houston, at the time international executive director of the Lausanne Committee for World Evangelism, told a plenary session of Lausanne II in Manila in 1989:

> There are six saving acts of God in Jesus Christ.... The Incarnation ... the Cross ... the Atonement ... the Resurrection ... the ascension ... Pentecost ... the Second Coming of Christ. Now all these churches (Anglican, Roman Catholic, Lutheran, Evangelicals, Orthodox, Pentecostals) believe in all these six saving acts. ... Let us make it our unflinching goal to stay together ... as reflected in the Lausanne Covenant.[8]

So at last we learn from the previous director himself that from the beginning the Lausanne Covenant was intended to embrace Catholics and Orthodox! That revelation came as a shock to those participants who knew the heresies of Rome which Houston's speech denied. Delegates from Latin America, knowing Catholicism only too well, objected strenuously to the embrace of Catholics as Christians. Their protest was respected temporarily, but the momentum toward full fellowship with Catholics now seems irreversible.

## A One-Way Street

Evangelicals who imagine an equal partnership with Rome seem blind to the obvious. The term "separated brethren," as used in Vatican II and ever since then in Catholic ecumenical documents clearly indicates that "unity" can be attained only by non-Catholics joining that Church. This fact has also been declared in numerous papal pronouncements to the Catholic faithful even before Vatican II. Typical is the following from Pope Pius XII:

> We must not pass over in silence, or veil in ambiguous terms, the truth of Catholic teaching ... that the only

> true union is by the return of separated Christians to the
> one true Church of Christ.[9]
>
> For those who do not belong to the visible body of the
> Church . . . none can be assured of eternal salvation,
> because . . . they are still deprived of the helps and heav-
> enly favors found only inside the Catholic Church.[10]

Again we see Rome teaching that a person cannot simply
come to Christ and be saved through faith in His all-sufficient
sacrifice for sin. There are other "helps and heavenly favors"
which are necessary for one to be saved, and these are found
*only inside the Roman Catholic Church.* Fortunately, the day
has passed when this dogma had to be embraced under pain of
death. That day, however, will come again, and perhaps sooner
than we think.

Ecumenism is no equal partnership, but a one-way street to
Rome. There is an all-out effort by Catholic apologists to
refute the errors and inadequacies in evangelicalism. Thomas
Howard's book describing his journey to Rome was titled
*Evangelical Is Not Enough.*[11] Tapes and books of this type are
offered freely by Christian distributors and are carried without objection in most Christian bookstores. Yet many of these
same distributors and bookstores which handle Catholic mate-
rial refuse to stock books or tapes that are in any way critical of
Catholicism, even though they present the truth.[12]

## The New Strategy: Ecumenism

Having lost her status as the official state church in most
parts of the world, and no longer able to impose the death
penalty for nonconformance, Rome has adopted new tactics. It
was at her initiative, following the publishing of *Dignitatis
Humanae* ("Declaration of Religious Freedom") at Vatican II,
that the concordats in the few remaining countries where only
Catholicism was allowed were changed to grant freedom of
religion. This occurred in Colombia in 1973, opening the door
to all religions and separating church from state. The same
action was taken in 1974 in the Swiss canton of Valais, followed in 1975 by annulment of Article 24 in the 1940 Concordat with Portugal. Religious liberty was granted in Spain in

1976 by revision of the concordat to provide for separation of church and state, followed by similar action in Peru in 1980 and Italy in 1984. Finally, in July 1992, laws guaranteeing freedom of religion for non-Catholics at last went into effect in Mexico (though persecution and even killing of Christians by Catholics has continued). These moves did not reflect generosity on Rome's part but a clever strategy of taking the initiative to effect what was already inevitable in today's world.

Catholicism has become the ecumenical leader in a move to unite not only the "separated brethren" of Protestantism but all of the world's religions in a new world church. To large Hindu audiences in India in 1986 John Paul II declared: "India's mission . . . is crucial, because of her intuition of the spiritual nature of man. Indeed, India's greatest contribution to the world can be to offer it a spiritual vision of man. And the world does well to attend willingly to this ancient wisdom and in it to find enrichment for human living."[13] What an astonishing commendation of Hinduism!

One of the world's most influential Hindu leaders, Sri Chinmoy, known as "the guru of the United Nations" (where he holds twice-weekly meditations for staff), has been praised by more than one pope. Chinmoy's 80-plus meditation centers around the world have led millions into Hinduism's darkness, yet John Paul II considers him a friend and co-worker and has greeted him thus: "Special blessings to you . . . [and] to your members. We shall continue together." Pope Paul VI told Chinmoy, "The Hindu life and the Christian life shall go together. Your message and my message are the same." And now evangelical leaders are telling Rome that its gospel and their gospel are also the same!

Rome, of course, will be the headquarters of the new world religion, and the Catholic hierarchy will be in charge. Already she is preparing the way with amazing statements of acceptance of almost anything from voodoo to evangelicalism, while at the same time attacking the latter. During his 1993 tour of Africa the pope "sought common ground with believers in voodoo . . . suggesting that they would not betray their traditional faith by converting to Christianity."[14] Explaining that "the Catholic Church . . . wants to establish positive and cooperative relationships with . . . various faiths in view of a mutual enrichment," John Paul II declared that "the Second Vatican Council . . . recognized that in [all] diverse religious traditions there is something true and good, the seeds of the Word. It encouraged Christ's disciples to discover 'the riches which a generous God has distributed among the nations.' "[15]

Try to imagine Moses suggesting that Israel "discover the riches" to be found in the religions of the idol-worshiping pagans around them, or Paul suggesting that the Christians in Ephesus "discover the riches" of the pagan worship at the temple of Diana! Then what are leading evangelicals doing in becoming Rome's partners?

## Embracing All Religions

Like Mother Teresa, John Paul II praises all religions. Examples are legion, but we have space for only a few. In 1985, speaking to Muslims in Brussels, Belgium, the pope said: "Christians and Moslems, we meet one another in faith in the one God . . . [and] strive to put into practice . . . the teaching of our respective holy books."[16] Islam's Allah is not the God of the Bible, nor could any Christian commend the teachings of the Koran. Meeting with Muslim leaders in West Africa in 1993, the pope "called on Christians, Muslims and animists . . . to respect one another's religious beliefs. . . ."[17] How can one respect beliefs that lead people to hell? Far from asking us to "respect" pagan beliefs, the Bible condemns them.

Speaking to Shintoists and Buddhists in Tokyo in 1981, John Paul II commended the wisdom of their ancient religions which inspired them "to see a divine presence in each human being. . . . [As Christ's Vicar] I express my joy that God has distributed these [religious] gifts among you"[18]—an unthinkable statement in view of the errors of Shintoism and Buddhism! In Togo in 1985 the pope exulted that he had "prayed for the first time with animists."[19] A conservative Catholic critic of his Church's astonishing ecumenism writes:

> Originally, ecumenism was concerned with unity among Christians. But it is now, increasingly . . .

seek[ing] the union of all religions, Christian or non-Christian. On May 19, 1964, Paul VI officially launched a Secretariat for the non-Christians . . . [which] played an important role during the last two sessions of the Council [Vatican II]. . . . Some months later, Msgr. Wojtyla [who became Pope John Paul II] declared:

> Nostalgia for the unity of Christians makes common cause with that of unity for the whole human race. . . . This gives rise to the attitude of the Church towards the other religions, which is based on the recognition of their spiritual values, humans and Christians together, reaching out to such religions as Islam, Buddhism, Hinduism. . . .[20]

While the pope's embrace of all religions shocks conservative Catholics, it is actually consistent with history. From the very beginning under Constantine, when statues of Isis and Horus were renamed Mary and Jesus, and Pope Leo I (440-61) boasted that St. Peter and St. Paul had "replaced Romulus and Remus as [Rome's] protecting patrons,"[21] Roman Catholicism has always accommodated itself to the pagan religions of those peoples which it "Christianized." During a 1984 visit to New Guinea, Pope John Paul II presided over an outdoor celebration of the "New Mass" for natives. The Mass involved "dancers who pranced to the altar for the offertory procession, throwing up clouds of orange and yellow smoke, a pagan custom to ward off evil spirits . . . [while] an 18-year-old college student read a passage of Scripture at the papal altar wearing her traditional clothes [nude above the waist]." The *New York Times* said the Mass was indicative of—

> the Roman Catholic Church's efforts to make its services more universal by integrating into its ritual and liturgy elements of the cultures of the peoples to whom Western missionaries brought their religion.[22]

Such integration is as old as Catholicism. In Haiti every voodoo ceremony begins with Catholic prayers. There is a saying that Haiti is 85 percent Catholic and 110 percent Voudun.

The frightening spiritist cult of Santeria exploding across America is also a blend of African paganism and Catholicism involving "gods" passed off as Catholic saints who front for demons. Visiting the cemeteries in Rio de Janeiro on any religious holiday one finds the Catholic faithful there petitioning the spirits of their ancestors along with the Catholic saints. In Brazil and Cuba, spiritism and voodoo-related African religions of various kinds blend with Catholicism, and throughout Latin America native superstitions remain among Catholics. The use of images, holy water, and many of the rituals now part of Catholicism have been adapted from paganism.

## Paganism Within the Catholic Church

One finds every shade of New Age, occult, and mystical belief inside the Roman Catholic Church itself. *Catholic World* had an entire issue affirming the New Age movement, without a word of condemnation or correction.[23] Thousands of priests and nuns practice Yoga and other forms of Hindu or Buddhist mysticism. Catholic schools across the country, once looked upon as bastions of sound education, are as permeated with occult and New Age methods as are the public schools. *Spirituality of the Catholic Educator* presents a sampling of Catholic education today:

> New Jersey/New York area Catholic schools utilize a program titled *Energetics for Living: A Curriculum Enhancement Program for Peace Education*, developed by Sisters Vergilla Jim, O.S.F. and Claire Langie, O.S.U. Its purpose is "nothing less than the transformation of the child from within" through contact with the creative "energy" found "at the very center of their being" leading to an experience of "the interconnectedness and interdependency of all living creatures...." Contact with the child's "sacred center" is effected through "the regular practice of meditation, visualization, relaxation, breathing, etc."
>
> They have adapted the Hindu greeting "Namaste," which means "The God in me greets the God in you!"

Once the student sees that he and everything is God, "who would do violence to God or to any of his creatures?" asks Sister Loretta Carey, R.D.C., of Fordham University.

Sister Mary L. O'Hara, C.S.J., professor of philosophy at the College of Saint Mary, Omaha, specializes in promoting Buddhist and Hindu techniques for enhancing education in Catholic schools.[24]

Catholic retreat centers around the world mix "Christianity" with Hinduism, Buddhism, and all manner of New Age beliefs and practices. Typical is the Ashram Ya Azim, a Franciscan Sisters' Center for Meditation in Willard, Wisconsin, which seeks to reach "Christ consciousness" through various New Age techniques. In its defense, Virginia Barta, president of the Franciscan Sisters in the USA, explains: "We can be Catholic and at the same time open . . . to recognize the mystical truth in all religions."[25]

At the start of his first U.S. tour, the Dalai Lama, who claims to be god and the fourteenth reincarnation of the original Dalai Lama, was feted at New York's St. Patrick's Cathedral at what *Time* magazine called "an extraordinary interreligious festival" hosted by Cardinal Cooke. Declaring that "all the world's major religions are basically the same," the Dalai Lama was given a standing ovation by the overflow crowd.[26] Cardinal Cooke called the event "one of the dramatic movements of the Spirit in our time."[27] Surely not the Holy Spirit.

The entire May/June 1990 issue of *Catholic World* was devoted to Buddhism. The articles were all sympathetic, including favorable quotes from the pope. One article was even titled "The Buddha Revered As a Christian Saint"! John Paul II takes a broad-minded view of Buddhism and all other religions. He considers the Tibetan Buddhist Deity Yoga of his good friend the Dalai Lama, along with the prayers of witch doctors, spiritists, and every other religion, to be generating "profound spiritual energies" that are creating a "new climate for peace."[28] Similar examples could be multiplied. According to a *Los Angeles Times* news report:

> Pope John Paul II slipped off his shoes to sit quietly
> and solemnly with the supreme patriarch of Thailand's
> Buddhists at a Buddhist monastery in Bangkok. . . .
> The Roman Catholic pontiff later praised the "ancient
> and venerable wisdom" of the Asian religion.[29]

Try to imagine the apostle Peter attending a Buddhist temple ritual and praising Buddhism's wisdom! Or Paul telling audiences of Hindus, as John Paul II did during his visit to India, that he had not come there to teach them anything but "to learn from [their] rich spiritual heritage" and that the world needs to heed India's "spiritual vision of man."[30] The early Christians would never have been martyred had they taken a similar ecumenical approach to Rome's pagan practices.

## Why Ecumenical Popes are Popular

John Paul II seems to be in failing health. Whether he recovers his strength and continues or is replaced by another pope will have little effect upon the future. While John Paul II is the most blatant and effective ecumenist yet, he is only following in the footsteps of his predecessors, and his successor will continue in the same direction. Pope John XXIII (who opened Vatican II) and Pope Paul VI (who closed it) joined such notables as the Dalai Lama, Anwar el-Sadat (a Muslim), and U.N. Secretary General U. Thant (a Buddhist) to form The Temple of Understanding, known as the United Nations of religion. Catholics have been prominent ever since in the leadership of this major effort to establish a world religion.

As further proof of the ecumenism of John Paul II's immediate predecessors, Paul VI gave his blessing to the Second World Conference on Religion and Peace in Louvain, Belgium, in 1974. Under Catholic leadership, the Louvain Declaration stated:

> Buddhists, Christians, Confucianists, Hindus, Jains,
> Jews, Muslims, Shintoists, Sikhs, Zoroastrians and still
> others, we have sought here to listen to the spirit within
> our varied and venerable religious traditions . . . we have

grappled with the towering issues that our societies must resolve in order to bring about peace. . . .

We rejoice that . . . the long era of prideful and even prejudiced isolation of the religions of humanity is, we hope, now gone forever.[31]

It is interesting that the vast majority of Catholics, while refusing to follow papal dogmas in many respects, are only too eager to embrace the pope's ecumenism. And why not? The high percentage of Catholics who reject the basic teachings of the Church points toward a broadening "Christianity." A 1989 poll revealed that 25 percent of Catholics in America didn't believe in life after death, another 46 percent said no one really knows, and 55 percent believe they can dissent from official Church teaching while remaining Catholics. In a 1992 poll, 67 percent of Catholics favored ordaining women, 52 percent accepted abortion, 75 percent said priests should be allowed to marry, and 87 percent said married couples should make their own decision about birth control.[32] In an April 1994 poll, "less than 29 percent of those under the age of 45 agreed that the 'bread and wine are changed into the body and blood of Christ.' "[33]

In France and Italy the situation is even more amazing: 49 percent of French Catholics don't believe in the resurrection of Christ, 60 percent don't believe in heaven, 77 percent don't believe in hell, and 75 percent believe in neither purgatory nor the devil.[34] In fact, "two-thirds of Catholic theologians [express] disbelief . . . in the existence of Satan. . . ."[35] While 90 percent of Italians call themselves Catholics, only about 30 percent attend Sunday Mass; and national elections in Italy during the past decade have legalized both divorce and abortion in spite of pressure from the Church to the contrary.[36]

Catholics are not alone in apostasy. A poll early in 1994 indicated that "4 out of 10 [Americans] who call themselves evangelicals don't believe there is such a thing as absolute truth. [Is "evangelical," like "born-again," becoming a meaningless term?] Of all U.S. adults, 71 percent say there is no such thing as absolute truth."[37] Relativism and ecumenism go hand in hand. Those holding such loose views can easily be persuaded to join with almost anyone, provided the cause is compelling. Reviewing the book *Rome Sweet Home* (the story of Scott and Kimberley Hahn's conversion to Roman Catholicism), John W. Robbins wrote:

> [Scott] Hahn's defection is one of several similar defections. They are occurring, not because Rome is a true church, but because of the apostasy of "Protestantism." . . . Just when the preaching of the Gospel is most urgently needed, it is rarely heard in "Protestant" pulpits. . . . Only the grace of God can save us from another Dark Age and the church that Luther recognized as the slaughterhouse of souls.[38]

## Uniting Everyone in "Prayer"

Since taking office in 1978, John Paul II has moved ecumenism a quantum leap toward the coming world religion. One of the pope's major tactics for unity is getting religious leaders together for prayer. He wants to usher in the new millennium with an unprecedented day of prayer with Muslims and Jews on Egypt's Mount Sinai, according to a letter published by the Vatican.[39]

One of John Paul II's most amazing feats was the gathering at Assisi, Italy, in 1986 of 130 leaders of the world's 12 major religions to pray for peace. Praying together were snake worshipers, fire worshipers, spiritists, animists, North American witch doctors, Buddhists, Muslims, and Hindus, as well as "Christians" and Catholics. The pope declared that all were "praying to the same God." On that occasion the pope allowed his good friend the Dalai Lama to replace the cross with Buddha on the altar of St. Peter's Church in Assisi and for him and his monks to perform their Buddhist worship there.

The two most urgent causes, which will play an important part in uniting the world, are ecology and peace. It is increasingly believed that "peace" will be achieved by prayer to some higher power, and "any god will do," as Masonry says.[40] Inspired by the pope's example at Assisi, "Interfaith Councils" are springing up across the United States, where Christians meet for prayer and social action with the followers of all religions. The procedure at one of the meetings was described by a participant:

> Swami Bhaskarananda, a Hindu, chanted a prayer to God ... Ismail Ahmed, a Moslem, recited a short prayer to God ... as they stood in front of an altar adorned with pictures of Sri Ramakrishna, Jesus Christ and Buddha.[41]

Prayer has been uniting all religions worldwide, and even under evangelical leadership. At the 1993 National Prayer Breakfast in Washington D.C., Senator Kerry read John 3:1-21 (leaving out key verse 16), suggested that Christ was speaking of "spiritual renewal" and that "in the spirit of Christ ... Hindu, Buddhist, Muslim, Jew, Christian" were meeting together for that purpose. Vice President Al Gore said, "Faith in God, reliance upon a Higher Power, by whatever name, is, in my view, essential."

God said, "If *my people* who are called by *my name*" will pray "I will hear from heaven ..." (2 Chronicles 7:14). It was not an invitation to the worshipers of Baal and Ashtoreth and other gods to join with Israel in prayer. That would have been an abomination! Yet today's evangelicals are joining a mixed multitude to pray and to work for social justice and peace.

## Gathering Worldwide Momentum

It is amazing to what extent those who call themselves Christians are able to justify, for the cause of peace and ecological wholeness, participation in religious practices with those of all religions. There is a large movement in South America called "The First Assembly of the People of God of Latin America and the Caribbean" (APD) which is attracting a truly ecumenical groundswell of Catholics, Protestants, and pagans with the blessing of the Catholic Church. The phrase "People of God" comes from Vatican II, and the movement claims to have "brought to life the model of the pluralistic and service-oriented church outlined in Vatican II teachings." The *National Catholic Reporter* favorably reported on a recent convention in Brazil:

> One [leader] held a silver scepter of Candomble, the worship of African gods. ... Another, a Baptist minister,

displayed a drawing of the world traversed by a crucifix. . . . Beside him, a voodoo priest from Haiti raised a
pot of incense, spreading good energy over the crowd.
And a pastor from the United Presbyterian Church read
from Paul's letter to the Galatians.

The celebrants surrounded a Brazilian Catholic
brother who lifted up a priest's stole. Each kissed the
colorful band of cloth.[42]

A much larger but similar gathering, the Parliament of the
World's Religions, was held in Chicago in September 1993,
and was attended by about 6000 representatives of the world's
major faiths. One of the plenary speakers, the Dalai Lama,
called for a worldwide "spiritual awakening" that could be
heeded by all religions.[43] A major event of the Parliament was
the awarding to Charles Colson of the Templeton Prize for
Progress in Religion,[44] the world's most prestigious and lucrative (monetary value about 1.2 million dollars) ecumenical
award. It is given specifically for "encourag[ing] understanding of the benefits of each of the great religions." (Imagine
Elijah accepting an award for "encouraging understanding of
the benefits of Baal worship" or Paul on Mars hill "encouraging understanding of the benefits of paganism"!)

As always at such ecumenical milestones, Catholic leadership was much in evidence, including Chicago's Cardinal
Joseph Bernardin and Fr. Thomas A. Baima, director of the
Chicago archdiocese's Office for Ecumenical and Interreligious Affairs. Roman Catholic theologian Hans Kung was
"the main drafter of The Global Ethic . . . promoting interreligious cooperation" produced by the Parliament and signed
by most of the leaders present, including Rev. Wesley Ari-
arajah, deputy general secretary of the World Council of
Churches.[45] It was "the first time in history that representatives of all the world's religions—Buddhism, Christianity,
Hinduism, Islam, Judaism and 120 other religious groups—
reached common ground on ethical behavior. . . . Representatives from the Vatican and the National Conference of
Catholic Bishops were present" and reacted favorably. The
*Los Angeles Times* reported:

> Priests in Roman collars talked with saffron-robed Buddhist monks, and Rastafarians engaged in animated discussions with turbaned Sikhs. . . . On one night, followers of the neo-pagan Wicca [witchcraft] religion performed a full-moon ritual. . . .[46]

Roman Catholicism is proving to be the bridge that brings together all faiths. That fact alone is not surprising, but it is astonishing to see evangelical Christians stepping onto that bridge on one end while at the same time Hindus, Buddhists, and pagans of every stripe are stepping onto it from the other. If we are indeed in the last days, as seems apparent, it will not be long until all sides meet in the middle.

## A Stepped-Up Campaign

On September 16, 1980, John Paul II told the Catholics in Osnabruch, Germany, "Encourage in a charitable way your evangelical brothers [the Lutherans] to witness to their faith, to deepen in Christ their form of religious life."[47] Is the pope merely enticing the Protestants or is he really letting down the standard, as many Catholics fear? On February 6, 1983, he spoke of going "beyond misunderstandings . . . to find once more what is common to all Christians. . . ."[48] Such expressions of ecumenism have been common and have drawn fire from conservative critics within his Church.

There is no doubt that John Paul II has been breaking new ground in his pursuit of "unity." He knelt beside then Archbishop of Canterbury Robert Runcie at the Canterbury Anglican cathedral altar and the two leaders embraced. In 1981 the pope "invited Metropolitan Damaskinos to speak in his place. For the first time since the schism [A.D. 1054], an Orthodox prelate thus sat in the Chair of the Basilica."[49] The mutual anathemas between Rome and Constantinople had been lifted in 1965. On August 2, 1982, the pope resumed diplomatic relations with three Scandinavian countries that had not been recognized by the Vatican since they had broken with Rome at the Reformation. On December 11, 1983, John Paul II became the first pope in history to enter a Lutheran church. He did so in Rome, where he took part in the service and stated:

I am here because the Spirit of the Lord thrusts us towards ecumenical dialogue, to find complete unity among Christians.

In 1987, Patriarch Dimitrios I was welcomed into St. Peter's Basilica by John Paul II, who introduced him as "His Holiness, Dimitrios I, our well-beloved brother in Christ" and exhorted the congregation to "hear the words of the chief Patriarch. . . ." At the end of the Mass, Dimitrios returned to the altar "to bless the faithful."[50] The pope responded, "The Catholic Church and the Orthodox have been given the grace to recognize one another as sister churches and to walk together towards full communion."[51] On December 7, 1987, Patriarch Dimitrios I and John Paul II signed a declaration similar to the recent joint Catholic-evangelical agreement in the U.S.: "Each of our Churches has received and celebrates the same Sacraments [and] . . . we reject all forms of proselytism. . . ."[52]

## Strange Bedfellows

On January 31, 1994, Chinese Premier Li Peng signed into law documents 144 ("Regulations on the Management of Religious Activity of Foreigners Within China's Borders") and 145 ("Management of Places of Religious Activity Ordinance"). As *Wen Wei Po*, Hong Kong's major pro-Beijing newspaper, admitted, these regulations are intended to prevent "proselytizing" by foreigners. The Chinese government realizes the danger to Communism if evangelicals are allowed to obey Christ's command to preach the gospel to every person on earth.[53]

A similar but voluntary ban on "proselytism" is a key element in the accelerating ecumenical movement. Billy Graham's World Mission '95 involves such a pledge on the part of participating churches. The instructions for France, for example, for participation in this crusade that will be broadcast worldwide by satellite are clear: "All the denominations (Catholic, Orthodox, etc.) are to be kept advised and cooperation is to be mutual among all . . . in spite of differences in theology"—and there is to be absolutely "no inter-church proselytizing."[54] Ironically, the headquarters of the Mission in

France is in the town of Beziers, which readers will recall was wiped out by Pope Innocent III with the loss of about 60,000 lives as the "crowning achievement" of his papacy.

One of the most amazing displays of this "antiproselytism" compromise by evangelicals of Christ's command to preach the gospel in all the world *to every creature* (Mark 16:15) occurred in Colorado. In recent years the city of Colorado Springs has seen the influx of numerous evangelical ministries establishing their offices there. Evangelical youth were winning their Catholic and Jewish schoolmates to Christ, bringing complaints from Catholic and Jewish leaders. To bring peace to the community, evangelical leaders, among them James Dobson, Navigators director Terry Taylor, Young Life director Terry P. McGonigal, and local evangelical pastors, signed a "Covenant of Mutual Respect" with the local Catholic bishop and Jewish rabbi and others. The covenant itself was reproduced in the April 22, 1993, edition of the Colorado Springs *Gazette Telegraph* under the title "A Message to the People of Colorado Springs." It recognized the "Judeo-Christian heritage" common to all faiths represented by those signing the covenant and basically pledged to "learn from each other in a spirit of goodwill and mutual respect" rather than to evangelize. A Catholic newspaper reported triumphantly:

> "The effort to evangelize by some communities was creating an atmosphere of animosity," said Bishop Richard Hanifen of the Diocese of Colorado Springs. About a year ago, Rabbi Howard Hirsch of Temple Shalom and Bishop Hanifen both found that Jewish and Catholic youths were being evangelized at school by other students of different faiths. Terry McGonigal, director of the Institute of Youth Ministries for Young Life, agreed that other Christian youths were being evangelized in schools as well. . . .
>
> To curb misunderstanding and to facilitate understanding, religious leaders from community churches and organizations began meeting informally to discuss the situation. . . . Youth leaders attended the first meeting June 26, 1992, to discuss whether the evangelization efforts were a problem, and determined they were. . . .

Bishop Hanifen said in the future he hopes the group will explore all kinds of issues to learn the values of various faiths and how they view the Scripture. "Instead of trying to convince each other which way to settle issues, we hope to understand the processes of how we settle issues," he said. "I think with God's help, this will set the stage for the future for how our different traditions will behave, and that, I think, is very good for Colorado Springs."[55]

## The Charismatic Bridge to Rome

Oddly, at the same time that Rome is complaining about having Catholics evangelized, it is engaged in the largest evangelization program in history. "Evangelization 2000" is directed from the Vatican by Fr. Tom Forrest, to whom we have already referred. He organized a Worldwide Priests' Retreat which met at Vatican City in September 1990 to kick off the decade of evangelization. Interestingly, "The first purpose of the retreat [Forrest said] was to evangelize the priests." About 1000 of the 6000 priests attending responded to the call to "receive Christ as Savior and be filled with the Holy Spirit."[56] Why should such an appeal be necessary, especially to *priests*, if Catholics are saved? And how could these 1000 really "receive Christ as Savior" in the biblical meaning of that phrase without denying most of the Catholicism they have been trained to perpetuate? That Tom Forrest is still a Roman Catholic priest who celebrates the Mass, believes in purgatory and indulgences, and dare not say that he is eternally saved indicates that he has never accepted the biblical gospel. Yet evangelicals accept him as a partner in the gospel.

Forrest is a charismatic. Much of the responsibility for the growing partnership with Catholicism lies with certain leaders in the charismatic movement. Charismatics were the first to hold joint Protestant-Catholic conferences and to accept one another as Christians. About 10 million Catholics in America and 72 million in 163 countries worldwide now "speak in tongues."[57] That alleged ability was taken as proof by other charismatics that Catholics must be born again. The importance placed upon this experience caused even the most drastic differences in doctrine to be overlooked. The charismatic movement became the major bridge to Rome.

That there is a spurious "Holy Spirit" operating is evident. One of the first prophetic utterances in the Catholic charismatic movement (which began in the mid-1960s at Duquesne and Notre Dame Universities) was that "what Mary promised at Fatima is really going to take place."[58] Yet the apparition of "Mary" at Fatima was demonic, as we shall document in the next two chapters. The "gift of tongues" was received spontaneously by many Catholics as they were engaged in prayers to Mary: "With Tom N. it was as he was finishing his Rosary . . . with Sister M. it came as she knelt in silent prayer to the Blessed Virgin."[59] The general effect upon Catholics of their "baptism in the Spirit" has been increased devotion to Mary and greater zeal for the many heretical dogmas of Romanism.[60] The spirit that endorses such heresy will also endorse Antichrist.

On March 2-4, 1990, Robert Schuller hosted at his Crystal Cathedral the charismatic-Catholic-sponsored "6th Annual West Coast Conference on The Holy Spirit." The majority of the audience were Roman Catholics, as were about half of the speakers. The overwhelmingly Catholic audience was delighted to hear Schuller declare:

> When I had the dream of this cathedral, I didn't want to build it without the blessing of the Holy Father. So I made a trip to Rome and I met with the Pope. . . . I took a picture of the cathedral and I told him I was building this and that [I wanted it to] receive his prayers of blessing. A photograph, of course, was taken of us and I have it hanging on my 12th floor. . . . Then on the 30th anniversary of my ministry here I received the most beautiful full-colored photograph of the Holy Father bestowing his apostolic blessing upon my holy ministry, with a wonderful personal handwritten message. . . .[61]

Bible prophecy is being fulfilled before our very eyes. Christ warned that the nearness of His return to take His bride home to heaven would be heralded by religious deception such as this world had never known (Matthew 24:4,5,11,24). So great would it be that even the elect would be in danger of being deceived. Men would be accepted as Christian leaders, even workers of signs and wonders, who were not Christians at all (Matthew 7:22,23). Paul warned of the same deception and that it was the essential preparation for the Antichrist (2 Thessalonians 2:3,4), a preparation that has obviously been accelerating in our day.

In defense of his signing the historic document *Evangelicals and Catholics Together*, one Baptist leader exulted that it finally granted evangelicals recognition by Catholics as a legitimate religious group. The Reformers would hardly have been flattered by such "recognition." Moreover, the same status has long been granted to *all* religions by Rome. Nearly 30 years earlier Pope Paul VI had said:

> The Church has this exhortation for her sons and daughters: prudently and lovingly, through dialogue and collaboration with the followers of other religions, and in witness of Christian faith and life, acknowledge, preserve and promote the spiritual and moral goods found among these peoples. . . .[62]

This is Roman Catholicism, a "Christianity" that is able to accommodate itself to partnership with all religious beliefs and practices. The foundation is being laid for the world religion headquartered in Rome.

*There is no one, O most holy Mary . . . who can be saved or redeemed but through thee. . . .*
—St. Germanus[1]

*As we have access to the Eternal Father only through Jesus Christ, so have we access to Jesus Christ only through Mary. By thee we have access to the Son, O blessed finder of grace, bearer of life, and mother of salvation. . . .*
—St. Bernard[2]

*In thy hands I place my eternal salvation, and to thee do I entrust my soul. . . . For, if thou protect me, dear Mother, I fear nothing; not from my sins, because thou wilt obtain for me the pardon of them; nor from the devils, because thou art more powerful than all hell together; nor even from Jesus, my Judge himself, because by one prayer from thee, he will be appeased. But one thing I fear; that, in the hour of temptation, I may neglect to call on thee, and thus perish miserably. Obtain for me, then, the pardon of my sins. . . .*
—One of many prayers in the popular booklet *Devotions in Honor of Our Mother of Perpetual Help*[3]

*And it was told him [Jesus] . . . Thy mother and thy brethren stand without, desiring to see thee. And he answered and said unto them, My mother and my brethren are these which hear the Word of God and do it.*
—Luke 8:20,21

*And it came to pass [that] . . . a certain woman . . . said unto him [Jesus], Blessed is the womb that bare thee. . . . But he said, Yea rather, blessed are they that hear the Word of God and keep it.*
—Luke 11:27,28

# 27

# What About Mary?

We have identified the woman astride the beast as Vatican City and the false World Church which will eventually be headquartered there. But why a *woman* on the beast and not a man? Why is this false World Church seen as a *woman*? Again this criterion, like all of the others in Revelation 17, fits the Vatican perfectly. The most prominent figure by far in Roman Catholicism is a *woman*. She overshadows all else, including even God Himself. More prayers are offered to the Catholic Mary and more attention and honor is given to her than to Christ and God combined. There are thousands of shrines to Mary around the world (and hundreds of shrines to other "saints"), but scarcely more than a handful of minor shrines to Christ himself.

Some Catholic leaders even boast that in this day of burgeoning "goddess consciousness" and "women's liberation" the Catholic Church is right in tune with the times: A *woman* holds the position of highest honor and power. In Catholicism it is a *woman* through whom all graces, gifts, blessings, and power flow—a *woman*, who, as we shall see, has the amazing potential to unite the entire world, including even the Muslims, in one religion. This "perpetual Virgin," however, is a fiction that bears no relationship to the real Mary of the Bible, a woman who was not only Christ's mother but also Joseph's loving wife.

## Mary "Ever Virgin"?

The Bible teaches that Mary was a virgin until the time that Jesus was born. Subsequently she had a number of other children by Joseph, her husband. This fact is clearly expressed by the statement that Jesus was her "*first*born son" and that Joseph "knew her not *until*" Christ was born (Matthew 1:25). There are repeated references to Jesus' brothers and sisters, some of whom are even mentioned by name. The people who knew Jesus where He grew up in Nazareth "were astonished and said, Whence hath this man this wisdom and these mighty works?" They went on to argue:

> Is not this the carpenter's son? Is not his mother called Mary? And his brethren James and Joses and Simon and Judas? And his sisters, are they not all with us? Whence then hath this man all these things? (Matthew 13:55,56; cf. Mark 6:3).

Catholic apologists such as Karl Keating insist that these brothers and sisters were really Christ's cousins and that Matthew and Mark had to use the word for brother/sister because neither Hebrew nor Aramaic had a word for "cousin." There is no basis for such an unbiblical supposition. Furthermore, Matthew and Mark were written in Greek. Keating insists that although there was a word for cousins (*anepsios*) in the Greek, it was common for Jews writing in Greek to continue the Hebrew practice of referring to all relatives as brothers/sisters (*adelphos*). He cites examples from the Septuagint, but *none from the New Testament*, because there are none. In fact, *anepsios* is used in Colossians 4:10 to refer to the cousin of Barnabas. Moreover, the brethren of Jesus are usually mentioned as being in the company of Mary, indicating that they were *her children in her care* or, if grown, traveling *with her as part of the immediate family*.

The Catholic argument goes on to insist that for Christ to be born of a womb that would later conceive and give birth to other children would somehow contaminate Him. That argument, again, is not only without biblical basis but takes away from Christ's very humility in becoming a man. Peter de Rosa, as a Catholic, gives some interesting insights into why Rome can't allow Mary to have sexual intercourse even after giving birth to Christ:

> [W]e noted that priests, especially popes, have developed a cult of the Virgin Mary. For celibates, the ideal woman is an asexual being who gave birth to a child. Mary had a baby without sexual intercourse; that is perfection.[4]

If Mary had taken a vow of virginity, however, and that was what she meant by her response to Gabriel, then (as Martin Luther pointed out) by allowing Joseph to marry her she would have committed treachery and poured contempt upon the holy covenant of marriage. Even the Catholic Church doesn't allow a wife to take a vow of continence at her own pleasure, and the Bible is against it, declaring that the marriage bed is God's will for married couples (Genesis 1:28; 2:21-24; 1 Corinthians 7:3-5) and that it is honorable in all (Hebrews 13:4).

Clearly Mary's words to Gabriel "How shall this be, seeing I know not a man?" (Luke 1:34) refer *only to her condition at that time.* This was not a declaration that she had taken a vow of celibacy. If she had, she would not have been engaged to Joseph (verse 27). And if her perpetual virginity isn't true, neither are the other fantasies about Mary which Catholicism has invented (her immaculate conception, bodily assumption to heaven, etc.).

## Mary, "Mother of God"

The most authoritative book written on Catholicism's "Virgin Mary" is by Cardinal and Saint Alphonsus de Liguori. Titled *The Glories of Mary*, it is a virtual compendium of what the great "saints" of the Roman Catholic Church have had to say about Mary down through the centuries. The chapter headings are staggering, crediting Mary with attributes, abilities, titles, and functions that belong to Christ alone: "Mary, Our Life, Our Sweetness"; "Mary, Our Hope"; "Mary, Our Help"; "Mary, Our Advocate"; "Mary, Our Guardian"; "Mary, Our Salvation." Here is a sampling of Liguori's quotes of what the saints have said concerning Mary's role in salvation:

> Sinners receive pardon by...Mary alone. He falls and is lost who has not recourse to Mary. Mary is called ...the gate of Heaven because no one can enter that blessed kingdom without passing through her. The way of salvation is open to none otherwise than through Mary...the salvation of all depends on their being favored and protected by Mary. He who is protected by Mary will be saved; he who is not will be lost...our salvation depends on thee.... God will not save us without the intercession of Mary.... who would receive any grace were it not for thee, O Mother of God...?[5]

"Mother of God"? Yes, Jesus is God and Mary is His mother, but she is not the mother of Him *as God*, which He was and is from all eternity before Mary was even born. She is the mother of the *physical body* which the Son of God took when He became man, but she is not the Mother of God! The Scripture explains Mary's role:

> Wherefore when he [Jesus] cometh into the world, he saith...a body hast thou prepared me (Hebrews 10:5).

The incredibly unbiblical position to which Mary has been exalted by Roman Catholic tradition continues to be evidenced in the prayers offered to her. Those quoted at the beginning of this chapter are but a few of literally thousands which show that this false Mary is the very heart and life of Roman Catholicism. Yet Catholic apologists, sensitive of criticism in this regard, deny that Catholics pray *to* Mary. Peter Kreeft, for example, deceitfully writes, "Catholics [don't pray to saints, they] only ask saints to pray for them—just as we ask the living to pray for us."[6]

On the contrary, the most numerous and popular prayers in Catholicism are *to* the saints and especially *to* Mary, not to God or to Christ. Moreover, these prayers ask Mary to *do* for Catholics and for the entire world what she would literally have to be God (and, for some things, Christ) to be able to accomplish. At the close of the Sunday Mass in Denver in August 1993, John Paul II consigned all youth and the entire world to Mary's protection and guidance:

> Mary of the New Advent, we implore your protection on the preparations that will now begin for the next meeting [World Youth Day]. Mary, full of grace, we entrust the next World Youth Day to you. Mary, assumed into heaven, we entrust the young people of the world . . . the whole world to you![7]

Catholics only ask Mary to *pray* for them? If one asks prayer of a friend one doesn't say, "I implore your protection and entrust the whole world to you"! Yet such requests that only God could fulfill are typical of Catholic petitions of Mary, who is exalted to omnipotence and credited with caring for all who trust in her.

## "Mary, Queen of Heaven"

*Time* magazine comments that "according to modern Popes" Mary is "the Queen of the Universe, Queen of Heaven, Seat of Wisdom. . . ."[8] In the pope's September 1993 speech in Lithuania, he spoke of Mary as "Mother of the Church, Queen of the Apostles [and] dwelling place of the Trinity"! He told "priests and aspirants to the priestly life, men and women Religious" to "look to Mary . . . who is venerated here . . . in the shrines of Ausros Vartai and Siluva, to which I will go on pilgrimage! . . . To Mary I entrust all of you . . . !"[9] Such blasphemy is repeated in the most recited Catholic prayer, the Rosary. It concludes with this final petition:

> Hail, holy Queen [of heaven], Mother of Mercy! our life, our sweetness, and our hope! To thee do we cry, poor banished children of Eve; to thee do we send up our sighs, mourning and weeping, in this valley of tears. Turn, then, most gracious Advocate, thine eyes of mercy toward us; and after this our exile show unto us the blessed fruit of thy womb, Jesus; O clement, O loving, O sweet Virgin Mary.

Mary is our *life* and our *hope*? According to Scripture, *Christ* is our life (Colossians 3:4)! Why Mary is the Catholic's hope was explained by Bishop Fulton J. Sheen, whom Billy Graham admiringly called "the greatest communicator of the twentieth century":[10]

> When I was ordained, I took a resolution to offer the Holy Sacrifice of the Eucharist every Saturday to the Blessed Mother. . . . All this makes me very certain that when I go before the Judgment Seat of Christ, He will say to me in His Mercy: "I heard My Mother speak of you." During my life I have made about thirty pilgrimages to the shrine of Our Lady of Lourdes and about ten to her shrine in Fatima.[11]

What a pitiful expression of hope for eternity—that Mary will put in a good word for him because of his devotion to her! What happened to his faith in the Christ who died for his sins? In Catholicism, Christ and His sacrifice for our sins upon the cross are not enough. To be saved, one must have *Mary's* favor, for she decides who will be in heaven, as the many quotes above demonstrate.

Do Mary's "eyes of mercy" actually see everyone in the world? Is she really the "Mother of Mercy"? Didn't God's mercy exist long before Mary was even born? We read of the "God of mercy" (Psalm 59:17) and are encouraged to "trust in the mercy of God" (Psalm 52:8; Luke 1:78; etc.) but never a word is said in the entire Bible about Mary's mercy toward mankind.

Those who know *God's* mercy have no need of Mary's mercy. In fact, she would have to be omnipotent, omniscient, and omnipresent (qualities of God alone) in order to extend mercy to all mankind. Paul and John both refer to "grace, mercy, and peace" coming from *God* to believers (1 Timothy 1:2; 2 Timothy 1:2; Titus 1:4; 2 John 1:3), but nowhere is there a hint that mercy is bestowed by Mary on Christians. Yet the Rosary makes it seem that we depend upon *her* mercy rather than upon God's. Is it really her doing that brings believers into the presence of Christ? According to the Rosary, one would think so.

Mary is the "Queen of Heaven"? We are told in Scripture that Christ is the king, but never that there is a *queen* of heaven, much less that she is Mary. If there were a queen who shares Christ's throne it would be His bride, the church composed of the redeemed, yet the church is never referred to as the queen of heaven. The only "queen of heaven" mentioned in Scripture is an idol which was worshiped by the pagans and to which the Jewish women gave offerings, bringing the wrath of God upon them:

> The children gather wood, and the fathers kindle the fire, and the women knead their dough to make cakes to the queen of heaven, and to pour out drink offerings unto other gods, that they may provoke me to anger. . . .
> Because ye have burned incense [to the queen of heaven] and because ye have sinned against the Lord . . . therefore this evil is happened unto you (Jeremiah 7:18; 44:15).

Far from being embarrassed by such pagan connections, Rome flaunts them. Many Catholics boast that Mary has taken the place of "Maia, the nymph of Greek mythology, who was the mother of Hermes by Zeus, the sky god." The month of May was named after Maia, who was known as "the queen of May . . . [and] the Jesuit effort to turn the Queen of May into the Virgin Mary was successful. . . ."[12]

## The Multiple Marys

There are many Marys in Catholicism, "Our Lady" of this and "Our Lady" of that. Wherever "Mary" appears in various forms, that particular "Mary" develops a following. Most Catholics have their favorite "Mary." Some prefer "Our Lady of Medjugorje," others "Our Lady of Guadalupe" or "Our Lady of Lourdes." Pope John Paul II has two favorite "Marys": the "black Virgin" of Jasna Gora, the patron saint and protectress of Poland, and "Our Lady of Fatima." The latter allegedly appeared to him during his convalescence from the attempted murder (which took place on the anniversary of her supposed first appearance in Fatima, Portugal, on May 13,

1917). She had saved his life, she said, for a purpose and would give the world a sign that would cause it to bow to his supreme spiritual authority. *Time* reported:

> Devotion to Mary was ingrained in the Pope in his Polish homeland, where over the centuries the [black] Madonna has been hailed for turning back troops of the Muslim Turks, Swedish Lutherans and, in 1920, Soviet Bolsheviks. . . .
>
> John Paul [II has] made Mary's unifying power a centerpiece of his papal arsenal. He has visited countless Marian shrines during his globe trotting, and invokes the Madonna's aid in nearly every discourse and prayer that he delivers.[13]

The "Mary of the New Advent" to whom the pope referred in Denver is particularly associated with World Youth Day, which John Paul II has been promoting for some years. She was displayed at the all-night prayer vigil of pilgrims who walked to Cherry Creek Park (near Denver) to meet the pope, who came in by helicopter. A journalist who was present writes:

> It is well past 9 P.M. when the icon, the official one of World Youth Day, is presented. This part of the vigil is referred to as "Veneration [worship] of the image of the Virgin Mary: Our Lady of the New Advent" [which] the pilgrims now view for the first time . . . a painting of Mary with the child Jesus still in her womb. . . .
>
> The Lady of the New Advent is the most vulgar icon we have seen. . . . As the Colorado Chorus and the Youth Chorale sing the "Taize Magnificat," ten youngsters from Denver lift the icon of Our Lady of the New Advent and carry it around the aisles of the magnetometered area near the three-part stage. The crowd responds lavishly to it. Flashbulbs go off. . . . [Flower] petals are strewn around the icon. . . .[14]

The next day, Sunday, the pope returned in his helicopter. The pilgrims, shivering from the chill (having tried to sleep through the night on the ground), greeted him again with renewed excitement. There he celebrated Mass and 3000 priests took several hours to minister the wafers to the crowd of 375,000. Addressing Mary in heaven personally at times during his talk, the pope began:

> With my heart full of praise for the Queen of Heaven, the sign of hope and source of comfort on our pilgrimage of faith to the heavenly Jerusalem, I greet all of you who are present at this solemn liturgy. . . . This liturgy presents you, Mary, as the woman clothed with the sun. . . . O woman clothed with the sun . . . the youth of the world greet you with so much love. . . . In Mary the final victory of life over death is already a reality. . . .
>
> O Mary . . . as Mother of the Church, you guide us still from your place in heaven and . . . help us to increase in holiness by conquering sin.[15]

## The Cult and Worship of Mary

As early as 1854 Pius IX had sent up a papal infallibility trial balloon. It was well-received by the Church because it involved the ever popular "Virgin Mary." On his own initiative—by his own authority and standing alone without any Council or the *magisterium* supporting him—Pius IX pronounced as a dogma that all Catholics must accept the Immaculate Conception of Mary: that she was "in the first instant of her conception . . . preserved free from all stain of original sin. . . ." It was, in effect, a declaration of his own infallibility—that he did not need the support of the bishops or a Council but could define such binding dogmas on his own.

On November 1, 1950, Pope Pius XII made an allegedly infallible ex cathedra declaration in his Apostolic Constitution *Munificentissimus Deus* that "the immaculate Mother of God and ever Virgin Mary was at the end of her life assumed into heaven body and soul." In the Constitution the pope claimed that the dogma of the assumption had been unanimously believed in the Church from the very beginning and that it was fully supported by Scripture. In fact, the dogma was unknown to the early church and is unsupported by Scripture. Such papal declarations simply responded to the popular sentiment of Catholics and contributed to the growing cult of Mary.

The cult of Mary developed gradually as the apostasy gathered momentum. Commenting upon the adoration of Mary that took place during the pope's 1993 visit to Denver, a writer reminds us: "The *Encyclopedia Britannica* says that during the first centuries of the church there was no emphasis of Mary whatsoever.[16] The *Catholic Encyclopedia* concurs: ". . . there is no ground for surprise if we do not meet with any clear traces of the cultus of the Blessed Virgin in the first Christian centuries.' "[17] Von Dollinger explains:

> Neither the New Testament nor the Patristic writings tell us anything about the destiny of the Holy Virgin after the death of Christ. Two apocryphal works of the fourth or fifth century—one ascribed to St. John, the other to Melito, Bishop of Sardis—are the earliest . . . [suggestions] about her bodily assumption.[18]

The Roman Catholic Church denies that Mary is worshiped. She is supposedly only given *hyperdulia*, the other saints *dulia*, while Christ is given *latria*. But consider this prayer which is popular among Catholics: "Jesus, Mary and Joseph, I give you my heart and my soul." Why not only to Jesus? Why to anyone else? Only God demands—and surely only He deserves—one's "heart and soul." How can one give one's heart and soul to someone without worshiping that person? Can anyone in the same breath give *latria* to Jesus, *hyperdulia* to Mary, and *dulia* to Joseph?

Among devout Catholics, those who have dedicated themselves to serve Mary are legion. Typical is the Legion of Mary, which "began in Ireland on Sept. 7, 1921 . . . and is now in every country on the face of the earth. Mary's troops are everywhere!" The Legion has enjoyed the "commendation of five popes" since its inception. Pope Paul VI said, "The Legion of Mary is an army of those devoted and stalwart clients of Mary who are combatting the forces of evil in the world today."[19] It is an undeniable fact that devotion to Mary among Catholics far exceeds devotion to God or Christ.

## The Omnipotent, Omniscient, and Omnipresent Mary

*Soul Magazine*, "Official publication of The Blue Army of Our Lady of Fatima in the U.S. and Canada" (22 million strong) declares: "Mary is so perfectly united with the Holy Spirit that He acts only through [her] His spouse. . . . all our life, every thought, word, and deed is in Her hands . . . at every moment, She Herself must instruct, guide, and transform each one of us into Herself, so that not we but She lives in us, as Jesus lives in Her, and the Father in the Son."[20] Every thought, word, and deed of all mankind is in Mary's hands? She instructs, guides, and transforms each one of us into Herself? Then Mary is God!

Never does the Bible say that the Holy Spirit only acts through Mary! The Holy Spirit has been in action from eternity past, an eternity before Mary even was born. All our life is in *God's* hands, not Mary's. We are instructed and guided by *God*, not by Mary. And we are being transformed into the image of *Christ*, not the image of Mary. Nor does the Bible ever hint that Mary lives in the believers, while it assures us that Christ lives in us by His Spirit. To suggest that such promises are fulfilled in Mary is blasphemy of the vilest sort, which the real Mary would rebuke!

The Bible says repeatedly that Christ lives in the Christian (John 14:20; Colossians 1:27; Galatians 4:19) and the Christian in Christ (Romans 8:1; 2 Corinthians 5:17; Ephesians 2:10; etc.) but says never a word about anyone either being in Mary or Mary in anyone. For that to be true of Mary, as it is of God and Christ, she would have to be omnipresent like God. Amazingly, whatever the Bible promises God will do for us through Christ requires, in Catholicism, the intercession and intervention of Mary as an additional intermediary. What an abomination!

Consider "the Holy Father's [pope's] Prayer for the Marian Year." The pope asks Mary to comfort, guide, strengthen, and protect "the whole of humanity." To do so she would have to be all-powerful, all-knowing, and everywhere at once. Even worse, his prayer ends: "Sustain us, O Virgin Mary, on our journey of faith and obtain for us the grace of eternal salvation." This is blasphemy! Yet it is commonly declared that

"Mary is the refuge of sinners . . . the Gate of Heaven . . . our way to enter into paradise."[21]

Christ paid the debt for our sins and with His blood purchased our salvation, which is offered freely by God's grace to all who will receive it. There is no mention whatsoever of Mary in the gospel which Paul and the early church preached. To suggest that Mary must or even can in any way "obtain for us the grace of eternal salvation" is a denial of the sufficiency of Christ's sacrifice upon the cross for our sins and a rejection of the grace and love of God and Christ. Catholics try to explain it away, but the fact is that Catholicism's "Mary" is exalted above Christ and God.

## Maryology and Maryolotry

There are conservative Catholics who consider Pope John Paul II to be the betrayer of their Church because of his acceptance of other religions. Yet they are united with him in his devotion to Mary. The powerful exposé of the pope's ecumenism titled *Peter, Lovest Thou Me?* is dedicated "to the Immaculate Heart of the Most Holy Virgin Mary."[22]

For Mary's heart to be immaculate she must have been sinless. Yet the Bible unequivocally declares, "All have sinned and come short of the glory of God" (Romans 3:23). Mary herself rejoiced in God as her Savior (Luke 1:47), and only sinners need a Savior. Christ clearly said, "There is none good but one, that is God" (Matthew 19:17; Mark 10:18). No exception is made for Mary.

If the accusation were made that Mary is their chief deity, almost every Catholic would deny it vehemently. This is, however, the way it works out in practice. It is said that when Mary commands even God obeys.[23] What began as Maryology gradually became Maryolatry as the thousands of prayers to Mary, which attribute to her everything from salvation to omnipotence, testify. A popular tract, "The Rosary, Your Key to Heaven," declares:

> The Rosary is a means of salvation, because a true child of Mary is never lost and one who says the Rosary daily is truly Mary's child. . . . Mary is our all-powerful

> Advocate and she can obtain from the Heart of her
> Divine Son whatever is good for her children. . . . No one
> is beyond redemption if he but turns to Mary Immacu-
> late.

The fact that Christ died for our sins and offers eternal life as
a free gift of His grace means nothing without Mary. Though
the Bible never even hints at such a thing, and though Paul
never preached it or told it to anyone, yet for the Catholic,
Mary has become the essential conduit through which salvation and all grace flows. Jesus and God the Father play an
important role too, but it is *Mary* who brings everything
together and dispenses all God's gifts to those who through
devotion to her become "her children."

This blasphemous dogma is taught without any biblical
basis whatsoever. Nowhere does the Bible suggest that anyone
becomes a "child of Mary." According to the biblical gospel
we become "the children of God by faith in Christ Jesus"
(Galatians 3:26). Yet in Catholicism one becomes a "child of
Mary" with the promise that "no true child of Mary will ever
perish."[24] Again she has usurped the place of Christ.

Yes, Catholicism acknowledges that Christ is the one Medi-
ator between God and men (1 Timothy 2:5), but Mary is the
mediatrix between mankind and Christ, "the short road to
Jesus."[25] "Jesus is . . . the Reservoir of all graces, and Mary is
the Conduit whereby they are brought to us. . . . [Jesus] desires
that His own Mother be our immediate Advocate . . . to Whom
we entrust our wants, and She shall present them to Jesus. . . ."[26]
Thus prayers to God, though in Christ's name and through
Him, require Mary's intervention. Indeed, "all graces" come
by means of Mary's "powerful intercession":

> O God of infinite goodness and mercy, fill our hearts
> with a great confidence in our Most Holy Mother, whom
> we invoke under the title of the Immaculate Heart of
> Mary, and grant us by her most powerful intercession all
> the graces, spiritual and temporal, which we need.
> Through Christ our Lord. Amen.[27]

The Bible is very clear that we come to the Father through
Jesus Christ (John 15:16; 16:23). Never is there the slightest

suggestion that we must come to Christ through Mary, much less that Mary herself is to be petitioned and answers prayer on her own initiative and in her own power. Yet Mary's function as an intermediary to Christ and her powerful intervention on behalf of and protection of those who call upon her is both taught in Catholicism and testified to by Catholics.

A convict in prison who converted to Catholicism testified in Keating's *This Rock* magazine to the transformation in his own life and what "the Holy Spirit" did for other convicts who were also "converted." There is little about Christ (other than making the "sign of the cross"), but much about the Church and "Catholic community" and, of course, Mary. The article stresses the "spiritual fruits" of the prison ministry, demonstrated by the converted convicts all participating in an act of "total consecration"—not to Christ or God, however, but "to the Immaculate heart of Mary":

> I knew it was *Mother who had called them* [the converts] *to her heart....* I realized we could work things out so that the consecration could be made as a group in public when Archbishop Oscar H. Lipscomb was scheduled to be here for confirmation.
>
> The only time we could all get together for our group preparation was at 6:30 in the morning on the recreation yard, so that's what we did for 33 consecutive days. Murderers, rapists, burglars, drug dealers, and arsonists; these men sacrificed daily to meet *for the Mother of God*. Each day they withstood cold, wind, rain, and ridicule to prepare their hearts and souls for a total consecration *to the Mother* of the Perfect Prisoner.
>
> The big day came. Just before the apostolic blessing at the close of Mass, Archbishop Lipscomb allowed the public consecration. We filed past a borrowed *statue of our Lady*, each man stopping to *bow in her honor*, and lined up before the altar and then knelt. Since I led the consecration prayers, I couldn't see what was going on around me. I was told later that the Archbishop and the priests who accompanied him appeared to be fighting emotion during the ceremony. After all, before them knelt thirteen hardened criminals, converts all, who

had become innocent little children *at the feet of their Mother*[28] (emphasis added).

## Mary Crushes the Serpent's Head

Genesis 3:15 provides the first promise of the Messiah. God is speaking to the serpent (Satan): "I will put enmity between thee and the woman, and between thy seed and her seed; it [the seed of the woman, i.e., the virgin-born Messiah] shall bruise thy [the serpent's] head, and thou [Satan] shalt bruise his [the Messiah's] heel. Yet Catholic translations of Genesis 3:15 for years have said that "she [the woman] shall bruise thy head."

"The Rosary, Your Key to Heaven," cited above, says that Mary "will crush the serpent's head . . . all are in need of her help to get to Heaven." This abominable usurpation by the fictitious Catholic Mary of Christ's place as victor over sin and Satan persists as one of Catholicism's major perversions of truth. In Pius IX's 1849 encyclical, *Ubi primum*, he declared that Mary's "foot has crushed the head of Satan" and that it was Mary herself who "always has delivered the Christian people from their greatest calamities and the snares and assaults of all their enemies, ever rescuing them from ruin." Again, she would have to be God to do so.

On November 27, 1830, Mary allegedly appeared in Paris to Catherine Laboure with her heel on the serpent's head and ordered that a "medal" be cast with this depiction of her victory over Satan.[29] "Our Lady of the Miraculous Medal" became extremely popular. This medal is still worn around the necks of millions of Catholics for protection, many of whom swear that miracles have occurred for them as a result of wearing this amulet.

"Our Lady of the Miraculous Medal" is only one of literally thousands of alleged appearances of the Catholic "Virgin Mary" around the world and down through the centuries. Such apparitions have been multiplying and their frequency accelerating in recent years.[30] Some are not recognized by the Church as legitimate, but many are; and all, whether officially acknowledged or not, affect millions of Roman Catholics who look to them as evidence that the Catholic Mary is indeed the hope of the world.

It is a *woman* whom John saw astride the beast. Does that fact include intimations of the strategic role that Rome's fraudulent Mary will play in the preparation of the world for Antichrist? We must consider that possibility carefully.

*In an era when scientists debate the causes of the birth of the universe, both the adoration and the conflict attending Mary have risen to extraordinary levels. A grass-roots revival of faith in the Virgin is taking place worldwide. Millions of worshippers are flocking to her shrines, many of them young people. Even more remarkable are the number of claimed sightings of the Virgin, from Yugoslavia to Colorado, in the past few years.*

—*Time* magazine[1]

*There is no doubt that Paul VI, together with John XXIII and John Paul II, will be remembered as the three great Popes of Peace, pioneers of a momentous transcendence of the Catholic Church into the New Age.*

—Robert Muller, former U.N.
Assistant Secretary-General[2]

*On February 11, the liturgy of the Church recalls every year the apparition of our Lady at Lourdes.*

—Pope John Paul II[3]

# 28

# The Coming
# New World Order

*T**ime* magazine reports there have been so many sightings of the "Virgin Mary" around the world that "the late 20th century has become the age of the Marian pilgrimage" to the many shrines established to commemorate these appearances. There are 937 Marian shrines in France alone.[4] From 1961 to 1965 there were about 2000 visitations to northwest Spain's village of Garabandal accompanied by occultic phenomena and apocalyptic messages to the world. In 1983 hundreds of Palestinian Arabs "saw the Virgin Mary" near Bethlehem, Israel. She has appeared in every corner of the world:

> There is also Dozule...and Kibeho in Rwanda... apparitions of Our Lady at Akita in Japan...apparitions in Chile, in Australia and in Poland...in Canada... San Damiano [in Assisi, Italy], Cairo...Amsterdam, [New York, etc.].[5]

These apparitions have brought millions of people to faith in Catholicism's Mary. The shrine at Lourdes, France, attracts about 5.5 million pilgrims annually; Poland's Black Madonna draws 5 million; Fatima, Portugal, "draws a steady 4.5 million pilgrims a year from an ever widening array of countries." Since John Paul II visited the shrine of Mary at Knock, Ireland, "attendance has doubled to 1.5 million people each year.

To handle the influx, a new international airport was opened at Knock in 1986."[6] A "Mary, Queen of the Universe Shrine" has recently opened in Orlando, Florida. The shrine of Our Lady of Guadalupe near Mexico City "draws some 20 million visitors a year"![7]

Mary's powerful protection is celebrated around the world. Our Lady of Lanka, credited with preventing a Japanese invasion during World War II, has been the patron of Sri Lanka since 1948. Our Lady of Copacabana is "the patron of the Bolivian navy...Our Lady of Coromoto, patron of Venezuela."[8] Polish President Lech Walesa made a pilgrimage to Fatima, where he "offered prayers of thanks for the liberation of Poland."[9] John Paul II believes "Mary brought an end to communism throughout Europe."[10] Similarly convinced, Moscow's Archbishop Kondrusiewicz, in 1991, made a pilgrimage to Fatima that was carried on prime-time Soviet national TV. A shrine to "Our Lady of Fatima," who appeared in the Soviet Union just before the Berlin Wall came down, will soon be established in Moscow in gratitude for her defeat of Communism.[11] Kondrusiewicz wants her shrine to be a perpetual reminder of that great conquest.[12]

The apparitions consistently preach the coming world religion of Antichrist: All religions are basically the same and must come together for peace. Offering an ecumenical gospel that can be "accepted by Catholic, Protestant, Moslem or Jew,"[13] "Mary" declares: "Everyone worships God in his own way with peace in our hearts."[14] So says Our Lady of Medjugorje in Southern Bosnia-Herzegovina, where visionaries claim the Virgin has been appearing daily for the past 13 years[15] in the heart of Ustashi Croatia.

## Apparitions and Official Catholic Doctrine

Marian apparitions would hardly attract such a huge following if official dogmas did not support them. Catholics are taught to pray to Mary and are promised that she will protect them from every danger and supply their every need. Quoting Vatican II,[16] the new *Catechism of the Catholic Church* declares, "From the most ancient times the Blessed Virgin has been honored with the title of 'Mother of God,' to whose

protection the faithful fly in all their dangers and needs."[17]
Here is official Roman Catholic doctrine from the highest
level attributing to Mary authority and power which belong to
God alone! Amazingly, this reference is quoted in *This Rock*
(the premier Catholic apologist magazine) in an article arguing that although a large percentage of Catholics consider
Mary to be equal to God, that view is not official Church
doctrine.[18] But the quote proves it is. The "faithful fly [to
Mary for] protection . . . in all their dangers and needs." Could
anyone less than God give protection to all the faithful and
supply all their needs?

In the entire Bible there is *not one* prayer to Mary, not one
instance of her miraculously helping anyone, nor any promise
that she would or could. From Genesis to Revelation, protection and help are sought from, promised by, and found in God
and in Christ *alone*. This fact is attested by hundreds of verses,
of which the following are only a small sampling:

> The eternal God is thy refuge, and underneath are the
> everlasting arms (Deuteronomy 33:27); God is our ref-
> uge and strength, a very present help in time of trouble
> (Psalm 46:1); In God is my salvation . . . my refuge is in
> God (Psalm 62:7); The Lord . . . is my refuge . . . in him
> will I trust (Psalm 91:2); Fear not . . . I will help thee,
> saith the Lord, and thy redeemer, the Holy One of Israel
> (Isaiah 41:14); Lord [Jesus], save me! (Matthew 14:30);
> Lord [Jesus], help me! (Matthew 15:25); Let us therefore
> come boldly unto [God's] throne of grace, that we may
> obtain mercy, and find grace to help in time of need
> (Hebrews 4:16).

The infinitely powerful and loving God, and Christ (who is
one with the Father), have protected, as promised, all who
trusted in them through the centuries. Then why would anyone
call upon Mary? Is she mightier than God or more compassionate or more reliable or quicker to respond? Though most
Catholics would deny it, Mary subtly displaces the Christian
Trinity. The image of Our Lady of Guadalupe was credited
with miracles during its recent tour of the United States. Some
of the honor she receives in Mexico includes:

Public buses in Mexico City suburbs have flower-adorned shrines to the Virgin on their dashboards, Mexican factories often post pictures of the Virgin to discourage bad behavior and tens of thousands of annual pilgrims to the Basilica finish their journey crawling on their knees.[19]

To beseech Mary for help and protection implies that she is at least equal to God in power and is preferred over God and Christ. This is not the Mary of the Bible, but the woman who rides the beast. Faith in Catholicism's Mary, supported by her thousands of apparitions, prepares the way as perhaps nothing else could for a world religion, a New World Order, and the reign of Antichrist.

## A Unique Role for the Amazing Mary

Worldwide, today's women are asserting themselves as never before in history. Contrary to popular opinion, "women instigate most domestic violence [and] hit men more frequently and more severely [than men hit them]" and violence is far more frequent in lesbian relationships than between husband and wife.[20] Women are taking over what were once men's jobs, and there is a growing acceptance of women at the highest levels of leadership in business, government, and religion. Only God could have given John, 1900 years ago, a vision that so fits our day—a *woman* in control.

From current trends, it seems inevitable that a *woman* must ride the beast. And of all the women in history, none rivals Roman Catholicism's omnipotent, omniscient, and omnipresent "Mary." Could it be that in preparation for her unique role in the New World Order astride the beast she is now appearing to millions around the world in a dazzling display of power? The script is ingenious! John Paul II has said:

Mary...should inspire all who cooperate in the Church's apostolic mission for the rebirth of humanity....The Church journeys through time...along the path already trodden by the Virgin Mary.[21]

The ecumenical power of this Mary is found in the fact that she provides a new deity to whom the followers of all religions can look—a female deity in step with the spirit of our age. Even Protestants find her appealing. At a women's conference in November 1993, "more than 2,000 participants recited a liturgy to . . . a female deity . . . [and] in a ritual that resembled holy communion, the women partook of milk and honey to honor the goddess." A far-out New Age gathering? No, "most of the participants represented mainline Protestant denominations. . . ."[22]

A woman Lutheran pastor "boasted that Jesus Christ's name was never mentioned" while another church leader urged attendees to overthrow "the patriarchal image of [a] Father God." Korean theologian Chung Hyun Kyung "urged Christians to adopt a 'new Trinity' composed of Buddhist, Hindu and Filipino goddesses."[23]

Catholicism is a jump ahead. Its "Mary," a goddess suitable for all religions, is already adored by a quarter of earth's population. Moreover, her ability to command the loyalty of multitudes has been demonstrated on a national level for centuries:

> Mary was "declared Queen of the Ukrainian people" in 1037, and Hungary was dedicated to her by King St. Stephen at about the same time. "Richard II solemnly consecrated England to Mary as 'her Dowry' . . . in 1381." France was consecrated to Mary in 1638 by the order of Louis XIII, who said, "We consecrate to her particularly our person, our State, our crown and our subjects"; Poland in 1656 by King Casimir. All of the "South American Spanish colonies were dedicated to Mary through a 'solemn consecration' in 1643 at the command of King Philip IV"; and in 1664 the same "was done for Portugal and all her colonies at the instigation of King John IV . . . Austria the following year" etc. In 1846 the bishops of America wrote, "We . . . place ourselves and all entrusted to our charge . . . under the special patronage of the holy Mother of God. . . ."[24]

## Mary and Islam

It is easy to imagine Buddhists, Hindus, New Agers, and liberals—as well as both Catholics and Protestants—uniting in a world religion, but the billion Muslims pose a special problem. Mary, however, seems to be the unique one through whom even they could be united into a universal faith. A British Catholic magazine reports that "a Marian revival is spreading throughout Africa, with alleged apparitions of the Virgin Mary finding a following among Muslims. . . ."[25] African Muslims themselves are seeing apparitions of the Virgin Mary and "are not required to become Christians" to follow her.[26] *Our Sunday Visitor* pointed out the honor given to Mary in Islam's Koran and the intriguing connection between her and Muhammad's favorite daughter, Fatima.[27]

Bishop Fulton J. Sheen wrote an interesting book in which he predicted that Islam would be converted to Christianity "through a summoning of the Moslems to a veneration of the Mother of God." He reasoned thus:

> The Koran . . . has many passages concerning the Blessed Virgin. First of all, the Koran believes in her Immaculate Conception and also in her Virgin Birth. . . . Mary, then, is for the Moslems the true *Sayyida*, or Lady. The only possible serious rival to her in their creed would be Fatima, the daughter of Mohammed himself. But after the death of Fatima, Mohammed wrote: "Thou shalt be the most blessed of all the women in Paradise, after Mary."[28]

Sheen goes on to say how remarkable it was that "our Lady" had the foresight to appear in the Portuguese village of Fatima (named after Muhammad's daughter during the Muslim occupation) and thus become known as "Our Lady of Fatima." It is a fact that when a statue of "Our Lady of Fatima" is carried through Muslim areas of Africa, India, and elsewhere, Muslims turn out by the hundreds of thousands to worship her. In two days an estimated 500,000 came to give their respects to this idol in Bombay, India.[29]

## Mary and John Paul II

No one is more convinced of the validity of the Fatima visitations than the present pope. Nor is anyone more devoted to Mary. John Paul II, who has "dedicated himself and his Pontificate to Our Lady,"[30] bears the M for Mary in his coat of arms; his personal motto, embroidered on the inside of his robes in Latin, is *totus tuus sum Maria* (Mary, I'm all yours). The pope has unusual personal reasons for this special devotion. The assault upon his life occurred on May 13, 1981, the anniversary of the Virgin's alleged first appearance on May 13, 1917, at Fatima, Portugal.[31] In a vision during his convalescence she told him that she had spared his life for a special mission he must fulfill in bringing peace.[32]

Returning to the Vatican after his recovery, John Paul II prayed at the tombs of his immediate predecessors and declared, "There could have been another tomb, but the blessed Virgin . . . has willed otherwise."[33] He added gratefully and reverently, "For everything that happened to me on that day, I felt that extraordinary Motherly protection and care, which turned out to be stronger than the deadly bullets."[34] Why would you need God when you have Mary's protection?

The thankful pope made a solemn pilgrimage to Fatima on May 13, 1982, where he "prayed before the statue of Our Lady of Fatima. Thousands heard him speak and consecrate the world to Mary as she had requested." On at least three other occasions, "on October 16, 1983; on March 25, 1984; and on December 8, 1985 . . . he consecrated the world to our Lady"[35] with "special mention" of the Russian people. Now that the Berlin Wall has come down and Soviet Communism has unraveled throughout Eastern Europe, credit is being given to Our Lady of Fatima for fulfilling her promise that if the popes and bishops would consecrate the world and Russia to her Immaculate Heart, "My Immaculate Heart will triumph, Russia will be converted, and there will be peace!"[36]

Such a statement is in the fullest opposition to the clear teaching of the Bible, which offers "peace with God through our Lord Jesus Christ" (Romans 5:1) as a free gift of God's grace—a peace that was bought "through the blood of his cross" (Colossians 1:20). Individual peace comes by faith to all who believe the gospel. World peace will only be established when Christ returns to reign from Jerusalem as the prophets foretold.

Yet Catholicism's Mary has taken the place of Christ as the one through whom peace will come, and the present pope and his Church support this heresy. Today's world (including those who call themselves Christians) is only too willing to accept a solution to its problems that leaves out Christ. That the woman is astride the beast seems to indicate that this pseudo-Mary of the apparitions will play a key role in the false peace by which Antichrist "shall destroy many" (Daniel 8:25). Declaring that the Lord had "confided the peace of the world to her," the apparition that appeared as the Virgin of Fatima offered its own peace plan in the place of Christ:

> Say the Rosary every day to obtain peace for the world. . . . Pray, pray, a great deal, and make sacrifices for sinners, for many souls go to Hell because they have no one to make sacrifices and pray for them. . . .
> God wishes to establish in the world the devotion to MY IMMACULATE HEART. If people do what I tell you, many souls will be saved and there will be peace.[37]

Souls "go to Hell because they have no one to make sacrifices"? Christ has already made the only saving sacrifice!

## A Seducing Spirit

Here is a blatant denial, accepted and promoted by Rome, that Christ's sacrifice paid the full debt for sin. Every pope in the last 60 years has honored Our Lady of Fatima.[38] Devotion to a mythical "Immaculate Heart" substitutes for devotion to God and Christ, and obedience to "Our Lady" brings peace. The apparition is surely not Mary! Claiming for itself the authority and attributes of Christ, the apparition at Fatima also declared:

> I will never leave you. [This is the promise of Christ to His disciples, and it presupposes omnipresence, an attribute of God alone.] My Immaculate Heart will be your refuge and the way that will lead you to God. . . .
> Sacrifice yourselves for the conversion of sinners [only Christ's sacrifice avails for sinners], and in reparation for the sins committed against the Immaculate Heart of Mary. . . .

> I promise to assist at the hour of death with all the graces necessary for salvation all those who, on the first Saturday of five consecutive months, go to Confession and receive Holy Communion, recite five decades of the Rosary and keep me company for a quarter of an hour while meditating on the mysteries of the Rosary with the intention of making reparation to me.[39]

This counterfeit Mary's offer of "the graces necessary for salvation" and her promise to "lead you to God" is one more denial of the sufficiency of Christ's finished work upon the cross, a denial which is implicit in Catholic dogma and rituals. It is to *Mary's* heart that the world must make reparation for the evil it has done *against her*—another blasphemous teaching. David said, "Against thee, *thee only*, have I sinned" (Psalm 51:4). Sin is against *God*, not against any of His creatures. Thus to teach that *reparation* must be made to Mary for *sins against her* is again to put her in the place of God. This elevation of the woman not only fits John's vision but also blends paganism and "Christianity" as foretold.

"Say the Rosary every day to obtain peace. . . ." A popular Catholic television program advertises, "There is no problem that cannot be solved with the Rosary," and gives an 800 number to call for further information. To say the Rosary one must repeat The Lord's Prayer and "Glory be to the Father . . . Son . . . and Holy Spirit" six times each and the "Hail Mary, full of grace" 53 times. Yes, the *woman* dominates. The world is being prepared for the one who rides the beast, and even evangelical leaders and their flocks are being deceived. (One popular evangelical prophecy expert known for his Bible memorization repeatedly praises the pope on TV and quotes "Our Lady of Fatima" as though she speaks the truth.)

Clearly these "apparitions" oppose the biblical gospel of salvation by grace through faith in the finished sacrifice of Christ, and glorify a counterfeit Mary in His place. A "seducing spirit" (1 Timothy 4:1) is at work. Yet John Paul II has said, "The message of Fatima is addressed to every human being and is more relevant and more urgent than ever."[40] The offer of a pseudopeace is given by apparitions everywhere. Consider the following ad in *The Dallas Morning News* by the local "Queen of Peace Center":

PRESCRIPTION FOR PEACE. *A Voice Cries Out in the Wilderness . . . a woman's.* This event has been reported in the *New York Times, 20/20, Life, Time* Magazine and *The Wall Street Journal,* etc. Millions of people have visited this site and most have returned home with a renewed faith in God, peace in their hearts, and a desire to live the Gospel message . . . we're talking about the appearance of the Virgin Mary in Medjugorje, Bosnia-Herzegovina as well as dozens of locations around the world.

WHY THE VIRGIN MARY? The Blessed Virgin Mary was the vessel that brought Jesus into the world the first time. Could it be that she is heralding His second coming? . . . "Begin by first creating peace within your own hearts," she says, "then in your families and in the world."[41]

## Catholicism's Jesus: Subordinate to Mary

The apparitions are given credit for pointing people to Jesus, yet there is little sign of real devotion to Christ among pilgrims to Marian shrines. It is *Mary* who has the honor. The Rosary is prayed over and over, the talk is all about Mary rather than Christ or God, the devotion is to her, and pilgrims see themselves as her servants doing her bidding. Mary, not Christ, is the one who will bring peace. It is *her* peace plan for the world, reparation must be made to *her* for the sins committed *against her,* and she must hold back the hand of her son from judgment. Mary, not Christ, is glorified.

Moreover, the Jesus promoted in the apparitions is a counterfeit who is always subordinate to Mary. The visions of "Mary" at Fatima, Portugal, which have meant so much to all of the popes since then and especially to John Paul II, are very explicit in their diminishment of Christ and the elevation of Mary in His place. The false gospel of salvation through Mary is even endorsed by a demon posing as Jesus who accompanies Mary. The official account of the apparitions of "Our Lady of Fatima" declares:

On the 10th of December, 1925, the Most Holy Virgin Mary appeared to Lucia, with the Child Jesus by Her side, elevated on a cloud of light. [Jesus is no longer a *child!*]

Our Lady rested one hand on Lucia's shoulder, while in the other hand She held a heart surrounded with sharp thorns. At the same time the Child Jesus spoke:

Have pity on the Heart of your Most Holy Mother. It is covered with thorns with which ungrateful men pierce it at every moment, and there is no one to remove them with an act of reparation.[42]

On February 15, 1926, "the Child Jesus" appeared again and urged Catholics to "spread this devotion of [and] reparation to the Immaculate Heart of His Holy Mother," declaring that *reparation must be made to the Immaculate Heart of Mary for mankind to be saved!*[43] Here again is blasphemy of the worst kind. It would never be uttered by the real Mary or by Jesus.

Christ is no longer a child and thus could not possibly appear in that form—and why should He even if He could? A mature man when He died for our sins, He is now in a resurrected, glorified body at the Father's right hand. It defies all bounds of rational thought and reality to imagine that Christ is still a babe accompanying His mother. Yet those who find no problem believing that millions of different wafers can each be the true physical body of Christ, "whole and entire," have no difficulty believing that Christ, while a mature man in heaven in His resurrected body, can and does at the same time appear as a babe on earth.

Furthermore, the real Jesus, after His resurrection, told His disciples that "repentance and remission of sins should be preached in *his name* among all nations" (Luke 24:47). In his preaching, Paul declared that *"through this man* [Jesus] is preached unto you the forgiveness of sins, and *by him* [not Mary] all that believe are justified from all things, from which ye could not be justified by the law of Moses" (Acts 13:38,39). The Bible contains no hint of reparations being made to Mary, much less that this is essential "for mankind to be saved."

All of the apparitions boldly offer a false gospel of salvation through Mary and the usual sacramental Catholicism of purgatory, ritual, and works. "Our Lady of Medjugorje" has said:

> There are many souls . . . who have been in Purgatory for a long time because no one prays for them. (7/21/82)
>
> God has placed His complete trust in me. I particularly protect those who have been consecrated to me. (11/6/82)
>
> At Christmas the greatest number of souls leave Purgatory. There are in Purgatory souls who pray ardently to God . . . [and] God permits them to manifest themselves . . . to their relatives on earth in order to remind them of the existence of Purgatory . . . (Spring, 1983).

Clearly we are seeing what Paul warned would occur in the last days: "Some shall depart from the faith, giving heed to seducing spirits and doctrines of devils" (1 Timothy 4:1). What these apparitions teach are definitely doctrines of devils that deny the sufficiency of Christ's death for our sins, that deny His position as Lord of all and exalt a false Mary above Him. She becomes the way to Jesus and the door to heaven (standard Catholic doctrine but not biblical). Typical is the following excerpt from a letter from the Office of the Bishop, Diocese of San Angelo, Texas, concerning a shrine to be built to "Our Lady of Guadalupe":

> When our Blessed mother appeared to Juan Diego on the hill of Tepeyac in 1531, Mary asked that a shrine be built in her honor so that through her, God's love, compassion, help and assistance could be poured out on the pilgrims who would come to this sacred place. . . .
>
> Let us pray for the guidance of the Holy Spirit . . . and ask our Blessed Mother to give us her guidance. [signed] Your servants in Christ and Mary, Most Reverend Michael D. Pfeifer, OMI, Bishop of San Angelo and Rev. Domingo Estrada, OMI, Pastor, Our Lady of Guadalupe.

The Shrine Offering slip enclosed said, "Yes! I want to help build a shrine to honor Our blessed Mother so all can be comforted by her presence." But earlier shrines to "Our Lady of Guadalupe" exist. There are thousands of Marian shrines around the world. Can her presence be at all of them simultaneously? She would have to be God for that to be true. In fact, the Catholic Mary promises to be with each individual Catholic worldwide. It is undeniable that Catholics look to Mary as though she were even greater than God and certainly more merciful and likely to favor them than God or Christ. As goddesses dominated in the past, so this goddess will play a dominant role in the immediate future.

### Ancient Rome's Religion Revived

Clearly, along with a worldwide revival under Antichrist of the Roman Empire there will be a revival of its religion which, as we have seen, was paganism surviving under a thin veneer of Christian terminology. It eventually became known as Roman Catholicism.[44] Statues of the fertility goddess were renamed Mary. Images had been made of the Roman emperors, and all who refused to bow to the images and worship the emperors as gods were killed. As the successors to the Roman emperors, the popes also killed those who refused allegiance to them and their religion. This is irrefutable history, which the Bible says will repeat itself under Antichrist:

> [They will] make an image to the beast [Antichrist]
> ...and cause that as many as would not worship the
> image of the beast should be killed (Revelation 13:14,15).

A pope will not be the Antichrist, but will be his right-hand man, the false prophet of Revelation 13:11-17; 19:20; 20:10. At current papal appearances, however, one observes adoration like that which the world will give Antichrist when it worships him as God. Consider this eyewitness account from the 1993 World Youth Day at Denver. Pilgrims who had fasted and walked the 15 miles to Cherry Creek Park for an all-night vigil before "Our Lady of the New Advent" awaited the pope's return the next morning. What followed was almost terrifying to the few Christians present:

> Suddenly, the whirring of the white-topped helicopter is
> heard above the music. "It's the Pope! Papa!" ... The crowd

becomes ecstatic . . . people press forward. Some are clutching rosaries . . . crying . . . [others] cheer . . . the orchestra begins the *Abba Ojcze Fanfare*, the Pope's entrance music.

The crowd noise now is deafening as the small figure of Pope John Paul II walks out from the stage . . . smiles and waves to the crowd. . . . The adoration of this man by these people is amazing to behold. . . . In his presence people lose ordinary defenses. They are vulnerable under this high-caliber "spirituality." He smiles with approving eyes, hugging and kissing those he can reach. . . .

John Paul II in his white attire approaches the steps leading to his chair, a throne-like structure of oak. He waves again to the standing pilgrims then climbs the steps and sits down. . . . The music continues softly as a young person from the International Youth Forum reads from offstage: "Behold a great multitude which no man could number, from every nation, from all tribes and peoples and tongues, standing before the throne and before the Lamb, clothed in white robes, with palm branches in their hands, and crying out with a loud voice, Salvation belongs to our God who sits upon the throne, and to the Lamb!"

The implication of that particular Scripture in this setting . . . induces a sense of alarm and dread from Protestants. The Scripture is from Revelation 7:9-10 and presents a view of Christ on his throne in heaven. "The great multitude which no man could number" is the true church, the Bride. . . . However, at Cherry Creek Park the pope sits on a throne among youths of many nations and tongues. They cry out to him as this Scripture is read.

Is this pope insinuating that he is Christ on his throne and the youths below him are his sheep . . . ? . . . The arrogance is overpowering despite John Paul's seeming humility. However, those unaware of Scripture and the translated meaning of the Polish hymn neither see nor sense arrogance. They see and sense love.

Pope John Paul II definitely has an enormous spirit of seductiveness . . . respond[ing] to *Abba/Father* while sit[ting] in white vestments on a throne. . . .

Youths dressed in native costumes and representing each of the continents come forward carrying their national flags. They proceed up the center steps and place their flags at the podium, literally at John Paul's feet.[45]

## Here We Go Again!

Pagan Romans who worshiped the emperor were not narrow-minded. They had many gods and tolerated a wide range of beliefs. Christians were not persecuted because they believed in Jesus Christ but because they believed in Him *alone* and would embrace no other gods, but *only* the God of the Bible. Catholicism is similarly tolerant of every religion and allows its members to practice everything from Yoga to voodoo so long as they remain in the Church. Both popular opinion and legislation are solidifying similar attitudes.

"Hate laws" are coming on the books in Canada and the United States (and elsewhere) which will make it a crime to suggest that anyone is wrong in his religious or moral beliefs or practices. Likely, it will soon be against the law to say that homosexuality is sin or that any religion is wrong. The "Genocide Treaty" signed by the United States and many other nations (though not yet enforced) already makes it a crime to suggest that someone's religious belief is false and to try to convert others to what one considers to be the truth.

Oddly enough, Roman Catholicism, while claiming to be the one true Church, at the same time embraces all religions, as we have seen. On this count as well, the Vatican qualifies uniquely as the woman astride the beast in Revelation 17. We have seen John Paul II's embrace of all religions and his claim that all gods are the same, while at the same time denouncing fundamentalist Christians. His friend and admirer, televangelist Robert Schuller, presents similar ideas from an alleged evangelical perspective: The way to "tell the good religion from the bad" is whether it is "positive." Schuller urged "religious leaders . . . whatever their theology . . . to articulate their faith in positive terms . . . in a massive, united effort by leaders of all religions [to proclaim] the positive power . . . of world-community-building religious values."[46]

"World-community-building religious values" acceptable to all religions? Antichrist couldn't improve upon that New Age doubletalk! Yet Schuller is commended by evangelical leaders and has the largest audience each Sunday morning of any televangelist. Schuller's embrace of Roman Catholicism and his advocacy of Protestants "coming home" to Rome has been well-documented.[47]

The coming world religion will be subtly, not blatantly, anti-Christian. It will, like Hitler's National Socialism, pose as *positive* Christianity and will be irresistibly appealing to the whole world. Like so much that we are already seeing even within evangelical circles, it will be a perversion of Christianity in the name of Christ. The same acceptance of all religions is preached by the apparitions of Mary and by the most appealing Catholic evangelist, Mother Teresa, whom no one dares criticize because of her outstanding charitable deeds of self-sacrifice.

The worldwide fame of Mother Teresa of Calcutta has given Catholicism acceptability with Protestants, who rightly admire her life of sacrificial charity. Rome calls her "one of the world's greatest evangelists."[48] Yet her "evangelism" leads no one to Christ but encourages trust in whatever god they believe in:[49]

> [T]hey brought [us] a man with half his body eaten away. Worms crawled all over him. . . . I went to clean him, and . . . he asked, "Why are you bothering to do this?"
>
> "I love you..," I said. "For me you are Jesus coming in his distressing disguise . . . I am only sharing the joy of loving you, and loving Jesus in you."
>
> Then what did this Hindu gentleman say to me? He just said, "Glory be to Jesus Christ." . . . He realized that he was someone loved.[50]

This Hindu gentleman was not told the most wonderful evidence that "he was someone loved": that this "Jesus Christ," who is God, became a man to die for his sins and thereby paid the debt demanded by God's justice, so that he could be forgiven and receive eternal life as a free gift of God's grace. He was not evangelized in the biblical meaning of that term at all. He was left a Hindu with all of his superstitions and false beliefs intact—left in his sins to die without Christ, a Hindu who was "loved," but not loved enough by "one of the world's greatest evangelists" to be told the truth that would rescue him from hell! Such is Catholicism's new "evangelism" that proposes to "convert" the world by the year 2000. "I love all religions," says Mother Teresa, an idea that fits the coming world religion perfectly.[51]

## The Vatican and the New World Order

The new world religion will be similarly tolerant of all beliefs which are willing to unite with one another in the charitable rescue of mankind. Uncompromising Christians will be put to death for standing in the way of unity and peace. David Koresh was a false Messiah, but the massacre at Waco shows how easily the Antichrist could justify the destruction of any who deviate from the world religion. President Clinton said:

> I hope very much that others who will be tempted to join cults and become involved with people like [David] Koresh will be deterred by the horrible scenes they have seen [of the immolation of the Branch Davidians at their Mount Carmel compound near Waco, Texas]. . . . There is, unfortunately, a rise in this sort of fanaticism all over the world. And we may have to confront it again.[52]

It is almost frightening that the President of the United States commends the massacre at Waco as the "justice" deserved by religious fanatics. In contrast, governments cultivate partnerships with Roman Catholicism. This was so not only in past centuries, but today as well. John Paul II's relationship with Reagan, Bush, Gorbachev, Arafat, et al is wellknown. His willingness to ignore injustice to keep such relationships was demonstrated early in his pontificate. He visited Argentina's "three-man ruling junta [but] refus[ed] to grant an audience to the relatives of about 20,000 people who were abducted by the military and 'disappeared.'"[53]

One reason for Antichrist's close partnership, at first, with the Vatican is seen in the importance which every nation on the earth puts upon good relations with "the most extensive international organization in the world outside of the United Nations."[54] U.S. Ambassador to the Vatican Raymond Flynn has said, "The Vatican relationship to the United States is extraordinarily important . . . it is in the national interest of the

United States of America to have strong diplomatic relations with the Vatican."[55]

President Clinton considered his meeting with the pope in Denver to be of the utmost importance. He met several times with Ambassador Flynn in preparation for that meeting, and Flynn flew out with him in the presidential plane for continuing consultation. Less than a year later Clinton journeyed to Rome to meet with the pope in the Vatican. The whole world recognizes the importance of this relationship (and so will Antichrist):

> From Rome to Washington, geopolitical analysts are talking about a "new alliance" between the world's chief military power, the U.S., and the world's chief spiritual leader, the pope.[56]

Soon the alliance will be between the *world ruler* and the Vatican. Indeed, the woman will ride the beast, so vital will be her role. Antichrist will know there can be no political peace without religious peace. Until all religions are willing to embrace one another as partners in working toward common goals there can be no global peace—and the pope, for the reasons we have documented, will be essential to establish full ecumenism. Robert Muller, a Catholic and former U.N. Assistant Secretary-General and Chancellor of the University for Peace, has said:

> We need a world or cosmic spirituality. . . . I hope that religious leaders will get together and define . . . the cosmic laws which are common to all their faiths. . . .
> We must also hope that the Pope will come before the year 2000 to the United Nations, speak for all the religions and spiritualities on this planet and give the world the religious view of how the third millennium should be a spiritual millennium. . . .[57]

When finally the religious leaders and political leaders unite to accomplish the same goals, the kingdom of Antichrist will have arrived. Such was the situation (in imperfect union) under Vatican leadership for more than a thousand years in the past.

And so it will be again, but this time with the terrifying full control that only today's computers and spy satellites can effect.

## A Solemn Warning from Heaven

How could religious leaders and their followers tolerate such totalitarianism? Consider the example of a 266-member delegation of America's National Council of Churches (NCC) which visited the Soviet Union in June 1984. They toured 14 cities and visited numerous state-licensed churches. The *New York Times* reported that the NCC delegation offered "praise for the status of religion in the Soviet Union and condemnation of the United States' role in the arms race . . . [and] voiced irritation that the harmony of their visit had been marred when two demonstrators, demanding religious freedom, held up banners [reading 'This is not a free church'] during a Baptist church service."[58] The NCC delegation's leader, Bruce Rigdon of McCormick Theological Seminary in Chicago, "expressed offense at the protest and admiration for the Soviet authorities who suppressed it."[59]

In Santiago De Compostela, Spain, during August 4-13, 1993, the World Council of Churches (WCC) held its Fifth World Conference on Faith and Order. Roman Catholics were official and full participants for the very first time at any WCC meeting. The goal toward which participants were working was a world church—and not one which is united so much by *faith* as one which is *visibly* united in the eyes of the entire world. The delegates adopted the statement:

> There is no turning back . . . from the single ecumenical movement that unites concern for the unity of the church and concern for . . . the struggles of the world.[60]

That significant declaration recognizes that the world church must operate in partnership with the world government. WCC Central Committee Moderator Aram Keshishian declared in his address that the WCC "must relate its doctrinal work more closely to social ethics. . . . Faith and Order cannot ignore the socio-political and economic dimension in its quest for church unity. . . . Any dichotomy between Christian Faith and political involvement, between unity of the church and struggles for justice, is an ecumenical heresy."[61]

That goal will be realized. The marriage of convenience, however, between Antichrist and the false World Church won't last indefinitely. When the honeymoon is over, Antichrist will turn on and destroy the "whore" (Revelation 17:16), effecting God's will in the process (verse 17). One of the most damning indictments God makes against the woman on the beast is that she will have trafficked not only in costly "merchandise of gold and silver and precious stones" but also in "slaves and souls of men" (Revelation 18:12,13). We have documented that as well.

In the meantime, there is a "voice from heaven" saying in awesome tones:

> Come out of her, my people, that ye be not partakers of her sins, and that ye receive not of her plagues. For her sins have reached unto heaven, and God hath remembered her iniquities.
>
> Reward her even as she rewarded you, and double unto her double according to her works; in the cup which she hath filled fill to her double.
>
> How much she hath glorified herself and lived deliciously, so much torment and sorrow give her, for she saith in her heart, I sit a queen, and am no widow, and shall see no sorrow.
>
> Therefore shall her plagues come in one day: death and mourning and famine; and she shall be utterly burned with fire, for strong is the Lord God who judgeth her (Revelation 18:4-8).

May all those who love Christ and His gospel come together in compassion and true union to rescue as many as possible from this dire judgment.

*The truth has been divinely revealed that sins are followed by punishments. God's holiness and justice inflict them. Sins must be expiated. This may be done on this earth through the sorrows, miseries and trials of this life and, above all, through death.*

*Otherwise the expiation must be made in the next life through fire and torments or purifying punishments. . . . The punishments with which we are concerned here are imposed by God's judgment, which is just and merciful. The reasons for their imposition are that our souls need to be purified, the holiness of the moral order needs to be strengthened and God's glory must be restored to its full majesty.*

—Vatican II[1]

*If anyone says that after the reception of the grace of justification the guilt is so remitted and the debt of eternal punishment so blotted out to every repentant sinner, that no debt of temporal punishment remains to be discharged either in this world or in purgatory before the gates of heaven can be opened, let him be anathema.*

—The Council of Trent[2]

# APPENDIX A

# Purgatory

A s the quotations opposite indicate, Catholicism teaches that while Christ's death made it possible for sins to be *forgiven*, the pardoned sinner must himself suffer some undefined pain or torment of unknown intensity and duration in order to be *purged* and thereby made fit for heaven. While Catholicism says it is theoretically possible to be cleansed through the sufferings of this life and one's death, no one, not even the pope himself, can know whether that has occurred. Consequently, almost all Catholics expect to spend some unknown length of time in purgatory. Failure to accept the doctrine of purgatory brings automatic excommunication from the Roman Catholic Church.

Both Trent and Vatican II speak of those who, even though Christ suffered for their sins, "must still make expiation [for their sins] in the fire of purgatory."[3] Here is Vatican II's further explanation of this doctrine:

> The doctrine of purgatory clearly demonstrates that even when the guilt of sin has been taken away, punishment for it or the consequences of it may remain to be expiated or cleansed. . . .
> [I]n purgatory the souls of those who died in the charity of God and truly repentant but who had not made satisfaction with adequate penance for their sins and

omissions are cleansed after death with punishments *designed to purge* away their debt.[4]

What is *adequate* penance? No one knows. The Church has never defined it. Where does the Bible say that punishment *purges* from sin? It doesn't.

## The Impossible Doctrine

The doctrine of purgatory does violence to both logic and Scripture. Romans 6:23 says, "The wages of sin is death [i.e., eternal separation from God]" not a limited time in purgatory. We would be lost forever apart from Christ's sacrifice for our sins. Nor is sin of such a makeup or quality that *suffering* of any kind can purge it from the heart and soul. Sin is part of mankind's very nature. Suffering may indeed alter one's attitude temporarily, but once the pain has passed, the old tendencies return because the heart has not been changed. It takes a miracle of God to purge the soul of sin—a miracle which must both leave intact man's power of choice and satisfy the demands of God's infinite justice.

The Bible declares unequivocally that there is only one way for the soul to be cleansed: through the blood of Christ poured out upon the cross in payment for sin, and by a new birth of God's Spirit in the soul through faith in Christ and His finished redemptive work. Thus on two counts the doctrine of purgatorial sufferings is false: 1) It is *impossible* for suffering to cleanse the heart of sin; and 2) It is *unnecessary* for the pardoned sinner to suffer for his sin because Christ has already paid the full penalty demanded by God's justice. On that basis alone is a person cleansed.

The Bible declares that Christ, "when he had by himself *purged* our sins, sat down on the right hand of the Majesty on high" (Hebrews 1:3), indicating that the *purging* is finished. And again, "The blood of Jesus Christ, [God's] Son, cleanseth [purges] us from *all* sin" (1 John 1:7). Scripture is very clear in stating that it was the shedding of Christ's blood in death under the judgment of God that purged us. Moreover, "without shedding of blood is no remission [of sin]" (Hebrews 9:22). Purgatory isn't said to be a place of blood-shedding, but of "purifying fire." The only possible purging of our sins was accomplished by Christ; it is accepted only by faith; it is effected in the heart only by the grace of God.

There is a further reason why suffering either on earth or in purgatory by the sinner himself cannot purge from sin: The one making the sacrifice for sin *must himself be without sin.* Sixty-two times in the Old Testament we are told that the animals that were offered had to be "without blemish" (Exodus 12:5; 29:1; Leviticus 1:3; etc.). These were "types" or symbols of Christ, the sinless, holy "Lamb of God" who would "take away the sin of the world" (John 1:36,29). Thus no amount of suffering by a sinner, here or in purgatory, could ever purge him or anyone else from sin. Only a sinless sacrifice can suffice.

Of Christ we are told, "[He] did no sin" (1 Peter 2:22), "[He] knew no sin" (2 Corinthians 5:21), and "in him is no sin" (1 John 3:5). Absolute sinlessness was essential or else Christ could not have died for our sins; He would have been under the penalty of death for His own sins. So Peter said of Christ that He "the *just* [suffered] for [us] the *unjust* that he might bring us to God [i.e., to heaven, not to purgatory]" (1 Peter 3:18). He added that those who lack this assurance have forgotten that they have been "purged from [their] old sins" (2 Peter 1:9). If we have trusted Christ as our Savior, we are to accept by faith the fact that God has purged us through Christ's finished work.

### The Origins, Development, and Purpose of This Doctrine

The idea of purgatory, a fictitious place of final purgation, was invented by Pope Gregory the Great in 593. There was such reluctance to accept the idea (since it went contrary to Scripture) that purgatory did not become an official Catholic dogma for nearly 850 years—at the Council of Florence in 1439. No doctrine has so increased the Church's power over its members or added so much to its income. To this day the threat of purgatory hangs over Catholics, who therefore give repeated offerings to the Church for its help in getting them out of that place of torment.

Rome promises that if its decrees are followed one will eventually be released from purgatory and enter heaven. Yet the Church has never been able to define how long any person must spend in purgatory nor how much that time is shortened by any means it offers. It is utter folly to trust one's release from purgatory to a Church which cannot even define how long one must spend there for each sin or how much each ritual or act of penance reduces purgatorial suffering. Nevertheless, offerings are given by Catholics to the Church and large sums left in wills (remember Henry VIII) to have multiple Masses said on one's behalf. That process never stops, "just in case" more Masses are needed.

The Council of Trent, Vatican II, and the resulting *Code of Canon Law* contain many complex rules for applying the merits of the living, and especially Masses, to the dead in purgation of their sins and to reduce time in purgatory:

> The Church offers the Paschal Sacrifice for the Dead so that . . . the dead may be helped by prayers and the living may be consoled by hope.
>
> Among Masses for the Dead it is the Funeral Mass which holds the first place in importance. . . . A Mass for the dead may be celebrated as soon as news of a death is received. . . .[5]

A major developer of this horribly false but ingeniously profitable doctrine was an Augustinian monk named Augostino Trionfo. In his day (the fourteenth century) the popes ruled as absolute monarchs over both heaven and earth. By their power to bind and loose they not only established and deposed kings and emperors, but it was believed they could open or shut the gates of heaven to mankind at will. Trionfo's genius extended this authority, at the behest of Pope John XXII, to a third realm. Von Dollinger explains:

> It had been said before that the power of God's vicar extended over two realms, the earthly and the heavenly. . . . From the end of the thirteenth century a third realm was added, the empire [rule] over which was assigned to the Pope by the theologians of the *Curia*—Purgatory.[6]

## Problems with Support from 2 Maccabees

Gavin tells how in his day (the early eighteenth century) it was still commonly taught that there were eight levels in purgatory. The poor were in the lowest level, where the fire was coolest, with kings in the highest level, where the fire was hottest. God in His goodness had supposedly planned it that way because kings and nobles were able to pay more to the Church to get their souls out whereas the poor had little to pay. He tells of poor people who, upon being told that a relative who had just died was among the beggars in purgatory, scraped together the money to say enough Masses to get them moved up to a higher level. Though the torment was greater, they would be in better company. So the priests charged money both to make the torment in purgatory greater and to get poor souls out of it!

Neither the word "purgatory" itself nor the idea of purgatory is to be found even once in the entire Bible. Nor is it so much as hinted at by Jesus or the apostles. Apologist Karl Keating admits that the doctrine "is not explicitly set out in the Bible."[7] The one verse always cited in support of purgatory comes from Apocrypha: "It is a holy and wholesome thought to pray for the dead, that they might be loosed from their sins" (2 Maccabees 12:45)

There are three obvious problems with this verse. First of all, there is not one example in the entire Bible of anyone praying for the dead. The Bible clearly states that "it is appointed unto men once to die, but after this the judgment" (Hebrews 9:27). It is too late for prayer after death; all that follows is judgment. Therefore this verse contradicts the Bible.

Secondly, those of whom this was said had been guilty of idolatry: "But under the tunic of each of the dead they found amulets sacred to the idols of Jamnia, which the law forbids the Jews to wear" (2 Maccabees 12:40 New American Bible). Idolatry was a mortal sin and, according to Catholic doctrine, would have landed these men not in purgatory but in hell, from which there is no release. Thus the idea of praying for them was both blasphemous and a waste of time, hardly the basis for accepting the doctrine of purgatory.

Finally, the very book of Maccabees itself declares that there were no prophets at this time and thus the inspiration of God had ceased: "There had not been such great distress in Israel since the time prophets ceased to appear among the people" (1 Maccabees 9:27 NAB). And again: "The Jewish people and their priest have, therefore, made the following decisions. Simon shall be their permanent leader and high priest until a true prophet arises" (1 Maccabees 14:41 NAB). Thus the two books of Maccabees can only be regarded as historical accounts at best but certainly not as Scripture, inasmuch as God was not inspiring anyone among His people. Obviously, then, one cannot support any true doctrine by a quote from this source. No wonder it contradicts the Bible!

## What About Paul's Suffering?

Catholic apologists attempt to be biblical by basing the doctrine of purifying sufferings upon Colossians 1:24, where Paul says, "Who now rejoice in my sufferings for you and fill up that which is behind of the afflictions of Christ in my flesh for his body's sake, which is the church." That Paul's suffering, however, had nothing to do with purging sin, either his own or anyone else's, is clear from the fact that Christ's sufferings had completed that work. Only a sinless sacrifice and the shedding of blood would avail.

Then what did Paul mean? Rather than suffering to effect the purification of his or anyone else's soul, Paul was suffering for the sake of *bringing the gospel to others* ("my suffering for you"). He referred to the persecution which "all that will live godly in Christ Jesus" would suffer (2 Timothy 3:12). Jesus told His disciples they would be hated and persecuted by the world (John 15:18,19). There is an "offense of the cross" (Galatians 5:11), and Paul said we must be willing to "suffer persecution for the cross of Christ" (Galatians 6:12).

It is not that Paul, like Christ, was suffering for sins in order to make up for what Christ's suffering *upon the cross* lacked, for there was no lack in that. The suffering that Paul endured and all other Christians true to the Lord must endure comes because we identify ourselves with Christ and live Christlike lives that condemn the world and reveal its evil. Therefore the world hates us as they hated Christ. In fact, Christ said that Paul must suffer greatly "for my name's sake" (Acts 9:16). In Acts 5:41 the disciples rejoiced that they "were counted worthy to suffer shame for his name." The suffering that true Christians endure is at the hands of those who hate their Lord and are offended by His cross.

Philippians 1:29 says it is a privilege to suffer because of the hatred the world has toward Christ: "Unto you it is given in the behalf of Christ not only to believe on him but also to *suffer for his sake*." Second Thessalonians 1:5 speaks of "the kingdom of God, for which ye also suffer." First Timothy 4:10 says that we "labor and suffer reproach because we trust in the living God." Peter also referred to the suffering that comes to every Christian who is true to the Lord (1 Peter 3:14; 4:13,16). Many other verses express the same thought.

In Philippians 3:10 Paul expresses his passion to know Christ "and the fellowship of his sufferings," which he says helps to bring him into conformity with the death and character of Christ. It is clear that Paul referred to sufferings for Christ's sake here upon earth at the hands of sinners, not to suffering in a future purgatory to be cleansed of one's sin. Paul writes in Romans 8:18 that "the sufferings of *this present time* are not worthy to be compared with the glory which shall be revealed in us." Certainly there is no thought of purgatory. We go from the sufferings of this world into the presence and glory of Christ and God.

## Other Serious Problems with Purgatory

The doctrine of purgatory errs in a number of other ways. It forgets that we have offended God's infinite justice. James says that even the smallest sin makes a sinner "guilty of [breaking] all" of the commandments (James 2:10). Why? Because any sin is rebellion against God, which separates the sinner from God for eternity. We are finite beings and could never pay the infinite penalty demanded by God's justice. Consequently there is no escape from hell, but the sinner must suffer there eternally. To "expiate" one's sins by suffering is therefore impossible.

Of course, in theory God could pay the infinite penalty demanded by His justice against sin, but that wouldn't be just because He isn't one of us. So God became man through the virgin birth. Being a sinless man and infinite God in one Person, Christ was able to satisfy the claims of His own justice so that "whosoever believeth in him should not perish but have everlasting life" (John 3:16). The only expiation of sin comes as a free gift of God's grace; any attempt to earn or merit it constitutes a rejection of God's offer of mercy to unworthy sinners. Moreover, the thought that there is any suffering at all left for a Christian to endure in payment of his sins after Christ suffered the full penalty and cried "It is finished" (John 19:30) is a blasphemous denial of the redemption that Christ effected and the salvation that He offers.

In the teaching of purgatory we see once again that Roman Catholicism does not accept God's offer of salvation by His grace, but insists upon adding human works to what Christ has done. Although Catholicism does affirm that salvation is ultimately by grace through faith, it also states that good works (though by God's grace operating in the individual) are essential for salvation. We quote again from Vatican II:

> From the most ancient times in the Church good works were also offered to God for the salvation of sinners...[by] the prayers and good works of holy people...the penitent was washed, cleansed and redeemed....
>
> Following in Christ's steps, those who believe in him have always...carried their crosses to make expiation for their own sins and the sins of others...[to] help their brothers to obtain salvation from God....[8]

## A Fatal Contradiction

Only blind submission to the Church prevents the Roman Catholic adherent from seeing that the doctrine of purgatory contains an obvious and fatal contradiction. On the one hand we are told that the sacrifice of Christ is not enough to get one to heaven, but in addition to Christ's sufferings on the cross the forgiven sinner must himself suffer torment to be purged of his sin. On the other hand, however, and in direct contradiction, it is said that the Mass, which is the representation or perpetual renewal of Christ's sacrifice, reduces (by some unknown amount) one's suffering. Presumably, if enough Masses were said one would be *purged* by the *expiation* of all sins without any suffering at all. So one doesn't have to suffer, after all, to be purged.

If one truly had to suffer before heaven's gate could open, the Church would have nothing to offer and would lose a major means of income. The same would be true if Christ's sacrifice for sin, as the Bible teaches, were enough to purge the sinner. The Catholic Church would again be out of business. Therefore, to keep the Church operating and its coffers full, it is taught that one may be purged of sin by certain means which the Church can provide, and that Christ's sacrifice on the cross was insufficient to purge of sin, so that the Mass, for which the Church receives income, can be credited with reducing suffering in purgatory and opening the gate of heaven. How amazing that what Christ's suffering on the cross could not effect, the alleged repetition of that suffering reenacted on Catholic altars can accomplish.

Moreover, the sufferings of others also are said to reduce the time needed for purging in purgatory. The stigmata of Padre Pio and the sufferings of the "saints" can thus accomplish what the sacrifice of Christ on the cross could not. Here it is again: "Following in Christ's steps, those who believe in him have always . . . carried their crosses to make expiation for their own sins and the sins of others." Christ's cross could only *forgive* but could not *purge* sin; yet the crosses carried by others can *purge* sin and thus can do more than the cross of Christ!

So the doctrine of purgatory contains a fatal contradiction. It declares that one *must suffer* in order to be purged of one's sins; yet at the same time it says one *need not suffer* if certain rules are followed. The major means of escaping suffering is through the repetition of the Mass, but there are many others. The reduction or elimination of suffering in purgatory is also effected through "indulgences." That doctrine is explained in Appendix B.

*An indulgence is a remission before God of the temporal punishment for sin the guilt of which is already forgiven, which a properly disposed member of the Christian faithful obtains under certain and definite conditions with the help of the Church which, as the minister of redemption, dispenses and applies authoritatively the treasury of the satisfactions of Christ and the saints.*

*An indulgence is partial or plenary in as far as it frees from the temporal punishment due to sin either partly or totally.*

*The faithful can gain partial or plenary indulgences for themselves or apply them for the dead by way of suffrage.*

—The Code of Canon Law[1]

*For God's only-begotten Son ... has won a treasure for the militant Church ... he has entrusted it to blessed Peter, the key-bearer of heaven, and to his successors who are Christ's vicars on earth, so that they may distribute it to the faithful for their salvation. ...*

*The "treasury of the Church" ... is the infinite value, which can never be exhausted, which Christ's merits have before God. ... This treasury includes as well the prayers and good works of the Blessed Virgin Mary. They are truly immense, unfathomable, and even pristine in their value before God. In the treasury, too, are the prayers and good works of all the saints [who] ... attained [by such good works] their own salvation and at the same time co-operated in saving their brothers. ...*

—Vatican II[2]

# APPENDIX B

# Indulgences

Can Bible-believing Christians really accept such an obviously false gospel and join with those who preach it in evangelizing the world? Can evangelicals, in good conscience, direct inquiring souls to a Church which preaches purgatory and indulgences, and agree that its members are Christians and not to be evangelized? A Church which claims to control the gate to heaven and opens it to those who put themselves in her hands?

In fact, she glories in her claim to be "the minister of redemption" (Canon 992 says the same). Rome unashamedly admits that the salvation she offers must be received in partial installments and that its efficacy is derived not only from "Christ's merits" but from the surplus "good works of all the saints" beyond what they needed to "attain their own salvation."

How astonishing that evangelical leaders could credit Roman Catholicism with being Christian and propose to evangelize the world as her partner in the gospel! We can only assume that they are ignorant of her true teachings and have been deceived by the many misrepresentations emanating from Catholic apologists. How else could those who otherwise seem to be stalwarts of the faith say that evangelicals and Catholics are in agreement on the fundamentals of the gospel?

Vatican II goes on to say, "To gain indulgences the work prescribed must be done."[3] Here is further proof, if it were needed, that Rome preaches, promises, and practices salvation by works. And yet, oddly enough, the person himself doesn't have to do the good works. The good works of others may be credited to one's account in Rome's contrived ledger, which, when balanced out by its specious reckoning, opens the gate to heaven.

## The Origin and Development of the Doctrine of Indulgences

The very concept of indulgences comes from paganism: the idea that the infliction of pain, the recitation of formulas, or the pilgrimages to shrines and sacrifices to the gods are meritorious and influence the gods in one's favor. The idea that saying so many Hail Marys or kissing a crucifix and repeating a formula could reduce purgatorial suffering which Christ's sacrifice on the cross could not reduce is bad enough, but the teaching that an indulgence may be applied to the *dead* carries the blasphemous absurdity a quantum leap further. The idea that "time off for good behavior" could be credited to someone in purgatory who has not done the necessary "work prescribed" betrays again the fraud of Romanism. Anything is possible for a financial offering.

The gospel of indulgences is one of Rome's most blatantly unbiblical and illogical doctrines coming out of the Middle Ages, and it is still in force today. The pagan concept of indulgences gradually became defined as part of Roman Catholicism over the years and eventually became the papacy's greatest moneymaking scheme. Theoretically it should take only one Mass to release every soul from purgatory; Mary, whose power is infinite, could do it in a moment; and the popes, whose power is also unlimited, could empty purgatory with the stroke of a pen by simply devising an indulgence to do so. Why not, then? Do they have no love for souls? The answer is obvious. Von Dollinger writes:

> [Augostino] Trionfo, commissioned by John XXII to expound the rights of the Pope, showed that, as the

dispenser of the merits of Christ, he could empty Purgatory at one stroke, by his Indulgences, of all the souls detained there, on the sole condition that somebody fulfilled the rules laid down for gaining those indulgences.

He advised the Pope, however, not to do this... [though] the Pope's power is so immeasurably great, that no Pope can ever know the full extent of it.[4]

To empty purgatory would stop the inflow of offerings for more Masses and endless graces and favors. Instead, the requirements for getting out of purgatory were made ever more complex, necessitating ever greater services from the Church. The doctrine of indulgences was at last declared an official Church dogma by Pope Clement VI in 1343. Clement reasoned that "one drop of Christ's blood would have sufficed for the redemption of the whole human race." The remainder of that blood shed on the cross, its virtue "increased by the merits of the Blessed Virgin and the supererogatory works of the saints" (above and beyond the good works needed for their own salvation), constitutes the "treasury" referred to above. By papal bull in 1476, Pope Sixtus IV "extended this privilege to souls in purgatory [reducing their time of suffering there], provided that their living relatives purchased indulgences for them."[5]

Out of this "treasury of the Church" salvation/redemption is dispensed a bit at a time by the Catholic clergy through the seven sacraments. There is no way to know how much credit is granted for each deed, ritual, or indulgence, or how long this process must continue. Never is sufficient grace given to assure one of heaven. Always more Rosaries must be said, more Masses performed, more offerings given in order to obtain more grace from the Church. Peter, whom Catholics say was the first pope, warned of such "false teachers" who would "bring in damnable heresies . . . and through covetousness shall they with feigned words make merchandise of you" (2 Peter 2:1,3). Merchandise indeed! No gold mine could compare.

In Catholicism, one never passes "from death to life" as Christ promised (John 5:24) but is always in the process of earning salvation with the Church's help and with the expectancy of finishing the "purging" process in purgatory. In fact, excommunication is the penalty for a Catholic to say he is saved and knows that he has eternal life through faith in Christ's finished work. The very heart of the gospel that evangelicals affirm is denied by Catholicism in its official catechisms, canons, decrees, and dogmas, and those who dare to affirm the biblical gospel are anathematized.

## Meriting Grace

There is almost no limit to the ingenious "means of grace" which popes and their assistants have imaginatively invented. One of the most popular ways to merit grace (a contradiction of terms) is through wearing the brown scapular of Our Lady of Mount Carmel (to which we have earlier referred). The " 'Sabbatine' [Saturday] Privilege is based on a bull allegedly issued March 3, 1322, by Pope John XXII . . . [declaring] that those who wear the Scapular and fulfill two other conditions . . . will be freed from Purgatory [by the Virgin Mary] on the first Saturday after death."[6]

In spite of the heresies and evil of Pope John XXII, many other popes (Alexander V, Clement VII, Pius V, Gregory XIII, etc.)[7] have confirmed his teaching about the brown scapular, which in itself is so obviously contrary to Scripture. Pope Pius X declared, "I wear the cloth; let us never take it off." Pope Pius XI "joyfully professed: 'I learned to love the Scapular Virgin in the arms of my mother. . . .' " Pope Paul V affirmed that "the Blessed Virgin will aid the souls of the Brothers and Sisters of the Confraternity of the Blessed Virgin of Mount Carmel after their death. . . ." Pope Benedict XV offered a "partial indulgence for kissing the Scapular." And in 1950 "Pope Pius XII wrote the now-famous words concerning the Scapular: 'Let it be your sign of consecration to the Immaculate Heart of Mary, which we are particularly urging in these perilous times.' "[8]

We have already noted the fatal contradiction that indulgences are designed to shorten suffering in purgatory; yet that very suffering is supposed to be essential in order to be purged for entrance into heaven. It makes no sense. Moreover, one can only wonder how and why an indulgence obtained by means of adoring a crucifix or having a Mass said is even more potent than Christ's actual death on the cross and how such representations of Calvary can accomplish what Christ's death could not. Again it makes no sense, but the Catholic has been taught not to reason why but simply to accept what the Church says.

Vatican II has a large section containing 20 complex provisions revising previous rules concerning when and how an indulgence may be obtained. One is reminded of Christ's denunciation of the rabbis in Matthew 23 for devising a labyrinth of rules that kept the people dependent upon their spiritual guidance. Rome has done the same. It would take a lawyer specializing in the Church's Canon Law to unravel the intricacies of how and when to maximize the various offers of "grace." The following is illustrative:

> The faithful who use with devotion an object of piety (crucifix, cross, rosary, scapular or medal) after it has been duly blessed by any priest can gain a partial indulgence. But if this object of piety is blessed by the Pope or any bishop, the faithful who use it with devotion can also gain a plenary [full] indulgence on the feast of the Apostles Peter and Paul, provided they also make a profession of faith using any approved formula. ...
>
> The way [partial indulgences] have been determined hitherto, by days and years, is abolished. Instead, a new standard for measuring them has been laid down. From now on a partial indulgence will be indicated only with the words "partial indulgence" without any determination of days or years.[9]

If Rome was wrong in its rules concerning indulgences in the past, how can anyone be certain that she is correct now? And what of those who relied upon the previous rules? Of course, knocking off so many days or years in the past didn't really mean anything because the Church could never say in the first place how much time had to be spent in purgatory. Nor does an indulgence under the new rules have any understandable significance today. And what kind of "God" would bend His justice for such contrivances, measuring out "grace" depending upon whether the deed was done on a certain "feast" day and whether a priest or bishop had "blessed" the supposedly sacred object!

The major means of acquiring an indulgence of unknown benefit is, of course, through the Mass. Canon 904 states: "Remembering that the work of redemption is continually accomplished in the mystery of the Eucharistic Sacrifice, priests are to celebrate frequently...."[10] As we have already noted, instead of being a memorial to an accomplished redemption, each Mass takes another tiny step toward full redemption. No one knows how tiny that step is, but it must be miniscule indeed judging by the millions of Masses that continue to be celebrated with uncertain results.

### Salvation for Sale

It was the sale of indulgences more than anything else that roused Luther's ire to such an extent that he nailed his 95 theses to the door of the Wittenberg castle chapel and sparked the Reformation. As we have seen, salvation was sold in many other ways beside indulgences, and still is to this day. Though the fee is today called an "offering," in fact money changes hands, with the promise of salvation as the incentive for the "gift." Historian Will Durant's comments are of interest:

> Almost as mercenary as the sale of indulgences was the acceptance or solicitation, by the clergy, of money payments, grants, legacies, for the saying of Masses supposed to reduce a dead soul's term of punishment in purgatory. Large sums were devoted to this purpose by pious people, either to relieve a departed relative or friend, or to shorten or annul their own purgatorial probation after death. The poor complained that through their inability to pay for Masses and indulgences it was the earthly rich, not the meek, who would inherit the kingdom of heaven; and Columbus ruefully praised money because, he said, "he who possesses it has the power of transporting souls into paradise."[11]

What fraud, as though God could be bought off for money! In Spain the annual papal Bull of the Crusade had to be purchased by everyone of seven years and older at least once each year. No one could be buried without the current Bull in the coffin. Upon purchase of the Bull, the pope immediately granted indulgences and absolution from all sins except heresy and the vow of chastity. A Catholic observer in eighteenth-century Spain, with reference to this Bull, made this damning comment:

> Let us say that we may suspect that this Bull sends more people into hell than it can save from it; for it is the greatest encouragement to sin in the world. A man says, I may satisfy my lusts and passions, I may commit all wickedness, and yet I am sure to be pardoned of all by the taking of this Bull for two reals of plate [silver]. By the same rule, their consciences cannot be under any remorse nor trouble; for if a man commits a great sin, he goes to confess, he gets absolution, he has by him this Bull, or permission to sin, and his conscience is at perfect ease, insomuch that after he gets absolution he may go and commit new sins, and go again for absolution.[12]

Well-known Catholic apologist Peter Kreeft claims that "the Church soon cleaned up its act and forbade [shortly after Martin Luther's defection] the sale of indulgences...."[13] Charles Colson erroneously claims the same.[14] Of course, that simply isn't true. But even if it were, one cannot dispense so easily with the gross deceit that milked the faithful of their money and robbed them of salvation in the process. The sale of salvation had deceived millions for centuries by the time of the Reformation. Were there any refunds given by the Church? Of course not. Any remedy for those who had passed into eternity thinking they had bought their salvation? No. Tragically, the fraud continues to this day.

Kreeft, like other Catholic apologists, omits the fact that the false and evil doctrine of indulgences remains an integral part of present Catholicism, and that money is still given to secure salvation. As we have earlier noted, Vatican II declares: "The Church. commands that the usage of indulgences... should be kept... and it condemns with anathema those who say that indulgences are useless or that the Church does not have the power to grant them . . . [for] the task of winning salvation."[15]

It is no good to plead that the abominations of the past are no longer practiced by Rome. Of course they are, and quite openly, especially in Roman Catholic countries, though less so in the United States. Yet even here, salvation (in baby steps toward heaven, of course) may be purchased by offerings to the Church. One friend of the author whose father died recently in the United States said that more than 2000 dollars was expended for Mass cards at his father's funeral, which would allow for a number of Masses to be said on his behalf to help get him out of purgatory.

Rome has given her people a gospel of despair. Multitudes of Catholics live in dread of committing a mortal sin, of failing to reveal all in confession, of falling short of the rules and regulations their Church has set for salvation. As a consequence, they are completely at the mercy of the Church, looking to it for salvation rather than resting in God's rich grace and in Christ's finished work at Calvary.

*[T]he Apostolic See ... transferred the Roman Empire from the Greeks to the Germans in the person of Charlemagne. [And] the princes ... recognize, that the right and authority to examine the person elected as king—[or] Emperor—belong to us, who anoint, consecrate and crown him.*

—Pope Innocent III, *Decretal "Venerabilim fratrem,"* March, 1202[1]

*John, by the grace of God king of England, lord of Ireland ... to all faithful Christians who shall see this present charter, greeting. ...*

*We ... offer and freely concede to ... our Mother the Holy Church, to our lord Pope Innocent and to his Catholic successors, the whole kingdom of England and the whole kingdom of Ireland ... for the remission of our sins and of the sins of all the members of our family, living or dead; and receiving them and holding them, from now onwards, from God and the Roman Church as a vassal, we now do and swear fealty to the aforesaid our lord Pope Innocent, to his Catholic successors and to the Roman Church. ...*

—King John Lackland's *Infeodation to Pope Innocent III*, May 15, 1213[2]

*The Catholic Apostolic Roman religion shall continue to be the sole religion of the Republic of Ecuador, and ... no other dissident form of worship or any society condemned by the Church shall at any time be allowed within the Republic of Ecuador.*

—*Concordat between Pope Pius IX and the Republic of Ecuador* September 26, 1862[3]

# APPENDIX C

# Dominion over Kings: Further Documentation

Akey element in John's identification of the woman astride the beast is the statement that she is a city *which reigns over the kings of the earth.* We have carefully documented the fact that papal Rome fulfilled this prophecy and that she alone meets all the other criteria as well which John presents for identifying the woman astride the beast. We challenge anyone to find any other city beside Rome and its successor, Vatican City, which meets all the identifying characteristics set forth in Revelation 17.

Undoubtedly Christ's revelation to John that a religious body professing to be the bride of Christ would enter into unholy alliances with kings and even reign over them is one of the most remarkable prophecies in all of Scripture. Several books in their entirety could be filled with evidence that this prophecy was fulfilled in the Roman Catholic Church. However, we can only take space to present a small amount of additional documentation for those who may be interested.

## Judge of All and Judged by None

Pope Leo X (1513-21) forbade the courts in every country to try anyone for a crime from which they had been absolved by the Church in payment of the fee set for each offense. If any judge tried to circumvent this dictate, he was summarily excommunicated. To be put out of the Church meant loss of citizenship as well, inasmuch as the civil authorities were required to accept the Church's decrees.

Pope Paul IV (1555-9), inquisitor par excellence, unrivaled torturer of Christians and persecutor of Jews, was so foulmouthed that his expressions could not be believed except as sworn to by witnesses. He quarreled constantly, even with the only two friends of the papacy at that time, Kings Charles V and Philip II, because in his mind a major purpose of the papacy was "to tread under foot kings and emperors."[4] Just before his death in 1559, in response to the growing Protestant schism, which by now had reached alarming proportions and threatened to invade the Congress of Cardinals itself, Paul IV issued the bull *Cum ex Apostolatus Officio*.

As "Roman Pontiff, Vicar on earth of God and our Lord Jesus Christ, holder of plenitude of power over nations and kingdoms, judge of all men and judged by no one in this age," Paul IV declared that he had unlimited power to depose every monarch and to take anyone's possessions without legal process. Anyone trying to assist those thus dispossessed would be excommunicated. His decree stated:

> [A]ny persons whatsoever who shall be detected, acknowledged or proved to have departed from the Catholic Faith . . . or fallen into heresy, or have entered into, fomented or ordered schism, shall incur the aforesaid penalties [excommunication and dispossession of property], whatever position, rank, order, condition or preeminence they may enjoy, even if they . . . possess the worldly authority and honour of a Count, Baron, Marquis, Duke, King or Emperor. . . .
>
> It is permitted to no man to challenge this statement. . . . But if any one should presume to attempt this, let him know that he will incur the anger of Almighty God and of His blessed Apostles Peter and Paul.
>
> Given in Rome at St. Peter's, in the year of the Lord's Incarnation 1559 on the fifteenth day (before the) Kalends of March, in the fourth year of our Pontificate.[5]

Pope Sixtus V (1585-90), who rewrote the Bible to conform to his own peculiar ideas, declared that he had not only religious but civil jurisdiction over all kings and princes and that he could "appoint or dismiss anyone any time he pleased, including emperors." This was no idle threat. In those days it was commonly believed that outside the Roman Catholic Church there was no salvation. Thus to be threatened with excommunication by the pope made emperors tremble, for it was tantamount to being sentenced to eternity in hell.

Pope Clement XI in his 1715 Bull, *In Coena Domini*, excommunicated all who failed to obey the Holy Father and especially all who did not pay him their taxes. The bull declared that the pope held supreme authority over all men (including sovereigns) and their affairs, secular or religious. Subsequent popes reconfirmed this dogma. Rome has never abrogated it.

## Maintaining Papal Dominance

The Vatican has been called "one of the world's most magnificent repositories of art" and "the most remarkable treasure house in the world." Part of that treasure is now on world tour (including Michelangelo's *Pieta*), a tour which began in Denver, Colorado, to coincide with Pope John Paul II's visit there in August 1993. Next on the tour was Buenos Aires. The treasure is not expected to return to the Vatican until the year 2000, "in time for the celebration of Christian millennium." One of the treasures being displayed is the tiara of Pope Pius IX, convener of Vatican I. Its description includes:

> The crown is the symbol of the sovereignty of the papacy. . . . The tiara is adorned with pearls and precious gems and is inscribed in Latin, which translates as: "To the infallible Vicar of Christ; To the Supreme Governor of the world on earth; To the father of Nations and Kings."[6]

Such claims to "reign over the kings of the earth" fulfill John's vision, as we have seen, and have never been annulled by Rome, which still sees the popes as the ultimate monarchs who rule the world for God. The demise of monarchies, however, left the popes with no more kings to rule. The succeeding republics and democracies put government in the hands of the people and gradually (in most countries at least) gave equality to all religions. We have documented the fact that, as the popes saw their power in danger of eroding, they did everything they could to undermine the new governments. Their consistent suppression of basic civil rights is an undeniable matter of record.

Past papal power has not, however, diminished as much as would appear at first sight. The Roman Catholic Church continues to teach its subjects (some 980 million around the world) that loyalty to her comes first and that she can absolve any of her subjects from loyalty to civil rulers. This fact and the dangers it posed for civil governments was recognized by the State of Missouri more than 100 years ago. As a consequence, the State Constitution of Missouri was amended in 1864 to "require that all clergymen take an oath of loyalty to the State of Missouri and therefore to the United States. At this crucial moment in the Civil War, the Roman Catholic Archbishop of St. Louis sent a pastoral letter to all his priests condemning the required oath" and encouraging them to defy the government.[7]

## Justifying Totalitarianism

On September 20, 1870, General Raffaele Cadorna's forces of a newly united Italy broke through Rome's Aurelian walls at *Porta Pia*. The pope's forces under General Hermann Kanzler could do little more than put up token resistance. Not only Rome but what was left of the papal states was now taken over by the new Italy. Savoring their long-sought independence, the citizens' attitude became openly hostile toward the Church which had so long ruled vast territories with an iron fist. When Pius IX (who had rammed papal infallibility through Vatican I) died a few months later and his casket was carried with great pomp through the streets and up to St. Peter's, mobs of Italians filled the square, throwing stones and shouting:

> Death to the Pope! Death to the Priests! Throw the pig in the river! Throw the beast in the Tiber!

Only the police prevented the mob from making good its threat. This antipapal attitude on the part of the man in the street had been developing for some years in response to the suppression of basic freedoms under papal rule. Five years before the First Vatican Council opened, the pope had issued his infamous encyclical *Quanta cura* in which he denounced "the proponents of freedom of conscience and freedom of religion . . . [and] all those who assert that the Church may not use force."[8]

The papacy had ruled by force for centuries and the popes were fearful of the new winds of freedom that were bringing a desire for basic individual rights. Such an atmosphere was repugnant to papal pride and ambition. The pope had been certain that the dogma of papal infallibility, officially decreed by a council of bishops from around the world, would have put an end to such nonsensical dreams of freedom. As one highly regarded nineteenth-century historian explained:

> The pain of death for offences against religion was [still] part of the penal code; to the Church was still permitted the relic of medieval lawlessness—the right of asylum for criminals; to the parish priest were left all civil registers; to the Jesuits the right to penetrate everywhere—to rule the royal household, the private homes of citizens, the public institutions, the schools, etc.; so that the country was absolutely subject to the priestly power.[9]

In reading the astonishing record of papal power and oppression executed through its clergy one marvels how thoroughly it was accepted as part of life, not only by the ordinary people (who were helpless to oppose it) but by civil rulers as well. Nor did the obvious evils and injustices perpetrated for centuries by the Church seem to cast any doubt upon the validity of papal decrees. Von Dollinger gives this astonishing picture:

> God's Vicar upon earth, it was said, acts like God, who often included many innocent persons in the punishment of the guilty few; who shall dare to contradict him?

> He acts under Divine guidance and his acts cannot be measured by the rules of human justice. . . .
>
> Paradoxical as it may sound, it is an historical fact that the more suspicious and scandalous the conduct of the Popes . . . appeared to pious men, the more inclined they felt to take refuge from their own doubts and suspicions in the bosom of Papal infallibility . . . [having] been taught from youth that the Pope is the lord and master of the Church, whom none may contradict or call to account. . . .
>
> Peter Cantor, as early as the end of the twelfth century . . . [acknowledges] that the Papal corruptions [have] no scriptural justification . . . but then it would be sacrilegious to find fault with what the Pope does.[10]

The false doctrine of papal dominion over kings may be summarized in these words written to the patriarchs of Constantinople by Pope Innocent III: "The Lord left to Peter the governance not of the church only but of the whole world."[11] Nor has the Roman Catholic Church, by papal bull or concilliar declaration, ever backed away from that position.

*At the beginning of the fourteenth century...
the nature of the church's inerrancy was still
ill-defined. The idea that the pope might be
personally infallible was too novel, too contrary
to all traditional teaching, to find any widespread acceptance.*

—Brian Tierney in *Origins of Papal
Infallibility*[1]

*Rome has spoken, the dispute is at an end.*

—St. Augustine (354-430)

# APPENDIX D

# Papal Infallibility and Apostolic Succession

I n order to promote the necessary blind faith in the pope's infallibility and in the dogma that salvation is obtainable only in the Roman Catholic Church, its hierarchy has hidden the facts and rewritten history. One example is the quote by Augustine on the facing page. If, as the argument goes, Augustine, the greatest theologian of the Church, was willing to submit to whatever Rome (i.e., the pope and hierarchy) decreed, then surely ordinary Catholics ought to do the same. Such submission, however, is not what Augustine proposed. In context, the quote means something else. Two synods had ruled on a disputed matter and the Bishop of Rome had concurred, which "appeared to him [Augustine] more than enough, and so the matter might be regarded as at an end. That a Roman judgment in itself was not conclusive, but that a *'Concilium plenarium'* was necessary for that purpose, he had himself maintained. . . ."[2]

Nowhere else in his voluminous writings did Augustine even come close to suggesting that the Bishop of Rome had the final say on issues of faith or morals. In fact, Augustine said that the African Church had been correct in rejecting Roman Bishop Stephen's (254-7) opinion on settling a baptismal dispute. Never once, in all the arguments he proposed on many issues, did Augustine suggest that the Bishop of Rome should be consulted as the final arbiter of orthodoxy, or even that he should be consulted at all.

Interestingly enough, though the Council of Nicea in 325 decreed that the three Bishops of Rome, Alexandria, and Antioch (the concept of a "pope" was still unknown) be designated as "superior" to other bishops of less important Christian centers, the Bishop of Rome at the time refused to accept such a distinction for himself. Historian Lars Qualben comments further:

> The General Council of Constantinople in 381 designated the bishop of that city a patriarch; and the General Council of Chalcedon in 451 gave the same title to the bishop of Jerusalem [leaving out the bishop of Rome] . . . [and] the patriarch of Constantinople [not of Rome] was voted the chief bishop of the entire church.
>
> After the Western empire was destroyed in 476, the emperor of Constantinople became the sole emperor of the world, and this new dignity naturally added some prestige to the patriarch of that city. . . . The bishop of Rome and the patriarch of Constantinople became leading rivals for church supremacy.[3]

## A Doctrine First Declared by Emperors

Emperors had, in fact, declared the supremacy of the Bishop of Rome over the *Western* Church (but not over the Church universal) and called him "the Roman Pope" as early as the fifth century. An edict of the Emperors Valentinian III and Theodosius II in 445 declared: "We decree by this perpetual Edict that it will not be lawful for the bishops of Gaul or of other provinces to attempt anything contrary to ancient custom without the authority of that venerable man the Pope of the Eternal City."[4]

It must be noted that this recognition of papal authority comes from emperors, not from an ecumenical council representing the Church. The purpose on the part of the emperors was not to conform to Scripture but to maintain unity in the empire—and unity among the rival bishops and their followers was essential to that end. Rome, being the capital, had to be the center of ecclesiastical authority even as it was of civil.

Moreover, for a Catholic to take comfort in such declarations, he must also accept the fact that at the same time the emperors honored the Bishop of Rome's authority they made it clear that they were above him. The Emperor Justinian, for example, in his edict of April 17, 535, on the "Relations between Church and State," declared: "There is, indeed, a recognition of the distinction between the clerical and lay elements in Christian society; but, for all practical purposes, the Emperor is to be the controller of both, exercising, as he apparently is to do, a supervision over the 'moral wellbeing' of the clergy."[5]

It would be centuries before the popes would establish their authority over emperors and kings and even longer before papal infallibility and dominion over the entire Church would be thoroughly established. In fact, councils asserted their authority over popes. More than one council deposed rival claimants to Peter's throne, who were simultaneously insisting that each was the one true vicar of Christ. Though now and then the Bishop of Rome, for his own selfish reasons, attempted to assert his authority over the rest of the Church, it was not accepted by Christendom in general until near the second millennium, nor could he point either to tradition or to conciliar decrees to support the idea.

The claim was finally made to stick in the West 19 years after the Great Schism, when, in 1073, Pope Gregory VII forbade Catholics to call anyone pope except the Bishop of Rome. Before then, many bishops were fondly addressed as "pope" or "papa." Though the Roman Catholic Church lists "popes" going back to the very beginning, and all of the alleged Bishops of Rome are now commonly referred to as such, in actual fact this title was not commonly accepted in its present meaning prior to 1073.

### Saving Infallibility by Denying It

We have shown that the manner in which many popes attained that office (through military might, the maneuverings of prostitutes, purchase, patronage of emperors, mob violence, etc.) disproves the claim that the papacy has come down from Peter by an unbroken line of apostolic succession. That more than one pope occupied "Peter's Chair" at one time, each claiming to be the one true, infallible pope, supreme head of the Church and each using his alleged power to excommunicate the others, also proves the theory of apostolic succession to be a fiction. The last time more than one aspirant made simultaneous claim to the papacy the issue was settled in a manner which in fact also pulls the rug out from under any valid claim by the popes to infallibility.

Early in the fifteenth century there were three men who each claimed to be pope. They were Gregory XII (1406-15), whose first pontifical act was to pawn his tiara for 6000 florins to pay his gambling debts; Benedict XIII (1394-1423) of Avignon (one of a number of popes who resided in Avignon's papal palace during a schism that lasted more than 100 years, with rivals in Rome and Avignon each claiming to be the true pope and excommunicating each other); and Alexander V (1409-10) whose chief pastime was feasting and who was attended in his regal palace by 400 servants, all females. The latter pope was poisoned by Baldassare Cossa, who took the pontificate in his place as John XXIII (1410-15).

These three were all deposed by the Council of Constance, until then the largest council in the West, with 300 bishops present, 300 doctors, and the deputies of 15 universities. Although he is now shown as an "antipope," it was Pope John XXIII who formally opened the Council on All Saints' Day 1414. Such was the intrigue surrounding this gathering of Church leaders that some 500 bodies ended up in nearby Lake Constance in the four-year course of that allegedly holy convocation. It was also reported that 1200 prostitutes had to be brought in to keep the bishops and cardinals and their assistants in good humor. Yet this same council condemned Jan Hus to the flames in 1415 for preaching that there was no higher authority than Holy Scripture, which all men, even priests and popes, ought to obey by living Christlike, holy lives.

Of the three above-named popes who each claimed to be the one true vicar of Christ, only Gregory XII is now shown on official lists as a legitimate pope (though he was deposed by this Council), the other two as antipopes. When in 1958 Pope Pius XII's successor took the name John XXIII, more than one Catholic cathedral, finding that its list of popes already contained a Pope John XXIII, had to make a hasty correction. The original Pope John XXIII has been described as a "former pirate, mass-murderer, mass-fornicator with a partiality for nuns, adulterer on a scale unknown outside fables, simoniac *par excellence*, blackmailer, pimp, master of dirty tricks."[6]

In a twist worthy of a soap opera, Pope John XXIII, who opened the Council with great pomp, was condemned by it to prison. He was treated far more lightly than he deserved, the original 54 charges against him being reduced to a mere five. Edward Gibbon wrote sarcastically in *The History of the Decline and Fall of the Roman Empire*: "The most scandalous charges [against John XXIII] were suppressed; the Vicar of Christ was only accused [and found guilty] of piracy, murder, rape, sodomy and incest." Whereas incorruptible Jan Hus had been burned at the stake by the Council of Constance for pleading Church reform, John XXIII was given a mere three-year prison sentence for his numerous and appalling crimes.

Cardinal Oddo Colonna was named the new pope by the Council of Constance and called himself Martin V (1417-31). Upon former Pope John XXIII's release from prison, Pope Martin V reinstated this master criminal and murderer as Bishop of Frascati and Cardinal of Tusculum. Thereafter, exercising the power of the Roman Catholic Church, Cardinal Baldassare Cossa ordained priests and solemnly turned the wafer and wine into the body and blood of Christ—at least that was what the faithful believed. As a cardinal, the former Pope John XXIII, now an ex-convict, was qualified to cast votes for new popes along with fellow cardinals, many of whom were not far behind him in the list of their crimes as well.

Ironically, the Council of Constance saved the Church from three rival popes by asserting its authority over the papacy. The vote was unanimous in establishing the following principle:

> Every lawfully convoked Ecumenical Council representing the Church derives its authority immediately from Christ, and every one, the Pope included, is subject to it in matters of faith, in the healing of schism, and the reformation of the Church.[7]

Had papal infallibility as it is known today been accepted then, this solution to the dilemma of three rival popes would have been impossible. The very dogma of papal infallibity, which was established at the First Vatican Council in 1870, is a denial of the authority which a previous council, the Council of Constance, had asserted over popes in order to save the Church.

Von Dollinger's comments are of interest, especially since his book came out a few weeks before Vatican I would contradict Constance on the important issue of conciliar versus papal power:

> Gregory XII and Benedict XIII had been deserted by their Cardinals, and all that could be held to constitute the Roman Church took part in the Council [of Constance]. If a Pope is subject to a Council in matters of faith he is not infallible; the Church, and the Council which represents it, inherit the promises of Christ, and not the Pope, who may err apart from a Council, and can be judged by it for his error. . . .
>
> And they [the Council's decrees] deny the fundamental position of the Papal system, which is thereby tacitly but very eloquently signalized as an error and abuse. Yet that system had prevailed in the administration of the Church for centuries, had been taught in the canon law books and the schools of the Religious Orders, especially by Thomist divines, and assumed or expressly affirmed in all pronouncements and decision of the Popes, the new authorities for the laws of the Church. And now not a voice was raised in its favor; no one opposed the doctrines of Constance, no one protested![8]

# APPENDIX E

# Papal Heretics, the Bible, and Galileo

As we have noted, heresy brings automatic excommunication. Even one papal heretic, if he were not restored by repenting of his heresy, would break the line of alleged apostolic succession back to Peter. As we have shown, there were many popes who were accused of heresy by other popes and by the councils, and a number were formally excommunicated.

Pope Adrian VI (1522-3), who personally pronounced Pope Celestine III (1191-8) a heretic, declared that John XXII was only one in a long line of papal heretics.

## A Long Line of Papal Heretics

Among the earliest known heretics to sit on Peter's alleged throne was Liberius (352-66). Forced into exile because of a quarrel with the emperor, Liberius was offered repatriation if he would denounce Athanasius, who had led the fight against the Arian heresy. No stickler for doctrine, Liberius obliged the emperor and thereby sided with those who said that the Son was less than the Father—an opinion which the Church has consistently denounced as heresy of the worst sort.

Heretical popes came along quite regularly. Innocent I (401-17) and Gelasius I (492-6) proclaimed that babies went straight to hell (not Purgatory) if they died, though baptized, before receiving communion. After all, if one takes John 6:53 literally—"Except ye eat the flesh of the Son of man and drink his blood, ye have no life in you"—as Catholicism teaches, then these popes were correct. That view was condemned as heresy by the Council of Trent.

During the last two years of his pontificate, Sixtus V (1585-90) rewrote the entire Latin Bible, adding phrases and sentences at whim, leaving out entire verses, changing the titles of the Psalms, and inventing his own system of chapters and verses. In a Papal Bull *Aeternus Ille* (an allegedly infallible declaration on faith and morals to the entire Church), he declared by "the fullness of Apostolical power" that this new "translation" of the Bible must be "received and held as true, lawful, authentic and unquestioned in all public and private discussions, readings, preachings and explanations." Anyone who disobeyed was to be excommunicated.

Of course, when the clergy saw the pope's astonishing handiwork, which instantly had made obsolete the Council of Trent's approved Latin Bible and all textbooks based upon it, they were horrified. Fortunately, Sixtus died a few months later and a cover-up was devised by Bellarmine. As de Rosa explains:

> A Bible had been imposed with the plenitude of papal power, complete with the trimmings of excommunication, on the whole church—and it was riddled with errors. The academic world was in turmoil; Protestants were deriving enormous pleasure and amusement from the predicament of the Roman church.
>
> On 11 November 1590, Bellarmine returned to Rome. . . . Personally relieved that Sixtus, who had wanted him on the Index [of forbidden books and authors], was dead, he feared for the prestige of the papacy. . . . Bellarmine advised the [new] pope to lie. Some of his admirers have disputed this. Their task is formidable.
>
> The options were plain: admit publicly that a pope had erred on a critical matter of the Bible or engage in a cover-up whose outcome was unpredictable. Bellarmine proposed the latter.[1]

Bellarmine and a group of dedicated scholars sworn to secrecy went to work and in about six months corrected the past pope's errors. A new edition of the "Sixtus Bible" was published as though it were merely another printing of the same, and a massive effort was made to recover the original copies of the heretical publication, which were then destroyed. As one would suspect, a few copies escaped the search and have been preserved (one in the Bodleian Library in Oxford). These "Bibles" constitute one more proof that popes are not infallible and that to maintain this lie the Church is willing to tell other lies as well.

## Galileo and the Inquisition

Further evidence, if it were needed, that popes are not infallible is found in the tragic/comic case of Galileo. In defense of Church dogma, Pope Urban VIII (1623-44) threatened an elderly and very ill Galileo with torture if he would not renounce his claim that the earth revolved around the sun. Declaring that this belief was contrary to Scripture, the pope had Galileo on his knees, in fear for his life, recanting of this "heresy" before the Holy Office of the Inquisition! The geocentric view remained official Catholic dogma for centuries, with infallible pope after infallible pope affirming it: The earth was the center of the universe, and all heavenly bodies, including the sun, revolved around it.

It was not until 1992 that the Vatican, after a 14-month study, finally admitted that Galileo had indeed been right. That admission was at the same time an acknowledgment that the many popes who had affirmed that Galileo was wrong were themselves fallible creatures capable of making false interpretations of Scripture. Yet Vatican II reaffirmed the dogma that only the *magisterium* led by the infallible pope may interpret Scripture and that all the faithful must unquestioningly accept their interpretation.

No wonder Vatican II limits its endorsement of biblical inerrancy to matters of faith and morals! It states, "The books of Scripture firmly, faithfully and without error teach that truth which God, for the sake of our salvation, wished to see confided to the sacred Scriptures."[2] A Knights of Columbus edition paraphrases this section thus: "Hence the Bible is free from error *in what pertains to religious truth revealed for our salvation*. It is not necessarily free from error in other matters (e.g., natural science) [emphasis in original]."[3] Apparently the God who created the universe and who inspired the Bible doesn't know natural science!

The *magisterium*, which claims to be infallible and the only interpreter of Scripture, is obviously far from infallible and must therefore have an excuse for the scientific errors it makes. Thus it puts the blame on Scripture. In denying individuals the personal, moral responsibility of heeding God's Word (rather than what some hierarchy says about it), the Roman Catholic Church clings to the last vestiges of authority which it once exercised over the lives and consciences of all men and governments.

# APPENDIX F

# What About Tradition?

Roman Catholicism does not claim to rest upon the Bible alone but also upon "tradition" allegedly passed down from the apostles. However, there is absolutely *no* Catholic tradition which can be traced back to the apostles. *None!* Catholic traditions arose much later than that era, and the idea of infallibility was one of the latest traditions of all. The very concept of ex cathedra pronouncements, so central to infallibility, was not even imagined before the sixteenth century.

Moreover, it is admitted that tradition has gone through many changes. Vatican II acknowledges: "Tradition that comes from the apostles makes progress . . . there is a growth in insight into the realities and words that are being passed on."[1] It continues:

> Sacred Scripture is the speech of God as it is put down in writing under the breath of the Holy Spirit. And Tradition transmits in its entirety the Word of God which has been entrusted to the apostles by Christ the Lord and the Holy Spirit. . . . Hence, both Scripture and Tradition must be accepted and honored with equal feelings of devotion and reverence. . . .
>
> It is clear, therefore, that, in the supremely wise arrangement of God, sacred Tradition, sacred Scripture and the Magisterium of the Church are so connected and

associated that one of them cannot stand without the others. Working together, each in its own way under the action of the Holy Spirit, they all contribute effectively to the salvation of souls.[2]

Serious problems with this view are immediately apparent: The Bible is not sufficient in itself, it cannot stand alone, and it does not have all the truth we need for salvation, but it must be supplemented by tradition and interpreted by the "Magisterium of the Church." Neither the Roman Catholic Church with its *magisterium* nor its tradition existed during the 2000 years of Old Testament times, and obviously God's Word of that era (which continues today and is larger in volume than the New Testament) had no need of either. We have seen how thoroughly this Catholic idea that the Bible is "insufficient" contradicts what the Bible itself says. Nor do the problems end there.

Without a tape recording of what was said it would obviously be impossible to trace any oral tradition back even ten years, let alone 1900 years back to the apostles. Oral statements leave no permanent record that can be verified. The problem wouldn't be eliminated even if someone early in the second century, a mere 50 or 100 years after the apostles, wrote down what he claimed had been their oral teaching, for that would still leave a gap of oral transmission without verification. It is a simple fact that the Roman Catholic Church, for all its talk about apostolic tradition, cannot prove that even one of its traditions comes from the apostles!

Christ quoted from the Scriptures and said that all must be fulfilled (Mark 14:49; Luke 24:44). Never once did He quote tradition or suggest that it would be fulfilled—a strange omission if tradition is an essential part of Scripture. Paul assures us that all *Scripture* is "given by inspiration of God" (2 Timothy 3:16; cf. 2 Peter 1:20,21). No such assurance is given for *tradition*. In fact, the opposite is implied. Paul tells Timothy to "preach the word... reprove, rebuke, exhort with all longsuffering and doctrine" (2 Timothy 4:2). He never said to preach tradition—again a strange omission if tradition is essential or even valid.

There is no Old Testament Jewish tradition which existed from Moses or David or Isaiah and which was to be observed in addition to God's Word. Christ had nothing good to say about Jewish tradition, but denounced it as having perverted and rendered ineffective God's Word (Matthew 15:1-9). He surely wouldn't require the church to depend upon easily perverted oral tradition but would give her, as He gave Israel, all the instruction she needed in writing.

## Scriptural References to Tradition

The words "tradition" or "traditions" occur 14 times in the New Testament. Eight references (Matthew 15:2,3,6; Mark 7:3,5,8,9,13) are Christ's statements in the Gospels, and all of these are derogatory of Jewish traditions, as noted above. Paul makes five references, two of which are clearly derogatory (Colossians 2:8; Galatians 1:14). Peter's one reference (1 Peter 1:18) is also derogatory. That leaves three favorable references by Paul: "Now I praise you, brethren, that ye remember me in all things, and keep the traditions as I delivered them to you" (1 Corinthians 11:2); "Therefore, brethren, stand fast, and hold the traditions which ye have been taught, whether by [our] word or our epistle. . . . Now we command you, brethren, in the name of our Lord Jesus Christ, that ye withdraw yourselves from every brother that walketh disorderly, and not after the tradition which he received of us" (2 Thessalonians 2:15; 3:6).

Upon these latter three verses Catholicism's entire case for tradition rests. Yet none of these verses refers to Roman Catholic tradition as it has developed through the centuries since the days of the apostles. Paul was obviously speaking of things that he and/or the other apostles had already personally taught. He was not referring to traditions that might develop under the influence of unknown church leaders at some time in the future. Therefore, unless it can be demonstrated that present Roman Catholic tradition was first taught by the apostles and has remained pure to this day, no support for it can be found in these verses. And we have already shown that it is impossible to trace any present tradition back to the apostles.

Moreover, Roman Catholic traditions contradict the clear teaching of Scripture and thus could not possibly have been taught by the apostles. There are even contradictions within Catholic traditions themselves. In his *On the Study of Sacred*

*Scripture*, Pope Leo XIII (1823-9) wrote that the Church Fathers "have sometimes expressed the ideas of their own times, and thus made statements which in these days have been abandoned as incorrect." We have seen, too, that false decretals were manufactured and that they became the basis of much tradition and even of canon law that remains to this day.

## Oral Tradition, a Temporary Expedient

While the New Testament was in the process of being written there was obviously a time when the early church relied upon the oral teachings of the apostles. We have every reason to believe, however, that whatever teaching the Holy Spirit inspired which was intended for all believers down through history would have been put into writing. This is true for the reasons already outlined: 1) There was no oral tradition passed down from Old Testament times from Moses, David, Samuel et al for Israel, so why would there be for the church? 2) Christ condemned all oral tradition developed by the rabbis as having perverted the written Word of God, so why would He want the church to have the same corrupting influence? 3) It is impossible either to trace oral tradition back to its source or to be certain of its accuracy. 4) Oral teaching must inevitably be corrupted in the process of transmission from one generation to the next. 5) Not everything that Paul or the other apostles ever said was on the level of Scripture and intended for believers in all ages, and the only sure way to make a distinction would be to put permanent teachings into writing.

That apostolic oral teachings which were intended for all time were put in writing is indicated by the apostles themselves. We have such evidence in Paul's writings. In 1 Corinthians 11:23 he states that he is presenting in writing what he had previously taught them orally: "that which also I [earlier] delivered unto you. . . ." In 2 Thessalonians 2:5 Paul states the same thing: "Remember ye not, that, when I was yet with you, I told you these things?" He was giving them (and us) in writing what he had previously told them orally; and at the same time he was elaborating upon it and providing further understanding. The same thing is true of the tradition to which he refers in 2 Thessalonians 3:6. Again he points out, "When we were with you, this [same thing] we commanded you [orally] . . ." (verse 10). Peter says the same: "Moreover I will endeavor that ye may be able after my decease to have these things always in remembrance" (2 Peter 1:15). In other words, he put in writing what he had earlier taught them orally so they wouldn't forget or corrupt it after his death.

Paul was deeply concerned about false doctrine. Much of his writing was to correct heresy. He warned the Ephesian elders: "For I know this, that after my departing shall grievous wolves enter in among you, not sparing the flock. Also of your own selves shall men arise, speaking perverse things, to draw away disciples after them" (Acts 20:29,30). It would be unreasonable, then, to imagine that Paul would not put into writing all that the Holy Spirit had inspired him to teach. If men would even pervert the written truth, how much easier to pervert what was oral, as memories failed and new generations came which had never heard the original teaching.

## What About Written Tradition?

The written tradition in Catholicism comes from works of the so-called Church Fathers. Unfortunately, a great deal of fraud is mixed in and is often indistinguishable from fact. These frauds became the source of ideas that remain as established dogmas today, such as the saying attributed in the *Isidorian Decretals* to Pope Julius about 338 that "the Church of Rome, by a singular privilege, has the right of opening and shutting the gates of heaven to whom she will" and that the popes inherit "innocence and sanctity from Peter" and are therefore holy and infallible and all Christendom must tremble before them.[3] Such statements are clearly not biblical. From his exhaustive studies of the original historic documents, von Dollinger informs us:

> Towards the end of the fifth and beginning of the sixth century, the process of forgeries and fictions in the interests of Rome was actively carried on there. Then began the compilation of spurious acts of Roman martyrs, which was continued for some centuries, and which modern criticism, even at Rome, has been obliged to give up. . . .

While this tendency to forging documents was so
strong in Rome, it is remarkable that for a thousand years
no attempt was made there to form a collection of canons
... more than twenty Synods had been held in Rome
since 313, but there were no records of them to be
found.[4]

Spurious tradition was manufactured and eventually became the basis for almost the entire papal system and much
canon law. It was the false *Decretals*, revised and elaborated
upon century after century, which formulated Roman Catholicism as it is today. Von Dollinger informs us further:

Gregory VII ... regarded himself not merely as the
reformer of the Church, but as the divinely commissioned founder of a wholly new order. ...
Gregory collected about him by degrees the right men
for elaborating his system of Church law. ... Anselm
may be called the founder of the new Gregorian system
of Church law, first, by extracting and putting into con-
venient working shape everything in the Isidorian
forgeries serviceable for Papal absolutism; next, by alter-
ing the law of the Church, through a tissue of fresh
inventions and interpolations. ...
Clearly and cautiously as the Gregorian party went to
work, they lived in a world of dreams and illusions about
the past and about remote countries. They could not
escape the imperative necessity of demonstrating their
new system to have been the constant practice of the
Church, and it is difficult, if not impossible, to distinguish where involuntary delusion merged into conscious
deceit. Whatever present exigencies required was selected
from the mythical stores at their command hastily and
recklessly; then fresh inventions were added, and soon
every claim of Rome could be shown to have a legitimate
foundation in existing [fraudulent] records and decrees.[5]

The *Decretals* were used to build up fictitious sayings of the
popes (which thereafter became the law) and to put tradition
(and false tradition at that) on a par with Scripture. Moreover,
unlike the Bible, which is readily available in one volume,

tradition is contained in many volumes of the alleged writings of the Church fathers and the decrees of the Councils. Voluminous and not accessible to the average person, it consists of: at least 35 volumes of Greek and Latin church fathers, usually ending with Gregory I in A.D. 604; another 35 volumes of Church council decrees; about 25 volumes of the popes' sayings and decrees; about 55 volumes of the alleged sayings and deeds of the saints, some 150 volumes in all. Richard Bennett, former Catholic priest, explains further:

> The ordinary Roman Catholic bishop or priest, let alone the ordinary Catholic, can never find all of his tradition, or read it since it is in many dead and foreign languages. Even if all were available in translation, a person could never master 150 volumes in such a way as to be one with the Bible. To declare, therefore, that [the Bible plus] sacred tradition forms a single deposit of Scripture is absurd.[6]

Clearly, by its sheer volume, Catholic "sacred tradition" far outweighs the Bible by about 150 to 1. Thus the average Catholic doesn't have access to the greater part of what the Church calls "the Word of God." Moreover, unlike the Bible (which much of it contradicts), written tradition and official dogma of the Church have frequently changed, even propounding contradictory ideas on such important topics as abortion. Most Catholics are not aware that the infallible Church and popes have changed their minds several times on this topic— unthinkable from today's perspective.

From the fifth century onward, Aristotle's view that the embryo goes through stages from vegetable to animal to spiritual was accepted. Only in the final stage was it human. Thus Gregory VI (1045-6) said, "He is not a murderer who brings about abortion before the soul is in the body." Gregory XIII (1572-85) said it was not homicide to kill an embryo of less than 40 days since it wasn't yet human. His successor, Sixtus V, who rewrote the Bible, disagreed. His Bull of 1588 made all abortions for any reason homicide and cause for excommunication. His successor, Gregory XIV, reversed that decree. In 1621 the Vatican issued another pastoral directive permitting abortion up to 40 days. As late as the eighteenth century the Church's greatest moral theologian, St. Alphonsus de Liguori, still denied that the soul was infused at conception and allowed for flexibility, especially when the mother's life was in danger. Finally, in 1869, Pius IX declared that any destruction of any embryo was an abortion and merited excommunication—a view that remains to this day.

# APPENDIX G

# John Paul II
# Asks "Forgiveness"

The front page of *L'Osservatore Romano* (the official Vatican newspaper) for March 15, 2000, carried this headline: "HOLY FATHER CELEBRATES 'DAY OF PAR-DON.'" The commentary leading into the Pope's speech declared, "On Sunday, 12 March, the First Sunday of Lent, Pope John Paul II celebrated Holy Mass in St. Peter's Basilica and asked the Lord's forgiveness for the sins, past and present, of the Church's sons and daughters." *Sons and daughters* only, but not the Church itself? Yes, and that is the official position which is consistently presented throughout all of the documents.

Said the Pope, "We are all invited to make a *profound examination of conscience...* the recognition of past wrongs serves to *reawaken our consciences to the compromises of the present...*" (emphasis in original). Surely the profound examination and reawakening of conscience the Pope professes would uncover specific details of at least many if not most wrongful deeds actually committed. Yet no acts of evil are described in the Pope's call for repentance or in any of the other associated documents.

When a Catholic comes to confession, the priest requires specifics and will even probe the penitent's conscience with leading questions (which, sadly, have polluted the minds of innocent children for centuries with things they have never imagined) to make certain that all sins have been enumerated: "All mortal sins of which penitents after a diligent self-examination are conscious must be recounted by them in confession, even if they are most secret...." [1] The Pope needed only to consult history to obtain exhaustive details of the multitude of crimes committed by his predecessor popes and their Church. We have recounted some of these wicked acts in the previous pages of this book, many of which rival those attributable to the worst secular tyrants. Yet the Pope never described even one specific act but spoke only in generic generalities about:

> ...*infidelities to the Gospel committed by some of our brethren*...the divisions which have occurred among Christians...the violence some have used in the service of the truth...the distrustful and hostile attitudes sometimes taken towards the followers of other religions...our responsibilities...regarding atheism, religious indifference, secularism, ethical relativism, the violations of the right to life, disregard for the poor in many countries.
>
> We humbly ask forgiveness for the part which each of us has had in these evils by our own actions, thus helping to disfigure the face of the Church. At the same time...*let us forgive the sins committed by others against us* (emphasis in original).

Such vague categorizations containing neither the names of the guilty nor an honest account of their misdeeds could hardly be called a confession of sins. Yet this whitewash of a Church "drunk with the blood of the martyrs" was hailed by the media and even by many evangelical leaders as an act of great courage, integrity, and humility. In fact, the Pope's "act of contrition" must be considered by any impartial observer to be little more than a ploy to bury in the past, as supposedly confessed and dealt with, the horror of persecution, torture, and murder perpetrated by the Roman Church through much of her history.

This pretended apology insults our intelligence and mocks the memory of the millions of victims of papal Rome throughout the ages. There was not a word of sympathy or contrition for the victims of her inquisitions, no mention of her crusades against innocent Jews and Christians throughout Europe, papal wars of extermination against Hussites, Albigensians, Waldensians, Huguenots, and countless other victims of such cruelty that would make even a Hitler blush. Nor was there a word about the crimes of numerous unbelievably villainous popes, some of which we have revealed in previous pages. Instead of admitting that many popes, on the basis of their deeds, could not be considered Christians at all (much less Vicars of Christ!), the Vatican unashamedly includes their names in that long line of alleged "apostolic succession" through which Pope John Paul II claims his authority today.

We have documented in these pages the specifics of many of the outrages against God and man committed century after century by the Roman Catholic Church. But the Pope admits nothing in his supposed "confession." How can there be an examination and awakening of conscience and a valid confession without explicit recital of specific evils perpetrated through the centuries by his Church through its leaders? The Pope has engaged in hypocrisy of the highest degree, sweeping centuries of brutal wickedness under the carpet of a pretended "confession" while admitting nothing.

The transparency of John Paul II's attempt to exonerate his Church is exposed in his attributing the unnamed sins he "confesses" to her "sons and daughters." In fact, these crimes (though many were indeed executed by "the children" of the Church) were done in obedience to and under the leadership (indeed, the insistence and urging) of the Church itself through its popes, cardinals, bishops, and priests.

The inquisitions were conceived and directed by the popes themselves and involved diabolic tortures which were forever being ingeniously "improved" to make them more excruciating, the better to exact confession and recantation of alleged heresies of which multitudes were falsely accused. Some of the torture chambers with their cunning instruments for exacting the most agonizing suffering are still available for viewing by curious tourists throughout Europe. Eighty supposed Vicars of Christ, one succeeding the other, supervised and insisted upon this horror. It was the popes, aided by the bishops, cardinals, and priests, who inspired and directed the Crusades (both to the Holy Land and against evangelical Christians in Europe) which brought about the slaughter of millions of innocent Christians,

Jews, and Muslims—even offering special indulgences to those who would execute this mayhem.

These horrors committed by papal Rome in the name of Christ are indisputable history. Yet the Roman Catholic Church has never admitted to, repented of, or asked forgiveness for these crimes, nor did John Paul II choose to be the first Catholic leader to do so. And who dares—or cares—to hold Rome responsible? Apparently no one. The complicity of evangelical leaders in this sham through their praise for the Pope and their condoning of Catholic heresies is scandalous.

The Pope's hypocrisy reached new heights in his claim that "a thorough and fruitful reflection" of sins had "led to the publication...of a document [the product of 'numerous meetings of the subcommission and...plenary sessions...held in Rome from 1998 to 1999'[2]] of the International Theological Commission, entitled: "Memory and Reconciliation: The Church and the Faults of the Past." That title's lofty promise is immediately dismissed by the document's Introduction, which declares its purpose to be "not to examine particular historical cases but rather to clarify the presuppositions that ground repentance for past faults." True to that pledge, that 19,000-word statement, like the Pope's supposed confession, deliberately avoids even mentioning, much less describing, any actual deeds. Obviously, however, to pretend a confession without a clear recital of sins is to perpetrate a giant hoax. Yet nearly everyone accepts it as something commendable!

The entire document reflects the same hypocritical avoidance as in the Pope's alleged confession of any culpability on the part of the Church. All is blamed—and without identifying the sins—on "the past and present sins of her sons and daughters...faults committed by the sons and daughters of the Church...past acts imputable to the children of the Church...the Church should become ever more fully conscious of the sinfulness of her children...John Paul II's appeal to the Church to mark the Jubilee Year by an admission of guilt for the sufferings and wrongs committed by her sons and daughters in the past...," and so on.[3]

Furthermore, the unwillingness of the Church to admit any sin on its part is defended as a matter of long-standing and justifiable policy:

> Indeed, in the entire history of the Church there are no precedents for requests for forgiveness by the Magisterium for past wrongs...the occasions when ecclesiastical authorities—Pope, Bishops, or Councils—have openly acknowledge the faults or abuses which they themselves were guilty of, have been quite rare. One famous example is furnished by the reforming Pope Adrian VI who acknowledged publicly in a message to the Diet of Nuremberg of 25 November 1522, "the abominations, the abuses...and lies" of which the "Roman Court" of his time was guilty, "deep-rooted and extensive...sickness...extending from the top to the members." Adrian VI deplored the faults of his times, precisely those of his immediate predecessor Leo X and his curia, without, however, adding a request for pardon.
>
> It will be necessary to wait until Paul VI to find a Pope express a request for pardon addressed as much to God as to a group of contemporaries. In his address at the opening of the second session of the Second Vatican Council, the Pope asked "pardon of God...and of the separated brethren" of the East [i.e., Orthodox] who may have felt offended by us...Paul VI [referred] solely to the sin of the division between Christians....[4]

To the above can be added Vatican II's vague statement that "the Council 'deplores' the persecutions and manifestations of anti-Semitism 'in every time and on whoever's part.'"[5] These are the only three incidents of even a halfhearted admission of some guilt on the part of the Church or its leaders. Even then the references are nebulous and confined to mourning the "division" in Christendom so as to clearly imply that the Church of Rome is the one true church and that "unity" means rejoining her ("regret for the 'sorrowful memories' that mark the history of divisions among Christians...methods of violence and intolerance used in the past to evangelize"). Even that admission is weak and lacks any request for forgiveness. Always the Pope and supporting documents distinguish "between the indefectible fidelity of the Church and the weaknesses of her members... between the Bride of Christ 'with neither blemish nor wrinkle... holy and immaculate,' and her children....."[6]

In "Memory and Reconciliation" Pope John Paul II is quoted offering "hope that the Jubilee of 2000 will be the occasion for a purification of the memory of the Church from all forms of 'counter-witness and scandal' which have occurred in the course of the past millennium." The Pope seems to have accomplished that "purification of memory" without confessing to anything, so eager is the world and even the evangelical church to overlook the evils of Roman Catholicism in the interest of a false "unity."

This document from the International Theological Commission of the Roman Catholic Church to which the Pope refers with such approval is cunningly crafted to avoid the damning truth. The torture and slaughter of millions of Christians, Jews, and Muslims is passed over as "the use of force in the interest of truth" by which it is suggested that the "separated brethren...may have been offended by us (the Catholic Church)." Pretentious phrases such as "historical judgment... historical evaluation...ethical discernment...the principle of conscience...moral responsibility...the principle of historicity" mask the cruel reality with a façade of self-serving pharisaical piety.

Reference is made to "the hostility or diffidence of numerous Christians toward Jews...[and] anti-Jewish prejudices embedded in some Christian minds and hearts...a call to the consciences of all Christians today, so as to require an act of repentance...as well as to keep a 'moral and religious memory' of the injury inflicted on the Jews." Such platitudes only add insult to injury in light of centuries of not mere anti-Semitism but virulent persecution and wholesale murder perpetrated by the Roman Catholic Church against those whom the Bible refers to as God's chosen people and Christ's brethren. The Pope has managed to portray an allegedly spotless and guiltless Church which is sincerely concerned over some undefined guilt attached to her "sons and daughters." Amazingly, the media buys the delusion, and evangelical leaders, in their eagerness to support ecumenism's counterfeit unity, credit the Pope with laudable contrition.

# APPENDIX H

# John Paul II's Visit to Israel

Early in the afternoon of March 20, 2000, after a four-hour flight from Rome in his special plane, the last leg escorted by Mirage jets from the Jordanian air force, Pope John Paul II arrived in Amman, Jordan. King Abdullah II greeted the Pope as he stepped form the plane, and the two walked together down a long red carpet to meet waiting dignitaries. How odd it is that heads of state, high officials, celebrities, and crowds of cheering thousands and even hundreds of thousands greet the Roman Pontiff wherever he travels, whereas the Christ whose Vicar he claims to be was "despised and reject of men" (Isaiah 53:3).

Christ promised His disciples that they, too, would be treated by the world exactly as He was: "The servant is not greater than his lord. If they have persecuted me, they will also persecute you..." (John 15:20). And so it was. The apostles, true to their Lord and to His Word, were martyred. Peter was crucified, traditionally upside down. How odd, then, that Peter's supposed successor, who even claims to be Christ on earth, is loved, lauded, consulted, and feted by the world's most powerful leaders. Something is amiss!

In his formal speech John Paul II recalled the "great desire" he had often expressed since the beginning of his pontificate in 1978 "to make a pilgrimage to the Holy Land." He referred to Christians, Jews, and Muslims as "believers" in the one God and urged them to consider themselves to be "one people and one single family."

In contrast, Christ said that the "single family" to which all mankind belonged had the devil for its father (John 8:44), that to enter the family of God required a new birth by the Spirit of God through faith in Christ and His redemptive sacrifice upon the cross (John 3:3-17), and He called all mankind to repent or perish (Matthew 9:13, Luke 13:35).

The Pope went almost immediately about 15 miles southwest of Amman to Mount Nebo's summit in the heart of Jordan to see the view Moses had of the Promised Land from that vantage point of 2,500 feet elevation. There he was welcomed by Franciscan monks, the Catholic bishops of Jordan, and entertained by a children's choir. The following day the Pope celebrated Mass in a downtown Amman stadium before about 35,000 people, including 2,000 children participating for the first time.

After a half-hour flight from Amman, the Pope's plane touched down at Tel Aviv's airport, where the Pontiff was ceremoniously welcomed by Israeli President Ezer Weizman and Prime Minister Ehud Barak. In his speech the Pope referred again to his long-standing desire to visit the Holy Land and stressed that his was a "personal pilgrimage" by the Bishop of Rome "to the origins of our faith in the God of Abraham, Isaac, and Jacob." Once again, apostate Judaism and pagan Islam were acknowledged as true faiths serving the one true God. In fact, Allah is a heathen deity and both Islam and Judaism reject the triune God of the Bible and Christ as the Son of God and Savior of sinners. Indeed, Islam claims that rather than Christ dying in our place for our sins, another died on the cross in His place while He was taken to heaven alive, from whence He must return and die at last as a man on earth.

On hand to greet the Pope as part of the welcoming ceremony were leaders of the Israel government, rabbis and leading Catholic clergy from Jerusalem, along with Muslim leaders. President Ezer Weizman praised the Pope's "contribution to the condemnation of anti-Semitism as a sin against heaven and against humanity" as well as his "plea for pardon for the past actions committed against the Jews by members of the Church." As we know, it was the Church itself that persecuted Jews, and the "plea for pardon" avoided any specifics; but Israel is seeking friends and in that pursuit is willing to close its eyes to the well-known truth. From Tel Aviv the Pope went to spend the next several nights in the residence of the Vatican's representative to Israel known as the "apostolic nuncio," a term and position completely foreign to anything taught or experienced either by Christ or His apostles.

The Himalayan hypocrisy of the papal visit was evident in the Pope's repeated references to the Israelis as God's people and to the Promised Land, while at the same time upholding the claim of non-Jews to parts of that land and supporting the claims of the international community to control the destiny of Jerusalem. The Pope repeatedly referred to Jerusalem as holy to Muslims in spite of the fact that it is not mentioned even once in the Koran and never was considered a holy site to Muslims until very recently as a ploy to expel the Jews. In contrast, Jerusalem is mentioned over 800 times in the Bible and God Himself repeatedly calls it the City of David and the place where He has placed His name forever.

Conspicuous by its absence was any admission by the Pope or referenced by his Israeli hosts to his Church's consistent anti-Semitism throughout the centuries. Missing also was any reference by either party to the resolute resistance on the part of the Roman Catholic Church to the very birth of Israel. Further, the Pope and the Israelis maintained a strange conspiracy of silence also concerning the Vatican's consistent opposition to Jerusalem as the Israeli capital. Political correctness was carefully honored. Throwing that facade aside, let us look briefly at only a part of the record.

Pope Urban II, who inspired the First Crusade in 1096, called the Jews "an accursed race, utterly alienated form God." The Pope urged the crusaders to "start upon the road to the Holy Sepulchre to wrest that land from the wicked race and *subject it to yourselves.*" Urban II's offer of full forgiveness of sins for participants brought forth hordes of volunteers who, under the banner of the cross, massacred Christ's earthly brethren, the Jews, by the thousands all along the route to Jerusalem. The Crusade leader, Godfrey of Bouillon, vowed to avenge the blood of Jesus upon the Jews, leaving not one alive. Upon taking the city of David, the crusaders chased the Jews into the synagogue and set it ablaze.

In 1205, Pope Innocent III said that the Jews, "by their own guilt, are consigned to perpetual servitude." In 1311, the Council of Vienna forbade all intercourse between Christians and Jews. The Council of Zamora ruled that Jews must be kept in strict subjection. In 1434, the Council of Basel confined the Jews to ghettos and forced them to wear a distinguishing badge.

In 1555, Pope Paul IV reduced Jews to slaves and rag merchants. Marriage between a Catholic and a Jew was punishable by death. One synagogue was allowed in each city; the others were destroyed, seven out of eight in Rome suffering that fate. Succeeding popes treated Jews as lepers without rights, among them Pius VII, Leo XII, Pius VIII, and Gregory XVI. Addressing the Roman Curia in 1873, Pope Pius IX branded all Jews as "money-lusting enemies of Christ and Christianity." As late as 1882, Rome's Jesuit journal, *Civilta Cattolica,* claimed that Judaism required crucifying Christian children and using their blood in ceremonies.

In his diaries Theodore Herzl relates that when in 1904 he asked Pope Pius X for his support of the Zionist movement, the Pope refused with these harsh words, "We cannot prevent the Jews from going to Jerusalem, but we could never sanction it. As head of the Church, I cannot recognize the Jewish people...if you come to Palestine we will be ready with churches and priests to baptize you." The Pope placed himself solidly among the enemies of God by refusing to sanction what God had repeatedly promised!

In 1919, Cardinal Pietro Gaspari, Vatican Secretary of State, wrote that "the danger that frightens us the most is the creation of a Jewish state in Palestine." In hundreds of Old Testament prophecies God promised to return His chosen people to the land He had given them. How could fulfillment of God's solemn promises be both opposed by Roman Catholicism and the very thing which it found most frightening? Yet this proposition to the Jews worldwide and to the restoration of the Jewish state in Israel has been the consistent pursuit of Roman Catholicism throughout history. No further proof is needed of the anti-God and anti-Christ nature of this false religious system.

For centuries anti-Semitism was an integral part of Roman Catholicism. A large part of that attitude can be traced to the Roman Catholic dogma that Catholics, not Jews, are God's Chosen People, a dogma which is maintained to this day. A 1928 Vatican decree referred to Jews as "the people formerly chosen by God." It is commonly acknowledged that Hitler could not have created a national hatred of Jews in Germany leading to the Holocaust without centuries of Church-inspired anti-Semitism.

On April 26, 1933, the Führer reminded Vatican representatives Bishop Berning and Monsignor Steinman that for 1,500 years their Church had regarded Jews as parasites to be killed and that he intended a "final solution to the Jewish problem."

Before he became Pope Pius XII, Cardinal Eugenio Pacelli, papal nuncio to Germany, had given Vatican money to Hitler to help start the Nazi Party. The 1933 Vatican Concordat Pacelli negotiated with Hitler gave the Nazis a certain legitimacy and, in Hitler's words, was a great help in the "struggle against international Jews." Upon becoming Pope, Pacelli sent a condescending message to the Führer assuring him of the Vatican's good will. In part it said:

> To the Illustrious Herr Adolf Hitler, Führer and Chancellor of the German Reich!
> We recall with great pleasure the many years we spent in Germany as Apostolic Nuncio, when we did all in our power to establish harmonious relations between Church and State. Now...how much more ardently do we pray to reach that goal...

This was 1939 and Hitler's abuse of and intention for the Jews had been fully exposed to the world. In January of that year, Hitler had warned that the outbreak of war would "result...in the extermination of the Jewish race."

On June 22, 1943, with the smoke of incinerated Jews hanging in the air across Europe, Pope Pius XII once again reiterated his Church's continual opposition to God's promises to His chosen people. In a blunt letter to President Roosevelt, the

Pope rejected making the Promised Land of Israel (which he called Palestine) a Jewish homeland:

> It is true that at one time Palestine was inhabited by the Hebrew Race, but there is no axiom in history to substantiate the necessity of a people returning to a country they left nineteen centuries before. If a "Hebrew Home" is desired, it would not be too difficult to find a more fitting territory than Palestine. With an increase in the Jewish population there, grave, new problems would arise.

No axiom in history, indeed. But what bearing does that have upon what God has promised in literally hundreds of biblical prophecies! Pius XII never spoke out publicly against the Holocaust, nor did he attempt privately to dissuade Hitler from annihilating the Jews. The Nazi archives have yielded no letter from the Pope to Hitler opposing the Holocaust or supporting Jews. The American archives, however, contain proof that Pius XII took the time and had a firm enough conviction to express himself forcefully to President Roosevelt against the return of the Jews to the land which God had given them as a heritage forever.

In 1947, the United Nations, troubled by a rare tinge of conscience in the wake of the Holocaust, partitioned "Palestine," giving 18 percent to the Jews and 82 percent to the Arabs. The Vatican used its influence to insist that UN Resolution 181, giving the Jews this meager part of the land God had promised them, included the provision that Jerusalem must remain an "international city." It must not be under the domain of Israel, though it had been their capital since Jerusalem's founding by David nearly 3,000 years before.

Again one is overtaken with astonishment that the supposed true church which claims to represent God and Christ could so firmly oppose and even be frightened by the prospect of God fulfilling His promises to bring His chosen people back into the Promised Land. It is equally astonishing that after this long history of opposition, Pope John Paul II could pretend that the Roman Catholic Church is the friend of Israel. Even the Pope's current words and deeds belie fiction.

The Second Vatican Council in 1965 affirmed the centuries-old claim that Roman Catholics had replaced Jews as God's chosen people: "the church is the new people of God...." Catholic Rome calls itself the Holy City, the City of God, the Eternal City—titles God gave Jerusalem. Indeed, it was not until 1994, a long 46 years after Israel's birth and 16 years into John Paul II's pontificate, that the Vatican, having consistently sided with the Arabs against Israel, finally gave reluctant recognition to the existence of the Jewish state.

By helicopter the Pontiff flew from Jerusalem to Bethlehem. At his presidential palace, Yasser Arafat enthusiastically greeted his friend the Pontiff, returning the favor of the warm receptions the Pope has on many occasions given the PLO leader in Rome. These cordial encounters date back to the days when Arafat was known to the whole world as one of the worst terrorists and mass murderers in history. Instead of rebuking Arafat for his publicly and repeatedly outspoken passion to annihilate Israel and for his anti-Christian Islamic beliefs, the Pope has been a warm friend and supporter.

John Paul's trip to Bethlehem was in response to Arafat's prior invitation to join him there to celebrate "our Jesus Christ." *Our* Jesus Christ? Arafat says Jesus was a Palestinian freedom fighter against Israel, and the Pope smiles and blesses him!

Visiting the Palestinian Dheisheh refugee camp, the Pope "stopped in a cinder-block schoolroom to make his remarks about the 'degrading' conditions in which the refugees have now been living for more than half a century." Said the Pontiff, "Only a resolute commitment on the part of the leaders of the Middle East, and of the international community in general, can solve the causes of your current situation." The Pope particularly "singled out [for praise] the Catholic services and the UN's Relief and Works Agency for Palestinian Refugees, which helps to administer dozens of camps...."[1] There was no rebuke for the Arab nations with their oil billions for keeping the original 350,000 refugees in squalid camps (where a high birth rate has multiplied their numbers into the millions) nor any question why, in contrast, the tiny and impoverished new-born nation of Israel had been able very quickly to absorb over 800,000 refugees of its own pouring in from Arab states where they had been persecuted since the advent of Islam. These genuine refugees had left everything behind to reach a haven of safety which had never before existed for them.

Surely the Pope could not be ignorant of the fact that the Arabs themselves had created the Palestinian refugees, having rejected the 1947 UN partition of Palestine, determined that the Jews would not possess any part of it. Israel had been content and only wanted to live at peace. The new state of Israel had instantly been attached with the overwhelming force of the regular armies of six Arab nations. The Arab High Command had broadcast orders over radio day and night for all Arabs to get out while its armies drove the Jews into the Mediterranean.

As for the international community and the UN's vaunted administration of the refugee camps, it is no secret that Israel would solve the problem of the refugees under its control, but the Arabs and the UN will not allow it to do so. More than a million Palestinians in refugee camps came under Israeli control as a result of the 1967 Six-Day War. Israel offers them state land, electricity, sanitation, streets, and schools and has built nine residential projects housing 10,000 families. Arab nations oppose Israel's help for the refugees. The United Nations annually adopts the following astonishing resolutions which betray its hypocritical double standard:

> The General Assembly...demands that Israel desist from the...resettlement of Palestine refugees in the Gaza Strip...
> The General Assembly...calls once again upon Israel...to refrain from any action that leads to the...resettlement of Palestine refugees in the West Bank....

John Paul II held to a busy schedule, traveling throughout Israel for several days. On March 24, he celebrated Mass on a hillside overlooking the Sea of Galilee. In a demonstration of the Pope's immense popularity, more than 100,000 young people attended, probably the largest gathering of any kind in Israel's history. They included pilgrims from around the world, about 17,000 from Italy, 9,000 from Spain, 10,000 from America, 1,000 from Asia, and many other from Israel and the surrounding Arab countries. In places of heavy Muslim concentration, such as Nazareth, John Paul II rode in his famous Pope-mobile accompanied by heavy security. There, too, on March 25, he celebrated Mass at a Catholic basilica.

That same day found the Pontiff once again back in Jerusalem for an ecumenical meeting with religious leaders hosted by the Greek Orthodox Patriarch of Jerusalem. Welcomed by Patriarch Diodoros I to "the throne room" of the Orthodox patriarchate, the Pontiff issued another strong ecumenical call to the leaders of the various branches of traditional Christianity, declaring that "it is essential to overcome the scandalous impression caused by our dissension and our controversies." Of course, it has been repeatedly made very clear that "unity" will not allow any compromise on Rome's part. There can be no revision of her dogmas, but recognition of the Pope's sovereignty is required by all. Unity means uniting with Rome. The infallible declarations of her popes and dogmatic pronouncements of her councils will not allow it to be otherwise.

On March 26, his final day in Jerusalem, the Pope met with the ancient city's leading Muslim officials. He held talks with Sheikh Idrimah Sabri in the Al Aqsa mosque on the Temple Mount, then visited the Western Wall. There he prayed silently and inserted in a crack between the stones a small paper containing the same prayer he had recited in St. Peter's Basilica in Rome during the "Day of Pardon" ceremony—a prayer asking God's forgiveness for sins committed against Jews, not by his Church and predecessor popes and bishops, but by "Christians." No specific deeds or perpetrators were mentioned. Presumably God knows the evil committed and by whom, and indeed He does and it will be judged righteously in that Day.

# The Lutheran-Catholic Joint Declaration Justification

O n October 31, 1999, in Augsburg, Germany, representatives of the Lutheran World Federation (LWF) and of
the Roman Catholic Church (RCC) signed a Joint Declaration of
Justification (JD), disclaiming previous differences. Headlines
such as "JOINT DECLARATION VIRTUALLY ENDS REFOR-
MATION ARGUMENT" appeared around the world. Seemingly,
Luther had been deceived into thinking he had discovered "justification by faith," when, in fact, the Catholic Church believed it all
along. The Reformation had been a blunder fought over a semantic
misunderstanding. Catholic/Lutheran differences had been put
behind them. Peace and unity had been restored at last.

That the JD was signed on the very day (October 31) that
Martin Luther, in 1517, publicly nailed his 95 Theses to the door
of the Wittenberg Castle chapel could hardly have been a coincidence. Nor could it have been by chance that the document was
signed at the very place where (in the absence of Luther, who
dared not appear for fear of his life) the Augsburg Confession
(composed by Melanchthon in consultation with Luther) was
read June 25, 1530, before 200 dignitaries of Church and state.

Condemned by Rome at that time and ever since, the Augs-
burg Confession was foundational to Lutheranism for 469 years.
Apparently, that is no longer the case, at least for the LWF.
Lutheran leaders have now joined Rome in betrayal of the very

truths for which Luther suffered so greatly. Rome has been vindicated at last.

Upon the 49-member LWF Council's earlier unanimous vote to accept the JD, the Evangelical Lutheran Church of America's Presiding Bishop H. George Anderson (an LWF vice president) led the Council in singing "Now Thank We All Our God." Swedish Archbishop K.G. Hammar called it a "big day for the Lutheran world." Indeed, what could be bigger than renouncing the Reformation and discrediting Luther?

The JD was the fruit of 30 years of dialogue between Lutheran and Catholic leaders. If justification by faith in Christ is that complicated, who can be saved? When the Philippian jailor cried in Acts 16:30, "Sirs, what must I do to be saved?," Paul did not reply, "Do you have about 30 years for me to explain?" He simply said, "Believe on the Lord Jesus Christ, and thou shalt be saved" (Acts 16:31) with not a word about the many complex rules and rituals Roman Catholicism has subsequently made essential to salvation.

In signing the JD, Lutherans surrendered; Catholics changed nothing. The Vatican has refused to rescind any of the more than 100 anathemas still in effect against those who proclaim justification through faith in Christ without Roman Catholic sacraments. Yet many Protestants and Catholics are now convinced that Luther misunderstood true Catholicism and that both sides are now in agreement on the crucial point of justification by faith alone. In fact, Martin Luther was not the only one who misunderstood Catholicism, if that was the problem. There were many contemporary reformers such as Calvin, Zwingli, Denck, Hess, von Amsdorf, Zutphen, Propst, Esch, Voes, and a host of others. In fact, they understood Catholicism very well and knew exactly what they were protesting and why. To imagine otherwise is to embrace a lie.

Furthermore, for 1,000 years before Luther, Europe saw persecutions, burnings, and drownings of evangelical Christians who had never been Catholics and were not called Protestants. That epithet would only later be attached to those excommunicated from the Church for protesting its evils.

A movement among priests and monks calling for a return to the Bible began many centuries before the Reformation. The reformation movement within the Roman Church can be traced as far back as Priscillian, Bishop of Avila. Falsely accused of heresy, witchcraft, and immorality by a Synod in Bordeaux, France, in A.D. 384 (seven of his writings which refute these charges have recently been discovered in Germany's University of Wurzburg library), Priscillian and six others were beheaded at Trier in 385. Many martyrdoms followed through the centuries.

Jumping ahead to the late 1300s, John Wycliff, "moring star of the Reformation," championed the authority of the Scriptures, translated and published them in English (and almost as fast the Catholics burned them) and preached and wrote against the evils of the popes and Catholic dogmas, especially transubstantiation. Jan Hus, a fervent Catholic priest and rector of Prague University, was influenced by Wycliff. Excommunicated in 1410, Hus was burned as a "heretic" in 1415 for calling a corrupt church to holiness and the authority of God's Word. We have already quoted the letter from Pope Martin V commanding the King of Poland in 1429 to exterminate the Hussites—almost 100 years before the Protestant Reformation.

Such early reformers set the stage for Martin Luther. Luther himself said, "We are not the first to declare the papacy to be the kingdom of Antichrist, since for many years before us so many and so great men...have undertaken to express the same thing so clearly,...." For example, in a full council at Rheims in the tenth century, the Bishop of Orleans called the Pope the Antichrist. In the eleventh century, Rome was denounced as "the See of Satan" by Berenger of Tours. The Waldensians identified the Pope as Antichrist in an A.D. 1100 treatise titled "The Noble Lesson." In 1206, an Albigensian conference in Montreal indicted the Vatican as the woman "drunk with the blood of the martyrs," which she continued to prove.

Provoked by the licentiousness he had seen among the Pope and clergy in his visit to Rome, and by the sale of indulgences as tickets to heaven (financing the construction of St. Peter's basilica), on October 31, 1517, Luther nailed his "Disputation on the Power and Efficacy of Indulgences" (known as "The Ninety-Five Theses") to the door of the Wittenberg Castle

Church. Copies translated from the original Latin were widely distributed, inciting heated debate all over Europe about selling forgiveness of sins.

On October 12, 1518, arrested and summoned to Rome by order of Pope Leo X, Luther was held at Augsburg for trial before Cardinal Cajetan. Refused an impartial tribunal, Luther fled for his life by night. On January 3, 1521, a formal bull was issued by the Pope consigning Luther to hell if he did not recant. Summoned by the Emperor, who pledged his safety, Luther appeared before the Imperial Diet in Worms on April 17, 1521. Asked to retract his writings, Luther replied:

> I am bound by the Scriptures I have quoted and my conscience is captive to the Word of God. I cannot and will not retract anything...here I stand; may God help me.

Now an outlaw by papal edict, Luther fled again and was "kidnapped" on his way back to Wittenberg by friends who took him for safekeeping to Wartburg Castle. From there he disseminated more "heresy" in writings that further shook all Europe. Rome's determination to eliminate Lutheran heresy, as expressed in March of 1529 in the second Diet of Speyer, provoked a number of independent princes to assert the right to live according to the Bible. They expressed this firm resolve in the famous "Protest" of April 19, 1529, from which the word "Protestant" was coined.

The Imperial Diet was convened in Augsburg for a thorough examination of Protestant heresies. On that occasion the Augsburg Confession was first read. It delineated the clear differences between Lutheranism and Catholicism. In particular, Article IV declared that men "are freely justified...their sins are forgiven for Christ's sake, who, by His death, has made satisfaction for our sins." Article XIII declared that "the Sacraments were ordained...to be signs and testimonies" and condemned "those who teach that the Sacraments justify by the outward act...." Article XV admonished "that human traditions instituted to propitiate God, to merit grace, and to make satisfaction for sins, are opposed to the Gospel and the doctrine of faith. Wherefore vows and traditions concerning meats and days, etc., instituted to merit grace and to make satisfaction for sins, are useless and contrary to the Gospel."

How shocked the Reformers would be to know that in the same city of Augsburg, Lutherans recently signed a new document proclaiming agreement with the Roman Catholic Church on justification. This is all the more shocking in view of the fact that Roman Catholicism remains the same as in Luther's day. In spite of signing the JD, the Roman Church continues to teach and practice the very things which the Augsburg Confession specifically rejected.

Undeniably, the belief and practice of 1 billion Roman Catholics around the world (ignored by the JD) remain precisely what they always were. That fact renders the JD's careful and complex theological language meaningless. Catholics still flagellate themselves and offer good works and suffering to earn their salvation. They still pray to Mary for salvation. One still finds Roman Catholics at Marian shrines around the world walking on their bruised and bloody knees to earn God's grace. This is not the Middle Ages but present day Catholic "salvation" as practiced worldwide.

Catholics still believe that the "merits and graces Christ won on the cross" can only be received in small installments that never fully save and are dispensed only through Mary and through the sacraments and dispensations of the Church. And they still believe, and their Church continues to insist, that to these "merits and graces of Christ" have been added the merits earned by Mary and the saints through their prayers and good deeds. All of these together make up the "treasury" the Church possesses and from which it dispenses salvation in installments along with indulgences.

Catholics still wear scapulars and medals to open heaven's door, they still look to Mother Church to offer masses after their death to release them from "purgatory." Official Roman Catholic dogma still holds, in denial of abundant Scripture attesting to Christ having died once for all time on the cross, that Christ is being perpetually immolated as sacrifice on their altars. They still pray to "saints" such as Padre Pio, whom they believe suffered to pay for others' sins and thereby redeemed multitudes through the stigmata he bore for 40 years. Indeed, several hundred thousand of the faithful filled St. Peter's Square May 2, 1999, when Pope John Paul II beatified Pio on the way to making him a "saint."

This is Catholicism as it has been practiced for 1,500 years, unchanged by the JD or ETC. Wittingly or not, evangelicals who sign such documents are endorsing these pagan practices and encouraging a billion Roman Catholics in a false hope.

The very practice of offering indulgences (which opened Luther's eyes to the evil of Rome's gospel), which he denounced and against which he labored so diligently, is still a vital and official part of Catholicism. Yet that fact is strangely ignored by evangelicals in their current endorsement of Rome and acceptance of Roman Catholics as "brothers and sisters in Christ." Even while Lutheran/Catholic negotiations were being finalized, the Pope was promising special Jubilee indulgences for the year 2000 and continuing to make dogmatic pronouncements in support of this gross heresy. For example, in the General Audience of August 4, 1999, at the Vatican, the Pope explained again that "we cannot approach God [i.e., enter heaven] without undergoing some kind of purification [through one's personal suffering in addition to what Christ suffered on the cross]. Every trace of attachment to evil must be eliminated, every imperfection of the soul corrected...and indeed this is precisely what is meant by the Church's teaching on *purgatory*." Protestants signing the JD and ECT are thus mocked in the very act.

On Christmas Eve 1999, John Paul II opened a "holy door" in St. Peter's (and subsequently three others in Rome) through which pilgrims coming from around the world have been walking in order to gain the promised forgiveness of sins. John Paul II boasts that this practice was begun in 1300 by Pope Boniface VIII. In "Unam Sanctam," in 1302, in infallible bull still in force today, Boniface made absolute obedience to the Pope a condition of salvation. To this the JD and ECT are also blind.

As we explained earlier, Boniface was so evil that Dante buried him in the lowest depths of hell. He simultaneously had both a mother and her daughter as his mistresses. He utterly destroyed the beautiful city of Palestrina with its priceless art and historic structures dating back to Julius Caesar, reducing it to a plowed field which he sowed with salt after killing its 6,000 inhabitants. Why? Palestrina's ruling family, the Colonna, had made themselves the Popes enemies, and he gave indulgences (yes, *indulgences*) to those who helped defeat them. John Paul II must know all this, yet he and his Church trace his alleged "apostolic succession" back through such monster popes, of whom Boniface was by no means the worst.

It seems more than ironic that although the Reformation began over indulgences, and that Roman Catholicism continues to promote indulgences and to anathematize those who will not accept them, Romanism has now been declared not only by liberal Lutherans but by leading evangelicals to preach the true gospel of salvation by grace through faith in Christ's finished work. The treatise Martin Luther nailed to the door of the Wittenberg Castle chapel October 31, 1517, though popularly referred to as his 95 Theses, was originally titled by him "Disputation on the Power and Efficacy of Indulgences." While it appears that at the time Luther was still struggling with and had not yet fully rejected the false doctrine of purgatory, he denounced indulgences in no uncertain terms as offered then and now by the Church of Rome. Among his 95 theses were the following:

21. Thus those indulgence preachers are in error who say that a man is absolved from every penalty and saved by papal indulgences.

24. For this reason most people are necessarily deceived by that indiscriminate and high-sounding promise of release from penalty.

37. Any true Christian, whether living or dead, participates in all the blessings of Christ and the church; and this is granted him by God, even without indulgence letters.

45. Christians are to be taught that he who sees a needy man and passes him by, yet gives his

money for indulgences, does not buy papal indulgences but God's wrath.

52. It is vain to trust in salvation by indulgence letters, even though the indulgence commissary, or even the pope, were to offer his soul as security.

62. The true treasure of the church is the most holy gospel of the glory and grace of God.

76. We say on the contrary that papal indulgences cannot remove the very least of venial sins as far as guilt is concerned.

82. Why does not the pope empty purgatory for the sake of holy love and the dire need of the souls that are there if he redeems an infinite number of souls for the sake of miserable money with which to build a church?

83. Why are funeral and anniversary masses for the dead continued...?

90. To repress these very sharp arguments of the laity by force alone, and not to resolve them by giving reasons, is to expose the church and the pope to the ridicule of their enemies and to make Christians unhappy.

As we have explained elsewhere and shown from the Bible, the doctrines of purgatory and indulgences are a denial of the sufficient efficacy of the finished work of Christ upon the cross and deny the very words that Christ cried in triumph to all the world, "It is finished!" Roman Catholic forgiveness of sins was not procured through the once and for all sacrifice of Christ, a forgiveness received alone by faith in Him, but it is earned by Catholics' personal good works and sacrifices according to their Church. The Pope has made the year 2000 a unique Jubilee of forgiveness during which he offers special indulgences, even granting forgiveness of sins for giving up cigarettes for a day. The following are excerpts from his "Bull of Indiction of the Great Jubilee of the Year 2000":

The coming of the Third Millennium prompts the Christian community to lift its eyes of faith to embrace new horizons in proclaiming the Kingdom of God. It is imperative therefore at this special time to return more faithfully than ever to the teaching [not of the Bible, but] of the Second Vatican Council....May the ecumenical character of the Jubilee be a concrete sign of the journey which, especially in recent decades, the faithful of the different Churches and Ecclesial communities have been making. It is only by listening to the Spirit that we shall be able to show forth visibly in full communion the grace of divine adoption which springs from Baptism....

We recall the year 1300 when, responding to the wish of the people of Rome, Pope Boniface VIII solemnly inaugurated the first Jubilee in history...[and] offered abundant remission and pardon of sins to those who visited Saint Peter's Basilica in the Eternal City...a pardon of sins which would not only be more abundant, but complete....On the occasion of this great feast, a warm invitation to share our joy goes out to the followers of other religions, as it does to those who are far from faith in God. As brothers and sisters in the one human family, may we cross together the threshold of a new millennium....

I therefore decree that the Great Jubilee of the Year 2000 will begin on Christmas Eve 1999, with the opening of the holy door in Saint Peter's Basilica in the Vatican...and the opening of the holy door in each of the other Patriarchal Basilicas of Rome....Another distinctive sign, and one familiar to the faithful, is the indulgence, which is one of the constitutive elements of the Jubilee.... Free and conscious surrender to grave sin, in fact, separates the believer from the life of grace with God....It is precisely through the ministry of the Church that God diffuses his mercy in the world, by means of that precious gift which from very ancient times has been called *indulgence*....With the indulgence, the repentant sinner receives a remission of the temporal punishment due for the sins already forgiven as regards the fault....*Every sin, even venial*...must be purified either here on earth, or after death in the state called Purgatory. This purification frees one from what is called the *temporal punishment of sin*....

I decree that throughout the entire Jubilee all the faithful, properly prepared, be able to make abundant use of the gift of the indulgence, according to the directives which accompany this Bull.... The nations will never grow weary of invoking the Mother of mercy [Mary] and will always find refuge under her protection. May she...guard the steps of all those who will be pilgrims in this Jubilee Year....Given in Rome, at Saint Peter's, on 29 November, the first Sunday of Advent, in the year of our Lord 1998....

Then follows the rules for obtaining the Jubilee Indulgence.

By the present decree...expressed in the Bull of Induction...by the same Supreme Pontiff, the Apostolic Penitentiary defines the discipline to be observed for gaining the Jubilee Indulgence...[it] can also be applied in suffrage to the souls of the deceased [in purgatory]....Then too, the rule that a plenary indulgence can be gained only once a day remains in force during the entire Jubilee year....

Participation in the Eucharist, which is required for all indulgences, should properly take place on the same day as the prescribed works are performed.... With regard to the required conditions, the faithful can gain the Jubilee indulgence:

1) In Rome, if they make a pious pilgrimage to one of the Patriarchal Basilicas...take part devoutly in Holy Mass or another liturgical celebration...or some pious exercise (e.g., the Stations of the Cross,

the Rosary...)...prayer to the Blessed Virgin Mary....

2) In the Holy Land, if....

3) In other ecclesiastical territories, if they make a sacred pilgrimage to the Cathedral Church...there spend time in pious meditation....

4) In any place, if they visit for a suitable time their brothers and sisters in need or in difficulty....

The plenary indulgence of the Jubilee can also be gained through actions which express in a practical and generous way the penitential spirit which is, as it were, the heart of the Jubilee. This would include abstaining for at least one whole day from unnecessary consumption (e.g., from smoking or alcohol, or fasting)....

There can be no doubt that Catholicism today, as in Luther's day, denies salvation through faith alone in Christ and equally denies the sufficiency of His finished sacrifice upon the cross for our sins. This is the same Catholicism practiced in Luther's day and for centuries before him. It is still in practice today, a fact which makes mockery of the documents deceived Protestants and evangelicals join Catholic theologians in signing. As always, today's Roman Catholicism adds works to faith as a condition of gaining heaven and claims that forgiveness of sins is dispensed only through the Church, through her priesthood and rituals and in accord with her dogmas. Paul would pronounce the same anathema upon today's Catholicism as he pronounced upon the Judaizers in Galatians chapter 1. We can only conclude that those crediting Roman Catholicism with preaching the true gospel have renounced not only the Reformation but the gospel itself.

# Glossary

### Anathema

Excommunication from the Roman Catholic Church pronounced upon heretics or gross sinners. The consequence is eternal damnation unless the one anathematized repents and returns to the Church. The Council of Trent pronounced the anathema more than 100 times upon those who accepted the beliefs of the Reformers; Vatican II reconfirmed those anathemas and added one of its own; and thus Roman Catholicism damns to eternal hell all evangelical Christians today. The only remedy is repentance of evangelical doctrines (heresies to Rome), entrance into the Roman Catholic Church, and submission to her decrees. Thus all "dialogue" or cooperation between Catholics and evangelicals must, by very definition in Catholicism, lead to the evangelicals ultimately joining the Roman Catholic Church—for their own salvation, of course.

### Bull, papal

The common name by which important decrees of the popes in past centuries were called, though no longer used today. In Latin the word *bulla* signifies a seal, and the papal bulls were known for the wax or lead seal attached to each, of which many examples have been preserved.

### *Code of Canon Law*

The codification in 1983 into one large volume (more than 1000 pages) of the canons and decrees of the Second Vatican Council, which itself incorporates those from past councils as well as the pronouncements of popes. The *Code* also contains detailed commentary explaining the proper implementation of the 1752 canons of law to which Catholics are subject in obedience to their Church. The last previous codification was done in 1917.

### Concordat

A treaty or agreement defining relationships and duties between the Vatican and secular governments. This is only possible because Vatican *City*, unlike any other city on earth, is recognized as a state on a par with secular nations and thus able to enter into politico-religious agreements and ex change ambassadors with them.

## Decretal

A papal letter issued in response to a question facing the Church that requires an official position. Many such decretals, collected and attributed to individual popes and relied upon in the past, are today recognized as "false decretals." Nevertheless, many of the beliefs and practices first established by reliance upon such forgeries were never extricated from the body of Catholic tradition and remain an integral part of it today.

## Encyclical

A letter written by a pope expressing the official view of the Church on a certain matter of importance.

## Eucharist

A special form of bread (tiny wafer or host) and ordinary wine which is believed to be the literal Body and Blood of Jesus Christ by having been consecrated by a priest and thus having been "transubstantiated" through a special formula and power which Catholic priests alone possess. The offering of this miraculously constituted "Christ" upon Catholic altars is the principal part of the ceremony or ritual known as the "Sacrifice" of the Mass and is believed to be efficacious in the remission of sins.

## Indulgence

The "remission before God of the temporal punishment due to sins forgiven as far as their guilt is concerned, which the follower of Christ with the proper dispositions and under certain determined conditions [decided by the Church hierarchy] acquires through the intervention of the Church, which, as minister of the redemption, authoritatively dispenses. . . ." So says the "Apostolic Constitution on the Revision of Indulgences" decreed by Pope Paul VI on January 1, 1967, and included as one of the post-conciliar documents of Vatican II.

The doctrine of indulgences arises from Catholicism's strange and unbiblical insistence that Christ's sufferings for our sins upon the cross at the hands of man and God could only obtain forgiveness of guilt but still left the "forgiven repentant sinner" under the obligation of suffering for his own sins either in this life or most likely in the "purifying flames of purgatory." An indulgence presumes, through the power given to the Church, to reduce the time or intensity of the suffering in purgatory by some unknown length or amount. (See Appendix B for further details.)

## Interdict

A penalty imposed by the popes upon a city or even an entire country prohibiting the practice of the Roman Catholic religion. Thus the sacraments which bring salvation could not be practiced and the entire populace would be without the means of forgiveness of sins and entrance into heaven. It is a mortal sin not to attend Mass at least once a week, and that would be impossible under an interdict. Thus any person dying during an interdict would be under mortal sin and without the means of forgiveness through confession and the sacrament of the Anointing of the Sick or last rites and doomed to hell. No wonder kings and emperors trembled when threatened with such a penalty by popes, a penalty which gave popes a power against which no mortal could fight and which made Catholic Rome that "city which reigneth over the kings of the earth" (Revelation 17:18).

## Liberation Theology

A movement within the Roman Catholic Church originating in Latin America which puts the main emphasis upon social justice. Thus to be theologically orthodox one must oppose verbally and by actions any oppression of the poor and lower classes by both Church and state. In fact, the proof of one's salvation is in such opposition to oppression rather than in acceptance of the gospel and affirmation of the doctrines of the faith.

## Mass

The offering upon Catholic altars of the alleged Body and Blood of Christ (in an "unbloody manner") there created through the professed miracle of "transubstantiation." This "sacrifice" is declared to be efficacious for the forgiveness of sins and shortening one's suffering in purgatory. Its deadly error is that it downgrades the sacrifice of Christ upon the cross to a partial payment for sin with the continuance of that sacrifice endless times upon Catholic altars essential to at last bring about full pardon of sin and entrance into heaven. What Christ's death upon the cross (which the Bible says was done only once for all time and was all-sufficient) could not do, by Catholic doctrine, the Mass can eventually accomplish if it is repeated enough times. The Church, however, has failed to define (in fact, doesn't know) how many such "sacrifices" of the Mass it will take to get a given individual out of purgatory and into heaven. Therefore, the faithful Catholic hopes that after his death a sufficient number of Masses will be paid for by relatives and continue to be said in his name.

## Purgatory

That place of "purging" where the Catholic believes those who die without having made sufficient restitution ("expiation") for their sins (even though Christ suffered for them) must spend some time of suffering in order to be made clean enough to enter heaven. The flames of purgatory are said to differ from the flames of hell in that the goal of purgatory is to cleanse the soul for heaven, whereas the flames of hell only torment for eternity.

## Scapular

For those in religious orders it consists of two strips of cloth (one in front, one in back) joined across the shoulders and worn as an outer garment. For the laity it consists generally of two small pieces of cloth joined by strings and worn about the neck under the clothing. There are some 18 varieties of blessed scapulars approved by the Church. The wearing of the scapular, along with meeting certain other conditions, confers protection and privileges, even, in some cases, reducing or entirely eliminating one's time in purgatory.

## See: Apostolic, Holy, First

The "Holy See" or "See of Peter," etc., is a designation for Rome and more specifically Vatican City as the residence of the pope and headquarters of the Roman Catholic Church with its many offices. In fact, it indicates that the pope is the leader of the one true Church, which is the depository of the true faith of Christ committed to Peter and to be carried by his successors to the world.

## *Te Deum*

An ancient Latin hymn, *Te Deum Laudamus*, sung at the conclusion of the Office of Readings on Sundays and special occasions. It is especially used for thanksgiving to God for unusual blessings—and was so used (sung) in Catholic cathedrals for the birthdays of Hitler, his escape from plots upon his death, Nazi victories in the field, the coming into power of Ante Pavelic as head of the Croatian Ustashi government, etc.

# Notes

**Overturning the Reformation**
1. *Moody*, May 1994, p. 62.
2. *Charisma*, May 1994.
3. *New York Times*, March 30, 1994, p. A8.
4. *New Evangelization 2000*, Issue no. 23, 1994.
5. "Roman Catholic Doubletalk at Indianapolis '90," *Foundation*, July–August 1990, excerpts from talk by Fr. Tom Forrest to the Roman Catholic Saturday morning training session.

**Chapter 2—Reason to Believe**
1. Will Durant, *The Story of Civilization*, vol. VI, *The Reformation* (Simon and Schuster, 1950), p. 727.
2. Peter de Rosa, *Vicars of Christ: The Dark Side of the Papacy* (Crown Publishing, Inc., 1988), p. 194.
3. Durant, op. cit., vol. VI, p. 729.

**Chapter 4—An Unfolding Revelation**
1. *Strong's Exhaustive Concordance*, Greek Dictionary of the New Testament, p. 12; *Webster's New Universal Unabridged Dictionary*, p. 2035.

**Chapter 5—Mystery, Babylon**
1. *Brownson's Quarterly Review*, January, 1873, vol. i, p. 10. Brownson had been a celebrated skeptic and outspoken critic of the priesthood before his conversion to Rome some 30 years previously. See William Hogan, Esq., *Popery, As It Was and As It Is* (Hartford, 1854), pp. 500-530ff.
2. J.H. Ignaz von Dollinger, *The Pope and the Council* (London, 1869), p. 19; see also R.W. Thompson, *The Papacy and the Civil Power* (New York, 1876), p. 419.
3. R.W. Thompson, *The Papacy and the Civil Power* (New York, 1876), p. 460.
4. Dollinger, op. cit., p. 21; see also Sidney Z. Ehler and John B. Morrall, *Church and State Through the Centuries* (London, 1945), pp. 299, 314.
5. Dollinger, op. cit., p. 23.
6. Emmet McLoughlin, *An Inquiry into the Assassination of Abraham Lincoln* (The Citadel Press, 1977), p. 70.
7. Ibid., pp. 80-82.
8. *The Catholic World*, July 1870, vol. xi, p. 439.
9. Peter Viereck, *Meta-Politics: The Roots of the Nazi Mind* (Alfred A. Knopf, Inc., 1941, 1961 ed.), pp. 317-18.
10. Franz von Papen, *Memoirs*, trans. Brian Connell (London, 1952), p. 279.
11. Guenter Lewy, *The Catholic Church and Nazi Germany* (McGraw-Hill, 1964), pp. 160-61
12. Ibid., pp. 100, 106.
13. Ibid., p. 105.
14. Ibid., pp. 106-09.
15. Ibid., p. 108.
16. Ibid., p. 211.
17. Viereck, op. cit., p. 282.
18. Jean-Michel Angebert, *The Occult and the Third Reich* (New York, 1974), p. 201.
19. William L. Shirer, *The Rise and Fall of the Third Reich* (New York, 1959), p. 330.

**Chapter 6—A City on Seven Hills**
1. *The Catholic Encyclopedia* (Thomas Nelson, 1976), s.v. "Rome."
2. Karl Keating, *Catholicism and Fundamentalism: The Attack on "Romanism" by "Bible Christians"* (Ignatius Press, 1988), p. 200.

3. *Catechism of the Catholic Church* (The Wanderer Press, 1994), p. 279, para. 1075.
4. Sidney Z. Ehler, John B. Morrall, trans. and eds., *Church and State Through the Centuries* (London, 1954), pp. 153-59; *Hakluytus Posthumus* (William Stansby for Henrie Fetherstone, London, 1625) as cited in Avro Manhattan, *The Vatican Billions* (Chino, CA, 1983), p. 90.
5. *Our Sunday Visitor*, December 5, 1993, p. 3.
6. John A. Hardon, S.J., *Pocket Catholic Dictionary* (Image Books [Doubleday], 1985), p. 99.
7. *Our Sunday Visitor's Catholic Encyclopedia* (Our Sunday Visitor Publishing Division, 1991), p. 842.
8. Ibid., pp. 175, 178.
9. Robert Broderick, ed., *The Catholic Encyclopedia* (Thomas Nelson, Inc., 1976), pp. 103-04.
10. Ibid., p. 466.
11. William Shaw Kerr, *A Handbook of the Papacy* (London: Marshall, Morgan & Scott), p. 241.
12. J.H. Ignaz von Dollinger, *The Pope and the Council* (London, 1869), pp. 307-08.
13. Nino Lo Bello, *The Vatican Empire* (Trident Press, 1968), p. 167. See also David A. Yallop, *In God's Name* (Bantam Books, 1984); Richard Hammers, *The Vatican Connection* (Penguin Books, 1983).
14. James A. Coriden, Thomas J. Green, Donald E. Heintschel, eds., *The Code of Canon Law* (Paulist Press, 1985), Canon 1273.
15. *The European*, April 9-12, 1992, p. 1.
16. Peter de Rosa, *Vicars of Christ: The Dark Side of the Papacy* (Crown Publishers, 1988), pp. 396-97.
17. R.W. Thompson, *The Papacy and the Civil Power* (New York, 1876), p. 82.
18. De Rosa, op. cit., p. 172.
19. Kerr, op. cit., pp. 239-40.
20. Emelio Martinez, *Recuerdos [Memoirs] de Antano* (CLIE, 1909), pp. 105-06.
21. De Rosa, op. cit., pp. 20-21.
22. E.g. Guenter Lewy, *The Catholic Church and Nazi Germany* (McGraw-Hill, 1964), pp. 300-04. The same facts have been documented by many other authors and historians as well.
23. De Rosa, op. cit., p. 5; Lewy, op. cit., p. 111.
24. Dollinger, op. cit., pp. 10-12.
25. Walter James, *The Christian in Politics* (Oxford University Press, 1962), p. 47.
26. R.W. Southern, *Western Society and the Church in the Middle Ages*, vol. 2, Pelican History of the Church series (Penguin Books, 1970), pp. 24-25.
27. Cormenin, *History of the Popes*, p. 243, as cited in R.W. Thompson, op. cit., p. 368.

**Chapter 7—Fraud and Fabricated History**
1. James A. Coriden, Thomas J. Green, Donald E. Heintschel, eds., *The Code of Canon Law* (Paulist Press, 1985), Canons 1404, 1405, and 333, sec. 3, pp. 951, 271.
2. J.H. Ignaz von Dollinger, *The Pope and the Council* (London, 1869), p. 3.
3. *La Civilta Cattolica*, 1867, vol. xii, p. 86.
4. Austin Flannery, O.P., gen. ed., *Vatican Council II: The Conciliar and Post Conciliar Documents*, rev. ed. (Costello Publishing, 1988), p. 380.
5. *The Catholic World*, August 1871, vol. xiii, pp. 580-89.
6. Coriden, et al., op. cit., Canon 212, Section 1.
7. Flannery, op. cit., vol. 1, p. 412.
8. Ibid., pp. 379-80.
9. Ibid., pp. 365-66.
10. Karl Keating, *Catholicism and Fundamentalism: The Attack on "Romanism" by "Bible Christians"* (Ignatius Press, 1988), pp. 215-18.
11. Dollinger, op. cit., p. 59.
12. Peter de Rosa, *Vicars of Christ: The Dark Side of the Papacy* (Crown Publishers, 1988), pp. 205-06.
13. Ibid., pp. 248-49.
14. Ibid., p. 25.
15. August Bernhard Hasler, *How the Pope Became Infallible* (Doubleday & Co., Inc., 1981), p. 48.
16. W.H.C. Frend, *The Rise of Christianity* (Philadelphia, 1984), p. 773.

17. H. Chadwick, *The Early Church* (Wm. B. Eerdmans, 1976), p. 243.
18. Frend, op. cit., p. 707.
19. Dollinger, op. cit., p. 62.
20. Ibid., pp. 76-77.
21. R.W. Thompson, *The Papacy and the Civil Power* (New York, 1876), p. 372.

**Chapter 8—Unbroken Line of Apostolic Succession?**
1. Austin Flannery, O.P., gen. ed., *Vatican Council II: The Conciliar and Post Conciliar Documents*, rev. ed. (Costello Publishing, 1988), vol. 1, pp. 357, 376.
2. *New Catholic Encyclopedia* (Catholic University of America, 1967), vol. 1, p. 632, s.v. "Antipopes."
3. Sidney Z. Ehler, John B. Morrall, trans. and eds., *Church and State Through the Centuries* (London, 1954), p. 48.
4. E.R. Chamberlin, *The Bad Popes* (Barnes & Noble, 1969), p. 21.
5. James A. Coriden, Thomas J. Green, Donald E. Heintschel, eds., *The Code of Canon Law* (Paulist Press, 1985), Canon 332, p. 270.
6. T.A. Trollope, *The Papal Conclaves* (1876), cited in Peter de Rosa, *Vicars of Christ: The Dark Side of the Papacy* (Crown Publishers, 1988), p. 98.
7. Chamberlin, op. cit., p. 172.
8. Peter de Rosa, *Vicars of Christ: The Dark Side of the Papacy* (Crown Publishers, 1988), p. 104.
9. Edward Gibbon, *The Decline and Fall of the Roman Empire* (London, 1830), chapter xlix.
10. J.H. Ignaz von Dollinger, *The Pope and the Council* (London, 1869), p. 81.

**Chapter 9—Infallible Heretics?**
1. Peter de Rosa, *Vicars of Christ: The Dark Side of the Papacy* (Crown Publishers, 1988), p. 204.
2. James A. Coriden, Thomas J. Green, Donald E. Heintschel, eds., *The Code of Canon Law* (Paulist Press, 1985), Canon 1364, p. 920.
3. J.H. Ignaz von Dollinger, *The Pope and the Council* (London, 1869), pp. xv, xvii.
4. D. Antonio Gavin, *A Master-Key to Popery*, 3rd ed. (London, 1773), pp. 113-14.
5. August Bernhard Hasler, *How the Pope Became Infallible* (Doubleday & Co., Inc., 1981), p. 36.
6. Ibid., from the introduction by Hans Kung, p. 9.
7. De Rosa, op. cit., p. 180.
8. Ibid., p. 212.
9. Ibid.
10. Dollinger, op. cit., p. 275.

**Chapter 10—Infallibility and Tyrany**
1. National Catholic News Service, ed., *John Paul II, "Building Up the Body of Christ," Pastoral Visit to the United States of America* (Ignatius Press, 1987), p.9.
2. Ibid.
3. Ibid.
4. Sidney Z. Ehler, John B. Morrall, trans. and eds., *Church and State Through the Centuries* (London, 1954), p. 273.
5. Evangelical Confederation of Columbia, Bulletin No. 50, June 26, 1959.
6. J.H. Ignaz von Dollinger, *The Pope and the Council* (London, 1869), pp. 337-38.
7. "The Reformation Not Conservative," *The Catholic World*, Sept. 1871, p. 736.
8. Peter de Rosa, *Vicars of Christ: The Dark Side of the Papacy* (Crown Publishers, 1988), pp. 175-76.
9. Cormenin, *History of the Popes*, p. 243, as cited in R.W. Thompson, *The Papacy and the Civil Power* (New York, 1876), p. 244.
10. Gerard Dufour, *La Inquisicion Espanola* (Montesinos, 1986), p. 32.
11. Comte Le Maistre, *Letters on the Spanish Inquisition* (Boston, 1815), preface, p. xvi.
12. Pope Pius IX, *The Syllabus of the Principal Errors of our Time...*, III.15.
13. Cormenin, op. cit., p. 206.
14. Ibid.
15. R.W. Thompson, *The Papacy and the Civil Power* (New York, 1876), pp. 51-53, also Appendix B, pp. 718-20.

16. Ibid., p. 53.
17. Ibid., pp. 43-52.
18. Count Charles Arribavene, *Italy under Victor Emmanuel* (London, 1862), vol. II, p. 366, as cited in Emmet McLoughlin, *An Inquiry into the Assassination of Abraham Lincoln* (The Citadel Press, 1977), p. 205.
19. Thompson, op. cit., Appendix C gives the entire text of "The Encyclical Letter of Pope Pius IX," pp. 721-27, see especially p. 722.
20. *The Catholic World*, December 1872, vol. xvi, p. 290.
21. Arribavene, op. cit., pp. 93-94.
22. Emmet McLoughlin, *An Inquiry into the Assassination of Abraham Lincoln* (The Citadel Press, 1977), p. 94.
23. Arribavene, op. cit., vol. II, p. 389.
24. G.S. Godkin, *Life of Victor Emmanuel II* (London, 1880), p. 76.
25. August Bernhard Hasler, *How the Pope Became Infallible* (Doubleday & Co., Inc., 1981), p. 64.
26. Ibid., pp. 66-67.
27. Ibid., p. 74.
28. Ibid., p. 29, and inside back jacket.
29. Ibid., from the introduction by Hans Kung, p. 14.
30. Ibid., pp. 97-98.
31. Ibid., pp. 68-69, 78.
32. Ibid., p. 80.
33. Ibid., pp. 71-72.
34. Ibid., pp. 93-94.
35. Loraine Boettner, *Roman Catholicism* (The Presbyterian and Reformed Publishing Company, 1982), p. 246.
36. Dollinger, op. cit., 71.
37. Hasler, op. cit., p. 153.
38. Dollinger, op. cit., pp. 52-55.
39. Hasler, op. cit., pp. 121-22.
40. Ibid., pp. 126, 133.
41. Ibid., p. 189.
42. Ibid., pp. 136, 143-44.
43. Ibid., pp. 124-27.
44. Guillermo Dellhora, *La Iglesia Catolica ante la critica en el pensamiento y en el arte* (Mexico City, 1929), p. 248.
45. Frederico Hoyos, S.V.D., *Enciclicas Pontificias* (Buenos Aires, 1958), p. 179.
46. De Rosa, op. cit., pp. 34, 45.
47. *USA Today*, December 8, 1993, p. 17A.

## Chapter 11—Upon This Rock?

1. Austin Flannery, O.P., gen. ed., *Vatican Council II: The Conciliar and Post Conciliar Documents*, rev. ed. (Costello Publishing, 1988), vol. 1, p. 454.
2. J.H. Ignaz von Dollinger, *The Pope and the Council* (London, 1869), p. 74.
3. Peter de Rosa, *Vicars of Christ: The Dark Side of the Papacy* (Crown Publishers, 1988), pp. 24-25.
4. Dollinger, op. cit., pp. 53, 66, 74.
5. Cormenin, *History of the Popes*, p. 243, as cited in R.W. Thompson, *The Papacy and the Civil Power* (New York, 1876), p. 248.
6. August Bernhard Hasler, *How the Pope Became Infallible* (Doubleday & Co., Inc., 1981), p. 8 in the introduction.
7. Dollinger, op. cit., pp. 65-66.
8. De Rosa, op. cit., p. 250.
9. H. Chadwick, *The Early Church* (Wm. B. Eerdmans, 1976), p. 245.
10. Eusebius, *Oration on the Tricennalia of Constantine*, 5.4.
11. Will Durant, *The Story of Civilization* (Simon and Schuster, 1950), Part III, "Caesar and Christ," p. 656.

12. De Rosa, op. cit., p. 43.
13. Durant, op. cit., Part III, p. 656.
14. Philip Hughes, *A History of the Church* (London, 1934), vol. 1, p. 198.

## Chapter 12—Unholy Mother
1. *USA Today*, December 8, 1993, p. 17A.
2. J.H. Ignaz von Dollinger, *The Pope and the Council* (London, 1869), pp. 89-91.
3. Peter de Rosa, *Vicars of Christ: The Dark Side of the Papacy* (Crown Publishers, 1988), pp. 395-96.
4. R.W. Thompson, *The Papacy and the Civil Power* (New York, 1876), p. 443.
5. De Rosa, op. cit., pp. 402-03.
6. Will Durant, *The Story of Civilization* (Simon and Schuster, 1950), vol. VI, p. 18.
7. Ibid., vol. V, pp. 155-56.
8. Ibid., pp. 157-58.
9. Ibid., pp. 159-60.
10. *Inside the Vatican*, April 1994, p. 55 under the heading "23 May."
11. De Rosa, op. cit., pp. 404-05.
12. Harry J. Margoulias, *Byzantine Christianity: Emperor, Church and the West* (Rand McNally, 1982), pp. 103-04.
13. De Rosa, op. cit., p. 405.
14. Ibid., p. 119.
15. Thompson, op. cit., p. 443.
16. Ibid., p. 444; see also de Rosa, op. cit., p. 412.
17. Frederic Seebohm, *The Oxford Reformers* (London, 1869), pp. 70-71, 74-76, 110.
18. Durant, op. cit., vol. V, p. 576.
19. Francesco Guicciardini, *Storia*, I, 20, as cited in E.R. Chamberlin, *The Bad Popes* (Barnes and Noble, 1969), p. 173.
20. *Inside the Vatican*, November 1993, pp. 55, 57.
21. E.R. Chamberlin, *The Bad Popes* (Barnes and Noble, 1969), p. 198.
22. E.g. *Our Sunday Visitor*, February 27, 1994, p. 5; *National Catholic Reporter*, January 7, 1994, p. 9.
23. *National Catholic Reporter*, September 3, 1993.
24. Patricia Nolan Savas, "Misconduct by clergy is no surprise," *USA TODAY*, December 8, 1993, p. 17A.
25. *Times* (St. Petersburg, FL), February 11, 1994, p. 3A.
26. *National Catholic Reporter*, January 7, 1994, p. 9.
27. Ibid., p. 3.
28. *Our Sunday Visitor*, February 27, 1994, p. 5.
29. *National Catholic Reporter*, January 7, 1994, p. 3.
30. Ibid., September 17, 1993, p. 7.
31. Ibid., October 1, 1993, p. 7.
32. Ibid., September 17, 1993, pp. 6-7.
33. William Hogan, Esq., *Popery As It Was and As It Is* (Hartford, 1854), p. 37.
34. *Inside the Vatican*, November 1993, cover story, "After the Encyclical: Ratzinger," p. 4.
35. *Times*, op. cit.
36. *Dallas Morning News*, October, 1993.

## Chapter 13—Seducer of Souls
1. Austin Flannery, O.P., gen. ed., *Vatican Council II: The Conciliar and Post Conciliar Documents*, rev. ed. (Costello Publishing, 1988), vol. 1, p. 71.
2. Ibid., pp. 35, 193.
3. *Fidelity*, December 1993, p. 2.
4. *Our Sunday Visitor*, December 5, 1993, p. 3.
5. J.H. Ignaz von Dollinger, *The Pope and the Council* (London, 1869), pp. 238-39.
6. Ibid., pp. 241-42.
7. *Catholic Encyclopedia*, 1907-23 edition.
8. Padre Pio Foundation of America (24 Prospect Hill Road, Cromwell, CT 06416), 1993 Appointment Calendar with daily readings—the month of April has a picture of the Padre

with his hands held up to show the stigmata with the caption: "The wounds of the crucifixion. Padre Pio bled daily for 50 years."

9. Newsletter, The Padre Pio Foundation of America and the Mass Association (Holy Apostles Seminary, Cromwell, CT 06416), August or September 1988.
10. Flannery, op. cit., vol. 1, p. 65.
11. E.R. Chamberlin, *The Bad Popes* (Barnes and Noble, 1969), p. 12.
12. *The Pope Speaks*, March/April 1990, vol. 35, no. 2, "Icons Speak of Christian History, pp. 130-31.
13. Charles Colson, *The Body, Being Light in Darkness* (Word Publishing, 1992), p. 271
14. Flannery, op. cit., vol. 1, pp. 62-79.
15. Ibid., p. 77.
16. *Inside The Vatican*, April 1994, p. 55 under 19 May.
17. Chamberlin, op. cit., p. 69.
18. Dollinger, op. cit., pp. 250-51.
19. Sidney Z. Ehler, John B. Morrall, trans. and eds., *Church and State Through the Centuries* (London, 1954), pp. 122-24.
20. Dollinger, op. cit., pp. 258-59.
21. Raynald, *Annal.* anno 1438, 5.
22. Dollinger, op. cit., p. 275.
23. Ibid., p. 269.
24. Ibid., p. 278.
25. Ibid., p. 284.
26. Ibid., p. 280.
27. Chamberlin, op. cit., p. 69.
28. Will Durant, *The Story of Civilization* (Simon and Schuster, 1950), vol. VI, p. 920.
29. Dollinger, op. cit., p. 298.
30. Psalmaei, *Coll. Actor.*, in Le Plat, vii. ii. 92, cited in Dollinger, op. cit., pp. 299-300.
31. Dollinger, op. cit., pp. 298-99.
32. *Storia del Conc. di Trento*. v 425 (ed. Milano, 1844).
33. Durant, op. cit., vol. VI, p. 453.
34. Ibid., pp. 453-57.
35. *National Catholic Reporter*, August 27, 1993.
36. From a transcript of "PrimeTime Live" (ABC), January 6, 1994.

## Chapter 14—An Incredible Metamorphosis

1. Augustine, *de cat. rud.*, XXV, 48.
2. Tertullian, *Apology*, 40.2.
3. Tertullian, *To the Nations*, I.4.
4. *Epistle of Diognetus*, V. 4-11.
5. Clement, *Miscellanies*, II.20.125.
6. William Byron Forbush, ed., *Foxe's Book of Martyrs* (Zondervan, 1962), p. 14.
7. Ibid., p. 17.
8. Philip Hughes, *A History of the Church* (London, 1934), vol. 1, p. 165.
9. H. Chadwick, *The Early Church* (Wm. B. Eerdmans, 1967), p. 118.
10. Hughes., op. cit., p. 172.
11. Will Durant, *The Story of Civilization* (Simon and Schuster, 1950), vol. IV, p. 75; vol. III, p. 657.
12. Peter Brown, *Augustine of Hippo* (University of California Press, 1967), p. 213.
13. Peter de Rosa, *Vicars of Christ: The Dark Side of the Papacy* (Crown Publishers, 1988), pp. 34-35.
14. August Bernhard Hasler, *How the Pope Became Infallible* (Doubleday & Co., Inc., 1981), p. 35.
15. J.H. Ignaz von Dollinger, *The Pope and the Council* (London, 1869), pp. 14-15.
16. Austin Flannery, O.P., gen. ed., *Vatican Council II: The Conciliar and Post Conciliar Documents*, rev. ed. (Costello Publishing, 1988), vol. 1, p. 800.
17. Dollinger, op. cit., pp. 339-40.
18. De Rosa, op. cit., p. 98.

19. Dollinger, op. cit., pp. 245-46.
20. Ibid., p. 184.
21. Ibid., p. 187.
22. Ibid., p. 184.
23. James A. Coriden, Thomas J. Green, Donald E. Heintschel, eds., *The Code of Canon Law* (Paulist Press, 1985), Canon 1404.
24. Flannery, op. cit., vol. 1, p. 380.
25. Ibid.

**Chapter 15—Unholy Alliances**
 1. Guillermo Dellhora, *La Iglesia Catolica ante la critica en el pensamiento y en el arte* (Mexico City, 1929), p. 248.
 2. Maurice Keen, *The Pelican History of Medieval Europe* (Pelican, 1969), pp. 14-15.
 3. Colman J. Barry, O.S.B., ed., *Readings in Church History*, vol. 1, *From Pentecost to the Protestant Revolt* (The Newman Press, 1960), p. 223.
 4. Eusebius, *Oration on the Tricennalia of Constantine*, 2.4, 3.5-6.
 5. *National Catholic Reporter*, October 22, 1993, p. 3.
 6. *Time*, July 26, 1982, p. 35.
 7. *New York Times*, June 4, 1985.
 8. August Bernhard Hasler, *How the Pope Became Infallible* (Doubleday & Co., Inc., 1981), p. 257.
 9. Ibid., p. 256.
10. John Toland, *Adolf Hitler* (Ballantine Books, 1977), pp. 431-32.
11. Ibid., p. 623.
12. Ibid., p. 724.
13. *Time*, February 24, 1992, pp. 28-35.
14. *World*, March 6, 1992.
15. *Columbia*, June 1990, p. 8.
16. *Christi Fideles* brochure, "How Can Catholics Reclaim America?" advertising a conference on October 17, 1993.
17. Austin Flannery, O.P., gen. ed., *Vatican Council II: The Conciliar and Post Conciliar Documents*, rev. ed. (Costello Publishing, 1988), vol. 1, pp. 364-65.

**Chapter 16—Dominion Over Kings**
 1. Cormenin, *History of the Popes*, p. 243, as cited in R.W. Thompson, *The Papacy and the Civil Power* (New York, 1876), p. 369.
 2. J.H. Ignaz von Dollinger, *The Pope and the Council* (London, 1869), p. 35.
 3. Ibid., p. 339.
 4. Cited in R.W. Thompson, *The Papacy and the Civil Power* (New York, 1876), pp. 414-15.
 5. Rev. Peter Geiermann, C.SS.R., *The Convert's Catechism of Catholic Doctrine* (Tan Books and Publishers, Inc., 1977), Imprimatur Joseph E. Ritter, S.T.D., Archbishop of St. Louis p. 24.
 6. Walter James, *The Christian in Politics* (Oxford University Press, 1962), p. 47.
 7. Dollinger, op. cit., pp. 214-18.
 8. Freeman, *The Norman Conquest*, p. 320, cited in R.W. Thompson, op. cit., p. 441.
 9. Thompson, op. cit., pp. 410, 557.
10. Ibid., p. 466.
11. Dollinger, op. cit., pp. 87-89.
12. Peter de Rosa, *Vicars of Christ: The Dark Side of the Papacy* (Crown Publishers, 1988), p. 253.
13. Ibid., p. 73.
14. Cormenin, op. cit., p. 459.
15. Hallam, *The Middle Ages*, p. 287, cited in Thompson, op. cit., p. 559.
16. Sidney Z. Ehler, John B. Morrall, trans. and eds., *Church and State Through the Centuries* (London, 1954), p. 50.
17. Ibid., p. 52.
18. Ibid., pp. 73-76, for a copy of this document.
19. Thompson, op. cit., p. 559.
20. Ehler and Morrall, op. cit., p. 51
21. Ibid., p. 53.

22. *National Catholic Reporter*, July 3, 1992.
23. Avro Manhattan, *Murder in the Vatican* (Ozark Books, 1985), pp. 5-7.
24. Cormenin, op. cit., p. 275.
25. Colman J. Barry, O.S.B., ed., *Readings in Church History*, vol. 1, *From Pentecost to the Protestant Revolt* (The Newman Press, 1960), pp. 470-71.
26. De Rosa, op. cit., pp. 99-100.
27. D. Antonio Gavin, *A Master Key to Popery: In Five Parts*, 3rd ed. (London, England, 1773), p. 154.
28. Ibid., pp. 157-58.
29. Emmet McLoughlin, *An Inquiry into the Assassination of Abraham Lincoln* (The Citadel Press, 1977), p. 70.
30 De Rosa, op. cit., pp. 26-2ı
31. Nino Lo Bello, *The Vatican Empire* (Trident Press, 1968), p. 186 and jacket.
32. *National Catholic Reporter*, October 22, 1993, p. 11.
33. Lo Bello, op. cit., p. 186

## Chapter 17—Blood of the Martyrs

1. Jean Antoine Llorente, *History of the Inquisition*, as cited in R.W. Thompson, *The Papacy and the Civil Power* (New York, 1876), p. 82.
2. Comte Le Maistre, *Letters on the Spanish Inquisition* (Boston, 1843), p. 22 as cited in R.W. Thompson, *The Papacy and the Civil Power* (New York, 1876), pp. 82-83.
3. Peter de Rosa, *Vicars of Christ: The Dark Side of the Papacy* (Crown Publishers, 1988), p. 180.
4. Ibid., p. 35, and jacket.
5. Will Durant, *The Story of Civilization* (Simon and Schuster, 1950), vol. IV, p. 784.
6. De Rosa, op. cit., p. 179.
7. J.H. Ignaz von Dollinger, *The Pope and the Council* (London, 1869), p. 195.
8. Durant, op. cit., vol. IV, pp. 773-74.
9. Le Maistre, op. cit., p. 39, as cited in R.W. Thompson, *The Papacy and the Civil Power* (New York, 1876), p. 83.
10. Ibid.
11. De Rosa, op. cit., p. 175.
12. Dollinger, op. cit., pp. 190-93.
13. Samuel Vila, *Historia de la Inquisicion y la Reforma en Espana* (CLIE, 1977), p. 48.
14. Dollinger, op. cit., p. 193.
15. Durant, op. cit., vol. V, p. 527.
16. Ibid., vol. IV, p. 680.
17. St. Thomas Aquinas, *Summa Theologica* (Louis Guerin, Barri-Ducis, 1857), vol. 4, p. 90.
18. Cormenin, op. cit., pp. 116-17, as cited in R.W. Thompson, *The Papacy and the Civil Power* (New York, 1876), p. 553
19. D. Antonio Gavin, *A Master Key to Popery: In Five Parts*, 3rd ed. (London, England, 1773), p. 253.
20 *The Tablet*, November 5, 1938.
21 Rev. John Foxe, M.A., *Book of Martyrs; or, a History of the Lives, Sufferings and Triumphant Deaths, of the Primitive as well as Protestant Martyrs: from the Commencement of Christianity, to the Latest Periods of Pagan and Popish Persecution* (Edwin Hunt, 1833), from the introduction to the 1833 ed., p. iv, based upon the 1824 ed. (improved by important alterations and additions by Rev. Charles A. Goodrich).
22. De Rosa, op. cit., p. 20.
23. Dollinger, op. cit., pp. 313-15.
24. De Rosa, op. cit., pp. 182-83.
25. Durant, op. cit., vol. VI, p. 211.
26. Gerard Dufour, *La Inquisicion Espanola* (Montesinos, 1986), p. 32.
27. Durant, op. cit., vol. VI, pp. 410-15.
28. De Rosa, op. cit., vol. 175.
29. Emmet McLoughlin, *An Inquiry into the Assassination of Abraham Lincoln* (The Citadel Press, 1977), pp. 27-28.
30. Gavin, op. cit., p. 212.

31. Sidney Z. Ehler, John B. Morrall, trans. and eds., *Church and State Through the Centuries* (London, 1954), p. 7.
32. *De Planct. Eccl.* ii.28, cited in Dollinger, op. cit., p. 185.
33. E.H. Broadbent, *The Pilgrim Church* (London, 1931), pp. 88-89.
34. Durant, op. cit., vol. IV, p. 772.
35. Du Pin, *The Inquisition*, vol. ii, pp. 151-54, cited in R.W. Thompson, *The Papacy and the Civil Power* (New York, 1876), p. 418.
36. R.W. Thompson, *The Papacy and the Civil Power* (New York, 1876), p. 418; see also de Rosa, op. cit., p. 73.
37. Broadbent, op. cit., pp. 88-89.
38. J.H. Merle D'Aubigne, *History of the Great Reformation of the Sixteenth Century in Germany, Switzerland, and c.* (New York, 1843), vol. II, p. 398.
39. Muston, *History of the Waldenses*, vol. i., p. 31, cited in Thompson, op. cit., p. 489; see also Broadbent, op. cit., pp. 100-01.
40. Plass, *What Luther Says*, vol. 1, p. 36.
41. *The Complete Writings of Menno Simons c.1496-1561* (Herald Press, 1956), p. 7 (translated from the Dutch by Leonard Verduin and edited by J.C. Wenger, with a biography by Harold S. Bender).
42. Ibid., p. 16.
43. Thieleman J. van Braght, *The Bloody Theater or Martyrs Mirror of the Defenseless Christians Who Baptized Only Upon Confession of Faith, and Who Suffered and Died for the Testimony of Jesus, Their Saviour, From the Time of Christ to the Year A.D. 1660* (Herald Press, 1950 ed., originally published in 1660), p. 984.
44. Ibid., pp. 984-85.
45. *Time* magazine, December 6, 1993, p. 58.
46. *National Catholic Reporter*, December 10, 1993, p. 5.
47. Ibid., June 19, 1993.
48. *Our Sunday Visitor*, January 23, 1994, p. 5.
49. *Inside the Vatican*, November 1993, p. 35.

**Chapter 18—Background to the Holocaust**

1. "Zum 20.April," by J.S., *Klerusblatt*, April 12, 1939, pp. 221-22.
2. *Katolicki Tjednik*, May 25, 1941.
3. Peter de Rosa, *Vicars of Christ: The Dark Side of the Papacy* (Crown Publishers, 1988), p. 34.
4. G.T. Bettany, *A Popular History of the Reformation and Modern Protestantism* (London, 1895), p. 4.
5. Rabbi Yoel Schwartz and Rabbi Yitzchak Goldstein, *Shoah, A Jewish perspective on tragedy in the context of the Holocaust* (Mesorah Publications, Ltd., 1990), pp. 159-61.
6. Ibid., pp. 163-65.
7. Will Durant, *The Story of Civilization* (Simon and Schuster, 1950), vol. IV, p. 388.
8. Ibid., *Reformation*, p. 729.
9. *La Civilta*, vol. iii, p. 11, 1862.
10. De Rosa, op. cit., p. 158.
11. Gerard Dufour, *La Inquisicion Espanola* (Montesinos, 1986), pp. 16-17.
12. De Rosa, op. cit., pp. 194-95.
13. August Bernhard Hasler, *How the Pope Became Infallible* (Doubleday & Co., Inc., 1981), p. 293.
14. *Orange County Register*, May 26, 1994, front page; see also the *Jerusalem Post*, May 26, 1994.
15. *Jerusalem Post*, May 27, 1994.
16. Guenter Lewy, *The Catholic Church and Nazi Germany* (McGraw-Hill, 1964), p. 273
17. Jules Isaac, *Jesus et Israel* (Paris, 1948), p. 508.
18. Lewy, op. cit., p. 16.
19. Ibid., pp. 25, 30-31, 38-40.
20. H. Rauschning, *The Voice of Destruction* (New York, 1940), p 53.
21. Lewy, op. cit., pp. 45-46.
22. Ibid., p. 55.
23. G.S. Graber, *The History of the SS* (New York, 1978), p. 11

24. Ibid., p. 12.
25. Ibid., pp. 76, 205.
26. Ibid.
27. *Los Angeles Times*, April 17, 1993, p. A10.
28. Cited by Hans Askenasy, *Are We All Nazis?* (Secaucus, NJ, 1978), p. 25.
29. Lewy, op. cit., p. 274.
30. Ibid.

## Chapter 19—The Vatican, the Nazis, and the Jews

1. Manfred Barthel, *The Jesuits: History and Legend of the Society of Jesus* (New York, 1984), p. 266.
2. Guenter Lewy, *The Catholic Church and Nazi Germany* (McGraw-Hill, 1964), p. 287.
3. John Toland, *Adolf Hitler* (Ballantine Books, 1977), p. 424.
4. Cited by Hans Askenasy, *Are We All Nazis?* (Secaucus, NJ, 1978), p. 76.
5. Ibid., p. 27.
6. Toland, op. cit., p. 961.
7. Lewy, op. cit., p. 279.
8. Ibid., pp. 272, 279.
9. Ibid., p. 282.
10. Ibid., p. 285.
11. Ibid., p. 159.
12. Ibid., p. 277.
13. Yehuda Bauer, *A History of the Holocaust* (Franklin Watts, 1982), p. 136.
14. Ibid., p. 137.
15. Lewy, op. cit., p. 152.
16. Peter Viereck, *Meta-Politics: The Roots of the Nazi Mind* (Alfred A. Knopf, Inc., 1941, 1961 edition), p. 319.
17. Michael Berenbaum, *The World Must Know: The History of the Holocaust as Told in the United States Holocaust Memorial Museum* (Little, Brown & Company, 1993), p. 156.
18. William L. Shirer, *The Rise and Fall of the Third Reich* (New York, 1959), p. 58.
19. *Newsweek*, February 8, 1954, p. 49.
20. Lewy, op. cit., p. 306.
21. Avro Manhattan, *The Vatican in World Politics* (Horizon Press, 1949), p. 126.
22. *Time* magazine, December 6, 1993, p. 60.
23. Peter de Rosa, *Vicars of Christ: The Dark Side of the Papacy* (Crown Publishers, 1988), p. 198.
24. Lewy, op. cit., p. 341, cited also in Askenasy, op. cit., p. 61.
25. Lewy, op. cit., p. 289.
26. Ibid., p. 304.
27. *America and the Holocaust, Deceit and Indifference*, part of "The American Experience" PBS series, April 6, 1994.
28. Lewy, op. cit., p. 321.
29. Ibid.
30. *Humani generis*, August 12, 1950 encyclical of Pius XII.
31. *Bend Bulletin* (Oregon), January 25, 1994.
32. *Washington Post*, December 30, 1993, p. A1; *Los Angeles Times*. December 31, 1993, p. A8.
33. Austin Flannery, O.P., gen. ed., *Vatican Council II: The Conciliar and Post Conciliar Documents*, rev. ed. (Costello Publishing, 1988), vol. 1, p. 367.
34. Ibid.
35. Lewy, op. cit., p. 308.

## Chapter 20—The Slaughter of the Serbs

1. Magnus Linklater, Isabel Hilton, and Neal Ascherson, *The Nazi Legacy: Klaus Barbie and the International Fascist Connection* (New York, 1984), p. 187.
2. Scott Anderson, Jon Lee Anderson, *Inside the League* (Dodd, Mead & Company, 1986), subtitle, front cover.
3. Ibid.
4. Ibid., pp. 291-92.
5. *Nedalja*, April 27, 1941.

6. Avro Manhattan, *The Vatican's Holocaust* (Ozark Books, 1986), p. 9.
7. Anderson and Anderson, op. cit., p. 292.
8. Linklater, et al., op. cit., p. 188.
9. Anderson and Anderson, op. cit., pp. 27-28.
10. *Los Angeles Times*, January 19, 1988, Part I, p. 22.
11. Anderson and Anderson, op. cit., p. 28.
12. *Newsweek*, February 8, 1954, p. 49.
13. *Los Angeles Times*, January 19, 1988, Part I, pp. 20, 22.
14. Anderson and Anderson, op. cit., p. 296; see also Mark Aarons and John Loftus, *Unholy Trinity: How the Vatican's Nazi Networks Betrayed Western Intelligence to the Soviets* (New York, 1991), p. 102; and *Los Angeles Times*, January 19, 1988, part 1, pp. 20, 22.
15. *Nasa Nada*, April 23, 1958.
16. *Los Angeles Times*, January 24, 1988.
17. Robert D. Kaplan, "Why Yugoslavia Exploded," *Reader's Digest*, March 1993.
18. *Seattle Times*, August 8, 1991, p. A10.
19. *Los Angeles Times*, March 14, 1993, editorial.
20. *Our Sunday Visitor*, April 10, 1994, p. 3.
21. *Los Angeles Times*, January 17, 1993, p. A39.

**Chapter 21—The Vatican Ratlines**

1. Airgram from Cabot, Belgrade, to Washington, 12 June 1947, USNA, RG 59, 740.00116EW/6-1147, cited in Mark Aarons and John Loftus, *Unholy Trinity: How the Vatican's Nazi Networks Betrayed Western Intelligence to the Soviets* (New York, 1991), front.
2. Mark Aarons and John Loftus, *Unholy Trinity: How the Vatican's Nazi Networks Betrayed Western Intelligence to the Soviets* (New York, 1991), preface, p. x.
3. Ibid., from caption beneath photo 3 in center of book.
4. Ibid, pp. xii-xiii.
5. Ibid., p. 92.
6. Scott Anderson, Jon Lee Anderson, *Inside the League* (Dodd, Mead & Company, 1986), p. 39.
7. Gita Sereny, *Into that Darkness . . . the Mind of a Mass Murderer* (Picador, London, 1977), p. 289.
8. Hudal, *Römische Tagebucher*, p. 21 as cited in Aarons and Loftus, op. cit., p. 37.
9. Aarons and Loftus, op. cit., p. 108.
10. Anderson and Anderson, op. cit., p. 39.
11. Ibid., p. 295.
12. Ibid.
13. Magnus Linklater, Isabel Hilton, and Neal Ascherson, *The Nazi Legacy: Klaus Barbie and the International Fascist Connection* (New York, 1984), p. 190; see also Aarons and Loftus, op. cit., pp. 27-28, 40-45, 86, 93-95, passim.
14. For example, see the *Seattle Times* and *Tribune/Herald*, February 15, 1992.
15. *San Diego Union-Tribune*, December 14, 1993.
16. Aarons and Loftus, op. cit., pp. 102-03.
17. Ibid., comment under photograph 12 in center of book.
18. Linklater, et al., op. cit., pp. 188-89.
19. Aarons and Loftus, op. cit., p. 104.
20. Ibid., p. 109.
21. Ibid.
22. Ibid., pp. 109-12.
23. Aarons and Loftus, op. cit., pp. 254-55; see also Linklater, et al., op. cit., pp. 189-92.
24. Aarons and Loftus, op. cit., pp. 102-03.
25. Anderson and Anderson, op. cit.; Aarons and Loftus, op. cit.; see also newspaper articles e.g. the *San Diego Union-Tribune*, December 14, 1993, *New York Times*, February 4, 1992, *Orange County Register*, May 31, 1993, pp. 34-35.
26. Anderson and Anderson, op. cit., p. 40.
27. *Orange County Register*, May 25, 1989, p. A18.

28. Ibid., February 7, 1992; see also *Morning News Tribune* (Tacoma, WA), February 4, 1992, p. A-1.
29. Aarons and Loftus, op. cit., pp. 282-83.

## Chapter 22—Sola Scriptura?

1. *The Canons and Decrees of the Council of Trent*, trans. and introduced by Rev. H.J. Schroeder, O.P. (Tan Books, 1978), p. 274.
2. J.H. Merle D'Aubigne, *History of the Great Reformation of the Sixteenth Century in Germany, Switzerland, & c.* (New York, 1843), vol. II, p. 392.
3. Austin Flannery, O.P., gen. ed., *Vatican Council II: The Conciliar and Post Conciliar Documents*, rev. ed. (Costello Publishing, 1988), vol. 1, p. 379.
4. Ibid., p. 755.
5. From Harold S. Bender, *A Brief Biography of Menno Simons*, p. 5, at beginning of *The Complete Writings of Menno Simons, c.1496-1561* (Herald Press, 1956) (translated from the Dutch by Leonard Verduin and edited by J.C. Wenger, with a biography by Harold S. Bender).
6. Pope Pius XII, *Divino Afflante Spiritu*, no. 34-35, 1943.
7. George Martin, "Is There a *Catholic* Way to Read the Bible?" *New Covenant*, June 1993, p. 13.
8. Flannery, op. cit., vol. 1, pp. 764-65.
9. *The Pope Speaks*, March/April, vol. 39, no. 2, 1994, p. 93.
10. *Time*, December 6, 1993, p. 60.
11. Flannery, op. cit., vol. 1, p. 755.
12. *Cateschisme de L'Eglise Catholique* (Libreria Editrice Vaticana, 1993), p. 32. (Taken from the French ed., trans. privately by Yves Brault—the English edition was not yet available.)
13. *Inside the Vatican*, April 1994, pp. 50-52.
14. Emelio Martinez, *Recuerdos [Memoirs] de Antano* (CLIE, 1909), p. 390.
15. *Our Sunday Visitor*, June 5, 1994, p. 6.
16. *New Covenant*, June 1993, p. 12.
17. *Our Sunday Visitor*, June 5, 1994, p. 6.
18. Henry Clarence Theissen, *Introduction to the New Testament* (Wm. B. Eerdmans, 1943), p. 26.
19. W.H.C. Frend, *The Rise of Christianity* (Philadelphia, 1984), p. 135.
20. Karl Keating, *Catholicism and Fundamentalism: The Attack on "Romanism" by "Bible Christians"* (Ignatius Press, 1988), pp. 125-27.
21. Rev. Peter Geiermann, C.SS.R., *The Convert's Catechism of Catholic Doctrine* (Tan Books and Publishers, Inc., 1977), Imprimatur Joseph E. Ritter, S.T.D., Archbishop of St. Louis), pp. vi, 25-27.
22. This teaching is all through Vatican II. E.g. see Flannery, op. cit., vol. 1, pp. 365, 381.
23. Keating, op. cit., pp. 125-27.
24. Ibid., pp. 140-41.
25. *Christianity Today*, September 20, 1985.

## Chapter 23—A Question of Salvation

1. H.J. Schroeder, O.P., trans., *The Canons and Decrees of the Council of Trent* (Tan Books, 1978), p. 52.
2. Austin Flannery, O.P., gen. ed., *Vatican Council II: The Conciliar and Post Conciliar Documents*, rev. ed. (Costello Publishing, 1988), vol. 1, pp. 65, 68.
3. Ibid., p. 755.
4. From a letter signed by James W. Jewell for Colson dated May 23, 1994, to T.A. McMahon, quoting a public statement by Colson made elsewhere.
5. Flannery, op. cit., vol. 1, p. 412.
6. Schroeder, op. cit., p. 44.
7. Ibid., p. 46.
8. Flannery, op. cit., vol. 1, p. 378.
9. Ibid., p. 799.
10. Ibid., p. 1.
11. Ibid., pp. 4, 6.
12. Letter on file.
13. Flannery, op. cit., vol. 1, p. 915.
14. Ibid., p. 917.

15. Emelio Martinez, *Recuerdos [Memoirs] de Antano* (CLIE, 1909), p. 404.
16. Peter Kreeft, *Fundamentals of the Faith: Essays in Christian Apologetics* (Ignatius Press, 1988), p. 273.
17. Rev. John Ferraro, *Ten Series of Meditations on the Mystery of the Rosary.*
18. St. Alphonsus de Liguori, *The Glories of Mary* (Redemptorist Fathers, 1931), pp. 161-62, 170.
19. Ibid., pp. 166-67.
20. Ibid., pp. 237-43.
21. Ferraro, op. cit.
22. "Heaven Opened by the Practice of THE THREE HAIL MARYS," Imprimatur: Francis Cardinal Spellman, Archbishop of New York.
23. From a brochure published by Aylesford Lay Carmelite and The Scapular Center, Darien, IL 60559-0065.
24. Liguori, op. cit., p. 235.
25. Ibid.
26. Brochure, op. cit., Darien, IL.
27. John A. Hardon, S.J., *Pocket Catholic Dictionary* (Doubleday, 1966), p. 249.
28. Flannery, op. cit., vol. 1, p. 72.
29. Kreeft, op. cit., p. 277.
30. David W. Cloud, *Flirting with Rome, Volume 2, Key Men and Organizations* (Way of Life Literature, 1219 North Harns Road, Oak Harbor, WA 98277, 1993), p. 5.
31. Flannery, op. cit., vol. 1, pp. 364-65.
32. From his papal bull, *Unam Sanctam*, A.D. 1302.
33. *Catechisme de L'eglise Catholique* (Service des Edition, Conference des eveques catholiques du Canada, 1993), p. 184, para. 837.
34. Ibid., p. 186, para. 846.
35. Flannery, op. cit., vol. 1, p. 366.
36. Ibid., pp. 365-66.
37. *Catechisme*, op. cit., p. 186, para. 846.
38. James A. Coriden, Thomas J. Green, Donald E. Heintschel, eds., *The Code of Canon Law* (Paulist Press, 1985), p. 698.
39. Flannery, op. cit., vol. 1, p. 367.
40. Ibid., p. 365,
41. Ibid., p. 366.


**Chapter 24—Sacrifice of the Mass**
1. Austin Flannery, O.P., gen. ed., *Vatican Council II: The Conciliar and Post Conciliar Documents*, rev. ed. (Costello Publishing, 1988), vol. 1, pp. 104, 107, 109.
2. Ibid., pp. 101, 104, 249; see also the new universal *Catechism of the Catholic Church* (The Wanderer Press, 1994), p. 285, para. 864 (French ed.); and James A. Coriden, Thomas J. Green, Donald E. Heintschel, eds., *The Code of Canon Law* (Paulist Press, 1985), Canon 897
3. John A. Hardon, S.J., *Pocket Catholic Dictionary* (Doubleday, 1966), p. 132.
4. *The New Saint Joseph Baltimore Catechism*, No. 2 (Catholic Book Publishing Co., New York, 1969), p. 171. See also the new universal *Catechism of the Catholic Church* (The Wanderer Press, 1994), pp. 284-304.
5. Ibid., p. 168, see also Vatican II and the new universal *Catechism*.
6. Flannery, op. cit., pp. 114, 1.
7. Ibid., vol. 2, p. 36.
8. Hardon, op. cit., p. 249.
9. Ibid.
10. Mother Teresa, *In the Silence of the Heart.*
11. Flannery, op. cit., pp. 132-33.
12. *New Covenant*, February 1994, pp. 16-17.
13. D. Antonio Gavin, *A Master Key to Popery: In Five Parts*, 3rd ed. (London, England, 1773), pp. 184-88.
14. Guenter Lewy, *The Catholic Church and Nazi Germany* (McGraw-Hill, 1964), p. 272.
15. Flannery, op. cit., vol. 1, pp. 102-03.
16. James A. Coriden, Thomas J. Green, Donald E. Heintschel, eds., *The Code of Canon Law* (Paulist Press, 1985), p. 646.

17. Flannery, op. cit., vol. 1, p. 102.
18. John M. Drickamer, "The Real Presence," *Christian News*, February 21, 1994, pp. 5, 11.
19. Hardon, op. cit., p. 248.
20. Ibid., p. 250.
21. *Catholic World Report*, April 1994, p. 38.
22. Hardon, op. cit., p. 271.


## Chapter 25—The Reformation Betrayed

1. David Beale, *Southern Baptist Convention, House on the Sand?* pp. 142-43; *Dallas Morning News*, August 19, 1978.
2. *McCall's*, January 1978.
3. Michael de Semlyen, *All Roads Lead to Rome?* (Dorchester House Publications, England, 1991), p. 178: (see also *Time*, Oct. 15, 1979; *Christianity Today*, Nov. 3, 1979; *Saturday Evening Post*, Jan.-Feb. 1980.)
4. *Cleveland Plain Dealer*, March 27, 1994, p. 4-B, "Catholics, Protestants work for Graham crusade."
5. Citing *Halley's Bible Handbook*, Billy Graham Crusade ed., special ed. printed by permission of Zondervan Publishing House for the Grason Company, 13 S. 13th St., Minneapolis, Minnosota, cited in Wilson Ewin, *Today's Evangelicals Embracing the World's Deadliest Cult* (Quebec Baptist Missions, Box 113, Compton, Quebec, Canada J0B 1L0, 1994), p. 57.
6. Henry H. Halley, *Pocket Bible Handbook* (Chicago, 1944), pp. 608-13.
7. D. Antonio Gavin, *A Master Key to Popery: In Five Parts*, 3rd ed. (London, England, 1773).
8. Will Durant, *The Story of Civilization* (Simon and Schuster, 1950), vol. VI, pp. 531-32; see also E.H. Broadbent, *The Pilgrim Church* (London, 1931).
9. Durant, op. cit., vol. VI, pp. 530-31.
10. Ibid., pp. 529-30.
11. Ibid., pp. 543-48.
12. Ibid., pp. 549, 576-77.
13. Ibid.
14. Ibid., pp. 577-78.
15. Ibid., p. 577.
16. Ibid., p. 591.
17. Rev. John Foxe, M.A., *Foxe's Book of Martyrs*, ed. William Byron Forbush (Zondervan, 1962), pp. 207-08.
18. R. Tudor Jones, *The Great Reformation* (InterVarsity Press), p. 164.
19. Ibid.
20. *Foxe's Book of Martrys*, ed. Forbush (1962 ed.), op. cit., pp. 247-49.
21. Ibid.
22. Durant, op. cit., vol. VI, pp. 598-601.
23. Sidney Z. Ehler, John B. Morrall, trans. and eds., *Church and State Through the Centuries* (London, 1954), pp. 180-83.
24. Semlyen, op. cit., p. 148.
25. Ibid., p. 150.
26. *Washington Times*, February 24, 1994; *The Catholic World Report*, April 1994, pp. 20-21.
27. Peter Kreeft, *Fundamentals of the Faith: Essays in Christian Apologetics* (Ignatius Press, 1988), p. 107.
28. *Seattle Times*, May 8, 1990, "Pope warns against sects."
29. *Moody Monthly*, November 1993.
30. *Foundation*, Jan./Feb. 1987, pp. 5-6; Ibid., May/June 1989, p. 10; "Celebration 2000 Letter," Oct. 14, 1993; advertisement of speakers at the International World Convention of the FGBMFI, *Charisma*, May 1991; *Charisma*, April 1988, p. 86; *Full Gospel Business Men's Voice*, March 1987, pp. 3-9; *Foundation*, Nov./Dec. 1990, pp. 8-9; *Christianity Today*, Mar. 5, 1982; *Charisma*, August 1993, p. 78; "1993 Consultation on Evangelization of the Catholic World," brochure produced by Youth With A Mission (Dublin, Ireland).
31. Flannery, op. cit., vol. 1, p. 380.
32. E.g. *Wanderer*, June 30, 1994, interview with Patrick Madrid, cited in *Christian News*, July 4, 1994, p. 2; "Roman Catholic Doubletalk at Indianapolis '90," *Foundation*, July-August 1990; Pope Pius XII, *De Motione oecumenica*, December 20, 1949.

33. David W. Cloud, *Flirting with Rome, Volume 3, The Southern Baptist Convention* (Way of Life Literature, 1219 North Harns Road, Oak Harbor, WA 98277, 1993), p. 23.
34. Ibid., p. 29.
35. From a tape of "Praise the Lord" (TBN), October 17, 1989.
36. *The Southern Cross*, January 13, 1994, p. 11.
37. Kenneth Kantzer, *Christianity Today*, November 18, 1988.
38. E.g. *The Tidings* (official newspaper of the Catholic Archdiocese of Los Angeles), vol. 97, no. 32, August 9, 1991, p. 9; *St. Louis Review*, July 12, 1991, pp. 1, 8.
39. *The Portland Catholic Sentinel*, September 25, 1992.
40. "Billy Graham Crusade Scheduled for Nassau Coliseum: Assistance Sought from Catholics," *Charismatic News Notes*, published by the Diocese of Rockville Centre, 129 Broadway, Hicksville, NY 11801, May 1990, p. 1.
41. *St. Louis Review*, September 27, 1991.
42. *Gastonia Gazette*, November 22, 1967.
43. *Newsweek*, June 23, 1969.
44. *Southern California Christian Times*, vol. 5, no. 1, January 1994, Orange Co./L.A. ed., p. 1.
45. Kreeft, op. cit.
46. *Foxe's Book of Martrys*, ed. Forbush (1962 ed.), op. cit., pp. 233-37; Jones, op. cit., pp. 164-65.

**Chapter 26—Apostasy and Ecumenism**

1. Cited in Michael de Semlyen, *All Roads Lead to Rome?* (Dorchester House Publications, England, 1991), p. 183.
2. "Praise the Lord" program, Trinity Broadcasting Network, October 17, 1989, hosted by Paul and Jan Crouch—guests were two Catholic priests, Fr. John Hamsch and Jesuit Fr. Herbert De Souza, and leading Catholic laywoman, Michelle Corral.
3. *Los Angeles Herald Examiner*, September 19, 1987, Religion page.
4. Billy Graham, *The Saturday Evening Post*, January-February 1980.
5. *Focus on the Family Citizen*, January 1990, p. 10.
6. From page 23 of the final draft of the joint declaration.
7. "What Separates Evangelicals and Catholics?" *Christianity Today*, October 1981.
8. *World Evangelization*, November/December 1989, January 1990.
9. Pope Pius XII, *De Motione oecumenica*, December 20, 1949.
10. *Mistici Corporis*, June 29, 1943.
11. Thomas Howard, *Evangelical Is Not Enough* (Ignatius Press, 1984).
12. We could give a long list of stores and distributors but will refrain from naming them in the hope that they may change their policies.
13. "Spiritual Vision of Man," Pope John Paul II, *L'Osservatore Romano*, February 10, 1986, p. 5.
14. *Los Angeles Times*, February 5, 1993.
15. *L'Osservatore Romano*, February 10, 1993 as reprinted in *The Christian News*, August 2, 1993, p. 22.
16. Abbe Daniel Le Roux, *Peter, Lovest Thou Me?* (Australia: Instauratio Press, 1989), p. 140.
17. *National Catholic Reporter*, February 19, 1993, p. 11.
18. Le Roux, op. cit., pp. 144-45.
19. *La Croix*, August 23, 1985.
20. Le Roux, op. cit., p. 45.
21. H. Chadwick, *The Early Church* (Wm. B. Eerdmans, 1967), p. 243.
22. *The Roman Catholic*, June-July 1984, p. 32.
23. *The Catholic World: The New Age, a Challenge to Christianity*, May/June 1989
24. *Momentum*/April 1990, special section, *Spirituality of the Catholic Educator*.
25. *Chicago Sun Times*, December 24, 1989.
26. *Time*, September 17, 1979, p. 96.
27. *Newsweek*, September 17, 1979, p. 115.
28. *Our Sunday Visitor*, November 13, 1988.
29. *Courier-Journal*, May 11, 1984, p. A7.
30. "Spiritual Vision of Man," op. cit., p. 5.
31. Alan Geyer, "Religious Isolationism: Gone Forever?" *The Christian Century*, October 23, 1974, pp. 980-81.
32. *The Oregonian*, June 20, 1992, p. C12; see also *National Catholic Reporter*, September 4, 1992, p. 15; see also *National Catholic Reporter*, June 17, 1994, p. 7 and *Our Sunday Visitor*, June 19, 1994, p. 2.

33. *Our Sunday Visitor*, June 19, 1994, p. 19.
34. Le Roux, op. cit., p. 49.
35. *The Catholic World Report*, July 1992.
36. *New York Times*, June 4, 1985.
37. *National and International Religion Report*, February 21, 1994, p. 2.
38. John W. Robbins, "The Lost Soul of Scott Hahn," *The Trinity Review*, March 1994, p. 4.
39. *Orange County Register*, April 16, 1994.
40. *Little Masonic Library* (Macoy Publishing and Masonic Supply, 1977), vol. 4, p. 32.
41. Carol M. Ostrom, "Trust is key, interfaith group agrees," *Seattle Times* (Seattle, WA), March 11, 1987.
42. *National Catholic Reporter*, October 9, 1992, p. 13.
43. E.g. *Washington Post*, September 4, 1993, pp. A1, F8; *Minneapolis Tribune*, August 29, 1993; *Orlando Sentinel*, September 5, 1993, p. A-16; *Seattle Times*, WORLD, September 1, 1993; *Christian News*, September 6, 1993, p. 14; *National Catholic Reporter*, September 10, 1993, pp. 4, 3 and September 24, pp. 11-14.
44. *The 1993 Parliament of the World's Religions*, registration information, p. 2 listed under "Glimpses of the 1993 Parliament, and p. 3 listed on the official schedule of the "1993 Parliament of the World's Religions" for Thursday night in the time slot (8:00) occupied by plenary sessions on every other night. This was the major Parliament event for that day, with the different location (Rockefeller Chapel) than normal listed because of the additional crowd anticipated. All Parliament registrants were bused from the Palmer House to the Rockefeller Chapel.
45. *The Orange County Register*, September 4, 1993, Religion page, Metro 9.
46. *Los Angeles Times*, September 5, 1993, p. A1.
47. D C of December 2, 1980, p. 910, as cited in Le Roux, op. cit. p. 110.
48. D C of February 6, 1985, p. 136 as cited in Le Roux, op. cit., p. 111.
49. Le Roux, op. cit., p. 122.
50. Ibid., p. 124.
51. Ibid., pp. 124-25.
52. D C of January 17, 1988, p. 80, as cited in Le Roux, op. cit., p. 125.
53. Reported in *The Voice of the Martyrs*, June 1994, p. 6 (P.O. Box 443, Bartlesville, OK 74005).
54. *Bulletin d'information #1*, Novembre-Decembre 1993, Mission-Mondiale '95 France, BP 3017, 16, Impasse Bourdelle, 34500 Beziers, France.
55. *The Catholic Herald*, June 2, 1993, pp. 3, 12.
56. *Calvary Contender*, January 1, 1991. See also *Charisma*, December 1990.
57. *New Covenant*, January 1993, pp. 8-9.
58. Edward D. O'Connor, C.S.S., *The Pentecostal Movement in the Catholic Church* (Ave Maria Press, 1971), p. 58.
59. Ibid., p. 128.
60. Ibid., e.g. pp. 166-67.
61. From a tape of "Praise the Lord" program (TBN), March 7, 1990—a rebroadcast from the ceremony. (Schuller, Crouch, and Hayford on tape together.)
62. Pope Paul VI, *Nostra Aetate*, 2, para. 6.

## Chapter 27—What About Mary?

1. St. Alphonsus de Liguori, *The Glories of Mary* (Redemptorist Fathers, 1931), p. 171. De Liguori was a cardinal and saint and recognized as authoritative concerning Mary. He quotes the great saints of the Church on this subject in his book.
2. Ibid.
3. *Devotions in Honor of Our Mother of Perpetual Help*, official ed. (Liguori Publications, undated), pp. 46-47.
4. Peter de Rosa, *Vicars of Christ: The Dark Side of the Papacy* (Crown Publishers, 1988), p. 427.
5. De Liguori, op. cit., pp. 82-83, 94, 160, 169-70.
6. *Bookstore Journal*, "Official Publication of the Christian Booksellers Association," February 1992, p. 30.
7. *NRI Trumpet*, October 1993, p. 14.
8. *Time*, December 30, 1991, p. 62.

9. *The Pope Speaks*, March/April, vol. 39., no. 2, 1994, p. 105.
10. Quoted in numerous advertisements for videos of Fulton J. Sheen's television shows.
11. Fulton J. Sheen, *Treasure in Clay*, p. 317.
12. *The Catholic Sun*, May 26, 1993.
13. *Time*, December 30, 1991, p. 64.
14. Kathleen R. Hayes, "All-Night Prayer Vigil Becomes Devotion to Lady of the New Advent, a Heavenly Goddess," *NRI Trumpet*, October 1993, pp. 6-14.
15. Ibid.
16. *The Encyclopedia Britannica*, vol. 15, p. 459.
17. Hayes, op. cit.
18. J.H. Ignaz von Dollinger, *The Pope and the Council* (London, 1869), pp. 28-29.
19. *Catholic Family News*, April 1993, p. 13.
20. *Soul Magazine*, Nov.-Dec. 1984, p. 4.
21. *Catholic Twin Circle*, August 26, 1990, p. 20.
22. Le Roux, op. cit., dedication page.
23. This has been stated explicitly by some of the "saints" of the Church and it is implicit throughout the entire teaching of calling upon Mary from whom help is obtained more quickly than by calling upon God or Christ directly. See Liguroi, op. cit., e.g. pp. 40, 130, 137, 156, 157, 174.
24. *Devotions in Honor of Our Mother of Perpetual Help*, back cover.
25. *Catholic Twin Circle*, August 26, 1990, p. 20.
26. *The Fatima Crusader*, Winter 1992, p. 16.
27. Prayer on a card published by The International Fatima Rosary Crusade, RD 1, Box 258, Constable, NY, 12926 bearing the Imprimatur: February 21, 1961, Francis Cardinal Spellman, Archbishop of New York.
28. Russell Ford, "Criminal Rehabilitation—Catholic style," *This Rock*, February 1994, p. 17.
29. John J. Delaney, ed., *A Woman Clothed with the Sun* (Doubleday, 1961), pp. 63-88.
30. *Time*, December 30, 1991, pp. 62-63.

**Chapter 28—The Coming New World Order**
1. *Time*, December 30, 1991, p. 62.
2. *NRI Trumpet*, October 1993, p. 3.
3. Daughters of St. Paul, eds., *Servant of Truth: Messages of John Paul II* (St. Paul Editions, 1979, reprinted by permission of *L'Osservatore Romano*), vol. 2, p. 384.
4. *Time*, December 30, 1991, p. 62.
5. Brother Michael of the Holy Trinity at the Sorbonne, "Messages from Heaven to Earth: Fatima, Medjugorje, Kebeho and Charismatic Renewal," *The Catholic COUNTER-REFORMATION in the XXth Century*, November-December 1985, p. 1.
6. *Time*, December 30, 1991, p. 62.
7. *The Christian News*, September 13, 1993, p. 3.
8. *Our Sunday Visitor*, February 7, 1993.
9. *The Catholic World Report*, March 1994, p. 20.
10. *Time*, December 30, 1991, p. 64.
11. *The Catholic World Report*, March 1994, p. 20. See also *Houston Chronicle*, July 27, 1991.
12. *The Catholic World Report*, March 1994, p. 23.
13. *Miracle at Medjugorje*, April '88, Wayne Weible, p. 8.
14. *Christian News*, January 2, 1989, p. 4, quoting an interview with "Seer Vicka Ivankovic" in the *St. Louis Dispatch*, December 25, 1988.
15. *New Covenant*, November 1993, pp. 7-11.
16. Austin Flannery, O.P., gen. ed., *Vatican Council II: The Conciliar and Post Conciliar Documents*, rev. ed. (Costello Publishing, 1988), vol. 1, *Lumen Gentium*, 21 November 1964, 66, p. 421.
17. *Catechism of the Catholic Church* (Libreria Editrice Vaticana—In the USA, The Wanderer Press, St. Paul, MN, 1994), section 971, p. 253, *Imprimi Potest* Joseph Cardinal Ratzinger.
18. *This Rock*, May 1994, p. 11.
19. *National Catholic Reporter*, January 29, 1993, p. 3.
20. *USA Today*, June 29, 1994, p. 15A.

21. Pope John Paul II, *Redemptoris Missio*, 86, 92.
22. *Charisma*, May 1994, p. 76.
23. Ibid.
24. *Soul Magazine*, March-April 1993, p. 19.
25. *The Tablet*, February 29, 1992.
26. *The Christian World Report*, May 1992.
27. *Our Sunday Visitor*, May 29, 1994, p. 5.
28. Fulton J. Sheen, "Mary and the Moslems," *The World's First Love* (Garden City Books, 1952); see also Malachi Martin, *The Keys of this Blood: The Struggle for World Dominion Between Pope John Paul II, Mikhail Gorbachev and the Capitalist West* (Simon and Schuster, 1990), p. 285.
29. *The Fatima Crusader*, Winter 1992, front cover and p. 3.
30. Ibid., November/December 1986, p. 9.
31. *St. Louis Review*, November 4, 1988, cited in *Christian News*, November 14, 1988, pp. 10-11.
32. Malachi Martin, *The Keys of This Blood: The Struggle for World Dominion Between Pope John Paul II, Mikhail Gorbachev and the Capitalist West* (Simon and Schuster, 1990), pp. 626-27; see also interview with Malachi Martin, *Washington Times*, September 28, 1990, p. B6.
33. *La Croix*, August 17, 1981, as cited in Abbe Daniel Le Roux, *Peter, Lovest Thou Me?* (Australia: Instauratio Press, 1989), p. 18.
34. Cited on back of card with photo of Pope bowing to a statue of Our Lady of Fatima. "This prayer card was published to commemorate the visit of Pope John Paul II to Fatima on May 13, 1982, and especially for use during the worldwide All-Night Vigil sponsored by the Blue Army of Our Lady of Fatima [Washington, NJ 07882] on May 12-13, 1982."
35. *The Fatima Crusader*, November/December 1986, p. 9.
36. *Our Lady of Fatima's Peace Plan from Heaven* (Tan Books and Publishers, 1983), inside back cover.
37. Ibid., back cover.
38. *The Fatima Crusader*, November/December 1986, p. 1 of letter of appeal inserted in middle of the magazine, which starts, "Dear Fellow Catholic."
39. *Lucia Speaks on the Message*, pp. 26, 29-31, 47.
40. Quoted at the beginning of each "Heaven's Peace Plan," a daily Catholic radio program produced by the International Fatima Rosary Crusade, hosted by Fr. Nicholas Gruner, who publishes *The Fatima Crusader* magazine (with an estimated 1 million readers). The radio program claims to reach millions of people in the United States and Canada each week "with our Lady of Fatima's urgent message." The claim is also made at the beginning of each program: "It is only by obedience to our Lady of Fatima's message that we here in North America shall avoid being enslaved by Communist Russia. It is only by prompt obedience to our Lady of Fatima's message that the world will have peace...."
41. *The Dallas Morning News*, June 25, 1993.
42. *Lucia Speaks: The Message of Fatima According to the Exact Words of Sister Lucia, Published by the Most Reverend bishop of Fatima* (Washington, NJ: Ave Maria Institute, 1968), p. 46.
43. *Lucia Speaks on the Message of Fatima* (Washington, NJ: Ave Maria Institute), pp. 26, 30-31, 47.
44. See Dave Hunt, *Whatever Happened to Heaven?* (Harvest House Publishers, 1988), for a comprehensive account of how this came about.
45. Hayes, *Trumpet*, October 1993, op. cit.
46. *Orange County Register*, April 25, 1993, editorial, L01.
47. E.g. *Tidings*, October 20, 1989; *Los Angeles Herald Examiner*, September 19, 1987, Religion page.
48. *New Evangelization 2000*, first issue, July-August, 1987, p. 15.
49. Desmond Doig, *Mother Teresa: Her People and Her Work* (Harper and Row, 1976), p. 156.
50. *New Evangelization 2000*, is. 9, pp. 11-12.
51. *Time*, December 4, 1989, p. 12; *Masterpiece*, Winter 1988, p. 6.
52. Bill Clinton, President of the U.S., April 20, 1993, at press conference, *The New American*, September 6, 1993, p. 24.
53. *National Catholic Reporter*, June 19, 1992, p. 4.
54. *Our Sunday Visitor*, January 24, 1993, p. 2.
55. *Inside the Vatican*, October 1993, p. 41.

56. Ibid., p. 37.
57. *World Goodwill Newsletter*, 1989, no. 4, pp. 1, 3.
58. *The New York Times*, June 21, 1984.
59. *The New American*, September 6, 1993, p. 27.
60. Cited in *Foundation* magazine, July-August 1993, p. 7.
61. Ibid.

### Appendix A—Purgatory

1. Austin Flannery, O.P., gen. ed., "Apostolic Constitution on the Revision of Indulgences," *Vatican Council II: The Conciliar and Post Conciliar Documents*, rev. ed. (Costello Publishing, 1988), vol. 1, p. 63.
2. *The Canons and Decrees of the Council of Trent*, ed. and trans. H.J. Schroeder, O.P. (Tan Books, 1978), Sixth Session, Can. 30, p. 46.
3. Flannery, op. cit., vol. 2, p. 394.
4. Ibid., pp. 63-64.
5. Ibid., p. 205.
6. J.H. Ignaz von Dollinger, *The Pope and the Council* (London, 1869), pp. 186-87.
7. Karl Keating, *Catholicism and Fundamentalism: The Attack on "Romanism" by "Bible Christians"* (Ignatius Press, 1988), p. 190.
8. Flannery, op. cit., vol. 1, "Apostolic Constitution on the Revision of Indulgences," II 5., III 6, pp. 65, 68.

### Appendix B—Indulgences

1. James A. Coriden, Thomas J. Green, Donald E. Heintschel, eds., *The Code of Canon Law* (Paulist Press, 1985), Canons 992-94, pp. 698-99.
2. Austin Flannery, O.P., gen. ed., "Apostolic Constitution on the Revision of Indulgences," *Vatican Council II: The Conciliar and Post Conciliar Documents*, rev. ed. (Costello Publishing, 1988), vol. 1, pp. 66-70.
3. Ibid., p. 72.
4. J.H. Ignaz von Dollinger, *The Pope and the Council* (London, 1869), pp. 186-87.
5. Earle E. Cairnes, *Christianity Through the Centuries: A History of the Christian Church* (Zondervan Publishing House, 1981), p. 282.
6. "About the Brown Scapular," pamphlet put out by The Blue Army of Our Lady of Fatima, Washington, NJ 07882.
7. St. Alphonsus de Liguori, *The Glories of Mary* (Redemptorist Fathers, 1931), p. 235.
8. "About the Brown Scapular," op. cit.
9. Flannery, op. cit., vol. 1, pp. 77-78.
10. Coriden, et al., op. cit., p. 646.
11. Will Durant, *The Story of Civilization* (Simon and Schuster, 1950), vol. VI, p. 24.
12. D. Antonio Gavin, *A Master Key to Popery: In Five Parts*, 3rd ed. (London, England, 1773), p. 141.
13. Peter Kreeft, *Fundamentals of the Faith: Essays in Christian Apologetics* (Ignatius Press, 1988), p. 278.
14. Charles Colson, *The Body, Being Light in Darkness* (Word Publishing, 1992), p. 271.
15. Flannery, op. cit., vol. 1, pp. 71, 74.

### Appendix C—Dominion Over Kings: Further Documentation

1. Sidney Z. Ehler, John B. Morrall, trans. and eds., *Church and State Through the Centuries* (London, 1954), p. 70.
2. Ibid., pp. 73-75.
3. Ibid., pp. 273-75.
4. J.H. Ignaz von Dollinger, *The Pope and the Council* (London, 1869), p. 339.
5. Ehler and Morrall, op. cit., pp. 173-80 for a copy of the Bull; see also Dollinger, op. cit., pp. 311-12.
6. *Our Sunday Visitor*, August 22, 1993, pp. 10-11.
7. Emmet McLoughlin, *An Inquiry into the Assassination of Abraham Lincoln* (The Citadel Press, 1977), p. 45.
8. Cited in August Bernhard Hasler, *How the Pope Became Infallible* (Doubleday & Co., Inc., 1981), p. 245.

9. G.S. Godkin, *Life of Victor Emmanuel II* (London, 1880), pp. 76-77.
10. Dollinger, op. cit., pp. 236-37.
11. *The Encyclopedia Britannica* (1910 ed.), p. 579.

**Appendix D—Papal Infallibility and Apostolic Succession**
1. Brian Tierney, *Origins of Papal Infallibility, 1150-1350: A Study on the Concepts of Infallibility, Sovereignty and Tradition in the Middle Ages* (Leiden, Netherlands, 1972), p. 144.
2. J.H. Ignaz von Dollinger, *The Pope and the Council* (London, 1869), p. 58.
3. Lars Qualben, *History of the Christian Church.*
4. Sidney Z. Ehler, John B. Morrall, trans. and eds., *Church and State Through the Centuries* (London, 1954), pp. 7-9.
5. Ibid., pp. 9-10.
6. Peter de Rosa, *Vicars of Christ: The Dark Side of the Papacy* (Crown Publishers, 1988), pp. 93-94.
7. Dollinger, op. cit., p. 244.
8. Ibid., pp. 244-45.

**Appendix E—Papal Heretics, the Bible and Galileo**
1. Peter de Rosa, *Vicars of Christ: The Dark Side of the Papacy* (Crown Publishers, 1988), pp. 217-19.
2. Austin Flannery, O.P., gen. ed., "Dogmatic Constitution on Divine Revelation," *Vatican Council II: The Conciliar and Post Conciliar Documents*, rev. ed. (Costello Publishing, 1988), p. 757.
3. Vatican II, "*Vatican Council II, Divine Revelation* (Knights of Columbus paraphrase ed.), III.11e.

**Apendix F—What About Tradition?**
1. Austin Flannery, O.P., gen. ed., "Dogmatic Constitution on Divine Revelation," *Vatican Council II: The Counciliar and Post Conciliar Documents*, rev. ed. (Costello Publishing, 1988), vol., p. 754.
2. Ibid., pp. 755-56.
3. J.H. Ignaz von Dollinger, *The Pope and the Council* (London, 1869), pp. 78-93.
4. Ibid., pp. 99-106.
5. Ibid., pp. 83-85.
6. Richard Bennett, *Appraisal Kit on Roman Catholicism*, available from Berean Beacon, P.O. Box 55353, Portland, OR 97238-5353.

**Appendix G**
1. *Catechism of the Catholic Church* (Libreria Editrice Vaticana, 1994), par. 1456.
2. *L'Osservatore Romano* weekly edition in English, 15 March 2000, "International Theological Commission—Memory and Reconciliation: The Church and the Faults of the Past," p. 1.
3. Ibid., pp. 1,2,3, and following.
4. Ibid., pp. 1-2.
5. Ibid., p. 2.
6. Ibid.

**Appendix H**
1. *The Catholic World Report*, May 2000, p. 37.

# Index